THE ROAD TO SEPTEMBER 1939

THE TAUBER INSTITUTE SERIES FOR THE STUDY OF EUROPEAN JEWRY

The Tauber Institute Series is dedicated to publishing compelling and innovative approaches to the study of modern European Jewish history, thought, culture, and society. The series features scholarly works related to the Enlightenment, modern Judaism and the struggle for emancipation, the rise of nationalism and the spread of antisemitism, the Holocaust and its aftermath, as well as the contemporary Jewish experience. The series is published under the auspices of the Tauber Institute for the Study of European Jewry—established by a gift to Brandeis University from Dr. Laszlo N. Tauber—and is supported, in part, by the Tauber Foundation and the Valya and Robert Shapiro Endowment.

For the complete list of books that are available in this series, please see www.upne.com.

Jehuda Reinharz and Yaacov Shavit
The Road to September 1939: Polish Jews, Zionists, and the Yishuv on the Eve of World War II

Adi Gordon
Toward Nationalism's End: An Intellectual Biography of Hans Kohn

Noam Zadoff
Gershom Scholem: From Berlin to Jerusalem and Back

*Monika Schwarz-Friesel and Jehuda Reinharz
Inside the Antisemitic Mind: The Language of Jew-Hatred in Contemporary Germany

Elana Shapira
Style and Seduction: Jewish Patrons, Architecture, and Design in Fin de Siècle Vienna

ChaeRan Y. Freeze, Sylvia Fuks Fried, and Eugene R. Sheppard, editors
The Individual in History: Essays in Honor of Jehuda Reinharz

Immanuel Etkes
Rabbi Shneur Zalman of Liady: The Origins of Chabad Hasidism

*Robert Nemes and Daniel Unowsky, editors
Sites of European Antisemitism in the Age of Mass Politics, 1880–1918

*A Sarnat Library Book

JEHUDA REINHARZ AND YAACOV SHAVIT

THE ROAD TO SEPTEMBER 1939

POLISH JEWS, ZIONISTS, AND THE YISHUV ON THE EVE OF WORLD WAR II

Translated by Michal Sapir

Brandeis University Press
Waltham, Massachusetts

BRANDEIS UNIVERSITY PRESS

Manufactured in the United States of America
Designed by Eric M. Brooks
Typeset in Skolar by Passumpsic Publishing
First paperback edition 2019
ISBN for the paperback edition: 978-1-68458-007-1

Originally published in Hebrew in 2013 as *Haderekh leseptember 1939: Hayishuv, yehudei polin, vehatenuah hazionit erev milhemet ha'olam hashniyah* (Tel Aviv: Am Oved Publishers).

The Library of Congress cataloged the hardcover edition as:
NAMES: Reinharz, Jehuda, author. | Shavit, Yaacov, 1944- author.
TITLE: The road to September 1939: Polish Jews, Zionists, and the Yishuv on the eve of World War II / Jehuda Reinharz and Yaacov Shavit.
OTHER TITLES: Derekh le-September 1939. English
DESCRIPTION: Waltham, Massachusetts: Brandeis University Press, [2018] | Series: The Tauber Institute series for the study of European Jewry | Includes bibliographical references and index.
IDENTIFIERS: LCCN 2017035956 (print) | LCCN 2017037964 (ebook) | ISBN 9781512601541 (epub, mobi, & pdf) | ISBN 9781512601534 (cloth: alk. paper)
SUBJECTS: LCSH: Jews—Poland—History—20th century. | Jews—Europe—History—20th century. | Zionism. | Holocaust, Jewish (1939–1945)—Poland.
CLASSIFICATION: LCC DS134.55 (ebook) | LCC DS134.55 .S4313 2018 (print) | DDC 305.892/4043809043—dc23
LC record available at https://lccn.loc.gov/2017035956

5 4 3 2 1

We are sleeping, we are sleeping,
Like buildings late at night
Without knowing what is looming—

Israel Stern, "When the Surgery
Is Over," *Haynt*, September 1, 1939

CONTENTS

PREFACE

"THE BIRDS LEFT EARLY"

On Monday, September 4, 1939, the management of the Tel Aviv Zoo announced the birth of a female fawn and the arrival of a desert rat (also called a gerbil). In addition, the zoo acquired seventeen hoopoes in a pitiable state: they were rescued from an Arab who had captured them and plucked their wings, and were therefore unable to fly. The authorities confiscated the birds and handed them over to the zoo. The children's newspaper *Davar Leyeladim* wrote: "The hoopoes and the other birds were captured in our country on their migratory route from Europe. This year the birds left early for the warm countries, perhaps indicating that winter has come early this year. And maybe the birds are also fleeing the war in Europe?"[1]

About a week earlier, at the end of August, Brunia Reitberger, a housewife from Tel Aviv's Mazeh Street, and Sarah, her ten-year-old daughter, traveled to visit the mother's family in Piotrków Trybunalski, a town sixteen miles south of Łódź, home to around 18,000 Jews (which amounted to about a third of the town's population). Worried relatives, friends, and neighbors tried to dissuade Mrs. Reitberger from going: everyone knows that a war is about to break out any day now! But she insisted. They were only going for a short family visit and will return right after the holidays. Ahead of the trip they got Sarah a new red coat and a red velvet hat and filled a suitcase with presents for the relatives. The mother and daughter sailed on the ship *Har Zion* to the port of Constanta in Romania, and on the night of September 1 alighted at Warsaw's train station.

The platform was packed with people looking for a way to get out of the city. One of them turned to the mother and said: "Madame, go back to Palestine. Now!" She did not follow his advice: they were so close to their destination and would not turn back. On the morning of Saturday, September 2, 1939, not a living soul was waiting for them at Piotrków's train station. The mother and daughter traveled by cart to 5 Old Warsaw Street, where they received a chilly welcome; no one noticed Sarah's coat and velvet hat: "Why did you come now? A war has broken out and the Germans are bombing us. It's dangerous here and we must leave."

The flight from the town had already begun, and the road to Sulejow was jammed with "innumerable carts," which were attacked from the air. Sarah found herself on a horse-driven wooden cart packed with family members, pillows, and quilts. "What happened? Where are we going? [. . .] There was no answer."[2] Piotrków was taken by the German army on September 4. In the following days, around 2,000 Jews managed to flee eastward, only to be replaced by a large number of refugees from the neighboring towns. Approximately 25,000 people were crammed into the first ghetto in Poland, which was established on October 8. The process of transferring them to the ghetto continued until the end of January 1940.[3] Sarah and her mother had to endure three months of terror and hardship before they made it back to Tel Aviv.

At the beginning of September, a few hundred women and children from Palestine were waiting at the port of Constanta in Romania for ships to take them back from their summer visits to see their families. Among them were Dvora Gertz and her five-year-old daughter Dalit, who had visited the parents of Dvora's husband in Białystok. They got to Constanta by train because they could not find seats on the flight from Warsaw to Lod, Palestine, and had to wait at the port for three days. Far away in Kalisz, Mr. Freger soothed his frightened wife, saying that the Germans were only trying to terrorize Poland, "but the Poles are strong enough to withstand these German attempts."[4]

In 1938, at the request of the New Zionist Organization, founded by the Revisionist Zionist movement (which three years earlier had seceded from the Zionist Organization), a lawyer from Krakow, Dr. Yohanan (Jan) Bader, one of the leaders of the Revisionist movement, prepared a "working paper" on the Evacuation Plan—a plan for an organized mass emigration of Jews from Poland to Palestine to be carried out over ten years, until 1948. Now Bader heard from some military people that the pace of the fighting armies' movements would be similar to that of the First World War; that is, a slow pace. Confident of the Polish army's ability to defend the border, Bader believed that the German army would divert most of its forces to the western front. Therefore, "it would take a while before the enemy gets anywhere near Krakow," and he had enough time to decide what to do.[5]

Another leading member of the Revisionist movement, Dr. Wolfgang (Binyamin Zeev) von Weisl, who had been among the passengers on the airship *Graf Zeppelin* flight from Germany to the Middle East on Purim in March of 1929, acted differently. Von Weisl was a journalist and a prolific writer who had served as an artillery corps officer in the Habsburgian army and was awarded the Iron Cross for his service. When he heard the Austrian chancellor Kurt Schuschnigg announcing on Austrian radio that there would be a referendum on Austria's future, von Weisl told his wife: "Pack the suitcases immediately, take what you can, tonight we go with the children to Paris." His surprised wife replied: "You must be running a fever!" and Dr. von Weisl answered: "Never mind." The von Weisls and their two young children left Vienna for Paris with no luggage on March 12, 1938, the day after the Nazis entered the city. The following morning, Gestapo officers knocked on the door of their house on 48 Kirschengasse, but found their apartment empty.[6]

In his autobiography, Bader reflected on why he did not leave Poland like von Weisl, despite the warnings of Zeev Jabotinsky, the founder and leader of the Revisionist movement, who foresaw what was in store for the country's Jews, and confessed: "Maybe I was also too busy with my professional work, with the matters of the movement and the weekly, with photography, with reading books and with going to cafés and to the theater, and forgot the main thing: Jabotinsky's warning. I deluded myself: we still have time."[7] He did not believe that Poland was destined for a similar fate as Austria and Czechoslovakia.

Wiktor (Avigdor Wilhelm) Chajes from Lviv (Lvov, Lemberg), a banker, loyal Polish patriot, a leader of the Jewish community, and political wheeler-dealer who defined himself as "both Jewish and Polish," and who at the beginning of the 1930s was awarded several distinguished honorary decorations by the Polish government, wrote on August 16:

> We seem to be on the verge of a historic moment. War? Revolution? If so, where? It has to be said that among us the situation is tense, but there is no nervousness. Everyone is ready to defend. Hitlerism is running riot. Hurling insults, lies and threats in the press and on the radio. Adolf himself is secluding himself in Brechtesgaden and keeping silent. Holding talks, making plans, preparing something. In the last month I've been reading *Mein Kampf*. He wrote it about fifteen years ago and has been systematically paving the way for his theses and doctrines. He is consistent. The more I read his *Mein Kampf*, the more I fear him. But he will lose, he will surely lose.[8]

Two days later, on August 18, Dr. Willy Cohn, a historian and teacher in Breslau, put the blame on tensions in Poland. (In February he wrote in his diary, "I cannot say that Germany, in its fight to obtain living space for itself, is unjust."[9])

Jabotinsky, the leader of the Revisionist movement, was relaxed: "There is no reason to believe in the possibility of a war. [. . .] The world looks a peaceful place from Pont-Aven, and I think Pont-Aven is right."[10] Illa (Lili) Lubinsky-Strassman, a member of the Irgun (Etzel) delegation, visited him in the town of Vals-les-Bains, where he was vacationing, on her way to the Twenty-First Zionist Congress in Geneva. She was worried that if war broke out she would not be able to return to her family in Warsaw, but Jabotinsky soothed her: "There is not the remotest chance of war. Nobody wants it. [. . .] See you in a few days in Paris and we will go on a spree (*fera la bombe*)."[11]

On August 29, in Dresden, Victor Klemperer, a converted German-Jewish scholar, wrote: "The last few days pulled and still pull too much at my nerves. The unconcealed mobilization without any mobilization being announced (people, cars, horses), the pact with the Russians and the incredible turnabout, confusion, the incalculable situation, the balance of forces *after* this volte-face. [. . .] The maddest thing was the hand-in-hand picture of Ribbentrop and Stalin. Machiavelli is a babe in arms by comparison."[12]

"It seems that Poland allows itself anything under England's auspices," wrote Willy Cohn on August 26 in Breslau, fed by the German propaganda, and two days later he added that Poland was not ready to give up the corridor or Danzig without a war.[13]

On August 30, Chaim Weizmann, president of the Zionist Organization, wrote from London to his brother Feivel in Haifa: "We all live on a volcano and every minute expect the appearance of enemy aircraft over London or Paris. It will be as Providence decides. Personally, I am calm and do not believe in a final catastrophe. However, nerves are on edge."[14]

The Palestine press reported the signs of imminent war: the express train from Vienna and Berlin failed to arrive in Paris on August 29, the streets of the French capital had been darkened, the schools were getting ready to evacuate the pupils to the provinces, and even the animals in the zoo at Bois de Vincennes were transferred to zoos in provincial towns. Despite these signs of war, an ad published in the Palestine newspapers on August 30 invited tourists from the country to take a dream vacation in France: "Visit France, the land of beauty. It offers convalescence in its warm spas, relaxation in the mountains, joy of life on the beaches and in its sea resorts. Details, brochures and hotel prices can be found at any important news agency."

When the Twenty-First Zionist Congress in Geneva dispersed, Dr. Moshe Kleinbaum (Sneh), leader of the Zionist movement in Poland, flew to London, despite his fear that if war broke out he would not be able to return home. Every day he visited the offices of the Polish airline LOT, where he learned that the flights to Warsaw were full and that there would be no available seats for the next few days. On one of his visits he got lucky: he heard that a seat had become unexpectedly available on a flight leaving for Warsaw on Thursday, August 30. In a letter to Nahum Goldmann, Kleinbaum explained that he had decided to return to Warsaw despite the dangers, because he was "too attached to Poland and to the Jews of Poland, I cannot become an emigrant." Kleinbaum left for Warsaw on August 30, on the last flight from London to the continent. After a few stopovers, he arrived home on the evening of August 31 and rushed to join the military unit in which he served as a physician.[15]

The historian Dr. Emanuel Ringelblum, a delegate at the Twenty-First Zionist Congress for the Poalei Zion Leftist party in Poland, wrote in his diary about the grueling journey that he and his friends had to endure on their way back from Geneva to Warsaw: "We are on a thirty-hour train ride in a sleeping car to Warsaw. Air raid siren. [. . .] Hanging on the cars, on the roofs. Some are trying to break into our car. Manifestations of antisemitism in the country. Civic awareness made us decide to return to their country. Those who wanted to stay in the country."[16]

At 4 p.m. on August 29, a LOT Polish Airlines plane landed at Lod Airport, having taken off from Warsaw at 1 a.m. Worried citizens were waiting for the ten passengers who got off the plane near the offices of Orbis, the company representing the Polish airline, on Montefiore Street in Tel Aviv. The passengers reported that the Polish population showed courage, and that the general attitude was that Hitler must not be surrendered to and that not even one inch of Polish land nor the merest Polish stake in the "corridor" to Danzig (Gdansk) conceded.[17] You could feel the tension in the air, they told the waiting people, who were yearning for firsthand information, but there were no particular signs of panic. Life in Poland was not disrupted, there was no shortage of food supplies, the banks were open, and Jewish organizations took part in preparations for air-raid defense.[18] *Hazofe*, the Hamizrachi religious national party newspaper, proudly informed its readers that "hundreds of orthodox Jews with beards and earlocks are working shoulder-to-shoulder with Polish citizens" in digging protective ditches.[19]

Early in the morning of September 1, Nazi Germany's armored columns crossed the border into Poland. The Second World War had begun. It is hard to avoid the shadow of the "end"—which in August 1939 was impossible to foresee—that hangs over this month with all its weight. It is also difficult to ignore the heavy cloud of accusations and counter-accusations that hangs over this month: whose eyes were blind, even on the eve of war, to the impending disaster? Who was naïve, and who was completely in the dark? What could have been done and was not, and why?

August 1939—as well as, of course, its preceding months and years—looks like a voyage on a "ship of fools" whose passengers are occupied with needless quarrels and useless arguments, absorbed in everyday trifles that the events following September 1 would reveal in all their futility and pointlessness, even shamefulness. An almost obvious question arises: how is it possible that in the course of that month Jews in Palestine and in Poland carried on with their ordinary lives? One explanation can be found in a letter Berl Katznelson (a leader of the Labor movement) wrote from London at the beginning of October 1938: "We live here from one upheaval to the next. Not every upheaval erupts, not every decree that we face sees the light of day, but here you live every calamity, even before it materializes, and even when the calamity is miraculously postponed, either for one hour or for a long time."[20]

This book serves as a sort of collective diary of statesmen, social and political activists, and ordinary people whose first-person eyewitness accounts were recorded in personal diary entries, letters, and memoirs, along with daily newspaper accounts. These accounts are a record of what they knew, thought, and felt in "real time." In their focus on the vicissitudes of everyday life, rather than on the big questions of the hour, they bring to life this crucial moment in Jewish history and illuminate more effectively than some traditional histories the events that lead up to World War II and the Holocaust.

We do not intend to describe the events by reading history backward. We have tried not to read the story from its endpoint, but rather to tell it as much as possible in the "present." Before August 1939, as well as during that month, no one really knew what was in store. It is only a retrospective reading that determines that the events moved inexorably toward an unequaled calamity and that it was impossible to halt their course. A fog of uncertainty and lack of knowledge shrouded that month. And in any case, even if everyone had known where history was heading, they would have been helpless to divert the ship toward a safe haven. The processes that preceded the breakout of the Second World War have been reconstructed and analyzed in numerous books, some of them recording and reconstructing the behind-the-scenes occurrences that were unknown to people at the time. The history of the Jewish people, the Zionist movement, and the Yishuv, the Jewish community in Palestine prior to the establishment of the State of Israel in 1948, in the 1930s have been the subjects of an extensive body of literature. This book could not have been written without consulting it.

The reader of this book will find almost no German Jews in it.[21] Likewise, it will not discuss the fate of the Jews of Romania, Hungary, or France, for example. The choice to focus on Polish Jews seems obvious to us. Poland was home to the largest Jewish population in the world—around 3.5 million Jews in 1939—and after 1924 it was the main source of Jewish emigration across the Atlantic and to Palestine. From 1921 to 1938, more than 400,000 Jews left Poland. Initially, most of them went to the United States, but from 1924 onward the rate of those immigrating to Palestine increased. Between 1929 and 1935, Palestine absorbed around 43.7 percent of the total Jewish emigration, whereas the United States absorbed 10.9 percent.

If in 1929 Palestine took in less than a tenth of Jewish emigration from Poland, then in the years prior to the Second World War it became the principal destination for that emigration. In 1935, Palestine absorbed around 80.6 percent of the emigrants, and in 1937, 32.2 percent.[22] Between 1919 and 1939, around 140,000 people emigrated from Poland to Palestine—around 35 percent of its total Jewish population. During the Mandate period, Poland was thus the large source of immigration to Palestine and the main source for the Yishuv's demographic growth. In addition, a large part of the private capital that was imported to Palestine belonged to Polish Jews, who made a considerable contribution to the national funds (the "national capital").

In the middle of the 1930s, as the pressure to leave Poland grew and Palestine became the almost exclusive destination, the British government imposed new restrictions on Jewish immigration. As a result, the country's gates were shut to many who wanted to emigrate to it. The Zionist movement and its institutions had to lay the bridge on which at least some of the Polish Jews would cross over to Palestine. The Yishuv's political future and its power were now intertwined with the fate of Polish Jews. The fate of Polish Jews, however, as opposed to the fate of German Jews and later that of Jews under the Third Reich, was not on the public and international agenda. It did not occupy any place in British or international policy considerations, because Polish Jews had not been expelled and did not become asylum-seeking refugees. The countries of the free world had no interest in resolving Poland's internal problems by opening their gates to a large Jewish immigration.

The Zionist movement found itself in a difficult dilemma. On the one hand, putting the need for Jewish emigration from Poland on the international agenda was welcomed. On the other hand, directing this emigration to different countries in Africa or South America meant that Zionism would become irrelevant. In October 1936, for example, Weizmann wrote to Moshe Shertok (Sharett), director of the Jewish Agency's political department, that Poland had put the question of Jewish emigration from Eastern Europe on the international agenda. "The recent pronouncements of the Poles have made a very great impression. The Polish problem transcends the ordinary boundaries and makes it patent to everybody that our misfortunes will soon grow to a first-rate international calamity for which we cannot take the responsibility and which may affect vitally the state of affairs in the East and South East Europe."[23]

This led to the conclusion that it would be possible to spur the governments and the world's conscience to see finding a solution for the Jews' plight as a lofty conscientious duty. This was also accompanied by a belief that the power of the Jewish world could not be reduced to its plight. Weizmann, however, did not mean that putting the subject of Jewish emigration on the international agenda would include alternatives to Palestine. He — and others — believed that when it would become clear that there were no such alternatives, Palestine's status as the only destination would be reinforced.

However, it would be a mistake to describe the history of Polish Jews between the two World Wars only from a Zionist or a Palestinian perspective. Most of the Jews in Poland were not Zionists, and many of them opposed Zionism or were indifferent to it. Nor did many Zionists show an urgency or eagerness to immigrate to Palestine. Polish Jews had a rich and multifaceted existence as an integral part of Polish life and under its influence. The shadow of a possible war weighed on them without being necessarily tied to the future of the Jewish Yishuv in Palestine, and even in isolation from it.

At the end of a dinner held on February 22, 1938, at the house of Leopold Amery, the Secretary of State for Dominion Affairs from 1924 to 1929, Ben-Gurion told Sir Harold MacMichael, who was appointed High Commissioner for Palestine in 1938 (and held the position until 1944), that the Zionist movement wanted "to save the young generation of Eastern and Central European Jewry — and it's possible. It's a question of two million Jews." MacMichael replied that the Jews were "rushing things." Ben-Gurion wrote in his diary: "And again I saw that we are hitting a wall. The Englishman doesn't know what time means for us."[24]

What was the Zionist "dimension of time" in the 1930s? Can we distinguish between rhetoric and plans of actions, wishes and means? The research literature, and even more so the political and public debate, have been suffused for over fifty years with a bitter disagreement around the question to what extent Jews in general, and the political leadership of the Zionist movement in particular, were aware that time was pressing. Did the "awareness of time" change between 1935 and 1939? What was done under the pressure of time in order to break through the "wall," and did the Jews of Poland and of the Yishuv share the same "concept of time"?[25]

Various plans and solutions were mooted and discussed publicly and behind closed doors, stirring up the debate and creating polarization. Plans can testify to the sense of time and to a will to act. But they do not indicate that those who thought up the plans had the power and the means to carry them out. As will become apparent in the narrative that follows, individuals and organizations within the Zionist movement feared for the fate of the Jews of Europe and did what they could within the fog of uncertainty and with limited resources. Once the war broke out, however, the fate of European Jewry was virtually sealed.

The 1930s found European Jews and the Yishuv on two sides of a chasm, over which only a very narrow bridge could be laid. From the end of 1939 they lived in different worlds. Only the migrating birds could leave Europe as if there were no borders in the world as a war down on earth unfolded like none before it.

THE ROAD TO SEPTEMBER 1939

Emigrate, emigrate! They are calling the Jews even from the seats of the Sejm. But where to? Who will take in two million "superfluous" Jews?[1]
Wiktor Chajes, December 14, 1938

A curse lies on the relationship between the Poles and the Jews.[2]
Yitzhak Gruenbaum, January 1940

1

"A MILLION SUPERFLUOUS JEWS" —AND MORE

On May 13, 1935, the grief-stricken Wiktor Chajes, a leader of the Jewish community in Lviv, wrote in his diary: "The Marshal has passed away. Died yesterday (Sunday, May 12, at 10 p.m.) of cancer," and added:

> My poor homeland. Something has ended in Poland. A new historical era will begin. Why should we delude ourselves, he was Poland. [. . .] The whole country is crying. [. . .] For me the Marshal was everything. He was the homeland. I fear that now I shall become a citizen who fulfills his duties to the state and nothing more. [. . .] If I could cry and wish Poland strength, order, peace, unity and harmony.[3]

The sixty-eight-year-old Marshal Józef Piłsudski (1867–1935), whose death Chajes was bemoaning—the "grandpa" (*dziadek*), as he was called by his devotees—had been the founder and leader of the Second Polish Republic. After the military coup of May 1926 he became an almost omnipotent ruler, although he did not hold any official title. He died of stomach and liver cancer on the night of May 12, 1935, and at midnight the government ministers arrived to honor the dead leader of the "revived Poland" (*Polska odrodzona*) at the Belweder Palace, formerly the Royal Palace.

The news of his death spread rapidly. Army officers went around Warsaw's restaurants and cafés and ordered any music playing to be stopped.

The following day public institutions were closed and the streets were covered with White Eagle flags flown at half-mast. Crowds of mourners, their hats in their hands, gathered in front of the palace. The president of the Republic, Ignacy Mościcki, eulogized him as "The Greatest Pole." The journalist Dr. Yehoshua Gottlieb wrote in *Der Moment*: "We have lost a man who was the symbol of Poland, the new liberated Poland."[4] Zeev Jabotinsky, the founder and leader of the Revisionist movement, who was staying in Lutsk, sent Ignacy Mościcki, the Polish president, a telegram "on behalf of the Revisionist Zionist movement, its youth movement, and its ex-legionnaires and soldiers." The telegram read:

> I ask Your Excellency to accept our sincere commiserations on the sad and grave loss suffered by Poland, the Polish people, and Poland's friends all over the world.
>
> At this time of grief I wish to express our firm belief in the future of the idealistic people, whose heart was revealed to us by Marshal Piłsudski.[5]

The Federation of Polish Jews in the United States also sent a telegram of condolences, expressing that "[We as] Jews respected Marshal Piłsudski as a man whose whole life was dedicated to right and justice, whose unswerving objective was the destiny of Poland, and whose thought embraced all of Poland's children, regardless of race or creed."[6] The historian Professor Meir Balaban wrote on May 15: "We were afraid to even think about it [Piłsudski's death], and whenever we heard news of his grave illness, we were consoled by the hope that this man, whose will was strong, would overcome this illness and continue to hold the helm of the renewed Poland in his strong and pure hands."[7]

On the morning of May 17 the funeral procession took place in Warsaw. The coffin, to which around 800,000 members of the public had come to pay their respects, was placed on a gun carriage led by six pairs of white horses; the Marshal's sword was laid on the coffin, which was followed by army units and numerous delegations. After the wake at the church, airplanes flew above the thousands-strong crowd in an aerial salute. Piłsudski had willed his brain to scientific research, his heart to be buried in Vilna under his mother's ashes, and his body to be buried in Krakow. His wish was interpreted as symbolizing his legacy for subsequent generations: his appreciation of science, his profound affinity with Vilna, and the campaign to liberate Poland from the yoke of the Tsarist Empire, which had begun in Krakow on August 6, 1914.[8]

"The whole of Poland is in mourning," wrote Chajes. "I'm going to Krakow for the funeral, and the day before I'm organizing Jewish participation in a procession of honor here [in Lviv]. Europe is aware of the size of the blow that has struck Poland."[9] On May 18 the Marshal's body arrived by train in Krakow and was placed in a glass coffin in the chapel of the Wawel Cathedral, the burial place of the Polish kings. Two hundred thousand people walked past the coffin during one day and two nights. A rumor spread that Hitler intended to honor the deceased and attend the funeral. The Fuhrer did not come, but sent a large wreath with his deputy Hermann Goering and three generals.[10] Chajes wrote: "The funeral was a once in a lifetime sight. [. . .] Some hundred and fifty ministers and generals came from all over Europe. Patton, Laval,[11] Goering. [. . .] A hundred and fifty to two hundred and fifty thousand people came to Krakow. The procession was meticulously organized. The ceremony lasted from seven in the morning to one in the afternoon. [. . .] All of Poland is crying. All of Europe is aware of the magnitude of the disaster."[12]

The Marshal's funeral was an impressive event, unprecedented in the history of Poland. It was also the burial ceremony of the Polish Republic, though the latter did not know in May 1935 that it was nearing its death. Piłsudski's death not only marked the end of an era in the history of independent Poland but also the beginning of a new chapter—the last chapter before the Holocaust—in the hundreds of years of Jewish existence in Poland. Since gaining its independence, and even more so from 1935 to 1939,[13] Poland had been in the grips of a debate about the character of the republic and the relations between "state" and "nation" in it: was Poland a country "only for Poles" (which also belonged to Poles in the "Diaspora"), with the ethnic minorities having no part in it but only living as second-class citizens, or was it a multinational country, the Jews being one of its nations, as Piłsudski had thought, believing in "the state's supremacy over the nation"?[14]

The "Jewish Question" played a significant role in the political struggle between Piłsudski's camp, the "Sanacja" (healing) camp on the one hand, and the nationalistic and antisemitic camp of the national-democrats (the "Endecja," Narodowa Demokracja), on the other. Many Poles saw the approximately three and a half million Jews who now lived in Poland (around 10 percent of the population) as a millstone around the republic's neck and as a real cause for its domestic troubles, and the nationalist camp demanded that at least some of them be removed. The claim of the leader of the nationalistic antisemitic camp, Roman Dmowski, that the existence of Jews in Poland was "lethal to our society and we must get rid of them"[15] if Poland was not to become a "Judeo-Poland," became the rallying cry of his followers. They likened Polish Jews to "a well-organized swarm of locusts" that was eating anything and everything in its path. Therefore, "they should be shown the door" so that Poland could remain free of Jews. Nazi antisemitism found its ardent supporters in the Endecja camp, which saw the actions of the Nazi regime as a first positive step toward solving the "Jewish problem" not only in Germany, but in Poland as well.

After Piłsudski's death, his successors adopted the opinion that a large Jewish emigration was necessary in order to "heal" Poland. They started voicing it on any possible diplomatic stage, searching for territorial destinations, including Madagascar, Angola, Ecuador, and Northern Rhodesia, to which the "surplus of Jews" could be transferred. Foreign Minister Beck wrote to his ambassador in Washington that it should be stressed "that Polish Jews are a better colonizing element than German Jews."[16]

In any event, the Polish government's efforts to raise the subject of Jewish emigration onto the international agenda were in vain. Although the plight of Polish Jews and their possible emigration did appear on the international agenda along with the question of Jewish refugees from the "Reich," Western governments continued to see the situation of Polish Jews as an unfortunate but mainly an internal Polish matter.

Jewish delegations from numerous cities and representatives of various Jewish organizations attended Piłsudski's funeral. In synagogues across Poland they eulogized the dead leader, and communities sent telegrams of condolences. The Committee of Rabbis in Poland wrote: "Out of the deep sadness that has engulfed all the citizens upon the death of the builder and the man to whom Providence had given Poland, we pray that his soul may come to rest and that his dreams for Poland may be fulfilled [. . .]." The committee announced four weeks of mourning, and a council of representatives from various Jewish organizations formed a committee to commemorate his name. On returning to Lviv, Chajes (who had met Piłsudski twice in the early '20s) founded a library holding 5,000 books and named after the Marshal, donated 2,000 złoty for a prize in a competition to write a poem about him, and donated another 1,000 złoty to erect a monument in the city. At the end of June he installed in his elegant house a bust of the Marshal, made by the sculptor Nathan Rapoport:

> Piłsudski's head is wonderful. A royal forehead, sad thoughts, powerful and great. Every morning I pay my respects, and pass by him several times a day. Formidable. [. . .] In these great days of the Olympics,[17] as a

Jew I feel miserable. As a Pole I fear the possibility that soon the Prussian snake will slither its way to Silesia and Gdansk. In the Marshal's days no one was afraid of anything or anyone. I look at the leader's bust and ask for calm. But you know what? The bust is no more alive than he is, and those who are in power now are small. Ah, so small.[18]

At Isaiah (Sevek) Krotoshinsky's school in Łódź, the teacher wrote on the blackboard a poem in memory of the dead Marshal, and Isaiah conducted the class chorus, which filled him with great happiness.[19]

Manifestations of grief, as well as consternation over the future, could also be seen in Palestine. The Polish consulate was flooded with telegrams, representatives of institutions and organizations came to offer consolation, and in various places, including the Catholic church in Jaffa, memorial ceremonies were held. The Committee of the Associations of Polish Immigrants held a funeral prayer at the Great Synagogue on Tel Aviv's Allenby Street, attended by the Polish consul, representatives of the Chief Rabbinate, representatives of the national institutions, and so on.

On Sunday, May 19, the thousand or so passengers of the ship *Polonia* gathered on deck. Rabbi Shaul Taub of Modzhitz (the Yiddish name for the Polish town of Dęblin) recited the "El malei rachamim" (God of Mercy) and the ship's captain thanked his passengers for sharing in Poland's grief. In the Zionist Labor movement, the left wing of the Zionist movement, the mourning over Piłsudski's death was moderate and reserved, because the workers' parties did not sympathize with his autocratic regime. *Davar*, which reported extensively on the funeral, the burial ceremonies, and the reaction of Polish Jews, wrote: "We have no reason to relate to the Polish Marshal with any sympathy,"[20] but admitted that there was no doubt his death had marked a turning point in the situation of Polish Jews.

Beyond the displays of grief and mourning there were worry and anxiety over what was to come. Some described Piłsudski's Poland as "a kind of island," in which the Jews had been protected from the raging storms outside, which they might not be able now to withstand. Ben-Gurion claimed: "Without Piłsudski's influence — the National Democratic Party would have had the same violently antisemitic regime in Poland [as in Germany]."[21] *Hayarden*, the Palestine organ of the Revisionist movement, founded by Jabotinsky in 1925 and advocating a maximalist form of Zionism, tried to instill calm: "There is no room for shock as a result of Piłsudski's death," and promised that Poland's situation was more secure than ever thanks to the set of treaties it had signed. It too, however, was not blind to the new reality.

The whole Jewish community in Poland, the newspaper wrote, was anxious over the possibility that in the wake of the Marshal's death citizens would see an intensification of "the evil wind of fierce hatred for the Jews" among the opposition parties.[22] Earlier, after the synagogue in a town near Sosnowiec had been burned, *Hayarden* had already warned: "The destruction of Polish Jewry is an actual fact, and its terror will be seven times as great as the destruction of the Jewry in Germany, whose wealth, after all, stands them in good stead in times of trouble."[23]

Yitzhak Gruenbaum, until recently (1931) the leader of the Zionist movement in Poland, called Piłsudski "the hero of his generation," and drew a balanced portrait of the dead leader: in the first period of his reign the Marshal was "a symbol of the decent treatment of national minorities and Jews. Though in his first years the terror against Jews increased and he did nothing to stop it; whether he did not want to or could not — cannot be determined at this moment in time." Those years, Gruenbaum noted, "saw the emergence and development of the legend about Piłsudski, who wanted a Poland built on freedom for all its peoples, on social fairness, and on the people's rule." Piłsudski's autocratic rule was based on the notion of the state's supremacy, a notion designed to restrain the "monster of anarchy" ingrained in the Polish people and to strengthen Poland against its great enemy: the USSR. At the same time, he instated a democratic regime in Poland, "and who knows if his successor, who will now replace him, will be able to preserve this legacy?"[24] Faced with the new situation, Gruenbaum believed that from then on it was not only German Jews that one should be worried about: "We should not only use the situation of Polish Jews in our diplomatic war but also use the funds and the immigration certificates to help Polish Jews. By doing so we will prove to Polish Jews that we take an interest in their situation and do our best to come to their aid." Dr. Ephraim Fischel Rotenstreich, one of the leaders of the "General Zionists B" party, maintained that a few hundred additional immigration certificates would save the Jewish youth in Poland from the claws of Communism and that although "clearly, with 500 additional certificates we will not save the Jews of Poland [. . .] we shall thus prove to them that we are lobbying on their behalf."[25]

Polish Jews clung to Piłsudski's legacy, which now signified days that would never return, days like those in September 1933, when the Krakow Jewish community participated in collecting funds for a new national museum in the city, in order to, through this act, "express the bond and the solidarity of feeling that have connected us for thousands of years to the

Polish public [. . .] and may this monumental building, which will be built through this joint effort, testify to the inextricable link between all the citizens of the new independent Polish state."[26]

On July 28, 1935, delegations of Jews from all over Poland arrived in Krakow and carried earth in wheelbarrows to the big mound that had been erected in memory of Piłsudski on the north bank of the Vistula River. Some brought clods of earth from the tomb of pułkownik (regiment commander) Berek Joselewicz, a Jewish officer who served in the 5 Mounted Riflemen Regiment of the Duchy of Warsaw and was killed in May 1809 near Kock[27]: "In the presence of Krakow's Jewish community, earth was scattered from an artistic bronze urn, and afterward, as has become the custom, they joined the construction of the earth mound."[28]

The newspaper *Nowy Dziennik* (the New Daily), which was founded in Krakow in July 1918 by "a group of Jewish citizens tied with bonds of love to their people" in order "to combine feelings of Polish patriotism with love for their people and cope with enemy attacks," reported on a spontaneous manifestation of mourning by Krakow Jews. They erected two "tombstones" made of cardboard boxes and wooden planks, covered with black cloth and adorned with the national colors: "It had the Marshal's portrait and a bronze statue on the front, chains all around, and a permanently lit bulb on top and two burning candles on the sides. It was covered all around with greenery and flowers."[29] The Revisionist newspaper *Trybuna Narodowa* (the National Stage), published in Krakow, wrote that the dead Marshal was the symbol and model of an uncompromising struggle and an iron will.

Chajes returned to Krakow on May 25 and also pushed a wheelbarrow full of earth to the mound. "The place by the mound—wonderful," he wrote in his diary. Chajes described the speech given by Jabotinsky, whom he called "the leader of the radical or fascist Jews," in Warsaw on May 29 as a "fine speech" and a "precious revelation." The speech interpreted the situation of Polish Jews. It became clear to Chajes that both he and Jabotinsky had been reared on Polish romanticism and had grown up in the shadow of the double tragedy of the Poles and the Jews.[30]

For the members of the Revisionist movement in Poland, Piłsudski was not only a great leader but also a symbol and model of national leadership.[31] The movement expressed its grief in various ways, culminating in a memorial rally on August 10, 1935. Thousands of members from Brit Hahayal (an organization of ex-Polish army soldiers) and Betar (an acronym for Brit Yosef Trumpeldor, a Revisionist youth movement founded by Jabotinsky in 1923), wearing their brown uniforms—"the color of defense and of the earth of the Sharon" — marched in a large procession through the streets of Krakow. At 10 p.m. Jabotinsky gave his speech, which drew a resemblance between the two "Jozefs" — Józef Piłsudski and Yosef Trumpeldor: tomorrow, said Jabotinsky, when the Betar members visit Piłsudski's grave in Sowiniec, and lay on the fresh tomb a symbolic bag of earth brought from Trumpeldor's grave in Tel Hai, these two will talk to each other "about the profound secret hidden in their souls: it is the secret of loving one's homeland, of making the eternal sacrifice for it, and of a life dedicated to the national interest." *Hayarden* wrote: "The spellbound crowd remained standing there for a few minutes after Jabotinsky's speech ended," and then the procession dispersed to the singing of "Hatikva." The next day the Betar members held a special prayer in memory of the deceased in the old synagogue in Kazimierz,[32] in the presence of many of the city's dignitaries, and from there the procession left for Sowiniec. The Betar commissionership officers who led it carried a bag of earth, shaped like a cannonball and wrapped in blue and white, and a decorative scroll carrying the Hebrew and Polish inscription: "To the venerated leader of the Polish people Józef Piłsudski, from the National Hebrew movement that seeks to liberate its people and its land — earth from Yosef Trumpeldor's battlefield." At the end of the ceremony, the Betar commissioner in Poland, Aaron Propes, emptied the bag of earth onto the grave, and the assembly stood at attention for five minutes. *Hayarden* promised that after the participants returned to their homes across Poland they would keep an indelible impression of the ceremony in their hearts.[33]

The members of the Revisionist movement in Poland saw a resemblance between the Marshal and Jabotinsky. The latter testified that "he had never seen or heard Piłsudski,"[34] and in 1928 even warned not to over-trust him, because he was a ruler without a party and when he left the stage, the political system in Poland would revert to what it had been before him.[35] Now, after the Marshal's death, Jabotinsky portrayed him as a leader whose life's mission was to remold Poland, to save it from the "anarchy" that had characterized its history and to turn it into an orderly state: "*His* Poland should have been orderly, clean, punctual, active and resourceful, fair; in short: 'Western.'"[36] In the Jewish context, Jabotinsky saw Piłsudski as a leader who had purged Poland of its antisemitic shadows and turned it into an island of political freedom for Jews, who had enjoyed absolute liberty to act in the public and political spheres. And what would happen now, after his death? And what would be the relationship between the Revisionist movement and the new Polish regime? In Jabotinsky's view, Piłsudski's successors, the "colonels," were the last chance for Polish Jews to find some honest allies who would stand firm against the antisemitic camp.[37]

After Piłsudski's death, responsibility for the "Jewish issue" moved from the Ministry of the Interior to the Ministry of Foreign Affairs. This change suggested that in the eyes of the new government, the "Jewish issue" was not just an urgent "internal problem," but also an "international problem," because the "Jews make up the only very large minority not possessing their own territory." Thus, Poland must reduce their percentage to the Polish population.[38] In the memorandum submitted to the League of Nations' Council in Geneva by the Polish delegate on September 18, 1935, the "Jewish question" and the "Palestine question" were explicitly linked: the emigration of Jews to Palestine was an urgent economical exigency for Poland in order to ease the density of its population.[39]

It was no coincidence that on September 1935 the New Zionist Organization (the NZO) was founded as a rival—and, in fact, an aspiring alternative—to the Zionist Organization founded by Herzl, which since 1931 had been dominated by the Zionist "left." The propaganda campaigns run by Jabotinsky in the months prior to the NZO's inaugural congress in order to recruit supporters seemed to his followers like a victory parade. He went from city to city escorted by an "armor-bearer" wearing a khaki-colored military jacket, riding pants, and black shiny boots: "His clothes sported glittering buttons and a strap made of silver threads. On his head he wore a round hat whose visor was adorned with a broad sliver stripe."[40] Over 150,000 members of the movement voted in a poll held by the Revisionists in favor of seceding from the Zionist Organization, and around 700,000 declared their support for the new movement.

The thrilled Jabotinsky felt that a new—sixth—era in his life had begun.[41] He was "suddenly young again," he wrote, "bathing in a fountain of youth" (*bain de jeunesse*).[42] He wrote to a friend that he had shed twenty years of his age and 80 percent of the Diaspora and was leading his supporters out of a stifling cave into the purified air of fields and hills.[43] Now, he believed, the Revisionists would be able to work independently and freely to attain the longed-for hegemony in the Zionist movement and represent it in the international political arena in general and in Poland in particular. It was in his view no less than "the preliminary step to the revolution that will save Zionism."[44]

The founding of the New Zionist Organization was marked on June 13, 1936, by a large mass rally in Warsaw, where it was announced that the

Directorate of the new organization would sit in the Polish capital—"the center of Jewish life and Jewish hope"—and that its role would be to organize a national congress of "all the Jews working for the revival of the nation and the state in Palestine."[45] "Time is on our side and not against us," wrote Jabotinsky from his vacation spot in the "Nice" hotel in the Italian spa town of Montecatini Terme in Tuscany.[46] To Abba Achimeir, one of the leaders of the movement's "maximalist" radical group,[47] whom he had invited to join the Directorate of the New Zionist Organization in Warsaw (Achimeir arrived in November 1938 to run the movement's offices), Jabotinsky wrote in November 1935: "Only in Poland do we have such immense power on the Jewish street; power which, if joined by the prestige of a world institution, no other party or movement could compete with; and that would compensate to a large extent for our weakness in London and Jerusalem."[48] The Revisionist movement was transitioning from the "heroic" phase to the "practical" phase, he stated.[49]

Apart from intensive organizational activity, Jabotinsky now embarked on extensive propaganda tours and wide-ranging diplomatic activity: countless lectures, speeches, meetings, and talks, which yielded mainly expressions of sympathy and support.[50] The representatives of the Jewish Agency and Zionist Organizations in Poland likewise began to maintain frequent contacts with the Polish authorities and even to cooperate with them, under the assumption—or rather, the illusion—that because Poland and the Zionist movement had a shared interest, Poland was a vital ally for the main Zionist concern: immigration.

As we shall see, the issue of Jewish emigration from Poland was the central issue in relations between the Polish government and the Zionist movement. The Polish government was interested in encouraging massive immigration of Jews to any possible destination. It thus supported the efforts of the Zionist movement to direct immigration to Israel and was therefore perceived by all camps in the Zionist movement as a crucial ally in the struggle against British policy, but, at one and the same time, the Polish government knew that Palestine could not absorb a massive emigration—not within the boundaries of the Mandate, and certainly not within the borders of the Partition Plan, and it therefore sought other destinations for immigration.

The Zionist movement, for its part, feared that acquiescing to destinations other than Palestine, even if tacitly, would weaken its political struggle and that its failure would only increase antisemitism in Poland. At the same time, it was very anxious about mass immigration to Palestine, both because of its sociocultural makeup and because of the knowledge that such a massive immigration would prove to be difficult to manage. In any case, expectations vis-à-vis the Polish government led the heads of the Zionist movement, and especially Jabotinsky, to assert that the need for mass Jewish migration from Poland was not related to antisemitism but was instead an objective aim of societal development and that it was in Poland's interest and therefore important for Poland to intervene with the British government.[51]

Could the Zionist movement really guarantee that the "million superfluous Jews" would be able to immigrate to Palestine? After Piłsudski's death it became clear that the Polish government expected the Zionist movement to encourage a large Jewish emigration to Palestine—a lot more than the number of immigrants from Poland in the previous twenty years. From 1919 to 1939, around 140,000 people emigrated from Poland to Palestine (making up around 40 percent of the legal immigration to the country). In the second half of the 1930s, as the emigration pressure from Poland grew in parallel to the increased pressure from those wishing to emigrate to Palestine from the Reich countries, the number of certificates allocated to Polish Jews decreased. The inevitable consequence was that the number of emigrants from Poland to Palestine decreased considerably compared to previous years.

Even before that, the scope of the immigration was not that significant relative to the size of the Jewish population in Poland (and to its natural growth rate, around 40,000 per year), and the Polish Foreign Ministry did not conceal its disappointment. In that period, the emigration of any Polish residents to the United States almost ground to a halt, following the law that was passed in Congress in 1924 limiting emigration from all countries to 153,000 emigrants per year. In total, 244,000 people emigrated from Poland to the United States after 1921, most of them before 1924. From 1931 to 1940 the number of emigrants decreased to around 17,000.[52] The total emigration of Poles, Jews and non-Jews, from 1931 to 1938 was about 515,000—about 23 percent were Jews—of which about 164,000 migrated overseas, and only a small portion migrated to other countries in Europe (especially France and Belgium).[53]

The number of Jewish emigrants from Poland to the United States and to other countries (mainly to South America) decreased considerably, and there was no immigration to other countries in Europe. At the same time, from 1937 onward the number of immigration certificates to Palestine decreased. Until summer 1937, the number of immigrants was determined by a yearly quota that the Mandate government allocated according to the country's "economic absorption capacity."

The immigrants were divided into several categories: workers (C); "capitalists" (A—divided into four subcategories); students and religious practitioners (B); and "dependents" on local residents (D). Until summer 1937, a "capitalist" Jew with at least a 1,000 Palestine pounds could get a certificate in the British consulates without having to wait for a permit from the Immigration Department in Jerusalem.[54] In 1935 around 30,000 people emigrated from Poland (52 percent of the total number of immigrants), in 1936 around 13,000 people (around 47 percent), in 1937 3,708 people (37 percent), in 1938 3,642 people (29 percent), and in 1939 4,532 people (18 percent).[55]

In the Zionist context, this led to a struggle over the distribution of certificates to immigrants belonging to the "workers" category among those wishing to emigrate from the different countries, and among the political camps, a struggle that engaged the Zionist movement until 1937. "[Voters] come to us," wrote Ben-Gurion with cold disillusionment in summer 1933, "because they see us as the channel for immigration. If we do not provide this channel, they will go elsewhere: our ideas used to attract the youth in previous years; at the moment, there is also a totally different factor: immigration. And these people will go to whoever has control over immigration."[56]

The certificates, accused Dr. Werner Santor, director of the Jewish Agency's Immigration Department, in May 1936, were sometimes sold by the parties that had received them.[57] This struggle revolved around the distribution of, at the most, several thousand or even several hundred certificates, "fought" over not only by would-be emigrants from Poland but also from the Reich. The latter were favored by the British authorities. The dark forecasts about what was in store for Polish Jews expressed genuine concern but were also part of the fight over the distribution of immigration certificates among those wishing to emigrate from Poland and those wishing to emigrate from the German Reich, and intended to support the demand to increase the number of certificates allocated to Polish Jews.

The leaders of the Zionist movement knew that the Polish government did not pin its hopes only on emigration to Palestine, and therefore it was not enough to try and convince it that Palestine was the one and only destination for emigration. Polish authorities also had to be convinced that the Zionist movement wanted massive immigration to Palestine and was able to persuade Polish Jews to emigrate—as well as to organize this emigration.

Even if the Zionist politicians had been able to sway the British to increase the immigration quotas, it would not have been enough to satisfy the Polish expectation "to get rid of the surplus of Jews."

Moreover, the Polish government's attempts to encourage the emigration of Poles to other countries as a solution to the economic problems in Poland did not help much to solve the economic crisis, and it is difficult to say that the emigration of a million Jews over the course of ten years was a real cure for Poland's economic woes.

When Weizmann agonized at the Twenty-First Zionist Congress in Geneva about "hundreds of thousands of Jews destined to suffer pogroms and poverty," and about "tens of thousands of our people homeless, tossed from shore to shore, blown around like chaff in the wind,"[58] he probably did not envisage more than three million Jews living in Poland under the murderous oppression of Nazi Germany; he certainly did not foresee in his wildest dreams a quarter of a million Jews or more running for their lives to the eastern regions of the country taken by the Red Army on September 17, 1939. "The torrent of calamities" that Weizmann feared was focused on the fate of the refugees and deportees from the Reich—from Germany, Austria, and Czechoslovakia.

In August 1939 Polish Jews were neither tossed "from shore to shore" nor persecuted, deported, imprisoned, or murdered. Although their situation had become very unstable in the five years that preceded the war, they were fighting for their rights in the public arena. Poland had not confiscated their property, isolated them from society, deprived them of all their civil rights, or thrown them in jails and detention camps, and they were not facing the danger of expulsion. About a month before Marshal Piłsudski's death, Gruenbaum wrote that the situation in Germany was not comparable to the situation in Poland: "In Poland there are three million Jews and there is a possibility of a political war. Not so in Germany: there, there is no possibility of war and the situation of German Jews is tragic."

Gruenbaum believed that the Poles would not be able to subscribe to the idea of "driving the Jews out of the country [Poland] without damaging the country itself" and would not be tempted to believe that Poland stood to gain economically from such expulsion. If the Zionist movement encouraged a massive exodus of Jews from Poland, Gruenbaum warned, "We who are building the land can expect torrents that would be self-inflicted."[59] This warning that "a torrent of immigrants" would jeopardize the Zionist project in Palestine, which was not an isolated opinion, came from someone who knew well and understood which way the winds were blowing in the Polish government and public.

Polish Jews were divided in their opinions about their status and their impending future, and about the best ways to fight for their rights and respond to their deteriorating situation. Both those who believed that the struggle would succeed and those who estimated that the hourglass of Jewish existence in Poland was running out—and therefore the only solution was massive emigration—saw themselves as Polish patriots. Many of them spoke about "romantic love" for the Polish homeland. And in any case, no strain in Jewish public life doubted that the Polish Republic was a stable political entity, whose independence and sovereignty were not at risk, and which would know how to defend itself when necessary. The majority of Polish Jews supported the position of *doikeit*—"staying put."

Thus, it was not the nightmarish vision of occupation by Nazi Germany that made the alarm bells ring and warn of the Jews' deteriorating situation. It was rather the view that internal processes were pushing Poland down the slippery slope of nationalistic antisemitism, an antisemitism whose aim was to disrupt and even put an end to hundreds of years of Jewish existence in the country.

Warning signs for what was in store appeared even before Piłsudski's death. Toward the end of his reign, in January 1934, Poland signed a Non-Aggression Pact with Nazi Germany, and in September 1934 it rescinded the articles in the Treaty of Versailles that protected minorities' rights. The new constitution, ratified in April 1935, about a month before Piłsudski's death, restricted these rights considerably.

Being a Polish patriot, Chajes justified the disavowal of the Treaty of Versailles signed in June 1919. Poland, he claimed, should not keep the agreement that was forced on it and obliged it to protect national minorities, like the other states that were not bound by it: "Poland is in the right!" he wrote, and did not hide his delight over the Non-Aggression Pact that Poland had signed with Germany. This pact, he hoped, would diffuse the tension between the two countries over the "corridor" to Danzig.

His view changed when in the elections for the Sejm, the Polish parliament, held on September 8, 1935, and boycotted by the leftist parties, only five Jewish delegates were voted in. Now he wondered what was in store for the Jews in post-Piłsudski Poland. Brokenhearted, Chajes concluded that he had been right in his gloomy forecast that the departure of the venerated Marshal would lead to a profound crisis: Poland was no longer striving to assimilate the Jews, he wrote in his diary, and "the Pole of the Mosaic faith" was a thing of the past.[60] Now he started documenting acts of violence against Jews: "Sometimes my palace no longer brings me any joy. My bourgeois abode sometimes fills me with fear. Each time I identify more with those beaten up in the parks. The Corporations' caps make me anxious. In the universities in Lviv, Warsaw, and Vilna the students do not hesitate to attack even Jewish girls."[61]

Piłsudski's death released many forces that had been reined in in his lifetime and waited for a chance to erupt. The new government was too weak to oppose them.[62] Chajes constantly lamented the Marshal's death and mourned the death of the "real" Poland. The Polish Jewish patriot, the deputy mayor of Lviv, even found himself accused in court of abusing public funds to pay for various expenses of the Jewish community. Although the investigation was scrapped, Chajes wrote bitterly: "A Polak-Jew [*Polak-Żyd* —Polish-Jew] has become a museum piece."[63] Some Jewish activists believed that the pact resulted from the weakness of the German policy, but others saw it as expressing a calamitous blindness. Neither the former nor the latter could foresee the immediate impact that the pact, and the government's unilateral decision to rescind its commitments vis-à-vis the minorities treaty, would have on the situation of Polish Jews.[64]

On October 26, 1933, after returning from a trip to Poland, Ben-Gurion wrote Weizmann that he saw

> these days as *yemei mashiach* (messianic times), and not at all in a mystical and religious sense, but in a real and practical sense. Judaism is being destroyed and strangled. [. . .] I have seen the situation of the Jews in Poland, in Lithuania, in Latvia. We cannot go on like this. Germany is only a prelude. Not only the poverty, the lack of livelihood opportunities, the political pressure, the intensifying antisemitism—the terrible thing is the total lack of hope. The Jews in these countries have nothing to hope for any more. Everyone knows that the situation can only get worse, and there is nothing more terrible in a person's life than a lack of hope.[65]

Ben-Gurion added, however, that he did not envisage an immigration of millions or hundreds of thousands—rather of tens of thousands—and soon perhaps more.[66] His main concern was for the Jewish youth in Poland, because "obviously Palestine does not yet offer a solution for all Polish Jews. Immigration to Palestine is necessarily limited, and therefore there is need for selective immigration."[67]

Two and a half years later, in March 1936, about a year after Piłsudski's death, Ben-Gurion wrote from Warsaw: "At the moment we need a great political effort to put the *catastrophe of Polish Jews* on the agenda."[68] He did not explain what he meant by "put on the agenda," and a chasm lay between the force of the alarm bell and the feeble response he offered.

The Federation of Polish Jews in the United States was likewise unable to do more than lament the situation. Polish Jews had fought for Poland no less than the Poles, and now the Poles were repaying good with evil: "Poland tortured her Jewish citizens a few years ago by pogroms and excesses, and today by economic suppression. [. . .] The lording Poles of today are interested in only one thing: to ruin, and if possible, to annihilate all the Jews who live in Poland."[69]

This helplessness did not diminish in the next three years, but rather intensified in the face of deepening discrimination and poverty, waves of physical attacks, an economic boycott, pogroms, and antisemitic incitement. Antisemitic postcards in the *Der Stürmer* vein were common.[70] The anti-Jewish campaign was buoyed by what was happening in Germany, and in the second half of the 1930s became an inseparable part of the lives of Jews in Poland. They became, the newspaper *Nowy Dziennik* wrote, "despised, ridiculed, misunderstood, and often persecuted."[71]

As the nationalist and antisemitic Endecja party increased its power and advocated forced emigration of masses of Jews, the government's policy undermined the Jews' livelihood opportunities to the extent that many of them were deprived of "any chance of making a living." A clear expression of this was economic boycott of Jews, which received backing from the prime minister and minister of Internal Affairs, General Felicjan Sławoj-Składkowski. He announced at the Sejm's opening session on June 4, 1936: "Causing injury to any person in Poland is forbidden. [. . .] An economic boycott (*bojkot ekonomiczny owszem*), certainly, but we will not allow any injury."[72]

The word "certainly" (*owszem*) was interpreted as expressing a sympathetic neutral stance toward the boycott, and even as a green light from the government for the economic boycott against Polish Jews. The boycott took various shapes, such as vociferous propaganda, vigils next to Jewish stores, and violence against farmers who sold produce to Jews: "Terrorism, dispossession, boycott, and law [forbidding kosher slaughter]." Jewish workers were fired from their workplaces under pretext of "mistrust and insecurity." Chajes noted: "At the Sejm, Sławoj promises that he will not allow Jews to be beaten up, but he has nothing against economic war. That's good. No killing, only starving. What naivety. Starving the Jews won't satiate the rest. Certainly."[73] The Polish ambassador to the United States justified the acts: it was a case of "free economic competition," he claimed, and anyway, the situation of Polish Jews was far better than that of Polish farmers.[74]

"We are facing a catastrophe in the lives of Polish Jews," warned Gruenbaum in March 1936. "We are heading toward a new catastrophe in the life of our people, a catastrophe that will be greater than that of German Jewry."[75] That month he reported to Nahum Goldmann, representative of the Zionist Executive to the League of Nations and founder of the World Jewish Congress, that the danger in Poland was "great. [. . .] If we cannot overturn the situation it will reach a catastrophe similar to that of Germany, but the difference is that in Germany there were 600,000 Jews and in Poland 3 million."[76] The Yiddish writer Sholem Asch wrote: "The core of the Jewish situation is not in Germany but in Poland."[77] When Ben-Gurion met with the High Commissioner on April 2, 1936, in the Government House in Jerusalem, he said that the most pressing concern was

> our people's dead-end situation in several countries, and especially in Germany and Poland. [. . .] You may still remember what I told you two years ago, that only Piłsudski stood between Polish Jewry and a catastrophe that might be worse than in Germany. Piłsudski is dead, Piłsudski's opponents have yet to take power, but Piłsudski's party, which is still at the helm, is facing increasing antisemitic pressure. [. . .] The Polish government worries about what would be said about it in the Polish opposition newspapers, and abandons the Jews to pogroms and dispossession. And the Jews' situation, which is never good, has now become desperate, both politically and economically. One by one they lose their economic positions and must starve to death or flee. But where can they go? If it were possible to transfer Polish Jews to America or Argentina, we would do it despite our Zionist ideology. But the whole world is shutting its doors. And if there had been no place for us even in Palestine there would have been no choice for our people but to take its own life.[78]

Jabotinsky, as noted earlier, had more trust in Piłsudski's successors. In 1933 he declared: "I know all the dark sides of this country [Poland] but I also know the other side of the Polish nature. [. . .] And he [Piłsudski] saved his country, set it in order and planted the seed of fairness within it. Were I a Polish Jew I would say: 'My friend, Marshal Piłsudski's group, his faithful followers, are your last hope of finding honest allies.' I wander all over the world, from country to country, looking for allies for our cause. And I can tell you that I do not see allies more suitable and more realistic than this group of Piłsudski's followers."[79]

Eliyahu Dobkin, head of the Histadrut's Immigration Department, described his impressions at the end of October 1936 in a more moderate tone. Although he had seen Jews being beaten on a Lviv street, "still you cannot compare the atmosphere in Poland to the deeply depressing feeling of Jewish helplessness and humiliation."[80] In contrast, a grim picture was painted in June by the Histadrut envoy in Galicia, Yona Kossoy (Kesse), who reported his impressions from a tour of Galicia: "It is beyond human capacity to describe the situation. No scientific definition or economic and sociological analysis can help us imagine the horrific devastation. [. . .] Everything, everything is guided by a malicious hand towards destruction and annihilation. [. . .] Economic terrorism, fear, pogroms and actual pogroms, overt mass hatred on the street, on the train, in every establishment and on every corner — this is the atmosphere in which Polish Jewry lives, or rather, is suffocated."[81]

Zionism, said Weizmann in spring 1935, "is aimed at eternity, and compared to that, saving thousands of Jews is merely aimed at the present moment."[82] Around two years later he admitted in his testimony to the Peel Commission (The Royal Commission) that it would be difficult to overcome "the Polish tragedy." The Polish foreign minister, Colonel Beck, Weizmann reminded the members of the Commission, declared several times that "Poland has a million Jews too many." These were Jews who had been connected "with the fate and destinies of Poland for well nigh a thousand years. They went through all the vicissitudes through which the Polish nation went. They are out to make their contribution to Poland, good, bad, or indifferent, as everybody else. Why should they be singled out as being a million too many?" Weizmann protested.[83] This number, a million "superfluous Jews," was already cited in the mid-1920s by Gruenbaum — and had been repeatedly mentioned ever since.[84]

Weizmann was compelled to apologize for attributing the remarks about a million superfluous Jews to Beck. In a letter to the Polish press attaché in London, he wrote that in his testimony before the Peel Commission he "obviously was operating under a misapprehension in quoting Colonel Beck on this point." All the same he noted that there were many calls in Poland today to remove as many Jews as possible, citing as proof the Polish representative to the League of Nations speaking of the "necessity and urgency of finding new outlets for Jewish emigration. Poland had a large Jewish community which has to be enabled to settle abroad."[85]

In 1937, when the hope that Piłsudski's successors would follow in his footsteps had already faded, Jabotinsky was still convinced: "Marshal Piłsudski's group — his loyal followers" — is looking for "a fair solution to the question of the Jews in Poland, and they are the last barrier between the Jews and an all-out crusade that might have been conducted against them."[86] This defense of the colonel's regime stemmed from the assumption that only cooperating with it, on the basis of a common interest, would make it possible to promote the plan for a great emigration ("evacuation") of Polish Jews to Palestine. Therefore, the Revisionists sought to address the Polish interest, which was also a Jewish interest, and consequently Poland was perceived as Zionism's important and vital ally in the struggle over Palestine's future.

At the same time, Jabotinsky did not ignore the fact that the colonel's regime did not have the power — or perhaps the will — to stand against "the strong forces" of antisemitism in Poland, a country he had begun to describe as "the most tragic of all the world's ghettos."[87] Some twenty-five years earlier (in 1910), he had presented Poland (under Tsarist rule) as a country in which there were two peoples, and which belonged to two peoples — a statement that drew harsh criticism,[88] whereas now he began to warn that the near future for Polish Jews was black, and that a great disaster was about to befall them: "The volcano will soon start to emit its annihilating flames. [. . .] I see a terrible picture. The time to save you is running out. I know that you cannot see this, because you are occupied with day-to-day concerns. Listen to me at this hour, the midnight hour, for God's sake: let each person save himself, as long as there is time, because time is running out."[89] Jews were facing, warned Jabotinsky, "days of terror and pogroms. Days of disgrace and hopelessness."[90]

The fear of a massive immigration from Poland that would "flood" Palestine still prevailed. Until the early 1930s, most Polish Jews were perceived by many in the Zionist movement as "unsuitable" for immigration to Palestine, and therefore mass immigration seemed not only impossible, but also undesirable. During the fourth wave of immigration (the Fourth Aliyah, 1924–1926), the middle-class immigrants from Poland were perceived as bringing with them inferior culture, profiteering, and small businesses, which turned Tel Aviv, the first Hebrew city, into a city of shops. They were described as immigrants with no Zionist zeal, who would not advance the Yishuv's development and reinforcement.

Particularly harsh words against the "unorganized immigration" from

Poland that had begun in 1924 were written by Uri Zvi Greenberg (who was not yet identified with the Revisionist movement, which was yet to be founded—it was established in April 1925): "Now that the gates to all the countries are shut, the dark hour has come; the Polish peddlers have finally remembered Palestine, the end to all exiles. It is a sign that all hope is lost." Greenberg believed that it was merely a craze that had taken hold of the masses, who after hundreds of years of "natural adaptation to the climate, the language and the customs of a Slavic homeland," had suddenly found themselves torn from it and heading "without any training or ideology to Palestine, in order to establish the same Nalewkian peddlery, [and all] because [Władysław] Grabski [an economist and statesman who served as prime minister of Poland in the years 1924 and 1925 and who enacted legislation that prompted a mass emigration to Palestine known as the Fourth Aliyah] had implemented his economic reform and America had instated a quota."[91]

Such expressions of distaste were not uncommon in the 1920s, and even in the second half of the 1930s one could still hear people supporting the principle of selection, that is, giving preference to "pioneers" and "workers," and the image was still prevalent of the lower-middle-class Polish Jew who was "a little bit of a matchmaker, a little bit of a tout and a little bit of a trader."[92] The two large movements, on the Right and on the Left, preferred the immigration of young people who had had pioneer (or "military") training rather than a "popular" immigration. However, from the early 1930s the "selection principle" was adhered to only in theory, in the rhetoric. In practice, no policy of "selective immigration," preventing the exit of many of Poland's Jews, was implemented. Berl Katznelson, a leader of the Zionist Labor movement and its spiritual guide, suggested at the Twenty-First Zionist Congress that immigration was now about refugees "escaping the inferno and trying to break into Palestine,"[93] reflected the situation faithfully. Not only did the leaders of the Workers movement not stop the immigration of "bourgeois capitalists"—they encouraged it and gave it precedence.

In an attempt to imitate the "Transfer" agreement signed with the German government in 1933, and in order to encourage middle-class immigration, in 1936 the Jewish Agency's Directorate proposed to the Polish government to sign a "Clearing" agreement. The agreement was meant to enable the transfer of Jewish capital from Poland—a necessary condition for the absorption of a large immigration in Palestine—by way of purchasing Polish goods. The agreement came into force on March 1, 1937, but only very few Jewish "capitalists" showed any interest in it, and in August 1938 it was terminated. The "Evacuation" plan brought forward by the Revisionist movement also mentioned the organized liquidation of Jewish assets as a condition for the organized emigration of 750,000 Polish Jews over ten years. However, the movement did not encourage the Jewish middle class to use the window of opportunity that was open until summer 1937 and emigrate, and many of its activists preferred to stay in Poland. The immigration potential of middle-class Jews from Poland was thus not realized until 1937.

In the second half of the 1930s, a large number of Jews were knocking at the doors of the Palestine offices in Poland in order to receive certificates. Nevertheless, many of those who expressed interest chose to remain in Poland or sought other preferred emigration destinations. Not all the "capitalists" used the certificates allotted to them out of the total quota, which was now determined by the political criterion of preserving the "desirable" numeric ratio between the Jewish and the Arab population, and sometimes there was a small surplus of certificates for "capitalists" left in Poland.[94] The riots that broke out in Palestine in April 1936 added to the fear of immigrating to Israel, where the security situation seemed dangerous and alarming. Chajes wrote on June 14: "In Palestine the Arabs are on strike. The rioting has been going on for a month. The only refuge for Jews is under threat."[95] The father of Henya Heiman (Elkind), who got a student's certificate, tried at the last minute to dissuade her from boarding the train, shouting that she must not go because "in Palestine they are killing Jews."[96]

In fact, even before the riots began, many Polish Jews saw Palestine as a backwards and dangerous country. Miriam Saadia's grandfather immigrated from Łódź in 1935, and sometime later was joined by Miriam's uncle Meir and her aunt Renya, a dentist by profession. Shortly before the outbreak of war Renya returned from Tel Aviv to Poland, explaining that she could not stand the terrible weather. Her grandfather sent letters from Palestine telling his family about the hardships of living in the country and about the riots. Miriam's father, a doctor at the Jewish hospital in Łódź and who also had a private clinic, wrote to his father in Palestine that it would be a mistake for him to abandon everything just because of some incidents of antisemitism, whereas her mother never even considered emigrating, because she felt deeply embedded in Poland's cultural life: "I well remember her enthusiastic and pathos-filled speech [at the graduation ceremony of the private school in which her brother studied], praising our dear homeland, Poland!"[97]

Yaacov (Jack) Werber, a fur and textile merchant in Radom, and his wife

Emma, received letters from friends in Palestine urging them to immigrate there. But they kept postponing their trip, because despite the flagrant antisemitism, the status of second-class citizens, and the economic difficulties, "few were willing to leave their families and communities behind in Poland."[98] Sarah, the mother of Lily Folman, a Zionist activist, had always dreamed of immigrating to Palestine to follow family members who had done so in the 1920s. Her father, the secretary of the Great Synagogue in Warsaw, even traveled to Palestine to explore the possibility of emigrating, but "came right back and stayed in Warsaw. It was not easy for him to give up a good job, a comfortable apartment and a prominent social status."[99]

Polish Jews' contribution to the development of the Jewish Yishuv in Palestine manifested itself not only in emigration[100] but also in capital transfers. There is no available data as to what part of the private capital that arrived in Palestine in 1924–1939 came from Poland, and what was the share of Poland's Jewry in donations to the national funds at that time.[101] Certainly, until the middle of the 1930s the rate of capital imports from Poland out of the total imports to Palestine was the highest. On the other hand, at the Nineteenth Zionist Congress, held in Lucerne in summer 1935, Nahum Sokolow, the Polish-born journalist and Zionist leader, who in 1931 took over from Weizmann as president of the Zionist Organization, claimed that many Polish Jews were surviving thanks to the financial support they were receiving from Palestine. The pioneers, "who are working hard and earning money," were sending small amounts of money to their families, and tens of thousands of families in Poland were subsisting thanks to Palestine.[102]

Sokolow, however, gave no data. The real aid came from the Jews in the United States. Since the end of the First World War, United States Jewish aid organizations had instituted various economic and philanthropic projects. In 1938 the Joint—the American Jewish community's relief organization, founded in 1914—invested around $1,245,000 in Poland, and in 1939 the organization invested around $845,000.[103]

The links between Palestine and Poland were close. Family members in Poland sent their relatives in Palestine various food products, such as sausages, goose fat, mushrooms, and alcoholic drinks, and immigrants returned to visit their family members in Poland and stayed there for long periods.[104] They kept in contact through newspaper reports and mutual visits. Envoys and party activists from Palestine worked in Poland regularly.[105] In the years prior to the Second World War, Aba Achimeir wrote, "Jewish Warsaw was teeming with leaders of the Hatzohar and Betar movements in Palestine. Larger than the number of Hatzohar and Betar activists in Poland who [im]migrated to Palestine was the number of this movement's activists who returned from Palestine to Poland. [. . .] And why? [. . .] The lure of the masses. [. . .] in Nalewki and the adjacent street in Warsaw there were more Jews at the time than there were in the whole of Palestine."[106]

The link with Palestine was maintained by sea: sailing to one of the Black Sea ports (or to Trieste in the Adriatic Sea) and from there continuing by train to Poland. Usually travelers sailed on Romanian ships, which were "always full of 'common folk,' and slept in crowded, airless cabins holding twenty beds," and had to "plead every single day in order to get some raw cucumbers and tomatoes. Sometimes they even managed to get—if they kept asking—some roasted potatoes or poached eggs and even a piece of fish from a sardine can." When the "common folk" travelers boarded the train in Bucharest, if they managed to squeeze into the car, "they [stood] upright, crammed very tight together."[107]

The price of sailing on the Constanta-Haifa line (with a fast train to Lviv), without food and in fourth class, was 6,300 Palestine pounds (Pp) in June 1935. With food and in third class the traveler paid 8,500 Pp. On the *Har Zion* and *Har Carmel* ships, a second-class ticket cost 16,500 Pp. There were many complaints about the traveling conditions on the Romanian ships *Dacia* and *King Carol*: "There is no ventilation, you suffer greatly from the lack of air and the dirtiness [. . .] Most of the passengers are forced to sleep on the crowded deck to avoid the suffocating hall."[108] In December 1938 a new passenger line was opened, which ran two more ships that sailed once a fortnight. The Polish ships *Kościuszko* and *Polonia* sailed regularly between the Black Sea ports and Palestine.

In 1937 the Polish airline LOT started to operate flights from Lod Airport. At the request of a pupil at the Hatehiyah elementary school in Brisk (Brześć—Brest-Litovsk), which he visited on his journey to Poland, Yitzhak Yatziv, editor of *Davar Leyeladim*, told the school's pupils about the wonder of flying on an airplane—"a big aluminum bird with 14 comfortable seats"—from the airport (aerodrome) in Lod, which was still being built. Yatziv described the flight as easy and comfortable, the changing landscapes seen through the window, and the stopovers: in Rhodes (under Italian rule), in Athens, in Thessaloniki, in Sofia, and in Bucharest, and finally in Lviv and from there to Warsaw. In total, the flight took twenty-seven hours.[109]

Many Polish Jews believed that mass emigration intended to "put an end to the Diaspora" was not realizable, or that the calls for a great exodus from Poland were irresponsible, encouraging the elements that sought to drive out all the Jews and undermining the struggle against discrimination. This was not opposition to Jewish emigration itself but to emigration directed by the government.

At a press conference he held at the beginning of August 1936, Gruenbaum suggested that although there was no solution other than emigration, that solution did not rule out the continuing struggle for equal rights in Poland itself.[110] Ben-Gurion argued: "Fueling Poland's wish to get rid of the Jews might push" it to seek overseas colonies "or send the Jews to Madagascar and other islands." He had no special affection for Poland and presented a realistic position: "Poland is not interested in Jewish immigration to Palestine — it is interested in the Jews leaving, and that is it. Poland is not capable of transferring hundreds of thousands of Jews to Palestine. It does not hold the key to the country, it cannot force England to accept a massive number of Jews."[111]

The evacuation plan, Ben-Gurion argued, would weaken the Zionist movement when it became apparent that Palestine was incapable of absorbing the immigrants from Poland. In other words, the plan was both a dangerous "adventure" and hardly realistic.

The fear that Poland would find "islands" to send the Jews to as an alternative to Palestine was unfounded. When Józef Lipski, the Polish ambassador to Berlin, heard from Hitler that it was necessary to organize the emigration of Jews to some overseas colony, he responded that if Hitler succeeded in finding such a solution, they would erect a grand monument in his honor in Warsaw. A decisive stance against the claim that Palestine was the only destination for immigration was presented by the Bund (founded in Poland in 1920). One of its leaders, Heinrich Erlich, protested that as someone who had left Poland, Gruenbaum had no right to tell the Jews that "it is better to get shot in the head in Palestine than to get stabbed by a knife on the streets of Warsaw."[112]

The Bund never stopped believing that its role was to lead the struggle for equal civil rights for Polish Jews, which would be achieved after the political regime would be changed. In contrast to the Zionists, who saw themselves as "conditional citizens," the Bundists saw themselves as "connected in life and death to their homeland Poland,"[113] although the party did not oppose emigration and even helped those of its members who decided to leave.[114]

The Haredi Agudat Yisrael (founded in 1916) was no less up front in its opposition: "The Jews in Poland are fighting for our existence, in the place where we live and that we do not want to leave. [. . .] A home in which we have been residing for hundreds of years and in which we have built a life and an existence."[115] For the Bund, calling the Jews to leave Poland in droves meant that "the antisemites were not wrong."[116]

Despite his bitter disappointment over what was going on, when Chajes found out in November 1937 to his great surprise that he had won the "Golden Cross" decoration for his services to Poland, he could not contain his excitement: "In return, I gave my love to Poland and to its people. With decent and devoted work. Never with genuflecting or obsequiousness."[117] The life of a lover like Chajes was hard and bitter. "Farewell dear Poland," he wrote in June 1938, "he who is about to die, a Pole of the Mosaic faith, salutes you. [. . .] I love Poland, my homeland, which unfortunately has always played the peacock and the parrot [a quotation from Juliusz Słowacki], and is now mimicking the Hitlerites and thinking it is doing the right thing." Sometimes he was filled with hope: "Common sense, justice and clear reflection should prevail"[118]; usually, however, he was gripped with despair: "If Poland had some luck and was led by a proper chief like Piłsudski, it could stun the world."[119]

The critical attitude and the despair intensified in the second half of the 1930s. This is what the teacher Chaim Kaplan wrote in his diary on November 11, 1936:

> Today is the national holiday (independence day) of the Polish state. I see happiness on every face. But it means nothing to me, and I, as a Jew, am like a mourner among merrymakers. My mood is sad and despondent. This is not because I hate the Polish people and begrudge them their happiness and success. I do not hate any people, and especially not the people with whom I share the same homeland and the same civil concerns. But I cannot stand a "beggar on horseback" [. . .] who rules and tramples over the earth. When they were beggars, tormented and oppressed by those who were more violent and stronger, their poets dreamed of the "saving Messiah," and now that they have prevailed they want first of all to be "saved from the Jews" they hate. [. . .] Ever since they gained independence, their only life is power.[120]

The key to Palestine was not held by the Zionist movement, and certainly not by the movement in Poland, which formed the heart of Zionism. Between the two World Wars, and especially during the 1930s, its membership (including East and West Galicias) grew very rapidly:[121] In 1931, around 283,000 shekel-payers [those buying a certificate of WZO membership] voted in the elections for the Zionist Congress; in 1933 there were around

310,000 voters, in 1935 around 350,000 voters (a number that disappointed Ben-Gurion, who said: "In Congress Poland [the central area of the country] — the country of poverty, pressure and large immigration to Palestine — the number of shekel-payers reaches only 10 percent of the total Jewish population"),[122] in 1937 there were around 264,000 voters (out of around 928,000 shekel-payers), and in 1939 (four years after the secession of the Revisionist movement and its supporters from the Zionist Organization) there were around 182,000 voters (out of around a million shekel-payers).[123]

The movement was very active in all areas of the political, cultural, and educational spheres. Its Hebrew-Zionist-oriented cultural activity was extensive: educational institutions, youth movements, pioneer training, literature, and so on. Its political life manifested itself, among other things, in a deep polarization and even some violent confrontations within the movement itself, and in a struggle against the non-Zionist and anti-Zionist movements (the Bund and Agudat Yisrael) that operated within the Jewish population in Poland.[124]

Poland was also an important arena in the struggle for hegemony in the Jewish Yishuv in Palestine. The number of Zionist voters in Poland greatly influenced the balance of power between the various political movements in the Zionist Organization. The battle over the Polish "Jew's soul" and over his vote gained not only an ideological dimension, but at times even an eschatological dimension, and was seen as a struggle over the right way to salvage Jewish existence. This internal dispute was sometimes bitterer and harsher than the confrontation with the non-Zionist movements. The struggle for the Zionist vote, said Ben-Gurion, who in August 1932 embarked on a propaganda tour across Poland ahead of the election campaign for the Eighteenth Zionist Congress, demanded traveling from city to city and from town to town: "The most important thing in the whole war: to visit places. [. . .] The main thing: to visit places directly. [. . .] We have people, but there are no volunteers for the required trips. Most of the Jews [live] not in the metropolises and the big cities, but in towns. Each of the comrades must make, between today and the elections, a certain number of visits. If the Revisionists have created a movement, it is because they have understood this need."[125]

Ben-Gurion's busy schedule was dedicated to organizing the fight against the Revisionist movement, which had started to gain momentum; there was almost no mention in his diary of any encounter with Polish Jews.[126] As the elections for the Eighteenth Zionist Congress in Prague in April 1933 neared, Ben-Gurion returned from Poland to lead the crucial fight against the Revisionists. The latter enjoyed great support, he wrote, among "the Jews on the street" and the masses who "want to go," that is, leave Poland. He contrasted "the Jews on the street"—the "simple" Jewish public—with the "ideologically engaged" Zionist public.[127] Ben-Gurion accused the Revisionists of hoping "for a world war and a military adventure so that one of the sides would declare a Jewish state [. . .]." He wondered: "Do we want a world war, in which Jews would be slaughtered, quite apart from the risk of universal destruction that would threaten Europe?"[128] In his view, Poland was the center of pioneer emigration and the great reservoir of supporters for the workers' parties in the elections for the Zionist Congresses, and therefore also the arena in which "a fateful war" was fought against the Revisionist movement, which he described as "Zionist Hitlerism," and this was "a bitter and desperate war."[129] At the same time he ignored the situation of "the Jews on the street" and failed to warn against the dangerous future awaiting them.

The political struggle that was brewing in the Zionist movement was also described by Nahum Sokolow. In five letters he sent from Warsaw to Berl Locker, a member of the Zionist Directorate in London, he described his impressions (which later appeared under the title *A Journey to Poland in 1934*). Sokolow knew the reality in Poland, his birthplace, but what troubled him in 1934 was mainly "the partisan stupidity." He was referring to the political factionalism that was tearing the Jewish public from within,[130] and the negative role played by the sensational press, which was propagating "fictional reality" and spreading false rumors and false hopes.

The accusation of instilling false hope was laid mainly at the Revisionist movement and its leader. These false hopes, he believed, fed on the distress and the wish to leave Poland. Revisionism was inflaming the Jewish street by encouraging uncontrolled and even dangerous emigration, and was toying with the idea of cooperating with Poland's militaristic circles. In response, Sokolow proposed to publish a proper Zionist newspaper in Hebrew disseminating "propaganda for wholesome Zionism instead of sickly imaginary visions." What he appraised as the quasi-hysterical situation of Polish Jews was therefore not only the result of objective conditions, but also the product of a psychic state that gave rise to delusions. The Polish government led by Piłsudski had fought the rioters and the manifestations of antisemitism. Although Piłsudski's death might, in Sokolow's view, lead to the takeover of "a kind of Polish Hitlerism" and a wave of antisemitism, he pinned his hopes on a strong regime that would suppress such phenomena. "There is a world of difference," he wrote, between Fascist Italy and

Poland. The latter may be a Catholic country with a tradition of romantic revolutionism, and its hatred of Jews may come "from the bottom," from the masses, but its government rejected nationalism and race theories; it idolized the state and the military, and did not contain "the soil from which can grow an antisemitism which basks in the cult of descent and race, in dreams and delusions of a Polish national uniqueness."[131]

Sokolow directed his criticism not only toward Jabotinsky, but also toward the delusional picture painted by the poet Uri Zvi Greenberg: "Polish Jewry, sad and worried for its daily bread, is not marked by degeneration. It is marked by the sign of royalty, if in Jewish cities and towns can rise (today!) such a popular movement as 'Brit Hahayal,'[132] evoking a longing for heroism like that of the ancient conquerors of Canaan."[133]As he watched the Betar members march through the streets of Warsaw, Greenberg wrote with exhilaration: "The Jordan Guard has risen on the banks of the Vistula; the Hebraic battalion which will grow from tens of thousands to hundreds of thousands strong."[134]

Eschatological visions are one thing, and political activity another. Although Poland did not hold the "key" to Palestine, it seemed able to influence the key's holder: the government of Great Britain. The political future of Palestine had become "a Polish problem," and the Zionist movement was hoping to gain the support of the Polish government in the corridors of power in London and in the League of Nations in Geneva. The Polish government oppressed the Jews and flirted with the Zionists, wrote Chajes in May 1934; its political line was "an agreement with the Zionists."[135]

The helplessness of the Jewish society in Poland in the 1930s was caused neither by the deep rift in Polish Jewish society nor by the debate within the Zionist movement. The bitter irony was, in the words of Ezra Mendelsohn, "During the inter-war period Poland seemed to be the ideal environment for Jewish politics."[136] Indeed, all camps and factions of Polish Jewry had substantial freedom of action until the last moment, but none of them had a response to the reality of the 1930s, and especially not to the situation that took hold on September 1, 1939.

Who were the "million superfluous Jews"? "Where are the [real] Jews?" wondered the German Jewish writer Alfred Döblin (whose parents were born in Poland), author of the novel *Berlin Alexanderplatz*, about his Jewish acquaintances in Berlin, because the Jews he knew around him did not strike him as "genuine" (that is, authentic) Jews. "In Poland," was the answer he got.[137] At the end of September 1924, Döblin went out to "discover the Jews" and see whether there was any truth in the opinion that the millions of Jews living in Poland and Galicia were a cohesive group. He traveled for around two months all over Poland, and on returning to Berlin published his impressions in the book *Journey to Poland* (*Reise in Polen*).

Döblin discovered that the Jews were not only recognized as a national minority, but they indeed formed a real nation: "The Jews have their own costumes, their own language, religion, manners and mores, their ancient national feeling and national consciousness."[138] His description, however, depicted a multifaceted Jewish society, divided by classes, parties, and factions, as well as by areas. He uncovered the roots of the tension between the "old" and the "new," and described the alienation felt by a large number of Jews toward the Polish culture and the poverty and deprivation of many of them.

Döblin was not alone. Travelogues from the 1920s and 1930s chose to highlight the bleak parts of Jewish life in Poland. "Their lives are hell on earth. They all want to escape," wrote the French journalist Albert Londres at the end of 1929. In a series of pieces he published in the newspaper *Le Petit Parisien*, Londres portrayed a dreary life of poverty and hardship, describing an imaginary scene: if King David II had arrived on Warsaw's Nalewki Street, the main street in the Jewish quarter,

> 360,000 kaftans with short boots, flat caps, and flapping beards, emerge from cellars and underground corridors in which no gentile ever stepped foot, stumble up hundred-year-old rickety staircases, springing from ditches, alleys, dead ends, emerging from yards, leaving markets, leaving stores, abandoning their houses of worship with their prayer shawls still on their heads and their phylacteries still on their foreheads and part of their arms, their hands swaying like blossoms, bursting into Nalewki [Street] and crying out: "Long live the King! Long live King David the Second!"[139]

Descriptions of degenerate poverty and degradation can frequently be found in memoirs from the period. This is, for example, how Binah Bojman described her grandfather's house in Warsaw:

> The only room served during the week as a kitchen, dining room, workplace for grandpa and the two unmarried daughters, and living space for seven people; the kitchen and the stove stood in one dark end, a dining table stood in the middle of the room, and along the walls and windows stood the beds. The room also contained a bucket of water for washing—the tap and the restroom were in the courtyard—and two sewing

> machines, and various belongings scattered around. The room was humble and very cramped, and held the family get-togethers.[140]

The small house where Mordechai Peltz lived as a child in the village of Mośćiska contained two rooms: in the spacious room there were a big bookcase, a wide sofa bed, and next to it a simple and large table. In a second room stood two old beds and a linen trunk, and opposite them, up against the wall, an old wardrobe. The kitchen contained a brick oven and stove. Opposite it stood a kind of table: a few planks attached to a stand. Water was carried in two buckets attached to a yoke from around 400 yards away, and a few tens of yards away from the house was the restroom—a rickety shed exposed to the rain and the snow, with a hole in the ground covered by a wooden board.[141] Jack Werber's family, a family of nine plus a maid, lived in a three-room apartment in Radom:

> A living room, a bedroom and a kitchen, an apartment that was considered quite fancy in those days. I slept in the room in which my sisters had slept until they got married, and the maid slept in the kitchen. We were quite well-to-do, but most of the Jews in the city struggled. Large families with six or seven children often lived in one room. Running water was rare in the houses, and they would usually have one pot with clean water and one pot with used water. Common outdoors restrooms served all the apartment buildings' residents.[142]

Later their situation improved and the family moved to a three-story building on Radom's main street. Indeed, many lived in one-room apartments, basement apartments, and attics; sometimes several people shared a single bed. Some of the descriptions of poverty and squalor served ideological purposes, but not all of them were exaggerated. Most Polish Jews were self-employed and did not keep any employees; working youths earned very little, and the rate of those classed as economically inactive in the Jewish population was around 60 percent. Jewish hired workers were employed in workplaces where the salary was low, and the number of people needing aid and charity reached around 25 percent of the Jewish population. However, the grim descriptions presented only one aspect of Jewish life. Jewish society in Poland also included a middle class of professionals, big industrialists, and merchants.[143] This, for example, is how Yohanan Bader described his affluent family's house in the center of Krakow:

> Their large apartment and our office were on the first floor, and our apartment was on the second floor. My parents' apartment was like a

museum. Antique furniture, eighteenth-century china, pictures by famous painters, and in the living room two antique carpets. [. . .] Our apartment (1722 sq. ft.) had four rooms. [. . .] Modern furniture alongside antiques in the cupboards. Parquet floor—oak floorboards, covered with Persian rugs. [. . .] My wife would sometimes host big receptions for 20, 30, 40 guests.[144]

The apartment of the Kleinboims, who got married in October 1933, in the Praga district on the northern bank of the Vistula, was more modest. It was in a large apartment building and had four rooms, including a spacious study, which also served as a reception room.[145] The apartment of the Folman family, parents and three daughters, was a typical middle-class Warsaw Jews' apartment. They had a live-in Polish maid who was in charge of the housework, and after she served the meal she would sit down to eat in the kitchen, where she also slept on a folding bed. Once a month came a professional laundress who did the laundry on the stove in the kitchen in a large tin tub.[146]

Döblin and Londres were also interested in the future awaiting Polish Jews. Döblin cited the Zionists' position, but his sympathy lay with his interlocutors, who opposed Zionism. He thought that Zionism only offered a solution for the very few, overlooking the millions of Jews living within the borders of the Polish Republic, as they were determined after the First World War and the Russia-Poland war (which ended with the Treaty of Riga, on March 1921).

Another travel book, the novel by the modernist writer and poet Jacob Glatstein, is clouded by a vague and uncertain future. In summer 1934 Glatstein visited his hometown of Lublin, twenty years after having left it to immigrate to the United States. In a novel first published in installments in the Zionist weekly *Der Yiddisher Kemfer* (*The Zionist Fighter*), and then in the book *Ven Yash Iz Gekumen* (*The Glatstein Chronicles: Homecoming at Twilight*, 2010: p. 226),[147] he described a mosaic of Jewish characters. One of them, Finkel, says: "They are pogromists by instinct. They'd be happy to bathe in our blood . . . They hate us for observing the Sabbath and they hate us for violating the Sabbath. They hate pious Jews and they hate freethinkers who eat lobster. They hate our capitalists and they hate our beggars. They hate our reactionaries and they hate our radicals, those who earn their bread and die three times a day from starvation."[148]

Another character, the lawyer Neifeld, says:

Believe it or not, I was once an ardent Polish patriot. In fact there was a time when all the Jewish youth was patriotic. When Poland gained its independence, we became confident and held our heads high. The Polish soil of our grandfathers and great-grandfathers seemed doubly dear to us. But soon we saw our mistake. We began to be persecuted at every step, pushed and kicked around, hard enough to make us realize that Poland was not freed for us, that Polish independence did not include ours.[149]

In April 1938, Glatstein published the poem "Good Night, World" (A Gute Nakht, Velt), a bitter farewell to the cruel and degenerate world of the "gentiles" and a call to return to the ghetto, to the Jewish world: "World, I stride with joy to the quiet ghetto-light [. . .] I kiss you, disheveled Jewish life. Within me weeps the joy of returning." In the novel, the lawyer Neifeld describes Polish Jewry as "a burning bush." Dan Miron, who translated the book into Hebrew, wrote in the afterword that Glatstein saw Polish Jewry as standing on the edge of a precipice, though not as a dying community, but rather as "a community whose very cries, out of poverty and fear, testify to the plenitude of life."[150]

"The plenitude of life" in all areas of Polish Jewish lives did not manifest itself only in "cries." Until September 1939, they continued to maintain a wide variety of communal, party-political, and autonomous cultural activities. They had the political freedom to organize and act in both the autonomous Jewish context and the nationwide Polish one. Until the end of August 1939, Poland was the arena of some fierce internal struggles, which were conducted both in the general Jewish public and within the Zionist movement. A sense of impending annihilation was to be found mainly in apocalyptic literature and prophecies of doom.[151]

Visitors from Palestine often saw a one-dimensional picture of Jewish life in Poland. In his travel notes from the early 1930s, the educator David Hacohen called Poland "my motherland" and "the cradle of my childhood," for which upon returning he felt "the great pain of the son who returns home to be met by a stepmother" (Polish Jews, wrote Jabotinsky in a similar vein, were an organic part of the soil and the air in Poland).[152] Hacohen described, for example, a conversation with a Jew living in Volye, who told him:

Our sons who [im]migrated to Palestine begged us to follow them, but we were deeply tied to this land. What have the gentiles not done to us? They destroyed, robbed, massacred and abused us. But we are like this tree with its many branches: they came at us with saws and axes, they felled the trunk, and the root remained. We sprouted again, we grew again, and it is hard to uproot us. But these Poles are turning the tree up on its roots. And as the Jew spoke in his grainy language, full of figures and color, I saw before me a great forest, whose trees had been uprooted by cruel hands, turning the roots on their heads.[153]

The only ray of hope that Hacohen found in Poland was "Palestine in Warsaw" — the Grochów training farm of the Hechalutz and Hashomer Hatzair, not far from the capital; by contrast, Jewish Warsaw struck him as resembling "a ruined ants nest":

> Like herring in a barrel, the three hundred and fifty thousand Jews live in crammed and crowded conditions on a few Warsaw streets. And the insult cries out: gentile Warsaw is so spacious, full of greenery, light and air, that you cannot feel the masses of people living in it. And against it Jewish Warsaw — crammed, crowded, full of filth and squalor, containing neither garden nor tree, and resembling a ruined ants nest [. . .] And if on the Jewish streets there is still some regard for order and cleanliness — then inside the courtyards (and some courtyards serve hundreds of people) what a terrible mess, dirtiness, degeneration and neglect. In this filth run around the children of Israel, with their pale faces and black eyes. I pity you, the poor children of Polish Jewry.[154]

Between September 25 and October 27, 1933, Berl Katznelson also made a roughly month-long trip to Poland. Prior to that he spent a ten-day vacation in Munkács, Czechoslovakia, where he enjoyed spas and massages. In one of the training farms in Poland he slept "on a bed shared with 20 young men" and saw slums, "poor and dirty Jews," and children covered with rags "like kittens." "All these will be lost," he wrote, "if we cannot offer them swift refuge in Palestine. All the sources of their livelihood — both material and spiritual — are drying up. And we are still very far from knowing how to save them."[155]

The demographer Yaacov Leszczynski saw the Jewish Poland of 1937 as a world of "two realities": at times a depressing and disintegrating world, and at others a colorful and lively one. On the one hand — assemblies, demonstrations, protest marches, and revolutionary songs. In one week, he wrote, there were around 400 rallies attended by at least 200,000 Jews, criticizing the government's policy. On the other hand he described Poland as a country in which Jews were being attacked and their property plundered: in the first three weeks of September, around 500 Jews were injured. One reality is "abstract and spiritual," and the other "concrete and practical, a reality of blood." Leszczynski had no doubt that the first reality would end up triumphing. The question was only "how to bear the other, bitter reality, how to hold on until salvation comes?"[156]

The journalist and activist Mendel Singer, who visited Poland in 1937, described the influence of rising antisemitism on Jewish students as no less tragic than the fate of Jewish youth in Nazi Germany: the difference was that in Poland there were no pogroms but a "collective lynching."[157]

Yitzhak Yatziv arrived in Poland in summer 1937, having left it around twenty-five years earlier. His impressions from the trip are infused with melancholy:

> How do they walk—these Jews—on Polish soil keeping this appearance, a foreign, fearsome appearance, so that someone who has not seen them grouped together for many years is shocked to his core on first encountering them, as I was when I walked from Marszałkowska Street to Nowolipie Street on the day I arrived in Warsaw. The same Jews, when they walk around in Jerusalem, and even more so in Tel Aviv, with their satin clothes on the Sabbath, their talliths under their arms, their sashes on their waists—they are different people, relieved of their terrifying appearance and filled with colorful expansiveness. How are things in Warsaw? Frayed nerves, restlessness, flared tempers, fear, despair, hopelessness. It all seems bad. Every conversation with the locals adds to the bleakness.[158]

Yatziv spoke about the pogroms in Brisk in May 1937 and about the spread of antisemitic propaganda shared by the "street," the courts, and the "regime": "The air is stuffy and suffocating."[159] When he returned to Palestine, he was asked as he got off the plane in Lod: "Is the situation of the Jews in Poland really as bad as the newspapers describe it?" His answer was: "Comparatively speaking, their condition is much more difficult than the situation of German Jews. The financial reserves dwindled a long time ago, they are being deprived of their economic positions, prevented from gaining new ones, the incitement against them and the abuse are like Hitler's, with the addition of pogroms and an economic boycott—that is, a hot and cold pogrom."[160]

On February 24, 1938, Arthur Ruppin, an economist and sociologist who directed the Palestine office of the Zionist Organization beginning in 1908, arrived in Poland, staying there until early March and returning at the end of the month for a short visit, which he described, ironically, as a "victory tour." Ruppin was struck by the manifestations of antisemitism, but more than that by the manifestations of poverty. On March 29 he visited the Jewish slum in Warsaw and saw "a market of rags and old shoes, rusty locks, apartments in tiny dark basements. Unbelievable." The following day he visited the town of Grójec, about an hour and a half's ride from Warsaw, where he was also struck mainly by the poverty. The solution he proposed was to appoint a committee of economic experts, "which will draw up a plan to improve the situation in the long run. [. . .] A lot can be achieved through better organization of the Jewish economy," he assessed.[161]

On the ship on which Yitzhak Tabenkin, a Labor Zionist leader and leader of the Kibbutz Hameuchad movement, sailed at the beginning of September 1938 from Haifa to Brindisi, on his way to the Hakibbutz Hameuchad convention in Józefów, there were also around thirty Arabs, from Iraq and Palestine, some in uniform, on their way to a Nazi gathering in Nuremberg. They distributed among the passengers a brochure in English against the Jews in Palestine. Poland itself, Tabenkin wrote, "is constantly under the threat of Nuremberg." And the Jews "of course, for now, are getting on with their lives. Making a living is their main concern."[162] During this visit, Tabenkin learned "the value of Aliyah Bet [illegal immigration to Palestine]. Without it there is almost no life for the movement, because there is no air to breathe." He was mainly preoccupied with the question of uniting the pioneers' movements. He saw the main value of illegal immigration in ensuring the continuing existence of the movement in Poland.

In order to avoid taking a German plane displaying a swastika, Moshe Shertok (Sharett), at the time the head of the political department of the Zionist Executive, took off on the morning of April 17, 1939, about a month after the St. James Conference ended with a Zionist defeat, on a special flight that inaugurated the British Airways London-Warsaw line. The plane took off at about noon, and at four in the afternoon landed for a short stopover in Berlin. He remembered: "During the half hour we were held there I was horrified. Any clerk or policeman seemed like a kind of bird of prey, a creature from the underworld, outside the human realm. To exacerbate the impression I was placed in a fenced-in area designed for passengers in transit, and in this enclosure I felt like I was in a detention camp. It was a nightmare, a terrifying dream in broad daylight."

At 6:30 p.m., Shertok landed at Warsaw Airport. The purpose of his trip was to discuss the Clearing agreement with Polish foreign ministry officials. Bodyguards from the Sadran organization led him "to the poor Jewish corners," where he saw "a gloomy Jewry." More than the scenes of old age, frailty, and pernicious poverty, he was dismayed by "the deathly paleness of the children's faces. Eyes and no more!"[163] The Zionist politics in Poland also filled him with despondency: "I have never seen such a face of Zionism in my life. Although from everything I had read and heard—especially from Sokolow's letters, which I remember well—I knew what to expect, nevertheless my unmediated encounter with this Zionist reality shocked me."

There was unruly, rebellious behavior, and a vengeful joy at the Directorate's expense for its political failure at the roundtable conference. Shertok visited a school belonging to the "Tarbut" education network, where he found a "decent poverty," as well as the offices of Keren Hayesod and Keren Kayemet and the Hechalutz premises in Warsaw and Łódź. On April 21 he returned to London, and on the way was "racked with self-criticism"—perhaps he had not said what he should have said. His first encounter with "East-European Diaspora" made him reflect: "I was too worried about fortifying the public for the blow that is about to befall them and stirring them towards trust in their own powers and towards self-action, and I failed to call for revolt against the new policy and for a sharp response. I failed to point out the malaises of Polish Zionism itself and was not firm enough in fighting against them."[164]

The reflections of a temporary guest, whose familiarity with Polish Jewry was superficial, led him to believe that if only he had spoken straightforwardly he would have led his listeners to a decisive and effective political action to preserve their rights.

In July 1939, Yehuda Helman, a member of Kibbutz Gvat and an envoy of the Hechalutz movement in Poland, recorded his impressions from a tour of the movement's training farms, from Pinsk to Gdynia: "This is the first time I am visiting many cities and seeing large numbers of Jews, and what a terrible picture is emerging of Jewish life. For the most part they are ashamed and scared to speak Yiddish. On the train they are scared to read a Jewish newspaper, so as not to attract attention, lest they be recognized as Jews. Fear is everywhere."[165]

In his bitterness over the opposition to the Evacuation Plan, Jabotinsky protested in an open letter, "A word to Polish Jews," which he published on November 6, 1936, in the Revisionist weekly *Unzer Velt*, that Polish Jews preferred to continue living "in their narrow and shabby alleyways" and were ignoring his warnings: "Polish Jews! You should be ashamed of yourselves before God and man."[166]

On August 30, Anthony Biddle, United States ambassador to Poland, wrote to Cordell Hull, the U.S. secretary of state, that in Poland, like in Romania, Hungary, and other countries, the Jewish problem had become a major social, economic, and political issue. He added that Beck, the Polish foreign minister, had stated that this was a problem that "our generation must solve," because the future looked ominous. The Secretary of State replied that if Western countries encouraged emigration, they would only hasten decrees whose sole aim was to abandon masses of people to the mercy of the world. This problem had no global solution, he argued.[167]

Sir Howard Kennard, the British ambassador to Warsaw, wrote in November 1938 to Foreign Secretary Halifax that most of the Poles "regard it as inevitable that in order to induce a state of mind favorable to emigration among the Jews, their position here must be made less comfortable. [. . .] Local excesses — not organized, as recently in Germany, but more or less spontaneous — are of not infrequent occurrence."[168]

Around seven years earlier, in November 1931, the German representative in Warsaw had explained to the Foreign Ministry in Berlin: "As is well known, hatred for the Jews is rooted in the ideology of Polish National-Democracy." Therefore, he concluded, Piłsudski's fight against this ingrained antisemitism stood no chance.[169] In a similar vein, Weizmann explained to Rabbi Stephen S. Wise, a communal leader and leading American Zionist: "I think the Polish situation is worse than even the German. There we deal with a people which are used to make pogroms, entirely uncontrollable, and with a Jewish community which is more numerous than the German one, and with much less power of resistance; they are already half starved."[170]

Martin Buber, who arrived in Poland for a lecture tour under the auspices of the Hebrew University in March or April 1939, suggested after returning to Jerusalem that the deep hatred for the Jews in Poland was not the result of "a propaganda campaign directed from above," as in Germany, but was ingrained antisemitism.[171]

As noted earlier, Jabotinsky analyzed the situation differently. German racist antisemitism was an "endemic disease" that lurked in the "German's nature," whereas Polish antisemitism was an unfortunate result of an "objective" state of affairs. It was an unavoidable consequence of the fact that the large Jewish population posed competition in the employment market, thus giving rise to hostility and actions designed to push the Jews to the periphery of the economic activity.[172] In Poland, Jabotinsky claimed, antisemitism was stirred up and stoked by the demagogy of the right wing camp (the "Endecja") under the influence of the racist antisemitism in Germany. However, a large part of the Polish public was not drawn to this antisemitism. It could be fought, he estimated, and even weakened. Jabotinsky's view of Polish antisemitism did not change even after the war broke out. He wrote: "The author has never found the merest trace of resentment among Jews who have emigrated from Poland towards the Polish people, nor even towards the Polish state."[173]

It is unclear whether Jabotinsky truly believed that there was no "authentic" Polish antisemitism or was simply catering to the ears of the Polish government. Moreover, many Polish Jews, including some who did not feel any deep affinity with Polish history, concurred: there was no comparison between Poland and Germany. At the beginning of 1938, the Society of Polish Jews for the League of Nations presented a memorandum to the Federation of League of Nations Societies' Minorities Commission. The memorandum described the question of Polish Jews as a problem that required a radical solution within an international framework. The reason for the Jews' situation, the memorandum said, was the large disproportionate concentration of Jews on Polish soil. Not only could they not be assimilated, but they actually did their best to not be assimilated. Most of the Jews did not see themselves as Poles but as citizens of Palestine, and "the Polish nation will never accept the fact that a foreign element makes up such a high percentage of its population as the Jews currently do." The Jewish question in Poland was not therefore "inherently a question of race or religion, but first and foremost a question of political economy." The only solution for it was to demand that Western countries take in a large Jewish immigration.[174] The authors of the memorandum disagreed with Jabotinsky on a fundamental point: the possible destination for immigration. On the other hand, in the Jewish press in Poland, Nazism was portrayed as a primeval phenomenon of "bloodthirsty hunters," which was taking Europe back to the Middle Ages. The Yiddish poet Kadia Molodowsky, for example, described Nazi Germany as "crouching like a pig over Europe" — Poland included.[175]

The debate about the reasons for antisemitism was academic.[176] In February 1937, the Camp of National Unity (OZON: Oboz Zjednoczenia Narodowe) was founded, and the "popular" antisemitism turned into policy. "The Polish government says that if there is no Jewish emigration from Poland, it would have to move from biological antisemitism to active revolutionary antisemitism, and it says this out of friendship," remarked Ben-Gurion at the Mapai Central Committee meeting on December 15, 1938.[177] The concern that Ben-Gurion showed for the fate of Polish Jews was no less than Jabotinsky's, but his words were said in closed forums rather than public speeches or printed in the press.

The antisemitic incidents and anti-Jewish legislation in Poland were a source for concern, which manifested itself in the frequent use of words such as "extinction," "annihilation," and "calamity." This catastrophic rhetoric fed on a series of violent antisemitic attacks, preceded by a propaganda and incitement campaign in the Sejm and in the media. Violent incidents against Jews, in which many Jews were injured, took place as early as the end of 1931 and continued in the following years. These incidents caused despair and alarm: "[Polish Jews have] nothing to live on today and no hope for tomorrow."[178]

After Piłsudski's death the pogroms multiplied, and from 1935 to 1937 a wave of violence swept across Poland, especially in the towns. Reports of pogroms in Poland during 1936 and 1937, as well as autobiographies written years later, portray a Jewish community permeated by a powerful sense of mortal danger, an awesome fear that gave rise to apocalyptic rhetoric that talked of Jews living on an active volcano that was likely to erupt at any moment. More than a hundred attacks on Jewish communities as well as many hundreds of attacks on individual Jews were reported in those years.

The Jews of Poland, as well as the Jews who followed events in Poland, had reason to be concerned. In Grodno, a pogrom started on June 7, 1935, after an altercation between a Jew and a Pole who had fought over a young woman's favors at a nightclub, in which the Jew stabbed his rival, and he died of his wounds. Hasia Bornstein-Bilitzka testified: "On midday on Friday, at the end of the funeral, the mourners, around one thousand strong, left the cemetery armed with axes, clubs and butchers' knives, and started rioting in the city center. All along Dominikanska Street, the city's main street, they smashed shop windows and looted stores owned by Jews. From there they continued to the cross and parallel streets and started attacking Jewish houses in the neighborhood." The riots in the city went on for several more days, and during them two Jews were murdered and more than forty injured: "Nothing was ever the same again. We returned to live in the house, to speak with our Polish neighbors, but the rupture could not be healed."[179]

On March 9, 1936, on market day, there was a pogrom in the town of Przytyk in the Kielce Voivodeship. The Jews made up around 87 percent of the approximately 2,500 residents of Przytyk. An incited mob of peasants from the vicinity attacked Jewish stalls and destroyed several of them, and the riots spread across the town. Houses and stores belonging to Jews were looted. The riots resulted in three Jews killed, twenty-two injured, and great damage to property. Boris Smolar, an eyewitness, sent this report on March 11: "The mob, previously incited by antisemitic leaders [. . .] gathered in the marketplace, shouting anti-Jewish epithets. Polish police attempted to halt the mob from invading Jewish streets, but retreated when they failed, leaving a free hand to the rioters."[180]

The Jews of Przytyk defended themselves with weapons and drove away the attackers. A Polish peasant was killed by a gunshot. The Polish police, who arrived after the event, searched for weapons in Jewish houses. Fourteen were charged and sentenced to long periods in prison (the Jew who shot the pistol was sentenced to fourteen years and six others to five and six years). The rioters, by contrast, were let off with light punishments, and four of them were released due to lack of evidence.

In response, the Bund's Central Committee announced a national protest strike on March 17, which was joined by a massive number of Jews. The riots in Przytyk became a symbol of the Jewish right to self-defense and the Jews' determined public reaction in defense of their lives and property. A. S. Yuris, the Histadrut envoy to Poland, wrote: "Przytyk—not only riots, but also uprising and self-defense. In this sense the situation of Polish Jews is not like that in Germany. In Poland you can organize the resistance of 4 million Jews."[181] Following the trial, the carpenter and poet Mordechai Gebirtig (Marcus Bertig) from Krakow's Kazimierz district, whose poems were bought in 1921 by the Jewish-American impresario Molly Picon and distributed all over the Jewish world, wrote his poem "Undzer shtetl brent" (Our town is burning), a poem mistakenly attributed to the Holocaust period: "The whole town's up in flames / And you stand there looking on / With futile folded arms / [. . .] With your blood douse the fire, / Don't stand there, brothers, looking on [. . .]."[182] Not everyone, however, thought this was "a pogrom in the full sense of the word."

The wave of riots continued through 1936. A pogrom took place between June 1 and June 5 in the town of Mińsk, Mazowiecki, about twenty-five miles east of Warsaw, after a sergeant in the Polish army was shot dead by a demobilized Jewish soldier because of a personal dispute. Dozens of Jews were injured, many hid in basements, and more than 3,000 fled to Warsaw. In the course of 1936 there were around 180 organized riots and sporadic attacks, in which around 3,000 Jews were hurt. The violent antisemitic incidents continued in 1937—in May in Brisk, in June in Czestochowa around 125 miles southwest of Warsaw, and in other places. Around fifty Jews were murdered.[183] According to a memorandum drawn up in June 1937 by the Eretz Israel Association for the League of Nations, sixty Jews were injured in a pogrom in Brest-Litovsk on May 13, and two of them died of their wounds; stores and apartments were robbed and destroyed, and the entire Jewish quarter was set on fire. In 1936, 341 attacks on Jews took place in the

Białystok region. This grave situation, the memo asserted, called for international intervention.[184]

In July 1936 and at the end of 1937, Leszczynski wrote two detailed reports that described the "pogroms and riots, the attacks and assaults on Jews in Poland in 1935–1937," and were based on accounts in the Jewish press. The reports were submitted to the World Jewish Congress, and when their contents became known to the Polish consul in Geneva, he threatened that if they got published, the activities of the Jewish Congress in Poland would be banned. The Executive Committee decided to forego the publication in order not to risk its continuing activities in Poland. The reports were shelved in the organization's archive and were destroyed with the rest of the archive on the eve of the Nazi occupation of France. Leszczynski reconstructed them in 1952.[185]

Around 150 nationalists (inspired by the "March on Rome" led by Mussolini in October 26–27, 1922) marched to the town of Myślenice near Krakow to free the town from its Jews, attacked the police station, and burned Jewish-owned stores. They also tried to set fire to the synagogue before fleeing to the surrounding woods. The leader of the rioters was arrested, and in his defense claimed that he was demonstrating against the connection between foreign tycoons "serving the Jews" and the Marxist parties and trade unions.

"The fall is approaching," wrote Chajes in September 1937, "here and there we witness attacks on Jews. Here and there the authorities interfere and try to prevent them. But the situation is not good."[186] Two months later, on November 29, fall turned into winter: "The situation is getting worse. In the universities there are clashes with the Jewish youth. Afterwards—smashing shop windows, shouting and demanding a ghetto for the Jewish students." The Polish traders "demand precedence, pressure, the eradication of Jewish trade."[187]

On January 12, 1939, Gruenbaum wrote to the Polish prime minister that although it was true that the government defended the state from the antisemitic factions "who wish to follow in the footsteps of Germany, Hungary or Italy," this was mainly passive defense. It was also true, he wrote, that the Polish government and the Zionist movement had a joint interest in the Jews leaving Poland, "however it does not mean that I agree that the throngs of dispossessed Jews should be goaded by laws that restrict their rights, terror on the streets of cities and towns, and an economic boycott, and that their numbers should be artificially and systematically controlled."[188]

To express the Yishuv's solidarity with Polish Jews, the National Committee organized a mass assembly at Beit Haam in Tel Aviv on March 15, 1936, which was attended by around 2,000 people. The main speakers, Gruenbaum and the writer Sholem Asch, devoted their speeches mainly to the "slaughter decree"—a law that was proposed at the beginning of 1936 and passed in a toned-down version in January 1937, and that allowed kosher slaughter only for domestic consumption. The law was perceived as symbolizing the dispossession of Polish Jews, a process "which is making the lives of millions of Polish Jews impossible, and will lead to a flight that will cause a terrible catastrophe for hundreds of new refugees."[189] It was seen as an ongoing pogrom, at once economic, physical, and religious. All the assembly could offer was a declaration "that the Yishuv will not rest or be silent until the world responds to our call and ensures the lives and rights of the Jews in Poland."[190]

In Poland, in stark contrast to the situation in Germany, Austria, and Czechoslovakia, the Jews were not deprived of their civil rights, and they defended themselves, formed aid committees, and went on protest strikes. Polish Jews protested against discrimination, antisemitic incitement, and violence at the universities. Not all the Jewish press saw the pogroms as an existential danger, and it highlighted the organization of self-defense and of political and public protest (on October 19, 1937, a partial strike was called in the Jewish community) and brought optimistic news. In July 1939, for example, the Municipal Committee of Dobromil, following the suggestion of one of its Jewish members, decided to name one of the town's streets after Chaim Nachman Bialik, the most influential Hebrew poet in modern times, to mark the fifth anniversary of his death.[191]

The attacks against Jews came in other guises. Avraham Zelig Kalkstein began his studies in Germany in the early 1930s. In 1936, Nazi students persecuted him in order to expel him from the university and falsely accused him of stealing books from its library. He was charged based on false testimonies and sentenced to six months in prison. After being charged with "racial defilement," Kalkstein fled to Poland. The German authorities approached the authorities in Poland and demanded he be put on trial, and he was sentenced in Warsaw's Municipal Court to three weeks in prison. Kalkstein appealed and was completely exonerated. The prosecutor appealed again, and the trial was transferred to the Supreme Court, which reversed the decision and returned the case to the Municipal Court.[192]

Many other Jewish students suffered incitement and humiliations, and their numbers decreased "alarmingly" following the "numerus clausus" policy.[193] In September 1937, the Polish education minister published "the ghetto benches decree," which enabled universities to oblige Jewish students to sit in specially assigned seats. Students who refused to abide by the decree were expelled or punished.[194]

On November 29, 1938, the Jewish student Karol Zellermeyer was stabbed several times at Lviv University and died. Around 40,000 Jews attended his funeral, but only the university's rector and two professors showed up. The "Endecja" militias prevented Jewish students from entering, "and the rector watched it all from his office."

On the same day a Jewish soldier was killed in a clash with Czech soldiers. He was buried in the town of Cieszyn with great ceremony, and the pułkownik (colonel) who eulogized him called him "comrade" and "spoke from the bottom of his heart about equality etc."[195] On December 6, Shmuel Probler, a student at the Lviv Technical College, died of knife wounds he had sustained two weeks earlier. Throngs of Jews from all over Poland arrived for his funeral, and again the rector and a few professors were kind enough to go to the cemetery. When Rabbi Ezekiel Levin eulogized the murdered student and blamed the university authorities for not giving minimal protection to the Jewish students, the rector and the professors left.[196]

Many professors protested the "ghetto benches" law, but many others agreed with the policy or acquiesced silently. In any event, this policy became common practice.[197] On November 10, 1936, the Bund and the Jewish trade unions announced a strike in protest against the "ghettoization." In the following years the incitement intensified and the violent attacks and murders at universities multiplied. Protests and resistance from the Jewish students were to no avail.[198]

The decrease in the number of students, wrote *Haaretz*, "has this year [1939] become so dramatic, that there are grounds to fear that in a few years Jewish students will almost completely disappear from institutes of higher education in Poland."[199] In several academic establishments there were violent attacks, and three Jewish students were killed. An even graver discrimination was registered in the employment of Jewish lecturers.

The decrease in the Jews' share in institutions of higher education—from around 21 percent in 1925 (double their share in the population) to 8.2 percent in 1938–1939[200]—was the main reason for the increase in the number of those enrolling at the Hebrew University in Jerusalem. In the 1930s, around 2,800 holders of certificates from the B category—which also included students—immigrated to Palestine and were admitted to the Hebrew University in Jerusalem. Some of them left in organized groups. Their exodus continued after war broke out.

Lily Folman finished her studies at the Hebrew gymnasium "Yehudiya" in Warsaw in May 1938 and sent her matriculation diploma to the Hebrew University in Jerusalem. In summer 1939 the Palestine Office in Warsaw informed her that she had been granted a certificate, but during the bombing of Warsaw the office was hit and her certificate was burned. On November 23, she sent a letter to Palestine through the Dutch consulate, but the reply was delayed, and in the meantime the certificate had expired. Finally she received notice from Hebrew University that she had been admitted and that a new certificate was waiting for her in Trieste. However, the Italian border had been closed. With around thirty other immigrants she waited in Vienna and reported to the Gestapo offices until the visa to Turkey arrived. When she wrote her parents about it, they rushed to her and suggested she return to Warsaw: "Just as we get by here, you'll get by; just as long as you don't have to travel to unfamiliar and dangerous distances." After a long journey through Yugoslavia, Greece, and then Syria and Lebanon, Folman arrived in Haifa in June 1940.[201]

Similarly, Ella Goral (Dobshin) managed to get out of Dvinsk (Latvia) after war broke out, but because the occupation of Poland blocked the route to the port of Constanta, she traveled to Königsberg and from there to Berlin, Budapest, and Bucharest, and in mid-November disembarked at the port of Haifa.[202]

The wave of riots in Poland was concurrent with the "riots" in Palestine. Chajes wrote on June 14, 1936:

> In Palestine, for a month now, the Arabs have been striking at the Jews. Ambushes, arsons, sabotages, dozens of victims, a boycott, a small revolution. They do not want the Jews. They fight without hatred, but they want to stop, by fire and sword, the building of the Jewish state. In Poland the youth in the cities do the same thing. And in the towns—the peasants. With hatred, with force, they want to hasten the destruction of Polish Jewry. They are starting to starve the Jews. From above—expulsions. From below—clubs, arsons, attacks, eight against one. It is bad.[203]

On April 15, 1936, a few armed Arabs blocked the road near Tulkarm, stopped a truck transporting chickens to Tel Aviv, made the passengers get out, and shot them. A seventy-year-old poultry store worker from Jaffa, Yisrael Chazan, was killed on the spot, and the other two were wounded. One of them died of his wounds five days later. The murdered man's funeral in

Tel Aviv turned into a mass demonstration. The next day groups of Jewish youths beat up Arabs who happened to be in town for work.

On Sunday morning, April 19, not far from Hassan Bek mosque in Jaffa, Eliezer Bitchotzky, a partner in a soda drinks factory in Jaffa, was beaten to death with an iron rod and wooden clubs. He was the first casualty in what would soon be called the "1936 riots." On that day nine Jews were killed in Jaffa and the Manshieh neighborhood, and forty were wounded. The British police intervened and killed two Arabs.

By April 23, around 7,000 Jews had fled from Jaffa to Tel Aviv. They were housed in dozens of basements, unfinished buildings, and garages. The National Committee called the week starting on April 19 "the days of terror." Sixteen Jews were killed that week in Jaffa and its environs. Between April 19 and October 12, 1936, eighty Jews were killed (as well as thirty-six British soldiers and policemen and ninety-five Arabs). The violent incidents continued almost every single day. The situation in which Jews were murdered in Palestine in larger numbers than in the Diaspora was seen, not only by Zionist right-wing circles, as an insupportable and unforgivable humiliation of the national honor, and therefore as a reality that demanded response. The poet David Shimonovich (Shimoni) wrote:

> Our blood is like water all over the world . . .
> But here we will not be like withering leaves,
> Leaves that are blown away by the wind—
> Here we will not meet our death like meek sheep![204]

The poet S. Shalom wrote:

> Shut the window and door
> And turn off the light.
> Like islands in the world's sea—
> Under siege in the night.
>
> Listen for an hour or two
> Suddenly—a shot is heard!
> Eyes stare in the dark,
> Heart anxious and scared.
>
> Was the guard shot at?
> Was a brother murdered from the back?
> Did the desert savages
> Rise from the ambush and attack?[205]

On May 5 the poet and doctor Shaul Tchernichovsky miraculously escaped a bullet that was shot at a car in which he was returning from seeing a patient in Rishon Lezion. A father and two of his sons were murdered on the night of August 12, and two days later four Jews were murdered on Mount

Carmel. On May 16, two nurses who were working at the government hospital in Jaffa were murdered. Terror against Jews turned into revolt against British rule, and was forcefully repressed by the army.[206] Ruppin reacted to the violent events with equanimity:

> I myself am facing these days with supreme serenity and level-headedness. I have developed a theory: naturally and necessarily, the Arabs' resistance to Jewish immigration will from time to time find its release in such outbursts; we are destined to live in a state of continual warfare with the Arabs, and fatal sacrifices are inevitable. Perhaps this is an undesirable situation, but this is the reality, and if we wish to continue our work in Palestine against the Arabs' will—we shall have to take such sacrifices into account.[207]

The Yishuv became embroiled in a bitter debate over how to react to the riots,[208] and the Jewish press in Poland and other countries seethed. Large rallies were held in various cities. The Zionist Organization and Jewish Agency Directorates published a pamphlet "To the Jewish People," in which they expressed concern for the Yishuv's safety:

> In these difficult, trying times, we find solace in the knowledge that Jews all over the Diaspora are anxious about the fate of the revival project in our land, which is not only the project of the Jews in Palestine, but that of the Jewish people as a whole. We are sure that it is not only the concern for the safety and lives of the 400,000 Jews living in Palestine, but the deep fear for the historical hope of the nation in its homeland, that is at this time driving all the sections of Judaism.[209]

On April 30, despite the general strike that had been announced by the Arabs in Palestine on April 22, the fourth Orient Fair opened on a 25-acre site that had been inaugurated a year earlier near the Yarkon estuary in Tel Aviv. The fair featured 1,986 exhibitors from sixteen countries. The High Commissioner, Sir Arthur Wauchope, spoke at the fair on May 25, British Empire Day, promising: "No strike and no act of violence will make the government stray even one iota from its firm decision to fulfill its Mandate commitments in full." However, the number of visitors at the fair was smaller than expected, and some of the planned events were canceled.

At noon on May 18, accompanied by three British Coast Guard boats, the first ship put down anchor in the Tel Aviv Port—the Yugoslav freight ship *Civerty*, carrying 950 tons of cement. The first export cargo left the pier on

June 7 in two Jewish-owned ships: *Attid* and *Richard Burchard*. In 1938, 116 ships anchored at the port. On May 28, 1936, the fair held its Sea Day, attended by sailors from the three Jewish-owned ships: *Tel Aviv*, *Har Tzion*, and *Attid*. At the end of October the British Secretary of State for the Colonies, William Ormsby-Gore, reported to Parliament about the 190 days of the riots, in which 187 Arabs, 80 Jews, and 21 British had been killed. According to the data collected by the Jewish Agency Directorate, by the end of October, 91 Jews had been killed and 369 injured.[210]

In 1933 the Polish government did not prevent Jewish anti-German activities in Poland, nor did it prohibit the boycott on German goods announced by Jewish economic organizations. On May 5, Jabotinsky was even allowed to speak on Warsaw Radio. In his speech he called for "a boycott on the products of Hitler's Germany," because this was an interest common to both Poland and the Jews. This freedom to act made Jabotinsky believe that he would lead the Jewish people "to a campaign against Hitler" and "a war against the German nation."[211]

The mobilization of the Jewish public crossed party lines. Across Poland around, 170 committees were formed to organize the boycott, Jewish storeowners removed German products from their shelves, and the German export to Poland duly suffered. The boycott spread into other countries. In Britain, for instance, it was organized by local committees. In October 1933, around a thousand Jewish delegates gathered in London, calling for a boycott on German goods. The *Daily Express* maintained that the boycott "has revived the Jewish people and sparked a renaissance,"[212] whereas other newspapers estimated that the boycott was reinforcing the antisemitic myth about an international Jewish conspiracy. Some even believed that such a conspiracy was not a "myth."[213]

The boycott movement troubled the Nazi regime, for which the demonic image of the Jews as a political and economic force that moves the world was an inseparable part of its worldview. The movement provided the Nazis with "proof" that the demonological picture of an international "Jewish conspiracy" conducting economic war (*ökonomische Abwehr*) against Germany was correct. German diplomats and secret agents in Poland and elsewhere regularly reported back to Berlin about the extent of the Jewish public's willingness to join the boycott, and about the violence with which it was sometimes imposed.[214]

The German monitoring of Jabotinsky's activities began as early as 1927 and continued after the Nazis came to power. An urgent dispatch to Berlin from the beginning of April 1933 described propaganda and organization activities all over Europe—it called it "Jewish terrorism"—and reported on Jabotinsky's visit to Poland to promote the boycott. A report from Warsaw sent on May 2, 1933, said that the Jewish camp was divided and unorganized and was strong mainly in districts where the rabbis had a robust public influence. Conversely, assimilated Jews and big merchants did not join the boycott. The report cited one of the "agitators," who described the boycott "as our answer to Hitler's barbarism. We have set off an anti-Hitler reaction in the Polish districts. The whole of world Jewry is on our side."

In western Europe, the report believed, the boycott movement stood no chance, but in Poland not only did the government not forbid it, but it even sanctioned the forming of the Central Committee Against Germany. On April 10, Berlin was informed about assemblies in more than 700 synagogues that had not been banned by the Polish government.[215] A Gestapo agent who followed the movements of Jabotinsky, who was described as "a deadly enemy" (*Todfeind*) of Nazi Germany, reported in February 1935 on the second Betar World Congress, which was held in January in Krakow, and said that it included incitement against Germany.[216]

At first the Polish government regarded the boycott favorably, which led the German ambassador to Poland to note with surprise that Poland—"the classic country of anti-Jewish pogroms"—had placed itself in the role of advocate for Jewish interests, and was supporting a boycott on German goods. The foreign minister, Józef Beck, who was asked to clarify the policy on this matter to the Polish ambassador in London, stated that the government did not restrict Jewish reaction to anti-Jewish acts that took place in Germany, "in accordance, of course, with international custom and internal order." However, after Poland and Germany signed the Non-Aggression Pact on January 26, 1934, and an economic agreement in November 1935, Jewish organizations were banned from campaigning for a boycott on German goods. In June 1936, the Central Committee for Anti-German Economic Boycott stopped its operations under government orders.[217]

The idea that Poland's economic and demographic troubles would be solved by establishing Polish colonies in Asia and Africa, with the help of the League of Nations, emerged as early as 1918. In response to the calls for Polish Jews to emigrate, Chajes now reflected on the great contribution the Jews could have made to Poland's prosperity: "If they had used the Jewish resources wisely, Palestine could have been a Polish colony today."[218]

As mentioned earlier, when it became clear in the middle of the 1930s that Palestine was not going to become "a Polish colony," the Polish regime started to look for destinations for Jewish emigration in the African continent. The plan to settle Jews in Madagascar was raised by the Polish foreign minister, and gained the cooperation of the French government. A three-man expedition, including two Jews, went out at the beginning of May 1937 to examine the conditions in Madagascar. It toured the island for around ten weeks, and came back reporting that it would be possible to colonize it with a few hundred families at most. The plan came to nothing, and it seemed that the Polish government had not pinned much hope on it to begin with. It therefore hastened to declare that the plan did not impinge in any way on Poland's positive stance regarding Jewish settlement in Palestine.[219] The Polish government showed increasing interest in the "Palestine question."

Roman Brandstaetter, a Polish-Jewish writer (who converted after the Second World War), compared Polish Jews to a "blind generation," fast asleep and oblivious to the impending threat of an unprecedented disaster. In a satirical-allegorical feuilleton titled "A Jewish Republic at the North Pole," which he published in February 1938 in the periodical *Nowy Głos*, he described the settlement of Jewish refugees at the pole: an amazing city called Tel Vivant (in Polish: *Hurray*) was built on the shore of the ice sea, and a parliament, a government building, and a university were built on top of Bear Mountain. Several months after the founding of the colony it held parliamentary elections. The feuilleton proceeded to describe how doctor Hannibal Pomerantz founded a party and a militia, and took control of the pole's supply of frozen water under the slogan "The state is the leader, the leader is the water!" The water became an economic, ideological, and messianic asset. Soon Hannibal also founded a police force and an army of spies and provocateurs, but he faced a difficult problem: the polar bears did not accept the Jewish settlement, and violent clashes erupted between the Jews and the bears, clashes that sparked disagreement within the Jewish public on how to react to them. The solution was proposed by one of the archaeologists of the "water party" (*Dlaczegowy*). He discovered the remains of an ichthyosaur from the Flagstone Age, and concluded that the prehistoric creature had Semitic roots: next to it he found an object resembling an umbrella and the remains of prehistoric shoes resembling boots. In his book he wrote: "The bears must finally recognize that this land has always been Jewish land. It has always been Jewish, and Jewish it will remain!"

The bears acknowledged the claim and moved to the northern part of the pole. After the Jewish republic gained international recognition from the League of Nations, thanks to the connections of its representative in

Geneva (styled after Weizmann), who obtained it during a meal with his British friends over a plate of herring and cream, Hannibal, the leader of the republic, became a dictator and sent his political rivals to concentration camps. This provoked fierce opposition from a new party, the "climate party" (*Klimatowców*), and Hannibal was assassinated. Having come to power, the opposition started working on changing the pole's climate —and indeed, the ice started to melt. The tropical climate from the pole reached Warsaw and all the other European countries, creating international tension.

Under the influence of the climatic changes, some people changed their political opinions, while others were overcome by madness. Antisemitic demonstrations started in Warsaw, calling on the Jews to return to Poland. The Jews refused, but offered to sell the Europeans cheap refrigerated rooms. On the other hand, Europeans started immigrating to the pole. The immigrants lived in ghettos, wore long coats and black skullcaps, grew beards and strange curls called "*peot*," and in time developed their own jargon. The Jews did not welcome the immigrants. Pogroms broke out, and Jews armed with whips and razor blades attacked the immigrants. One old and gray-haired European man rolled his *peot* and said: "The Jews want to do away with us," and started crying; 16 million Europeans cried with him on the polar shore.[220]

This satirical feuilleton, of which we have cited only a small part, derided both Zionism and Polish antisemitism, but most of all it described the impossible situation in which Polish Jews had found themselves trapped. Brandstaetter could not foresee, of course, that three years later the idea would come up to settle Jewish emigrants from the Reich in Alaska.

In mid-April 1939, after the Zionist movement's defeat at the St. James Conference, Shertok arrived at the Foreign Ministry in Warsaw for discussions. He was greeted by Deputy Foreign Minister Mirosław Arciszewski ("some say he is of Jewish descent," wrote Shertok in his diary). Arciszewski confirmed that it was Poland's policy to encourage Jewish emigration, but promised nothing about the "Clearing" agreement, and in particular failed to promise that the Polish government would change the restrictions on the maximum amount an emigrant was allowed to take with him in foreign currency—500 złoty (around 19 Palestine pounds). The Revisionists' shadow hovered over the conversation. Arciszewski, wrote Shertok, "let the cat out of the bag and said that the sympathy in Polish government circles towards the Revisionist movement, in terms of ideological affinity, hindered the tightening of relations between the Polish government and the Agency."[221]

The conversation was unsuccessful, and on April 21 Shertok flew to London. The doors of the Polish Foreign Ministry, where the prevailing opinion was that a mass emigration of Jews should be organized, were indeed open to Jabotinsky.[222] The Foreign Ministry saw the Revisionist movement as a dynamic element that should be supported, although it had doubts over its capabilities.

In 1935, when Jabotinsky was no longer the leader of the opposition in the Zionist Organization, but the leader of a new and independent Zionist organization, these doors opened to him and he met Foreign Minister Beck on June 9, 1936, and again in early July, during the League of Nations session. After this meeting he wrote to Beck (in French), apologizing for writing by hand, as his secretary had left with the typewriter. He suggested that Poland, being a friendly government, should urge the Mandate government in the name of "humanitarian principles and its own political interests" to adopt a constructive plan for a large settlement of Polish immigrants in Palestine. He did not hesitate to mention that this kind of Polish support would bring Poland the support of influential Jews everywhere. The government that would take on such an initiative would immediately achieve the status of a moral leader, the ramifications of which would reverberate on the international stage.[223]

On September 9, he dined at the Foreign Ministry officials' club in Warsaw's Europejski Hotel, one of the most upscale hotels in the city, with a group of senior government officials and tried to convince them that his organization would revive the Zionist ideals. He and his interlocutors reveled in the words of Count Michał Lubienski, the Foreign Ministry's director-general, "that only our Piłsudski was able to delve so incisively into the hidden depths of problems." Jabotinsky also met the prime minister, General Sławoj-Składkowski, who wore his military uniform in his guest's honor.[224]

On June 21, Jabotinsky sent a long memorandum to Beck explaining the Evacuation policy. He wrote the deputy director of the Foreign Ministry's political department, who was a converted Jew, that the evacuation would turn Zionism "from an amusement to a rescue plan" and that the country that would take it upon itself to carry it out "would be walking on a magic carpet."[225] "The need for evacuation," he explained, "has nothing to do, or almost nothing to do, with the conscious and active antisemitism of the masses or the Christian governments. In fact it has to do with a certain objective tendency in social development, which is almost independent of private desires." Furthermore, active antisemitism, and especially government-directed antisemitism, could only stop the evacuation: "It would create panic, and it is well known that in an atmosphere of panic it is very hard to find the way out."

In his memo, Jabotinsky listed the main points of the plan and stressed that it would not be realizable without the British government's cooperation. In order to "soothe" the Polish foreign minister, he explained that he did not expect the Polish government to intervene in favor of the plan in London, but that he was talking about a "friendly petition."[226] A week later he sent Beck, who was in Geneva, a handwritten letter, and this time he was more frank: he hoped, or expected, that the Polish government, which was a "friendly government," would approach the British government both "in the name of humanitarian principles and for its own political interest, [and] propose to the Mandate authorities to adopt a constructive plan for the large-scale settlement [of Polish Jews in Palestine]." A government that would act in that way, Jabotinsky promised, would gain the ardent support of the entire Jewish people: not only parties and political organizations, but also "all the moral, political, [and] financial forces," and all "the influential Jews who are scattered in the press, in literature, in banking, in parliaments, and who knows where else. All of them will rise unanimously in both hemispheres to welcome such an initiative."[227]

It was not only Jabotinsky and his aides who were involved in the campaign to persuade and intercede with the Polish foreign minister. On October 2, 1936, Nahum Goldmann likewise met Foreign Minister Beck for a long talk, and both, as Goldmann wrote Weizmann, spoke frankly. Beck explained that the Polish government was doing its best to fight against antisemitism. However, defending the equal rights of the Jews would not solve "the Jewish problem," which stemmed from the Jews' (and Poles') natural growth and diminishing means of subsistence. According to Goldmann, Poland had enormous difficulty securing the means of existence for the Polish population. The yearly population surplus was extremely large and did not find any provisions; the children of the farmers went to the towns, where most of the jobs were occupied by the Jews. In addition, the Jewish population had a high natural growth rate, for whom in present-day Poland there was surely no means of existence available.

Hence, the Polish government supported Jewish emigration to Palestine and the Zionist movement's demands, but Palestine could clearly not absorb all the Jewish emigrants. Therefore, other destinations had to be found. At the same time, Beck was skeptical about the chances of Poland receiving overseas colonies in the foreseeable future. Goldmann thanked Beck for his sympathetic support for the Zionist cause and added that the Zionist movement was not opposed to the emigration of Polish Jews to other countries. The Zionist movement, Goldmann said, "admits that Palestine by itself cannot absorb all Jewish emigrants and therefore one should still find other destination countries." Moreover, its immigration policy was guided by the assumption that not all those wishing to emigrate were suited for Palestine, and therefore the policy was based on the principle of selective immigration. In light of this, the cooperation between the Zionist Organization and the Polish government should be based on two principles: first, a declaration that the immigration policy would in no way impinge on the rights of Polish Jews. Second, that the Polish government would act in cooperation with the Zionist Organization, and "cherish no illusions with regard to the actual possibilities" of the Evacuation plan of Jabotinsky and his movement.

When the Polish government officially received Mr. Jabotinsky and thus gave the impression that it consented to his fantastic and completely illusory program for the evacuation of 1.5 million Polish Jews within ten years, it hung its hopes on a movement that lacked the support of the Jewish public and that had no chance to manifest itself in reality. This, it was believed, "would bring heavy damage to the prestige of Poland in the Jewish and gentile world."[228]

The two rival camps within Zionism pinned their hopes on Poland. Ultimately, both accepted Beck's diagnosis regarding the need to encourage a mass emigration of Jews from Poland. While Jabotinsky advised a large emigration plan, which had no chance of being actualized, his opponents hoped for Polish assistance with a small-scale emigration.

The meetings continued in October 1937, and Jabotinsky used them to explain the rationale behind the Revisionist movement's opposition to the Partition Plan: within the partition borders it would not be possible to absorb the mass immigration of Polish Jews. He saw the situation in Europe—the "terrible storm"—as a "propitious storm," which would put the wind back in Zionism's sails. He quoted the poem by the American poet Ella Wheeler Wilcox, "The Winds of Fate": "One ship drives east and another drives west / With the selfsame winds that blow; / 'Tis the set of the sails / And not the gales / That tells them the way to go."[229]

On June 8, 1938, Antoni Paprocki, an adviser at the Polish Foreign Ministry's consular department, came to Łódź to meet Jabotinsky. Their conversation lasted three hours. Jabotinsky presented his main views and demands. The immigration possibilities to Palestine had been blocked, he told his interlocutor, and therefore new ways should be sought to get half a million or one million Jews from Poland to Palestine. To achieve this aim they would have to work toward changing the country's formal status from a mandate to a condominion (even a Polish one), and simultaneously organize some Jewish pressure: convene a "Sejm of Zion," a new Jewish parliament, which would represent two million Jews who would declare their readiness to immigrate to Palestine. In his report on the conversation, Paprocki wrote: "Jabotinsky struck me as a very good, but disappointed and psychically broken man." The Foreign Ministry chiefs made it clear to Jabotinsky that an overt call for illegal immigration would force the authorities to impose constraints, both because of pressure from Britain and because such immigration would bring little benefit. The British government's intention to stop Jewish immigration, Jabotinsky told the Foreign Ministry chiefs, led by Arciszewski, on October 10, 1938, required vigorous counteraction from the Polish government.[230]

Such action was not forthcoming. While the Polish authorities were willing to help illegal immigration in various ways, it was not about to increase the amount of foreign currency the emigrants were allowed to take out of Poland. They also disapproved of organizing rallies against the British policy, arguing that they had no practical use and that their failure would only provoke a wave of antisemitism.

Despite the common interest, the Polish Foreign Ministry was well aware that the Revisionists lacked the financial resources to carry out plans such as to purchase the passenger ship *Polonia* for a million złoty (40,000 pounds sterling). Since 1933, the 15,000-ton ship had sailed regularly from Constanta, via Istanbul and Piraeus, to Palestine. It was taken out of service in summer 1938 (its last outing on this line was in February 1938, and in 1939 it was sold for scrap).[231] Nothing came of the negotiations for the ship's purchase, conducted by Revisionist activists through intermediaries.[232]

Jabotinsky's companions were very impressed by the willingness in Polish government circles to help the illegal immigration,[233] but it was a "marriage of convenience."[234] The Polish prime minister described it figuratively: "He is not choosey about where he buys good quality products for a cheap price, even if the seller is Jewish . . ."[235] His companions were impressed not only by the warm welcome that the movement's leader received from his Polish interlocutors, but also by his trips around Poland, in which he was greeted in every town by a guard of honor composed of Brit Hahayal and Betar members. It was the movement's clout and Jabotinsky's leadership, they believed, that convinced the Polish administration that the

Zionist movement—represented by the Revisionists—was ready to attain political independence in Palestine by its own means.

What Jabotinsky failed to take into account was Poland's weakness and its dependency on Britain. He saw Poland as a powerful country that knew how to protect its interests and its honor, and whose urgent interest it was to solve the "Jewish question" in any way possible. Therefore he deluded himself and his movement's members into believing that Poland was capable of pressuring the British government to open Palestine's gates to masses of Jewish emigrants. In private he was skeptical about Poland's power to influence the British government. He wrote his friend (and later his biographer) Joseph Shechtman on February 28, 1939, following Beck's visit to London, that although Britain saw Poland as a big and important power, Poland was dependent on Britain, rather than the other way around. Therefore, even if Polish pressure were exerted in London, it would be useless if it contradicted British interests.[236]

The Polish disappointment at the Revisionists' inability "to deliver the goods" was great. The Poles saw the "plans" to "take Palestine" by force of arms as figments of the imagination. On February 7, 1939, Witold Hulanicki, the Polish consul in Jerusalem, recommended that the Foreign Ministry in Warsaw give preference to helping the Revisionists because they were more active in getting illegal immigrants to Palestine.[237]

In early May, Paprocki arrived in Palestine, among other things to verify the Polish consul's reports about the Revisionists' power. Ben-Gurion, who met him, got the impression that Paprocki did not like the Revisionists and therefore it was advisable to speak to the Ministry of Interior Affairs (because the Ministry of Foreign Affairs was subjected to British pressure) "about aid for immigration, military training and equipment," as well as to convince it that the Jewish Agency and the Haganah, the Jewish paramilitary founded in 1920 to protect Jewish communities from attacks by Arabs, would be more trustworthy and efficient partners. Ben-Gurion thus also toyed with the idea of cooperating with the Polish government: "We will promise the government that all the trained youths will be taken to Palestine—one way or another. We will also try to get permission to form a Jewish military unit, which will be sent to Palestine at the first opportunity."[238]

The Polish authorities were not impressed by Jabotinsky's Evacuation Plan—a term he used publically for the first time on June 13, 1936.[239] The Evacuation Plan—an exodus of Polish Jews—was a grand plan for the emigration of around a million and a half Jews from Europe over *ten years*, with around 700,000 of those coming from Poland.[240] It was supposed to be an organized exodus—"no panic, no flight—a kind of military campaign in which everything is planned in advance."[241]

According to the plan, the campaign was meant to spread over ten years (until 1948) and include mainly people between the ages of twenty-three and thirty-seven. Its execution was conditioned, as already mentioned, on the collaboration and aid of the Polish government, and of course on the approval of the British government. The preparations for the "campaign" included organizing a financial system that would enable the Jews to take their property with them, and raising international loans to fund the absorption and resettlement of hundreds of thousands of Jews over ten years. The British government was supposed to rezone some state land and reform its customs and tax policy.

Jabotinsky estimated the plan's cost between 30 million pound sterling and 47 million pound sterling (including 18 million pound sterling from private capital). In other words, the plan was based on the emigration of around 100,000 Jews per year. He was careful not to accuse the government publically of antisemitism, which did not prevent him from warning that Polish Jews were under great danger—not from a world war but from Polish antisemitism.

In a speech at a Warsaw rally in mid-May 1939, Jabotinsky urged his listeners to save themselves: "Now it has become clear that a great European war will not take place," but that did not mean that the danger to the Jews had gone. On the contrary, Poland was "one big cemetery."[242]

The great Evacuation Plan and its alternative, the plan for the emigration of a million Jews over two years,[243] were pipe dreams. When Jabotinsky called Polish Jews in summer 1939 to save themselves, the call came from the depth of his heart, but those Polish Jews who wanted to leave had nowhere to go. The key to Palestine was held by the British government.

The Evacuation Plan and its public propaganda campaign were highly controversial. Among other things, it was claimed that the plan involved cooperating with the antisemites, endangered Polish Jews, and encouraged the government to drive them out. In truth, there was nowhere to drive them out to. Jabotinsky and the Revisionist press defended the plan fiercely and passionately, and the Revisionist historiography describes its opponents as thwarting, out of blindness or malice, the possibility of saving Polish Jews. However, according to the Evacuation Plan, around two million Jews would have still been left in Poland in 1948. The speeches given by Jabotinsky between May 1 and 29, 1939, in Poland, Latvia, Lithuania, and Finland—on a tour his biographer describes as "a dramatic last tour"—and which were meant to arouse and alarm, would not have any real outcome. The warm welcome he received from heads of states and diplomats, a warmth that Jabotinsky's biographer illustrates by describing how Dr. V. Munters, the Latvian minister of foreign affairs, who met Jabotinsky in London, helped him put on his coat,[244] was to no avail. All the plans to accelerate an organized Jewish emigration from Poland came to naught.

As mentioned earlier, the common interest of the Polish government and the Zionist movement to increase the flow of emigration from Poland, and the recognition that there was no other destination for emigration except Palestine, created a basis for some overt and covert cooperation between different organizations. The cooperation began before the publication of the Partition Plan, which annulled the principle of "economic absorption capacity," and intensified after the White Paper's publication. It was manifested in providing passports; helping organize illegal immigration; selling weapons to the Haganah, a paramilitary organization, and to the Irgun Zva'i Leumi (Etzel), a Jewish underground organization of the Revisionists; and organizing military training led by Polish officers on Polish soil.[245]

The clandestine connections with the Revisionist movement were not initiated by the movement's leadership, but rather by Irgun's members, who acted in Poland independently and secretly. The initiative was led by Avraham Stern (Yair), a native of Poland, who did not pin much hope on Jabotinsky's political activity and found his own supporters at the top echelons of the Polish army. Dr. Henryk Strasman and his wife Lily (Ila) used their good connections in Polish government circles to open some doors for Stern and purchase weapons for the Irgun. In summer 1939, around 7,000 French rifles, Hotchkiss machine guns, explosives, and so on were transferred to the bonded warehouses on Warsaw's Cegielna Street. Some of the weapons were smuggled to Palestine inside the double side panels of lifts (shipping containers).[246]

Military courses were held in Andrychów in southwest Poland, in Zofiówka in the Lublin voivodeship, and in other places. They were kept secret not only for fear of British pressure on the Polish government to stop this activity, but also for fear of intervention from the Betar and Revisionist party chiefs. "The instructors were Polish army officers, who instructed us in the use of light weapons, rifles, machine guns, and explosives. For the first time in our lives we went to proper shooting ranges."[247] In May 1939, Stern came to the camp with a senior Polish officer and spoke to the twenty-six trainees at the end of the course parade. From Poland, he declared, will depart the "conquering army," sailing by sea to the homeland's shores.

This channel of activity and the far-reaching plans that accompanied it were further developed when it became clear that the plan for mass organized emigration from Poland to Palestine over ten years and the founding of a Jewish state on the two banks of the Jordan River was unrealistic, and that there was no chance of changing the British government's stance on the immigration issue. The Irgun had no choice but to pin its hopes on the weapons purchased in Poland and on the military training that, as the Irgun commanders believed, would help them take Palestine. The connections with Polish military officers and arms merchants and the military courses inspired the hope that Zionism was "about to take the subjugated Palestine by storm and break the yoke of foreign rule [. . .] and realize the delivering mass immigration."[248]

In the other Zionist camp the contacts were likewise not instigated by the political leadership. Thanks to these contacts, the Haganah held dozens of military courses for the Hechalutz members, led by Polish officers. Thirty-three male and female movement members took part in a course in Żielonka, an estate near Warsaw, that included some shooting training. On June 16, 1939, the course was attended by representatives of the Polish government's Military, Foreign, and Interior Ministries. On July 13, it was visited by journalists and guests, including Moshe Kleinbaum and Yitzhak Gruenbaum.

The Haganah envoys, headed by Yehuda Arazi, who had contacts in the top echelons of the Polish army and even compared the national aspirations of the Jews with the Polish struggle for freedom, managed to purchase some new weapons from a government source and send dozens of shipments to Palestine.[249] The purchases included 2,750 Mauser rifles, 225 RKM machine guns, 10,000 hand grenades, around two million bullets for rifles and machine guns, and a large number of pistols with their ammunition.[250] Some of the shipments were sent from the Constanta port in the hollow wheels of road rollers. Shaul Meirov (Avigur), the head of the Mossad LeAliyah Bet, the organization that arranged clandestine immigration, helped with the shipments' packing, which was done at night at the workshop of a Hungarian man on 160 Tcherinkovska Street, which was turned into a "roller factory" for the occasion. He later recalled: "We would normally finish work after midnight. Then we would take off our work clothes, rub our greasy hands in gasoline, put on our ties and walk out of the workshop into the deserted and silent street. We would go to one of the Warsaw cafés that stayed open late—and enjoy a strong and hot cup of coffee."[251]

Arazi introduced himself as the representative of the exiled *negus* (king) of Ethiopia, and said that the weapons were needed to liberate his homeland from Italian rule. On the shipments he wrote that they were intended for Arab buyers in Palestine, but it did not fool the British, who exerted heavy pressure on the Polish government to stop them. When the Zionist Congress convened in Geneva, the weapons acquisition activists in Poland were allocated 1 million złoty (40,000 Palestine pounds) from the funds' money in Poland. Arazi used this money to buy two airplanes and two gliders for the Aviron company. When he fled from Poland to Paris he left behind 500 rifles in the Warsaw warehouse.[252]

On December 6, 1938, Emanuel Ringelblum wrote to his friend the historian Raphael Mahler in New York:

> I have neither the strength nor the patience to describe for you everything that happened in Zbąszyń. Anyway, I think there has never been so ferocious, so pitiless a deportation of any Jewish community as this German deportation. [. . .] Zbąszyń has become a symbol for the defenselessness of the Jews of Poland. Jews were humiliated to the level of lepers, to citizens of the third class, and as a result we are all visited by terrible tragedy.[253]

As early as April 1934, Jews who were Polish citizens[254] were forced to leave Germany and go back to Poland, but the large-scale expulsion took place on October 27–29, 1938. At that time the German police raided the houses of around 17,000 Jews with Polish citizenship all over Germany in the middle of the night and handed them deportation orders. They were pulled out of their beds, ordered to get dressed quickly, and allowed to take only 10 marks per person plus hand luggage, but forbidden to take any valuables.

One of these deportees was Marcel Reich-Ranicki (later an influential literary critic in postwar Germany), born in the Polish town of Włocławek, who had come to study in Berlin and lived there in his aunt's house. In 1938 he was studying in the "Fichte" gymnasium in Wilmersdorf. Early in the morning of October 28 he was woken up by a policeman who examined his Polish passport, ordered him to get dressed immediately, and gave him the deportation order that said he had to leave the Reich within a fortnight. Reich-Ranicki was allowed to take 5 marks, a change handkerchief, and a book—he chose a novel by Balzac. The policeman escorted him through the still dark street to the police station, from where he was transferred with a group of fellow sufferers to the regional police station in Sophie-Charlotte-Platz. There they joined a few hundred Jews who were already waiting outside, and at dusk were led to a side platform at the Schlesischer Bahnhof train station. The hundreds of passengers who had been pulled out of their beds were trembling from the cold. However, he wrote in his memoirs, "compared to later transports, the conditions were still humane, yes, it was almost luxury."[255] He was lucky, because his parents and brother lived in Warsaw in a shared apartment. He was one of the deportees who had relatives or friends in Poland, and who received train tickets from the authorities for the remainder of their trip. Many others had no address to return to.

Train stations in the German cities were filled with deportees who were loaded onto freight cars for cattle; 724 Jews with Polish citizenship who lived in Dresden were assembled at the main train station in Dresden Neustadt and sent to the border town of Bytom in Silesia. There they were forced to cross the border to Poland. Those who lived near the border with Poland were marched there on foot, the policemen shooting in the air to make them walk more quickly.[256] Julius Rosenzweig, another deportee, recalled: "When we walked out into the street it was pouring with rain. On the roads and sidewalks people stood around and watched, others leaned out of their windows. They loaded us onto police cars and drove us to the station. There, again, people were watching us, but there were also some Jews who came to say goodbye."[257] Around 4,000 Jews were deported from Danzig to Gdynia by ship, and only around 1,500 of them were allowed by the Poles to come ashore.

The deportation operation, which was given the code name "Polenaktion," followed from the increasingly tense relations between Poland and Nazi Germany. It came as a response to the Polish government's decision on October 6, 1938, to revoke the citizenship of Poles who had been residing abroad for more than five years, unless they returned to Poland within a fortnight. In fact, the operation was aimed against the Jews. "Fifteen thousand Jews suddenly became pawns in the dispute between Germany and Poland," the Jewish press cried. The deportees were driven by train to the border and forced to cross it at gunpoint. The Polish border police opened fire on the trains, and several Jews were killed. Those who crossed the border in the Bytom area reached Katowice, Pomerania, and Zbąszyń in the western part of the Poznan district, on the border with Germany. "Trains crammed with deported Jews with their women and children," reported the

Hazofe newspaper on October 30, "are continuing to arrive from Germany to Poland, and thousands of deported Jews are stopped near the border since they do not have valid passports and are not allowed to travel to the Polish cities. Thousands of deported Jews are stuck in the fields between the borders." Some of the deportees received aid from Jewish organizations and from the Polish authorities, but in Zbąszyń around 8,000 of them gathered in a tent encampment erected by the Polish army in a disused cavalry camp: "Two hundred are sleeping outdoors in the cold and the rain, 1,200 have been housed in cowsheds with the cattle, five including an eighteen-year-old woman have lost their minds. [. . .] It is one calamity after another."[258]

Public opinion in Poland showed empathy—more out of hatred for Germany than compassion toward the Jews. The people of Zbąszyń and the surrounding areas provided the deportees with hot water. However, the Polish authorities prevented them from leaving the camp. The Joint and Aid Committees came to their help and fundraising events were held all across Poland. A fundraising campaign announced by the *Der Tag* newspaper raised around 50,000 złoty within a month, and an additional 3 million złoty were raised later.[259]

Among those coming to the deportees' aid was Emanuel Ringelblum. "In the course of those five weeks," he wrote, "we set up a whole township, with departments for supplies, hospitalization [. . .] a legal section [. . .] an independent post office [. . .], etc." Around 1,500 deportees found refuge in private apartments, with the expenses covered by the Aid Committee.

On November 18, 1938, the Polish ambassador to London was instructed by Foreign Minister Beck to convey to the British government that "any action in favor of German Jews must include the Jewish refugees deported to Poland." Beck also instructed the Polish ambassador to Washington to inform the American administration that Poland saw "a great urgency in starting a large-scale, constructive emigration activity." The ambassador, instructed Beck, should stress that "serious" Jewish circles also increasingly recognized the need for an emigration plan, and not necessarily to Palestine.[260]

In December, the Polish ambassador to the United States met with Lord Halifax, who was visiting Washington, and presented to him "the Jewish problem from our point of view. I stressed the gravely worsening situation in our Jewish sector due to the emigration pressure from German Jews, who are using all the available avenues in this regard." On December 3, the Intergovernmental Committee on Refugees in London examined Poland's request to discuss the matter of the Jews "who were forced to leave Germany, and whom Poland does not recognize as its citizens," and rejected it. Ten days later, the Polish government repeated its request and was denied again. When Heinrich Himmler visited Poland in February 1939, Foreign Minister Beck told him: "The Jewish problem in Poland is more complicated than in Germany. On the one hand [. . .] some of the Jewish population in Poland arrived in the past from Russia and has no connection to Poland, and should be gotten rid of first of all. On the other hand, there are many orthodox Jews in Poland whose lives run alongside us rather than together with us. [. . .] In any case the emigration of Polish Jews, which has slowed down recently, is more necessary than ever, and therefore we are presenting this case to the countries of western Europe in the most decisive terms."[261]

On June 10, 1939, the Polish ambassador to London asked the British deputy foreign secretary to see that the 25,000 certificates earmarked for refugees would include the Jews who had been deported to Poland from Germany.[262]

On November 1, 1938, the teacher Chaim Aaron Kaplan wrote:

> A stream of refugees from Germany has started to flow into "tolerant" Poland. [. . .] [It is a] deportation order because formally they are Polish citizens, although they have never seen their beloved "homeland" and are absolutely foreign to it. And lo and behold! The second evil kingdom in Europe, the revived Polish kingdom, which sees the Jews as its step children, [. . .] which restricts their movements, deprives them of their rights, and holds "vigils" outside their stores in order to starve them and make their lives a misery—this malicious government, whose majority is Hitlerite and minority democratic, has intervened in favor of its humiliated and persecuted Jews!!! This is politics!!! And where there is politics, even the hatred of Jews is forgotten and an enemy becomes a friend. True, political love is short-lived. When the interest is gone—the love is gone. But it lives in the moment.[263]

On November 3, Berta Grynszpan, who had been deported with her family from Hanover, wrote on a postcard to her brother Herschel in Paris: "We were allowed to go back home and at least take a few essentials. So I went there escorted by the 'schupo' [Schutzpolizei, the German gendarmerie] and packed some suitcases with the most needed clothes. That's all I managed to salvage. We don't have a penny to our name."[264]

On November 6, the deportees from Zbąszyń sent the president of Poland a letter: "We have now spent ten days in Zbąszyń, where we are forcibly held in old wooden stables under leaking roofs. We, our children, our elderly and our women are suffering from the freezing cold and lacking the most primitive conveniences (lighting and water), and are deprived of our personal freedom. We are unable to communicate with the outside world."[265]

Ringelblum wrote on November 14: "What I have been through is difficult to put in writing. [. . .] After a few days of work, I cried all night at seeing the suffering of these people. Now the situation is a bit better. Everyone has something to eat and a roof over their heads and some clothes to put on." "A whole town has been erected," he wrote in another letter, "but people have still been lying for five weeks on straw mattresses in large halls." Men whose families had remained in Germany received terrible news and were worried about what awaited them in Poland, when they got lucky enough to leave the camp. A finger of blame was pointed at the Polish government. *Haaretz* reported: "As a rule the German authorities' treatment of Polish citizens and Jews in general—has not been bad, relatively speaking. [. . .] Let's hope that the [international] intervention and the political leadership in Warsaw can at least fix, at the midnight hour, the injustice that has already been done."

In June 1939, some 3,000 to 4,000 women and children were still waiting at the camp for a permit to enter Poland. The newspapers reported that dogs were set on "the poor victims" and injured many of them. A woman and a child were murdered, and an elderly man died of exhaustion.[266] The British Foreign Office believed that many of the deportees had never been to Poland nor spoke any Polish. There were others like them in other countries, and therefore the Polish government allowed the Polish citizens to return to Poland; in the camp at Zbąszyń were left around 3,000 stateless deportees.

However, it was the German government, rather than the Polish government, that was responsible for this difficult situation. The British government, the Foreign Office officials maintained, had no "locus standi" (status) in this affair and therefore should not interfere in a matter that was not its business; moreover, the Polish government would not regard such an interference favorably.[267] To the appeal of the Polish ambassador to Britain, that Polish Jews be given preference in the distribution of certificates and in emigration plans to other countries, Secretary of State for the Colonies MacDonald replied that only those deported from Germany who had lost their Polish citizenship were entitled to be considered "refugees," whereas the others could resettle in Poland. Due to the number of illegal immigrants, which was deducted from the immigration quotas given to the Jewish Agency, the certificates quota would only be renewed at the end of March

1940. It should therefore be made clear to the Polish government, MacDonald said, that it was in its interest to stop the illegal immigration organized on Polish soil.[268]

The camp in Zbąszyń was closed only a few days before the outbreak of war. No one saw the event as a prelude to what was in store for Polish Jews a few days after it came to an end. However, it had an unexpected result somewhere far away. On November 7, 1938, the seventeen-year-old Herschel Grynszpan bought a revolver, took the metro to the Solférino station near the German embassy, and told the person at the reception desk that he had a document he wanted to give to one of the embassy's officials. The clerk at the reception desk offered to take the document and pass it on for him, but Grynszpan insisted on handing it in in person. Ernst vom Rath, the junior of the two embassy officials, who was not a Nazi, agreed to see him. Grynszpan entered his office, and according to his testimony, said to him: "You're a filthy Boche, and in the name of 12,000 persecuted Jews, here's your document." He pulled out his gun and shot the official five times from close range.

On the way to the police headquarters, Grynszpan explained that he had assassinated the German diplomat "in order to avenge my parents' misery in Germany." His parents, who lived in Hanover, were among those deported from Germany. As mentioned earlier, four days before the assassination he had received a letter from his sister Berta, describing how the police had driven them out of their house. He wrote a note to his uncle in Paris (in Hebrew), saying that he could not have acted otherwise: "My heart bleeds when I think of our tragedy and that of the 12,000 Jews. I must protest so the whole world hears my protest."[269] When news of the assassination reached Berlin, Hitler sent his personal doctor by plane to the hospital in Paris, but vom Rath died two days later, on November 9. That night was the beginning of Kristallnacht.

The cooperation between the Polish government and the Zionist organizations stopped in 1939. The political events moved quickly, and the Polish government had other things to worry about. The Zionists also understood that Poland's fate was on the line. Kleinbaum pledged his allegiance to Poland. Despite his harsh criticism of the government's policy toward the Jewish community, he vowed that "our arm is outstretched" and promised Poland the Jewish community's help in its war. In March, as tension mounted around the question of the "corridor," he wrote: "At the present moment, in which changes are obtained by force of violence near Poland's borders, Polish civil sentiment and Jewish national instinct dictate that we put all the powers and abilities of the Jewish community at the service of the state. Not only the Poles must be ready to fight for Poland's freedom and security, but all its inhabitants."[270]

Kleinbaum met Arciszewski in June and raised the idea of creating a "Jewish legion," whose soldiers would be Jewish young men who had not been drafted into the army. The deputy foreign minister did not reject the proposal out of hand, but he did not take it seriously. When he attended the Zionist Congress in Geneva, Kleinbaum informed Ben-Gurion of his talks and told him that his Polish interlocutors expressed the hope that Britain's policy was "temporary, a result of conjuncture."[271]

Later, in London, he discussed the subject with Weizmann and Lewis Namier, a pro-Zionist professor of history at Oxford, and argued that a Polish-Jewish legion would pave the way for recruiting Jews in other countries. Kleinbaum believed, or wanted to believe, that Poland now needed the outstretched arm of Polish Jews, who belonged to a nation of 17 million people, "which extends to all five parts of the world."[272] It is hard to believe that Kleinbaum and Ben-Gurion did not know, as Jabotinsky did, that Poland's dependence on Britain would prevent it from acting publicly in a way that might anger London. The leadership of the Revisionist movement also published a pledge of allegiance to Poland on March 29: "We shall all stand as one to defend the borders of the Polish state and its independence," it promised, and offered to form a "Jewish legion" that would fight for Poland. Hashomer Hatzair's leadership declared in a memorandum published May 1: "The danger of war is in the air. Fascism wishes to terrorize peoples and countries. There is no country today that is not endangered by it. [. . .] Poland also finds itself under threat to its independence and to the integrity of its borders. The workers' movement and the state's citizens shall stand as one in defense of their country's borders and its political independence from those who dare to assail its independence."[273]

After the Nazis rose to power in Germany in January 1933, the young Polish Republic found itself trapped between two giant enemies — the communist USSR to the east, and Nazi Germany to the west, which saw it as the "bastard of Versailles." Its allies, Britain and France, failed to offer any real help, and its relations with its small neighbors were tense. Czechoslovakia used the war between the USSR and Poland in 1920 to annex the important industry and transport region around the Olza River and the town of Cieszyn. Poland used the "Treaty of Munich" at the end of the 1930s to regain control over these territories. And it did not object to the dissolution of Czechoslovakia. Chajes wrote with patriotic enthusiasm on October 25,

1938: "Poland is powerfully riding the ocean waves of global politics. Beck is registering victories."[274]

This optimism relied on the fact that Germany had yet to raise any territorial claims concerning Poland. Carried by the patriotic wave that swept Poland following its firm stance in the dispute with Germany over the Baltic port of Memel (Klaipeda), Jabotinsky affirmed in May 1939: "I do not believe in the possibility of war. The belligerent grinding of nerves will be over in two [to] three months." The Revisionist press declared its unreserved allegiance to Poland and its full cooperation in the struggle for Jewish and Polish independence. These declarations were met with suspicion. They do not stem, the *Gazeta Polska* wrote in July 1939, from the Jews' love for Poland, but from their hatred for Hitler.[275] The sympathy accorded the Revisionist movement in large parts of the Polish press was not much help either.[276] Poland's rapid defeat in September turned all the ideas, plans, hopes, and disputes into parts of a bygone reality that no longer existed.

In September 1938, Jabotinsky told the Betar members that Palestine and Poland were worlds apart.[277] He tried to narrow this gap and pinned his hopes on those who had their own reasons for wanting to help but could not. Politicians, government officials, and Polish journalists could talk and write about the urgent and crucial need for Poland to "expel" its Jews, but these calls were in vain. The Jewish Agency and the Yishuv's leadership did not believe in the Polish government's ability to offer political help or a solution, and hoped that the British government would change its policy. However, even if they had managed to increase the quota of immigration certificates, it would not have sufficed to rescue most of the Jews from the impending disaster. For a while, it could have been hoped that the Partition Plan would lead to the founding of a Jewish state, which would open its gates to large-scale immigration. When that hope failed, illegal immigration remained a means of escape only for the few.

Those coming from Poland and other countries tell of the great joy that has seized the Jewish masses on hearing about "The Jewish State."[1]

Berl Katznelson, July 29, 1937

2

"THE DREAM OF A JEWISH STATE"

At the end of July 1937, more than two hundred men and women responded to the call made by Wilhelm Rippel, a lawyer from Warsaw, a former officer in the Polish army and an ardent follower of Jabotinsky, to travel on foot without visas or immigration permits from Poland through Czechoslovakia, Austria, and Italy to sail to Palestine. Although the Partition Plan, outlining the possible creation of a Jewish state, had already been published, Rippel refused to wait for the gates to open and claimed that he was acting in the spirit of Jabotinsky, even though the latter declined to meet him and his initiative was not supported by Hatzohar (Hatzionim Harevisionistim, the Revisionist political party) or Betar (the Revisionist youth movement). Rippel informed the Polish government that the aim of the march was to exert pressure on the British government.[2]

And thus, dressed in khaki uniforms and wearing blue hats, the members of the ephemeral organization "Front Młodożydowski" (Jewish Youth Front) embarked on their march, accompanied by a first aid wagon, a field kitchen, and a throng of onlookers. Near Piaseczno, around ten miles from the capital, the surreal march—whose intention was not really to march to Palestine but to raise public awareness—was stopped by the police. When the marchers refused to disperse, the policemen dispersed them with force. Many of them, including Rippel, who shouted, "Murderers! Murderers!" at the policemen, were arrested and charged. Rippel was sentenced to pay a fine of 300 złoty.[3] He did not despair and began to collect money to organize a new march, which never materialized.

Der Moment believed that the march revealed the tragic situation of Polish Jews. On the one hand they were being urged to emigrate, and on the other they were forbidden to leave. The newspaper called Rippel an adventurer, but such adventures sometimes generated tremendous events.[4] Chaim Lazar-Litai, who in 1938 was Brit Hahayal's (Union of Revisionist Polish Veteran Soldiers) head in Poland and a key activist organizing the Revisionist illegal immigration (the "Af-Al-Pi" Aliyah), met with Rippel, who offered him the help of "hundreds of his people." Lazar-Litai remarked that Rippel's initiative "resonated with people who did not want to consider the objective conditions, particularly among the unemployed on the Jewish street."[5] A year later, as we shall see, Jabotinsky mentioned the incident at the Betar World Congress in Warsaw as an example of delusional plans. Yitzhak Tabenkin, one of the leaders of the Labor Movement who had heard about the event from one of the Hakibbutz Hameuchad emissaries in Poland, wrote in his notebook:

> The enthusiasm that has seized our people's poor sections [in Poland] in particular is hard to describe. [. . .] A Revisionist madman [. . .] announced one fine morning that his group was leaving on foot to Palestine. More than a thousand young men responded to his crazy proposal. [. . .] They marched through the streets [of Warsaw] until the police dispersed them. [. . .] One poor porter in Warsaw jumped at a well-known journalist in the middle of the street, protesting: why was his newspaper "agitating" against partition? "We've had enough Tisha B'Av," the porter cried, "give us a *shtikl* [a little] Simchas Torah."[6]

Polish Jews anxiously awaited the Peel Commission's report. On July 4, *Der Moment* printed a poem called "A Letter from Germany." Its anonymous author called himself "Darkness":

> My body is in Germany
> My head — in the Jewish state.
> How can I have any rest
> How can I have any joy
>
> How can I eat, sleep
> And seek relief
> When my brain is feverish
> with the story of this partition
> [. . .]
>
> The small ancient map
> Of the country of happiness and suffering
> I am curious to know
> How it will be divided [. . .].[7]

When the Partition Plan was published on July 7 it made a big impression on the Jews of Poland. A late edition of *Der Moment* announcing it was sold out within minutes. Passersby stopped Jews on the street to ask them what was the news that had made them so happy. The newspaper wrote that despite the sadness of having to give up some important cities, the possibility that the near future would see the creation of a Jewish state in Palestine filled Jewish hearts with happiness. Many celebrated on the Warsaw streets until late at night, and in the cafés toasts were made for the Jewish state.[8] The wave of spontaneous excitement swept even the radical Zionist Left. The fact that Britain was proposing a Jewish state momentarily allayed their hostility toward "British imperialism." Chajes's enthusiasm was tempered: "England wants to give the Jewish people a state (part of Palestine). Will this help solve the Jewish problem? I do not know. But whatever happens—it will be a great, great thing."[9]

The happiness that gripped some of the Jewish community in Poland came not only as a reaction to the surprising possibility of creating a Jewish state, but also because at the time only Palestine was perceived as a realistic destination for Polish Jews who wished to emigrate.[10] As will be remembered, 1935 marked a turn for the worse in Polish politics, and in the following three years, in which the pressure on Polish Jews to emigrate increased, there was a sharp decrease in the number of immigrants from Poland.[11] The joy thus stemmed from the hope that a sovereign Jewish state, albeit within the narrow borders of the Partition Plan, would permit immigration on a large scale, put an end to the certificate system, and make the struggle for priority in the distribution of immigration permits among those wishing to emigrate from the different European countries redundant.

Not everyone, however, saw the plan as the answer. Those who rejected the Partition Plan were far from enthusiastic. They refused to believe that a state limited to the Partition borders would be able to absorb immigration on a significant scale and preferred the continuation of the British Mandate, on condition that it would permit large immigration. A "tiny corner" within the Partition borders, Jabotinsky wrote Winston Churchill on July 16, hoping to urge his intervention, would offer no answer to a "reservoir of distress" containing eight to nine million Jews. If the Partition Plan was carried out, he warned, it would not only fail to save the Jews of Europe but also give rise to an unprecedented antisemitic outburst. Even if the area in question were to be increased, it "offer[ed] no room for any considerable Jewish immigration," and "the moment this prospect becomes obviously impossible, an unprecedented outburst of anti-Jewish feeling is to be expected, and the government will be urged to follow the Nazi example of placing antisemitism in the statute book."[12]

There were thus those who not only failed to become excited by the vision of founding a sovereign Jewish state, but also saw it as a dangerous delusion. A state within the borders proposed by the Partition Plan would hardly be able to absorb a large immigration, and would therefore raise false hope. Its small size would deter immigrants on the one hand, and increase antisemitism on the other. Both factions of Zionist politics knew that accepting the Partition Plan would weaken Zionism's position before the Polish authorities. The latter would be able to claim that Zionism and Palestine were clearly unable to offer the destination for a large Jewish immigration.

The dilemma was by no means simple. In public, Ben-Gurion expressed his fear of "messianic fervor" following the partition proposal: "The [Peel] Commission's proposal has created more excitement in the Jewish people than anything done for hundreds and thousands of years. Some see this proposal as the destruction of Zionism—and some see it as the beginning of salvation."[13] His view was that the Zionist movement must not, by its own deeds and due to its own weakness, miss the historic opportunity, "which might never return." Nevertheless, he wrote Katznelson in a "messianic" spirit:

> Maybe I am gripped by madness—perhaps. But all my being is burning for the possible revival of the kingdom of Israel. For over a year now I have been worried that, God forbid, this "dream" would not come true. [. . .] Even after I saw the written announcement of a British Royal Commission and a British cabinet declaring the establishment of a Jewish state—I still worry that it will not come true.[14]

In the meantime, the British government fixed the immigration quota at 12,000 immigrants per year for the eight-month "transition period"—from August 1937 to March 31, 1938—from mandate to state. The emissaries from Palestine reported on an atmosphere of despair and apathy among the Hechalutz members, because the Partition Plan offered no immediate solution for those wishing to emigrate. The Zionist movement, they agonized, had nothing to offer the Jews; it was not even capable of organizing protests against the immigration restrictions.[15] The march organized by Rippel was one of the results of this frustration.

In summer 1937, the political circumstances obliged the Zionist movement to decide "whether founding the state is desirable or not for the Jewish people."[16] A state not as a vision for the distant future or as an "end goal" (*Endziel*), but in the here and now. The need to decide came as a result of the Partition Plan conceived by the Royal Commission headed by Lord William Robert Wellesley Peel, which was appointed in August 1936 following the riots that had erupted in Palestine in April. The Commission submitted its report to the British cabinet in June 1937 (it was published on July 7). The Peel Commission's appointment was announced at St. James's Palace on August 7, 1936. Jabotinsky was not concerned. I am "willing to bet my life on it," he wrote, that the English "would never dream of causing real damage to the Jewish progress in Palestine." All the proposals and plans that the British government was floating were nothing but a ruse "to distract the Arabs and lull them until we are ready."[17] Therefore, although he rejected the Commission's authority, he did not support boycotting it and intended to appear before it and throw the blame "on the failed governments in London and Jerusalem, and maybe also on the Jewish Agency," which might "be very useful for propaganda."[18] England, he wrote, tongue in cheek, had been transformed from Don Quixote to Sancho Panza.

The Commission members arrived in Palestine on November 11 and held the opening session of their deliberations the next day at the Palace Hotel in Jerusalem. The representatives of the Zionist movement appeared before the Commission toward the end of the month. The Zionist leadership's efforts to influence the Peel Commission's recommendations, and the debate that erupted within the Zionist movement on whether to accept or reject the Partition Plan, have been discussed in the research literature from a variety of aspects.[19] We shall focus here on one aspect, which is the main axis of our discussion: Did those in favor of partition offer a plan to prepare the Yishuv for the founding of a Jewish state, and in particular, in what ways did they propose to organize a large-scale Jewish immigration?

It soon turned out that although the "profound" and "formidable" debate that erupted in the Zionist movement after the report's publication, and that crossed partisan borders, was both fundamental and pragmatic, it was ultimately futile. It was not the argument within the Zionist movement that thwarted the plan, but the British government's renunciation of it not long after. The British reached the conclusion that it would not be possible to realize the intention of dividing western Palestine into two states, and that any such attempt would cause unrest among the Arabs in the Middle East and beyond, damaging vital strategic British interests at a sensitive time.

This conclusion delivered a fatal blow to the Zionist policy. Despite their criticism of the Mandate regime, almost none of the movement's leaders doubted that Zionism's political strategy and hopes hinged on cooperating with Britain. They understood very well that the desirable and necessary aim was to reach a "broad Jewish-English agreement" on continuing the cooperation and on implementing "fundamental changes in our favor concerning the scale of immigration, the land question and our share of government services."[20] The Zionist strategy was based, among other things, on an attempt to convince Britain that a large, strong, and loyal Jewish Yishuv would be "a military stronghold for England."

The Zionist political strategy, Ben-Gurion said in August 1936, required "procuring the help of the English."[21] This meant making efforts to convince not only the British cabinet but also British public opinion, which "is our crucial and main support outside the Jewish people."[22] On this matter there was no real disagreement between him and the leader of the opposing Zionist camp, Jabotinsky. The latter sent a letter in March 1934 to King George V, declaring that the Jews had always believed in the alliance with Great Britain, and in order for this belief not to be undermined, Britain needed to adhere to the "mandatory regime" and fulfill its commitments according to the Mandate commission.[23] The great fear was that the Partition Plan would not be ratified, thus leaving as its legacy not the "state" idea, but rather the conclusion that the Mandate administration had reached the end of its life.

The subject of Jewish emigration from Europe did not fail to come up in the Zionist leaders' testimonies before the Peel Commission. In his testimony of November 1936, Weizmann described the situation of millions of Jews in Europe who were turning into "human manure" and of the six million Jews suffering distress in Eastern Europe, two million of whom should be brought to Palestine over the next fifteen to twenty years: "Jews are being displaced," turning into "a sort of disembodied ghosts. They are doomed, they are exasperated, they are in despair," while in Germany, the Jews, who "have created modern Germany," have been destroyed "in one day, almost overnight."[24]

On the other hand, when Weizmann met Churchill at a dinner at the home of Sir Archibald Sinclair, the leader of the British Liberal Party and a Zionist sympathizer, on June 8, 1938, he quoted the "slightly lower" number of 50,000 to 60,000 immigrants per year.[25] This was the number of immigrants he mentioned to other British interlocutors. In private correspondence he wrote that preference ought to be given to labor certificates (permits for people without means of their own, or for agricultural workers) "and only on rare occasions to white-collar people." Jabotinsky spoke in his testimony on February 11 about "a disaster of historic magnitude in

Eastern Europe that obliged not only Britain, but the whole of humanity, to give the Jews a territory of their own."[26]

The conclusions Weizmann and Jabotinsky drew from this acute situation, however, were different: Weizmann was an ardent supporter of the Partition Plan, whereas Jabotinsky was its most trenchant opponent.[27] Even if they spoke of millions of immigrants—not to underscore the gravity of the European Jews' situation but as a realistic goal—no one in the Zionist movement's leadership presented this vision as a plan for the short term: they talked about a time frame of ten to twenty years. After all, the 1936 riots (the Arab Revolt) had also begun as the Palestinian Arabs' response to the Yishuv's rapid growth from 1933 onward. The year 1934 saw the arrival of around 42,000 immigrants, 1935—the record year of immigration to Palestine since the early days of Zionism—around 62,000 people, and 1936 around 30,000. In total, around 135,000 immigrants entered Palestine from 1934 to 1936. Capital imports also grew considerably, creating a boom in all areas of the economy. In 1936, the Jewish population in Palestine numbered around 400,000. Against this backdrop we can understand Weizmann's words at the Zionist Executive Committee's meeting in Jerusalem on March 31, 1935: "I fear that today we are substituting the concept of saving the Jews for the concept of salvation," adding: "When I see a ship carrying a thousand immigrants arriving at Haifa, and when I know what the ship left here [in Palestine], then I am glad as a human being, as a Jew. But when I consider whether these people are able to fit into the life we are building here, [. . .] I have to say openly, no. And what has been said here, that we are building on sand, may be true."[28]

A world of difference lies between Weizmann's statement in March 1935 and his speech at the Twenty-First Zionist Congress in Geneva. Ben-Gurion's words in April 1936 to Sir Arthur Wauchope, the British High Commissioner in Palestine, that "the whole world is shutting its doors. And if there had been no place for us even in Palestine there would have been no choice for our people but to commit suicide,"[29] failed to resonate with his interlocutor. At the same time, neither did Ben-Gurion see a "non-selective" large immigration as desirable. Around seven months earlier, in August 1935, he said at the Nineteenth Zionist Congress:

> A mass transfer to Palestine means first and foremost a mass transition to a life of work. Let us assume for a moment that we have around a quarter million Jewish families who are ready to move to Palestine right away (we can assume that in fact there are more). Let us also assume that

> the gates of Palestine have been miraculously opened and that the government allows this million to enter. And that we have enough ships to transport all these people immediately—clearly, a million Jews as they are in the Diaspora will not be able to subsist in Palestine.[30]

Reducing the immigration possibilities would make the Jews of Europe despair of Palestine, causing Zionism to be removed from the Jewish public stage as a political force, Ben-Gurion warned at the end of July 1937, at the World Council of Ihud Poalei Zion—Hitachdut (Mapai's global umbrella party organization), which convened in Zurich on the eve of the Twentieth Zionist Congress.[31] On the other hand, a sovereign Jewish state would allow the immigration of 100,000 people per year over the next fifteen years, and in the near future it would be possible to adjust the borders through the immigration of hundreds of thousands of Jews. About the situation of Germany's Jews, Ben-Gurion said: "Whoever says that Hitler has decreased our power does not tell the whole truth. The destruction of German Jewry has certainly weakened the Jewish people and reduced its political weight, but on the other hand—it has also increased the pressure of Jewish distress, and Jewish distress is also a political factor. Moreover, in time the Jewish state will be able to use force to enlarge its territory."[32]

When Shertok reported to the meeting of Mapai's political committee on December 10, 1936, on the Zionist representatives' appearance before the Peel Commission, he explained why it had been so difficult to convince the members of the Commission that the immigration quotas needed to be increased:

> If we intended to impress the "Commission" with our complaints, maybe we should not have started with the question of immigration. Certainly, for us the main complaint is in the area of immigration. But foreigners see things differently. In light of "schedules" [immigration quotas] that have been gradually growing in recent years and the large immigration in general, it is difficult to present this question as an outrageous complaint that leaves a strong impression on people from the outside.[33]

After the Commission left Palestine on January 19, 1937, the Zionist movement went through more than five months of tension, anxious waiting, and diplomatic activity—overtly, and mainly in the corridors behind the scenes. When the Royal Commission to Palestine's report was published, it turned out that it was full of praise for the Yishuv's development. It noted that the members of the Commission did not forget "what the Jews of Palestine never forget—the suffering of European Jews that forms a driving force and urges them to try and extend the borders of the national home as much as possible."[34]

But these words of praise for the achievements of the Zionist project concealed a sting: the Commission stressed the Palestinian Arabs' concern over the pace of the Yishuv's development and its impressive demographic growth. Therefore, it proposed canceling the immigration quotas ("schedules") in the transition period and allocating them not according to the existing principle of "economic absorption capacity," but according to a new principle: the principle of "political maximum," which would determine the demographic proportions between Jews and Arabs. The Commission wrote:

> The continuous impact of a highly intelligent and enterprising race backed by large financial resources on a comparatively poor, indigenous community, on a different cultural level, may produce in time serious reactions. The principle of economic absorptive capacity, meaning that considerations of economic capacity and these alone should determine immigration, is at present inadequate and ignores factors in the situation which wise statesmanship cannot disregard. Political, social and psychological factors should be taken into account. His Majesty's Government should lay down a political high level of Jewish immigration. This high level should be fixed for the next five years at 12,000 per annum. The High Commissioner should be given discretion to admit immigrants up to this maximum figure, but subject always to the economic absorptive capacity of the country.[35]

In other words, the Peel Commission envisaged a "transition period" of eight months and recommended also giving the High Commissioner the authority to fix lower immigration quotas during this period than the maximum recommended. On October 23, 1937, the Palestine government published a law that determined the maximum scope of immigration, including that of "capitalists." The quota for the months August 1937 through March 1938 was 8,000 immigrants.

On June 24, Edward Raczynski, Poland's ambassador to London, was instructed to approach the British government and stress the importance Poland accorded to allowing the Jewish state within the partition borders to take in a large Jewish immigration.[36]

On Wednesday, July 7, 1937, tension was at its peak. Everyone was waiting for the news broadcast on the Mandate radio, to hear the summary of the

Royal Commission's report concerning the solution to the Palestine question. In the days prior to the report's publication, Weizmann, who tried to find out its details from government officials, only managed to garner a few bits of information. "We are groping in the dark," he wrote to Wise on June 29, "and have pieced [the information] together from various conversations I have had, and cannot swear to it at first hand."[37] By July 7 the report was already on his desk, and his view was that "on the whole it is not bad . . . I have only read 'chunks' of the report. It is an intricate and complex document and must be digested slowly."[38]

On July 8, Weizmann wrote to Lord Peel to express his "deep gratitude for the tone and spirit in which the report was written."[39] Shertok heard the gist of the report two days before its publication, and his first reaction was that the Royal Commission showed decency toward the Jews and recognized the right of the Jewish people to determine its national aspirations.[40] However, a day after the report's official publication Shertok decided that the Royal Commission's conclusions "were highly worrying" and that the report was "an extremely disappointing document"—mainly because of its firm conclusion that "the Mandate is impractical."[41] At the same time, Shertok did not agree with the claim that "the state is not ready yet" and rejected Katznelson's strong words that it was like "pulling the fetus out with tongs in the fifth month."[42] Ruppin, who tried in vain, as he said, to imagine how the Partition Plan would actually take shape, concluded: "It strikes me as a trick of the imagination. It seems that the difficulties of implementing it would be almost insurmountable—due to the large numbers of Arabs in the Jewish state."[43]

Ben-Gurion sailed on April 29, 1937, on the *Marco Polo* to Venice, from where he continued to Paris to meet Weizmann, who was on his way to his vacation in the spa town of Merano in the Italian Alps.[44] Upon arriving in London, he met with British politicians in an attempt to influence them[45] and did not hide his fears, among other things, of what he described as the over-enthusiastic response of the Jews in Europe. On June 11, he spoke to Blanche Dugdale (Baffy), Lord Balfour's niece and Weizmann's right-hand woman, expressing his concern that Britain merely intended to throw the Zionist movement a morsel—but "we cannot house the Jews of Germany and Poland in 'skyscrapers' that we will build in Tel Aviv." A "chopped up" Partition Plan, Ben-Gurion told Dugdale, "would be a terrible catastrophe for the Diaspora Jews in their countries. Cutting down the immigration possibilities would cause a terrible wave of antisemitism and increased persecutions in all the countries of Eastern Europe."[46] After reading the report's summary several days before the publication of the full version, he wrote Shertok:

> I am worried that the Jewish people, at any rate the Jewish masses in Poland, Lithuania, Romania, and the rest of the countries of the Diaspora hell, would get too excited on hearing about the Jewish state. I myself am burning with this excitement, and am willing to give my life for the realization of this plan. But I fear that the Jewish masses will not see all the difficulties that still await us—before the plan comes to fruition—and the possible dangers of it failing to come true.[47]

Ben-Gurion received the full report in his hotel in London at the end of a tense week, in which according to him he had not slept even one night. He decided not to read it until the next morning, but "the trick did not work—even without reading the report I could not sleep."[48] More than anything he was troubled by "the dangers of the transition period"—that is, the period between Britain's practical withdrawal from the Mandate and the establishment of a Jewish state, a period in which, according to the Commission's recommendations, there would be a new policy of immigration quotas in place. Ben-Gurion also worried that the internal logic of the report's conclusion about the Mandate regime's unworkability might metamorphose into the claim that the Partition Plan was unworkable,[49] the result being neither partition nor Mandate.

After a few days Ben-Gurion reconsidered and reached the conclusion that such a historic opportunity might never return, and that Jewish state rule—that is, sovereignty—might perform wonders: a sovereign state would awaken dormant powers in the Jewish people. Now is the time, he wrote with exaltation and self-conviction, to do something revolutionary, not to waste time and not to give the British government the time and the pretext to change its mind. However, he added, success depended on Britain's adherence to the "transfer clause," that is, the transfer of the Arab population from the territories intended for the Jewish state: "The transfer clause is in my view more important than all our demands for additional territory."[50] On the afternoon of July 10, when he finished reading the Commission's report, he wrote that it required and deserved a second reading: "If its main practical conclusion does not fail to come true—this book will serve as the charter of our liberation, eclipsing the Balfour Declaration."[51]

On July 7, Jabotinsky, who had returned from a trip to South Africa, spoke at a meeting held at the "Alhambra" auditorium in Alexandria and declared that the Partition Plan was "drivel" (he used the Italian expression—

chiuchiuchiachia); the only thing left from it would be the official seal of approval for the idea of the Jewish state. He returned to London, appeared before members of Parliament, and detailed his main objections to the Partition Plan.[52] Jabotinsky's biographers emphasize his powers of persuasion and the influence of the numerous reasons he raised against the Partition Plan. However, they ignore the fact that although the policymakers in London reached the conclusion that the Partition Plan was unworkable, they rejected the alternative proposed by Jabotinsky. He, and other objectors to the Partition Plan, pinned their hopes on the vigorous opposition to the plan during the debate in the British House of Commons on July 21, led by Winston Churchill and Lloyd George.[53]

The opposing camp prevented a vote on the plan. At the end of the debate it was agreed that the government would first bring the Partition Plan before the League of Nations, and only after gaining its approval would the discussion of the plan return to the House of Commons. Those opposed to the partition also pinned their hopes on the disagreement that erupted between the Colonial Office and the Foreign Office. On the other hand, the Zionist leadership's activity focused on the attempt to promote the Partition Plan by convincing British politicians that they had no reason to fear the Arab opposition to the plan. The *Jewish Chronicle* wrote that it was a nightmare plan that would turn the national home into a national graveyard.

In a letter that Katznelson wrote to Leah Miron on July 29 from Zurich, where the Twentieth Zionist Congress had convened, he put the term *Jewish state* in brackets to emphasize his doubts over the purported political entity's ability to exist. On April 27, 1937, he wrote Weizmann that without the fulfillment of some basic conditions vital to the establishment of a state, the partition proposal was nothing but a caricature: "Neither a state nor Jewish."[54]

A month and a half later, on June 12, Katznelson explained in a letter he sent from London to the Mapai Central Committee in Tel Aviv that he rejected any "metaphysical opposition" to the idea of dividing Palestine into two states; his heavy doubts belonged to the political-realistic realm. That is, they stemmed from questions such as: What would be the partition borders and what could the Yishuv expect in the transition period "between one kingdom and another"—the time period between the withdrawal of the Mandate and the establishment of a Jewish state? The joyous picture of a sovereign state, whose gates would be open to unlimited immigration, and whose authorities would have the means and resources to organize and absorb immigration, seemed to Katznelson like a mirage: "The dream of an independent state and of glorious horizons opening up for immigration and action [. . .] might conceal, even from people who are versed with the real complexity of our lives, the existence of the conditions that might make our state abortive"; a state within the partition borders would be an "abortive state." The attraction for those who supported partition, he claimed, was independence and sovereignty and "the [Yishuv's] full ability to *bring in Jews, to settle and to defend* itself as it pleases." However, "even if the fundamental questions of Jewish independence were solved, our state could be shipwrecked on the rocks of the '*transition period*.'"[55]

Ruppin's view was that the partition idea was definitely worth discussing "if through it we achieve peace with the Arabs and guarantee a large immigration to the Jewish part."[56] On July 18, however, having studied the report while sailing on the ship *Galilea* from Brindisi to Trieste on his way to the Twentieth Zionist Congress in Zurich, Ruppin, his doubts deepening, wrote in his diary that the report "is of high quality [. . .], but regarding the results, if the Mandate rule continues—the conclusions for us are very depressing, and if some sort of Jewish state is established, the conclusions are too hazardous and uncertain for us."[57]

Weizmann was hoping for help from the Polish government. In July he held some talks with Raczynski, the Polish ambassador to Britain, and asked the Polish government to pressure the British government to expand the territory assigned to the Jewish state in the Partition Plan. If the Jewish Agency received special powers on immigration matters, Weizmann promised the Polish ambassador, it would be able to transfer 100,000 Jews from Poland to Palestine already in the first year. Weizmann even considered going to Warsaw in mid-September to meet Foreign Minister Beck, with whom he spoke in Geneva, two days before Beck spoke at the Council of the League of Nations on the Palestine issue.[58] On September 21, the Polish representative to the League of Nations claimed that a "partition" would not open Palestine to masses of Jews, but only to a "selected elite," and this was something to which Poland could not agree.[59]

The Revisionist movement wanted Poland to help abolish the Partition Plan entirely rather than merely use its influence to change its proposed borders or to increase the immigration quotas. In its view, the plan was a "third destruction [of the Temple]," and it pooled all its forces to wage war against "the tearing up of the homeland" with speeches, articles, and poems. Moreover, the Revisionist movement did not only object to the partitioning of "Western Palestine," but also advocated the creation of the Jewish state on both banks of the Jordan River, “threatening” to embark on a “world war” against both the Partition Plan and Britain. At the same time, the movement “promised” Britain that if it changed its policy, 17 million Jews would act as “bayonets and shields for the safety of the [British] Empire.”

The Revisionist press pointed out that it was not alone in its objection—Poland and Romania also opposed partition—and likened the Partition Plan to the Treaty of Versailles, which was “for Germany a *humiliation* [. . .], an injury to its pride and value—and therefore Germany was shaken, it quaked and fumed at the whole world and in the end spawned the fiend that has now become the downfall of the whole of humanity—Adolf Hitler.” Even more than Britain, according to the Revisionists, those responsible for the plan were “the internal traitors,” that is, the partition’s supporters,[60] headed by Weizmann, the main culprit for Zionism’s disgraceful political failure.

At times Jabotinsky was gripped by disappointment, concluding that the “British period” in the history of Zionism had come to an end; he did not, however, even for a moment lose the hope that Britain’s policy on the Palestine question could be changed. The mounting international tension only strengthened his belief that the British government would pull itself together, realize the strategic importance of a strong Jewish Yishuv, and open the country’s gates to one million Jewish immigrants. This belief inspired the relentless campaign he conducted from July 1937 against the Partition Plan.

The Evacuation Plan and his talks with various officials in the Polish administration relied, as we may recall, on the claim that Palestine could absorb the immigration of hundreds of thousands and even millions of Jews over ten years or more. Therefore, it was clear to Jabotinsky that he would have difficulty convincing his Polish partners that a large immigration was absorbable in the territorial borders delineated by the Partition Plan. In his book (published in Hebrew and Polish in 1937) *Medina Ivrit—Pitaron Sheelat Hayehudim* (*A Jewish State—Solving the Jewish Question*) Jabotinsky suggested: “A policy of planned and organized immigration should concentrate on those aged between twenty-three and thirty-nine. They are certainly capable of fulfilling a pioneering role; they will be even more capable if a proper system of preparation and training is finally established in the Diaspora.”[61]

Practically, an “organized immigration” meant setting up a financial system that would enable Polish Jews to take all their property with them. Jabotinsky was convinced that the naive idea, as he called it, that “the mass immigration would flood in from the east, but without any money, and the funds needed for their resettlement would be provided by rich Jews in Western countries," was an "utterly impossible" idea.[62] He estimated that around 47 million pounds sterling—an unimaginable sum—would be needed to carry out such a plan.[63] In other words, Jabotinsky maintained that a massive immigration would only be possible under a Mandate regime that would help create the necessary conditions in Palestine for the absorption and resettlement of massive numbers of immigrants.

The "partition debate"—the plans, the discussions, the questions, and the indecisions—barely included any concrete discussion of how the institutions of the Jewish state would be established and in what ways they would fulfill all the roles occupied by the Mandate government. In his testimony to the Royal Commission in November 1936, Weizmann merely said that the Jews did not object to the possibility that, even after partition, the responsibility for governance would remain with Britain.[64]

Ben-Gurion was more practical, and from April to August 1937 he detailed the numerous advantages of a sovereign state: a state knows where it can obtain weapons and does so openly; it buys ships and builds factories; the Jewish state would legislate its own land laws, determine its own customs tariffs, and sign its own trade agreements; a sovereign state would have "a Jewish army and a Jewish police force devoted to the country's security, [and] a Jewish administration that would see its role in building the state, with the help of the Jewish people around the world, which is devoted in spirit and soul to the kingdom of Israel." A state, Ben-Gurion added, would be able to bring in all the pioneers now in training "at once" and "dress them in khakis" and "invite gentile officers to teach them how to be soldiers [. . .] and within one month we would have good soldiers. A Jewish young man only needs one month of studying to become a good soldier. [. . .] The Jewish National Council cannot bring in weapons and form an army, but a state can."[65]

In order to show the British the Yishuv's military capabilities, on July 6 Ben-Gurion urged Pinchas Tarshish, a member of the Mapai Central Committee, to send him London photographs of Hechalutz members performing military maneuvers: "We will show them here to the people from the War Office and to several politicians. They make a big impression—and will benefit us. [. . .] Especially pictures of military maneuvers with guns."[66] On the same subject, he wrote in his diary on September 19, 1938, that in order to prepare the Yishuv for the war with Germany (that is, to defend the Yishuv) it would be necessary to recruit thousands of young men into the Haganah, coordinate food and raw materials, prepare air raid defenses, and organize a large immigration of young people. He did not elaborate as to how these preparations would be carried out.

Much was said in the following months about necessary and desirable borders, purchasing land, the need to control the water sources, the status of Jerusalem, and the transfer of the Arab population from the territories of the Jewish state to the future Arab state. The discussions in the Jewish Agency Directorate also revolved around more practical issues, such as manning government offices, setting up a legal system, structuring the budget and the tax system, defining the scope of state services (Shertok maintained that the burden of public services could only be taken on gradually), developing the economy, and organizing an army and a police force.[67] It was also determined that the Jewish state, once founded, would have diplomatic delegations in the important capitals.

These ideas, however, did not mature into a practical plan of action,[68] perhaps because in July 1937 the assumption was that the transition period from mandate to state would be gradual, and that Britain would not rush to withdraw from Palestine. Around seven months later, the Agency's Directorate submitted to the Partition Commission (the Woodhead Commission), appointed on January 4, 1938, twenty-three memoranda that elaborated its plans in the various areas in order to convince it that the Zionist movement and the Yishuv would be able to withstand the challenge of creating a state, with, as Weizmann put it, "a Jewish life, as we imagine it."[69] These memoranda, painstakingly prepared by around eighty experts, highlighted the importance of the Yishuv having its own seaport, but included no plan of action regarding the organization of mass immigration once the Jewish state was founded.

The Twentieth Zionist Congress, followed by the fifth session of the Council of the Jewish Agency, convened in Zurich from August 3 to 21, 1937, to discuss the Zionist response to the Partition Plan. There were 484 delegates from all over the world: Labor, with 216 delegates; the World Union of General Zionists, with 117 delegates; Hamizrachi, with 73 delegates; the World Alliance of General Zionists, with 40 delegates; and the Jewish State Party, with 9 delegates. There were also 29 delegates from Germany. Several hundred journalists came to cover the Congress (most of the sessions were closed to journalists). According to one estimate, around 5,000 visitors arrived in Zurich.

As in Geneva two years later, the Zurich Congress was preceded by conventions of various organizations, several exhibitions were held, and the sessions took place at ten different buildings. Four volunteer printers from Palestine saw that the publication of the daily Hebrew bulletin did not lag behind the German one, despite the less convenient technical conditions of its printing.[70] *Davar*'s delegate to Zurich, Bracha Habas, praised the city's authorities for their security arrangements: "Zurich is as quiet and pretty as ever. Its population is almost 2.5 times that of Tel Aviv, but it leads a tranquil life. [. . .] Some streets and corners feel like a remote village — and you are in the middle of a populous and bustling city."[71]

Tabenkin, who took a plane for the first time in his life, wrote in his notebook: "Between the clouds and the sea [. . .] the concept of the world expands [. . .] this perspective organizes reality [more] prettily."[72] Ben-Gurion and his wife Paula arrived in Zurich from Paris in a posh car — it was the first time, he wrote, that he had ever made such a long trip (twenty-four hours) by car: "Green and yellow meadows, greenish hills and alternating woods escorted us the whole way. Not one patch of land was uncultivated, not one hillock bare."[73] He stayed at the Eden au Lac hotel and began working immediately.[74] Weizmann arrived in Zurich on August 1 and stayed at the more expensive Grand Hotel Dolder. He knew that the Congress would be not only a test of his leadership but also a crossroads in the history of Zionism.

Two days later, at 8:15 p.m., around 2,500 people — delegates and guests — attended the gala opening session, which was held at the "Tonhalle," near Lake Zurich's outfall into the Limmat. The decorated hall could not hold everyone, and some of the audience sat in two adjoining halls equipped with loudspeakers. Weizmann, who was greeted with great applause, spoke in German and presented the burning problems on the Congress's agenda. There were also the customary welcome speeches.

On August 8, around 2,000 delegates took the train to Basel to mark the fortieth anniversary of the First Zionist Congress, which was held in the city in August 1897. The train tickets printed for the occasion carried a special inscription in Hebrew and German: "A special train for the 40th anniversary of the First Zionist Congress."[75] After the speeches, the crowd thronged to the Rhine Bridge, famous for the photograph of Herzl leaning against the rail, and observed a minute of silence in memory of the founder of the Zionist Organization and the visionary of the Jewish state.

On August 4, Weizmann spoke before the Zionist Congress for two hours, a speech in which he strongly criticized the Peel Commission's proposal to limit immigration to 12,000 immigrants per year. Without mincing words, he listed the alternatives facing delegates: "The choice we are facing is this:

a Jewish minority in the whole of Palestine — one can even say, in an Arab Palestine — or a region of a Jewish majority in part of the country." Above all, he stressed, stood the need to preserve the unity of the Zionist movement.[76] Weizmann struggled to overcome the burst of excitement that gripped him during his speech, and he needed a five-minute break. Dugdale wrote enthusiastically that it was a "great speech."[77]

Shmuel Katz, Jabotinsky's biographer, wrote that Weizmann was highly concerned over "the great stream of German Jews flooding Palestine." After his speech at the Congress Weizmann and a few other leaders went to the home of the Zionist political activist Shmaryahu Levin. There, according to testimony, Weizmann "spoke at length about the danger of land speculation and the development of an unwholesome economy," until Levin cried: "Chaim, have mercy on the Jews, let them first come and get their strength back. The rest will follow later." At which point, "Chaim fell silent."[78] This testimony, according to Jabotinsky's loyal biographer, supposedly proved Weizmann's distaste toward Eastern European Jews, showing that his ardent support for the Partition Plan — which he had helped conceive behind the scenes — stemmed from his fear of a great immigration of "undesirable elements" to the future Jewish state. He was, however, mistaken and misleading: these words were spoken by Weizmann during the Nineteenth Zionist Congress in 1935.

Behind the scenes, Weizmann tried to highlight the importance of the "transfer" idea, to fight against the immigration quota of 8,000 immigrants in eight months during the transition period, and expressed his hope that the transitional period could "be kept as brief as possible."[79] After the Congress, he reiterated that the state's survival required such borders that would guarantee its existence both strategically and economically.[80] Weizmann's speech, *Davar* wrote, "was peppered with humor and irony [and] was very enthusiastically received."[81] Katznelson got the impression that Weizmann "was at the peak of his artistic powers and in a good frame of mind." About Shertok's speech, which supported Weizmann's views, he wrote that it "even rose to the level of a student excelling in his exams."

Shertok had a much better opinion about his own speech[82] and, when he was done, returned to his seat "full of excitement and utterly exhausted." Some, he boasted in his diary, described his speech as "most brilliant."[83] In Katznelson's view, Shertok's speech was the best among the yeasayers, but was nonetheless unable to prove "that this [was] the way." Katznelson spoke on the morning of August 6, in Yiddish, claiming, among other things, that the assertion that without a state there was no immigration was meaningless: "On the subject of immigration we hear fine promises for the future, which without being realized *today* remain nothing but false promises," and who knew what would happen during the transition period.[84]

Shertok criticized Katznelson's speech and thought it lacked conclusions. Katznelson's wish to find a compromise, Shertok wrote, made his speech suffer from "a lack of internal balance" and created confusion in those still vacillating. However, he wrote his wife Tzipora that Katznelson had shown his wisdom at the Congress and managed to prevent an internal rift: "He is the most serious person at the Zionist Congress."[85] As for Ben-Gurion, he said in his speech that the territory assigned by the plan to the Jewish state did not have enough space "to absorb the masses of our people who need refuge."[86] Katznelson failed to get excited by Ben-Gurion's vision, and his impression from the speech was that Ben-Gurion sometimes reached "utter dejection, despairing even of himself."[87] Shertok thought that Ben-Gurion spoke endlessly and monotonously and wore the audience out.[88]

"What shall this vegetable called a Jewish state live on?" Menachem Ussishkin, a Russian Zionist leader and chairman of the Jewish National Fund (Keren Kayemet LeYisrael), mockingly asked the delegates of the Zionist Congress in Zurich, "Upon what shall we build our industry? [. . .] Where shall we find the economic foundation for a state in the form offered to us?" A Jewish state within the partition borders ("on the coastal strip"), he claimed, might create "an artificial pale for the Jews, which will only profit our speculators and the Arab land sellers in the Jewish territory."[89] He attacked those in favor of partition: "[They] were dazzled by the wonderful glow of 'the Jewish state,' a glow that is neither a great sun nor a great light, but [rather] a light that burns without warming or nourishing." The elderly leader promised that the world's 17 million Jews would be able to stand against the British Empire, and called on Weizmann not to be "a total realist, a total politician; do not be satisfied by waiting for the messiah, but fight for him to come in our time."[90] Ussishkin rejected out of hand the idea of forming any committees to discuss preparations for partition, saying they would amount to a recognition of the plan. He announced that he was "leaving this stage," and his words were greeted with "lengthy applause."[91] In the following months, he kept warning: just as Britain voided the Balfour Declaration of its content, so "will the name 'the Jewish state' become void in a very short time."[92] When he returned to Palestine he said that "Geneva affected me badly."[93]

On Friday, August 6, Ruppin went for a walk on a Zurich street. Two passersby saw the Congress symbol on his coat's lapel and, almost undetected, slipped "a travel ticket to Palestine" together with an antisemitic note into his pocket. Ruppin followed them, stopped them, and spoke with them for about half an hour about the Jewish problem. He found them "educated people aged twenty-five to thirty, equipped with all the arsenal of German racist antisemitism." The next day he wrote in his diary: "They behaved politely, but I found the conversation very disturbing. My interlocutors claimed that the Jews of Switzerland (17,000 in number!) are subjugating the government and forcing it to do their bidding. They spoke like fanatics, with honesty and conviction. Indeed the world faces grim prospects, when this youth comes of age."[94]

Groups of Nazis, some of whom must have come from outside Zurich, threw "tear bombs" into a café where delegates from Palestine were sitting and distributed leaflets: "Switzerland for the Swiss—out with the Jews!"[95]

The plight of the Jews of Germany and Poland hardly appeared on the Zionist Congress's agenda; it was usually mentioned as corroboration for Zionist arguments. Ussishkin claimed mockingly that the situation of Polish Jews served in the debate only as an empty argument, "here we go again: the Polish Jewry argument! We always resort to the Jews of Poland when we face an important turning point."[96] Kleinbaum was outraged: Polish Jews, who despite the pogroms continued to contribute to the Yishuv and who sent delegates to the Congress, he protested, "do not deserve to be discussed in the way they have been talked about here!"[97] The situation of Polish Jews was also mentioned by the Yiddish writer Sholem Asch at the Jewish Agency Council, which convened immediately after the Zionist Congress:

> Neither the Jewish people on its own nor Palestine on its own can solve the Jewish question. First of all we need to solve the Jewish question in each and every country. Each state on its own must solve the question of the Jews within it, and safeguard their lives. We must adhere to these principles, and understand that these days we cannot build a Palestine which would be able to take in the majority of the world's Jews, as Poland and Romania and other countries want—to somehow see all the Jews in their countries miraculously leave for Palestine. If we do not offer them this delusion, they will have to act seriously to solve the Jewish question in their own country.[98]

There were also some dissenting voices heard at the Jewish Agency Council. Dr. Judah Leib Magnes, president of Hebrew University in Jerusalem, must have riled many when he said: "One of the Jewish state's first actions would be to pass laws to restrict immigration, in order to prevent the catastrophe that an unlimited mass immigration could create in the country."[99] Albert Hyamson, a former director of the Mandate government's Palestine Immigration Department, wrote on August 18 in the *Times* that some in the Zionist Congress had spoken "hastily" about Palestine being able to absorb 100,000 immigrants per year—and in total another 1 to 2 million immigrants, without taking into account that it meant a population density of 1,250 people for every square mile—much more than in any country in Europe; "and after all Palestine is mainly an agricultural country."[100]

Jabotinsky arrived in Zurich secretly on July 7 to try and strengthen the hand of some of the leading opponents of partition, though he doubted their readiness to draw extreme conclusions in the event that it was accepted and to withdraw from the Zionist Organization. When he returned from Zurich he called for an alternative Congress and a large demonstration in London, demanding that the British government fulfill the Mandate Commission in both spirit and letter.[101]

Ben-Gurion questioned the Revisionists' opposition to the Partition Plan, writing in January 1938 that Jabotinsky avoided declaring outright that he rejected it: "Jabotinsky declares again and again that the Partition Plan will not be realized. He speculates as to the opposition of certain sections of the English government"—and thus, if the plan were canceled, he "will be able to boast that he had been a prophet once again." However, Ben-Gurion added, "it seems to me that if 'the Plan' becomes a reality, the Revisionists will become its supporters and Jabotinsky will find the way to not explain his fickleness. It would not be the first time."[102]

On August 14, 1937, Jabotinsky published a statement on behalf of the New Zionist Organization, saying that the majority decision in Zurich meant that the Jewish people might under certain conditions agree to the amputation of its homeland and its national home, thus in effect renouncing the idea of a Jewish state on both sides of the Jordan River—the only state that could address the true severity of the Jews' plight.[103]

The Congress ended with a compromise. The final resolution read: "The Congress rejects the unacceptable proposals raised by the Royal Commission as a way to fulfill the Mandate," and chief among them the definition of a maximum immigration quota for the eight months of the transition period. In addition, it said that the Zionist Congress rejected the Partition Plan. However, the Congress authorized the Zionist executive to negotiate with the British government on creating a Jewish state in Palestine. Any agreement reached would be discussed in the next elected Congress.[104] Two hundred and ninety-nine delegates voted in favor of this motion, whereas

160 delegates voted in favor of the minority motion (the naysayers), and 6 delegates abstained. The Congress thus rejected the Partition Plan in the way it had been proposed, but authorized the Zionist executive to "open negotiations aiming to examine the political conditions of his Majesty's government's proposal regarding the establishment of a Jewish state." Before the vote, Ben-Gurion was allowed to make a personal announcement: "I am in favor of a Jewish state not in the future but right now, as the beginning of salvation; and I am not afraid of Jewish independence even when it is limited," he declared amid protestations. "I am willing to give up under certain conditions only the British bayonets that accompany us on the way to Nablus and Jenin." Ussishkin called out to the session's chairman that it was a provocation.[105] For him, the Twentieth Zionist Congress was "a tragic Congress, but a momentous one."[106]

As for immigration, the Congress protested against the restrictions imposed by the government. Its only operative decision was to give 50 percent of the immigration permits to pioneering immigration, "taking into account the requirements of the country's efforts to continue building, which demand conquest of labor and pioneering efforts," and 15 percent of the immigration permits to skilled workers.[107] The Congress expressed its solidarity with "our persecuted comrades in Russia, in their heroic suffering for their loyalty to Zion." The budget of the Immigration Department for 1937 was 23,000 Pp, out of the Jewish Agency's total budget of 365,000 Pp.[108] Two days after the Congress ended, the Jewish Agency Council opened its sessions. The debate about the composition of the Agency executive ended by electing the previous executive. Ruppin concluded sarcastically: "There are more slaughterers than chickens."[109]

One of the leaders of the Palestinian national movement, Awni Abd al-Hadi, remarked that the Twentieth Zionist Congress displayed unity and tactical guile. Its final resolution, he said, showed that the Zionist movement accepted the idea of partition, but demanded wider borders: "The Jews' greedy ambitions [. . .] have no limit. The majority and the minority are united in one ambition—a Jewish state in Palestine."[110] And most importantly, the Zionist Organization managed to preserve its unity. Chajes wrote in his diary:

> The Zionist Congress in Zurich was held under the mark of the Jewish state. England wants to give up the Mandate (Balfour), and wants to establish in Palestine a tiny Jewish state. [. . .] Today I believe, as I have for many years, that the Jewish problem has two possible solutions—a radi-

cal and consistent exodus to Palestine (the Zionist idea) and a radical and consistent assimilation. The one does not exclude the other. [. . .] For many years I have been donating considerable sums to Keren Hayesod, the Palestine Building Fund, for the Jews. But to tell the truth, a Polish Gdansk or a huge Gdynia are more important and closer to my heart than the port in Tel Aviv. There you have it! And despite [. . .] the stupid and outrageous eradication policy against the Jews, despite the work done by Endecja [. . .] I am by a strange stroke of fate both Polish and Jewish.[111]

The Revisionists saw the resolution as a "betrayal," and Jabotinsky published a statement saying that the resolution meant that "the Jewish people might agree under explicit conditions to the dismantling of its homeland and its national home." Faithful to his belief that global public opinion was beginning to accept the idea of a national home on both sides of the Jordan River, he claimed that agreeing to the idea of partition in principle harmed the chances of finding political support and the possibility of providing a solution to the "plight of the Jewish masses."[112]

After the exhausting internal battle ended, some of the Zionist movement's leaders traveled to various holiday resorts. Ben-Gurion and his wife traveled to a vacation home offered to them by Israel Yefroykin, a socialist Zionist journalist and writer, a member of the Jewish Agency executive, and one of the founders of the World Jewish Congress in 1936 (as well as an activist in the boycott of Germany, which Ben-Gurion opposed) in the town of Pont-Sainte-Maxence, around thirty miles from Paris. Ben-Gurion described the place: "A lush garden with chestnuts and cypresses and oaks and fruit trees—a gurgling stream runs across the garden. The large, three-story house is surrounded by flowerbeds and a green meadow." He hoped for a few days of rest before sailing for the United States. On the bridge of St. Maxence, on the bank of the river Auge, he reflected, "We are on the verge of a Jewish state, but are still facing a struggle and maybe also some bitter surprises—or the opposite."[113] On July 28, he traveled to Cherbourg and sailed to New York; aboard the ship he finally got the rest he had hoped for.[114] He returned to Paris on September 17 and promptly flew to Geneva.

Katznelson traveled from Zurich to visit a youth camp in a small Czech village and later flew to Holland, visited the museums in Amsterdam, and from there traveled to Paris and London. He described the situation in which the Zionist movement found itself in September 1937 as in a "frozen fog."[115]

In reality, the Zionist movement found itself struggling in a fog against the British government's intention of withdrawing from both the Partition

Plan and the Mandate, and against the cancellation of the principle of economic absorption capacity. The battlefield moved to the League of Nations in Geneva, where the session of the Council of the League of Nations opened on September 10, and to its Mandates Committee. The representatives of the Zionist Organization met with the British colonial secretary MacDonald, the representatives of different countries, other personages, and journalists in an attempt to persuade them to oppose the abolition of this principle. Jabotinsky also came over, but met only with Professor William Rappard, the deputy chairman of the Mandates Committee. Shertok came to Geneva after traveling for one night and one day from Naples. First he stayed at the same expensive hotel as Weizmann, but later he moved to a cheaper guesthouse on Rue de Lausanne—a room with no breakfast or bath, but with a wonderful view of the lake and the mountains beyond.[116] One night he walked with a group of representatives to see the silent movie *The Green Pastures*, adapted in 1936 from a play written and later directed by Marc Connelly—"stories of Genesis and Exodus as they are imagined by Negroes." The newsreel screened before the film showed pictures from a mass rally in Nuremberg: "*C'est effrayant!*" (It's frightening!) cried a Swiss spectator sitting behind him.[117]

Despite the incessant rain, Ben-Gurion and Katznelson went with Nahum Goldmann on a trip to the mountains, whereas Shertok went to listen to the speeches at the Assembly of the League of Nations. He came out feeling that "we are out of bounds, beyond the fence."[118] More than that he felt stinging humiliation at the fact that "the representatives of 17 million people are sitting mute and ignored. And when an Arab gets up and speaks words of slander we have to hope for some gentile to say something in our favor. A disgraceful and humiliating fate!"[119]

Zionism gained the support of the Polish Foreign Minister, Józef Beck, who wanted Jewish emigration from Poland; in his speech at the Council of the League of Nations on September 14 described the Jews as "superfluous" in the Polish economy. But he had no influence on the discussions. Weizmann and Goldmann told Beck in their meeting with him on September 13 that he should not expect Britain to agree to the emigration of more than 25,000 people per year from Poland to Palestine. Beck answered that even the emigration of 30,000 Jews per year would improve the situation, and therefore he supported the Partition Plan.[120]

Jabotinsky, who tried during those months to move Poland to exert pressure on the British government, came out of his one-hour meeting with Marshal Rydz-Àmigły, the Polish defense minister, with a bad feeling: the prospects for Polish Jews, he said, were "extremely bleak." Geneva did not live up to the Zionist movement's hopes. The League of Nations' Mandates Committee supported an examination of the Partition Plan's feasibility, but rejected the idea that two states should be created immediately, suggesting that the transition period should be extended. Its decision was ratified in September by the Council of the League of Nations.

The political battle returned to London. The British government rejected the Polish arguments against the immigration restrictions. George Rendell, director of the Department for Central and Eastern Europe at the British Foreign Office, announced that his government would not change its policy, and in any case Palestine would not be able to absorb a large Jewish immigration.

On September 26, 1937, Arabs assassinated Lewis Y. Andrews, commissioner for the Galilee district, as he came out of Sunday service at a church in Nazareth (his bodyguard, a British constable, was killed as well). Andrews was perceived by the Arabs as a Zionist sympathizer, and Shertok predicted the impression that his murder would create: "The dejection in the valley, the joy of the terrorists, the terror that would grip the administration, the anger in the whole Yishuv. I foresaw the impression here—it's that bad, and all because of the Jews!" His fears were justified that evening, when he read the reaction in the *Evening Standard*, the paper owned by the press mogul Lord Beaverbrook, which said that the murder occurred because of the government's "absurd politics," and concluded: "The Partition Plan is dead and buried, we should accept the Arabs' demands!"[121]

The British government responded to the murder forcefully. The Arab Higher Committee and the Arab National Committees were outlawed and hundreds of Arab leaders were arrested. Thus began the second phase of the Arab Revolt, which extended from October 1937 through September 1939.[122] From July to October 1938 alone, 211 Jews were killed in Palestine, out of 520 casualties. And during all of 1938, 293 Jews were killed and hundreds injured. The terror was also directed at the British, in an attempt to take control of entire area. The facilities at Lod airport, which was under construction, were set on fire. The Arab Revolt became an armed anti-British rebellion. More than 50 Arabs were hanged.

On September 30, 1938, after a secret visit to Palestine by MacDonald, Secretary of State for the Colonies, the High Commissioner declared military rule and acted vigorously and with great force to suppress the revolt. This military decisiveness, however, was not part of the British government's willingness to use a large military force—two divisions, an armored battalion and an artillery regiment—to implement the Partition Plan. Its aim was to suppress the Arab Revolt and achieve calm in Palestine in order to secure Britain's strategic base in the Middle East. This aim was achieved. The large number of casualties and the destruction of property, however, did not make Palestine a safe refuge, and many saw Poland as a much safer place. Nevertheless, the pressure to emigrate from Poland grew, a pressure for which the Zionist policy had no answer.

The Zionist rhetoric spoke of acute distress, of masses seeking to leave, and of Zionism as the only savior. However, according to the Zionist timeline, in 1937 ten, thirty, and even forty years would be required for the immigration of 4 million Jews,[123] and in the short run the expectation was of 40,000 to 60,000 immigrants per year. In other words, the goal of the Zionist leadership's political struggle was in fact to leave the principle of "economic absorption capacity" in place and increase the immigration quotas, which also meant a gradual and controlled flow of immigration.

In this struggle the Zionist leadership suffered defeat. The new principle defined by the Peel Commission, the principle of "political maximum" for immigration, meant that in the following five years the Jewish Agency would receive a quota of no more than 12,000 immigration permits per year.[124] From October 1937 on, not only was the immigration of "workers" fixed by a quota, but so were the quotas of other types of immigrants. 1937 saw a worsening of the economic situation in Palestine. The number of people unemployed in the Jewish economy was estimated at around 12,000, and capital imports decreased considerably.

Already at the end of 1937, Weizmann expressed his concern that "the bad news one gets from Europe" had given rise to a new political orientation and the British government had started to doubt the possibility of realizing the Partition Plan. He remarked that the "government is beginning to waver in regard to the execution of the Partition Plan" and was doing nothing to promote the plan, and that the atmosphere of doubt and uncertainty encouraged disturbances in Palestine.[125] He saw this state of uncertainty as Zionism's greatest enemy. The opponents of the plan were trying to "strangle" Jewish efforts at national reconstruction and "throw us to the dogs."

In moments of optimism, Ben-Gurion continued to pin his hopes on Britain, which he described as the most reliable supporter the Jewish people and Zionism had in the world, and relied on the friendly British public opinion. The fact that the Peel Commission's report caused disagreement in the British government gave the Zionist camp hope that it would be possible "to save the partition" or alternatively preserve the Mandate. In light of the rumors that the British government intended to rescind the Partition Plan and give it a "respectable burial," and at the same time withdraw from the Mandate, Ben-Gurion sought in January 1938 to assuage the fears of the members of the Jewish Agency's executive: "I do not believe that English public opinion would *countenance* such a betrayal. After all, England is not a totalitarian state. There is the press and there is Parliament, and there is tradition, and we have friends, and there are promises and commitments and declarations; the English are not Jews. They do not get so easily confused and do not panic and do not change their tune every day."[126]

Although the Mandate was in danger, he said, it was not dead, and it would not be so easy to break it and withdraw from it.[127] In his diary he wrote that even the British Cabinet did not always know in advance how it would act in certain circumstances.[128]

Shertok joined those who warned against giving up on the Partition Plan, explaining that the logic that guided the resolution of the Twentieth Zionist Congress was that the Zionist executive could not reject the Partition Plan outright, but that if it succeeded in convincing Britain that the plan in its current form was "ridiculous," the alternative it would demand would be fulfilling the Mandate "unequivocally."[129] The test that Weizmann now faced was to persuade the British government to improve the partition borders. Ben-Gurion was skeptical as to Weizmann's ability to achieve a "good partition." Dugdale thought that there was a move to oust Weizmann from his status at the head of the Zionist movement.[130]

On January 1, 1938, Jabotinsky wrote James G. McDonald to "convey the deepest gratitude for the interest he is taking to save German Jewry." The simple, effective, and just solution for the Jews' situation, however, he wrote, would be to bring all the Jews of Germany plus around half a million Jews from the countries of distress into Palestine within the next two years, in order to resolve both the danger of spreading antisemitism and the question of Palestine. He added that the Zionists would be glad to submit to his excellency a rough draft of a scheme as to how a transfer of a million Jews in two years could be achieved.[131]

In March 1938, the British government appointed the Palestine Partition Commission, headed by Sir John Woodhead. Its members wrestled with the problem for four months, visiting Palestine between April 27 and August 3. In fact, the Commission's role was to provide the government with a ladder on which to climb down from the partition idea in a respectable manner.

Now the Zionist executive could only fight for the Mandate. Ben-Gurion wrote that Zionism had to "keep the Mandate with all our might as long as we do not have a state. [. . .] We have to fight for it as if there was no possibility or hope for a state."[132] Dugdale had no illusions. Britain was about "to sell the Jews" and withdraw from the Partition Plan, she wrote on September 19, 1938.[133] The next day, Ben-Gurion wrote Shertok about a conversation he and Weizmann had had with Colonial Secretary MacDonald, and admitted that the idea of mobilizing the Jews of Europe to fight Britain was hopeless: "Let us assume that we can recruit the Jews of Poland and Romania etc. for protest activities and for a political war. These are only the means. The end is pressure on the government. How will the protest pass through the different channels? Will it reach the government? Will Malcolm [MacDonald] or Neville [Chamberlain] read the article in the *Haynt* or hear a protest received in Pinsk?"[134]

Jabotinsky, whose movement organized a public campaign designed to pressure the British government (the "Petition Project"), was privately full of similar doubts about the chances of the petition having any impact, because the situation of Polish Jews did not bother the British government one bit.[135] Tabenkin counted on the strength of the Yishuv. He wrote on September 15 that Czechoslovakia had been wrong for pinning its hopes on a guarantee rather than on the willingness to shed blood. The situation in Palestine was different, he stated: here there were 400,000 Jews ready to give the English "trouble." "England must not be trusted [. . . it] betrayed Spain, betrayed Czechoslovakia and said explicitly what it intends to do in Palestine."[136] Weizmann brokenheartedly reached the conclusion that "the partition [was] dead."[137] The statements of long-standing allegiance to Britain — the "land of freedom," as Jabotinsky called it — were to no avail.

On March 12, 1938, the German army entered Austria and the following day its annexation (Anschluss) into the Reich was announced. Another approximately 250,000 Jews came under the rule of Nazi Germany. They were subject to humiliation, abuse, looting, confiscations, and arrest. Adolf Eichmann, an official in the Gestapo's Jewish Department in Berlin, was appointed in March to run the "Central Office for Jewish Emigration" (Zentralstelle für jüdische Auswanderung) in Vienna. In short order, he activated a mechanism of forced emigration and deportation, which gave a free hand to the organizers of illegal immigration and even pressured them with threats to accelerate their activities. The deportees' property was confiscated, and they were left with nothing but a transit visa. Many were driven to no-man's-lands on Austria's borders with its neighboring countries.

Wolfgang von Weisl, who left Vienna before the Anschluss and worked at the offices of the New Zionist Organization on de Bassano Street in the 16th arrondissement in Paris, noted that around 24,000 requests for entry visas to France were submitted to the French consulate in Vienna by April 26. On May 16, he wrote: "In fact all the countries in Europe have hastened to close their doors to Jews from Austria [. . . ,] especially France." Moreover, France was about to pass a law that would prevent the entry of Jews and threatened to deport around 10,000 refugees already residing in the country, including 2,000 Jews from Austria.[138]

Tens of thousands of Jews began to look for countries of refuge, obtaining fake documents and bribing border guards. The Palestine Office in Vienna stood helpless against the twofold pressure of the Nazi deportation apparatus on the one hand and the certificate seekers on the other. On July 27, during a debate on the refugee problem in the House of Lords, Viscount Herbert Samuel reported that the Nazis deliberately "endeavor[ed] to create a feeling of panic and terror among the Jewish population . . . in order to compel a speedy emigration." In recent weeks, he said, hundreds if not thousands of Jews had been arrested or sent to concentration camps. The consulates of Britain, the United States, and other countries were mobbed by hundreds and sometimes thousands of people, hoping to gain the longed-for visa that would enable them to escape the terror.[139] In this situation, Austrian Jews should have been top priority in the distribution of immigration permits available to the Jewish Agency according to the fixed quota. In 1937, 214 Jews emigrated from Austria to Palestine and 2,964 in 1938 (40.5 percent of the legal immigration). It was the Jews under the Reich whose plight the Zionist movement was called upon to respond to most urgently.

The initiative to seek alternative channels to the immigration quotas came in both Zionist camps from the grassroots level. Already in April 1934, Eliyahu Golomb, the senior figure in the Haganah organization, had summoned Yehuda Braginsky, who was about to be sent by the Hechalutz movement to Poland, and encouraged him to start organizing illegal immigration. Braginsky and his friends rose to the challenge. For that purpose, they leased the Greek 2,000-ton passenger ship *Vellos* ("fast"), which was built in 1906 and sailed under the British flag. They organized the transfer of 350 Hechalutz members—most from Poland—to Athens, with the knowledge and encouragement of the Polish authorities. The latter dispatched the train on which they traveled from Warsaw to Athens from a secondary station, for fear of British secret agents.

In Athens, Braginsky discovered that the group's organizers "were not too careful about choosing the human material, and thus in Greece we received Jews who were not at all ready for the ordeals that awaited them on their journey." After many hardships, the *Vellos* sailed from the port of Piraeus in July, and four days later arrived at the Kfar Vitkin beach. The immigrants were taken ashore by boats. One of those boats hit a rock and two of its passengers drowned. The stormy sea prevented the completion of disembarkation, and the ship sailed toward Tel Aviv. Katznelson, who was present with Golomb when the illegal immigrants were taken off the ship (an experience he would describe in his speech at the Zionist Congress in Geneva in 1939), wrote in his diary on July 31: "All night on the beach. Receiving the first ship. Sublime and horrifying. The capsized boat: the two who drowned."[140]

The *Vellos* sailed again, this time from the port of Varna in Bulgaria, with around 380 pioneers on board, and reached Palestine's shores on September 10. The military and the police were waiting for it on the beach. Only around 50 illegal immigrants managed to make it ashore at night. The *Vellos* wandered for a few days near the coast until it ran out of coal and food, and sailed to the Greek island of Sirius. The ship reached the island on October 17 and stayed there for eight days. The third disembarkation attempt, this time at the Tel Aviv Port, failed as well. The ship sailed to the port of Tripoli in Lebanon, replenished its water supplies, and sailed to Thessaloniki. It was forced to put down anchor outside the port for a few weeks because its passengers were not allowed to go ashore. The global press called the *Vellos* a "Jewish wandering ship" and a "ghost ship." Only after many efforts and appeals did the Romanian government agree to give the passengers transit visas, and on November 20 they were taken on the Romanian ship *King Carol* from Piraeus to Constanta. After 58 days without touching land, the illegal immigrants were taken on a special train—surrounded by police, secret agents, and soldiers—to the Polish border. They stayed there from November 25 to January 1935 in an old school building in the border town of Zaleszczyki. Eventually, they received immigration permits and made it to Palestine.[141]

Felix Fisher (Shefa), a young pioneer from Czechoslovakia who was one of the ship's passengers (and who immigrated to Palestine on January 23, 1935), wrote an illustrated diary in German during the voyage. Some of it was translated and published in Hebrew in 1982. In it he described the ship's odyssey and the failed attempts to put its passengers ashore. This is how he recorded the third landing attempt, near Tel Aviv:

We could clearly see the flickering lights of Tel Aviv. I could even discern a publicity [billboard] lit with red light. We drew nearer and our spirits were high. Suddenly a small boat passed next to us. I did not see anyone in it nor hear the beating of oars; quietly and with wonderful self-control, Dan [Shaike Trachtenberg] gave the order to go downstairs. The ship started sailing at great speed. No one was able to explain the appearance of the small boat. Suddenly our ship was lit as if by lightning, and at that moment we saw a signal rocket falling into the water and going off. Another signal rocket followed it right away, and in its green light I noticed a large motorboat passing close to our ship; at the end of the boat stood a soldier, who must have shot the signal rocket. My friend Hans asked me: "What's going on?" "It's the end," was my answer. Although people had not yet understood what was happening, or maybe because of that, they were totally quiet. Around five signal rockets were launched before the boat disappeared. It was quiet until the old man [the ship's owner] came and announced in broken English, "Finish Palestine."[142]

After the failed attempt to go ashore the ship wandered around at sea for about a month:

Life seemed to take on the old routine again: in the morning tea and a piece of hard, moldy bread. Supper was never even mentioned anymore. There were many illnesses, people became weak, they brewed cocoa—water from tins of concentrated milk. To strengthen the sick a little we cooked them some groats porridge but it was inedible; worse than the rice porridge we had been given. Once I got some noodles leftovers from one of the sailors and I gulped them down eagerly. Among the sailors there is one sailor-carpenter, a toothless old man, who only eats the soft part of the bread and there are many customers for the bread crust he leaves.[143]

The failure of the *Vellos*'s second voyage, the third attempt to get its passengers to their destination, which did not succeed because of some underhandedness by the ship's owner, and the big financial expenses, brought an end to Hechalutz's illegal immigration for around three years (Braginsky called them "three lost years").[144] The Jewish Agency executive reasoned that illegal immigration could not offer a solution for the plight of European Jews, all the more so because the British deducted the number of illegal immigrants from the allotted permits. The bitter experience also showed that illegal immigration attracted dubious characters, thieves and money grabbers, and that the immigrants' "quality" could not be controlled.

The Jewish Agency representatives who testified before the Peel Commission also spoke in two different voices: on the one hand, they expressed objection to illegal immigration—"because it involve[d] immigrants' exploitation and human trade" and because the Yishuv had to prove that it respected law and order—but on the other hand, they did not conceal their sympathy for the motives of the immigrants "who break laws that do not enable immigration."[145]

The illegal immigration was renewed only at the beginning of 1938, after Austria's annexation to Nazi Germany,[146] as a response to the British withdrawal from the Partition Plan and to the diminishing quotas of immigration permits. It was designed mainly to address the immigration pressure of the Hechalutz members, raising the question: Was it right to prefer them over other would-be immigrants? Now Ben-Gurion was resolute in his view that it was time to declare "war on England," war whose soldiers would be the thousands of refugees who would arrive at Palestine's shores and be incarcerated by the British "in detention camps."[147] Such a campaign, he claimed, would demonstrate the Zionist movement's determination to oppose the restrictions on immigration with all the forces at its disposal.

The search for an answer to the plight of the refugees and of "ordinary" Jews led to some private initiatives.[148] The Greek freight ship *Ionia*, organized by Revisionist movement members in Danzig, sailed in August 1934. The driving force behind this initiative was Zvi Herman Segal, the agent of the shipping company "Hamburg—South Africa" in Hamburg. Around sixty of the ship's passengers arrived after a troubled voyage at the port of Heraklion in Crete, where another group of some fifty passengers joined them and they sailed from Piraeus on the ship *Kapolo*. They did not manage to go ashore in Tel Aviv, and the captain dropped them off on one of the Greek islands, from where they managed to make their way to Crete. Meanwhile, the *Ionia* anchored on August 28 opposite the Tel Aviv shore, and most of its 117 passengers were taken off and dispersed across town. Only one boat, carrying seventeen immigrants, which was slowly making its way to shore, was discovered by a British patrol plane. They were captured and deported to Greece.[149]

In September, following the success of the *Ionia*'s voyage, some Betar activists in Poland bought the ship *Wanda*, which sailed from the port of Gdynia carrying around fifty Betar members on board. After a night of sailing on the stormy sea the ship sank, but all its passengers survived. These private initiatives stopped, and the illegal immigration connected to the Revisionist movement was only renewed in March 1937, once again not at the movement's initiative.[150]

In March 1932, Jabotinsky published an article called "Adventurism," in which he gave his "blessing" to Jews who crossed the border into Palestine illegally or who arrived in organized "tourist" groups and stayed in the country.[151] It seemed, however, that in "Adventurism" he meant crossing the border illegally on land rather than by sea. Jabotinsky became interested in immigration by sea only in August 1934, when he found out that "now Mapai is engaged with it with the help of the Jewish Agency." It turned out, he wrote, that no more than 5 to 10 percent of the immigrants were caught, while hundreds made it through, because "the regime turns a blind eye" and "the Jews are now willing to pay a fortune for the possibility of immigrating to Palestine; you can buy anything and even make a profit."[152] A few weeks later, Jabotinsky returned to the subject and proposed to appoint a person whose job would be to collect information in various port towns. This activity, he hoped, would hearten the Betar youth who were struggling to get certificates.[153] Nevertheless, the petition project (the "national complaint") remained, in his view, "the crucial project."[154]

In the summer of 1936, Moshe Krivoshein (Galili), a young resident of Palestine who had studied in Italy, where he met refugees from Germany, arrived in Paris. With the help of Dr. Kagan, a surgeon and the president of Maccabi in Paris, Krivoshein founded at Café de la Paix a public committee for a movement that was to be named "Af-Al-Pi" (in spite of). From Paris, Krivoshein went to Vienna, where he met Dr. Wolfgang von Weisl and told him about his plan. Von Weisl was suspicious but decided to introduce Krivoshein to the textile industrialist Hans Prutz, who gave Krivoshein 300 shillings.

Krivoshein and his partners in the Betar commission in Vienna had difficulty finding Betar members who would agree to join the mission, but in March they had a small group of fourteen immigrants who came to Piraeus and boarded a 50-ton ship that Krivoshein managed to purchase. The ship *Af-Al-Pi* sailed from the port of Piraeus and anchored off the port of Haifa on April 13, 1937. The engineer Kop-Tamir, Jabotinsky's brother-in-law, who worked at the Palestine Electric Corporation, managed to turn off all the lights downtown and in the port area, and the fourteen passengers disembarked without any problems.

The success filled the wind in Krivoshein's sails. Now he saw himself as an "admiral" commanding a navy of vessels. No less important, the success encouraged the Betar leaders to join the initiative and collaborate with him. The heads of Betar in Poland embarked on a recruiting campaign and assembled fifty-four Betarites who arrived by train at the port of Fiume equipped with tourist visas. The group marched to the port in a procession led by drummers, sailed on the ship *Af-Al-Pi B* to the port of Durrës in Albania and reached Tantura (Dor) beach in October 1937. This success made a big impression on the Betar circles, and in June 1938 they organized a convoy of 381 Betar members. The Gestapo in Vienna gave them one-off exit visas, and they traveled by train to the port of Piraeus and disembarked at Tantura beach on June 26.[155]

Hundreds of refugees thronged to the Revisionist movement's immigration office in Vienna. Krivoshein's arrogant behavior and his working methods angered the movement's immigration activists, in addition to some disagreements over money matters. The connection with him was severed, and his role in the history of illegal immigration relegated to the margins.[156] Now the Revisionists started to organize their immigration project and to establish a proper mechanism for recruiting the immigrants, preparing the convoys, and purchasing the vessels. Not only Betar members were allowed to join the voyages but also "ordinary" Jews (i.e., anyone in need), who paid between 700 and 800 gold coins. The illegal immigration activists used the Gestapo's permission to transfer the convoys of immigrants by trains and river ships on the Danube to the Black Sea ports. At the end of 1938, the ships *Daraga A*, *Daraga B*, *Eli*, *Geppo A*, and *Dalfa A* sailed with around 1,000 illegal immigrants on board, most of them from the "Reich countries."[157]

The chronicler of the Revisionist immigration wrote about an "endless flow of illegal vessels."[158] In fact, in 1937 and 1938, the Revisionist movement and its extensions brought to Palestine ten ships, which carried around 3,300 passengers (five of those ships in 1938, compared to the 140 immigrants who arrived on Palestine's shores in 1934), most of them refugees from the "Reich countries." This activity was perceived within the Revisionist movement as proof that illegal immigration was the way to break through the immigration permits barrier. In addition, in their view their activity in this area showed that they were not just talking about the need for Jewish emigration from Poland or waiting for the Polish government to adopt the Evacuation Plan, but also doing something about it. Therefore, they deserved to get the support and aid of the Polish authorities. This aid was indeed willingly granted: they received a discount of 50 gold coins on the price of a passport and 25 gold coins on the price of a train ticket. The Revisionists also saw the illegal immigration of Betar members as an important reinforcement of the movement's strength in Palestine. The immigrants were presented as "soldiers in the army for the military occupation" of Palestine. A popular song among the members of the Betar youth proclaimed:

> The ship almost full to the last
> From the bottom to the tip of its mast,
> Listing on the waves in the sun,
> Though without the raised muzzle of a gun.
>
> It is a warship of lions
> Carrying army battalions
> Powerful even with no weapons in their hand,
> Coming to build from scratch
> The future of our people on earth
> And to conquer and salvage our land![159]

This illegal immigration was therefore associated with the military training undergone by the Irgun members. A large part of the immigrants, however, had no connection with the Revisionist movement, and only made use of the immigration department for "ordinary Jews" that operated in the offices of the *Unzer Velt* newspaper in Warsaw, paying for the voyage with their own money. The success of the Revisionists' illegal immigration activity spurred the Haganah and its illegal immigration apparatus to renew, after "three years of paralysis," the activity that had been discontinued in 1934.[160] From January to November 1938, they brought five ships, with a little over 700 immigrants on board. This illegal immigration was the only way to offer help to some of the deportees and refugees from the German Reich and to some of those wishing to emigrate from Poland, who were not able to get an immigration permit as part of the quota.

A regular shipping route operated from the port of Trieste to Palestine. The authorities in Fascist Italy offered generous help to the refugees, and the office of the Jewish Agency's Immigration Department received much aid: 50,846 immigrants sailed from this port between 1931 and 1934—around two-thirds of the Jewish immigration in those years.[161] The route to Haifa was sailed by three ships belonging to the shipping company Lloyd Triestino—*Jerusalem*, *Galilea*, and *Palestine*—converted for passenger transport. They offered synagogues and libraries in Hebrew and Yiddish, and served kosher food. *Galilea*'s Jewish captain Umberto Steindler had his name inscribed in the golden book of the Jewish National Fund, and on the ship's hundredth voyage received a special commendation from the mayor of Tel Aviv, Meir Dizengoff.[162]

On December 6, 1938, the *Galilea* arrived at the port of Tel Aviv with 153 passengers, including around 80 elderly men and women from Germany, the "youngest" of them over seventy. The newspaper that reported their arrival wrote that the Nazis had disengaged the train car that took them to Trieste (where they waited seven days for the ship to sail) and abused the passengers. Even the Italian soldiers shed tears. The newcomers refused to answer any questions "lest it be harmful to those left behind in the Nazi hell." "It's best not to ask," they muttered. The poet Nathan Alterman wrote in *Haaretz*:

> [A]nd as the eighty stepped, tired and worn,
> onto the port's concrete platform,
> they fell face down on this land,
> and kissed the soil of this land [. . .]
> Then the country's gates, in the Kingdom's name,
> were soon locked again, as the system proclaims.
> And the elderly are yet to be told on authority,
> whether they kissed its soil by right or by charity,
> and whether this was within its absorption capacity.[163]

Would the illegal immigration be "selective" or was it designed for any Jew, whoever he was? The two Zionist movements that organized illegal immigration were required to answer this question before the Partition Plan, and all the more urgently once it was taken off the agenda.

Difficult days surround my people, clamoring like children 'round their father's sickbed.[1]
Israel Stern, "Der Boym" (The Tree)

3

"THE WAILING WALL IN ÉVIAN" AND KRISTALLNACHT

On February 14, 1933, Ruppin noted two events in his diary: the third (and last) volume of his book *The Sociology of the Jews* came out in Hebrew, and Hitler became Reichskanzler in Germany. He wrote:

> It is surely a sign of decline, if a demagogue like Hitler becomes the leader of the German people. Yet the blame is not to be laid only at the Germans, but also at the allies. They should have known that a nation of 65 million, which had been driven to its knees by the Treaty of Versailles, would not accept its defeat for long, and its situation would become fertile ground for the rise of demagogues and inciters. The situation of the Jews in Germany is horrifying from the moral standpoint. It is a catastrophic collapse of all the hopes of liberal Jews, who aspired to become integrated in the German people. Everything now hinges on the question —what would Hitler's positive actions be.[2]

A few weeks later, on March 26, responding to Hitler's speech at the Reichstag—an "informative, interesting, fascinating" speech—Ruppin wrote: "Terrifying rumors are circulating about the situation of the Jews in Germany [. . .]. They must be largely false, but to what extent? [. . .] A general feeling of dread and juridical insecurity—reminiscent of medieval times—is engulfing German Jews."[3]

In August 1933, Wiktor Chajes and his wife spent a holiday in the spa resort of Truskavets (Truskawiec) at the foothills of the Carpathians. Chajes contemplated the Jews' contribution to civilization, and particularly to Germany, and concluded that Nazism was a revolt against this very civilization and therefore "to hell with civilization and those party to it." Although he had not yet read *Mein Kampf*, what had happened in Germany since January was enough to prompt him to try and explain racial theory:

> Hitler continues to rise. They are not murdering each other yet. And the whole world is getting used to them. The Middle Ages are back. Civilization, culture, technical advancement—all these have been the idols for one generation. Now they are cursing these idols, because they have not brought happiness [. . .]. Begone, Jewish culture! Rise, the superior, pure German race. Even if you are ignorant. But pure, northern! Rise, Middle Ages, pure German, without hybrids, foreign blood, etc. A true tragedy for humanity.[4]

Willy Cohn, the teacher and historian from Breslau, wrote on August 29 in his diary: "We must arrive at a peace deal between the Jewish people and the German people. We must begin anew, without emotions getting in the way." Two days later he found a letter of dismissal from the Bureau of Education and at the end of September he wrote: "Everywhere livelihoods are being destroyed and people are being removed from their places of employment," but "nonetheless I am trying to retain my optimism." The Central Committee for the Relief of Jews Suffering through the War called on April 28 not to encourage "*uncurbed* emigration" because "no one will be saved by emigrating elsewhere, with no purpose and no chances of livelihood; [. . .] Do not just leave Germany!"[5] The German Jewish leadership predicted the emigration of 12,000 to 15,000 people per year.[6] Weizmann claimed at the Agency Directorate meeting held on November 2, 1935, that if 10,000 to 15,000 Jews per year emigrated from Germany to Palestine, "we would be able to answer history and say we did everything we could."[7]

The Revisionist *Hazit Haam* saw German Jews as responsible for their own fate. In a satirical poem it published on Passover Eve, 1934, it mocked their devotion to the German Diaspora. The poem "A life with no shame . . . ," signed simply by "Eldad," described a village customs official called Reb Chaim, "an honest and devout Jew," whose seder table regularly hosted the village policeman, who every year heard the seder end with a "great cry: 'Next year *in Jerusalem*.'" And then one year this cry was not heard, and the same happened the next year, after the riots that the village peasants, with the policeman among them, had perpetrated on the Jews. The village policeman asked for an explanation and was told that the cry was canceled on the Rabbi's orders,

But the old man turned away with shame,
As if the gentile had caught him stealing,
And he lowered his head to the ground,
And the tears fell from his eyes,
And he sighed and whispered:
My Lord! With deceit and lies
every year I cried
In the ears of this gentile the old cry:
Next year in the rebuilt Jerusalem!
And still I stayed in the despised Diaspora
Mired in slavery . . .

The poem's criticism was directed at the Jews of Germany:

The rich assimilated Jews of Germany
In the good and glorious days
Were calmly and quietly singing their songs:
"Deutchland, Deutchland above all!"
They refused to hear about "Zion,"
And erased it from their prayers,
And even those who were devout
Thought they were fulfilling their duty
By always crying out:
"Next year *in Jerusalem!*"

And if now, when things had gone from bad to worse, and the Nazi regime was lashing its whip to push them out to Palestine, they still settled for crying "Next year" rather than learning from their experience, then "surely it means they have neither honor nor sense."[8]

At the beginning of August 1937, Chajes and his wife returned from a month-long holiday in Carlsbad in Czechoslovakia. Chajes had talked with the local mayor about the Mickiewicz monument that had been erected in the spa town in 1897 and had since become neglected. In Carlsbad he met Jewish holidaymakers from Germany and felt little empathy toward them:

[They] behaved as if there was no Hitler. Well dressed, happy. Arrived in private cars. I would not be exaggerating if I said that out of 6,500 who arrived from Germany, 80 percent were Jews. Interesting! Are they reconciled to their fate? Have they lost their self-dignity? Have they never had any? Do I know? One thing is clear, materially speaking their situation is very good. Therefore only the ban on cooperating with Aryans is leaving its marks. So is everything being written about the oppression exaggerated? One gets the impression that Hitler cares more about the cultural-spiritual separation of the Germans from the Jews than that the Jews make less money. [. . .] He probably does not want any Jewish influence on the German culture, language and spirit. He wants to segregate them, to ghettoize, but not to starve. Either he is too weak for that, or they are more clever.[9]

In August 1933, on his way from the Eighteenth Zionist Congress in Prague, at Munich's train station, Ben-Gurion bought *Mein Kampf*.[10] His biographer, Shabtai Teveth, wrote that he was the only Labor movement leader who bothered to read the book, and was horrified by what he read. About six months later, in January 1934, Ben-Gurion said at the Histadrut Convention: "Hitler's rule puts the entire Jewish people in danger [. . .]. Who knows, perhaps only four or five years (if not less) stand between us and that terrible day."[11] In August 1934, at the Mapai Council, he was less adamant, arguing against the party members who were caught in a "defeatist mood" that although 1934 was "a year of madness in the world, the year of Hitler's government," "they are panicking over the German issue. They cannot see that Hitler can be opposed and that Revisionism can be opposed."[12] We should not infer from this comparison that political rhetoric and the equation of standing against Hitler with standing against the Revisionist movement weakened the Yishuv leaders' awareness of the German Jews' situation. "Now disaster has struck our people's most important cultural center, German Jewry," Ben-Gurion said to High Commissioner Wauchope at the end of July 1934.[13] Even prior to that Shertok had explained to Wauchope that German Jews were "gradually reduced to a state of absolute destitution. People who have some kind of profession or trade may be able to barely eke out a living, but the young generation has no hope."[14]

Weizmann read *Mein Kampf* before 1933 and reacted to the book in July of that year, when excerpts started to appear in *The Times*. He expressed not the slightest doubt as to what "the average Englishman . . . will think of those comi-manic perorations, those commonplaces, those pseudo-scientific biological and historical generalizations." There was no doubt, Weizmann wrote to the *Times* editor, what the opinion of any average neurologist would be about the state of the author's sanity. However, there was reason to fear that the published excerpts might lead the *Times* readers to conclude that Hitler was merely a radical politician, rather than someone who posed a great danger to Britain and its culture.[15] Weizmann told the delegates of the Twenty-First Zionist Congress that he had asked MacDonald whether he had read *Mein Kampf*, "not the 'kosher' version, which was published for the English public." When MacDonald answered in the affirmative, Weizmann claimed to have said: "In that case, I have no solution for you." He explained to the Congress attendees: "It was for the first time a kind of spotlight on the way of thinking about a person or persons, who holds our fate in their hands, who may have the best intentions, who may be the most honest and decent people, but are hostage to simplistic empiricism — a very dangerous thing in politics. And they do not see — either they see everything, or they see only halfway or partially — that there are two contrasting worlds facing each other."

Nazism was symbolized by "guns and wireless telegraph[s] and airplanes" and the other, the Jewish world was symbolized by morality. The gap between these two worlds could not "be bridged by throwing a kid in front of the leopard, or by deluding ourselves that the leopard will stop being a leopard when its skin is stroked." The conversation with MacDonald, Weizmann said, served as a warning that "we are indeed facing danger."[16]

The fact that the book filled Weizmann with deep concern, if not anxiety, could be gleaned from an "urgent and personal" letter he sent Benito Mussolini about six months after their meeting on February 17, 1934, in which he asked the Italian dictator to interfere with his Nazi ally in favor of the Jews of Germany. Weizmann did not know that the Italian ambassador to Berlin had advised the Führer on March 31, 1933, that his war against Judaism would not strengthen National Socialism from within, but rather increase the moral pressure on Germany and lead to economic acts of retaliation from world Jewry. According to the ambassador, Hitler screamed: "In 500 and 600 years, Hitler's name will still be praised everywhere as that of the man who rid the world of the curse of Judaism, once and for all."[17]

Weizmann had no doubt that Germany was lapsing into barbarism. When he visited Germany in February 1933 for the last time in his life, he advised Jews to escape from the country. How and where to — he did not say. The only hope he could offer them was that enlightened public opinion in the West would force the Nazi regime to act with restraint.[18]

Jabotinsky must have read *Mein Kampf* before Hitler's rise to power. On February 24, 1933, less than a month after Hitler was appointed Chancellor, Jabotinsky wrote the first of his articles dedicated to the situation in Germany, in which he defined the book as "simple":

> I once took the time to read the two volumes of his book *My Life* [thus was written in the article's Hebrew translation]. This masterpiece [said mockingly, of course] belongs, undoubtedly, to the type of literature we characterize as "simple"; lacking talent, naive, pedestrian ideas. [. . .] The book would have had better quality if it had been written by Goebbels, who can write brilliantly. [. . .] But [Hitler] is not stupid at all, certainly not. Hitler has common sense, he can reason, he can bring suitable examples from life and even from that part of world history that is studied at elementary schools. [. . .] [Hitler was] a decidedly average person, with the most ordinary mind: he does not have even one percent of Mussolini. He has no talent for governing, and he does not understand what is going on around him. Nevertheless those who believe his reign will be short-lived are wrong.[19]

After the "Night of the Long Knives," the purge of the Sturmabteilung (Nazi Storm Troopers, SA) in June and July 1934, Jabotinsky returned to the same subject. Hitler was not a fool, he diagnosed, "and one can spend an hour with Herr Chancellor in an interesting conversation, during which he would perhaps express several intelligent ideas." His book, however, was long and mostly boring, and Hitler himself had no charisma. At the same time, Jabotinsky believed that Hitler had a sense of reality and knew that all the promises he spread were "mere chatter, detached from life and from any actuality. Germany will not be able to achieve economic autarchy, will not be able to arm itself stealthily, and its army is no more than a large and strong police force." This was the real reason for the purging of Ernst Röhm and his SA. Jabotinsky wrote an imaginary dialogue between Hitler and Röhm:

> RÖHM: [. . .] In short, my good friend, you return to that groveling policy of Stresemann and Brüning.[20] Groveling before the higher nobility, groveling before the heavy industry, and—most bitterly—groveling before outside countries. You still try to coat the groveling with proud and tough words, however the content remains the same. And the young people, who have made you a dictator, are complaining not to you, but to us, to your enforcers: it is us they call traitors, it is us they urge to put an end to the groveling, it is us they mock, because they say that you have discarded us and replaced us with new friends. Forgive me, my dear, but such a thing—we cannot take and will not allow.
>
> HITLER: But, my friend, this is impossible.
>
> RÖHM: For you [it is] impossible.

This fictive conversation suggests that Jabotinsky thought that a ruling Hitler would be forced to be pragmatic: "The Third Kingdom [The Third Reich] is an absurdum: it does not exist and will never exist. Only one consolation remains; there is only one promise that can be fulfilled: the persecution of the Jews."[21] Did Jabotinsky read different things in *Mein Kampf* than Ben-Gurion or Weizmann had? The three of them found the book to be offering a bleak prospect for the future of German Jewry. Even if Hitler became "pragmatic" on questions of foreign policy, Jabotinsky wrote, his certain victims would be the Jews of Germany: "For the first time we the Jews are so starkly faced with the main question of our existence in the Diaspora: is it possible to pronounce a death sentence and nullify our influence on humanity's economic development?" *Haaretz* maintained that the Nazis would be preoccupied with reinforcing and stabilizing their rule, adding:

> Bad times have arrived for the Jews of Germany. The terror that has struck them in recent days will soon surely dissipate, as the new regime fortifies and stabilizes. Our brothers in Germany may not fear a "St. Bartholomew's Day," they may not suffer pogroms, and they may not be deprived of their civil rights in an official and legal way, but the regime has many ways to vent its anger on the Jews, to deprive them of basic human rights in practice, without annulling the "written" law. Instead of the pogrom of Russia and Ukraine we shall have a continuous social and economic pogrom. German Jews will be systematically removed from all their economic and social positions. The emancipation period is over. German Jews are facing a new "ghetto"—a ghetto whose pain and suffering will be great, since it will not be accompanied by the great and warm faith of our ancestors, who could learn to like their troubles and despise their enemy-persecutors out of their superior wisdom and their sense of self-worth.[22]

Doar Hayom had already expressed a similar view in the beginning of February 1933: "Hitler the Chancellor will be different from Hitler of the mass rallies," though this offered no consolation for German Jews. For them "begins a black chapter full of sorrow and hardship."[23] Although the newspaper believed that Hitler in power would be different from Hitler the demagogue, it added a caveat: "There is no doubt that something important and decisive is brewing in the kitchen of the Nazis and their cohorts."[24] The winds of war were starting to blow in Europe.

On March 17, 1933, the word "shoah" (catastrophe, "holocaust") appeared in the Hebrew press in the context of the Nazi's rise to power, perhaps for the first time ever. An article in *Hazit Haam* published by Yehoshua Heshel Yevin, physician, journalist, and writer, and a leader of the radical Revisionists, said that German Jews had had ten years to understand the roots of Nazism, "to get ready for the day of *Shoah* and also to save themselves from it in time." Nazism, Yevin wrote, was neither a "psychosis" nor a "momentary madness," but an all-out attack on the Jewish people "aimed to destroy and annihilate it. It is a total material and criminal annihilation that is taking place and will take place, if not through official pogroms than by eliminating any possibility of economic survival."[25]

An article titled "At the time of catastrophe (shoah) for German Jewry," published in *Davar* that same day, said that "German Jewry faces destruction. [. . .] [This Jewry] which only recently was affluent, might become a wretched, powerless community, ruined in terms of its economy, and perhaps also, in certain parts, broken in terms of its moral consciousness." The author of the article was concerned that the German Jews' capital might be lost, "not only for them, but also for the Jewish economy in Palestine," and pinned his hopes on the British government exerting its influence to save German Jewry: "The Jewish people *expects the will of the British government not to contrast with its ability*."[26]

On June 28, 1933, *Haaretz* wrote that even if Germany were all Nazi, it would not be able to carry out a "mad decision" such as confiscating the property of Jews who had arrived in Germany after August 1914. At the same time, the achievements of the Nazi party, "with all its ruthlessness and brutality," and the elections in Prussia, served as a warning that Germany was infused with "deep and dark hatred" for the Jews: the emancipation period was over and the Middle Ages were returning.[27] About six months later the newspaper changed its view, explaining to its readers that Hitler had failed because the German people was not made up only of "unenlightened masses," but also of many who had absorbed too much culture to be taken by the Nazi propaganda: he, "Hitler, poor lonely Hitler," had become "a neglected, confused and defeated man." Was this then, the writer wondered, "the end of his career?"[28]

Chaim Nachman Bialik was already pessimistic in May 1933, and in January 1934 admitted that although he could not foretell the future, from what he saw "the Jewry in the Diaspora—*in all* the Diaspora, not only in Germany—is on the verge of extinction."[29]

At the Nineteenth Zionist Congress, held in Lucerne from August 30 through September 3, 1935, and overshadowed by the economic crisis in Palestine and the cuts in the immigration quotas, the talk was about "the disaster" suffered by the humiliated German Jewry.[30] Nahum Goldmann reassured his listeners, predicting that the situation in Germany would change once the Nazi regime stabilized and Germany returned to its "sanity." What was happening in Germany was merely a manifestation of a recurring element in the life of the Jewish people in modern times — that is, a bad but passing event.[31]

Most German Jews held a similar view until the end of 1935. On June 21, 1933, the Association of German Jews sent a memorandum to the new Chancellor's office: "We would like, as part of the new state which has based itself on the principle of racism, to integrate our community into the general structure, so that in the sphere allotted to us we can take productive action for the homeland." The Agudat Yisrael rabbis in Frankfurt wrote Hitler on October 4: "We love the German homeland, the German soil, the German sun."[32] Both the former and the latter believed that German Jews must not give up their great achievements, but should henceforth keep to the isolated sphere outlined for them by the Nazi regime and wait for better days.

Polish Jews were aware of what was going on in Germany, and everyone — except the Bund, which thought it was not only Nazi antisemitism that should be condemned — called for a unified front to be formed against Germany. At a meeting of the Bund Council in spring 1934, Vladimir Kossovskii, one of the movement's leaders, prophesied: "War against Nazi Germany will mean the total annihilation of the entire Jewish population of Europe. The Germans will ruthlessly murder all the Jews, children and elderly, men and women." This dark prediction stemmed from the Bund's opposition to Poland's foreign policy. Kossovskii's conclusion from the nightmarish vision he described was that the Bund must not help Poland in its war preparations.[33]

April saw the foundation of "a united Jewish committee to fight against the persecution of Jews in Germany," and a protest meeting held on April 22 was heavily attended. Intellectuals, writers, and journalists tried to explain the essence of Nazism and its racist antisemitism.[34] The writer and essayist Yitzhak Katzenelson was especially blunt, describing Nazi Germany as Sodom and as "hell on earth," and the Germans as predators, vampires, "greasy criminals, loathsome creatures, slime bags who have risen from the depths to the surface, spread like a plague and infected people whose morality is frail and frightened with the Nazi virus." Hitler was described by Katzenelson as a pathetic sergeant-major, a criminal, and a Jew hater. He warned that the Nazi virus might spread surreptitiously, infect the entire Christian world, and cause its annihilation. At the same time, Katzenelson compared Nazi Germany to a frog blowing up its neck, of whom "finally nothing will be left but 'a piece of greenish-boggy skin dipped in slime.'" His advice to German Jews was not to lose their dignity and not to seek revenge: "It is better to be killed by rioters than to be one of them."[35]

Many failed to properly understand reality. Many were of the opinion that the Nazi regime was improvising as it went along, rather than implementing a systematic plan of action. Therefore, they ignored the consistent implementation of the Nazi regime's ideology and doctrine on both internal and foreign matters. This was, according to Bracher, the bitter mistake made by the non-Nazis in Germany and by the European countries. If there was dismissal, it did not necessarily stem from blindness, delusions, or the Nazi regime's success in concealing its intentions. There were enough reasons to believe that the Nazi regime was unstable and acting without a unified plan of action shared by all its authorities.

The two rival Zionist political movements, the Labor movement and the Revisionist movement, were quick to equate what was happening in Germany with the situation in the Yishuv and the Zionist movement. At the Mapai Council that discussed the fight against the Revisionists on August 24, 1934, Ben-Gurion said that there was no comparison between the situation of the workers' movement in Palestine and that of the German workers' movement.[36] Not only did he describe the Revisionists as "thugs who are imitating—in everything—the Nazis' tactics," but he also added that their danger could be withstood just like Hitler's.[37]

The Revisionists themselves did not hesitate to make such comparisons, calling the Labor movement "Hitlerite socialist-Zionists" who spoke "Hitler's language."[38] The only difference between an SS soldier and a "commander of the leftist squads" (Plugot Hapoel),[39] Uri Zvi Greenberg wrote, was that the former had a weapon but refrained from using it, whereas the latter refrained only because he had no weapon.[40] "The Reds in Palestine," wrote *Hazit Haam* on March 6, 1934, "are no less formidable than the Nazis. They are [their] equals in their ideology, their cruelty and their method." The Histadrut's control over the labor market was compared to Nazi Germany's "Aryanization" policy.[41] The Nazis were thus introduced into the rhetoric of squabbling and hostility that prevailed in the Zionist movement and the Yishuv through the front door. This unrestrained usage perhaps blunted the ability to comprehend the essence of the Nazi regime and its intentions.

On September 15, 1935, after the last of the rallies held in Nuremberg's main square as part of the annual gathering of the Nazi party, the city hosted a special session of the Reichstag. When Hitler finished his speech, his deputy Goering read out what is known as "the Nuremberg Laws," the laws that deprived German Jews of their civil rights and turned them into subjects of the state (Staatsgehörige), segregated from German society in all areas of life. The day after the Reichstag's meeting, Goebbels declared that the laws were designed to remove the Jews from German society, but "we do not have any island to which we can transport them."[42]

The aim of the Nuremberg Laws was not only to isolate the Jews "on an island" inside Germany, but also to encourage their "faster emigration" from Germany. To that end, an anti-Jewish economic campaign was launched in November 1935. Within three years, by November 1938, the economic existence of the approximately 360,000 Jews who still lived in Germany had become hopelessly precarious.

The ship on which Ruppin sailed to South America after the Nineteenth Zionist Congress anchored at the Barcelona port. Ruppin went ashore and read about the Nuremberg Laws in the newspaper. "I saw that Germany had introduced a new law—to remove Jewish children from general schools and educate them in separate schools. It is clear, then, that they want to push the Jews back into a spiritual ghetto."[43]

In November 1935, the intellectual and essayist Jean Améry, born to a Jewish father and a Catholic mother under the name of Hans Mayer, sat down at his regular café in Vienna. He opened the newspaper, read about the announcement of Nuremberg's race laws, and discovered that he was not what he had always thought he was and wanted to be, what his parents had taught him to believe he was: an Austrian citizen. The news piece had now officially determined that he was Jewish, or rather, "it had given me a new dimension to what I had already known earlier, but which at the time was of no great consequence to me, namely, that I was a Jew. A Jew, and moreover, only a Jew. When he entered the café, it was clear to him that he had a country and a life, but when he left the café he was without country and at best a likely victim."[44]

Jewish children who came to school in the morning, and their parents who arrived at their workplaces, discovered "that they were Jews." The first issue of the *Kinder-Rundschau*, the children's supplement of the *Jüdische Rundschau*, the journal of the Zionist Federation in Germany (the first issue was published on October 4, 1933, and the last on October 28, 1938), featured a story called "The Guest" (Der Gast). The story's protagonist, Fritz, returns home upset and looks up the word "guest" in the dictionary, explaining to his mother: "When I walked through the courtyard just now, I heard Kurt say to his brother, 'Fritz is our guest.'" In a piece titled "The Magic Box," published on November 30, 1934, Alice Pollack-Kostrolitz wrote about a boy named Joseph, who was prevented by his friends from joining their games "because I am Jewish, I do not belong with them anymore [. . .] and I am considered a stranger here." Even Willie, his best friend, had turned his back on him: "No, Joseph, I am not allowed to play with Jews anymore."[45]

The British newspapers had mixed reactions. The London *Times* believed that "the ghetto legislation" did not bode well, "but nevertheless it is also better than being a helpless minority." Other English newspapers described the Nuremberg Laws as a quarantine imposed on the Jews, who were treated as a source of contagious spiritual and physical diseases, and at the same time were segregated and slowly exterminated.[46]

On July 23, 1935, Ben-Gurion referred to the Nuremberg Laws in a speech he gave in Tel Aviv: "Comrades, we are on the eve of a second chapter in the new era for Zionism [and] for the workers' movement in Palestine." This new era, he said, had begun in 1933. It was

> a threefold change, a new phase in the history of the Jewish people, a new phase in the building of the land and a new phase in the Zionist watch. This year is also one of the most terrible and most calamitous years in our history. This year we have been deprived, in one of the large countries, of the human rights and human dignity that we had achieved over a hundred years ago. What happened this year in Hitler's Germany has no equivalent in the history of the Middle Ages and the Diaspora.[47]

Ben-Gurion asserted that what had happened in Germany had cast the history of the Jewish people in a new light: it had no future and no existence in the Diaspora, only in Palestine.[48] His main conclusion from this bleak prospect was that it was time to unite and close ranks among the Jewish people in general and in the movement and the Zionist Organization in particular, and use all their political power to accelerate the building of Palestine. In this last context, the picture painted by Ben-Gurion was optimistic. In contrast to earlier historical periods, he said, the current situation of the Jewish people offered something new and revolutionary: "Now we have a Zionist movement, the fruit of the last two generations. This is the new thing, full of hope and opportunities, which has emerged in our history in the last fifty years, and which signals a new turn in our fortunes."[49]

Levi Shkolnik (Eshkol), a member of the Haganah High Command, wrote Ben-Gurion in October 1935: "Nuremberg has heralded a return to Zion and *everyone* is holding their wandering sticks and who knows what tomorrow will bring. Everyone is looking for a way out, first of all for their property."[50] The priority that he thought should be given to those looking for a way out of Germany did not stem necessarily from the fear that their situation was graver than that of Polish Jews, but from the fact that their immigration would be accompanied by the transfer of Jewish capital to Palestine. The "utilitarian" consideration was an important one. Ben-Gurion believed that this was the first time in the history of Zionism that "an entire Jewish community, one of the richest Jewish communities in the world, has been faced with the danger of all its property being lost and is therefore willing to invest a large part of its capital in Palestine. [. . .] The disaster of German Jews should be met with a Zionist response: turn the disaster into a resource for building the land, save the life and the property of German Jews for the sake of Palestine."[51]At the same time, in a letter to Simon Marks, an entrepreneur, philanthropist, and one of the leaders of British Jewry, Ben-Gurion admitted, "Palestine cannot solve the Jewish question in its entirety."[52]

Ben-Gurion was not alone in thinking that the deep crisis suffered by German Jews signaled "a turn for the better," and that their tragedy could be leveraged for the building of Palestine. Saving Jewish life and property from Germany, said Ussishkin at the Jewish Agency Directorate's meeting with representatives of the Association of German Immigrants on November 23, 1935, was "for the country's sake."[53] Within the Zionist movement, the concern for the fate of German Jews was almost always accompanied with the question of how their situation would influence the movement and the Yishuv's future. Its institutions were caught up in a debate over which Jewish community suffered the most and which country should be top priority in the distribution of immigration permits — Germany or Poland.[54]

There were also those who had reservations about German Jews and who believed that "the human material resulting from permits being given to 'ordinary' refugees from Germany" was of a questionable quality.[55] Ruppin, for example, thought that action should be taken to prevent the immigration from "flooding the existing Yishuv in Palestine like a flame" and that therefore it was necessary to fix a quota for emigration from Germany. Shertok claimed that in certain circumstances Diaspora Jews should be dealt with ruthlessly,[56] and Gruenbaum believed that the greatest danger posed by the Nuremberg Laws was that the Polish government would learn from Nazi Germany and act in various ways to expel the Jews, in order to exploit the situation to develop trade and industry in Poland. Increasing the immigration quotas for refugees, he warned, would flood the Yishuv with a "deluge" of immigrants. Therefore, "the proper Zionist response" was an active war against Germany.[57] This "utilitarian" approach to emigration from Germany stood in striking contradiction to the warnings about what was in store for German Jews. In Ussishkin's view, "Hitler predicated his persecution on race rather than religion. In the latter case it would have led to the conversion of half of German Jewry."[58]

Similar voices were heard in the Revisionist camp. Uri Zvi Greenberg wrote:

> Because Hitler's regime excludes from the pure Aryan country even converts and sons of converts, our nation has regained some salvaged generations. Who knows what would have been the fate of those thousands of Jews, who in any case walked around like detached fragments, in the opposite situation, if the gates of the churches had been opened for their "personal salvation"? Conversion would have become a means of survival, and by the by they would have become gentiles. [. . .] Welcome back, our returning brothers. To share in our suffering and our joy.[59]

Willy Cohn in Breslau also found something "positive" in the Nuremberg Laws and wrote on September 16 in his diary that he understood from Hitler's speech that the steps being taken by the government could bring about a tolerable modus vivendi between the German people and the Jewish people and "from a Jewish perspective, I welcome the ban on mixed marriages."[60]

The day after the signing of the Munich Agreement on September 30, 1938, Ben-Gurion tried to explain the reasons for the Nazi regime's rise to power and to decipher its intentions. The German nation, he said, was "obedient and enslaved to its rulers more than any other nation in the world." Therefore, the German people would never rebel against their "leader-misleaders." At times Ben-Gurion hoped that even the spirit of that obedient nation would falter in the event of war, and that the German people would not be able "to stand against their formidable enemies in the west and in the east for long." Though it was true that Hitler and his murderous gang showed no regard for any "human reasoning," they too wanted to save their skins. Ben-Gurion repeatedly warned that the danger facing European Jews—who "would not be the last victims of a Nazi victory"—was the spread and intensification of a wave of antisemitism all over the world. Political amity with Hitler would lead to "sympathy" for Nazi ideology, he wrote: "The gentiles do not like us, and whoever likes Hitler will also like his antisemitic doctrine."[61]

On October 20, Ben-Gurion remarked that "Hitler [is] not only the enemy and destroyer of German Jewry. His sadistic and fanatic wish is to exterminate Judaism all over the world."[62] After Kristallnacht on November 9, his predictions became increasingly grim. In a speech he gave at the Yishuv convention organized by the Jewish National Council in Jerusalem on December 12, Ben-Gurion admitted:

> Of course we never underestimated the magnitude of the disaster that befell German Jewry and world Jewry in 1933—with Hitler's rise to power. But even the pessimists among us could not imagine what was to come from this evil and murderous regime, and the month of November 1938 marks a new date, or a new chapter, which is perhaps unprecedented in the history of Jewish martyrdom. Neither persecutions, nor deportations—this is organized extermination, physical extermination, accompanied by the sadistic abuse [. . .] [of] a whole Jewish community [. . . ,] [of] the 600,000 Jews of Germany and Austria. But it is more than that. The Nazi pogrom in November of this year is a signal for the extermination of the Jewish people all over the world. I wish I am proven wrong. But I fear that the German pogrom is merely the beginning. It started in Germany; who knows what will happen tomorrow in the Czech republic, [. . .] in Poland and in Romania and in other countries? Until now even the devil had not dared perpetrate such things. Now all the restraints have been removed. Our blood, our dignity, our property have become fair game—and there is no limit. There is no limit to what can be done to the Jews.[63]

Ben-Gurion did not hesitate to speak about "the extermination of the Jewish people all over the world." If war broke out and Hitler took over Europe, Ben-Gurion said in June 1939 to the Zionist Executive Committee, he would "first of all exterminate the Jewish people in Europe."[64] Ben-Gurion's main concern, however, was that Palestine would not be able to solve the refugee problem, a powerlessness that put Zionism in danger.[65]

Berl Katznelson, who had not read *Mein Kampf*, started as early as 1933 to warn against the destruction of German Jewry—"the destruction of its world." One fine morning the Jews will be removed from their respectable posts and "swept with the broom of conversion," he lamented at the Nineteenth Zionist Congress. At the beginning of 1939 Katznelson spoke cautiously, admitting that he did not dare guess the results of a second world war, but was thinking only of what would happen at the beginning of the war, "and here the calculation seems simple: the Jews in all the enemy countries are destined for extermination. They will be the first to be sent to the fire, and there will be no trace of them left."[66]

From January 1933 through August 1939, Jabotinsky regularly followed the events in Nazi Germany in commentary articles he published in the Revisionist press. In his first response to the Nazi party's ascent to power, he prepared for what was to come: "Perhaps we should doubt whether Hitler (even with a majority in the elected Reichstag) would pass laws against the Jews, but what good will it serve? Since the creation of the world, the main thing has always been not the law, but how it is interpreted."[67] Hitler in the role of Chancellor, he wrote, might become more clever, but in any case he would not stay in his role for long; and besides, after the anti-Jewish propaganda has put him in power, the "Jewish factor" will lose its importance.[68] Hitler, Jabotinsky predicted, "is destined from the outset for a disgraceful failure."[69] On April 14, 1933, he wrote: "The German crusade against the Jews is the most important and most serious event in the history of the last generations. If Hitler's regime remains in power, world Jewry faces destruction."[70] The Nazis could not stop their attack on the Jews, because without hatred for the Jews the regime would collapse. In his view, antisemitism was the only element of the Nazi ideology and platform that had any substance, whereas "the regime's other slogans have no substance whatsoever."[71] Moreover, because the Nazi regime would not be able to realize its belligerent slogans, its only consolation would be "declaring war on the Jews of Germany." This was why the Nazi regime declared "a war of annihilation against German Jewry." German antisemitism was not merely "street propaganda," but "part of the collective mood" of the German people —perhaps the most important part. Thus, while Jabotinsky dismissed Nazism's power to realize its aggressive intentions, he had no doubt about the seriousness of its intentions regarding German Jews. At the same time, full of confidence in the power of world Jewry, Jabotinsky proclaimed:

> Certain leaders of "The Third Reich" are threatening to take revenge against German Jews for the actions of world Jewry; to this there is only one answer: German gentlemen, it will do you no good, anything you do to our brothers will have only one effect: to amplify our vigor. We are not talking about one community in one country—we are talking about the existence of the Israelite nation.[72]

In August 1935, Jabotinsky described Nazism as no more than "gangrene that ends with surgery," explaining: "These new outbursts against the Jews have no connection at all to politics, not even to antisemitism."[73] About six months later, in January 1936, he predicted: "The Third Reich is nothing but a banal episode in the development of the Jews' plight." This "plight" had one solution: "To provide a place for all our refugees [. . .] the refugees of yesterday, of today and of tomorrow" in Palestine on both sides of the Jordan River.[74]

Despite his grim prediction regarding the future of German Jews, Jabotinsky found reason for optimism: the Jews were becoming a "tremendous global power" because they were defending a just cause. The tragedy of German Jews would lead to a general solution for the Jewish people. He added: "We predict for the Jewish people that this war will end with a total victory for the principles of justice and peace, and a necessary destruction of the regime that has raised its criminal arm against these principles."[75] Greenberg hyperbolized: "It is incumbent on us, Hatzohar and Betar, the real World Organization, to supply the leverage point for the war of the masses against Hitler's persecutions."[76]

The Revisionist movement did not bemoan the oppression of the workers' movement and saw Stalin as an enemy no less dangerous for the Jews than Hitler. It was not alone in this view. At a meeting of the Zionist Executive Committee in September 1933, Moshe Beilinson, a member of the editorial team of *Davar*, expressed his strict opposition to the Zionist movement joining the ban against German goods, reasoning that "there is no worse fate than that of Russian Jewry. [. . .] German Jews are still not in the situation of Russian Jews and I do not want to bring them to that situation."[77]

"The iron Chancellor speaks in elegies" was how Greenberg described Hitler's speech at the Reichstag in March 1933. Jewish journalists, he maintained, tended to dismiss the claim that Hitler threatened "to bring down the whole Tower of Babel that we are erecting all over the world to fight him." However, "his regime already conveys a sense of stability," and under the conciliatory rhetoric one could hear the whispering "flames of the swastika crusade." Thus, Jews had to "recognize the enemy in all his dangerous stature and use all our power to wage a concerted war against him. [. . .] Grand Zionism obliges us to be in the same situation as Marshal Piłsudski and Czechoslovakia's Masaryk." In other words, it was the Zionist movement's task to fight against Hitler's Germany, and it would win this war if it was led by the right sorts of leaders.[78]

Yehoshua Heshel Yevin wrote that the people could be saved from "total extermination" by action from the Archimedean point of the Jewish people: from the center of power on the shores of the Mediterranean, that is — Palestine.[79] On June 30, 1933, *Hazit Haam* wrote: "Nazism's anti-Jewish policy is not antisemitism. It is extermination. It is racial sadism that has received political validity."[80]

Greenberg sounded his warnings in April 1939 from the point of view of "grand," salvational Zionism. He described his words as "the voice of a lone Jew." The Jews, in his view, should not concern themselves with the tragedies of others — in Ethiopia, in China, in Czechoslovakia, in Albania[81] — as if they were "the hurting kinsmen of those stricken conquered territories: with exaggerated eagerness, with exaggerated pity, with exaggerated sorrow" — but with their own tragedy. That is, with the Arab Revolt and "with the burning home" in Palestine. Western Europe was surrendering to the armed German Amalek because it had been corroded by sweet pacifism, and its peoples would pay for this with "bitter slavery." "Europe" does not want war, "it is pacifism that wants war — the rotting socialism, because it dreams that the war will give it a blood transfusion."[82] A month later, after listening to one of Hitler's speeches on the radio, Greenberg warned of the danger of "the brown lava," that is, the danger that Hitler would realize his threat and expel the Jews from Germany.[83]

Some in the Revisionist movement were still convinced, even in 1939, that there was no reason to get excited over Hitler's declarations that he intended to annihilate the Jewish people. In two thousand years of exile, Jews have heard darker declarations, and furthermore, "war will sweep Hitler's medievalist regime aside!"[84]

Not all the movement's members shared the existential anxiety. In January 1939, the New Zionist Organization's conference in Palestine declared the complete failure of the Revisionist diplomacy and the need to separate the question of the Jews from the question of Palestine:

> No step of the Hebrew national movement should be decided on according to the status of the Jewish question in a certain country or according to this country's attitude to the Jewish question in the Diaspora, be it good or bad. No injury to local or partial Jewish interests, not even serious injury to vital interests, should make the movement lose its senses and divert even some of the nation's fighting power from the only fight for its aims. [. . .] Fighting antisemitism is a futile waste of energies and destined for failure in advance. It can only divert the attention and the warring forces from the only front relevant to the aims of the nation in its homeland.[85]

If war broke out in Europe, wrote Yitzhak Gurion, the editor of the Revisionist newspaper *Hamashkif*, at the beginning of 1939, it would sweep Hitler's medievalist regime aside.[86]

The belief that the Nazi regime was extremely unstable and liable to implode any minute, and that the Jewish people had an international moral and political power that could be harnessed in order to fight against Nazi Germany, to isolate it, to weaken and defeat it, was the driving force behind the international boycott movement against imports from Germany, which Jabotinsky and his movement helped organize. The boycott brought together two myths: on the one hand there was the Nazi demonology, which portrayed the Jews as controlling the world behind the scenes and stoked the Nazi regime's fear of the boycott movement. On the other hand there was the Revisionists' belief that the Jews had a moral power that would enable them to spearhead the resistance to Nazism and bring about its defeat.[87] The Revisionist movement saw the boycott as a "war between Germany and Judea," which it was spearheading. It was to be a "protracted global war," which could not "be conducted with global enthusiasm: it [could] *only* be conducted with the support of the World Organization."[88] Claims that the boycott movement endangered German Jews were dismissed by Jabotinsky:

> As for some of the German refugees settling in Palestine — this is a commendable plan, but it does not solve the terrible problem that has been so tragically revealed. By virtue of the crisis of German Jewry, we will demand the general solution of the Jewish tragedy [. . .] turning Palestine on both sides of the Jordan River into a Jewish state.[89]

Greenberg was even more enthusiastic: the Jews of 1933 were not the Jews of the 1929 riots. Although they did not have a navy or an armored corps, they were a people of 17 million that could "let Hitler's Germany feel the full force of its strike."[90]

The boycott began spontaneously, initiated by non-Jewish organizations, including American trade unions and others. On March 19, 1933, the Jewish War Veterans Association, which had around 250,000 members, announced it was joining the boycott, as did the World Jewish Congress. The boycott was joined not only by store owners and shoppers, but also by unions and dockworkers in western Europe and the United States.[91]

In November 1934, Zeev Karinsky, a financier in Vienna, defied the boycott's instructions and went to the cinema to watch a German "Hitlerite movie." When he was summoned to a "court of honor," he claimed in his defense that he only went there to accompany his wife, but the court fined him 25 guilders to help refugees from Germany; when he did not pay the fine, his name was published in the newspapers.[92]

In 1936, the United Boycott Council was formed by the American Jewish

Congress and the Jewish Workers' Committee. The boycott generated a lot of interest in the general press in the West, eliciting mixed reactions. Some believed that the boycott was a moral and effective weapon in the fight against Nazi Germany, while others saw it as confirming the opinion that the Jews retained great economic power.[93] Germany reacted with a propaganda campaign that described the boycott as another step in the war between the "new Germany" and "international Jewry." It thought the boycott could cause it some damage, because the Jews were scattered around the world and wielded tremendous economic power.[94]

It is debatable whether Germany was weakened by the international boycott, which troubled the Nazi regime much more than the boycott in Poland did. German representatives in Europe, in the United States, and in Palestine reported to Berlin on the boycott's expansion and its influence on exports from Germany. Some of these reports expressed concern over "the weapon of the boycott against Germany" (*die Waffe Boykotts gegen Deutschland*) organized by "world Jewry," over "their tremendous economic power" and over the possibility that the boycott movement would gather momentum and damage Germany's economy.[95] Hitler blamed the boycott movement for Germany's economic difficulties. The image of the Jews controlling the world economy and of a "global Jewish conspiracy" reliant on the Jews' dispersal around the world stoked this reaction and added fuel to the Nazi propaganda.[96]

Other reports reassured Berlin, explaining that the boycott had minimal effect.[97] Germany's general consul in New York communicated to Berlin on December 15, 1934, that American citizens—including U.S. Jews—were not cooperating with the boycott. The Gestapo tracked the discussions of the Zionist Congress in Prague in August and September 1933, as well as Jabotinsky's travels in western Europe, which aimed to boost the boycott movement. One of the reports called it "a wild attack on Germany."[98] Jabotinsky was depicted as a sworn enemy of Germany, a person who was full of hatred (*Heize*) toward the country and who declared that it was "an enemy of humanity [*Todfiend der Menschheit*]."

An American Jew named Mendel Wood wrote in the *Daily Herald* on October 11, 1934, that the economic crisis in Germany was caused by the persecutions of the Jews. Because a great leader was marked by his ability to admit his mistakes, it was only proper that Hitler, who was indeed such a leader, would admit his mistake and restore the civil rights of German Jews, and then the boycott would be called off and the Jews would help in Germany's recovery.

In an article published in the *Morning Post* on October 15, 1934, M. A. Davies and P. A. Horowitz, the chairmen of the General Jewish Council (an umbrella organization founded by the American Jewish Committee, the American Jewish Congress, B'nai B'rith, and the Jewish Labor Committee), reacted to the economic crisis in Germany and to Hitler's accusation that the Jews were responsible for it by stating, "American Jews would gladly join any efforts to rehabilitate Germany and contribute to its prosperity if all its citizens would be guaranteed their rights; Jews view with the gravest concern the possibilities of serious distress in Germany during the coming winter, and would gladly join any effort for restoration of prosperity, providing they could feel assured that in its achievement we shall see a Germany according to all her citizen full citizenship rights and opportunity." The German embassy in London was quick to forward the article to Berlin.

Jabotinsky extolled the Jews' power: "The millions of Jews are a political and economic force that you would not want to quarrel with."[99] In a speech on Warsaw Radio on April 26, 1933, Jabotinsky identified "as a traitor [. . .] any Jew in any country who buys goods that come from our persecutors' homeland."[100] Jabotinsky dedicated his speech, given in Polish and French, to the need to struggle against Germany. At the end of his speech he was offered the station's guestbook. This was his only appearance on Polish radio, which after the signing of the Non-Aggression Pact between Poland and Nazi Germany in January 1934 adopted the antisemitic line.

Although the boycott caused some damage to the German economy, it was powerless to take down the regime. Nevertheless, it was not the boycott's failure that led to the recovery of the German economy from 1936 onward, as Germany intensified the Aryanization processes and moved toward an autarchic economy.

As for the Zionist context, the boycott movement caused a profound internal rift, accompanied by insults and accusations of "betraying the Jewish people." The Transfer Agreement deepened the mutual hatred between the Labor movement and the Revisionist movement. The international boycott's disappointing results drove the Revisionists to concentrate on the Zionist arena. "We should focus our attacks on a point that still creates sensation," wrote Jabotinsky on August 17, 1934. "One such point is the 'Transfer Agreement,' [. . .] as a result of which Palestine has become one of the few countries to which German imports are on the rise."[101]

The boycott was supposed to give the Revisionist movement a leading status among the Jewish people. The Revisionists in Palestine organized large rallies against "the transfer disgrace" and accused the official leadership and Mapai of "holding their hand out to the robber" (Hitler) and thus revealing their true colors: "The transfer is a mark of shame with political value, which Hitler bought from the little Jews of Mapai and the Agency for the price of a commission."[102] The Zionist Directorate in London was accused of pressuring the organizers of the boycott conference in London to cancel it,[103] and the Revisionist press in Poland and Palestine published blacklists of boycott-breakers and harsh notices of condemnation:

> Jews! As you shop remember the persecution of the Jews in Hitler's country.
>
> Jews! Do you not fear the judgment of the next generations?
>
> Your grandsons and great-grandsons will say: "May our ancestors' bones rot in their graves for betraying their historic role and refusing to join the war against Hitler."
>
> Boycott German goods!
>
> Jewish public! How long will you support German products? How long will you continue to treat the cries of your plundered and persecuted brothers with indifference?![104]

Meanwhile, newly founded Committees for the Boycott on German Products pressured and threatened various institutions, such as stores and cinemas that screened films produced in Germany. In February 1935, the screening of *Our Kaiser* (*Unser Kaiser*) was approved because it was produced in Austria, but the screening of the film *Eve*, which was produced in Germany, was banned. The committees also attempted to charge a fee for issuing those permits. Factories received letters of warning, and the names of business establishments and importers who imported German goods to Palestine in return for Jewish capital were published in "blacklists" in the newspapers. Dr. Reichart, a Gestapo agent posing as a representative of the German news agency in Palestine, wrote to his superiors on March 30 that the boycott in Palestine could be broken and that the Transfer Agreement was the most effective means to do that.[105] By the end of 1935, the boycott movement's zeal had died down and so had the hope of uniting forces and efforts in order to make it effective. The Revisionists' attention was diverted elsewhere.

According to the Transfer Agreement formulated in August 1933, German Jews could transfer some of their capital—up to 50,000 reichsmarks per family—to Palestine by purchasing industrial products from Germany.[106] The Transfer Company received property and money from German Jews, and bought export goods in Germany according to the wishes of economic bodies in Palestine. In return for importing the goods, the immigrants received their money in Palestine pounds, minus 25 percent used to fund the absorption of immigrants with no resources who needed aid. The proprietors lost around 50 percent of their money. The immigrant was also required to pay the Reichsbank (the German central bank) up to 60,000 reichsmarks.

The fact that the Mandate government gave immigration permits outside the quota to "capitalists" who could present 1,000 Pp upon entering Palestine enabled part of the large wave of immigration called the Fifth Aliyah. By 1937, around 20,000 affluent Jews immigrated with some of their property. Around 40 percent of the emigrants from Germany in those years (around 45,000 people) required the transfer services. From 1933 to 1939, the net capital imports from Germany to Palestine through the Transfer Agreement came to around 8 million Pp, approximately 16 percent of the total Jewish capital imports in that period.[107] Only around a third of all the emigrants from Germany made use of the Transfer Agreement.[108]

As mentioned earlier, the Transfer Agreement caused a profound rift in the Zionist movement and the Jewish public. The Nineteenth Zionist Congress decided by a majority of 240 to 43 votes not to declare a boycott. The Zionist institutions in Palestine, Jabotinsky wrote in a manifesto "to the Jewish People" he published on April 25, 1935, "signed an agreement with Hitler's government. [. . .] And as a result Palestine became a destination for German exports."[109] The Revisionists accused Mapai of siphoning large parts of the transfer monies to the party's pockets, and claimed that Jewish capitalists whose businesses were connected with Germany attempted to thwart the boycott movement.[110] The Revisionist movement's Evacuation Plan included a Clearing Agreement with the Polish government, which was similar to the Transfer Agreement with Nazi Germany. The difference, at least in the eyes of the Revisionists, was that the Transfer Agreement reduced the chances of weakening the Nazi regime, whereas the Clearing Agreement with the Polish authorities intended to allow the emigration of mass numbers of Jews from the country.

To an extent, the Transfer Agreement did damage the boycott's effectiveness. Without this "collaboration" with the Nazi regime, however, it would not have been possible for Jews who owned property to emigrate from Germany to Palestine—an emigration that made a crucial contribution to the growth and consolidation of the Yishuv in the 1930s. It is hard to believe that the intensification of the boycott would have forced the Nazis to rescind the Nuremberg Laws and stop the policy of "encouraging" forced

Jewish emigration from Germany (of which the Transfer Agreement was a part). The representative of Rudolf Hess, Hitler's deputy, stated at an inter-ministerial consultation held on November 17, 1935, that the policy was to facilitate the Jews' emigration: "If they do not leave of their own free will, [. . .] he [Hitler] will force them out of Germany, and will not recoil from using any means of coercion to realize this decision."[111]

The question of how many Jews from the Reich could—and should—be brought to Palestine had been on the agenda since 1933. The sense of urgency, however, changed dramatically after November 1938. In 1935, Werner Senator, the head of the Agency's Immigration Department, claimed that it would be possible to bring 15,000 Jews per year from Germany to Palestine. Thus, German Jews would be given "the hope of salvation," and this would give them the power to hold on to their positions for years.[112]

The future of German Jews was tied to the future of the Zionist movement. Ben-Gurion wrote on December 31 that the fate of German Jews was in the hands of the Zionist movement, and it should bring at least the majority of them to Palestine. "Shall we scatter them to all the corners of the world, where their sons would become speculators and beggars and give rise to an antisemitic movement in their countries of refuge?" The question of German Jews, he added, "is a historic test case for Zionism. Either it wins here or it fails. Both the victory and the failure would be decisive." Victory or failure was also measured by Zionism's success in preventing another solution—that is, the immigration of German Jews to other countries. The aspiration, Ben-Gurion stated, was to absorb them "on a healthy land-settling basis so that they become a creative and cultural force, integrated within the Jewish people."[113]

In his testimony before the Peel Commission on November 25, 1936, Weizmann said that "there are in this part of the world six million people doomed to be pent up in places where they are not wanted, and for whom the world is divided into places where they cannot live, and places into which they cannot enter."[114]

In practice, the number of immigrants that the Zionist movement wished to bring to Palestine was in the tens of thousands. The economic prosperity in Palestine, leveraged by the imports of Jewish capital from Germany, led to an increase in the number of certificates. Immigrants from Category A—that is, immigrants with means ("capitalists")—received immigration permits outside the quota. In 1933, 8,300 emigrants arrived from Germany; in 1935 there were 8,460; in 1936 there were 8,664; and in 1937 there were

3,680. After the principle of "political maximum" was put forward in the Peel Commission's report, reducing the number of immigration permits to 12,000 per year, the number of emigrants from Germany reached 6,895 in 1938 and 16,400 in 1939 (65 percent of the total number of immigrants). By November 1938, a little under half of the Jews of Germany emigrated from the country—around 150,000 people.[115]

There were several reasons for this, including the profound affinity that some of the Jews felt toward Germany, the economic difficulty of losing a large part of their property (after November 1938, as mentioned earlier, it was almost impossible to take out any property), and the hope that the storm would nevertheless pass one day. Another explanation is the inability of most of the Jewish leadership, and especially of ordinary Jews, to comprehend a course of events that was fundamentally unpredictable.[116] Until Kristallnacht, there were still some voices calling on German Jews not to give up the struggle to restore the rights they had been denied.

Palestine could not compete with attractive immigration destinations in Europe or overseas. From 1933 to 1939, around 329,000 Jews (about 30 percent of the total number of Jews living in Germany, Austria, and the Sudetenland on the eve of the Nazis' rise to power) emigrated from the Reich. Around 60,000 of them immigrated to the United States, around 40,000 to Britain, around 30,000 to France, around 15,000 to Belgium, and around 8,000 to Switzerland. Others immigrated to Argentina, Brazil, Australia, and Canada.[117] Palestine absorbed around 55,000 immigrants from April 1933 to July 1939. From the Zionist standpoint, the fact that Palestine was the destination for only a relatively small part of the total number of immigrants was reason for concern. This concern was supplemented by the concern over the activities of Jewish organizations founded to deal with refugees from Germany, including the Jewish Refugees Committee, the Central British Fund for German Jewry, and the Council for German Jewry, in addition to the bodies already active in this area, the Joint and the JCA.

On January 25, 1939, counsel to the German Ministry of Foreign Affairs, Walter Schaumburg, wrote a memorandum to all Germany's delegations around the world, in which he summed up the expected results from the forced emigration policy: "The streaming of Jews to all parts of the world provokes resistance from the original population and this provides the best propaganda for Germany's Jewish policy. To encourage this antisemitic wave is the supreme task of German foreign policy. [. . .] As long as a Jew can find his livelihood in Germany, world Jewry will not give up its stronghold in Germany." In any case, the report added, the Jews were unwilling to emigrate unless they could take out the property they had stolen from the German people. The memorandum noted that the Évian Conference had proved that there were no countries willing to receive Jewish immigrants, and because Palestine was now closed to them as well, Germany could only hope that the Jews would not get a state in Palestine, but a reservation.[118]

The reasons for the Jewish emigration from the Reich until 1938 were mainly economic. Many of the emigrants believed it was "temporary emigration," until the storm passed. The boycott against Jewish trade (April 1933), the Nuremberg Laws (1935), and the Aryanization process increased the flow of emigrants, who received help from various Jewish organizations. Kristallnacht expedited the wish to emigrate from Germany at all costs. Emigration turned into flight. Some of the Jews of the Reich had the possibility of immigrating to Western countries, to the United States, or to other countries across the ocean, if they agreed to lose a large part of their property and capital. On the other hand, poor Jews or those with little property could not obtain passports or entry visas. The United States' immigration laws obliged those seeking entry visas to provide proof that they had the necessary financial means to ensure that "they do not become a burden on public funds" or to provide an affidavit from relatives or friends who guaranteed it financially. The immigration authorities in the United States checked the guarantors' ability to fulfill their guarantee.

On Friday, July 3, 1936, the fifty-six-year-old Czech Jewish writer Stefan Lux, who had moved from Germany to Switzerland in 1933, committed suicide. He entered the League of Nations' conference room in Geneva during a discussion about Fascist Italy's occupation of Ethiopia. When the Spanish representative spoke, Lux pulled out a revolver, shouted, *"C'est le dernier coup"* (It's the final blow), and shot himself in the chest. He died a few hours later in the hospital. The session was stopped for a while. Lux left behind a few letters: to the king of Britain, George VI, to the *Times* and the *Manchester Guardian*, to the secretary of the League of Nations, and to British foreign secretary Anthony Eden. He wrote Eden: "When a person speaks out before death—a calculated and voluntary death—he is entitled to be heard. I hope that the death of a young and almost unknown writer will help spread light and truth. With this feeling I hereby send you my warmest wishes which have until now been directed at you from some other party."[119]

Lux asked to be buried in a Jewish cemetery, and the funeral was paid for by the Jewish community in Geneva. The inscription on the gravestone at the cemetery in Veyrier, on the Swiss-German border, read "Martyr d'Israel" (martyr of Israel).

Lux's dramatic suicide did not leave a great impression on the League of Nations (the only result was that the security detail was reinforced). A committee dedicated to his commemoration was founded in Paris in 1938, in protest over the democratic states' indifference to the oppression of Jews in Germany. A news agency reported that before he committed suicide he said that his act was a protest against the way the Jews of Germany were being treated. The Nazi press called him "an idiot." *Der Stürmer* published the following lines under his photograph: "Kosher blood flowed at the League of Nations. A Jew shot himself as a gesture yesterday. He announced it to the outside world: the League of Nations has been shot."

The letter to Eden suggested that rather than to protest the persecution of Jews, Lux's intention was to get the West to recognize that Nazi Germany was being controlled by a dangerous group of criminals who were endangering world peace, and to abandon the policy of appeasement.[120] Public opinion and the governments of Europe, the United States, and other countries were aware that the "Jewish question" had now become "the Jewish refugees' question." Their concern grew after the Anschluss of Austria had imprisoned an additional 200,000 Jews under Nazi Germany's rule, and many of them started to besiege foreign consulates in the hope of obtaining the longed-for visas.[121] This pressure was one of the triggers for the initiative to convene an international conference to discuss the refugee question.

On January 1, 1938, Jabotinsky wrote James G. McDonald, former League of Nations High Commissioner, expressing appreciation for his efforts "to save the Jews of Germany." However, he added, the solution to the tragic problem was to bring all the Jews of Germany plus another half a million people from the troubled countries to Palestine over the next two years. This would prevent the danger of antisemitism developing further, as well as solve the question of Palestine, because an additional million Jews would relieve the British government of its responsibility for the country's internal security. World Jewry, he promised, was able to raise the necessary money to fund an immigration on this scale.[122]

On January 3, 1938, the motor ship *Poseidon* sailed from the port of Lavrion on the southern tip of the Attica peninsula, with 65 Hechalutz members from Poland on board, letting its passengers off at the Emek Hefer beach (it sailed again on May 17 carrying 65 pioneers, putting its passengers ashore on the 23rd). In April, the ship *Artemisia* sailed from the same port and its passengers also managed to make it ashore. In July it sailed again, bringing in its combined two voyages around 400 members of Hechalutz in Poland to Palestine. These voyages—and others—managed to bring to Palestine only a drop of the "ocean" of forced emigration initiated and executed by the Nazi regime. It was a forced emigration that turned the question of Jewish emigrants and refugees from the Reich into an international problem.

On April 16, 1938, Ruppin returned from his trip to Germany and Poland on the ship *Polonia*. It was the first passenger ship to put down anchor at the Tel Aviv port. During the voyage he recorded some of his impressions of Germany:

> It seems to me that many Jews in Germany still do not appreciate the full severity of what has happened to them. There are still some rich Jews who live on their interest—almost like in the old days. As long as they can buy foodstuff from the nearest grocer—they do not notice the disaster. They are unable to see that their children have no future in Germany, neither economically nor spiritually, and that they are destined to be considered ostracized—at least for a few decades.

Ruppin wondered: "It puzzles me that despite the unparalleled incitement in speeches and in the newspapers, there are no attacks on Jews on the streets or on the trains. [. . .] Even the officials, 90 percent of whom are Nazis, behave politely, and sometimes with willingness to help." Was it the German discipline that prevented the incitement from turning into violence?[123]

The refugee problem and the pressure on the American administration to increase the immigration quotas drove President Roosevelt to convene the Évian Conference in order to "relieve the pressure" and seek other immigration destinations. Hitler expressed satisfaction over the initiative: "I can only hope and expect that the other world, which displays such deep sympathy towards these criminals [the Jews], will show enough generosity and translate its sympathy into real aid. We on our part are willing to leave all these criminals in the hands of these countries; as far as I am concerned, even on luxury ships."[124]

Hotel Royal, in the resort, casino, and spa town of Évian-les-Bains on the French side of Lake Geneva, opposite the Swiss town of Lausanne, hosted the international conference on the refugee problem that took place between July 6 and 15, 1938.[125] The conference featured thirty-two countries and thirty-seven aid organizations, as well as various dignitaries (including the exiled Spanish cellist Pablo Casals). Nazi Germany refused to send any representatives. Ernst von Weizsäcker, director general of Germany's Foreign Office, wrote in his diary that the United States ambassador to Germany met him at a party and asked whether Germany would be willing to cooperate with the Évian Conference on the emigration of Jews: "I told him not to entertain any hopes." The emigration of Jews from Germany, said von Weizsäcker, was "an internal German problem."[126]

Around twenty Jewish delegations from various countries went to Évian, reported A. Alperin, the *Haaretz* newspaper's special envoy to the conference. They felt uncomfortable, he wrote, staying at the luxurious and elegant Splendid Hotel, which could be reached by funicular ("aerial train"). The hotel featured

> elegant vestibules and promenade gardens overlooking Lake Geneva—the utmost luxury—here, of all places, where governments' delegates have convened to talk about the persecuted and tortured, the refugees who have no roofs over their heads, who are driven away from shelter to shelter, from border to border. How can you compare this horror with the magnificence and beauty all around us? A terrible contrast.[127]

The *Haaretz* correspondent also heard that a few of the Zionist delegates took a liking to the place, and were thinking of approaching the Évian municipality to propose finding a suitable venue for the next Zionist Congress (in August 1939). His assessment that it was a nice idea that "'the Jewish state Congress' should draw power and optimism from the grace of this place" may have had a touch of sarcasm in it.[128]

The *Der Moment* correspondent at Évian, A. Hermann, reported that the changeable weather hindered the possibility of enjoying the "French atmosphere." The heat made it difficult to sit in the conference hall, and when there was time to walk around town, it was pouring with rain all day and the delegates were trapped in their hotels.[129]

It was not only the weather that instilled the town with a pessimistic atmosphere. Around 200 journalists went over to cover the conference. Among them was Hans Habe, a Hungarian-born Austrian journalist and writer, who wrote for the (Jewish owned) liberal newspaper *Prager Tagblatt*. In a novel he published in 1965, *The Mission* (*Die Mission*), he wrote: "[S]tatesmen have always . . . preferred to solve the problems of suffering mankind in the most pleasant and under the best possible touristic conditions."[130] Habe described Hotel Royal as a much more luxurious hotel than the Splendid. The former stood on the top of a hill, whereas the latter was located down the slope and resembled a first-class guesthouse.[131]

Around five years earlier, in September 1933, the League of Nations had appointed "A High Commissioner for Refugees" (not only Jewish ones). The role was given to the American diplomat James McDonald. The wave of refugees after the publication of the Nuremberg Laws, and the League of Nations' inability to offer any help, led to his resignation, and the British Sir Neill Malcolm was appointed to replace him. The organization's budget was funded by international Jewish organizations. In light of the wave of refugees and the tough immigration laws in the various countries, the creation of the Commissionership was a recognition of the fact that the refugee problem was an international one.

Shertok described the creation of the Refugee Commissionership at the Agency Directorate meeting in Jerusalem on August 21, 1938, as no more than a "gesture": the American government "is currently also easing the restrictions on Jewish emigration from Germany and Austria to the United States. It could have said to the British government that it is impossible right now to erase Palestine from the map of Jewish emigration countries. If things are said in the right tone and conveyed to the government in the same spirit they will have an effect."[132]

The *Haaretz* editor Moshe Glickson wrote optimistically that the conference broke the blockade of the refugees' terrible loneliness, and in its wake perhaps the Yishuv would break the "sloppy and bizarre wall of silence that added to the dejection and sorrow of our tortured brothers in Hitler's kingdom."[133]

In fact, Roosevelt had no intention of changing the American policy on immigration. The New Zionist Organization (NZO) did not reject Roosevelt's initiative out of hand. On the contrary, it could have been presented as a kind of "addendum" to the NZO's idea of convening an international conference to discuss the refugee question. The only difference, said Binyamin Akzin, a leader of the New Zionist Organization since the founding of the Revisionist movement in 1935, at a press conference in Tel Aviv in April 1938, was that the conference initiated by the U.S. president was going to deal with the question of how to solve the "problem of a few tens of thousands of Jewish refugees without shelter in their homeland." If they wanted to scatter them all over the earth, however, this in itself showed that there was no place of refuge for them. Therefore, the positive result of the conference would be for it to become "patently" clear that there were additional "*millions of Jews, potential refugees*" in Europe whose problem could be solved not by dispersing them, but by gathering them together in Palestine. The Évian Conference thus offered a "great opportunity for political Zionism."[134]

The United States had agreed to receive 27,000 refugees per year as part of its legal quota and reassured the countries invited to the conference that they would not be called on to fund the emigration nor asked to increase their own immigration quotas. In his opening speech, Myron C. Taylor, Roosevelt's personal representative, mentioned the refugee problem in general—wretched human beings whose fate was being discussed at the conference—but did not mention the Jewish refugees. Nevertheless, *Davar* wrote about the "surprisingly cordial tone of his speech."[135]

In the first week of July, a Palestine exhibition was held at Queen's Hall in London. It featured models of the Hebrew University in Jerusalem and of Tel Aviv, as well as a model of a "Wall and Tower" settlement: "Within four hours—from 6 a.m. to 10 a.m.—the defensive walls are erected around the settlement, and at noon the observation tower [the watchtower] is already standing." *Davar* reported, not without pride, that the *Manchester Guardian* journalist who covered the exhibition wrote: "Our authorities, who are responsible for safety measures against air-raids, and who are studying questions of population evacuation on a large scale, would do well to take a look at the exhibition at Queen's Hall" in order to learn the meaning of efficiency.[136]

Alas, life was not so calm in Palestine. During the Évian Conference violent events in Palestine followed one after the other. On Wednesday July 6, an Irgun terrorist attack at the downtown fruit market killed dozens of Arabs and wounded many. *Der Moment* reported on "terrible days in Israel" that claimed the lives of 130 victims in a "bloodbath in Haifa."[137] Then on July 11 the watchman Alexander Zaïd was murdered by Bedouins on his way from Sheikh Abreik to Kibbutz Alonim in the Valley of Jezreel. Although he was not the only Jew murdered that month, he was an individualist who built his own private farm, and he became an icon and a symbol in the Yishuv's collective memory.[138]

The opening session of the Évian Conference began at 4 p.m. on July 6 in the Grand Salon of the Hotel Royal:

> In the center of the room stood a horse-shaped conference table covered with green baize at which the chief delegates [. . .] had taken their seats, while their assistants occupied the two rows of chairs immediately behind them. [. . .] The hall was high, but only of medium size, a lounge that was not intended for such a serious, one might almost say macabre, occasion. The light walls, decorated in both the classicist and the secessionist style, were topped by a fresco ceiling [. . .]; the healing springs,

parks and promenades of the town of Évian-les-Bains were also depicted, half realistically, half idealized, leaving one with the impression of being in an emporium rather than a conference hall.[139]

The approximately 100 delegates plus around 100 advisors and aides did not doubt the severity of the German and Austrian refugees' plight. The delegates were asked to submit secret information about the number and types of refugees that their governments would be willing to take in, but they all explained the difficulty of allowing Jews to enter.

The representatives of the non-Jewish organizations wished to turn the attention to the plight of refugees from their countries. Zalman Rubashov (Shazar), a scholar, journalist, and at the time one of the leaders of Mapai and the Histadrut, described the opening session in *Davar*: "The representatives of the 33 governments sit around three tables set up in a kind of U shape [. . .] and around the tables of the countries' representatives sit the journalists, the envoys of all the famous telegraphic agencies and the special correspondents of all the big newspapers [. . .] and of course—the Jewish press in all its variety." At the end of the hall sat the "observers." The journalists were complaining, Rubashov added, that airmail "from the remote Évian" takes a week to arrive at its destination.[140]

The sessions were usually held in secret and were closed to journalists. Most of the delegates, Habe wrote, preferred to walk around the garden, where tables, chairs, and parasols were installed on the well-groomed lawns.

Despite the atrocities, the delegates dashed any remaining hopes of a mass emigration. The delegate from Peru said that the United States government had set an example for a "wise and cautious" immigration policy; the delegate from Australia declared that his country had no racial problem and had no intension of importing one; countries in Central America made it clear that they had no interest in "merchants and intellectuals"; Canada announced that it was willing to absorb only skilled agricultural workers; and Brazil wanted to receive only immigrants who had been baptized as Christians. The British government expressed its readiness to absorb 9,000 children without their parents, because a "sudden rush" of Jewish refugees might provoke antisemitic feelings. The United States was willing to take in 27,000 Jews from Germany. Only the Dominican Republic, which sought to earn "brownie points" from the American administration, declared its willingness to absorb 100,000 refugees.

The French delegate, Senator Victor Henri Bérenger, president of the

Senate's Foreign Affairs Committee, presented his country as the first to take in refugees: around 200,000 refugees from different countries had found sanctuary in France, which was loyal to its tradition as a country of refuge, but it had already fulfilled this duty to the maximum. The *Haaretz* envoy wrote on July 6 that his words were "the only phenomenon that brought satisfaction and encouragement."[141] Nevertheless, Julien Weill, the chief rabbi of Paris, reacted to anti-Jewish incidents that had taken place in Paris and some other cities by warning his fellow Jews not to gather in front of the synagogues during the holidays, and on November 19 stated that the Consistoire Central des Israélites de France, the central religious organization of French Jews, could not make "even the slightest contribution" to the refugee question, because France could not accept any more refugees.[142]

Lord Winterton, a British Member of Parliament, an anti-Zionist, and an advocate of the policy of appeasement, announced in a brief speech that his government would do all it could to help the United States and other countries for humanitarian reasons. Britain had taken in as many refugees as it could, and was examining the possibility of taking in Jewish refugees in its colonies in East Africa (their governors expressed their strong opposition to the idea). Lord Winterton maintained that even if Palestine's gates had been opened to unlimited Jewish immigration, the refugee problem would not have been resolved. In any case, the question of immigration to Palestine was not a subject that the conference was supposed to discuss.

Each Zionist organization from the various countries was given around five minutes to speak before a subcommittee. Norman Bentwich, one of the leaders of the Committee for German Jews in England, described the brief appearance on July 8 as a "humiliating process." The *Haaretz* correspondent found a glimmer of hope: "It [the conference] has a great moral value. The opening session itself looked like a strong demonstration against the persecutions in different countries. Representatives of the world's large democratic powers spoke forcefully, warning that such persecutions were a danger to civilization as a whole."[143]

Dr. Heinrich Neumann von Héthárs, an ear, nose, and throat doctor from Vienna whom the Gestapo sent along with von Neumann and Dr. Josef Löwenherz, leaders of the Zionist movement in Austria, brought to Évian a proposal from the Nazi authorities: they were willing to sell Jews for 250 dollars a head. If the conference turned down the proposal, he warned, 40,000 Austrian Jews would be sent to concentration camps.

A subcommittee headed by Professor J. M. Yepes, legal advisor of the Columbian government to the Permanent Delegation to the League of Nations, was appointed to discuss the proposal but failed to reach a decision. In the novel written by Hans Habe about this mission, on which there is scant information,[144] von Héthárs was called Heinrich von Bonde. He operated on Habe in his youth, and at the conference Habe took on the role of "protecting" him from the journalists who wanted to find out details about his mysterious mission. Von Héthárs appeared before the subcommittee. The rumor about his mission, he told Habe years later, "passed from table to table" between courses. The despairing von Héthárs was told that convening the conference would deter the Nazi dictator.

A memorandum was submitted to the conference by Lord Herbert Samuel, the first British High Commissioner in Palestine, demanding the renewal of the principle of "economic absorption capacity."[145] Returning to this principle, Samuel maintained, would allow Palestine to resolve part of the refugee problem. The representatives of the Zionist movement proposed that the countries taking part in the conference agree on an organized exit of Jews from the Reich over the next *ten years*, and not only to Palestine. They held talks, presented data and plans. Winterton, wrote Ruppin, greeted the Jewish delegation with extreme coldness and refused to hear about the emigration of Eastern European Jews. The brief meeting with him, he noted, was "like a slap in the face for us."[146] Dr. Benjamin Akzin, who came to Évian from Palestine as the representative of the presidency of the New Zionist Organization, said in his memoir that Winterton and Ruppin "ran around the corridors of the casino promoting their cause" and earned "honest and hypocritical" words of sympathy.[147]

Taylor, the conference chairman, promised Ruppin that Germany would understand that "dumping human beings on other countries was as inadvisable as flooding them with goods—and that it would allow the emigrants to take the necessary means of subsistence with them."[148] Ruppin believed that if German Jews could transfer their assets to Palestine, the country would be able to absorb 200,000 of the Jews of Germany plus another 100,000 Jews from Austria. He demanded that the debate include the Jews of Eastern Europe; otherwise, the elements interested in Jewish emigration from Eastern Europe would conclude that it could only be realized "by using Hitlerite methods." The Jews of Eastern Europe must not be completely absent from the conference's agenda, he argued, even if they were not included in it explicitly. Ruppin also insisted that emigrants must be allowed to bring out capital.[149]

In her autobiography, Golda Meyerson (Meir), one of the leaders of the Histadrut, wrote that during the discussions she sat in the audience and felt "a mixture of sorrow, rage, frustration and horror." On July 13, before returning to Palestine, she held a press conference in the dining room of Hotel Royal, in which she said: "There is only one thing I hope to see before I die [. . .] and that is that my people should not need expressions of sympathy anymore."[150] "The word 'Palestine' had not been mentioned yet at the conference," wrote Rubashov fumingly on July 8, "neither in the first session nor in the second."[151]

On July 9 the Jews of Vienna fasted and prayed in the synagogues for the conference's success. At the same time, the Nazis confiscated most of the Jewish institutions' buildings. Polish Jews did not send any delegates to the Évian Conference, and their issue did not appear on the agenda. On July 6, the Jewish organizations and the Zionist parties in Poland released a public statement in which they expressed Polish Jewry's profound gratitude to President Roosevelt. The representatives of Poland and Romania attended the conference as observers and protested that the issue of the emigration of Jews from Eastern Europe — though they were not refugees — would not be raised in it. The Polish foreign minister Beck told the United States ambassador to Warsaw that if the international conference restricted its discussions solely to refugees, it would intensify antisemitism in Poland, Romania, and Hungary. However, he added, in order to earn the cooperation of different Jewish circles (he meant mainly the two camps of the Zionist movement), it was necessary first to solve the problem of Palestine, because the Jews saw the proposals of alternative immigration destinations as a threat. Nevertheless, the Jewish leadership recognized that even if it obtained the maximum Palestinian territory, it would not solve the emigration problem.[152]

The Colonial Office was angry at the Polish government's request to give precedence in the distribution of certificates to emigration from Poland, because until 1938 the vast majority of immigrants had come to Palestine from Poland. The distribution of emigration permits was not the responsibility of Britain, but was entrusted to the Jewish Agency. The Office's officials maintained that Colonel Beck must not be given any information about His Majesty's government's plans concerning immigration control, but that he should be warned that Poland must not pin its hopes on Palestine as a solution to Poland's Jewish problem. On what should Poland pin its hope, then — the Colonial Office had no advice on this matter.

The Polish government had a clear interest that the conference also discuss emigration from Poland, and Polish diplomacy complained bitterly that its demand to include the question of Polish Jews in the conference's discussions rather than concentrate solely on Jews from the Reich had been rejected. The possibility that if a solution were found for the Jews of the Reich, hundreds of thousands of Jews from Poland would push to leave the country, was another pretext for the participating countries' refusal to open more than a crack. One of the results of the conference was that the Polish government tightened its cooperation with the Zionist bodies in search of alternative routes for immigration.

The Nazi regime's conclusion from the conference was that "all the countries participating in [the conference] [and] stubbornly holding on to the democratic idea justified in their practical policy the means taken by the leadership of the National-Socialist State against Judaism," and the conference showed the whole world that the problem of the Jews was by no means an internal German matter, but rather a pertinent problem with global political significance.[153] In other words, everyone pitied the Jews, but no one wanted them.

Alfred Rosenberg, the ideologue of the Nazi party, wrote in the *Völkischer Beobachter* that the refugees must not be allowed to immigrate to Palestine, because they would cause riots there. There were enough vast regions in the world where a Jewish state could be founded. He mentioned Uganda and Madagascar as possible destinations.[154] The real result of the conference was that the elements in the Nazi regime that preferred organized emigration over deportation were weakened.

Der Moment wrote that the representative of Colombia had said in his speech that Évian was the Wailing Wall of our time. After the conference ended, the journalist Y. Heftman wrote that you could say that the Wall had remained cold and hard. "The stones have stayed stones. The Wailing Wall of our time is much harder than the stone wall in Jerusalem." To him, the Évian Conference was a symbol of the destruction of European "progress."[155] The world's hypocrisy had been exposed, wrote Yitzhak Katzenelson, and if earlier he had called on the free countries to open their gates to Jewish refugees from Germany, after Évian he reached the conclusion that there was only one solution for the Jews: Palestine.[156] As a matter of fact, the conference led many countries to toughen their immigration laws.

The *New York Times* correspondent reported on July 8 that the various countries were playing poker, while the representative of *Davar* in Évian, Rubashov, wrote on July 12:

> One would have assumed that a unified front of the Jewish people at the Évian Conference was not an impossible demand. If regarding the dis-

tant future and a full solution to the Jewish Question there is disagreement among us, then on the current question of saving refugees, when all the roads are blocked and the demon of hatred is raging and any expedient with any substance will do—the organizations would find the way to negotiate and present one united delegation which would try to say some things to the countries' delegates. If not at this time and at this opportunity—then when?[157]

A telegram arrived in Évian from the Committees for the Defense of Palestine in Damascus, calling the conference attenders not to be influenced by the Jewish propaganda. The Arabs should not pay the price for the sins of Europe, which was exploiting the Jews. Countries that wished to help the Jews should open their gates to them. Jewish immigration to Palestine would only add fuel to the fire.[158]

A telegram thanking the president of the United States was sent by the conference. The conference concluded by appointing an Intergovernmental Committee for Refugees whose aim was to search for destinations for Jewish immigration in collaboration with the Nazi regime, but which failed to do much.

On July 12, 1938, *Haaretz* quoted a news piece published by the *Manchester Guardian* that said that the mayor of a German town on the border with Switzerland had decreed that the Jews could take care of their business and their private matters between 7 a.m. and 9 a.m., and go for walks between 6 a.m. and 9 a.m., but only on the street that ran along the Jewish cemetery. "Seven hundred Jews lived in this town before the Nazis came to power, and now there are only 60 elderly men and women left, confined to their homes like prisoners."

The Évian Conference was adjourned before noon on July 15, after ten days of discussions. In his concluding remarks, Lord Winterton said that Palestine had absorbed 300,000 Jews in the past years, and in light of the prevailing conditions the British government had decided to stop the immigration. The *Times* was satisfied: the conference did its job admirably, although the British delegation did not, in its view, earn the appreciation of the Jews who had pinned exaggerated hopes on Palestine's absorption capacity.[159]

Other British newspapers were a lot less enthusiastic. In the House of Lords, the "humanitarian spirit" of the Évian Conference and its results—and, of course, the role played by Britain—earned much praise in the debate on the refugee problem in July 1938. The importance of the conference, said Lord Samuel, was that "perhaps [. . .] it has brought out clearly before all the world the fact that this question of the refugees is not merely a matter of domestic moment in Germany, but is also of importance to all countries which may be directly or indirectly affected by the flood of humanity that has poured out from Central Europe."

At the same time, some of the speakers in the debate stressed that the conference acted with "realism" when it refrained from making proposals that would be unrealizable. Some mentioned different countries in Africa and Latin America that could theoretically serve as destinations for Jewish immigration, which would bring with it great benefits in both demographic and economic terms. On the other hand, some Lords explained that the Dominions were autonomous entities, and therefore Britain could not force an unacceptable policy on them, and in any case the Dominions would only be able to absorb a small number of immigrants.

This debate was also overshadowed by the fear that the refugees from the Reich might be joined very soon by massive numbers of refugees from the approximately 4.5 million Jews living in Poland and Romania. Therefore, the actions taken to solve the problem of refugees from the Reich might encourage the governments of Poland and Romania to increase the pressure on the Jews to emigrate. Some speakers did not forget to mention that the issue involved not only Jewish refugees, but also "non-Aryan Christians." Besides, the honorable Lords were of the opinion that the Nazi regime should contribute to solving the refugee problem by letting the emigrants bring out at least some of their property.[160]

From the end of the Évian Conference to the outbreak of the Second World War, 170,000 Jews would leave the territories of the Reich. Around 50,000 Jews left Austria in that period. From a Jewish point of view it was not enough, but the scale of the immigration provoked vigorous opposition in Western countries toward the Jews who were "coming in their droves." This opposition intensified greatly after Kristallnacht.[161] On October 5, all passports held by Jews in Germany were invalidated in order to prevent them from using them to cross the border into Switzerland. And in May and November 1938, the French government passed laws intended to close the borders to illegal immigrants and deport them.

In November 1938, the Jewish Emigration and Colonization Committee (JECC) (*Żydowski komitet emigracyjny i kolonizacjyny*), headed by the rabbi and scholar Professor Moses Schorr, was formed with the encouragement of the Polish government. The JECC approached the Intergovernmental Committee, requesting it include Poland in its activities. It warned that refraining from doing so would make it harder for the Polish government to stop violent antisemitism. The JECC also announced an appeal to raise funds for refugees, and managed to raise a million guilders.[162]

The Évian Conference did not earn approval within the Zionist movement.[163] Ben-Gurion was resolute in his negative attitude toward the conference. At the meeting of the Agency Directorate in Jerusalem to discuss preparations for the conference, he stated: "At this time the conference might cause tremendous damage to Palestine and to Zionism. [. . .] It might remove Palestine from the international agenda as a factor in solving the Jewish question. [. . .] For us it would be better to underplay the importance of the conference."[164] Neither did Ben-Gurion believe that Polish or Romanian diplomacy could be of much help. However, in light of the opposition to any "territorial" solution, he found it hard to ignore the fact that presenting Palestine as a destination for mass Jewish immigration could cause "tremendous damage" to both Palestine and Zionism. At the same time, he thought that the time was not ripe for presenting Palestine as the definitive answer, because there were "riots and every day they throw bombs and murder people and the country suffers from unemployment and is at an economic standstill"; this was not a country where "you solve a refugee question."

Gruenbaum also admitted that the Yishuv was not able to absorb "massive numbers of additional workers." At the same time, he predicted terrible dangers from the conference: "Palestine can disappear from the agenda as an immigration country."[165] Ruppin suggested demanding that the participating countries reach an agreement with Germany on an organized exit of the Jews along with part of their property, over ten years, with a third of them being absorbed in Palestine.[166] In the end, the Agency Directorate decided that Ruppin, Ussishkin, and Dr. Georg Landauer would go to Évian,[167] to be joined there by Nahum Goldmann and others. The non-Zionist delegations included the (British) Council for German Jews, the Committee of Community Representatives in England, representatives of Agudat Yisrael, and others. The conference was also attended by a few British Members of Parliament and friends of Zionism.

Ussishkin, as always, had forthright opinions about the conference's results: in Évian, Palestine was dealt a "blow" and was no longer considered relevant to the plans to save the Jews. "Our position at the Évian Conference was 'beggarly,'" he complained at the Agency Directorate meeting on December 11, 1938, because the Zionist delegates did not strongly insist that only Palestine could provide a solution to the refugee question.[168] He too probably knew that the conference rejected out of hand any discussion of the Palestine question, but chose to ignore that. The NZO chiefs went much further: not only did the Jewish Agency fail miserably, they claimed, but it also negotiated "on Jewish [im]migration to a faraway country, in order to prepare the ground for partition." Their answer to the "political failure" and the made-up story was to transfer the Agency's powers to an authorized institution chosen by all the world's Jews, which would be their sole representative in matters concerning Palestine.[169]

The Zionist Organization's weekly, *Haolam*, wrote on July 7 that thanks to Weizmann's appearance at the conference the movement would not be left "like sheep without a shepherd." After he met Lord Winterton on June 24, however, Weizmann reached the conclusion that Britain was going to try and separate the Palestine question from the refugee question at the conference.[170] On July 3 he wrote Jacobus Kann that he was waiting to see the results of the conference and he might join it for a day or two but did not pin his hopes on it. On July 14, Weizmann replied to Stephen Wise, who pleaded with him to go to Évian, that Malcolm McDonald had also invited him to speak at the conference, and therefore he might stop there for a few days before going on vacation. On Friday Weizmann bought tickets for the train from London to Paris, but a telegram from Nahum Goldmann advised him to delay his trip and wait for further developments. In the end, Weizmann did not go to Évian, writing on July 15: "Évian on the other hand has proved a grave disappointment, and its achievements have been almost negligible. Palestine figured hardly at all at the Conference."[171] Ruppin, who met Weizmann on his way to the spa town of Cauterets in the Pyrenees, found that "he looks unwell and his mood is dejected."[172]

Weizmann submitted to the Évian Conference a memorandum on behalf of the Jewish Agency, in which he distinguished between emigration and deportation by the state.[173] At the Twenty-First Zionist Congress Weizmann mentioned the conference and said that the various governments were willing to absorb 100,000 refugees, "but to our great detriment the realization of our proposals was interrupted."[174] Dugdale wrote in her diary on July 15 that Weizmann reacted to the conference's failure with an "apocalyptic program."[175]

Weizmann's mood in that period showed the distress in which not only he but the entire Zionist movement had found themselves. Already in November 1933 Weizmann wrote Felix Warburg: "The world is gradually, relentlessly and effectively being closed to the Jews, and every day I feel more and more that a ring of steel is being forged around us. [. . .] It is all inescapable, and every ounce of my energy [. . .] is going toward the consummation of that end [Palestine]. Everything else is a palliative, a half-measure, and merely postponing the evil day."[176]

On November 16, 1938, Weizmann claimed that there was no other solution to the refugee problem than Palestine. Their absorption in other countries was nothing but an "illusion."[177] At the same time, he doubted the Yishuv's ability to absorb a large immigration and the suitability of all the refugees to life in Palestine. Much of his diplomatic activity at that time was designed to increase the pressure on Nazi Germany to curb its policy.[178] His enthusiastic support for the Partition Plan also stemmed from the conclusion that the world's countries would lock their gates to Jewish refugees, and that only a Jewish state could offer them a solution. The failure of the Évian Conference proved that he had been right in his assessment that the willingness of the world's countries to absorb the refugees should not be relied on, and confirmed his claim that the world was divided into countries that did not allow the Jews to live in them and countries that prevented them from entering their borders.

However, the Partition Plan, on which he pinned his hopes, had also become a dead letter. The results of the conference refuted Ben-Gurion's fear that after Évian "the danger of territorialism would come not only from despairing Jews, but also from powerful countries that now tend towards 'the territorialist solution' at the expense of 'the Zionist solution' [. . .] and let us not be afraid to see things as they are: Zionism is in danger."[179]

There was likewise no grounds to Jabotinsky's belief that the conference showed that the Jewish question had no other solution but the one and only "territorial" solution — Palestine.[180] The Zionist fear that the Évian Conference would offer ways to further the emigration of Jews from Germany and Austria to other countries — rather than to Palestine — had nothing to rely on. The Intergovernmental Committee that had been established did not manage to do much.[181] Either way, the Zionist position did not and could not have any influence on the results of the conference. While in Paris, Ruppin wrote in his diary on July 18: "I stayed in Évian until Thursday, July 14. I did not wait until the closing session because the decisions were known in advance. [. . .] Palestine was not seen as a possible refuge for the emigrants except in a very limited capacity."[182]

At the Twenty-First Zionist Congress, Weizmann had warm words to say about the Évian Conference, initiated by President Roosevelt, "known for his generous spirit and sensitive heart." The conference had been "a noble initiative of historic importance" and was designed "to save around 100,000 Jews in a short time." Now, in August 1939, Weizmann tied the

Évian Conference with the White Paper, claiming that the initiative could have borne fruit if it had not been hindered by Britain's policy. Nevertheless, he was gracious to Britain as well: "The British government expressed its honest sympathy with the refugees' plight. Moreover the British people demonstrated in various ways its generous spirit towards the victims of racial persecution." The Évian Conference was not, therefore, according to Weizmann, only a futile conference, but "had a moral value which may increase with time," even though so far it had not yielded any results that "matched the tragic scale of the problem."[183]

For two and a half months, a small boat carrying sixty-two refugees from the town of Kittsee in the Burgenland region in East Austria anchored on the Danube. "While in Évian they discuss the fate of Jewish refugees," remarked the envoy Shlomo Lipsky (Tamir); these refugees were evicted from their homes on April 16, 1938, the seder night, by the SS, put on buses and led to the border with Czechoslovakia, where they were left in the middle of the cold and rainy winter in an open field. The Czechoslovakian border police brought them to Bratislava, from where they were deported to Hungary. From there they marched around twenty miles and were left in no-man's-land near the Hungarian town of Rajka on the border with Czechoslovakia and Austria. The refugees stayed outdoors in the cold and the wind for three days and nights, until the Bratislava Jews hired a tugboat and housed them in it. The boat was tied to the shore with a small wooden bridge. Hungarian sentries guarded the bridge, not letting the refugees descend to the bank of the Danube: "There was an opening on deck through which they shoved in all those Jews [who] lay crammed like sardines. [. . .] And meanwhile winter is approaching and they will freeze from the cold. They are eaten alive by worms and maggots."

Aliyah envoys who arrived on the scene found among the refugees thirty-five people "who should be brought to Palestine." "A mark of Cain shall stain us as long as we do not take care of this matter," the envoy Lipsky warned. "Bringing them to Palestine would symbolize the way to solve the Jewish Question."[184] He sent a memorandum to various institutions and public figures and published information on the refugees' situation in a letter that was printed in *Davar* and other newspapers,[185] but was told that there were no certificates. An approach had been made on their behalf to the Évian Conference. Jabotinsky told his audience in Warsaw about forty women and men of Polish Jewish origin who were deported from Germany and whom the Nazi authorities threw on an island in the Danube [. . .] stranded at the point where the borders of Czechoslovakia and Hungary meet. The forty are crying and calling for help—but no help comes from any direction. [. . .] We are full of anger and sadness. But [. . .] in a month or two, such sensational events will disappear, and the daily reality will remain.[186]

After a petitioning campaign, some financial aid from the Joint, and a fundraising appeal organized by Czechoslovakia, the Mandate government approved the issuing of special permits, and most of the refugees emigrated to Palestine.[187]

In July 1938 (as previously mentioned), Golomb and Jabotinsky met in London for a round of talks to discuss ways to fight the Arab Revolt. They debated whether it was possible to achieve unity in the Zionist movement. Golomb noted from memory: "He [Jabotinsky] thinks that the fear of war is exaggerated. There is no panic around the world and there will be no war. After a while they will return to seeking constructive solutions to many questions, including the question of the Jewish people. There will be a true Évian. For this we must prepare, for this we must organize a full representation of the Jewish people."[188]

From the vantage point of February 1940, Jabotinsky wrote about the Évian Conference: "Eighteen months ago, Évian was attended by around twenty Jewish delegations, each of course on behalf of some world institution or global movement. Each had five minutes to present its plans to those assembled." The failure could therefore have been anticipated, and now it was necessary to work toward the establishment, after the war, of a "national rescue committee" which would have to organize the emigration of 2 to 3 million Jewish emigrants "in the speed they move military forces across the ocean."[189]

Not only was the failure of the Évian Conference expected in his view; it was also a desirable failure, because the various plans to direct Jewish immigration to all the corners of the world were no more than "relief medicines" that diverted the mind from the main thing: they did not offer any solution to the situation of Jews in Eastern Europe and risked intensifying antisemitic outbursts. In the Revisionist movement's view, the only solution was to create a Jewish state that would absorb 200,000 Jews from other countries. In support of this view, they cited the Polish government's statement that it would not accept its interests—that is, the need for the emigration of a large number of Jews—being ignored.[190] The Revisionists saw the Évian Conference as "an attempt to relieve Jewish suffering through pain-relief, that is, without establishing a Jewish state" and believed that this explained why Palestine was not mentioned at the conference. They, meanwhile, had prepared a plan for the immigration of "around a million immigrants within a short time."[191] This plan—and others—were a cry in the dark.

On July 17, 1938, Shertok met Eric Mills, a senior official in the British Mandatory government, whose last role (from 1934) was director of the Department for Immigration and Statistics. Shertok proposed a magic solution for the Arab terror and the Irgun's counterterror: "The government will announce that it will allocate such-and-such number of Jewish immigration certificates for every Jew killed by Arabs" and deduct certificates for any innocent Arab killed by a Jew. Then "the two types of terror would stop."[192]

July was a month of bloodshed in Palestine. The day before Shertok's meeting with Mills, on Friday, July 16, at 1:15 p.m., an explosion shook the vegetable market on David Street in Jerusalem's Old City. The explosion happened shortly before the end of prayers at the nearby mosque, and the resulting shrapnel covered the market's walls. Ten Arabs were killed and around thirty injured. A rumor claimed that the explosion happened as Arab women were trying to transfer concealed weapons from one hiding place to another. A general trade strike was announced in Jerusalem and in other cities.[193]

On September 5, 1938, the first "race protection" laws were announced in Fascist Italy. Two days later all the Jews who had immigrated to Italy after January 1, 1919 (around 40,000 people, including around 6,000 from Germany and Austria), were ordered to leave the country within six months.[194] The next day, Walter Elliot, Britain's health secretary, told Weizmann that the Zionist movement must now, after the Anschluss of Austria and the race laws in Italy, accept any territorial proposal it was offered: "Make Tel-Aviv a second London—live in the streets, not fields, if need be—but live, not die. Make a City-State like Venice. Do not think of shattered hopes—think of getting out of present Hell."[195]

That same month Sir John Hope Simpson argued that the German government was placing other governments in a dilemma:[196] they could open their gates to hundreds of thousands of Jews, non-Aryans, and poverty-stricken political refugees, or they would have to close their gates and then bear the responsibility together with the German government for the way in which the Jews were treated in Germany.

Weizmann wrote to the leader of the Liberal Party, Sir Archibald Sinclair, on November 20 that the territorial plans were "dangling false hopes before the eyes of tortured people" and were merely "fanciful diversions."[197]

In any case, from March through September around 1,000 Jewish refugees from the Reich were allowed to enter a few of the "exotic countries" —the British colonies. On October 28, Weizmann, Ben-Gurion, and Orde Wingate, a pro-Zionist British Army officer, who in 1938 founded and led the British-Jewish counterinsurgency unit, dined as guests of the veteran Conservative politician Lord George Ambrose Lloyd and his wife. Ben-Gurion had already met him three days earlier and had tried to convince him that a Jewish state was also a British interest. Now he told Lloyd: "Precisely as a Jew I am more British than the British. You are strong, rich, confident, and you do not care if here and there you suffer defeat. For us England is our only friend in the world, and when England loses—we suffer more than the English do. The failure in Munich did not shake the Empire, it is still standing firm. For us it was a catastrophe."[198]

The British government did not intend to solve Nazi Germany's "dilemma." On November 9 the Woodhead Commission, the Partition Commission appointed to examine whether it was possible to implement the Partition Plan proposed eighteen months earlier by the Peel Commission, submitted its report. Its decisive conclusion was that the Partition Plan was unrealizable. That night, Kristallnacht happened in Germany.

On November 7, 1938, the seventeen-year-old Herschel Grynszpan shot the junior German diplomat Ernst vom Rath, who died of his wounds two days later, in the afternoon of Wednesday, November 9, 1938.[199] The traditional dinner party held at the Munich Town Hall (Alte Rathus) that evening to mark the anniversary of the failed coup of 1923 was attended by thirty-nine of those who had taken part in the Munich Putsch. Six of them sat at Hitler's table. During the dinner, Hitler and Goebbels whispered to each other, and at 10 p.m. Hitler left. Toward midnight the veterans of the failed coup rose from the table as well.[200] That night, Goebbels gave orders to start a pogrom against the Jews all over Germany and Austria, and the Judenpogrom known as Reichskristallnacht began around 2 a.m.: "Starting in the early hours of November 10, 1938, and continuing until nightfall, violence against the Jews of Germany was unleashed in a whirlwind of destruction."[201] In the town of Gross-Gerau in Hesse, for example, where only twenty-one Jews were living at the time, the Jewish public buildings were destroyed, all the Jewish men were arrested, and seven of them were sent to a concentration camp. They were loaded onto a truck, the sound of the motor merging with the sound of the arrestees' forced singing: "We sing to you, we sing to you our beloved, on our way out of town" (*Muss i denn, muss i denn zum Städtele hinaus, Städtele hinaus, Und du, mein Schatz, bleibst hier*).[202]

Betty Scholem, the mother of the Kabbalah scholar Gershom Scholem, wrote in March-April 1939 on her way to Australia on the vessel *Comorin*:

> The November action was planned to the last detail, like a military operation. They were merely waiting for a suitable opportunity, and were it not for the incident in Paris, they would have invented another excuse. Each member of the Hitler Youth and the SA had his role, and all the weapons were prepared in advance to express the "wrath of the masses"! "The people," just like the Jews, knew nothing about it, and silently watched the show. When we heard about the death in Paris, we immediately expected the worst. At night it started. The recruits arrived in trucks to all the stores owned by Jews. At the signal they attacked and broke the store windows, and the destruction spree began.[203]

She arrived at Sydney Harbor on April 18. Her husband, Arthur, arrived on May 27, 1939.

Kristallnacht had been planned in advance, and the assassination in Paris only served as its pretext.[204] It was the most extreme and violent step taken by the Nazi terror regime during its five years in power in order "to free Germany from the Jewish plague" by pushing the Jews out of Germany. According to one estimate, 100 Jews were murdered on Kristallnacht and another several hundred perished later in concentration camps, to which around 30,000 Jews were sent. Hundreds of synagogues were burned or destroyed and 507 stores looted and ruined. German Jews received a collective punishment of 1 billion reichsmarks (80 million Pp). The Jews were excluded from all the social and cultural networks, and even their driver's licenses were banned. Willy Cohn wrote in his diary on November 30: "The Jews are all talking about emigration and starting anew. I am very tired. Despite everything, I am tied to Germany where I have lived fifty years. I don't want to become a *shnorrer* [beggar] out there in the world and grovel. [. . .] For a spiritual man like myself that would be very difficult indeed."[205]

In Vienna, 7,800 Jews were arrested and 4,600 Austrian Jews were sent to the Dachau concentration camp (4,000 were released after they pledged to emigrate). Forty-two synagogues in Vienna were set on fire, and hundreds of apartments were confiscated. Twenty-seven Viennese Jews were murdered, and according to a report by the SD (the security service of the SS: Sicherheitsdienst des Reichsführers-SS), 680 Jews committed suicide. The SS newspaper *Das Schwarze Korps* announced on November 24 that Kristallnacht's aim was "the actual and final eradication of Jewry in Germany, its extermination without a trace." In "extermination" the paper meant the "cleansing" of Germany of Jews by driving them out in any possible way. In protest, the United States recalled its ambassador from Berlin.

On the night of November 10, Eliyahu Galezer, the Betar representative in Czechoslovakia since March 1938, arrived in Vienna. The taxi that took him to the Hotel de France, known as "the Jews' hotel," drove through empty streets. When it passed through the city center, Galezer noticed the reddening sky above a burning synagogue. At the Revisionist movement offices on 18 Stubenring Street he found the movement's immigration activists. The Agudat Yisrael representative, who also attended the meeting, promised that the Gestapo would not show up, because it wanted to get rid of the Jews. As he spoke, eight Gestapo men in civilian clothing broke into the room. Galezer showed them his Lithuanian passport and explained that he had come to Vienna to negotiate the hiring of vessels from the Danube shipping company in order to transfer emigrants to the Black Sea ports. He was ordered to return to his hotel. Galezer got on a tram to Berg, where a bridge over the Danube led to Bratislava in Slovakia, showed the bridge guards his passport, and after some nerve-racking moments crossed to the other side.[206]

The Palestine delegation to the meeting of the Zionist Executive Committee in London, held on November 11, 1938, sailed from Beirut to Alexandria and from there to Marseilles on the ship *Champollion*. The French vessel, wrote Shprintzak, carried "almost a microcosm of the whole nation. All the shades of the Yishuv are sailing to London. [. . .] All the classes are filled with the active heroes of the Zionist state." In the middle of the Mediterranean the passengers heard about Grynszpan's assassination attempt on the junior Nazi diplomat in Paris. Shprintzak, who was stunned by the news, said: "We are turning a new leaf of suffering." Ben-Gurion, on the other hand, heard that the pogrom "had put the German people off the Nazis."[207] It is unclear where this assessment originated. Although some reservations and criticisms regarding the events of Kristallnacht were voiced in Germany, they did not stem from the criminal acts that had been perpetrated, but from the fear that they might damage Germany.[208]

Ruppin wrote in his diary that day: "On November 9 there was a real pogrom in Germany. [. . .] Indeed our status in Germany is the status of a pariah with no rights!" Later he added: "Today I finished my book." Around a fortnight later, when further details emerged about what had happened, Ruppin wrote that he had proposed "to introduce a new Tisha B'Av, which would be observed by Jews all over the world—to commemorate this outburst of violent cruelty." Thousands of telegrams with requests for certificates, he recorded, had started to arrive in Jerusalem from Jews arrested in Germany, and he himself received hundreds of letters from all his acquaintances—"from people I met once in my life [. . .]. There are endless letters from Germany requesting immigration permits. All the acquaintances and relatives are contacting me."[209]

On November 20, Chajes wrote: "Hitler is running wild. [. . .] Taking revenge, inciting the masses, destroying the Jews. Imposing billions in taxes, imprisoning the Jews and confiscating their property. For a week now he has been raving and raging. It angers the whole world, provokes protests in England and America, but no one opens the gates to the Jews."[210] On December 7, he added: "Hitler is rampaging. Every day he is passing new anti-Jewish laws. Any day now the yellow badge from medieval times might return. But back then they were less brutal, not so ruthless, not so thirsty for blood and property."[211]

Chamberlain protested in reaction to Kristallnacht: Why should antisemitism be so brutal and cloud the relations between Britain and Germany?[212] The events in Germany shocked him, but he separated emotional reaction from practical politics, and said at the Cabinet meeting on November 14 that Britain was incapable of "scaring Germany" and putting pressure on it on this matter. The next day Chamberlain met a delegation of Jewish community notables, who were joined by Chaim Weizmann, and listened sympathetically to their reports about the desperate situation of German Jews. The prime minister, however, refused to increase the number of refugees allowed to enter Britain, and, needless to say, Weizmann's request for 6,000 immigration permits for the Jews interned in concentration camps fell on deaf ears.[213]

Britain's representative in Berlin reported on November 16 that the assassination in Paris had provided the Nazi regime with an opportunity to unleash "barbaric forces, like in the Middle Ages."[214] News about what was going on in Nazi Germany reached the West from various sources. In British government circles there were some who mistrusted the testimonies of "persecuted Jews, who are not perhaps entirely trustworthy witnesses."[215]

However, Kristallnacht and the following days were generally condemned by the Western press. The British parliament debated Kristallnacht on November 21 and condemned the events. The proposed motion did not mention the Jews explicitly, but recognized the suffering of specific religious and political minorities and the growing refugee problem.[216] The condemnation was harsh and general, but newspapers and conservative circles expressed concern that the persecutions in Germany and Austria might provoke a demand to open Britain's gates to more Jews still living within the Reich's borders. This concern rekindled futile plans to find overseas immigration destinations as substitutes for the "National Home." A motion to protest the events officially was rejected.

The organized brutal violence in Germany shocked the Jewish world. At the Jewish Agency Directorate meeting in London, Gruenbaum proposed to organize mass demonstrations and "break the windowpanes" in all the German embassies. He was especially concerned by the possibility that with no reaction, "tomorrow the fate of the Jews of Poland and Romania would be like the fate of the Jews of Germany today." The press reported the events extensively. On November 11, *Davar* wrote:

> Late last night, at the end of the celebrations in Munich to mark the 15th anniversary of the Nazi Putsch and upon hearing the news of Rath's death in Paris—the signal was given in Munich for pogroms against the Jews. The riots spread all over Germany and were perpetrated by the SA and SS and the Hitler Youth. The police stood by and the secret police arrested and tortured dozens of Jews in all the German cities. There are many whose fate is unknown. [. . .] Organized Nazi gangs raided the streets, broke windows in Jewish stores and threw out or looted the merchandise [. . .]. The plundering and arson attacks continued all day long.[217]

Haaretz wrote on November 13: "It turns out that in the provincial towns the pogrom was even more terrible than in Berlin and Munich, and the Jews' property was destroyed and ruined with exceptional cruelty. [. . .] All the local newspapers published an announcement saying that whoever did not go out to demonstrate against the Jews would be considered as their sympathizer."[218]

Yitzhak Katzenelson condemned the assassination, but called on the world to lend its ears to the desperate cry it gave a voice to. At the same time he wrote cynically that the world had taken note of the suffering of German Jews but ignored the existence of the concentration camps to which they were being sent.[219] All at once, the legislative violence had turned into life-threatening physical violence. Now the Jews' need and desire to emigrate from Germany had increased, but the number of the destination countries that were willing to take them in had decreased.

On November 16, Jabotinsky sent telegrams to the governments of several countries in Europe, asking for their help in arranging the "repatriation to Palestine within the coming years of all the German Jews plus half a million others from other countries where there is Jewish distress." The telegrams, it seemed, got no response.[220] On November 21, the British government agreed to take in around 10,000 Jewish children aged six to sixteen from Germany, Austria, and Czechoslovakia as part of what was called the Kindertransport. More than 7,000 children arrived in Britain by the end of August 1939.[221]

The session of the Zionist Executive Committee held in London on November 11, 1938, was mainly dedicated to the report that had removed the plan for Palestine's partition from the agenda. Its members mainly attempted to convince each other, while Shertok used the time to renew his knowledge of the Turkish language with a private tutor. The Executive Committee session had lost its relevance, he wrote, and now they had to wait for negotiations on convening a tripartite conference in London.[222] Ussishkin, one of the chief opponents of the Partition Plan, was happy with the report. Shprintzak shared his painful doubts with his wife: "Does the rejection of partition mean we have gained the entire country? Is this the conclusion of the Yishuv's fate and its future?"[223] On November 9, the day the Woodhead Commission's conclusions were published, the British government announced that the idea of dividing Western Palestine was unrealizable.[224] Ben-Gurion did not lose hope: "We keep talking about needing England's help, and not only do I still subscribe to this assumption, but I subscribe to it even more strongly." The Zionist response to the Woodhead Commission's report would be to organize a "rebellious immigration,"

> which would make England's life a misery, as is already done, though not with terror, but with an immigration that would rock the world [. . .] and I do not exclude the possibility that we will have to rise against England and conquer a Jewish state in part of the country. [. . .] After the negotiations in London, we shall be forced to start a war against England by organizing a rebellious immigration and taking control of Haifa by coordinating the immigration from it and transferring to it Jews from Tel Aviv and other places.[225]

If England did not change its mind, Ben-Gurion declared at the Mapai Central Committee on November 15, the Zionist movement would have to organize "ships that will bring massive numbers of young people to Palestine." How England would react? Ben-Gurion predicted, "It will sink our ships! [. . .] We will invite photographers who will photograph the English shooting at ships bringing Jewish refugees to Palestine and turning back Jews coming from Germany and Poland."[226] Yehuda Braginsky understood that Ben-Gurion meant a "war of immigration" rather than a "war over immigration." That is, he meant to organize an overt illegal immigration as a demonstrative act that would turn public opinion in Britain against the government.[227]

The Évian Conference and Kristallnacht presented the Zionist movement with a false dilemma: it was incapable of influencing Jewish emigration from Germany to western Europe or overseas, and it was unable to mobilize the existential threat hanging over the Jews of the Reich, and the tremendous pressure to emigrate, as a leverage for a "Zionist solution." The "window of opportunity" opened by the Nazi policy — to get as many Jews as possible out of the Reich — was utilized only partially. The Zionist movement had only two tools left to realize its goal: illegal immigration, and the immigration permits it received from the Mandate government. The order of priorities for distributing these permits became a sensitive issue that invited pressure, lobbying, and preferential treatment. It was like clutching at straws. Shlomo Rülf, a Nahariya resident who had been a rabbi in the Saar region from 1929 to 1935, wrote in his memoir:

> Suddenly the post from Haifa brought more telegrams and letters. Each telegram came from Germany, and in each there was a cry for help: "Get us a certificate!" It was more than the people of Nahariya could bear. They cried on the streets. "Last year I could still get a certificate for my brother," said one, "but now all the concessions have been canceled, and I don't know what to do." Another said: "When my mother visited us in 1937, I begged her: 'Mom, break up your business, you have enough! You can transfer a few thousand pounds and live with us without worries!' But my mother did not want to leave her excellent store."

The Nahariya residents managed to get a few certificates, including one for the mother, who at first refused to leave her store.[228]

On the eve of war there was another attempt to arrange an organized emigration of Jews from the Reich with the agreement and encouragement of the Nazi regime. George Rublee, an American lawyer and chairman of the Intergovernmental Committee for Refugees, negotiated with Hjalmar Schacht, the minister of economy responsible for turning the German economy into a war economy, in view of setting up an arrangement (the Wohlthat-Rublee plan) for the emigration of Germany's Jews partially funded by the world's Jewry.

Rublee had a strong sense of vocation and, no less importantly, was determined to succeed and driven by a great sense of urgency. He was convinced that it was possible to use the fact that Goering, rather than Foreign Minister Joachim von Ribbentrop, was in charge of the "Jewish issue" and strove to reach an agreement in which, among other things, the boycott on German exports would end, the emigrants would be able to receive compensation for the property they would leave behind over ten years, and the persecutions of Jews staying in Germany would stop. In addition, the plan intended to raise financial aid from Jewish organizations.

After many delays, Rublee arrived in Berlin on January 12, 1939, to meet with Goering and Schacht. Schacht wanted to improve Germany's foreign currency situation. Eight days later, Rublee discovered that the "moderate" Schacht was removed from the negotiations in favor of the more extreme von Ribbentrop. Nonetheless, on February 3, it seemed that Rublee had succeeded in reaching the following understandings: 25 percent of the monies still belonging to German Jews (1.5 billion marks) would be deposited in a trust fund. The world's Jews would donate a similar sum, and the Jews of Germany would redeem their share in the form of German goods.

President Roosevelt urged the Jewish organizations to establish the necessary fund, but the representatives of the organizations disagreed over the proposals, and the plan's funding ran into difficulties. More to the point, there were no countries willing to take in the emigrants.[229] The Zionist leadership was not party to these negotiations (nor perhaps even knew about them) and naturally could not thwart them.

In August 1938, Adolf Eichmann founded the Central Office for Jewish Emigration (Zentralstelle für jüdische Auswanderung) in Vienna. After the occupation of Czechoslovakia and the creation of the protectorate of Bohemia-Moravia, the principles that guided the deportation policy in Germany and Austria were applied to those areas as well. On November 12, a meeting was held at the German Ministry of Aviation headed by Goering, to discuss where to transfer all the Jews of Germany. The term that was used, *Endlösung*—"final solution"—meant total emigration "at all cost."

The Center for Jewish Emigration (Reichszentrale für jüdische Auswanderung) was founded in Berlin on January 24, 1939, under Goering's orders. It was headed by Reinhard Heydrich, deputy of the Gestapo commander Heinrich Mueller. Hitler announced at the Reichstag on January 30: "The world holds enough spaces suitable for the resettlement of Jews, and their emigration is an international question that demands a comprehensive agreement and the finding of emigration destinations." However, after the failure of the Évian Conference and the annexation of Austria, there was nowhere to direct the Jews' emigration and deportation.

In November 1938, responsibility for dealing with refugees arriving in Switzerland was transferred to the Aliens' Police (Eidgenössische Fremdenpolizei). Its commander, Dr. Heinrich Rothmund, saw the Jewish refugees as a "danger" that would lead to the "Jewification" of Switzerland, and implemented a policy of racial discrimination.[230] Paul Grüninger, the commander of the border police in the Swiss Canton of St. Gallen, brought forward the visa issuing date, faked other documents, and thus helped 3,600 refugees cross into Switzerland in April. He was fired after his actions were discovered, sentenced to pay a heavy fine, and denied his pension rights.[231]

On December 9, 1938, Horst Wagner boarded a train heading to Switzerland. Close to the border near Schaffhausen he left his belongings on the German train and passed through the restrooms to a Swiss train. People directed him to the Canton of St. Gallen, where Paul Grüninger was the chief of police. Rather than being deported back to Germany, he was sent to the refugee camp of Diepoldsau on the Swiss-Austrian border, where he stayed for around a year before emigrating to the Dominican Republic.[232]

The Nazi regime did not see the Évian Conference as a "theater" aimed to prove to the world that nobody wanted the Jews. However, the conference convinced it that there was no destination to which the Jews of the Reich could be pushed and forced to immigrate. After the publication of the White Paper in May 1939, it became clear that Palestine could not serve as an immigration destination either. The Polish government, disappointed that the question of Polish Jews was never discussed at the Évian Conference, likewise learned after the White Paper's publication that the plans to use Palestine as a destination for the immigration of Jews from the country had nothing on which to rely.

From April 1933 to July 1939, 329,000 Jews emigrated from the Reich. Around 153,000 of them immigrated to different countries in Europe. Around 176,000 people immigrated overseas,[233] around 55,000 of them to Palestine. On the eve of the war, about 331,000 Jews remained in the territories under the control of the Third Reich.

Historical writing and historical memory—mainly that of the Zionist movement—have focused on the "closing of the world's gates" and on the story of the immigrants and illegal immigrants to Palestine. This history failed to mention the tens of thousands of emigrant-refugees who were exiled and deported, who crossed the borders illegally where they could, paid bribes, benefited from acts of kindness, and drifted from country to country. They included, for example, the seventy-eight-year-old Moritz Jellinek and his wife Henriette, two of a few thousand Austrian Jews who crossed the border into Yugoslavia before and after it was annexed to Germany on February 13, 1938. On March 22, the couple traveled to the port town of Sušak near Rijeka (which the Italians called Fiume), a port of departure for several illegal immigrants' ships, and tried to cross the border into Italy. The Italian border police arrested them and returned the couple to Yugoslavia. The authorities there ordered them to leave the country within two days. Moritz Jellinek sank into a deep depression, slipped out of the hotel where he was staying, and tried to kill himself by jumping into the sea. He was pulled out of the water alive. Asked why he had done it, he replied: "Because he was deported from Vienna and was not wanted anywhere, he was fed up with life."[234]

A similar fate awaited the Jews living in one of the towns on the German-French border, who were rounded up on February 1939 and driven across the border in the evening. The French Gendarmerie refused to let them cross the border and they were sent to Dachau.

4

FUNERAL MARCH AT ST. JAMES'S PALACE

"THEY BETRAYED CZECHOSLOVAKIA, WHY SHOULD THEY NOT BETRAY US AS WELL?"

The Woodhead Commission's report was published on November 9, 1938 (late at night on the day Kristallnacht had begun in Germany and Austria). The members of the commission decided unanimously to reject the Peel Commission's partition plan but were divided over the possible implementation of an alternative partition plan. The conclusion the British Cabinet drew from the report was unequivocal: the idea of solving the Palestine question through territorial partitioning was impracticable. What's more, consideration of such a plan would jeopardize the relations with the entire Arab and Muslim world.

On October 24, the Cabinet Committee on Palestine rejected the Partition Plan. The Zionist leadership found itself losing out on all counts. The partition debate that had raged within the Zionist camp (as well as outside it) now seemed irrelevant: those who were in favor of partition were disappointed (though some of them were glad that it had ended that way and wanted to fight to restore the situation to the status quo ante), whereas those who were against it breathed a sigh of relief. Tabenkin, who arrived in London at the end of October, wrote in his notebook: "The subject of the State has now gone off the agenda [rather than the subject of partition]. [. . .] We must focus on ways to further Zionism rather than on the situation of the Jewish people."[1]

The only thing left for either camp was to believe — or hope — that the Zionist diplomacy would manage to change Britain's policy or that the Yishuv would be able to prevent this policy's realization. The Cabinet Committee that discussed the Woodhead Commission's report in October concluded that it proved that the Arabs were adamantly opposed to partition, and that if the British government stuck to it, it would lose the friendship of the entire Arab and Muslim world.[2] Again the Zionist camp pinned its hopes on the criticism hurled at the government by some members of the House of Commons, but the Czechoslovakia crisis tipped the scales. The British government abandoned the Partition Plan and, shortly after, the Mandate as well.

It was at the Twenty-First Zionist Congress that the Zionist movement sought to unite its forces in the fight against the White Paper. Around five months earlier, in February and March, its representatives had tried to persuade the British government to change its policy so that this fight would not be necessary. This attempt took place at St. James's Palace in London. The red-brick Tudor-style palace on Pall Mall had become the residence of the English monarchs in 1698. After part of it burned down in 1809, King George III moved to the nearby Buckingham Palace, and in the nineteenth century, as its status declined, St. James's Palace was used mainly to host formal events.[3]

The St. James Conference (known as the Round Table Conference) opened on February 7, 1939. Its goal was to find an alternative to the Partition Plan, which the Woodhead Commission's recommendations had termed impracticable. These recommendations were submitted to the British government on October 19 and published on November 9, 1938. The British Cabinet spent long hours debating the alternatives to be presented at the conference. In January 1939, the Cabinet decided that a Jewish state would not be created in Palestine and that Jewish immigration would be restricted to around 15,000 immigrants per year. In July 1938, Colonial Secretary Malcolm MacDonald had intended to propose an immigration of 300,000 Jews over ten years (that is, 30,000 immigrants per year), but during the conference the number of immigrants was being constantly reduced, reaching the threshold of 75,000 over five years, after which any additional immigration would depend on the agreement of the Arabs.[4]

Ben-Gurion was well aware that the international situation had put the Zionist movement in a quandary. A week after Austria's Anschluss to Nazi Germany in February 1938, he wrote his daughter Geula from London:

> The global situation is not in our favor. England is preoccupied with difficult global questions: war in China, war in Spain. Germany is swallowing Austria, and tomorrow it may be Czechoslovakia's turn. Everyone is

afraid of war. Mussolini is impudently trying to undermine England in the Mediterranean. The Arabs know this and are taking advantage of England's difficulties by warning that unless it stops its support of Zionism—either by retaining the Mandate or by creating a Jewish state—the Arabs will support England's enemies. But we too have friends, and our own power in Palestine and in the world is not negligible. But we are fighting a very tough war.[5]

Two days later, while dining at the house of the Conservative Parliament member Leopold S. Amery, Ben-Gurion told Harold MacMichael, who also attended the dinner: "Imagine that there was a world war—it is not so impossible and far-fetched. If there are many of us in Palestine—we can hold out and maybe even lend you some support. If there are few—we may be wiped out and you will not benefit either." From MacMichael's reaction Ben-Gurion concluded that his interlocutor did not reject his words, but that "on the question of pace I am afraid he will give us the usual difficulties we get from any Englishman, even when he is not an antagonist."[6]

Such an antagonist, for example, was the Conservative politician Lord Lloyd, who had served as High Commissioner in Egypt (and in 1940 would be appointed Secretary of State for the Colonies). In October 1938, Lloyd claimed that Britain had "sold the same horse twice"—to the Jews and to the Arabs, adding that any Jewish immigrants who arrived in Palestine would be "foreign Jews, from Poland, from other countries." If that place, strategically so vital to Britain, "will be in their hands—they will blackmail the British Empire."[7]

Support for the Zionist cause within the opposition was also qualified. Although during a debate in the House of Commons on November 24 Churchill sharply criticized the government and the Peel and Woodhead Commissions' reports, his alternative plan proposed that Jewish immigration would be restricted to 30,000 to 35,000 immigrants per year (the White Paper policy would be upheld during Churchill's time as prime minister, from May 1940 onward).[8]

On September 6, 1938, Shertok wrote that in France there was a mobilization and in Britain "there is a state of anxiety and preparation. Who knows if due to such events it will be possible to bring our affairs to a close; the British government's timetable may change and our interests postponed; the international entanglement may force Britain to shorten the front in order to save military personnel etc.; or they may conclude the opposite—that this is the moment to fortify."[9]

In other words, Britain may have no choice but "to opt for the Jews' help and recruit a Jewish force."[10] Ruppin wrote that same day: "Europe is awash with rumors about war. We hear that Runciman's mission in Prague has failed, and Germany has decided to annex the Sudetenland as it did Austria. It is impossible to guess the results of this war, which could develop into a world war. We could lose all our positions in Palestine if Britain is obliged to remove all its armed forces from here."[11]

Ten days later Ruppin wrote in his diary:

> The world was stunned yesterday morning to hear the news of the British Prime Minister Neville Chamberlain's flight to see Hitler. The meeting took place in Berchtesgaden [on September 15]. Its results are still unknown. History will pass its judgment on this extraordinary step, [. . .] history will decide whether Chamberlain's action helped prevent war and millions of human victims, or merely boosted Hitler's prestige and diminished England's. [. . .] If war does not break out and Hitler's demands are fulfilled—through British pressure on Czechoslovakia—Hitler will emerge victorious and be considered the strong man of Europe. This will undoubtedly add extra momentum to his anti-Jewish policy.[12]

Britain was up to its neck in burning problems, and Palestine was only one of them. Nevertheless, the time dedicated by the British Cabinet to discussing the future of Palestine in February and March 1939 attests to this question's centrality in the Empire's strategic considerations. On November 9, 1938, the British Intelligence informed the policymakers that withdrawing from the Partition Plan had weakened Arab hostility toward Britain. It was therefore advisable not to reawaken this hostility. The position of the General Staff was that Britain's uppermost strategic interest at the time was to sooth the Arabs' fears.[13]

The rich Jews can buy territories in North America and anywhere else, said Goering on November 12, 1938, and Hitler declared on January 30, 1939, at the Reichstag, which had convened to mark the anniversary of his rise to power: "The world has enough territories for Jewish settlement." He listed the likes of Tanzania, Madagascar, and Angola. He outlined his worldview:

> One thing I should like to say on this day which may be memorable for others as well as for us Germans. In the course of my life I have very often been a prophet and have usually been ridiculed for it. During the time of my struggle for power, it was in the first instance the Jewish race which only received my prophecies with laughter when I said that I would

one day take over the leadership of the state—and with it that of the whole nation, and that then, among other things, I would settle the Jewish problem. Their laughter was uproarious, but I think that for some time now they have been laughing out of the other side of their face. Today I will once again be a prophet: If the international Jewish financiers in and outside Europe should again succeed in plunging the nations into a world war, the result will be not the Bolshevization of the globe and thus victory for Jewry but the annihilation of the Jewish race in Europe.[14]

The fate of Czechoslovakia hung like a shadow over the Jewish delegation throughout the St. James Conference. Czechoslovakia's reputation was that of an exemplarily democratic country, free of antisemitic propaganda. Its image did not suffer even when in 1939 Czech border guards prevented Jewish refugees from Germany and Austria from entering the Republic. However, it was not sympathy toward Czechoslovakia, but the fear that the Czech crisis would prevent the British government from devoting its time to the Palestine question, that caused concern among the Zionists. After the Munich Agreement the concern grew that Britain would "betray Zionism" as it had betrayed Czechoslovakia, abandoning it to the mercy of Nazi Germany. Jabotinsky's conviction that Great Britain would neither disappoint the Czechs nor abandon them, because "her word is a rock and she will not let down the smaller nations,"[15] turned out to be illusory.

Ben-Gurion wrote Shertok on September 20: "Unfortunately, Czechoslovakia is to a large extent also our business." The comparison was clear. Britain had handed Czechoslovakia over to Nazi Germany, and now it had decided to hand the Yishuv over to the Arabs.[16] Shertok tried to allay these fears. With all the usefulness of analogies, he wrote, "In that they awaken us to the dangers [, . . .] what happened in Czechoslovakia's case does not have to happen in ours." Moreover, he convinced himself, there was a chance that Britain would not want to incur another moral stain—betraying the Jewish people.[17] Ben-Gurion was not blind to the changeable moods of the English public, and on September 27 he wrote in his diary that preparations for war were advancing at a feverish pace:

In Czechoslovakia the entire army and people have been mobilized. In France they are mobilizing the reserves. They are evacuating Paris; in London they are digging slit trenches in the parks, distributing gas masks to everyone, evacuating the schools, sending away the children. In Germany they are announcing a mobilization tomorrow, if until tomorrow at 2 p.m. they get no affirmative answer from Prague. And despite everything I find it hard to believe that there will be war now.[18]

In October he saw even more parallels between the fate of Czechoslovakia and the fate of the Jews:

> They distributed gas masks to everyone, removed the children out of London, spent days and nights digging trench shelters in Hyde Park, caused panic that in the next couple of days London will be bombarded by Hitler's planes, drafted the navy—and suddenly declared peace—and there was a big relief. No bombs, no destruction, no massacre, and the man on the street applauds the savior of peace. And the fate of Czechoslovakia, the fate of Europe—all this is distant, foreign, unreal. What you can touch with your hand—is peace. And now there is peace. And there is a chance to iron out the relations with Germany. At whose expense?—That is not interesting. [. . .] We, perhaps, are the first victim of this new turn. Not only the Jews of Czechoslovakia—all the Jews of Europe, and maybe also of Asia and America, will soon feel the triumph of evil, as the friendship with Hitler will see antisemitism spreading in Europe. [. . .] They betrayed Czechoslovakia—why shouldn't they betray us as well?[19]

Ben-Gurion was well aware of the fear of air raids that had gripped Britain, but did not perhaps know that England had started to prepare its armed forces for war.[20] He predicted that Hitler would get what he wanted and take control of the whole of Central Europe with threats and without war, because war would endanger his regime. Hitler was a bully, he wrote, but his General Staff would curb him. The clouds of war were dispersing, he estimated, and in the absence of war Britain would not need the Yishuv's help. Europe had been saved from the destruction that would have brought with it mass massacre, but peace had been salvaged for a heavy price. The despotic bully who ruled Germany was free to cut Czechoslovakia to pieces.[21]

At the beginning of October 1938, after the British prime minister had returned from Munich promising "peace for our time,"[22] Weizmann remarked that he would not be surprised if Chamberlain's appeasement method also got implemented in Palestine. He guessed that Britain would reach an agreement with the Mufti at Zionism's expense, as it did with Hitler at the Czechs' expense.[23] His gut feeling was that the British were "deceiving and betraying us as they did with Czechoslovakia."[24] Weizmann embarked on a battle, perhaps his toughest and bitterest yet, to convince Britain's leaders that the great power did not need to be afraid of the Arabs' opposition to the

Partition Plan. He tried to drum up political support for partition in London and other capitals. On November 27, he even went as far as Istanbul to sound out the Turkish government's position on the Palestine question.

On September 30, Yehuda Braginsky passed through Munich on his way from Warsaw to Italy. At that time Chamberlain, Daladier, Mussolini, and Hitler were meeting in the Führer-Hof building to discuss the future of Czechoslovakia. The road from the train station to the venue of the Munich Conference was guarded by the army, and the sidewalks where crowded with onlookers. Braginsky got the impression that the citizens of the Third Reich were in the grip of great anxiety and worried about the possibility of war. At the same time, he saw trains leaving for Italy full of German holidaymakers. He felt "that if we get reprieve this time, it will only be a short one. This is a crucial time, and we must accelerate our rescue project, or we will be too late."[25]

At the end of September, Katznelson met Jan Masaryk, Czechoslovakia's ambassador to Britain, who told him that he had suggested to Weizmann to purchase a three-story house in London: the first floor would be for Haile Selassie, the deposed emperor of Ethiopia, the second for Masaryk himself, and the third for Weizmann.[26] Masaryk thought that there was no greater illusion than to believe that after Hitler got what he wanted, he would not ask for more.[27] Katznelson wrote Leah Miron that he had no doubt that the meeting between Hitler and Chamberlain would "hand out one more blow, perhaps a death blow, to Czechoslovakia."[28]

Masaryk and the Zionist leaders were bound together by a shared destiny. On October 1, on the night following the signing of the Munich Agreement and the severing of the Sudetenland from Czechoslovakia, Masaryk, who had already quit his role as his country's ambassador to Britain, was a guest at Weizmann's house in London. During dinner Masaryk told his hosts, who included Ben-Gurion, Berl Locker, and Katznelson, "some illuminating and shocking details, how the Czechs had been led on and how much they had been deceived. [. . .] They were led on and lied to, step by step, and behind their back they were handed over to Hitler." Then Masaryk pointed at the puppy he had brought with him from Prague and said: "This is all I have left and believe me, I am ashamed to look him in the eye."[29] Ben-Gurion reported that at the dinner Weizmann had said that one could not expect the British to behave any more decently toward Zionism, and that "Malcolm MacDonald feigns friendship in order to hide the betrayal."[30]

Katznelson wrote Leah Miron about the conversation: Masaryk told them “with burning rage how they had been sold. Many things recall the behavior of the [Mandate] officials towards us.”[31] He then added sarcastically: “Jan Masaryk came and took revenge on the British in words.”[32]

Some four months after Czechoslovakia’s fate was sealed, on June 17, 1939, Dugdale dined with Jan Masaryk and Lord Israel Schiff and his wife at Masaryk’s home on Marsham Street. Masaryk prepared dinner and told his guests about a conversation he had had with Chamberlain and Foreign Secretary Lord Edward Halifax, whom he called “holy fox,”[33] in the days between the Bad Godesberg meeting (September 22, 1938) and Munich (September 29–30). Chamberlain had said to Masaryk: “Some people trust Mr. Beneš[34] — but I trust Herr Hitler.” He was probably hinting at the Alliance Treaty that the then-president of Czechoslovakia Edvard Beneš had signed with the Soviet Union in 1935. Masaryk rose angrily from his seat and said: “Mr. Prime Minister, I am merely my country’s servant; I cannot follow you to such heights!” Dugdale wrote in her diary: “If ever there was hate, it is the hatred of Jan for Chamberlain.”[35] After the St. James Conference Weizmann’s hatred for Chamberlain, and even more for MacDonald, was no less intense than Masaryk’s.

When Chamberlain’s flight to Munich became known, Ben-Gurion met with MacDonald at Weizmann’s home. The meeting lasted from 9 p.m. until midnight, during which Dugdale burst into tears — she was “depressed and insulted to the core not just by the shameful handling of Czechoslovakia, but as if personally hurt by her friends’ betrayal.”[36] MacDonald told his astonished guests that in the matter of the Sudeten “Germany has a case: the Sudeten belong to Germany.” He accepted the view, he added, that peace was guaranteed after Germany had annexed the Rhine area, Austria, and the Sudeten. Weizmann asked MacDonald whether he had read *Mein Kampf*, and Ben-Gurion mused: “Woe to the world whose fate is decided by these people!”[37]

After MacDonald left Weizmann’s house, the stunned president of the Zionist Organization told his wife Vera and Dugdale that he had no doubt that the English intended to abandon the Partition Plan: “They are going to sell the Jews also — give up Partition, for fear of the Arabs and the Germans and the Italians.” Ben-Gurion was more adamant, saying, “The Jews will fight, physically,”[38] but Weizmann did not react to this combative statement.

On October 12, Shertok met with General Sir Robert Haining, the general commander of the British forces in Palestine and Transjordan. The general said that there was no room for comparison between the “Czechoslovakian case” and the situation in Palestine: “The Czechs should not have been allowed to rule over the Germans. It was one of the fateful mistakes of the Treaty of Versailles. It is great that a war over Czechoslovakia has been averted." Shertok replied, "No one is happier than us that a new European massacre has been averted, which would have caused the total eradication of entire Jewish communities. I am terrified to think what could have been the fate of German Jews in the event of war [. . .]. Nevertheless the fact that war has been averted is not in itself enough to give us joy. The way in which the Czechoslovakia problem has been resolved is the triumph of force over justice." Then he underlined the fundamental difference between "the Czechoslovakian case" and "the Palestinian case": "The Czechs could bear their catastrophe with equanimity, because come what may, their existence as a people is assured. They are a united community well rooted in the land of its ancestors. Even if Czechoslovakia ceases to exist as an independent state and is ruled by a foreign power, the Czechs and the Slovaks as a people will not be destroyed. For us the situation is totally different. [. . .] The national existence of the Jewish people is at stake here."[39]

The fate awaiting German Jews after Kristallnacht was a source of profound and real concern, but the main fear was for the fate of the Jews in Palestine, who embodied "the national existence of the Jewish people."

In Lviv, Chajes did not know whether to be glad or worried. Poland had joined Nazi Germany in a bid to reclaim Těšín, a territory that the "Czechs stole from us [. . .] completely illegally. It is a painful shame that in this situation we are following Hitler"; however, Czechoslovakia's prime minister, Jan Syrový, was "probably a Bolshevik and a friend of Stalin's." The next day Chajes added: "This is the end of Czechoslovakia. A new entity will emerge. As long as it does not stand on flimsy foundations." His patriotism thus overcame his doubts: "Today the whole world is interested in Poland and in Beck, just as a month ago they talked about Chamberlain and Hitler."[40]

The Sudetenland was not the only territory torn off from Czechoslovakia in October 1938. The Nazis also won the ex-territorial road that connected Vienna, Breslau, and the Danube-Oder Canal. German army trains moved uninterrupted through Moravia. Poland got Těšín and the railway junction in Oderberg, which caused great enthusiasm in Poland and inspired calls in praise of Hitler.[41] Hungary received territories in southern Slovakia and Ruthenia. On October 5, Beneš resigned. Prague earned itself a few more months of dying throes.

Ilse Weber, who was later known as a Theresienstadt poet and in October 1944 voluntarily went with her husband and son Tommy to Auschwitz, where she perished, wrote to her friend:

> Never before have souls been sold out so dastardly! Hitler wanted "his" Germans. Fine! But why did England allow him to take so many hundreds of thousands of Czechs and Jews? [. . .] Why did they not think about the Jews there, in Munich? Did Chamberlain not realize the danger in store for the Jews when he sold us out to the Germans? What will all the poor people do, who have suddenly joined the many other "bothersome refugees?"[42]

Thousands of Jews and non-Jews from Germany and Austria had escaped to Prague, where they received shelter and aid. Now they were joined by thousands of refugees from the Sudetenland. The fate awaiting Czechoslovakian Jews could already be envisaged after September 30, 1938, the night the Munich Agreement was signed. The Czech government could not withstand the pressure and announced that it would dedicate itself to the "task of solving the Jewish problem."[43]

On March 13, 1939, the priest Dr. Jozef Tiso, the prime minister of Slovakia, who a week earlier had been sacked by Dr. Emil Hácha, the Czechoslovakian president (who had succeeded Beneš) because of his separatist leanings, flew to Berlin. He met there with Hitler and von Ribbentrop. The next day, when he returned to Bratislava, he convened the Slovak Assembly to a secret meeting, declared Slovakia's independence, and asked for the protection of Nazi Germany. Meanwhile, German radio conducted a propaganda campaign against the Czech government and broadcast military marches.

On the night of March 14, Hácha and Foreign Minister František Chvalkovský got off the train that had taken them from Prague to Berlin. The tragic farce began as they were greeted by an SS guard of honor. After midnight, they were led like sheep to the slaughter into the Führer's chambers, where Goering and von Ribbentrop were also present. Hitler informed them that the German army was about to invade Czechoslovakia at 6 a.m. and that any resistance would be ruthlessly crushed. Hitler left the room and Goering and von Ribbentrop described to the petrified guests how the German air force would take two hours to destroy Prague and turn it into ashes if they did not agree to the ultimatum to turn Bohemia and Moravia into a German protectorate.

The threats worked. Hácha, exhausted and suffering from a heart disease, fainted and needed two injections from Hitler's personal doctor. When he came to, he spoke on the phone with the members of his government, signed the surrender papers, and "entrusted the fate of the Czech people in the hands of the Führer of the Third Reich," who "agreed" to take the Czechs under its wings and promised them "autonomous development." Radio Berlin announced that the president of the former Czechoslovakia had "recognized the historical fact that Germany and Bohemia had been united for a thousand years. Germany is now the most formidable power in Central Europe."

The German chief of staff had warned that the Nazi Wehrmacht was not yet ready to attack, and the advance duly ran into difficulties. However, at 9 a.m. on March 15, in the middle of a snowstorm, the German army marched into Bohemia and Moravia. At 9:30 a.m. motorized units of the Wehrmacht entered Prague and took over the city's central buildings. Slovakia declared its independence and the Hungarian army invaded Sub-Carpathian Ruthenia. Czech Radio called on the army not to resist the invaders.

"The vultures came and pounced on the carcasses," wrote Ilse Weber. "Poland has taken away huge assets from us; the wonderful foundries of Trinec and all those coal mines, which were our lifeblood. And again the same injustice: Czech towns and villages were given away."[44]

On March 16, at dusk, Hitler drove through the Prague streets in a convoy of black cars and entered Prague Castle in the Hradčany district, which was lit by floodlights, accompanied by the defeated and humiliated president of Czechoslovakia and Prime Minister General Syrový. A German infantry company hoisted the German flag on the spire. For a moment Hitler appeared in the window and glanced at the beautiful city lying at his feet under night curfew.[45] He announced the creation of the Protectorate of Bohemia and Moravia. Thus, with no resistance, less than six months after the signing of the Munich Agreement, the Czechoslovakian Republic was erased from the European map. The Nazi newspaper *Westdeutscher Beobachter* wrote on April 5 that in Eastern Europe

> antisemitism is older than in Germany itself. It has been proved to act like a cure that can bring a unity of feelings and political wishes. The Munich Agreement has done a considerable service to the antisemitic policy that Germany and Italy have been working on in Eastern Europe. Masaryk's democratic state was not only a powerful military stronghold aimed against Germany, but also a fortified wall against antisemitism. Once this wall had been torn down the antisemitic movement can reach those parts of Eastern Europe that are not yet under its influence.

Due to the rain, the SS guards who were supposed to escort Hitler to Prague did not show up. Major Erwin Rommel, the guard's commander, offered to personally watch over the Führer, which he did.[46] The delays and hitches that the German army encountered—although the Czech army offered no resistance—reinforced the Polish leadership's confidence that the Nazi army was not as well equipped and well trained as it appeared to be. The Polish army would hold off the aggressor, they believed, if Hitler decided to attack. On March 21, the British Cabinet decided not to take any action to preserve the sovereignty of the Czechoslovakian Republic. By that time, it had already ceased to exist.

In March 1938, the Habima theater went on a European tour, performing two plays in Prague: *The Dybbuk* and *Uriel Da Costa*. One of the troupe members, Shlomo Brook, wrote: "When we were in Prague the situation of the Jews there was good. Prague is a lovely city [. . .]. It's hard to say goodbye to [. . .]. A city with high culture [. . .]. It's not for naught that the whole of Europe is worried for Czechoslovakia."[47]

On March 13, 1939, Yosef Katznelson, one of the organizers of the Revisionist movement's Aliyah Bet, arrived on the train from Budapest to Prague. Two days later he heard that the Germans were going to enter the city at noon. "The Czechoslovakians no longer exist," he wrote:

> We gather in one place. Where to? Unanimous decision—to Warsaw. Lucky we have a visa. German battalions are already moving through the streets. At the hotels German officers are waiting for available rooms. The few Germans in Prague are demonstrating on the streets. And the Czechs—what a disgrace! In the most remote Jewish town, two thousand years after the conquest of Jerusalem, there is greater mourning for the destruction of the Temple and the loss of independence than in Prague as it loses its sovereignty. Unbelievable ignominy.

A week later, already in Warsaw, Yosef Katznelson added: "In Poland, compared to Central Europe, it is so far paradise for the Jews. Order prevails, and they are standing up to the Germans like heroes."[48]

In Dresden, Victor Klemperer wrote in his diary on March 14:

> It is so obviously stage-managed from Berlin, in order to destroy Czechoslovakia completely and to open the way to the Ukraine. I told myself, even if England and France once again stand idly by, it would nevertheless be one more step in Germany's policy of aggression and so one more step towards the catastrophe. But now that according to today's evening paper the fixed game appears to have been so very swiftly and smoothly and completely won by Germany, while England and France take it all lying down, I feel as sick as a dog again.[49]

On March 14, the Nazi regime extended the validity of the Nuremberg Laws to the over 100,000 Jews of the Protectorate. The next day, on March 15, the day the Nazi army entered Prague, Shertok wrote with desperation: "We entered the conference hall like the delegation of a country defeated at war, called to hear the verdict of a fatal peace. But I believe we entered with our heads held high. In recent days I've been repeating to myself the English adage: in defeat—defiance!"[50]

When the representatives of the Jewish delegation got up to go to the tea table in the adjacent room with Colonies Secretary MacDonald and Foreign Secretary Lord Edward Halifax, Shertok taunted them: "Are we going to 'The Last Supper'?" hinting at the betrayal of Judas Iscariot. MacDonald failed to get the hint. On the contrary, his view was that the Jewish delegation had no reason to despair. Britain's own proposal meant that the Yishuv would grow to 600,000 people within five years. At that moment they could hear an orchestra playing in the nearby Buckingham Palace, where a reception was underway, and Shertok wondered aloud: "Is this our funeral march?" MacDonald, who was probably thinking of the bitter fruit of the policy of appeasement, replied: "Your funeral? What do you mean your funeral? It is my funeral."[51]

Chamberlain was asked at the British Parliament whether the British government had submitted an official protest to Berlin. The prime minister replied that Germany's actions could not be seen as corresponding to the spirit of Munich. The following day, he admitted that Hitler had deceived him. However, he claimed, "Nothing we could have done would have saved Czechoslovakia," and recalled Sir Nevile Henderson, the ambassador to Berlin, back to London. The *Daily Mail* wrote: "The process is natural" and "Europe has remained quiet," but the sense of relief over the ending of the Czechoslovakian crisis disappeared almost overnight. The wheels of European diplomacy were quickly set in motion to prevent Germany from making another move.

The occupation of Czechoslovakia took place as the St. James Conference was nearing its conclusion, and the Zionist delegation's attempt to persuade the British government to retract its intentions failed. Ben-Gurion wrote in his diary: "Today Hitler's armies entered Prague—and this evening the British government is submitting its proposals for the abolition of the national home policy."[52] Toward evening, Weizmann told him that Beneš, Czechoslovakia's former president, was to blame for its downfall, "because he should have fought . . ." We may guess that the three dots that Ben-Gurion inserted in his diary concealed what had passed through his mind on hearing Weizmann's burst of "combativeness." Dugdale was worried about a train loaded with 620 women and children that was on its way to Constanta port [she wrote: Gdansk]; it was not known yet whether the train managed to cross the border into Poland in time: "The men here are wild with anxiety."[53]

This train, carrying around 160 visa-holding immigrants with their families, left at 11 p.m. on its way to Ostrava in eastern Moravia, not far from the Polish border, crossed the border into Poland at 4 a.m. without delays and continued to the port of Constanta on the Black Sea coast.[54] The fifty-five-year-old writer Max Brod did not manage to get a visa to the United States. He booked himself and his wife seats in the sleeping car, and on March 6 wrote to Tel Aviv: "Here everything is going to work out[.] I will sail on the *Bessarabia* on March 16 from Constanta and on March 22 or 23 I will be in Tel Aviv. I have asked the Association of Czechoslovakian Immigrants to book me a room in a hotel or a guesthouse."[55] In his autobiography he recalled: "On the night the Germans took over the rest of Czechoslovakia we miraculously left our old country of residence, on the very last train leaving from the free zone. [. . .] Just after we crossed over, the border was closed behind us."[56]

Also on this train was Dr. Oskar Rabinowicz from Brno, the Moravian capital. He was one of the leading organizers of the Revisionist illegal immigration from Czechoslovakia, had good contacts at the top of the Czech government, and his name was associated with suspicions concerning the management of the organization's funds.[57] On the night of the Nazi invasion he got a message from London to board the train that left from Prague. While he was at the train station a Gestapo unit came to his apartment, which housed the offices of the German-language Zionist weekly *Medina Ivrit*, and searched the place thoroughly. In the middle of June his brother, Aaron Moshe Rabinowicz, a Betar activist who organized Aliyah Bet and transported refugees from Germany and Austria, traveled to Sulina Port in Romania, in an attempt to cross the border into Poland and from there continue to Constanta. At the Morawska-Ostrawa train station he was spotted by two soldiers who took him to their headquarters, where he was interrogated by an SS officer who showed surprising knowledge of the different historical approaches of the historians Graetz and Dubnov. Soldiers led Rabinowicz to the border, from where he made his way to Těšín. When war broke out he was in Katowice, trekked through the mountains to Rovno, reached Kiev, and went back to Rovno and Lviv. In November 1939, a Polish boy named Berco took him and another small group across the Dniester river to Czernovitz in Romania. He was jailed in the city and sent to prison in Bucharest. Confirmation of his admission to the Hebrew University in Jerusalem brought about his release. Rabinowicz sailed to Palestine on the ship *Transylvania*, which arrived at Tel Aviv port on the eve of Shavuot 1940.[58]

In the early hours of the morning of March 15, Eliyahu Galezer, the Betar representative in Czechoslovakia, woke up to the sound of strong knocks on the door of his room in the Excelsior Hotel on St. Wenzel Square. Oskar Rabinowicz, the chairman of the Revisionist movement in Czechoslovakia, told him that the Nazi army had crossed the country's borders and was going to enter Prague in about two hours. Galezer rushed to room 112, where he warned Yosef Katznelson and other immigration activists. Then he ran to the travel agency where he used to buy train tickets for illegal immigrants, and was told that the Nazis had closed the borders. He managed to get three tickets, including one for Katznelson, and the immigration activists boarded the train, which left at 2:15 p.m., toward the town of Bohumín. Twenty-four hours later they made it safely to Warsaw.

The Revisionist movement's Aliyah Bet office on 2 Benedykta Street continued to operate.[59] Early in the morning of March 15, the leaders of the Zionist movement, headed by the workers of the Palestine office, also woke up to the news that the Nazis had entered the city. They hastened to burn all the documents in their possession before the office closed. The headline of *Hamashkif*, the newspaper of the Revisionist movement in Palestine, on March 16 read: "A people that does not fight for its freedom—will end up a nation of slaves—the German monster has swallowed Czechoslovakia too."[60] In *Der Moment*, Dr. Joshua Gottlieb described Nazi Germany as the Golem of Prague: the Maharal stripped the Golem of its power when it started to pose a danger to the public, "but what will happen with the current Golem that is attacking the world? Who will send it back to its last place of rest?" The newspaper published an "interview" with the Golem:

> At the editor's request I went to see the Golem in Prague for a serious political conversation in light of the latest developments.
>
> I met the Golem on its little street . . .
>
> I: (waving my hand) Hello Golem!
> GOLEM: Heil! Sieg! Heil!
> I: What is this supposed to mean?
> THE GOLEM: What do I know? A kind of call . . . when you see a stranger.
> I: What will happen now? How do you intend to respond to the bad situation?

THE GOLEM: Me? It's none of my business. For this we have the Führer [. . .].

I: And what will become of the Jews?

THE GOLEM: The Jews must go, Jews out!

I: Ach, Golemtchik! This is how you thank the Jews? Don't you know that a Jew created you, otherwise you would have remained a piece of clay?

THE GOLEM (annoyed): What, a Jew created me? [. . .] I have a Jewish grandmother?

I: And who helped Czechoslovakia free itself if not Jewish friends?

THE GOLEM (thoughtful): You think you're so smart? Don't you know that all the Golem's power comes from the *shem* [one of the names of God] that you insert under its tongue? I used to have a democratic name in my mouth so I liked Jews. Now I have a racist name, a Nazi name, and I must be a racist.

I: Oylem Goylem![61]

On March 19, it was reported that "tens of Jews are committing suicide every day all over the country" and also that a first concentration camp had been built on Bohemian territory.[62]

On March 25 Ruppin wrote:

> Czechoslovakia no longer exists; Czechia has become a German "Protectorate," Carpatho-Rus has been annexed by Hungary, and Slovakia has remained an independent (?) country under German patronage. This violent move caused great resentment in England, France, the United States and Russia—yet it seems things will not go as far as war. In the meantime Hitler has also taken over the Memel district and returned it to the German Reich. What will be his next move? Will his hubris lead to his downfall, or will he be able to create a new "middle Europe"?[63]

In November 1938, after Kristallnacht, the British Parliament approved entry into Britain for Jewish refugees under the age of seventeen, provided that there would be someone to receive them and that 50 Pp would be deposited as a guarantee that they would return to their countries of origin when that became possible. Nicholas George Winton, a young British banker who arrived in Prague at the end of 1938, published a notice in Britain's newspapers seeking foster homes for 669 Jewish children, and sent them over in eight trains throughout the summer. The last Kindertransport dispatch, comprising around 250 children, was supposed to leave Prague on September 3, 1939. The Nazis did not allow it to leave.[64]

The annexation of Czechoslovakia raised concerns in Britain that another approximately 750,000 people would join the wave of refugees, which would then be followed by a much larger wave from Poland, Romania, Hungary, and Italy.[65] Samuel Hoare, the home secretary, said "candidly" in the House of Commons on November 21, 1938, that a large-scale entry of foreigners to Britain, where the rate of unemployment was high, would bolster anti-Jewish sentiments, therefore: "I have to be careful to avoid anything in the nature of mass immigration which, in my view, would inevitably lead to the growth of a movement which we all wish to see suppressed."[66]

It is difficult to know what the members of the Jewish delegation in London knew about what was happening in Czechoslovakia, and not only in the areas where there was a large German minority. The Gestapo confiscated Jewish-owned factories and banks, and synagogues were set on fire. On May 25, the Czech fascists held a demonstration on the streets of Prague, which the public reacted to with indifference. The majority of the Czech population showed sympathy for the Jews.[67]

Meanwhile, the Palestine Office renewed its activities on March 29, and several groups of immigrants embarked on their way to Palestine. "Most Jews," wrote Ruth Bondy, "did not feel as if a gaping abyss had suddenly opened before them, between yesterday and today; they did not consider the situation as unprecedented or unparalleled."[68] *The Jewish Chronicle* even expressed optimism: despite the Germans' attempts to spread antisemitism in Czechoslovakia, the Jews in Prague were getting on with their lives.[69] The *Times* correspondent reported to his readers that Christian customers were not boycotting stores owned by Jews despite the signs indicating "Jewish store." Czech citizens promised him that once they regained their independence, "the Jews-beating business will be sent back whence it came from."[70]

The Jewish press in Poland and Palestine told a different story: Prague was full of policemen, SS, and Gestapo, around 5,000 people had been arrested, a first concentration camp had been built in Bohemia, and dozens of Jews were committing suicide every day all across the country. In October 1938, Menachem Bader, the Jewish Agency emissary, wrote: "Now all the democratic plaster is cracking and falling off the face of Czech antisemitism." He proposed the announcement of a general hunger strike to awaken the world's conscience. In another memorandum, which he composed on April 17, 1939, Bader urged that time must not be wasted: if thousands of young Jewish people remained trapped they would increase the military capacity of Nazi Germany, which would use them as forced labor.[71] This fear was not without foundation. On December 20, 1938, the "Reich Institution for Work Placement and Unemployment Insurance" had issued a decree ordering all the unemployed Jews fit for work to register for forced labor.[72]

The news from Prague was not as horrifying as the news that had arrived a year earlier, after March 12, 1938, when the Germans entered Vienna. Although the Jews of Czechoslovakia suffered distress, humiliation, and separation from the general population, the German policy was designed to encourage their emigration. Adolf Eichmann, who arrived in Prague from Vienna in July 1939, founded the Center (Zentralstelle) for Jewish Emigration from Prague, transferring the methods he had used in Austria to Czechoslovakia. It is estimated that around 27,000 Jews managed to leave Bohemia and Moravia in 1938 and 1939.[73]

The pressure to obtain certificates grew, and with it the efforts to increase the illegal immigration. A year earlier, in August 1938, Martin Rosenblit, one of the leaders of the Zionist Organization in Germany, had written to the Palestine Office in Prague that he was "totally opposed to the organization of this illegal immigration and to the participation of Zionist circles, or of other Jews, in the [financial] expenses involved."[74] Now the situation had totally changed. British diplomatic representatives were ordered to warn the shipping agencies not to allow Jews without immigration permits on board. When King George VI heard from Lord Gort, chief of the imperial general staff (1937–1939),[75] that Jewish refugees were surreptitiously infiltrating Palestine, he replied that he was "glad to think that steps are being taken to prevent these people leaving their country of origin."[76]

In order to take these steps the British Navy was deployed to hunt down the ships.[77] A report on the refugee problem from September 1938 to June 1939 submitted by Sir John Hope Simpson estimated that if there was serious persecution of Jews in Bohemia, Moravia, and Slovakia, the number of refugees needing assistance would reach around a quarter of a million people, and they would be followed by refugees from Poland, Romania, Hungary, and Bulgaria.[78]

The occupation of Czechoslovakia, then, did not take the political leadership of the Zionist movement by complete surprise. Ben-Gurion, who followed the internal events in England, had long reached the conclusion that the English did not want war—not because of their pacifist spirit, but because of their fear of failure and of the aerial bombardment of their cities.[79] He feared that in the same way that Britain was abandoning Czechoslovakia to its fate, it might decide to abandon the Yishuv to its fate. With great conviction he wrote to a Zionist functionary in Poland in September 1938: "I am now filled with hope in our future as I have never been before," because in light of "the global upheavals England might need us."[80]

The Zionist leadership and the Jewish press followed the fight over Czechoslovakia's fate with deep affection toward the country. The way in which it fell victim and "paid the price" symbolized for them the bitter end that also threatened the Zionist movement. "These are sad days, because we have witnessed a bitter drama of great suffering. The shadow of war hovered above, an abyss of blood and fire opened below, and the peoples of Europe peered into its terrible gaping mouth — and the danger has seemingly passed, but at what price!" Ben-Gurion wrote to his daughter Renana at the end of September. "A small but decent and enlightened people has received a cruel and fatal blow. And not only from an enemy and a stranger, but also from its so-called friends [. . .]. France and England, supposedly ready to go to war to defend the sovereignty of the Czechoslovakian nation, collaborated with the tyrannical brute who is ruling Germany, and condemned it to be torn to pieces." Britain and France merely allowed Hitler time to strengthen his military, and "will he one of these days attack his prey like a predatory animal?"[81]

"The Palestine question" was more important to the British government and the British Empire than the fate of Czechoslovakia. MacDonald explained this position to the British Cabinet on November 14: the government needed to choose between its commitments to the Jewish world and its commitments to the Muslim world. True, the Jews of the United States wielded some influence, but the British Empire was in a certain sense a Muslim Empire. It was unthinkable that Britain would come into conflict with the Muslims within the Empire or with the Arab kingdoms in the Near East. Therefore, a Jewish majority in Palestine, even in the distant future, was inconceivable.[82] Jewish support for Britain would not make up for what it might lose if deprived of the vital support of the Arab and Muslim world.[83] The British government's decision to hold a roundtable conference in London provoked fear in the Zionist leadership that it intended to withdraw from its Mandate policy by concentrating united Arab pressure and weakening the Zionists' resistance.[84]

On December 17, Ben-Gurion flew to London. Due to the weather conditions, the flight experienced delays. The plane took off from Beirut to Corfu, and from there to Marseille. A storm forced it to land in Corsica. Ben-Gurion spent the evening reading "stories about past and present Mexican robbers." On the way to Paris "the poor plane kept swaying like a drunkard," and when it crossed the channel the passengers suffered bitter cold:

"Frozen and shattered and tired I finally got to the warm room in Mount Royal," his usual hotel in London. In the next two days he was struck by the atmosphere of anxiety over an impending war:

> They are seriously worried that *war will break out in March or April* [1939]. In the upper echelons here they mean it seriously. The news in the informed circles here is that Germany has decided to go to war against England before the latter arms itself too heavily. They are making feverish preparations to defend London and the other big cities against air raids. Some talk of war in March as a definite thing. [. . .] They explain Germany's position by its desperate economic and financial situation. Some also say that the regime's status has weakened. The annexation of the Sudeten seems to have caused disappointment, and has cost the loss of the alliance [signed] between Poland and Russia.[85] The pogrom [Kristallnacht], they say, has also turned the hearts of the German people against the Nazis. I do not know how correct these conjectures are—but *the danger of war in the coming months* is real. This news comes from an informed source. We must not spread this rumor in Palestine—but we must *prepare*.[86]

In the next few days the grave political situation in which the Zionist movement had found itself became painfully clear, and a disillusioned Ben-Gurion wrote that Britain needed the Arabs and not the Jews, because they were guaranteed the Jews' help in the event of war. Nevertheless, a British failure in the war would be "a catastrophe to Judaism as a whole."[87] There was no choice but to erect a united Jewish front against the emerging British policy. Ben-Gurion had no illusions. The Zionist movement would gain nothing from the talks.[88] A few months earlier Dugdale had already remarked that Ben-Gurion had "sadly" become anti-British.[89]

Most of the members of the Palestine delegation sailed on the Italian ship *Galilea* from Haifa to Brindisi. From there they took the train to Rome and from there flew to London. Katznelson was persuaded this time to catch a flight to Europe, which was easier than he had thought. Only he and one English passenger were on the plane, and it felt "as if we had taken a taxi to go overseas." The plane landed on the small island of Kastellorizo, off the coast of Turkey, and then continued to Athens and Brindisi. Katznelson boarded the train, crossed Italy, stopped in Zurich, and then continued to Paris. Then, he wrote, "I was alone in the car again, and I could think freely to the rhythm of the wheels."[90]

Yitzhak Tabenkin had already taken the French vessel *Champollion* on November 3 on his way to the Zionist Executive Committee's meeting in

London. The ship stayed overnight in Alexandria, where he went to the cinema to see the film *Snow White and the Seven Dwarfs* (the first animation film produced by Disney Studios in 1937). Later he described his impressions: "A childhood dream, beauty and love. A film that also speaks to adults. Everyone needs a fairy tale in place of [daily] life."[91]

The conference gave the Revisionist journalist Yosef Netz (Vinitzky) a chance to dip his pen in mocking sarcasm and a fair bit of Schadenfreude. He described how he sailed to London on the Italian ship disguised as an Arab and received excellent service. In London he got an enthusiastic welcome: the kingdom's leaders and officials greeted him, photographers pounced on him from all sides, and when he was asked whether the Arabs would help Britain in the war, he waved his hand as if to wave away a bothersome fly. The British press hastened to write about the need to make concessions to the Arabs so they would support Britain if war broke out. The Jewish delegation, he wrote, showed an astounding unity: "Everyone has united for the burial of Zionism."[92]

On January 15, 1939, Weizmann told Blanche Dugdale that he was considering retiring after the Twenty-First Zionist Congress and becoming an elder statesman, living in Rehovot and running the Sieff Institute. This would extend his life by another ten years, but "who knows what may happen between now and August 1st?"[93]

In January 1939, Victor Mallet, an advisor at the British embassy in Washington, wrote to the Foreign Office in London: "The Jews are now more interested in attacking Hitler. I hardly believe that they would be stupid enough to [start riots] against us when we are more or less the only friends they have left. [. . .] There are more and more people who say that the Jews are trying to push this country to war."[94]

On January 17, Colonial Secretary Malcolm MacDonald presented the main principles of the new policy in a secret memorandum he submitted to the Cabinet members:

> We cannot accept the contention that all Jews as such have a right to enter Palestine. It would clearly be absurd to admit that all the millions of Jews in the world have a right, which they should be allowed to exert if they wished, to settle in Palestine. We cannot avoid an eventual clash, if we continue to carry out the Balfour Declaration, between the forces of persecuted, desperate, brilliant, constructive Jewry in Palestine and the widespread pan-Arab movement which is rallying to the defense of its weakest brethren, the Arabs of Palestine.[95]

On January 21, 1939, Weizmann sent a special Code B cable to Ben-Gurion in New York, "Secret for closest friends only," to inform him that "imminent war seriously considered [in] highest quarters [and War Office] [is] urging upon Cabinet importance Arab friendship. Am making efforts influence them right direction."[96]

On February 1, Weizmann, Ben-Gurion, Shertok, Professor Selig Brodetsky, and Arthur Luria met with MacDonald at St. James's Palace to discuss the conference arrangements. Ben-Gurion wrote in his diary: "The conference room — spacious, a long table in the center with approximately 20 chairs around it. The chair in the middle is for the Prime Minister."[97] The delegation heard from MacDonald that the Palestinian Arabs would have two separate delegations, and that there was no risk that the Arab and Jewish delegations would run into each other on the stairs. Journalists would not be present in the meetings, and photography would be permitted only at the special opening session. At the same time, MacDonald tried to allay the Jews' fears, saying that while it was unlikely, it was not impossible that a Jewish state might result from all this.[98]

On February 3, the Archbishop of Canterbury published an appeal in the *Times* newspaper to all Christian churches to open Sunday prayers with a special prayer for the success of the talks. In the Jewish Agency Directorate opinions were divided on whether to take part in the conference. Some proposed refusing the invitation and waiting for better times.[99] But the British appeal could not be refused. All the Jews could do was prepare for the conference and present a united and strong front. The Round Table Conference, wrote *Hamashkif*, the mouthpiece of the Revisionist movement in Palestine, in that day's headline, was "a pure pan-Arab conference."[100]

The Revisionists followed the talks with concern and were certain of their failure — in fact, they expected it. *Hamashkif* quoted the liberal newspaper *Star*: "All the diplomats in London call the Palestine conference: 'contemptible and cheap, grotesque and imaginary.'"[101] The editorial published by *Davar* on October 12, 1938, similarly predicted the outcome: Palestine was coming under the influence of the Arab countries, "and after such a long period of trouble," this constituted "very dangerous news."

Along with the delegates from Palestine, the Jewish delegation to the conference included around forty representatives of Jews from the United States, Britain, France, Poland, and South Africa, who comprised an advisory panel that represented not only the Zionist movement and the Yishuv (eleven delegates), but also the representatives of American Jewry and a group of Lords, leaders of the Jewish community in Britain. The representatives of the Jewish Agency and the National Committee who took part in the conference included Weizmann, Ben-Gurion, Shertok, Yitzhak Ben-Zvi, Nahum Goldmann, Ussishkin, Katznelson, Yehoshua Suprasky, Ben-Zion Mossinsohn, and the two chief rabbis, Herzog and Uziel, as well as Rabbi Moshe Blau (representing Agudat Yisrael). Other participants were Stephen Wise (the head of the American delegation), the founder of the World Jewish Congress, Robert Szold, and Louis Lipsky. At the train station they were greeted by Secretary of State for the Colonies MacDonald, along with Weizmann, Ben-Gurion, and Shertok. Weizmann asked Wise not to instigate anti-British agitation in the United States, and Wise agreed because "you cannot fight England during Hitler's time."[102] The actual talks were conducted by Weizmann, Brodetsky, Ben-Gurion, Shertok, and Goldmann.[103]

The Jewish delegation rejected the British proposal to fund its stay in the city for the duration of the talks. Its task was to fight over the opinion of the public, the press, and the political circles. The Arab delegation represented the Palestinians (led by Mufti Haj Amin al-Husseini) and five Arab states—Egypt, Transjordan, Saudi Arabia, Iraq (whose representative was Nuri Said), and Yemen. They were invited after responding to the British government's call to intervene and put an end to the general strike that had been announced by the Palestinian Arabs on April 25, 1936, and had lasted 175 days, until October 11, 1936.

The Revisionist journalist Yosef Nedava wrote from London on February 7, 1939, that the Jewish Agency was responsible for the Arab countries' appearance at the conference, where they would serve as a "Trojan horse." The Agency was bending to any wind that blew in the British Foreign Office and hastening its own end, he predicted. He promised his readers that Jewish strength, based on "overflowing necessity and distress," would overcome pan-Arabism, which was "a meager force looking for comfort."[104]

On the morning of Tuesday, February 7, Shertok scrutinized Ben-Zvi's attire at the hotel and discovered to his chagrin that the chairman of the National Council had neglected to bring a tie. "I gave him one." Mossinsohn, on the other hand, had a tie that was "of the best quality and very proper."[105] Shertok managed to persuade Katznelson to put on a white button-down shirt with a stiff collar. "Considering the results that the government is preparing for us," wrote Katznelson, "it does not merit me dressing up in its honor." The subject of dress preoccupied him, and he wrote Leah Miron on February 20: "This time I am using my whole wardrobe. The thick overcoat, the old black suit—which I'm using instead of the tailcoat that others are wearing (I am allowed to show up in this garment, but Kunin [Ben-Zion

Kunin, a British Jewish doctor who looked after the delegates from Palestine during their London stay] insists that I also wear a shirt with a stiff collar so I can show my face in society."[106]

The following day Shertok noted with satisfaction that the *Evening Standard* had emphasized that while most of the Arab delegates had arrived at the palace in expensive cars, the Jewish delegates had used "ordinary taxi cabs." The members of the Jewish delegation got out at the palace gates wearing the obligatory top hats. The two delegations used separate entrances to the palace: the Arab delegation used the Friary Court entrance and the Jewish delegation used the Fairy Court entrance. The importance the British government accorded the conference was underscored by the participation of the prime minister, foreign secretary, colonial secretary, and high-ranking officials in the opening session. When the members of the Jewish delegation entered Queen Anne's room, Weizmann introduced them to the prime minister and his colleagues. Upon entering the room, Shertok wrote, "Chamberlain arranged his lips in a smile that remained fixed throughout the handshaking ritual and the obligatory rhetorical question 'how do you do.'"[107] The photographers took pictures of the delegation members sitting around the table and the conference opened at a quarter to twelve.

On the days leading up to the conference the heads of the Jewish delegation spent considerable time deciding the sitting order of its members. Arthur Luria, the political secretary of the Agency Executive in London, had to phone the Colonial Office member of staff in charge of the matter several times to inform him of changes in the seating order. After the meticulous preparations everything was ready for the first session, which was held at the Picture Rome, a hall whose walls proudly displayed the portraits of England's kings and queens. Shertok especially noted the portrait of King Henry VIII, "whose eyes [were] terrifying," and of "the righteous Queen Victoria, brimming with satisfaction and serenity." This is how he described the seating arrangement:

> There were four tables, a table across the width of the room, for the government; perpendicular to it on both sides [were] two long tables for the members of our delegations who are not members of the Agency Executive; perpendicular to those and parallel to the government's table —a semi-circular table for Weizmann and the Executive members. The distance between Chamberlain and Weizmann is not small, but we have chosen this arrangement to highlight the Executive vis à vis the government.[108]

Yosef Netz wrote mockingly: "Those who are talking about a 'round table' are mistaken—this term does not exist at all, it was 'aborted at birth.' The table first became two *tables*—one Jewish and one Arab, then three tables—one Jewish, one Muftish and one Nashashibish, and finally it turned out to be only one table, an ordinary *British table* made of hard oak."[109]

The Jewish delegation (Weizmann, Brodetsky, Ben-Gurion, Shertok, and Goldmann) and the Arab delegation sat in two separate rooms, and the British met each delegation separately. Chamberlain was forced to give his welcoming speech twice, once to the Jewish delegation and once to the Arab one. The discussions were chaired by Colonial Secretary MacDonald (whom Shertok nicknamed "The Tzadik" [the righteous one]), and from time to time were also attended by Foreign Secretary Halifax (whom Shertok, mimicking Masaryk, called "The Fox").

Four cameras documented the opening, and then it was time for the speeches: Chamberlain implored the Jewish delegation "to recognize the reality of the current situation," adding that the role of diplomacy in the face of a "stalemate" in the relations between two nations was to reach a compromise "on a just basis." He was followed by Weizmann, Ben-Zvi, and Wise. In his opening statement, Weizmann expressed his trust in the good will of the British and took the next two hours to present the unequivocal Zionist position: "Immigration is the main thing for us and without it there will be no agreement,"[110] stating that the Zionist movement had "certain vital interests which we cannot surrender, particularly at a time when the Jewish position in the world is more tragic" than two years ago. He did not hide the fact that the Partition Plan caused a "first-class controversy in our ranks" and "was a shock to Jewish public opinion." Zionism would reject outright the notion of a state in Palestine with an Arab majority and a Jewish minority:

> We are convening in a dark hour in our history and it will not be an exaggeration to say that the hopes and prayers of millions of Jews who are scattered around the Diaspora are concentrated now with unshakable confidence in the British good will. We believe that our project in Palestine compels us with cruel necessity to see the reality eye to eye, recognizing that there is no more bitter reality than the one the Jewish people has been faced with. Through all the difficult years we have tried to maintain our cooperation with the British government, which has always been the cornerstone of our policy. And we are approaching our present task with the same spirit.

He finished his speech with an emotional appeal: "I claim—and I believe I have the right to claim, with all respect and humility—that you should do justice to my people in this dark hour."

Weizmann also turned to the British government's "realpolitik" considerations: if war was indeed imminent—although he hoped that war would not break out—then if Western civilization lost to the Genghis Khan of our time (Hitler) the conference's decisions would be meaningless anyway; on the other hand, if it won, then the new set of circumstances would mean that there would be no need for Britain to surrender to the Arabs' demands. Britain must remember, he added, that it was guaranteed the unconditional loyalty of the Jews.[111]

Ben-Zvi spoke in Hebrew, with Luria translating his words. Shertok wrote, "Not only the Kingdom's seven officials but all the generations of English kings on the walls around us seemed astonished to hear this strange language."[112]

Eliyahu Golomb told Shertok that the writer Sholem Asch, a member of the United States delegation, came out of the opening session deeply moved: "With the current situation in central and Eastern Europe, the British government invites the representatives of the Jewish people and sits with them as equals . . . and the Jews have all come united," added Golomb sarcastically, "from Lord whatshisname to Sholem Asch." Shertok's view: "Of course the importance of the occasion should not be overstated," but neither should it be belittled. "It symbolized the fact that we are an independent political force."[113]

Ben-Gurion confided in his wife that the conference's results would be bad for the Jews, but this was not the final battle and they should get ready for the next one.[114] Weizmann used all his powers of persuasion sending long letters to MacDonald and Chamberlain explaining the reasons for the Jewish delegation's firm objection to the British government's proposals. However, he was aware that the occupation of Czechoslovakia had weakened the Zionist movement.

At the beginning of the conference, Katznelson, who confessed he was "too old" to be impressed by the blank faces of the "various 'gentile-boys' called ministers and deputy-ministers," had already reached the conclusion that the British government's intention was "'to reckon with reality,' that is: with the Mufti's power, with Hitler's power." On the other hand, he was happy to discover that the Jewish delegation was not a "strange menagerie," as he had feared, but a united group.[115] "We all live in a big and modern hotel, which I hate with a passion, although it's very comfortable," he told his wife.[116]

Gradually, Katznelson started feeling that "the delegation is being led by the nose" and that its members "are talking and talking incessantly. Talking also in moments when they should not. And the government is beginning to see us as people whose refusal is not a refusal and whose no is not a no: they will talk and refuse until we plead with them and they will acquiesce."[117] About six months later the writer Sholem Asch wrote about Weizmann's speech:

> In the big and grand hall [. . .] there is a tense and heavy silence. The kings and queens of England are looking down from the walls wearing royal garments and seeming to watch the proceedings. It is so quiet in the hall that you can hear a fly in its flight although the hall is full of people [. . .]. And the person speaking and riveting everybody's attention is Dr. Weizmann [. . .]. It is history speaking.

Asch seemed to hear them thinking to themselves: "The person sitting here before us, with his foreign Slavic Jewish appearance, with the forehead of a genius and a sculpted head, is one of us! What has he got to do with the Jews?" And one of the Englishmen even whispered in his ear: "Why doesn't he [Weizmann] go into English politics? If he wanted to, he could have been a second Disraeli."[118]

At times there was tension and disagreement among the members of the Jewish delegation, but they were all aware that the decisive hour was nigh. Ussishkin, who had initially refused to join the delegation, came along and immediately positioned himself as its right marker. He called the British "sellers of Christ," who were treating the Yishuv like they treated "the Czechs, the Ethiopians, the Chinese and the Spanish." Later he concluded: "Catastrophe has come!" In the sixth session, on February 17, he gave a tough speech ("today is my big day," he wrote)[119] against the British proposals, which Shertok translated into English "sentence by sentence." Ussishkin insisted they should get up and leave the negotiating table. When his view was rejected, he quit, as was his wont, and returned to Palestine on March 16 on the ship *Marco Polo*. Ben-Gurion described his quitting as "laziness" accompanied by "panic."[120]

Katznelson was becoming convinced that the British were leading the delegation on, and demanded to end the talks. Asch similarly predicted at the beginning of February, in a letter he sent to his wife Ethel in New York from the Park Lane Hotel: "We are in for big trouble." On February 17 he wrote again that the preceding week had been very sad. However, his view was that "the English need us in Palestine and they will help us." Asch was proud of Weizmann's words and noted that throughout his life there had been only four people in whom he had believed and from whom he had drawn strength: Ahad Ha'am, Bialik, Shmaryahu Levin, and Weizmann. Weizmann was a great man with a strong character, and the English loved him: "I believe in him with all my heart, and also in Ben-Gurion. We will get Palestine." As for his own speech, Asch was convinced that he had made a strong impression. He wrote his wife on February 17 that he was speaking every day: "You know me. I just get going and immediately get into it with all my heart. I feel I am needed here."[121]

Outside the conference rooms there was plenty of vigorous and very tense diplomatic activity, with a hubbub of consultations, informal conversations, meetings, receptions, tea parties, dinners, and press conferences. Among other things, the members of the Jewish delegation met the Arab representatives for official talks, talks that merely exposed the deep chasm between the sides. Four of the Yishuv's representatives—Ben-Zvi, Katznelson, Mossinsohn, and Suprasky—also met with Jabotinsky in the second week of February, rejecting his proposal to introduce cooperation between the Haganah and the Irgun on condition that the two organizations remained independent of the political institutions.[122]

The practical discussions began on the evening of February 8. The driver of the taxi that took Ben-Gurion, Shertok, and Goldmann to the palace muttered as they got off: "*Zol zein mit mazel*!" (good luck). After MacDonald's opening words Weizmann spoke, taking two hours to present "with great panache" the Zionist position that was not unfamiliar to the British. Long before the conference opened the British had known that the delegation would firmly object to the idea of creating an independent Arab state in Palestine, in which the Jews would be a minority. They also heard the warnings that the Yishuv would use all its force to resist the realization of such an intention, and that "only with British daggers will it be possible to stop immigration and create an Arab state in Palestine."

Words to this effect were also heard in the discussions. The spokespersons of the Jewish delegation made every effort at persuasion, describing the Yishuv as providing Britain with loyal military support in Palestine and the Jews as an unqualified ally in Britain's war against Hitlerism. It was to no avail. The astonished Weizmann, Ben-Gurion, and Shertok heard Halifax—who invited them to a meeting in his chambers overlooking St. James's Park and Green Park—propose that the delegation announce that for the benefit of peace and mutual understanding it would agree to a limited immigration for a certain number of years.

From the outset it was clear that the British government had no intention of withdrawing from its plan to end the Mandate regime. The compromise it suggested was that during the next five or so years—from 1939 to 1945—and on condition that Palestine's economic absorption capacity allow it, they would authorize the immigration of 75,000 Jews, 10,000 every year plus 25,000 refugees, especially children and dependents.[123]

On February 13, Shertok spoke and said that the main subject the conference had to deal with was immigration; Eastern European Jewry was ready to help in absorbing the new immigration, and the Yishuv in Palestine was dynamic and ready to receive it.[124] Ben-Gurion repeated these proposals in his meeting with MacDonald on February 18. He suggested that instead of determining the immigration quotas every six months, it was better to determine an overall quota for the next five years. Some governments were willing to help with Jewish immigration, he said. "Poland?"—asked MacDonald, and Ben-Gurion replied: "Yes, Poland, but not only Poland." When MacDonald pressed him, Ben-Gurion replied that the Yishuv would not be able to absorb 30,000 immigrants per year without having more lands at its disposal.[125] When Weizmann emphasized Britain's commitment to Zionism, MacDonald replied that Britain also had a moral obligation to the Arabs of Palestine.[126] Nonetheless, Dugdale wrote, Weizmann "wished to avoid a rift with the British government and 'may very well pursue his own line.'"[127]

That wish was soon tested. On February 15, 1939, the illegal immigrant ship *Atrato III*, purchased in Greece, sailed from Naples carrying around 300 illegal immigrants from Poland with entry visas to Panama. This was its third voyage. The entanglements involved in the ship's purchase and preparations illustrated the countless difficulties and obstacles faced by the organizers of illegal immigration. On February 20, three boats carried the illegal immigrants off the ship to Shfaim beach.[128]

Later in February, the British government reached the conclusion that efficient policing and naval measures were necessary in order to "prevent the smuggling of unauthorized refugees into Palestine through land or through the open sea." On March 2, 1939, Henderson, the British ambassador, called on the Nazi government to "check unauthorized emigration" of Jews from the territories of the German Reich.[129]

On February 16, Weizmann held a reception for the members of the Jewish delegation, which was also attended by MacDonald, who did not stay long; Halifax, a few high-ranking British officials, and some members of Parliament. The atmosphere very quickly turned "less friendly."[130] "The arguments and the conversations became tortuous,"[131] and on the morning of

February 18, Weizmann, Ben-Gurion, and Wise went to the prime minister's residence at 10 Downing Street. The three sat in the book-lined Cabinet conference room opposite Chamberlain and MacDonald and tried to convince them that the Jews could reach an understanding with the Arabs and that Britain had no reason to fear an Arab uprising. Ben-Gurion left the meeting feeling that Chamberlain would do more to defend Zionism in the Cabinet than MacDonald, whom he described as "useless support. Almost nothing can be hoped for from him."[132] Shertok believed that MacDonald's tactics were to intimidate the delegation: "Arabs upon you, the British Empire."[133]

On February 21, Weizmann, Ben-Gurion, and Shertok met with MacDonald and Halifax at the foreign secretary's office, whose walls were lined with caricatures of the British foreign secretaries in the nineteenth century. MacDonald listed his proposals, which included restricting Jewish immigration and dividing Palestine into three areas: in the first area Jewish settlement would be totally prohibited; in the second, restricted; and in the third, free. Ben-Gurion described the conversation as "a verbal duel that lasted more than two hours" between MacDonald and Weizmann, in which the colonial secretary had "the upper hand." Shertok also thought that MacDonald had displayed "great debating talent" in the duel between him and Weizmann, and wrote in his diary that the next day he found Weizmann "in a terrible mood," and that a chasm lay between Ben-Gurion and Weizmann: Ben-Gurion thought that the Arabs' claims should be disregarded and their resistance broken by force, whereas Weizmann believed that it was better to "seek a way for peace." The British government, wrote Shertok, agreed with Weizmann.

After the meeting at the Foreign Office, Weizmann, Ben-Gurion, and Shertok went for a walk in St. James's Park, encircling it several times. Weizmann apologized for his sudden weakness and wondered aloud whether it stemmed from a loss of direction or from the burden of fear. He said the words "loss of direction" and "the burden of fear" in Russian.[134]

On February 23, the Cabinet Committee on Palestine convened to hear MacDonald's proposals—that the British government would announce that it intended to create a Jewish state in Palestine and that Jewish immigration would continue, but would be capped at 80,000 immigrants over five years. That same day eight members of the Jewish delegation attended a first unofficial meeting with four members of the Arab delegation at St. James's Palace. The friendly atmosphere in the waiting room confused the British, "as it seemed as if the barriers between the Arabs and the Jews had fallen and they were much closer to each other than could have been imagined."[135]

However, the barriers between the delegations did not fall, and the verbal squabbling only revealed the depth of the chasm between them. Talks with the British government continued the next day, and the crisis seemed nearer than ever. Another meeting with the Arab representatives a day later over tea did not help. The rift with Britain became an undeniable fact.

The members of Mapai in the delegation got together to discuss the situation. Ben-Gurion thought that they should demand a Jewish state, and immediately. Katznelson was skeptical and said that he would settle for conditions that would enable a large immigration. The discussion ended with talk on the need to prepare the Yishuv for a future war.[136] MacDonald went to see Weizmann at his home to try and restore calm. In his room at the hotel, Ben-Gurion sat down to write a pamphlet addressed to the Yishuv. The Jewish Agency's news agency Palcor (established in 1933) published it in English and it appeared in Palestine on February 27:

> They are plotting to do away with the national home and hand us over to the gang leaders. This plot will not succeed! The heroism of the Yishuv, the distress of the Jewish masses in the Diaspora, the conscience of decent England, the moral and political help of the world's nations will thwart our enemies' ruses. Fear not! The people's representatives are standing guard here, with full confidence that each of you will stand the supreme test with loyalty, unity, discipline and strength.[137]

On February 26, the National Committee decided to hold a Yishuv assembly, which took place two days later. In the assembly it was decided to hold a general census of all the men aged eighteen to thirty-six and to form an emergency committee "to prepare the Jewish reaction."

On February 28, the talks in London reached a crisis point, prompting the suggestion to disperse the delegation and stop the talks immediately. Shertok, burning with a fever, wrote in desperation: "How quickly things have changed—in the wink of an eye! Positions that we considered well-entrenched have crumbled to dust. We now face the danger of an Arab state and a decrease in immigration [. . .] if not its complete cessation. A Yishuv of half a million people and no more."[138] At night he spoke with David Hacohen, who was about to return to Palestine. What should I tell them back home? Hacohen asked him. Two things, Shertok replied: "The order of the day is grab and salvage—any territory we acquire now may be the last. And don't be afraid of an Arab state—we are stuck like a bone in their throat, they can neither swallow us nor spew us out."[139] Asch wrote his wife on February 29: "The conference is in crisis, but the Jews are holding out and I'm proud of them."

On March 2 the Foreign Office sent Henderson, the British ambassador to Berlin, a telegraph informing him about "an unusually heavy traffic of Jewish refugees from Germany" who were setting off without entry visas and causing embarrassment to His Majesty's government as well as that of the United States. The ambassador was asked to bring the severity of the situation to the attention of the authorities in Germany and prevent the refugees from sailing on German vessels.

On March 8, the Foreign Office official, O. G. Rendel, suggested protesting to the Romanian government for having allowed around 850 Jewish refugees to leave the country on board the *Astir*. This old cargo ship was organized by the head of the Jewish community in Danzig, Dr. Kurt Itzig, and the Revisionist activist Zvi Herman Segal, who in 1934 had organized the sail of the ship *Union*.

The plan was supported by the Nazi authorities and helped by the Joint and the Revisionist immigration office in Warsaw. Around 470 immigrants received transit visas to Hungary and Romania, where they were joined by another group of immigrants. *Astir* sailed on March 6 from the port of Reni near the Danube delta in Romania. On March 13, it anchored in the Greek island of Samos to replenish its food supplies and on April 3 it reached Palestinian territorial waters, was captured by the British, and towed to the port of Haifa. On April 4, the immigrants were loaded onto the ship and it was sent back to sea. They were transferred to a small boat that attempted to let them ashore at the Ashkelon beach on June 28. The illegal immigrants on board were detained (some were released on July 4 and some later. Their number was deducted from the certificate quota).[140]

Besides his detailed diary, Ben-Gurion also kept a pocket diary, in which he wrote telegraphically:

4.3 Fell ill.
5.3 Didn't get out of bed.
6.3 10:30 Executive. In the morning changed rooms.
11.3 Chaim left for Paris.
12.3 At noon—Jabo.
21.3 a list of clothes he bought in Paris, along with their prices.
24.3 Left London with 5 dollars + 16 Pp + 27 Pp.
25.3 a list of the 18 books he bought in Paris.
27.3 8:45 train to Marseille.
2.4 Alexandria.
3.4 Tel Aviv.[141]

On March 1, contrary to Weizmann's view, Ben-Gurion demanded a withdrawal from the talks. A conversation at 10 Downing Street with Chamberlain momentarily changed his mind: maybe there was hope after all that the British would abandon the idea of an independent Arab state. The Jewish delegation returned to the negotiating table. On March 3, a talk was held in MacDonald's study. The large square table stood "empty and abashed and the kings [were] looking at each other rather than at us."[142]

Ben-Gurion wrote his wife Paula on March 3 that the St. James days were the toughest days in his life. In his diary he noted: "The pressure of the events, the talks with the government, the arguments among us, the tension that is increasing by the day and by the hour, the sleepless nights and the insomnia—all meant I had no physical or mental ability to continue with my notes."[143] The next day he fell ill with the flu and did not leave his room at the Mount Royal hotel. In a burst of combative fervor he made partly imaginary suggestions about arming the Yishuv, giving the members of the Hechalutz organization in Poland military training, and preparing "to create a Jewish army in Palestine, in America, in Poland, in France, in England, in the Dominions."[144]

"The Jews for their part," said Chamberlain to the Cabinet Committee on Palestine on March 6, "must be made to face up to the fact that a veto on immigration was inevitable after the initial period."[145] When on March 7 Weizmann said that for an agreement with the Arab countries the Zionist movement would be willing to slow down immigration, Shertok thought: "At such moments a person's hair turns white. I felt as if an abyss was opening at our feet."[146] This offer of compromise was to no avail, and the Arab delegation reiterated its position: a total stop to Jewish immigration to Palestine.

The talks and the exchanges were going around in circles with no chance of reaching an agreement. It was clear that the die had been cast and that the British government would not change its decision. Asch wrote to his wife: "The English, who can understand them? They want to take away what little they have given us in Palestine. [. . .] The Jews of Palestine will fight, they are ready for everything. Maybe tomorrow will be better. As for the English, you can never know. We are hoping for the best."[147] Ruppin wrote in his diary on March 12 that the British government wished first and foremost to stall. The Zionist movement, however, had to reject the interim agreement "which puts us under the rule of an Arab majority. No doubt we are destined for a few tough years in Palestine in that respect."[148]

March 14 was an especially sad day for Weizmann. He told Chamberlain that a chapter in his life was ending. It was the end of the collaboration between him and the British government. In the last speech he gave to the panel he promised that the British plan was nothing but "an episode in Jewish history," which had always had its ups and downs. It had also had brilliant hopes. Those hopes were now undermined, but "we will renew them. We will get through the difficult years ahead and come out into the open." Shertok wrote in his diary: "As in many moments in the past, on this hellishly difficult occasion we also felt that we were being addressed by one of the greatest Jews of his generation." The members of the delegation stood up and sang "Hatikva": "Some were moved to tears. There were many handshakes and goodbyes."[149]

On March 15, the ship *Atrato IV*, on its fourth voyage, arrived at Shfaim beach and let its 378 passengers ashore; 280 of them, Hechalutz members, had been organized in January in Germany and Vienna. They were joined by 120 local Hechalutz members.[150] The Gestapo obtained their transit visas to Yugoslavia as well as helped with the ship's purchase. The Mossad LeAliyah Bet invested more than 5,000 Pp in the voyage. The two groups left by train to the small Yugoslav port of Sušak near Rijeka, and after delays and some difficult moments at the borders reached the port. The Yugoslav authorities forbade *Atrato*'s embarkation due to safety reasons, and on March 7 the illegal immigrants boarded the coastal cruise ship *Colorado*, from which they moved to the *Atrato* outside Yugoslavia's territorial waters.[151]

Not everyone was impressed by this success. Eliezer Kaplan, the director of the Agency's Finance Department, said at the meeting of the Histadrut's Executive Committee in July 1939: "Aliyah Bet cannot take the place of Aliyah Aleph neither politically nor as regards Jews and Judaism."[152]

Weizmann and Ben-Gurion did not go to the closing session of the St. James Conference on March 15 to hear MacDonald present the British government's final proposal; this was the session that Shertok described as "The Last Supper." Years later Weizmann recalled: "The atmosphere of total futility that surrounded the conference was of course part of the atmosphere of the time."[153]

Ben-Gurion wrote to Paula the next day that the war that the delegation had been fighting for six weeks had not been entirely in vain: "For the first time in the history of Zionism—and in the history of the Jewish people after the Temple's destruction—we came through a difficult battle against an enormous force, and we came through it not through begging, asking for mercy or merely demanding justice. For the first time we used a new type of reasoning: our power in Palestine."[154] Three days later he was more disillusioned: "This week may be crucial. If the catastrophe of war materializes —many plans will be removed from the agenda, and our fate will depend on the course of the war and its results."[155] Still, on March 22, Ben-Gurion promised the Agency's Executive members in Jerusalem that the conference had carried "an internal blessing: in London we saw the creation of a united Jewish front, which I had not dared hope for."[156]

Shprintzak wrote from Tel Aviv to Shkolnik, who was in Los Angeles on a fundraising tour among United States Jews: "It is difficult to know what situation we will face in Palestine as a result of the London talks, but it appears that our lives and our project will come under a serious siege, which we will not be able to withstand if we cannot rely on the expedient help of our nation, the help of American Jewry—political help as well as funds." The news from the conference, he added, "reinforce the impression that our defeat this time in London is inescapable. Our struggle in London is one of the most dramatic in our history, and was conducted on our part with courage, with talent and with great wisdom. But it seems that reality is against us."[157]

Weizmann tried to lift the low spirits among the members of the panel: he praised the delegation's performance at the conference. Jews were still coming to Palestine, he declared, they could still buy land, found settlements, build industry, and with God's help they would do it now even more intensively. Despite the tragic aspects of the conference, it had revealed some positives as well: the representatives from Palestine would return home on the eve of Passover, the festival of liberty, and would continue to build the land.[158] Katznelson described the conference as "a victory, almost a miracle," because the Jewish delegation had kept its unity.[159] However, it was crystal clear to everyone that Britain had made up its mind to withdraw from the Mandate—though not from Palestine—and maintain a negative ratio between the Jewish and the Arab populations, even deducting the illegal immigrants from the quotas.

On March 17, Weizmann announced in an official letter that the Jewish delegation rejected the proposals of the British government. The Arab delegation rejected them as well. The Arab rejection worried the British government more than the Jewish rejection. MacDonald, who pushed to publicize the new policy without delay, said outright: "If we must offend one side, let us offend the Jews rather than the Arabs."[160] Sarcasm did not desert Netz, who wrote on March 17: "The Czechoslovakia business now seems like a kind of gesture, to prove to the Jews how strong the guarantees and assurances given by a great and respectable power are."[161]

All through the conference Shertok had not exchanged a single word with the old janitor in his hotel. On the morning of March 18, when he opened the door of Shertok's room for Reuven Zaslani (Shiloah), who had come to visit him, he suddenly said: "The gentleman is sick—probably out of sorrow over the results of the Palestine conference. Never mind! You cannot expect to get anything from this government. But this government will fall, there will be another government and then your situation will improve. We will get even with Hitler. We will see him shot. Let him just try to touch Britain."[162]

Ben-Gurion wrote in his diary on March 19 that in light of the international situation the Zionist movement would not even be able to "create a scandal": "Our hands are tied. The devil itself could not invent a more oppressive and menacing nightmare. They have put us in the dungeon, with our mouths gagged. We have been handed a sentence against which we cannot appeal. There may be a debate in Parliament—but whose heart will now be moved to defend an old promise to a helpless people, who cannot even hurt England with words?"[163]

Around noon on March 24, Ben-Gurion left London for Paris. Before leaving he was momentarily filled with optimism, noting: "A new ray of light has appeared in the London fog." He had heard from Dugdale that the Cabinet was divided, and that there was fierce opposition in Parliament to the government's policy. Meanwhile, he wrote, "the international situation has re-stabilized for a while. Memel has been taken. Romania has surrendered and has sold itself to Germany. Here they say that Hitler will not start a war before the end of the summer—before he accumulates enough oil and solidifies his conquests."[164]

In April 1939, Wiktor Chajes bought a new house in Lviv, in the area of "the established Polish intelligentsia." He called his attraction to this area of town "instinctive assimilation." Czechoslovakia's fate preoccupied him, but he was sure: "[Hitler] will have his Waterloo." A month later he wrote:

> A wonderful spring. The winds of war. We are starting to feel the Berlin gangster. He is used to being scared of war. That is, to being feared, and he sees as impudence the fact that each time he is feared less. Beck gave the proper honorable answer to his treacherous wriggling and attacks. Poland is now a topic that the whole world is talking about. It must be the right psychological moment. They were afraid of war, but now they are threatening Hitler with war. Therefore he, in turn, is starting to be afraid. He wants Pomerania and Gdansk. Hands up![165]

Most of the Zionist leadership saw the conference results as a fatal sentence imposed on a country defeated at war.[166] It was difficult to find solace in Weizmann's words that the conference was nothing but an episode in the history of Zionism.[167] On May 17, when the White Paper was published, a confrontation with Britain seemed inevitable. Two years of Zionist diplomatic activity had failed. However, between July 1937 and March 1939 the Zionist movement could point to some achievements in Palestine. The "riots"—the revolt of Palestine's Arabs that started in April 1936 with a general strike—neither weakened the Yishuv nor brought a stop to illegal immigration.

Yet the fight to increase the number of immigrants failed. It was not just a fight over the future of the Yishuv, but also over the fate of some of the Jews of Europe, whom the British government attempted to bar from Palestine.

Nevertheless, Weizmann insisted on believing that all hope was not lost. On March 24, on the eve of leaving for Palestine, he wrote Chamberlain a letter, describing the disaster that had befallen the Jews of Europe in a somewhat aggressive tone that smacked of weakness and desperation: "Any threat to our work and position in Palestine will be judged by Jews all over the world."[168] Simultaneously he promised that the Zionist movement would not stop its efforts to reach an agreement with the Arabs, and expressed his hope that Chamberlain would refrain in the last minute from adding more sorrow to "our tragic lot." About his departure he wrote, "never before have I left England with so heavy a heart. A cloud hangs over the relations between the Jewish Agency and British [government] ministers. Through all the ups and downs of more than 20 years I have found support in the thought that, to quote Lord Balfour's words, 'We are partners in the great enterprise,' an enterprise which means life or death to my people." These words made no impression on Chamberlain.

Stephen Wise's conclusion from the conference was that the Zionist movement should continue to build the national home. The members of the delegation reported to the meeting of the Administrative Committee of the Federation of American Zionists on March 19: "The spirit was excellent. There was not even a shadow of defeatism." Dr. Shlomo Goldman was more bullish, claiming that there was an opposition among American Zionists that supported mobilizing public opinion against Britain's policy.[169] He arrived in Geneva after a two-week visit to Palestine and accused the British officials and police of applying "Nazi methods" against the Yishuv.[170] Shertok wrote on March 22:

Hitler acts and Britain just talks. Instead of Germany being "surrounded" by Britain and its allies Hitler is gradually surrounding Poland. After the occupation of Prague and Memel Hitler can rest on his laurels for a while and has no need to provoke war. The only thing that could have maybe led to war would have been a British ultimatum for Hitler to exit Prague, but no one talks about this. In this situation it is very possible that the storm will subside in a few days and the British government will return to the agenda—that is, to us.[171]

The Weizmanns vacated the grand house on 16 Addison Crescent in which they had lived since 1918 and where they had played hosts to diplomats, politicians, and public figures; their departure seemed to symbolize the end of the era of cooperation that had begun with the Balfour Declaration.[172] Katznelson left what he called "the London fair" on March 19 on his way to Amsterdam, convinced that the conference had taught the British government that "you cannot fold us and put us in your pocket, as they thought previously." He spent four days on the Hachshara farm in Werkdorf in Holland, listened to Hitler's reception "on returning from his triumph in Prague" on the radio, and then left for Paris.[173]

On March 28 some of the participants in the St. James Conference, including Weizmann, Ben-Gurion, and Katznelson, sailed on the French ship *d'Artagnan*[174] from Marseille to Haifa. The weather became warmer by the hour, wrote Dugdale in her diary on March 31, and the sea grew calm. Ben-Gurion spent the day reading sociology books, and after dinner played chess with Yehuda (Lewis) Roaskin from Chicago, one of the sponsors of the Sieff Institute (later the Weizmann Institute of Science in Rehovot), and won. On April 3, Weizmann could not curb his anger toward Britain and expressed the hope that the Jews of the United States would join hands with the isolationists "to keep the U.S.A. from coming to the help of the British Empire." Dugdale was horrified, but said nothing. Weizmann struck Ben-Gurion as depressed, swaying between the hopes he had pinned on Britain and his bitter disappointment with its policy, and in fact, with his own failure. Dugdale told Ben-Gurion that Weizmann was planning to resign at the next Zionist congress and would retain his role as statesman. Ben-Gurion was quick to assure her that it was merely a passing mood: "I pray, hope, and believe that he is right," she wrote in her diary.[175]

They stopped over in Egypt, where they met Prime Minister Muhammad Mahmud and heard his noncommittal words about possible collaboration between the Yishuv and Egypt. During the voyage Weizmann did not write any letters. From Jerusalem he sent another of his futile letters to Chamberlain, warning against the grave consequences that might result from the British government's adherence to the White Paper's policy. He wrote Leopold Amery from Rehovot on April 25 that if the British government continued to ignore the plight of European Jews and was determined to hand Palestine over "to the Mufti's gang," it would encounter fierce opposition. No enlightened judge, he remarked, would indict a poor Jewish refugee who was escaping from the hell of Central Europe and making his way on an illegal immigrant ship to Palestine.[176] The British government increasingly resembled the tyrannical regime it was fighting against, Weizmann added, comparing Britain's treatment of the Jews to its treatment of the Czechs.

He could not have known that the Colonial Office would assert on July 22 that the idea held by some "Jewish circles," "that they are justified in trying to break the law by virtue of some super-legal higher morality, and in extenuation they cite the persecutions in Greater Germany, and the desperate plight in which many European Jews now find themselves" had to be rejected. Those circles were nothing but "lawbreakers" who think "only of themselves, and fail to realize that what they are doing is fundamentally anti-social—as anti-social as the German persecution of which they complain."[177]

Mordechai Bentov, the Hashomer Hatzair representative at the conference, traveled from London to Warsaw to visit his mother and they agreed that she would come and visit her children in Palestine like she used to do every two to three years, "and since war might break out—and wars usually break out in the fall, after the harvest—she will stay with us. And if the year goes by peacefully, she will be able to return to her home in Warsaw." His mother kept her promise. After his short visit to Poland, Bentov took the Orient Express through the Balkans to Aleppo in Syria, and in the restaurant car was surprised to meet Jamal al-Husseini, the Mufti's cousin and right-hand man. Bentov introduced himself as an American journalist returning from the Round Table Conference, and heard from al-Husseini that the Arabs had learned in London that the British government did not want the Arab revolt and the bloodshed in Palestine to continue, and that British public opinion was turning more and more toward the Arabs.[178]

Shertok stayed in England and in the second week of April took a vacation on the beach in Bournemouth. On April 17, he flew to Warsaw.[179] Netz could not find a place on the same ship that carried Weizmann and Ben-

Gurion, because "all the places on the ship were taken by the huge cargos of Weizmann's achievements and triumphs." He sailed on another ship, and when he arrived in Tel Aviv he was not surprised to discover that Jabotinsky had been right yet again: "During the baggage check at customs an old newspaper falls from my suitcase, I bend down to pick it up and find in it Jabotinsky's article from three months ago about the Round Table: total nonsense."[180] During the conference, Netz had hoped that Arab extremism would lead to its failure. To his joy, the Arabs did not disappoint him and Zionism was "saved" from the calamity of the Partition Plan and of the idea of creating a bi-national state.[181]

After arriving in Palestine, Weizmann visited Nahalal on May 5, telling the audience that had come to hear him that "the mistake of St. James" would be corrected, "just as they are correcting the mistake of Munich." It was the British government that had lost. The Zionist battle was not over. Some of his listeners, moved by his words, thanked him for his efforts: "Go to the people in the Diaspora who are waiting for you!"[182] Netz mocked his words: "Joy for the chickens of Bet-Alpha! Glee for the Dutch bulls at Ein-Harod! Delight for the horses in Nahalal—for your providers will come from afar, bringing their silver and gold with them."[183]

Weizmann's plan was to stay in Palestine until the start of the Twenty-First Zionist Congress in Geneva. But on May 10 he returned to London, stopping on the way for a brief trip to archeological sites in Athens. The day after his arrival he met with Chamberlain in a last attempt to prevent the White Paper's publication. On May 13 he met with MacDonald at his home in Great Waltham near Colchester. Dugdale and others asked him not to come, wrote MacDonald, "because I was such a monster [in his eyes]." The conversation was indeed difficult, and MacDonald said that although he knew that Weizmann hated and despised him, he had not stopped admiring him. According to his secretary and bodyguard, Weizmann left the meeting pale and trembling with rage, muttering that he had been confirmed in his opinion that the English were two-faced crooks.[184] A week later Dugdale visited MacDonald and accused him of ruining the love and loyalty of the Jews. MacDonald leaned on the table, covered his face with his hands, and admitted: "I have thought of all that."[185] Despite the difficult atmosphere, Weizmann—and the entire Zionist movement—would continue to need Britain's cooperation.

On April 6, 1939, the British Parliament held yet another debate about the refugee problem, focused on the possibility of finding destinations for Jews as well as other refugees abroad. Lord Winterton said the key question was where these people would go. Possibilities included Tanganyika, San Domingo, and Honduras, among others. Some members of Parliament evinced skepticism about these options: any attempt to "transplant" Jews from Central Europe to tropical countries was thought to be a hazardous experiment. Isaiah Wedgewood, a pro-Zionist British statesman, explained: Jews do not want to go to Gyana or Honduras, and any plan to direct them there was bound to fail.[186]

On April 20, the Cabinet Committee on Palestine held a final discussion. Chamberlain was decisive and set the tone: "If we must offend someone, we would rather offend the Jews than the Arabs," and this was the position that was adopted.[187] On April 28, Hitler annulled the Non-Aggression Pact with Poland and the naval agreement with Britain. Ruppin wrote the next day: "I concluded from this that Poland is siding with Britain. If Romania and Russia do the same, I doubt that the fascist countries will dare go to war."[188] Ben-Gurion wrote in his diary: "The global crisis is intensifying."[189]

Jabotinsky gave a series of speeches between May 1 and May 29, first in Poland, Latvia, and Finland and later in Romania, Yugoslavia, and Bulgaria. The enthusiastic receptions he got drove him to believe that he would be able to convene the "Zion Sejm"—a large Jewish assembly—and use it to influence the British government to change its policy. He soon realized that the Jews of Eastern Europe, who were like "a crowd of potential emigrants waiting on the beach for a boat," were waiting in vain: "Now Britain has announced that the ship will never reach their shore."[190]

On May 4, Edwin Samuel, son of the first High Commissioner for Palestine and deputy director of the Mandate government's Immigration Department, showed Ben-Gurion a poem by "a (gentile) English poet that was published in an American monthly: it should be published in every Jewish home. The poet is Wystan Hugh Auden, and it was printed in the *New Yorker*, April 1931." Ben-Gurion copied the poem "Refugee Blues" into his diary.[191] Here are a few lines:

> There's no place for us, my dear, yet there's no place for us. [. . .]
> Once we had a country and we thought it fair;
> Look in the atlas and you'll find it there.
> We cannot go there now, my dear, we cannot go there now. [. . .]
> The Consul banged the table and said,
> "If you've got no passport, you're officially dead."

At the beginning of July the authorities published the census that had been held in Germany and Austria on May 17. Of the approximately 560,000

Jews who lived in Germany in 1933, around 215,000 Jews had emigrated, around 30,000 were being held in prisons and detention camps, around 20,000 had committed suicide, and 8,000 had been murdered. Out of the 300,000 Jews of Austria, 145,000 were left in the country: 130,000 had emigrated, around 10,000 were imprisoned, a similar number had committed suicide, and 5,000 had been murdered.[192]

News of abuse and murder in the detention camps and of pogroms in Austria and Czechoslovakia were published regularly. On July 13, Britain's Secretary of State for the Colonies announced that in October the immigration would be stopped due to the scale of the illegal immigration. In response, a Jewish general strike was announced in Palestine from 2 p.m. until midnight. The National Council released a public statement calling on Britain to stop abusing the Jewish people. On July 20 the Union of Religious Organizations protested to the Tel Aviv mayor about "the shameful phenomenon seen on the Tel Aviv beach, as the bounds of modesty are breached by men and women bathing together, with no partition separating them, against all the rules of modesty. This phenomenon is shocking to the Jewish public in general and to religious Jews in particular."

The bloody events in Palestine continued. On July 23, Avraham Goldfaden's play *Mirale Efros* opened with Hannah Rovina in the leading role. At the end of July, the Swiss government forbade Jewish refugees from entering the country's borders. At the beginning of July, preparations were completed for the Twenty-First Zionist Congress in Geneva.

Palestine and the countries of the Jews' Diaspora are worlds apart.[1]
Zeev Jabotinsky, September 1938

5

A BRIDGE OVER THE WHITE PAPER?

On the night of May 13, 1939, Moshe Shertok and Dov Hoz (the Histadrut and Mapai emissary in London) went to see Weizmann in his London home. Shertok read out to Weizmann the summary of the White Paper, a copy of which had come into his possession. In his diary he wrote: "We found Chaim in a state of breakdown after his tremendously tense conversation with Malcolm [MacDonald]. He had poured out all his anger at him, accusing him of treason, comparing him to Hitler, until finally MacDonald lost his temper. They parted as overt enemies."[2]

That same night the German liner *St. Louis*, owned by the shipping company Hapag-Lloyd and running between Hamburg and America, set sail from Hamburg to Cuba. The voyage was organized as part of the Nazi policy of proving to the world that Germany was allowing Jews to leave. The ship, with a crew of 231, carried 963 emigrants, people of means who had paid good money for their sailing permit. All except six had entry permits to Cuba. The first-class passengers paid 800 reichsmarks and the tourist-class passengers paid 600 reichsmarks.

Yet behind the scenes of the voyage swirled a tangle of anti-Jewish propaganda, bribery, political intrigue, and lobbying. The Cuban authorities refused to let the Jews who held German citizenship disembark at the Havana port, where the ship anchored on May 27. On May 29, Boris Smolar, the foreign correspondent of the *Day*, wrote from Paris that the passengers "did not travel as refugees without a goal. They traveled as passport passengers, as immigrants with visas. [. . .] However sympathetic they may have been with the plight of the Nazi victims on the wandering ship, the half million dollars furnished for the *St. Louis* passengers has created a feeling in the minds of many non-Jews in Europe that the Jews are the richest people in the world. What nation can today afford to spend half a million dollars for less than a thousand people?" Smoler highlighted the reactions of refugees from Poland who complained that American Jews did not see fit to raise the same sum for them. The *St. Louis*, according to Smoler, had set a precedent. Other countries would also ask for ransom as a condition for the acceptance of Jewish refugees.[3]

The Cuban newspaper *Avance* wrote that a Jewish "invasion" of the Cuban homeland must be avoided by claiming that the emigrants' entry permits were not in order, thus preventing the Jews from enjoying the land conquered by the inhabitants' forefathers.

The *St. Louis* sailed on June 2 toward the U.S. coast. The U.S. government rejected all the appeals to allow the immigrants into the country, unwilling to set a precedent of immigrants' entry beyond the yearly quota (which was 25,957 immigrants from Germany per year). On June 5, the Cuban government agreed to allow the ship's passengers to go ashore in exchange for bonds worth $453,000, but the Joint was unable to raise the required sum (the organization expended around $1 million out of a budget of around $8 million in an effort to find the ship's passengers a harbor). Only 29 passengers were allowed to enter Cuba, and the *St. Louis*, which sailed between Havana and Miami, was ordered to return to Europe. On June 7, the readers of *Davar* were informed that the *St. Louis* had managed to let its 1,992 passengers ashore in San Domingo in the West Indies. The island's government intended to demand "$500 for each Jew," but later retracted its demand. Meanwhile, another news report claimed that 900 of the ship's passengers had been allowed to disembark on one of the islands of Isle de France and would be kept in a concentration camp until they received immigration permits from another country.

Alongside this "encouraging news" it was reported that the Polish immigration office had heard that the Latin American countries had begun hunting down illegal immigrants, and that the Brazilian government had instructed all its citizens aged eighteen to sixty who had arrived from Europe to register for monitoring purposes, and "the order spread panic around the country."[4] On June 11, Shertok told the members of the Jewish Agency executive about the 900 or so refugees on board the ship and about the proposal of Eliezer Kaplan, director of the Executive's Finance Department, that the passengers should go to Palestine. Ben-Gurion thought that they could be allocated some of the immigration permits, because "this immigration will be a very effective weapon in our political battle."[5]

The Joint asked the Jewish Agency to take 500 of the ship's passengers under its existing certificate quota, promising to fund their absorption

—£100 per person. The request was refused. The Agency executive saw it as "queue jumping" by immigrants who to begin with had no intention of going to Palestine. Its proposal that the British government assign them a special quota of certificates had no chance of being accepted.[6]

On June 17, the *St. Louis* put down anchor at Antwerp before returning to Hamburg, its home port. Two hundred and eighty-eight of the passengers received permission to go to Britain (where they were defined as "enemy subjects"), 224 were allowed to enter France, 181 were allowed to go to Holland, and 214 remained in Belgium. The rest went back to Germany.[7]

From January to May 1939, a few hundred more Jews, holding defective visas, sailed from Germany across the Atlantic on around a dozen ships on their way to South America. Most of them were allowed ashore in various countries.[8] In sum, from April 1933 to July 1939, around 36,000 Jewish immigrants from the Reich arrived in Latin America.

On April 6, 1939, as noted earlier, the British Parliament held another of its debates on the refugee problem, most of which was dedicated to the possibility of finding destinations for Jewish—though not only Jewish—immigration overseas. Earl Winterton reminded the members of the house of Rublee's negotiations with the Nazi regime, stating that the key question was: "Where are these people to go?" The answer: In any event not to Palestine, but to places like Tanganyika, San Domingo, Honduras, and other countries whose names had been mooted. Some Members of Parliament poured cold water on these proposals: any attempt to "plant" Jews from Central Europe in the tropical countries was hazardous; the Jews did not want to go to Guyana or Honduras, said Colonel Josiah Wedgwood, and any "schemes to direct these people to these countries is bound to fail."[9]

The three months between the close of the St. James Conference in March 1939 and the publication of Britain's new policy on the Palestine question (the White Paper) on May 17 were nerve-racking, full of frantic diplomatic efforts and fraught with rumors, proposals, and plans. The tension grew steadily as the publication was held back for weeks due to disagreements among the members of the British Cabinet. Nathan Alterman's poem "The White Paper and the People of the Book," published in *Haaretz* on May 14, 1939, reflected the expectant tension:

The people wait and expect
Told solemnly every day
About the very important text
Of English belles-lettres coming their way.

And it should be hoped indeed,
That in that fine literature's stocks
This text will honorably sit
Among the period's outstanding works.

And we, who from time immemorial
The People of the Book have been called,
Who better than us understands
The weight of the written word.

. . . .
This White Paper of course
Shall be added to the account,
And we shall keep it from being erased
And forever the story recount!

This black paper of course
Is reviving an ancient myth,
That to the glorious redemptive day
We shall cross on a paper bridge![10]

The next day, *Haaretz* printed another poem on the same subject, called "Definition":

What are we, idiots or fools?
Yesterday: a state, independence,
And today scorpions and whips.
Let's give it the right definition,
So things are brutally clear:
Arrogance, fickleness and deception.

They say that the Cabinet is of two minds
But we have only one,
And it won't back away or be scared
By the White Papers of Aram.[11]

The tense waiting period for the publication of the British government's policy, amid news of large concentrations of German armed forces near the border with Poland, did not disrupt the daily routine in Palestine. On May 9, a flower show opened in Tel Aviv, and in Jerusalem the medical center was inaugurated on Mount Scopus. The following day the city's "Edison" cinema held the "Youth Body Culture Celebration."[12] *Haaretz* reported: "The rush for a summer vacation has begun," adding that the Italian ship *Galilea* had arrived from Beirut to Tel Aviv to take around sixty passengers abroad. The rush to get away, the newspaper reported, was already evident, and around eighty passengers left for Europe on the Romanian ship *Transylvania*.[13]

On the morning of May 17, an armored car delivered copies of the White Paper from the government building in Jerusalem to the District Governor building in Jaffa. They were placed under guard before being distributed to the newspapers. At 8 p.m., a summary of "His Majesty's Government's Announcement on Palestine" was broadcast on the radio. The next day, the Tel Aviv municipality organized a strike to protest against the "restrictions on immigration." It also announced a blackout and a demonstration that would conclude with a rally at the Maccabiah Stadium. The municipality also announced a census of the city's residents aged eighteen to thirty-five.

On May 18 there were mass protest demonstrations in the towns and *moshavot* (rural settlements). In Tel Aviv tens of thousands of people thronged to the city's main streets, as groups belonging to the Revisionist movement marched along Allenby Street from the Mugrabi cinema to the Great Synagogue. Their chants included cries denouncing "Weizmann the traitor." The demonstrators carried banners and distributed leaflets. Some of them climbed the roof of the Land Registry Office on Allenby Street, hoisted a blue-and-white flag, and proceeded to smash the furniture and set fire to the premises. The police was called to the scene and a few demonstrators were injured in the brawl with the security forces.

During a mass demonstration in Jerusalem the next day, stones were thrown at the building housing the Mandate government's Immigration Department. The police and the army used batons against the demonstrators. More than a hundred of them were injured. A British policeman was killed by shots from a Haganah man's pistol. The Jewish Agency published a statement in which it rejected the White Paper outright and promised that the Yishuv would not give in.

The Jewish National Council (Vaad Leumi) appealed to the British nation, calling on it to display "its great moral power and put a stop to the abuse of the Jewish people, being burned at the stake of hatred and persecution and crying for help and salvation in its homeland." The Jewish National Council also announced a general strike, but appealed to citizens not to hold any rallies or gatherings.[14]

In Poland, a general protest strike proceeded as planned despite the Bund's attempt to prevent it. Tens of thousands of Jews turned out on the

Polish capital's streets. At Warsaw's Muranowska Square, crowds demonstrated in front of the British embassy. Mass rallies were organized at the community center on 26 Wialicka Street and elsewhere. Jabotinsky, giving his last speech on Polish soil, repeated his grim prediction about the future of Polish Jews. At the same time, he claimed that the international tension would soon subside, that Britain would stop being afraid of the Arabs, and that the Zionist movement—with the right leadership at the helm—would get the White Paper annulled. Illegal immigration was one of the means to achieve that, he said, because protests against a ban on immigration helped awaken the world's conscience to the injustice done to the Jewish people. Jabotinsky described Polish Jews as people sitting in a burning house and doing nothing to save themselves. The way to put out the fire, he suggested, was to create a parliament of Eastern European Jews (Zion Sejm).

On May 18, Weizmann spoke at the English Zionist Federation Conference, trying to project optimism: "We are assembled here tonight in a sad hour for the destinies of our movement and for the destinies of our people. But we Jews are used to adversity [. . .]. [It is] the blackest hour of Jewish history [. . .] a time when our enemies, cruel and relentless, seek to destroy the Jewish people body and soul, and when millions are literally living under conditions which can be called neither life nor death. [The White Paper is a] death sentence of the National Home." However, he assured his audience, "all decrees of humans, however mighty they may appear to themselves and at the time, are as naught; they will blow away like chaff before the wind."[15]

On July 22, 1939, the undersecretary of state for Foreign Affairs instructed the British embassy in Warsaw to keep exerting pressure on the government to stop illegal immigration, and to promise the government that Polish Jews would get the same opportunity as Jewish emigrants from other countries to immigrate to any prospective Jewish settlement in territories belonging to the British Empire.[16]

Exasperated not only with "the grand idea" of a massive Jewish immigration to Palestine but also with the idea of convening a "Zion Sejm," however, the Polish government advised the leaders of the New Zionist Organization "to postpone this show for the time being." In June it was made clear to them that calls for the Jews to leave only for Palestine did not coincide with Poland's policy of immigration to any available destination. All Jabotinsky could do was express his bitter disappointment. He had wanted "to organize, before the sleeping dogs awakened, a Jewish show of force that would exceed in its scale anything that had gone before, and demand that the gates be opened for mass immigration: not to convince the brutes or to win their hearts but to give those semi-friendly governments some argument they could use against the barking." Now, he wrote, "regretfully the attempt has failed, and the initiative for a Zionist revival will have to come from the antisemitic camp."[17]

Around a month later, at the seventh session of the Twenty-First Zionist Congress, Berl Locker pointed to the contradiction and hypocrisy in Britain's policy: on the one hand the colonial secretary promised to help the Polish government with Jewish emigration from Poland, but on the other he demanded that it didn't put a stop to illegal immigration. Moreover, he put "a heavy blame on the Jews of Poland, who [were] traveling to Palestine in contravention of the White Paper" and were trying to leave Poland, where, as was the case in other Eastern European countries, "there [was] a cruel politics of dispossession."[18]

Stefan Lux's suicide in Geneva may have given inspiration to others. On May 22, Shertok wrote in his diary that a young woman from Poland, a student at Oxford University, had come to see him and had offered to perform "an action" in the Parliament building in protest of the White Paper: to assassinate Prime Minister Neville Chamberlain or kill herself, or both. Walter Ettinghausen (later Walter Eytan, the first director general of Israel's Foreign Ministry), a lecturer in German at Oxford, was visited by a young Jewish student who offered to commit suicide in the Parliament building. He stipulated that he would only do it if he had Weizmann's approval.[19]

On May 23, six new settlements were established in the Lower Galilee and in Samaria. On May 29, the United States Consul General in Jerusalem reported mixed reactions to the White Paper: the Yishuv rejected it altogether, based "on a fundamental denial of its premises," while the Arabs distrust the British good faith.[20]

Jabotinsky described the White Paper as "something ephemeral"[21] that posed the Yishuv no danger; it was not "a real irreparable disaster" as long as Palestine remained under British rule. The main danger it posed was weakening Zionism in the international arena.[22] On June 9, 1939, he wrote the New Zionist Organization's presidium in Warsaw that the British regime would have difficulty overcoming active resistance to the immigration laws: "An immigrant ship can let passengers off at the Tel Aviv shore as long as there are 150,000 Jews in Tel Aviv who want it to happen."[23] Locker was similarly optimistic, telling the delegates at the Twenty-First Zionist Congress: "My feeling is that the White Paper is already losing ground. Because every single day the government itself breaches it in terms of immigration."[24]

Katznelson, on the other hand, was careful not to dismiss the White Paper so easily, and in his speech at the Congress he expressed great concern that the Congress would not only fail to declare war on the White Paper, but would even accept it, comparing it to a thunder that had already struck, "but as long as it does not make us fall, we do not admit to it." The grave meaning of Britain's policy was that the Balfour Declaration had been replaced by an "anti-Balfour" declaration.[25]

Jabotinsky was convinced that the Arabs would reject the White Paper—as indeed they did—but feared that in its wake the antisemitic atmosphere in Eastern Europe would intensify because it removed Palestine from the map of possible immigration destinations. Indeed, a memorandum written by the Polish Foreign Ministry duly concluded that the pressure on the Jews to emigrate should be increased: "The burden of searching for and finding emigration territories, as well as for financial means, should be placed on the Jews' shoulders,"[26] and Poland should not tie its emigration policy with the immigration quotas to Palestine. Even before the White Paper's publication, Jabotinsky already knew that Poland could not be relied upon because of its dependency on Britain, and now there was no choice but to look for a different political backer.

Avraham Stern (alias Yair, then one of the leaders of the underground Irgun Zva'i Le'umi [Etzel]), who pursued his own independent policy in Poland, saw things differently. Zionist policy—from both the Left and the Right—had collapsed, and it was time for a revolutionary change of direction: Poland would continue to provide a supporting rearguard and a training ground for a Jewish army that would conquer Palestine and create an independent Jewish state in the country.[27] During the St. James Conference, on March 6, Stern had held a press conference in Warsaw in which he presented his vision, which was in fact a declaration of mutiny against Jabotinsky's leadership. The latter threatened to resign, but later tried to smooth things over.

Stern's plan was adopted by Eri Jabotinsky, the Betar commissioner in Palestine and the movement leader's son, who wrote on March 13: "Aliyah Bet is becoming a 'popular craze'; a new crusade on a huge scale." He drew up a memorandum in which he proposed to organize the transport of 10,000 Betarites to Palestine's shores: five ships would set out on September 1, each carrying 2,000 people, who would land on the Tel Aviv beach at night—"but with no special secrecy."[28]

The atmosphere in the Revisionist movement had changed radically. Many believed, or wanted to believe, that such an operation could be carried out with the help of the Polish authorities or while they turned a blind eye. Representatives of the New Zionist Organization negotiated with a company that exported arms surpluses from the warehouses of the Polish army and with various middlemen. One of them, a Ukrainian engineer by the name of Ivashenko, the production manager at a steel factory in Polish Silesia, met Jabotinsky and was impressed; he donated 500 zloty (around $100) and promised that he could create a huge steam tank big enough to hide a canon. He even held a banquet to celebrate the occasion.

In May 1939, Stern arrived at the Andrychów camp with a senior Polish officer and addressed the trainees at the end-of-course parade: from Poland the "conquering army" would depart by sea to the homeland's shores.[29] On June 16, the Haganah military course in Zielonka was visited by representatives from Poland's army, as well as its Foreign and Interior Ministries. On July 13, it was visited by journalists and guests, including Moshe Kleinbaum and Yitzhak Gruenbaum and the representatives of the Irgun in Poland. The goal of these Haganah military training courses was not to get ready to take Palestine from Britain, but to prepare the trainees for the future struggle with the Palestinian Arabs.

In the second week of July 1939, Golomb and Jabotinsky met for further talks in London. Golomb tried to convince his interlocutor that the Irgun's acts of retaliation ("reactions") were endangering the Yishuv's military power and undermining its status in Britain. Jabotinsky offered to organize a Zionist roundtable, which would advance "the democratization of the Zionist Organization" and suggest "constructive solutions to many questions." On July 11, Jabotinsky reported on the talks to the NZO Directorate in London and expressed doubts as to the chances for an agreement between the Haganah and the Irgun.[30] He rejected any criticism of the Irgun's actions.[31] On the contrary, he gave these actions his full backing. On June 29, 1939, he had issued "a general directive" to the Irgun's headquarters in Palestine: "Public opinion, both Jewish and foreign, is in favor of the reactions, as long as there is no suggestion of deliberately targeting women. When engaging in *defense* one cannot distinguish between the sexes; but in a *reaction* one should avoid any step that might create such an impression [. . .]; the same goes for infants and the elderly."[32] However, in the article "Amen" that he published in *Der Moment* on July 19, Jabotinsky noted that in the First World War Britain reacted to the aerial bombing of its cities with similar raids on cities in Germany, which also harmed innocent people.[33] The effective and moral way to respond to the "shedding of Jewish blood in Palestine" and to put an end to it was to react. Any other way would reinforce the impression among the English that "we are weak and should not be relied upon as an ally in times of danger." These words came in response to the Irgun's actions in May 1939, chiefly an attack on the Arab village of Bir Ades near Petach Tikva on May 25. Several Arab women were killed in the failed attack.

The demonstrations and the violent protest did not change Britain's policy. Although the White Paper policy met with strong disapproval in the British Parliament, and not only from the opposition benches, Zionist diplomacy in London faced an iron wall. Shertok, who had returned to Palestine from London in the middle of June, reached the despairing conclusion that just as Chamberlain had sacrificed Czechoslovakia in Europe "for the sake of friendship with Germany," he was sacrificing the Jewish national home in Asia "for the sake of peace with the Arabs."[34] The United States offered no salvation either. The White House informed the British government that it would not oppose the new policy. The Zionist organizations refrained from instigating "a great war against Britain" and taking "desperate actions" to thwart the White Paper's publication. Louis Brandeis and Felix Frankfurter's meetings with President Roosevelt had no effect, and neither did the public protest.[35]

On June 10, 1939, the Polish ambassador to London submitted a memorandum to the British Foreign Office. It pointed out that the possibilities of Polish Jews immigrating to Palestine, which had been reduced in the preceding years, had been badly impaired following the White Paper. It reiterated the demand that at least 45 percent of the immigration quotas be allocated to Polish Jews, because the White Paper policy had impacted negatively on Poland's belief that the national home would be a natural destination for immigration. However, it added, this quota was not enough, and therefore Britain should assign a territory within its Empire for the settlement of Jews from Poland.[36] The reports on the situation of the Jews who had arrived from Prague to Poland failed to impress the Colonial Office, which in a memorandum it sent the British consuls in the United States on July 22 described the Jews from Poland and Romania as not being bona fide refugees and recommended that Colonel Beck "might be warned in general terms that it would be inadvisable for Poland any longer to rely on Palestine as a serious factor in the solution of Poland's Jewish problem."[37]

Because neither the Arab nor the Jewish delegations (in St. James) felt able to accept their proposals, and the conference did not result in an agreement, the governments were therefore free to formulate their own policy. The White Paper policy was based on three main principles: First, as soon as peace and order were sufficiently restored, including the transitional period in Palestine, steps would be taken to carry out this policy of giving the people of Palestine an increasing part in the government of their country. This arrangement would be determined by the present population data, which the restrictions on Jewish immigration were meant to freeze. After ten years Palestine would achieve complete independence. Second, Jewish immigration would stop, apart from a final quota of 75,000 immigrants over five years, subject to the country's economic absorption capacity. Further expansion of the Jewish National Home by immigration [would be permitted] only if the Arabs were prepared to acquiesce; in the next five years, immigration, if economic absorptive capacity permitted, would "bring the Jewish population up to approximately one-third of the total population of the country." Third, in around 95 percent of Palestine's territory the purchase of land by Jews would be banned or severely restricted.[38]

On April 28, the British published some new regulations that stated that the crews of illegal immigrant ships would be liable for two years' imprisonment and a heavy fine, and the ship captains for five years' imprisonment. On May 23, the British Parliament ratified the White Paper with a majority of 268 to 179. On June 14, a quota of 9,150 immigrants was set for the months May through September, and 696 permits were deducted for captured illegal immigrants, plus 568 uncaptured illegal immigrants.

At the Histadrut Executive Committee meeting on March 16, Pinchas Tarshish, the Histadrut emissary to Europe, said that there was no comparison between the situation of German Jews and that of Polish Jews: "At the moment we are beating ourselves up for not having done enough for Germany and not having ferreted enough people and money out. I hope we don't say these things in a short while to the Jews of Poland [. . .]. We must help the Diaspora, because the Diaspora is dying." His proposal was "to strengthen Zionism in the Diaspora."[39]

The drastic reduction of the immigration permits quota now intensified the pressure to accelerate illegal immigration and see it as a major weapon in the struggle against the White Paper and as a vital way to consolidate the Yishuv's strength. Eyes turned to the sea — the bridge between Palestine and the Diaspora.

Ben-Gurion returned from London on April 3 and shortly thereafter was hospitalized for three days for checkups. The high amount of sugar found in his blood was attributed to excitement and nervous tension. Even so, he had returned from the political battle in London with a greater fighting spirit than ever, and immediately started to mobilize the political system and the Yishuv's public opinion for a struggle against Britain's policy.

The events around the illegal immigrant ships the *Agios Nikolaus* and the *Astia* on April 2 and 4 reinforced his opinion that illegal immigration was the main weapon in both the struggle against immigration restrictions and the fight to prevent the creation of an Arab state in Palestine. He firmly believed that the Yishuv would be able to meet this task and that despite its navy and its guns, Great Britain would not be able to crush it; not because its was weak, but because "this is the British Empire and not Germany!"[40] The British government, Ben-Gurion claimed, would hesitate to use force to prevent illegal immigration. If "it were forced to build detention camps in Palestine, carry out mass arrests and even shoot at ships, it would find itself in a very difficult situation."[41] His practical conclusion was that the stopping of ships and the deportation of immigrants must be responded to, lest public opinion in the world got used to such acts; and "if they shoot at Jews trying to break into the country—the world will be outraged."[42]

Ben-Gurion failed to mention that news had already filtered through that the British government was considering building a detention camp for illegal immigrants in Cyprus. It was wishful thinking on his part when he said that the British police, navy, and air force had announced that they were powerless to fight illegal immigration.[43] On the contrary, the navy and the air force had accepted the task. Permanent patrols by four Royal Navy vessels began operating at the end of April, and a few days later they were joined by routine Royal Air Force patrol flights (only in the first week of August did it emerge that the warships would be stopping their pursuit of immigrants due to the deteriorating international situation). Katznleson disagreed with Ben-Gurion's view that a British government that would give orders to open fire on immigrants would not survive one week: "I am not confident of this," he said. "They have already shot at ships. And apparently people were injured, and I am not sure the English press reported it."[44]

On May 3, Weizmann wrote to the Jewish-Swiss (Corfu-born) author Albert Cohen, who at Weizmann's request had tried to set up a Jewish Legion Committee to recruit Jewish refugees in France. He described the suffering of the Jews—"a poor human cargo" as he called them—who were tossed around for weeks of unimaginable hardships far out at sea, were exploited, starved, and stolen from by pirate ship captains, but were ready to take it as long as there was a slim chance of getting to land, because "the poor souls have nowhere to go to; they are homeless, persecuted animals."[45] On June 5 Josiah Wedgwood said in Parliament that the British government's behavior was more appropriate for Hitler: MacDonald "may succeed in stopping this illegal immigration, but if he does the report of it will stink in the nostrils of posterity."[46]

In July 1939, the British government ruled that an immigration permit would cover only one additional dependent, a wife or a child. On July 26, the historian Professor Lewis Namier wrote a letter to the editor of the *Times* in which he reacted to MacDonald's announcement in Parliament a week earlier that 8,000 permits—the number of the illegal immigrants that had arrived and were expected to arrive in the next six months—would be deducted from the immigration quotas. MacDonald, Namier noted, did not even wait to see how many illegal immigrants would make it into Palestine; he added: "The Jews do not, and never will, acknowledge the legal validity of Mr. MacDonald's White Paper, but it now appears that neither does Mr. MacDonald himself." On August 5, Namier protested that the immigration regulations forced refugees to leave their families behind: "I ask once more: why can not the wives and children of refugees who received visas for Palestine be booked against the 25,000 whose admission is promised as soon as 'their maintenance is ensured'? In fact, Mr. MacDonald decided to exclude them under the White Paper." A campaign of pressure and lobbying succeeded in changing the policy, and in August 1939, during the Twenty-First Zionist Congress, the decision was repealed.

At dawn on January 12, 1938, at his hotel in Tel Aviv, Yehuda Braginsky received a note from Yisrael Galili, a leader in the Haganah headquarters, saying that the "tub" *Poseidon*, with sixty-five pioneers on board, had reached the Emek Hefer beach after a nerve-racking delay and that the disembarkation had been successful. Galili wrote: "It's done. God be praised."[47]

In 1938 Ben-Gurion vigorously opposed any illegal immigration that was organized without the Jewish Agency Executive's approval. When he heard that the illegal immigrant ship *Poseidon*, which had sailed on January 3 from the port of Lavrio on the southern tip of the Attica peninsula, had reached the shores of Palestine on January 12, carrying sixty-five illegal immigrants from the Hechalutz Hachshara in Poland who had been let ashore opposite moshav Avihail in Emek Hefer, he welcomed this success. Nevertheless, he was furious that the operation was carried out without authority and threatened to take its organizers to a disciplinary court (the ship sailed again on May 17 and once again managed to let its passengers ashore).[48]

During 1938 Ben-Gurion began to see illegal immigration as a vital political tool, and at the Mapai central committee meeting on December 15 he presented his plan for an "immigration revolt." Katznelson dismissed the idea: "Ben-Gurion talked about 'rebellious immigration.' I don't know how many ships will come; a few ships with a few thousand people will come and stand near the beach and not be allowed into the country." Although some party members supported Ben-Gurion, and Shlomo Levkovich (Lavi) called out to Weizmann, "Give the order!"[49] the call for an "immigration revolt" did not earn much backing or support. But Ben-Gurion did not abandon the idea, and after the White Paper's publication he wrote to Brandeis on June 6 that the British would not dare send boats carrying illegal immigrants back out to sea. Therefore the Yishuv must acquire ships, a task that would require great sums of money.[50] When he demanded that the Agency Executive increase the budget dedicated to immigration he met with the refusal of the Agency's treasurer, Kaplan, who thought that "Aliyah Bet cannot take the place of (the legal) Aliyah Aleph."[51] Few, if any, took Ben-Gurion's talk of immediately organizing the illegal immigration of a thousand illegal immigrants per week or founding a de facto Jewish state in the parts of Palestine populated by Jews seriously.[52]

The illegal immigration activists were not keen, to say the least, on a showy operation that would endanger both the immigrants and the immigration. They saw Ben-Gurion's words as no more than rhetoric. Tabenkin, who had returned from a visit to Poland in the fall of 1938, wrote that only there did he learn about "the value of Aliyah Bet. Without it there is almost no life for the movement, because there is no air to breathe."[53] His conclusion was: "There is no hope for legal immigration alone; what *Davar* should write is: any ship sent back will return, and Jews will keep coming night after night."[54] On his way to London in November 1938, Tabenkin had claimed that now that the subject of the Jewish state had come off the agenda, "We must focus on ways to further Zionism rather than on the state of the Jewish people." Four subjects were on the agenda: "immigration, land, weapons, ships."[55] The illegal immigration must continue, but *surreptitiously* rather than as a demonstrative act. On July 18, 1938, the Yishuv announced a general strike and a curfew to protest the curb on immigration.

Several more illegal immigrant ships arrived at Palestine's shores in 1938: the *Artemisia* sailed from the port of Lavrio on April 19, carrying 128 pioneers, and returned in July with another 158. The *Atrato* sailed on November 25 from the port of Bari in southern Italy and five days later let 300 pioneers from Poland ashore in Palestine. On April 1 the Greek ship *Assimi*, made for shipping cattle, sailed from the Constanta port carrying 268 pioneer members who were joined by some of the passengers of the *Katina*. It managed to let ashore 230 passengers before being stopped by the British coast guard and sent away from Haifa with around 240 illegal immigrants on board. On April 29, it approached Tel Aviv beach and let ashore another twelve passengers, before being discovered and sailing to the Greek island of Kea. On June 7 the ship returned to Palestine, and its passengers, who disembarked at the Naharia beach, were arrested and released after a week. The number of illegal immigrants was deducted from the official quota of certificates.

The Haganah organized large "spontaneous" demonstrations against the deportation in Haifa, with slogans and pamphlets distributed around town: "For every ship [turned away] a hundred will follow" and "the ships of despair will return." The *New York Times* described the *Assimi*'s story extensively on April 24, remarking that the sternest British judge could not treat the illegal immigrants as criminals and send them "back to hell."

On June 3 the United States consul general in Jerusalem reported on the arrival of the illegal immigrant ship *Liesel*, organized by the Maccabi association in Vienna; 921 immigrants from Poland, Romania, Germany, and Czechoslovakia had sailed on the Danube in two river vessels to the port of Sulina in Romania, where they embarked on the *Liesel* and set sail to Palestine on May 23. The British secret police tracked the ship's movements, a British reconnaissance plane discovered it on June 1 opposite Jaffa beach, and the ship was stopped and brought to the port. The consul general continued to report on the arrival of other illegal immigrant ships. The United States representative in Bucharest also reported that the *Liesel* had sailed and that the British ambassador to Romania was pressuring the Romanian government to stop the sailings.[56] In Jerusalem the Mandate government's Immigration Offices were set on fire. The immigrants were allowed ashore, and were deducted from the next quota of immigration permits.

There is no "immigration revolt" without ships. Ben-Gurion did more than just declare that "we should discover the sea" and express regret that in a Mediterranean bustling with all kinds of ships, "there is not even one Jewish ship."[57] His door was open to anyone who had an idea. In September 1937, Ussishkin had been thrilled by the arrival of the ship *Sarah I*, which carried the students of Betar's naval school in Civitavecchia to Tel Aviv. The ship had sailed on August 18, 1937, from Genoa and had anchored in Haifa on September 1. The Tel Aviv municipality organized a formal reception for the crew.[58] The excited Ussishkin declared that the Jewish National Fund would allocate a 25-acre area for a fishing village with naval schools and shipyards.[59]

On August 25, 1938, Ben-Gurion was visited by Major Frank Bearsted, an English shipping expert who proposed to set up four sea lines between Europe and Palestine. One of the lines would be an "immigration line" that would operate two 1,500-capacity vessels from the Polish port of Gdynia. Bearsted estimated that the cost of setting up the line would come to around 350,000 Pp.[60] In the early hours of the morning on April 22, 1939, Ben-Gurion was taken on a motorboat from the Tel Aviv port to inspect the shore between Tel Aviv and Caesarea and discovered an "empty beach." He envisaged creating tens of Jewish fishing villages, which would secure the shore and help the illegal immigrant ships. The following day he told the Agency Executive: "If the Jewish Yishuv in Palestine will eat Jewish fish there will be room for 4,000 fishermen. In addition to a livelihood for Jewish families, our shore will be Jewish."[61] He also proposed purchasing a radio-equipped ship for 5,000 Pp.[62]

These plans never materialized. On the other hand, the illegal immigration was renewed. In order to turn it into a "national project" that could bring "the maximum benefit,"[63] the responsibility for organizing illegal immigration was transferred from the Histadrut and Hechalutz to the Jewish Agency.[64] The illegal immigration apparatus required reorganization after the Greek government decided, under pressure from the British government, to close its ports to illegal immigrant ships, and the operation's center of activity moved from Athens to Paris. The Aliyah Bet activists settled in the modest Metropol hotel at 6 Victor Hugo Avenue, near the Arc de Triomphe, whence they oversaw the complex scheme. Shaul Meirov became the de-facto head of the Mossad LeAliyah Bet and Braginsky continued to coordinate activities.[65] The number of illegal immigrants who managed to leave Europe and make it into Palestine grew, but it was still a far cry from the enormous numbers that Ben-Gurion had envisaged. In February 1939 the British navy increased its presence along Palestine's shores and most of the illegal immigrant ships failed to make it ashore.

The renewal and institutionalization of illegal immigration by the Haganah were partly inspired by the success of the Revisionist movement, which continued the activity it had started a year earlier. The ship *Agios Nikolaus I* set sail on March 22. Hermann Flesch, head of the immigration office in Czechoslovakia and of the NZO immigration office in Brno, organized a group of 692 immigrants, including 150 Betar members, that sailed on two river vessels on the Danube as far as the Romanian port of Tulcea. There the group boarded the *Agios Nikolaus* and continued to the port of Sulina. The ship reached Palestine's shores on the night of March 31, but failed to let off its passengers. Two British warships and a police vessel ordered it to stop, and when it accelerated they opened fire. One of the passengers was killed. The *Agios Nikolaus I* was forced to return to the Aegean Sea.[66]

The ship *Astia*, purchased by an anonymous private individual, sailed with 699 refugees from Germany and Czechoslovakia on board, including around 100 women and around 50 children. It reached the Herzliya beach on April 2, after some four weeks of wandering at sea. Three coast guard boats opened fire and forced it to anchor in Haifa.[67] All the illegal immigrants were arrested.

On June 28, after a difficult journey, the ship *Astir*, organized by the Revisionist movement, reached Palestine's shores with 724 illegal immigrants from Danzig, Romania, Hungary, and Bulgaria on board. Britain offered the Romanian government financial aid to return the refugees to their countries of origin. Another proposal, to allow the refugees to stay in Cyprus temporarily, was rejected. The *Astir*'s passengers threw their Polish passports overboard, but because they had Romanian visas for "transit to Venezuela," Romanian authorities refused Britain's demand to prevent the ship from sailing. The ship sailed on March 6 from the port of Reni in Romania (today in western Ukraine), and on April 3 approached the Haifa port. A British warship opened fire, and the ship returned out to sea. Finally it anchored at the port of Lavrio, on the southern tip of the Attica peninsula. On May 18, the ship anchored at the island of Chios, and the passengers declared a hunger strike. On June 28, the *Astir* managed to reach the *Rishon* Letzion beach, but ran into two police vessels. Its passengers, who were transported to the Ashkelon beach on fishing vessels, were arrested (some of them were released on July 4 and the rest a little later, and their numbers were deducted from the quota of immigration permits).[68]

In October 1938 Jabotinsky met with the king of Romania in London. The king insisted that the meeting be kept secret (its existence was leaked to the press after it had taken place). Jabotinsky—who described the king as a "cultured antisemite" who was willing to "look for a fair way to relieve his country of a surplus of Jews"—obtained his agreement to allow river vessels passage on the Danube, an international waterway that did not necessitate transit visas, on their way to one of the Black Sea ports.[69] The hope that the Romanian king would persuade the British government to open Palestine's gates proved futile.

On October 14, 1938, the Af-Al-Pi Aliyah activists wrote to Jabotinsky in London about the great difficulties that were hampering their activities in Czechoslovakia, mainly for lack of money. After the required sum was received, at the beginning of January, around 750 refugees from Czechoslovakia and Betar members from Austria boarded a train in Brno (Moravia) and traveled to Balchik on the southwest shore of the Black Sea. There they boarded the ship *Katina*, which sailed on January 18 to Varna, where its passengers were joined by forty others. The sailing conditions were rough: the food store rotted, the drinking water spilled into the sea, many of the passengers fell ill, and four of them (plus one sailor) died.[70] When the *Katina* reached the Herzliyah beach, more than 200 of its passengers managed to get ashore in the fishing boat *Artemisia* before the coast guard discovered the ship. The British opened fire and captured nineteen illegal immigrants.

The ship returned out to sea. Coal was running out and a typhus epidemic broke out among the passengers. Jabotinsky phoned the immigration office in Prague from Paris, expressing concern for the passengers' fate. An envoy traveled to Athens to inquire after their condition. After delays and difficulties, the *Katina* sailed again, collecting near Crete the approximately 750 passengers of the ship *Geppo II* that had carried immigrants from Poland and Romania and had run aground and sunk on March 10. Now, with around 1,250 women, men, and children crowded on board, the *Katina* put down anchor opposite the Netanya beach and managed to let ashore around 700 immigrants before being discovered by patrol planes. The following night, when it approached the shore, the British shot at it and it escaped out to sea. Again its passengers suffered a few rough days before the ship returned to the Kfar Vitkin beach and let off around 360 of them.[71] The rest of the passengers were taken ashore on a sailboat, and only after desperate demonstrations on the vessel and protest demonstrations in Haifa were they allowed to go ashore, where they were arrested.

In November 1938, the Revisionist movement opened an immigration office in Poland, headed by Yosef Katznelson and Eri Jabotinsky. The office was designed, among other things, to offer an alternative to the private entrepreneurs who demanded great sums of money from the immigrants and handled them like "human traffickers."[72]

Following the White Paper's publication, Menachem Begin, who had been appointed head of Betar in Poland in March 1939, wrote that Britain could only stem the Jews' will to immigrate to Palestine by using brutal methods, similar to those that the Nazis used in Germany. The country's locked gates would not be brought down by an armed rebellion, but by "a spontaneous movement; to try and stop it would be like putting up a beam against a powerful stream."[73]

The ship *Parita* was purchased by the Revisionist movement's immigration office and sailed from the port of Sète near Marseille to the port of Constanta carrying around 80 refugees from Germany who had been smuggled across several borders on their way to Marseille. In Constanta they were joined by 644 Betar members from Poland and Romania.[74] Yaakov Ariel, one of the *Parita*'s passengers, published in 1944 a long description of the difficult voyage endured by the 1,200-ton vessel's 724 passengers:

> On the evening of July 12, 1939, we left Bucharest in two train cars. At 7 a.m. we arrived in Constanta. We were driven to the harbor in carts and carriages. After several minutes we saw from afar a ship with hundreds of men and women crowded on it. On two narrow ladders leading to the captain's bridge and at the ship's stern we saw two people wearing black boots holding thin sticks and giving orders. [. . .] Finally I discovered among the dozens of crammed people a hole in the deck and a ladder leading into the hull. I climbed down with my rucksack and suitcase and found myself standing on a filthy and slippery floor in which there was another hole like the one I had just climbed through. Around me I saw beds as narrow as wardrobes and made of planks. [. . .] Downstairs it was completely dark, because there was no electricity. We felt our way in the dark and found a long ledge made of planks and covered with mats, and half a meter above it there was another ledge made of planks similar to the one on the bottom. "Here," we were told, "will be your bunk!"

After describing the tough living conditions and the tension among the groups of passengers from different countries of origin, Ariel told about the forty days of the voyage, including the "military discipline" that the ship's commanders imposed on the passengers. A week after setting sail the situation on the ship worsened. On July 31 it anchored at the port of Rhodes, close to the passenger ship *Marco Polo*, lit by hundreds of colorful lanterns, anchored next to it: "We heard the sounds of dance music. We were just standing in line to get our supper. Our ship was dark. The iron stairs were slippery and damp, the aluminum bowls with the warm liquid burned our fingers." From Rhodes the *Parita* sailed to the port of Izmir, where it was forbidden to put down anchor. Only after great urging was the ship able to replenish its water and food supplies and sail on. At 3 a.m. on August 22 it reached the Tel Aviv shore.[75]

The illegal immigration organized by the Revisionist movement and by private entrepreneurs earned much criticism. In April 1939, Yitzhak Yatziv published a piece in *Davar* titled "Of the seafarers' hardships." He quoted the words of a "refugee" describing the voyage on one of the illegal immigrant ships (probably the *Astir*, which was organized by Z. H. Segal from Danzig and set sail on March 6, 1939, from the Romanian port of Reni), and remarked that the descriptions he heard were "similar to what we have read in stories about pirates." This illegal immigrant paid 80 pounds for the voyage (others paid more), and after many hardships boarded the ship:

> We saw a group of people in whom the wanderings, border smuggling and imprisonment had wreaked havoc. And if up until then we had been in the company of refugees who had mostly been affluent until the day they set off, here there were people on whom hardships had already left their mark. [. . .] We see our ship anchored in the harbor. We embark on it. We had just enough time to stretch our limbs after the cramped train car before we climbed a ladder down to the ship that promised to take us ashore. It was an average sized 2,000-ton ship. After climbing down I was soon disappointed. It was an old, neglected ship, full of filth and in visible disrepair. Into this tomb were gathered 750 people—including 250 women and 15 children. Inside, sleeping bunks on several levels. [. . .] Sacks filled with straw served as mattresses. Once you lay on your side you could not turn around again—the space was too narrow. But the hardest thing was the air down there. It was the rainy season, everything was covered—and the stuffiness was horrendous.[76]

Yatziv's "refugee" described the military discipline the ship's authorities implemented: from the first day they "punished and abused us" while they themselves enjoyed special privileges. Among other things, a man suspected of stealing food was hung for three hours on the mast, searches were conducted among all the passengers, and knives and flashlights were confiscated.[77] The British described the illegal immigration as a "dirty, sordid, crooked business" and the conditions on the ships as unbelievably filthy and crowded.[78]

Yatziv ignored the countless difficulties faced by the organizers of illegal immigration. Some of the people involved exploited the passengers' plight, ship owners and captains were often driven by greed, and government officials in the countries of origin either turned a blind eye or offered help, mostly for antisemitic reasons. However, some of those involved acted out of humanitarian motives. Moreover, Yatziv ignored the fact that despite the flawed organization, the hardships of the voyage and the suffering, several hundred refugees—including those who were transported like "cattle"—reached a safe haven in Palestine thanks to this immigration.

Katznelson told Jabotinsky when they met in Paris after the Twenty-First Zionist Congress that although on several occasions he had condemned the conditions on the ships organized by private individuals associated with the Revisionist movement, he could not "belittle people who even now are endeavoring to bring immigrant ships to Palestine."[79] The sea route was the route to salvation for many "ordinary emigrants," as Ben-Gurion described them — those who unlike the pioneers were not coming "to give to the country," and whom Katznelson described at the Twenty-First Zionist Congress as "human dust carried upon the seas," but "human dust which history has chosen to fulfill its mission."[80]

On May 18, 1939, the center of the Mossad LeAliyah Bet in Paris received a telegram in which it was asked to send — at any cost — a ship that would reach Palestine on May 19 "with no matter which immigrants on board." Braginsky reacted: "It is strange and saddening that people who knew that their telegram would only be received in Paris on Tuesday imagined that by the next day, Wednesday, an illegal immigrant ship from Europe would already have been organized and have reached Palestine's shores."[81] The Mossad had no choice but to increase the payment each pioneer/immigrant had to pay for the port expenses and for the voyage itself. It was also forced to take on "non-pioneers," eroding the principle that advised against bringing to Palestine "human material that cannot adapt to the country's harsh living conditions."[82]

The illegal immigration operation in all its various branches took advantage of the "window of opportunity" that had opened between the Nazis' takeover of Austria and Czechoslovakia and the outbreak of the Second World War, and of the temporary meeting of interests between the representatives of the Zionist movements and the policy of the Nazi regime and of other regimes in Eastern Europe (chiefly Poland and Romania) of encouraging illegal immigration and even expediting and helping it.

In May 1938, as mentioned, Eichmann arrived in Vienna at the behest of Reinhard Heydrich, head of the security police (SD), and set up the Zentralstelle (the Central Office) in the expropriated Rothschild palace. The office simplified the procedures for getting immigration permits, and Eichmann allowed the representatives of the Jewish organizations to put in place plans to get Jews out of the Reich. In some cases, Gestapo personnel escorted the trains to ensure their border crossing. After managing to get around 117,000 Jews out of Austria, Eichmann was sent to Prague to pursue a similar goal. In 1938 and 1939 around 258,000 Jews left the countries of the Reich. Illegal immigrants to Palestine made up 7.4 percent of all of Jewish emigrants.[83] In the month prior to the outbreak of war — August 1939 — eight ships sailed to Palestine, carrying more than 5,000 illegal immigrants, mostly from the Reich countries.[84]

The refugees' hardships made no impression on the British government.

It resented the Eastern European governments' wish to "get rid" of Jews by sending them to Palestine.[85] British secret agents tracked the organization of refugees and vessels and Britain's diplomatic delegates pressured the various governments to prevent any activity that aided illegal immigration.[86] At times the refugees' situation elicited a modicum of compassion among British government circles, but usually they portrayed them as lawbreakers, as people who were unsuitable to settling in Palestine, and even as spies. Warships and fast coast guard vessels that had arrived from Britain succeeded in the summer of 1939 in controlling Palestine's shores and stopping most of the illegal immigrant ships.

It is impossible not to see the similarity between Ben-Gurion and Jabotinsky's positions. Both believed that bringing ships crammed with illegal immigrants, which the British soldiers would overtake by force, would make a great impression on global public opinion. Ben-Gurion wanted the ship *Etrato*, which sailed from Constanta in May 1939, to put down anchor opposite Tel Aviv. When he found out on May 28 that the ship and the illegal immigrants on board it had been captured, he wanted to seize the ship at the Haifa port and release the illegal immigrants by force. The heads of the Mossad LeAliyah Bet did not comply with this dramatic outburst.[87] What Ben-Gurion saw as the Jewish public's indifference to the fate of the ships and the illegal immigrants also provoked the wrath of Jabotinsky, who in a speech at a mass rally in Warsaw that month called for active resistance to the illegal immigrants' deportation: "Where were the 50,000 Jews of Haifa? How did they allow them to be sent back?!" His words also referred to the fate of several other ships that had arrived at Palestine's shores the previous months. Now Jabotinsky withdrew his opposition to illegal immigration and called it a "national sport."[88] He saw this immigration as a way to overcome the pressing lack of certificates and prove to the Polish authorities that the Revisionist movement was doing everything it could to advance Jewish immigration despite the White Paper, and for the movement to become "the representative of the entire nation." Although he was aware of the sometimes suspect character of the private initiatives, which provided fertile ground for profiteering and extortion, he gave his blessing to the coordination of immigration by the movement's bodies.

At the Betar world conference in Warsaw in September 1938, upon hearing Begin's words on the need to take Palestine by force of arms, Jabotinsky could not help but interrupt, calling out: "Can he please tell me, how is he going to get the Betarite soldiers into the country without the charity of foreigners [that is, without British approval]?" Begin explained that it was "only an idea"; the way to realize it should be "discussed by the experts." Jabotinsky insisted: "Has he noticed the proportion of the Jewish military force in Palestine and the Arab military force?" Unsparing, he called the words of the rising young star in Betar in Poland "screeches" that should be "brutally suppressed." There was no comparison between Palestine and Italy or Ireland, he explained, because in the Jewish context it was the question of getting into the country that was at stake. His staunch opinion was that those who mistrusted the world's conscience were heading toward dangerous despair. Believing in the possibility of taking Palestine by force of arms meant Zionism's suicide. Therefore, those despairing were faced with two possibilities: jumping into the water of the Vistula or joining the Communist movement. Another possibility was "to do a (Wilhelm) Rippel and lead Jews on foot from Poland to Palestine. The bitter truth is this: Palestine and the countries of the Jews' Diaspora are worlds apart."[89]

Still, the success of bringing around 12,000 illegal immigrants to the shores of Palestine encouraged the leaders of Betar and the Irgun—who demanded priority for their people—to believe that they were capable of organizing a "fleet" of ships carrying military-trained illegal immigrants. These immigrants would land on Palestine's shores and take over the country: "The only route to salvation is to conquer Palestine, the route of war and blood." The Revisionist literature claims that on the eve of war the preparations to take over Palestine were "at an advanced stage" and the sailing of 10,000 trained and armed fighters had reached an operative stage.[90]

The plans for an "immigration revolt"—the declarations that "the Jewish Yishuv in Palestine, with the help of the Jewish people around the world, will take the organization of immigration to Palestine into its own hands"[91] and the plans for an "invasion from the sea" and the conquest of Palestine—were highly unrealistic. In reality, around 3,000 illegal immigrants arrived in Palestine in 1938, and 19,139 immigrants in 1939, of whom around 12,000 were illegal.[92] As mentioned above, as of the middle of 1939 the number of illegal immigrants who were caught was deducted from the official quotas.[93] From March to September 1, 1939, around twenty ships, carrying around 9,000 illegal immigrants, were caught. The majority of the immigrants were refugees from the three countries of the Reich, while a minority came from Poland.[94] Five thousand immigration permits were allocated by summer 1939, but many of those who received them did not manage to leave their countries of origin in time.[95]

In a memorandum written on September 21, the U.S. consul general in Jerusalem listed the illegal immigrant ships that had arrived in Palestine since June 1939, carrying around 5,000 immigrants. Now, he wrote, they would be joined by many illegal immigrants fleeing Poland. Britain would find it harder to stop this immigration, he estimated, because its organizers were using new tactics.[96]

Five ships that sailed to Palestine between March 1939 and spring 1940 —the *Astir*, the *Parita*, the *Naomi Julia*, the *Skaria*, and the *Pancho*, carrying around 3,800 illegal immigrants—were organized by the Revisionist movement. During the same period, the Mossad LeAliyah Bet organized ten voyages, carrying around 4,800 immigrants, and between May and the end of August 1939 the Mossad sent three ships: the *Colorado*, the *Dora*, and the *Tiger Hill*. During the same period private entrepreneurs organized seventeen voyages, carrying 9,086 illegal immigrants.[97] The talk of a "fleet of ships" that was starting to stream toward Palestine's shores was an exaggeration.[98] Nevertheless, despite all the difficulties and restrictions, from 1934 to 1939 around fifty ships arrived at Palestine's shores, bringing 20,000 to 35,000 illegal immigrants. Around two-thirds were organized by the Revisionist movement, by movement activists together with private parties, or by people acting on their own initiative.

Does this number prove the Revisionist movement's inability to carry out its elaborate plans? Does it prove the Jewish Agency Executive's failure to turn illegal immigration into a national enterprise because of its wish to avoid risking relations with Britain? Would it be right to claim that the organization of illegal immigration after the Second World War indicates that it was also possible to purchase more vessels and bring more immigrants before the war?[99]

Perhaps if the Revisionist movement had managed to raise more funds and if the Mossad LeAliyah Bet had had a larger budget it would have been possible to increase the number of vessels, overcome the numerous obstacles, and save more Jews. The Revisionist movement, which saw itself as an alternative Zionist organization and forestalled the Jewish Agency in creating an organizational setup for illegal immigration, invested a great deal of effort and resources in its organization, and was more successful in this area than the Jewish Agency.[100]

Private initiatives were also more successful: from September through December 1939, for example, the Zionist activist from Bulgaria, Baruch Confino, organized the immigration of more than a thousand illegal immigrants from the port of Varna. Even an illegal immigration on a bigger scale, however, would not have been able to build a bridge of ships over the White

Paper and move Poland closer to Palestine. It could only have offered a lifeline to a small number of people.

From April 1936 to September 1939, 520 Jews were killed as a result of the Arab Revolt (and around 2,500 more people were injured). In his lecture tour in Poland, at the invitation of the country's Friends of the Hebrew University, which included some twenty lectures in various towns, Martin Buber spoke about the "eternal spirituality" that underpinned the Jewish people's existence, about the need to combine universal humanist values and national values, about the fact that many Jews would not be able to make it to Palestine, and about the subsequent need to instill them with the spirit of "ghetto-pioneering."[101] In August 1939, about five months after returning from his tour in Poland, Buber wrote a short piece, titled "The Samsons," condemning the Irgun's actions: in the Jewish Yishuv there were "young men who imagine themselves as Samsons, they consider placing mines in front of vehicles carrying innocent and defenseless strangers and attacking houses populated by innocent families of strangers as Samson-like acts." They annoyed Britain "less than a mosquito annoys a busy man" and in fact were committing suicide. If their way became accepted "we will not leave our children a free and pure country, but they will live in a bandits' cave [. . .] and a bandits' cave is what this Yishuv will be for generations to come."[102]

The elections for the Twenty-First Zionist Congress were held on July 30, 1939. In Palestine around 106,000 voters (about 70 percent of those eligible to vote) voted for six parties. The elections campaign was not particularly passionate. The Revisionists called on their supporters to ban the elections, and in Poland the Zionist movement had difficulty bringing voters to the polls. Only around 138,000 shekel payers out of some 323,000 people eligible to vote turned up to cast their votes.

6

THE FORGOTTEN CONGRESS (GENEVA, AUGUST 16–25, 1939)

Early in the morning on Thursday, August 24, 1939, the 527 delegates, 46 Zionist Executive Committee members, and more than 1,000 guests who had come to the Twenty-First Zionist Congress in Geneva from thirty-five countries[1] had almost no doubt that the news arriving from Berlin and Moscow suggested that war was imminent. The fear of war had increased after the Nazi takeover of Czechoslovakia on March 15 and had intensified in light of the growing tension between Germany and Poland. At the end of September 1938, "after a day of numerous shocks," Katznelson wrote from London: "For several hours it felt as if we were already at war. Hundreds of thousands rushed to leave London, everyone had equipped themselves with gas masks, in the parks there were already workers digging shelters. And the fear of death could be seen on every face in this big metropolis."[2]

In the course of 1939 the level of fear, anxiety, and hope fluctuated. "We are fortunate [he must have meant: 'destined'] to live in a period," wrote Katznelson, "when the events of each day are bigger than the next's, and every event is enough for a whole lifetime."[3] In August 1939 no one could tell whether war would break out and when, and whether it would be a "local war"—between Nazi Germany and Poland—or a pan-European one.

In any case, there is a difference between waiting for war and knowing for certain when it will break out. The Zionist Congress delegates—and not only they, of course—could not have known what was happening behind the scenes of the diplomatic efforts and the military preparations, and could certainly not have known that the wheels of war were moving quickly and would not be stopped at the last minute on the brink of the abyss. They convened in Geneva for what was for them "a Congress held in reaction to the British government's criminal paper [the White Paper]."

The rising tension in Europe led to proposals to cancel the Congress, but these proposals were rejected because the heads of the Zionist Organization believed that the Congress would offer an important stage on which to demonstrate the Zionist camp's unity in terms of its firm opposition to the White Paper published by the British government approximately four months earlier, on May 17, and the ways to fight it. Thus, despite the atmosphere of uncertainty, the anxiety, and the fear that war was imminent, it was decided to hold the Congress as planned. We can only assume that if the Congress participants had known that war would break out at the beginning of September, they would not have come from all over the Jewish world to Geneva and risked finding it difficult and maybe even impossible to return to their countries. On August 16, the opening day of the Congress, none of those attending could have foreseen that following the events of the coming days the Congress discussions would come to be perceived as expressing the terrible impotence of the Zionist movement, tragically demonstrating the Zionist camp's penchant for quarrels and useless arguments even under the shadow of catastrophe.

The atmosphere on the eve of the Congress was far from festive. David Ben-Gurion, chairman of the Jewish Agency Executive since 1935, described the Zionist movement as a "broken, disintegrating movement consumed by hatred. Unjustified hatred, due not only to actual disagreements, but to an exaggerated and sick hatred" among all the parties. This hatred, he explained, fed on the weakness of the Jewish people, "on the state of helplessness we find ourselves in, and on the fact that we have no state institutions and no power of coercion."[4] Ben-Gurion was referring, among other things, to the fact that the Congressional elections that had been held at the end of July had taken place amid claims of fictitious distribution of shekels ("the shekel market") and of vote rigging,[5] as well as to arguments over organizational matters. Could such a torn, weak movement, whose morale was at its lowest ebb, "withstand the hard and possibly protracted struggle on which we are embarking?" Ben-Gurion wondered.[6] *The Jewish Chronicle*, the mouthpiece of English Jewry, asked: will it be "Congress—or Cackle?"—would it be held in a spirit of optimism and confidence, or would they hear inane and useless condemnations of the British government: "Let us hope that the delegates assembled will not be fobbed off with a lot of silly denunciations of the British government—over which they have, as [we have seen] practically no influence."[7]

During the Congress the delegates were able to glean some of the political and diplomatic events from press reports about the international tension that seemed to be coming to a head. They could not have known, however, that in Berlin, despite the hesitations and delays, the decision had already been taken to invade Poland, and the date had been set: August 26.

On August 13, Field Marshall Goering, who was acting behind the scenes to try and reach a compromise with Britain, revealed to Nevile Henderson, the British ambassador to Germany, that Poland was destined to be divided between the "two lions."

A week later, on August 19, the first wave of the German army, comprising around 1.8 million troops, moved toward the border with Poland. On August 24, its divisions were in place and ready to attack.[8] On that day Stalin gave a secret speech at the Politburo explaining the considerations guiding him: if the Soviet Union signed an agreement with Britain and France, Germany would seek to reach an agreement with them and war would be averted, whereas if the USSR signed a Non-Aggression Pact with Germany, the Germans would attack Poland and the Western powers' intervention would be inevitable. Such a war would lead to disorder and riots in France and Britain, and the situation would allow the Communist movements to capture power in those countries. It was in the Soviet Union's interest to create the conditions for a war that would exhaust Britain and France. To the question of whether a victory for Nazi Germany would not put the Soviet Union at risk, Stalin replied that this was not an imminent danger, because the western front would exhaust Germany: "Comrades! It is in the interest of the Soviet Union for a war to break out between the Reich and the Anglo-French capitalist block. We must do everything to make sure it lasts as long as possible to exhaust both sides. That is the reason we must agree to sign the treaty the Germans offer us and to work to make sure that war [takes place] . . . and to prepare for the time it ends."[9]

Suspicious of the intentions of Britain and France, which had been party to Hitler's appeasement at Czechoslovakia's expense, Stalin sought to gain time for the Soviet Union and push Nazi Germany away from its border by dividing Poland. Thus, while an Anglo-French military delegation was conducting futile talks in Moscow, the Kremlin agreed on August 12 to open political talks with Nazi Germany. On the evening of August 20, Hitler sent a personal missive to Stalin asking him to receive his foreign minister, von Ribbentrop, on August 23 at the latest. Stalin reacted quickly, and on the evening of August 21 announced that he would see von Ribbentrop on Wednesday, August 23. Albert Speer, "Hitler's architect" (and from the beginning of 1942 the minister of armaments), recalled in his memoirs that Stalin's affirmative answer was received while Hitler was staying at his Berchtesgaden residence in the Alps, and that he cried: "I have them! I have them."[10]

At 11 p.m. the German radio announced the breaking news, and the next morning the Soviet news agency TASS announced von Ribbentrop's expected visit to Moscow. On August 11, Hitler had told his inner circle: "If the West is too stupid and too blind to comprehend" that everything he undertakes was directed against Russia, he would be forced to reach an understanding with the Russians; strike the West first, and after their defeat, turn back against the Soviet Union.[11] Now on August 22 he told his generals: "I had already made this decision [to attack Poland] in the spring, but I thought that I would first turn against the West in a few years, and only after that against the East. But the sequence of these things cannot be fixed [. . .]. I wanted first of all to establish a tolerable relationship with Poland in order to fight first against the West. But [. . .] it became clear to me that, in the event of a conflict with the West, Poland would attack us."[12]

At 4:20 a.m. on August 23, von Ribbentrop and his thirty-two-strong entourage took off in two Condor aircraft from the airport near Salzburg for a snap twenty-four-hour visit to Moscow. The planes were delayed for about two hours because of unexpected fire from the Soviet aerial defense. At 1 p.m., the German delegation landed at Moscow airport, which was decorated for the occasion with swastika flags. It was greeted with a guard of honor, but the national anthems were not played. Von Ribbentrop did not expect to meet Stalin himself, and was very surprised when at 6 p.m. he was invited to have a light supper with the Soviet leader and his foreign minister, Molotov. Stalin agreed with von Ribbentrop that only the stupidity of the other countries allowed Britain to rule the world. Nazi Germany's foreign minister felt in Moscow, as he told Hitler, "like among old party members." Stalin raised a toast to the Führer and said that he knew how much the German nation loved him.[13]

Von Ribbentrop immediately informed Hitler about the agreement, and champagne glasses were raised in the Eagle's Nest in the Bavarian Alps. Hitler was delighted: "Now I have Europe. The others can have Asia." Twenty-four hours after its arrival, the German delegation left Moscow satisfied with their achievement, and Hitler flew to Berlin to greet von Ribbentrop. Robert Coulondre, the French ambassador to Moscow, reported to Paris that the Non-Aggression Pact would contribute greatly to boosting the Nazi regime's confidence in the strength of the German army.[14] Ivan Maisky, the Russian ambassador to London, who believed that Chamberlain wanted a "new Munich" but was too late because Hitler's appetite had grown so rapidly, was surprised by the agreement and wrote in his diary: "Our policy is obviously undergoing a sharp change of direction, the meaning and consequences of which are not yet entirely clear to me."[15]

Ostensibly the Ribbentrop-Molotov Pact was a treaty of non-aggression between the Soviet Union and Nazi Germany, but in fact it was an agreement to divide Poland. Article 2 in the "secret protocol" appended to it said that if war broke out, Poland and the Baltic states would be divided between Germany and the USSR. The map that was attached to the agreement showed the borders of Poland's partition between the occupiers and the areas of "Restpolen," which included the ethnic Polish regions on both sides of the Vistula. A second agreement signed on September 29 moved the dividing line from the Vistula to the Bug River, in fact abandoning the idea that Restpolen Article 2 in the pact gave Germany a free hand to attack Poland and was based on the assumption that England would not go to war, because after the Soviet Union would seize its part of the Polish territory, England would refrain from declaring war on it.[16] The Intelligence Department of the German army's High Command promised Hitler that Britain and France would protest against a German attack on Poland but would refrain from taking any military measures. On August 23, Poland reacted to the pact with a general mobilization of its army.

The newspapers in Europe and in Palestine reported von Ribbentrop's flight to Moscow on August 23: "Von Ribbentrop will fly from Salzburg to Königsberg and from there to Moscow," and on Wednesday morning will be received for an interview with Stalin and Molotov, wrote *Haaretz*. The newspaper proceeded to explain that the visit would conclude with the signing of a Non-Aggression Pact between Germany and the Soviet Union: a pact that did not contradict the defensive pact among the Soviet Union, Britain, and France. Nevertheless, the editorial thought that the agreement could have a terrible influence on the international situation: "The astonishing news of a conspiracy between Stalin and Hitler, through von Ribbentrop and behind the backs of the military delegations from England and France, regarding a non-aggression pact between Germany and the Soviets has put an end to all the illusions about a broad and active 'peace front' against the aggressive plots of the Rome-Berlin axis."[17]

In Lviv, Wiktor Chajes wrote in his diary:

> Surely history knows nothing similar. Hitler has changed direction and is walking hand in hand with Stalin . . . Only a month ago they called each other names: lepers, dogs, crooks—and now they have signed a non-aggression pact. [. . .] It seems to me that there is no method in Adolf's madness, and he is starting to be soft in the head. He succeeded in a few moves, and therefore even the wise men around him totally believed him. But now they may sober up and see that they are being led by a con-

fused madman. [. . .] We may be calm. Time is on Poland's side. Beck is taking good care of his business.[18]

The Nazi-Soviet agreement struck the world like a bolt out of the blue. The Soviet Union's devotees in the Zionist movement were shocked, and as devout believers had to explain and make excuses for the agreement that the Communist power had signed with its sworn enemy. Dugdale, whom Ben-Gurion called "Chaim's prophetess,"[19] wrote in her diary: this day is a "day of deepening mystification as far as outside world is concerned."[20]

The Congress delegates, she wrote, had been arguing all day about the agreement's meaning. Her view was that its immediate result would be that by the weekend someone else would be occupying the seat of the British prime minister, Neville Chamberlain, whose policy had suffered a major blow. Dugdale could not have known, of course, that at 3 p.m. on that day the British Cabinet had convened and announced that the Soviet-Nazi Non-Aggression Pact would not influence Britain's commitment to Poland, and that the British prime minister would repeat these strong words in a personal letter to the Führer.

On August 22, Willy Cohn wrote in Breslau: "I think that Germany wants to create a fait accompli in the East before the western powers could interfere [. . .] it is possible that at this very moment, Germany and Russia have reached an agreement to divide Poland again!" Later that day he wrote: "A massive realignment has occurred in our politics. What some had long presumed has now occurred. An agreement has been signed between Germany and [the] Soviet Union, initially in the area of trade policies, although a non-aggression pact will follow! And so, Poland will have to bend to German will, and perhaps there will now be progress in pacifying the world."[21]

Nevile Henderson, the British ambassador to Berlin, flew from Berlin to Berchtesgaden to hand Hitler the letter on August 23 at noon. Britain began mobilizing the Royal Air Force reserves and issued blackout instructions. As noted above, however, Hitler's moves were based on the assumption that Britain was too weak to help Poland in practice, and the tough-talking letter failed to impress him. The Reuters news agency reported that Hitler informed the British ambassador that he had no intention of heeding Britain's guarantees for Poland's safety. Henderson privately thought that the guarantees that Great Britain had given Poland were restricting British diplomacy.[22]

Arthur Ruppin wrote in his diary on August 24: "Yesterday's news about the signing of a Non-Aggression Pact between Russia and Germany fell like a bombshell. [. . .] It was unexpected and is completely inexplicable. The rumors of war are more and more frequent. Mrs. Dugdale promised me today that the war will break out within two days."[23]

Weizmann wrote years later in his autobiography:

> An atmosphere of unreality and irrelevance hung over the Twenty-First Zionist Congress which sat in Geneva from August 16 to August 25, 1939. We met under the shadow of the White Paper, which threatened the destruction of the National Home, and under the shadow of a war which threatened the destruction of all human liberties, perhaps of humanity itself. The difference between the two threats was that the first was already in action, while the second only pended; so that most of our attention was given to the first, and we strove to assume, at least until the fateful August 22, when the treaty was signed between Germany and Russia, that the second might yet be averted, or might be delayed. But on that day, when Hitler was relieved of the nightmare of having to wage war on two fronts, even the most optimistic of us gave up hope. The Jewish calamity merged with, was engulfed by, the world calamity.[24]

Geneva, in the French southwest part of Switzerland, straddles both sides of the Rhône River, on the shore of Lake Geneva. Its international character was forged after the League of Nations (Palais des Nations) headquarters was built there in 1937. The old city is located on a plateau on the Rhône's left bank and boasts many ancient buildings: a cathedral, city hall, the college founded by the religious reformer Jean Calvin, the Museum of Art and History, and so on. Jewish and Zionist institutions also established their European offices in the city: the Jewish Agency, the World Jewish Congress, the Joint (American Jewish Joint Distribution Committee), and Ort (a society for the promotion of skilled trades that had been founded in Petrograd in 1880 and in 1921 moved to Berlin, Paris, and finally Geneva). The city was well known to many of the Zionist movement's leaders and activists, and in 1936 hosted the first convention of the World Jewish Congress. About a year prior to the Zionist Congress, in July 1938, an international conference was held in the resort town of Évian, on the French side of the lake opposite Lausanne, in an attempt to find destinations for Jewish emigration from the German Reich; it was doomed in advance to fail. Now the beautiful and elegant city was invaded by around 1,500 Zionist party activists and guests. Before and during the Congress it hosted the conferences of various political and public organizations, such as a meeting of the board of trustees of the Hebrew University in Jerusalem and the Jewish Physicians Convention.

Now, in the months prior to the Zionist Congress the question arose whether Geneva was the appropriate venue for the event. Some suggested it should be held in Palestine. Shertok suggested holding it in the United States, because if it were held in Europe it would not get much attention. However, because transporting so many delegates to the United States would have doubled the expenses, it would have been necessary, in Shertok's view, to reduce the number of delegates. The proposals were rejected, and the number of delegates and other Congress attenders who traveled from Palestine was large enough for the shipping companies to offer competitively reduced charges. We have no estimate of the Congress's costs, but according to one calculation the travel expenses of a delegate from Palestine came to around 60 Pp, making the overall cost of only the hundred delegates who came from Palestine around 6,000 Pp. To that should be added the cost of accommodation in Geneva. The travel and accommodation cost around 100 Pp, and of all the delegates from there at least 11,500 Pp; plus there was the cost of organizing the Congress and running it, which must have reached a much higher sum. Indeed, there were those who claimed: "We must not squander the Jewish people's money with such profligacy right now! At a time when thousands of Jewish refugees are starving on the seas and the plains; in Poland, in Romania etc. etc. people are going hungry—it is an unpardonable sin to waste thousands of pounds on bestowing false honors."[25] On the other hand, the sum allotted by the Congress to the Jewish Agency's Immigration Department was 23,000 Pp (out of an overall budget of 365,000 Pp per year).

Yosef Shprintzak wrote about the trip to his wife: "For the first time I saw the new arrangement at the airport in Lod—an airplane station that is better than the one in Alexandria and even than those I have seen in European cities." From Alexandria he sailed to Italy on an Italian ship. The journey was comfortable, the sea was very quiet, but none of the passengers, wrote Shprintzak, was clear on "how to go about things in Geneva, in today's circumstances in the world, in Judaism, regarding England's attitude towards us and in the personal relations among those at the top and those who are candidates for the top."[26]

Other delegates sailed on the French ship *Mariette Pacha* from Beirut to Alexandria and on to Marseille. Ruppin had a small but well-aired first-class cabin. If before leaving he believed that in light of the risk of imminent war the trip was an adventure, now he thought: "The international situation has improved a little, in any case for the time being." During the voyage Ruppin read Edgar Ansel Mowrer's book *Germany Puts the Clock Back*, which came out in 1933 and analyzes the emergence and character of Nazi Germany.[27] He wrote in his diary: "Despite all the likely explanations—the very fact of Hitler's rise in 1919–1933 is astonishing. Can you really capture an entire people with just speeches, half-truths and relentless propaganda?" On July 24 he wrote in Chamonix-Mont-Blanc, at the foot of the 9,000-foot-high Aiguille du Midi: "The risk of war seems to have diminished. Hitler has announced that he would not go to war over Danzig [. . .]. Rainy weather."[28] Golda Meyerson (Meir), a member of the Zionist Organization's Executive Committee since 1934, "tiredly" explained to her children that she had to go abroad again, this time to the Zionist Congress, "where monumental issues that concerned the life of the Yishuv were going to be thrashed out."[29]

Yosef (Vinitzky) Netz, the correspondent of the Revisionist newspaper *Hayarden* in Geneva, described the voyage as a mirage: here he was sailing from an English port (Haifa), on a Fascist (Italian) vessel in the company of "Socialist Mapai functionaries" dressed in "bourgeois clothes" and "carrying in their round bellies the troubles of the entire Jewish people." They were all going to Geneva to agree on another cut in the partition map —and eventually they would agree to accept Uganda instead of Palestine. This Congress, he predicted, would be "the Congress of suffering and bereavement." He added sarcastically that one should not forget the unimaginable suffering of the functionaries, who every year migrated from the homeland to the Diaspora, unable to find themselves a resting place: "Here I am looking at them, these poor people [. . .]. Every feature in their faces proves how concerned they are for our poor nation. They are so depressed that they cannot even go to the ship's kosher kitchen, and they eat in the non-kosher one."[30]

By contrast, Bracha Habas, the correspondent sent to the Zionist Congress by the Histadrut's newspaper *Davar*, waxed lyrical:

> Switzerland has greeted the early arrivals to the pre-Congress conferences in its usual way: with plenty of greenery, enviable waterfalls, snowy mountains, and also . . . persistent and melancholy rain. We were therefore greatly encouraged by the sudden appearance of a blue-and-white ribbon at one of the stations before Lausanne, which we reached by train at dawn. Every face tired from a sleepless night and blackened by the abundant Italian soot broke into a smile. The ribbon's owner was a young Jewish woman who spoke all the languages, including Hebrew.

Long lists of addresses and prices suggested that she was the Congress's accommodation representative. Indeed, as the train started moving again she turned to her work. Welcoming the guests with rooms in advance, this is one of the useful arrangements that the Congress organizers have implemented this time round.[31]

Netz saw Switzerland in a different light: "The whole of Switzerland is ready for it [the Congress], the sun seems to shine just for us, the sky is spread out for us, the Swiss' *wallets* are ready to receive our money, the stars and the shiksas are all waiting just for us."[32]

Geneva was chosen as the venue for the Twenty-First Zionist Congress because Zurich was hosting the Swiss National Exhibition at the time, and Basel was too close to the German border. Because tourism was down due to the threat of war, rooms were easy to find, and the Geneva municipality was generous with its hospitality. It provided the Congress with several buildings free of charge, most notably the Grand Théâtre on the Old City's Place Neuve, a majestic opera hall inaugurated in 1879 and holding 1,400 seats. This was where the representatives of the Zionist movement intended to discuss mainly the ways of fighting the White Paper of May 1939. The blue-and-white flag was hoisted on a tall mast on the building's roof, and a banner in Hebrew and English above the columns of its entrance read: "The Twenty-First Zionist Congress."[33]

The writer Samuel (Sammy) Gronemann, who had emigrated to Palestine from Germany in 1936 and served as president of the Congress's law court, told the delegates that he had recently visited the painting exhibition brought to Geneva from the Prado museum in Madrid, and had seen "some beautiful pictures, sometimes in small and cheap frames. It is we who have to create the frame for the Congress, and you who have to fill it. I would like the picture of this Congress to be pleasant and very very beautiful."[34]

The number of shekel-payers in fifty-one countries — that is, the number of those eligible to vote in the Congressional elections — reached a record of approximately 1.4 million, and around 300,000 voters took part in the elections. The Congress delegates (264 were elected in electoral districts and 268 represented districts where no elections were held) arrived from nearly all the corners of the Jewish world. There were delegates from Morocco, South Africa, the United States, Canada, and Uruguay, as well as Palestine (133), Poland (109), Austria (12 delegates), Slovakia (6), and Nazi Germany (16), where there were still around 190,000 Jews left (80,000 Zionist shekels were distributed in the country).[35]

The correspondent of the Revisionist newspaper *Der Moment*, who reported derisively on the "Congress festivities," noted that most of the delegates were official or unofficial representatives of the Jewish Agency and that the number of invited guests was so small that it might be necessary to rush over some guests from other Swiss cities.[36] *Davar*, on the other hand, reported with sadness that many familiar faces would be missing this time, most notably the representatives of the Zionist movement in Czechoslovakia, "which has been destroyed and repressed." As a matter of fact, ten delegates did arrive from Prague, after depositing their family members' passports with the Gestapo as a guarantee of their return. The Nazi regime wanted these delegates to try and obtain immigration permits (certificates) or ways to leave Czechoslovakia for the country's remaining Jews.[37] Hebrew was going to be the principal language at the Twenty-First Zionist Congress, *Davar* reported, because the delegations from Germany and Austria were small and the German language "had lost its flavor."

The delegates from Poland endured a grueling journey. Because the German consulate in Warsaw refused to give them transit visas they had to travel to Switzerland via Hungary, Yugoslavia, and Italy. The historian Emanuel Ringelblum described their long journey from Warsaw to Geneva in his diary: "The travails over getting a passport. Not individual passports, but rather collective ones for groups of ten people. The agent promised that war would not break out in September. The fear of traveling in that country [Germany]. Difficulties in securing entry visas which were denied to some of us [. . .]. The pleasant attitude toward us on the train, we could not sense at all the mood of war or hatred toward us. I will eat well in the food car."[38] Ringelblum's party, Poalei Zion Left, which had decided to attend the Congress after a debate at the party conference in May 1938, sent five delegates to Geneva.

The Congress organizers made great efforts to confer it with prestige and respectability. A competition was held to choose the official Congress symbol.[39] The winning design, by the graphic designer David (Heinz) Gumbel from the Bezalel art school, showed a hand with three of its fingers raised and under it the verse "If I forget thee, O Jerusalem."

The commercial department of the insurance company Lloyd Palestine-Egypt in Jerusalem published an illustrated anthology to celebrate the Congress. The organizers rented apartments for delegates and guests (Weizmann and his entourage stayed in luxurious apartments on 12 rue de St-Victor, not far from the Museum of Art, made available by a Swiss friend); organized exhibitions; and published pamphlets in Yiddish, English, German, and Polish. The presidency administration was allocated thirty rooms in the Grand Théâtre building, and another seventy halls and rooms were hired for the different parties in seven adjacent buildings, with a kosher restaurant opening nearby. The delegates were able to use a special telephone service with six main lines. Seventy staff and forty ushers and guards from the Securitas firm were in charge of security and order. The city's hospitality was exemplary, and as a mark of appreciation it was registered in the Golden Book of the Jewish National Fund.

Der Moment's[40] correspondent to Geneva was unimpressed by the organization, telling his readers in Poland that he had heard the townspeople in the cafés talking disparagingly about the Jews. And not because Geneva was an antisemitic city—on the contrary—but because the private firm hired by the Zionist executive to organize the Congress rented all the cheap rooms in town and demanded that the landlords pay them 10 percent for each deal, which had angered them. Such terms were not common in a town as "congress welcoming" as Geneva, he wrote. In any case, the Swiss, who had a developed business sense, took the opportunity to raise the room prices.[41] Shprintzak wrote to his daughter: "This is my fourth day in Geneva. Many delegates are already filling the streets of this lovely city. The various political parties have already started their conferences [. . .], and yet the usual element the eve of Congresses is still missing—a spirit of enthusiasm and expectation; and there is nothing on which to base a guess as to the future of the Geneva gathering and its results."[42]

The first to arrive were the delegates of the Hapoel Hamizrachi movement. Rabbi Simcha-Bunim Feldman, the Hamizrachi leader in Poland, who had immigrated to Palestine in 1924, published in Poland on the eve of the Congress a brochure called *The Fatal Mistake: A Word to Religious Judaism*, in which he called on religious Jews of Poland to vote in the Congressional elections: "Remember, the fate of all of you and your children and your brothers and sisters is in your hands. The Zionist organization is a democratic organization [. . .]. Therefore it is a mitzvah for every religious Jew to purchase a shekel for himself and for any adult in his family. [. . .] Only thus can religious Jews atone for their fatal mistake in the last thirty years."

They were followed by the delegates of Young Wizo, the General Zionists delegates, and the Mapai delegates. The cafés, especially those around the theater building, filled with delegates and guests exchanging views about the desirable nature of the Congress, but offering no practical ideas. *Der Moment* showed a great love for anecdotes, its correspondents sharpening their pens to mock the Congress. They reported mainly on what struck them as futile talk and grumblings. At the stormy opening session of the Hamizrachi conference, for example, the newspaper's correspondent listened to passionate speeches against Mapai and accusations against the Jewish Agency and Weizmann. "A flood of words flowed forth," he wrote. He also wrote that the delegates of "Hamizrachi savored the report about the new yeshiva that had opened in Tel Aviv, serving 300 students, and a generous donation to build another yeshiva." He added ironically that most of the café-goers in Geneva were displaying optimism; after all, Chamberlain himself had promised Weizmann at the Round Table Conference in London (the St. James Conference)—at least this was what the delegate Haim Licht had told the Warsaw-based journalist—that in a few years the Jewish people would rule over the entire Near East. And if this was what the future held, why should they start fighting against Great Britain? They should just wait patiently, and everything would be all right. The journalist from Warsaw saw the Congress as a "charade": the members of Geneva's Jewish community did not take part in it because the admission fees were too expensive: 25 to 35 francs (30 to 40 zloty) for one session and 60 to 100 francs (80 to 120 zloty) for the whole Congress. The journalists too, he remarked, did not conceal their resentment when they had to pay 2 francs for their press card. The representative of a large French telegraph agency left the building in a huff and said he would not cover "a Congress of merchants." His words caused a commotion and a representative of the Congress management rushed to mollify him.

On the eve of the opening session a distinguished delegate from France, the writer Yehoshua Yehuda, exchanged blows at the Lyrique Café near the opera building with Mr. Waldman from the Congress office because he found out that he had been allocated a seat in the third gallery with "all the plebs," rather than in the press circle. Mr. Waldman said what he said, and Mr. Yehuda responded with two slaps. Emanuel Ringelblum wrote: "The delegates spend more time in the Café Lyrique . . . than in the plenary hall." The cafés were teeming and buzzing, with journalists and delegates exchanging views about highly important matters as well as jokes.[43]

Other journalists asked themselves how the Zionist leadership could have left Palestine at a time when the country was awash with blood. This accusation came from the fiery pen of the radical poet Uri Zvi Greenberg: 133 delegates from Palestine, he wrote, had traveled to Geneva at the public's expense to enjoy Switzerland's views, while the beautiful Sea of Galilee and the sad Jordan River were going to stay in the "Palestine protectorate."[44] Two days later, Greenberg lamented that the Divine Spirit had not gone to

Geneva with the delegates — who in the last twenty years had "devoured the body of the Messiah." The Revisionist press stated that the Twenty-First Congress was not "a Zionist Congress but a gathering of traitors and incompetents." Conversely, the *Forverts*, the newspaper that had been founded by the Bund in New York in 1897 and in the 1930s changed its tack to support Zionism, wrote that the Twenty-First Congress was facing the greatest crisis in the history of Zionism, adding that a plan to create a Jewish fleet (and an airline) was being discussed in Geneva.

Der Moment quoted some of the jokes heard in the café:

> "The delegates from Germany were appointed by the Gestapo; those from Palestine — by Mapai."
>
> "If Hamizrachi boycotts the Congress, Zrubavel will shave his beard."

There was also some activity behind the scenes. The illegal immigration activists, for example, met in a modest restaurant to discuss organizing refugee convoys and setting up contacts. "A shocking tragedy is revealed to us in all its horror whenever we speak with the representatives of the persecuted communities in the face of an impending catastrophe," wrote the immigration activist Yehuda Braginsky in his memoirs. The detached and unrealistic nature of the discussions on the subject astounded him.[45]

Few of the Congress delegates' testimonies dealt with speeches or political matters, and there was almost nothing in them to satisfy a reader expecting or wishing to know what took place behind closed doors, or even how the delegates spent their spare time. Ruppin, who stayed on the fifth floor of the Beau Rivage hotel, "in a room overlooking the wonderful view of the lake (12 Swiss francs for the room including breakfast)," wrote in his diary that he used to go and swim in the lake: "Yesterday [the 23rd] and today I swam in the lake again and had lunch there for 1.50 francs."[46]

A faint ray of optimism had emanated from Geneva around two months earlier. In June 1939, the League of Nations' Mandates Commission devoted eleven meetings to discussing the White Paper published by the British government about a month before. Some of the meetings were attended by Britain's colonial secretary Malcolm MacDonald. Weizmann had also come to Geneva at the end of May and had had a long talk with the Swiss representative, William Rappard, the vice chairman of the Mandates Committee.[47] After protracted discussions, the committee decided by a majority of votes (those of the representatives of Belgium, Holland, Norway, and Switzerland) that the policy enunciated in the White Paper "did not conform to the interpretation that the committee—in agreement with the mandatory power and the [League's] council—had given to the British Mandate."[48] The Jewish Agency believed that it had gained a moral victory. However, the League of Nations was a broken reed. Berl Katznelson estimated soberly:

> The Mandates Committee criticized the White Paper. We are obviously grateful for any expression of sympathy for our plight, and we have nothing but gratitude and respect for these gentlemen, who faced with the pressure of a great power have shown courage and defended the rights of a downtrodden and humiliated people. But do we have any certainty that the League of Nations' Council will also muster the strength not to surrender to the pressure of the great power, and will not turn the White Paper into a document certified by international approval?[49]

The war prevented the League of Nations Council meeting that was supposed to discuss the White Paper policy from going ahead. Another source of hope was the fact that in the British House of Commons debate on May 22 and 23, only 268 out of the 413 government supporters voted in favor of the White Paper, while the 179 members of the opposition and around 20 of the government's supporters voted against it (110 members abstained). Even the internal opposition, however, did not prevent the White Paper from becoming a done deal.

The *Jewish Chronicle* wrote on August 11 that the Czechs were barely impacted by the forced injection of the beastly Nazi poison: "They declare quite openly that as soon as they receive back their independence, the Jew-baiting business will be sent whence it came." On August 14, it was reported that a pogrom had taken place in Bratislava (Slovakia), and that in the previous night a deportation order had been issued to around 8,000 Jews who were ordered to leave by the end of the month. A decree published that same day ordered a complete segregation between the general population and the Jews and forbade Jews from entering public parks, hotels, beaches, restaurants, and cafés. Victor Klemperer wrote in his diary: "The same tension for weeks, always growing and always unchanged. Vox populi: He [Hitler] will attack in September, he will partition Poland with Russia, England-France are impotent. Natscheff and some others: He does not dare attack, keeps the peace and stays in power for years. Jewish opinion: bloody pogroms on the first day of the war. Whichever of the these three things may happen: our situation is desperate."[50]

On August 14, the Italian ship *Palestina*, which sailed regularly from Trieste to Palestine, brought 102 immigrants, mostly youth Aliyah teenagers and children from Germany and Czechoslovakia. Other ships brought immigrants and returning residents from Marseille and Constanta. The next day Rivka Gurfein's piece in *Dvar Hapoelet*, the mouthpiece of the Women Workers' Council, harshly criticized the rough conditions on the ships that sailed under private initiative:

> We carry on with our daily lives — and near us, around us, at a small distance from us, every day new chasms open their dark maws and continue to devour precious prey, physical and spiritual lives. [. . .] More tender Jewish children orphaned in a strange and cruel way solicit alms of home and pity on the doorsteps of Europe, while their fathers hover between madness and suicide in a world that no longer has any room for them — and new convoys carry those without a foothold on shoreless ships, subject to the whims of our own "executioners," who rob them of their remaining human dignity and faith and hope. [. . .] Nowadays the animal in man has been set free and it emerges everywhere from its dark lair.[51]

Weizmann arrived in Geneva, the city where at the beginning of the century he had spent three years as a chemistry lecturer, from his holiday resort in the spa town of Vichy, where he had stayed almost the whole of July in the hope of getting some rest before returning to the political arena. Shaul Meirov, the head of the Mossad LeAliyah Bet, had visited him in the spa town to ask for his help in an urgent matter: the *Dora*, a small and old 584-ton vessel that had been recently purchased in Copenhagen and sailed under a Panamanian flag, sailed on July 15 to Antwerp with some 300 illegal immigrants on board. One hundred and twenty Hechalutz members from Germany plus sixty from Belgium waited for the ship in Antwerp. Alarmed at the ship's condition, the representative of the committee of Jewish refugees in Holland demanded the disembarkation of 100 passengers. The Dutch press protested that the government was allowing a "death ship" to go out to sea. The departure was delayed, and Meirov went to Vichy to ask Weizmann to intervene. Weizmann agreed and gave Meirov a letter for the representative of the refugee committee, in which the representative was asked to put his full trust in the Mossad LeAliyah Bet's emissaries.

After some delays the *Dora* sailed with around 480 passengers on board, and was spotted by the British observation post in Gibraltar. Under pressure from the British government the Turkish authorities refused to allow it to drop anchor at the port of Mersin, and only after days of hardships and a mutiny of the Greek sailors did the *Dora* arrive on August 12 at the beach of Shefaim north of Tel Aviv. A police boat that was patrolling the beach failed to notice it. The *Dora* was one of the only ships that managed to evade the British naval pursuit, and after dropping off its passengers ashore it sailed to Rhodes.[52]

On August 15, rumor spread in Geneva that Weizmann intended to resign from the Zionist movement's presidency or that he had decided not to give the opening speech to protest the attacks on him and his policy. In the preceding months, Weizmann had told his close associates that sixty-five was the right age for retirement, and therefore after the Congress he would not continue in his role.[53] His mood in those days was also low due to the death of his mother on July 30, which he had experienced as "a great shock."[54]

The rumors about his resignation, however, were false. On the evening of August 16, the brightly lit theater building was surrounded by tight police guard, as the *Der Moment* correspondent described the opening night, and the hall began to fill up: first came "the low-ranking Agency officials, and then the delegates. The leftists wearing gray work jackets (*rubashkas*) and the women with deep cleavages." The photographs from the occasion show delegates wearing suits and ties. At 8:30 Weizmann struck Herzl's gavel—behind his back hung a large picture of the Zionist visionary flanked by two blue-and-white flags—and after words of greeting from Mr. Lachenal, the president of the Conseil d'État of the Geneva canton, and other distinguished guests, he stood up to give the Congress's opening speech. An audience of around 1,500 awaited his words.

An emotional Weizmann spoke of the regime of evil and cruelty that was sweeping over Europe and of the destruction of great Jewish centers—he was referring to Germany, Austria, and Czechoslovakia—and predicted a grim future: "The shadow hanging over Israel has grown darker. Hundreds of thousands are destined for cold pogroms, torments of body and spirit, poverty and want [. . .]. An enemy [Hitler] has openly declared his aim to annihilate the Jews" and "large centers of learning and culture have been swept aside with the broom of annihilation. [. . .] The shadows surrounding the Jewish people have become thicker." Weizmann did not hide his anxiety over the fate of European Jews: "Tens of thousands of our people are homeless, tossed about from shore to shore, hunted like chaff in the wind." The consolation Weizmann offered was that there was no use lamenting, but it was necessary to unite in order to defend the Zionist enterprise.[55] He dedicated most of his opening speech to Zionism's ways of struggling against the White Paper, the future relations with Britain, and a vigorous rejection of the criticism that his policy had proven a total failure. On the contrary, he said: "Britain, which loves freedom and abhors injustice and persecutions, has always been our friend. This friendship is dear to us, and we will retain our gratitude to England despite the disappointment over the new policy." Weizmann firmly rejected his critics' claims: "The view that our policy has come to naught is baseless. Our policy has not failed. We have not failed. Others have failed. We trusted Great Britain. We trusted its honesty, and we still want to trust it. Is it our fault that some of its representatives see some sort of benefit in betraying this trust? We are not to blame, surely, and are not the ones to be condemned." Weizmann had not lost his trust in Britain or his hope that it would change its policy.[56]

Weizmann's voice was quiet and hoarse. To the hostile *Der Moment* correspondent he seemed tired and exhausted. According to the latter, Weizmann read his words like someone who had nothing new to say, and mainly defended himself against the accusations that his policy had failed: "The delegates looked at the walls with embarrassment. The speech gradually faded until Weizmann's voice was barely heard." The only speakers praised by the journalist from Warsaw were the guests Justin Godardt, a former minister and a present member of the French senate, and the British MP Tom Williams, who attacked his government's policy. The delegates from all the parties, added *Der Moment*'s envoy, who after the opening event flocked to the Lyrique café, decided almost unanimously that Weizmann's speech was a resounding failure. Weizmann's supporters blamed it on his illness and promised that he would present his political vision the following day.

Shprintzak was impressed: "Weizmann is endlessly lucky. The audience received him with universal enthusiasm and cordiality. Even though his speech this time was not brilliant, he found the right formula for affable expression and contact with the Congress."[57] The *Zionist Review* described the speech as "an impressive opening address."[58] "The opening of the Congress is usually a formal, boring and tiresome ceremony," wrote Ben-Gurion in his diary. "The opening tonight was no exception—although there was more formal ceremony than boredom." As opposed to the journalist from Poland, he singled out for praise Weizmann and Nahum Goldmann's addresses.[59] And the *Forverts* interpreted Weizmann's speech as a call to intensify the struggle against England.

Weizmann continued his speech the next day, dealing mainly with the relations with Britain. He reassured the delegates: "Never has Jewish power been fully revealed to such an extent and never has all the good and exalted in us been displayed with such magical force, as when we have been faced with difficulties. We are in distress, and I am sure we will not put our past to shame. And when we meet at the next Congress, we will be able to say that we have moved forward."[60] The words were greeted with lengthy applause.

Dr. Nahum Goldmann, who since 1933 had been the representative of the League of Nations' Committee of Jewish Delegations, and since 1935, after having his German citizenship revoked, the representative of the Jewish Agency, spoke during the opening session in French. He said that the Congress was "convened at an almost unprecedented time in the history of the Jewish people, which is quite rich with tragic moments and crisis periods." The present crisis, Goldmann said, confirmed that there was no other solution to the Jews' plight than the Zionist solution, which was not "a partial and poor solution, valid for ten years or one generation." The world was closed to the Jews, but the plight of the Jews in Central and Eastern Europe could not be discussed solely under the shadow of the refugee problem:

> Woe be to our people if the world starts to see us as a nation of refugees, a nation of beggars for whom some place of refuge should be found. [. . .] The refugee problem is not identical with the Jewish question. The refugee problem is only a partial and special expression of the large Jewish question that has existed for hundreds of years. And even if there are hundreds of thousands of refugees for whom a place of refuge must be found right away or as soon as possible, still our nation is not a nation of refugees. [. . .] Our refugees are entitled to escape to any country—it is natural and obvious, and we shall offer them our help; but our nation as a nation will not follow in their footsteps. Their national path is a return to the homeland and not flight and escape. The nation knows only one path, the path that leads to Zion.[61]

Emigration, said Goldmann, "was the main means, and maybe the ideal tool in our war of survival. [. . .] Without this phenomenon the Jewish people would not have been able to hold on." Goldmann, wrote *Der Moment*, could speak with great verve, but in truth he only embellished his banal words with combative-sounding noises. Yosef Burg, a Hamizrachi delegate, got the impression that Goldmann "claimed categorically" that war would not break out.[62]

On August 17, the Zionist Federation published an ad in the London *Zionist Review* calling readers not to miss a golden opportunity to celebrate the High Holidays in Palestine and join a "special Rosh Hashanah tour"—a fourteen-day visit to Palestine costing 36 guineas. The ad promised that the visitors would stay in first-class hotels with full board.

The Twenty-First Zionist Congress was an arena of conflict between

Weizmann and Ben-Gurion, and to some extent also between Ben-Gurion and Berl Katznelson. The conflict revolved around illegal immigration. Ben-Gurion arrived in Geneva on August 15. He had flown from Haifa to Athens, from where he continued on an Italian airplane to Marseille. From there he made his way to Geneva by train because he refused to fly to Switzerland, as the only plane making that flight was a German plane. On the day of his arrival, Ben-Gurion presented his political doctrine at the meeting of the Jewish Agency Executive, stating that Zionism's present goal was to fight the White Paper. The dilemma he presented was the following: how to fight Britain and at the same time pin all of Zionism's hope on it. His answer was: by organizing illegal immigration on a large scale, preparing and training a military force in Palestine, and seizing strategic positions.[63]

Even before the publication of the White Paper on May 17, 1939, Ben-Gurion was full of fighting spirit, and his positions hardened after its publication. On August 18, at the Congress's general assembly, Ben-Gurion spoke more moderately. He promised his listeners that the rift with Britain was neither absolute nor long term, and that the White Paper had no roots in the English tradition. In any case, he said, it was in the Yishuv's power to fight the White Paper's decrees, and the Jews in Europe had no choice but to break through Palestine's gates: "Only with warships and machine guns can England [. . .] block the way to the homeland."

That same day, at another Labor party meeting, Ben-Gurion tried to convince his comrades that Britain needed the Zionist movement's agreement to its policy. The proof was that Colonial Secretary MacDonald himself, who was one of the greatest crooks in England—according to Ben-Gurion—had used all his charms on a Jew from Pinsk (Weizmann) trying to obtain his agreement to the White Paper. At a meeting held the next day he reiterated at length the need to prepare for an armed revolt if Britain tried to implement the White Paper, detailing the means of struggle available to the Yishuv: not by military means, because whoever proposed to defeat Britain with military means was "either a crook or an idiot."[64]

On August 21, Ben-Gurion appeared at the meeting of the Congress's political committee in his combative mood and presented the main points of his plan: to carry out a grand immigration operation (an "immigration revolt") while "taking strategic positions" along the coast.[65] Britain, he insisted, would not be able to impose a foreign (Arab) rule on Palestine by force of arms. Ben-Gurion warned the members of the political committee to watch what they said and not divulge anything from the discussion: "If the things that we discuss here are published in any way, it puts the freedom of many people in Palestine at risk." He added that the debate at the general assembly of the Congress suffered from the fact "that they could not call the whole thing by name, and here [in the closed meeting] we can talk freely only if we are absolutely sure that all the participants in this meeting have not only the good will, but also the ability to keep a secret." What the members of the political committee were required to keep secret was the "revolt plan," lest it reach British ears — the very same ears that the Zionist diplomacy was seeking to convince that the international tension required military cooperation between Zionism and Great Britain. However, the British government received regular reports on the movement of illegal immigrant ships, and there was no doubt that a large-scale organization of illegal immigration would not have escaped their knowledge.

In any case, Ben-Gurion did not explain how the big immigration enterprise would be carried out. His words did not surprise the Mapai delegates, who had already heard him suggest similar plans, and they were far from impressed.[66]

Weizmann was horrified by Ben-Gurion's aggressive tone. He himself had not given up faith in the ability of the Zionist diplomacy, in which he was engaged before and after the White Paper's publication, to turn back the wheels of Britain's policy on the Palestine question. A large-scale illegal immigration, Weizmann claimed, was not a realistic prospect, thus the right way to fight the White Paper was to appeal to the conscience of British public opinion.[67] Perhaps he hoped that heartrending words about refugee ships being tossed about at sea would move and shock this public.

Kleinbaum declared at the general assembly that it was impossible for the Jews in the Diaspora and in Palestine to be free as long as Hitlerism existed in the world. The Congress was "in a tragic tangle: the British Empire is the force that wishes to destroy Hitler, but at the same time it has published the anti-Zionist White Paper." Zionism had no choice, said Kleinbaum, just as the international proletariat had no choice but to stick by Britain, which was standing at the forefront of the struggle against Nazi Germany. Another part of his speech was devoted to the need to fight "Jewish gangs," that is, the Irgun.[68] The representatives of the Left faced a tough dilemma that Yaakov Hazan, one of the top leaders of Hashomer Hatzair and a delegate on its behalf, solved by making a distinction between the imperialist British Empire that wished to ensure "its rule over the world" on the one hand, and "the England of the English worker, whose sympathy for our project is growing," on the other.[69]

Netz derided the fighting talk: in Palestine the Congress delegates were "ashes and dust," and in Geneva they became bold and spoke vainly and boastfully. The *Jewish Chronicle* reported that the Congress had become ruled by a hysterical atmosphere and irresponsible talk.

Ben-Gurion's seeming two-facedness epitomized the dilemma that the Zionist movement found itself in after the Partition Plan had been taken off the agenda and after the St. James Conference (February–March 1939) had signaled the end of the Mandate regime. In previous years, Ben-Gurion had praised the Pax Britannica, a regime that allowed the Zionist enterprise to be built in Palestine,[70] but in his speech at the political committee meeting he claimed in the heat of the moment that Britain would only be able to prevent illegal immigration if it used warships and machine guns against the illegal immigrants (which it did; from 1939 onward the warships and fast coast guard vessels managed to take control of Palestine's shores and prevented most of the illegal immigrant ships from getting close to shore).

These confrontational words were uttered by Ben-Gurion throughout 1938 and 1939. The plan of action he conceived became known as "combative Zionism."[71] It consisted of declaring war on England "not with guns and bombs, not with terror and murders like the Arabs" — but by organizing "mass immigration to Palestine, by transporting thousands of refugees — despite the government's interdiction — to Palestine's shores, an act that would tie the refugee question to Palestine." According to his plan, preparations for the immigration revolt would include establishing an organizational apparatus, purchasing vessels and creating a network of smugglers, overtly and clandestinely bringing thousands of young people from Europe, strengthening their hold on Haifa, and preparing to take the port by force: "From Haifa we will declare the foundation of a Jewish state. Will they shoot at us?"[72]

Ben-Gurion's combative words met with vigorous opposition even in his own labor party. Marie Syrkin, daughter of the Zionist-socialist thinker Nachman Syrkin and a delegate of Poalei Zion in the United States, wrote: "A great speech and one of the two most moving at the Congress by a small, white-haired man with an *idée fixe*, the speech of a fanatic, and in the last analysis, the speech of a great man, with vision, with tenacity, and above all with a plan of action."[73]

One may assume that an action taken against British targets, such as the one carried out on August 9, was not met with the approval of most of the Congress delegates, though it was never mentioned: at 3 a.m. on August 9 the British police boat *Sinbad II*. which tracked down illegal immigrant ships, was blown up at sea. It was a state-of-the-art 60-ton motorboat, equipped with machine guns, searchlights, and radio.[74] Israel Norden, a Dutch Jew who worked on board the ship as a mechanic, volunteered to sabotage it without endangering the lives of the crew. The blast tore the boat in two and it sank within several minutes. The boat's commander was killed and the rest of the crew managed to swim to the shore near Hadera.[75]

Yitzhak Gruenbaum, leader of the Zionist movement in Poland until 1932, who addressed the Congress on Friday, August 18, spoke passionately about "the Zionist solution," while firmly rejecting the heated proposals to declare a campaign of "civil disobedience" or "war" against Great Britain. These slogans, he claimed, were suitable for a people living in their own land.[76] The only way open to Zionism was to implement the Partition Plan, because "the divided country is not a living body for us: so the partition knife cuts through a living body other than our own. Do not borrow terms from other nations. If they cut up Poland, they cut up its living body with a knife, since the Poles live in Poland. However, when they cut up Palestine the knife does not cut through our own body."

The seventy-six-year-old Menachem Mendel Ussishkin, president of the Jewish National Fund, arrived in Geneva from the Vichy spas. A few months earlier he had asked not to represent the General Zionists B party, because he had had bitter disagreements with most of its members, and only Ben-Gurion's words had persuaded him to attend the Congress. In his speech, Ussishkin called for unity in the struggle against the White Paper. The following days he fell into depression, but managed to pass the motion calling to continue "redeeming the land."[77]

In the evening of Saturday, August 19, the Allenby cinema in Tel Aviv premiered the film *The Little Man and the Great War*,[78] described as "a movie about the Great War with neither war nor espionage." The ad said: "This film [has] earned special attention in these times." The movie was preceded by a Carmel newsreel "dedicated to the harvest in the Valley."

Katznelson's speech on August 20 was eagerly awaited. He spoke in Yiddish and focused on the internal arguments within the Zionist movement about the ways to fight the White Paper. He touched only briefly on the immigration policy in light of "the great catastrophe" that had created "masses of Jewish refugees from the hell of Germany, Austria, and Czechoslovakia," and on the fate of "tens and hundreds of thousands of our brothers" who "will be the first to fall in a war that is not theirs, to fall not for the sake of their own people and freedom, but on behalf of their tormentors and bitter enemies."[79] Not only the civilized world, he said, was showing signs of sympathy with the immigrants and the refugees; "the sea too sympathizes with them and pities them." Katznelson told the delegates the story of the ship *Rim*:

> I read in *Davar*, on the eve of its closure by the authorities, that five boats had arrived, only one of them a motorboat, carrying 160 refugees, including pregnant women and thirty children. Thirty kilometers from shore the captain lowered them into boats and left them to fend for themselves. And the sea took pity on them and brought them to our shore. If the sea had been relying on distinguished Jewish community leaders it may have acted differently.[80]

Davar was shut down by the censors on August 17 (because on August 11 it had published a piece protesting the creation of "concentration camps for Jews in the country of their national home") and renewed its publication on August 23. In the days of its closure it was replaced by a newspaper called *Hegeh*, which reported on August 20 that early in the morning the coast guard had discovered a motorboat, a cargo ship, and a sailing ship approaching the Netanya beach, with around 800 illegal immigrants on board. The British army blocked the access to the disembarkation site and occupied the beach, and the immigrants were arrested. According to the newspaper, the British soldiers gave the immigrants cigarettes and many of them had tears in their eyes. The *Zionist Review* also praised the British soldiers' and policemen's humane behavior, which "impressed the Yishuv." The journal reported that the British waded into the surf toward the boat and carried the women and children to the shore. They also emptied their pockets of cigarettes and food and gave them to the ravenous wanderers.[81]

The old 522-ton river vessel *Rim* sailed from Constanta on June 26 carrying two groups that together numbered around 690 illegal immigrants. The first group included 151 refugees from Austria and from other countries. Each family of refugees paid between 600 and 1,500 German marks for the journey. Shortly after they got to Constanta, some of them contracted scarlet fever. The Romanian authorities placed the group under quarantine and threatened to send it back to Austria. The Viennese Jewish community's council refused to help.

On March 23 the engineer Emil Petushenko wrote to Jabotinsky: "So far we have borne with patience and discipline the troubles that have befallen us, such as living in a basement, sleeping on a stone floor, scarcity, contagious diseases." The refugees, he wrote, had in effect been abandoned by their senders and therefore expected Jabotinsky to save them before it was too late. Jabotinsky's secretary noted on the letter's margins: "The President [of the NZO] hopes for a quick and positive solution."[82]

The solution for the predicament was found by a Revisionist functionary from Romania, the engineer Michael Gorenstein, and the Romania travel agency, which leased the *Rim* and had brought it to Constanta, where the second group organized by Gorenstein was waiting. The night before sailing some desperate Jewish refugees tried to force their way onto the ship, and after a struggle some of them managed to get on board. The *Rim* sailed on June 26 carrying around 690 immigrants and anchored in Rhodes on June 29. On the island, the Italian authorities forced it to take on another 260 refugees and local immigrants. On July 6, after the ship sailed out to sea, it crashed against some rocks, caught fire, and started to sink. The Italian police boat *Fiume* rescued the passengers and brought them to the island of Symi, from where they were transferred by two Italian warships to Rhodes. They were kept under quarantine in a military tent camp, where they stayed for over six weeks. A delegation from Palestine brought them some money, food, and clothes. Finally, some of them boarded the *Agios Nikolaus* and others got into three boats that were tugged by the ship. On August 18, the *Agios Nikolaus*'s 814 passengers descended into the tugged vessels some thirty miles from the Netanya beach. They were arrested and transferred to the detention camp in Sarafand and released after a short while.[83]

In previous years, Katznelson had had reservations about the quality of the immigrants and had encouraged the illegal immigration of Hechalutz members. Now at the Congress he spoke adamantly in a different vein: "They tell us: unselected immigration, bad elements, it is well known. [. . .] I hear them and think: when did you become so picky?" In the past people had accused the Zionist Organization of preferring "people of work and courage," whereas now "that the great catastrophe has come and the Jewish refugee escaping the hell of Germany and Austria, Czechia and Slovakia breaks into the country, you start demanding selection." No one knew why history had chosen to fulfill its mission "through Jewish refugees, through human dust carried on the seas [. . .]. But it is not for us to change it. This is what history has decided, and we have no choice but to obey it and follow its choice: the refugee."

The fighting spirit that permeated Katznelson's speech, which went on for about an hour, excited the audience. He claimed that the White Paper was not a decree like any other, and that it should be fought through illegal immigration. He recalled the night of July 30, 1934, when he had watched from shore a chain of young men and women standing in the water and transferring immigrants from the ship *Vellos* to the shore.[84] He imagined it as a continuous chain stretching from Judah Halevi to the present days: "If you will it or not, if you help or hinder, the afflictions of the Jewish people will drive the boats out to sea."[85] Moreover, Katznelson expressed his confidence that even a great power like Britain would not be able to remain indifferent to the troubles and suffering of massive numbers of human beings. He wrote to his wife Leah Miron that his speech had earned praise "both from the rabbis of Hamizrachi and from the Left." Indeed, Dugdale described the speech as "moving and beautiful," and Marie Syrkin described it years later: "Without oratory, without any of the stock in trade of the supposed 'eloquent' speaker, he stirred the Congress as no one else had done. He stood on the platform, a short stocky man, speaking rapidly between gulps of water, pausing to look at his notes and he held his audience tense."[86] Ben-Gurion complimented Katznelson and thought his speech was "the best Zionist speech made here,"[87] though Katznelson had rejected his view that illegal immigration was mainly a symbolic weapon of propaganda.

Katznelson's praise for illegal immigration and his refusal to see it as a demonstration of political revolt was met with broad agreement. Many of the Congress delegates stood up and applauded him. Moshe Krone, a Hamizrachi delegate from Palestine, wrote in his memoirs: "I remember the strong impression made on the Congress by the 'cold and passionate' analysis of Berl Katznelson, who demanded to break the blockade on Palestine by increasingly intensifying the illegal immigration."[88]

But Ben-Gurion's words, and especially Katznelson's, also provoked disapproval. Weizmann believed that they had been guilty of carelessness on delicate matters and had damaged the Zionist policy.[89] On the way to Eaux Vive for lunch, Weizmann's eyes "looked like small stones [. . .]. Chaim [was] angrier than ever at this." He threatened to "pack his things" and resign from the movement's presidency. His anger stemmed from the fact that he saw political danger in talking publically about a rift with Britain and about a "revolt."

Although in political committee discussions behind closed doors Weizmann said he had told Chamberlain that "the Jews will swim to Palestine," his view was that the organization of the illegal immigration should be entrusted to experienced hands; and in any case, this meant actions that might be "good for a year or for five years, and maybe only for two or three months." If illegal immigration was indeed the only means available to the Zionist movement, Weizmann thought, then "our movement's situation is pitiable."[90] At this time in his life he was prone to disappointment, and he seemed to have lost his influence.[91] Weizmann refused to agree with the characteristically extremist Ussishkin, who asserted that the Zionist cause would benefit more from bringing 30,000 immigrants illegally than from bringing 40,000 immigrants legally.

A completely different trend could be sensed in the words of other speakers. A Hamizrachi representative stated at a meeting on August 18: "We are standing on the brink of salvation." Dr. Abba Hillel Silver, the representative of the U.S. General Zionists, who together with Solomon (Shlomo) Goldman led the American delegation that had come to the Congress in a dejected mood due to the growing power of the isolationist and conservative elements and the antisemitic surge in the United States,[92] warned against hasty actions that would lead to a conflict with Britain and against plans to organize illegal immigration. The Jews of the United States, he warned, would not be willing to raise money to fight against Britain. He expressed total support for Weizmann's political line, which meant resisting the White Paper with all "the classic Jewish means, and continuing to work towards annulling the White Paper." "The whole of humanity is suffering today, not only the Jews," declared Silver.[93]

In a private letter, Katznelson described Silver as "a rude fool," but in public he watched his words for fear of damaging the fundraising efforts in the United States. When Silver wondered about the somber mien of his old friend Dr. Emanuel Neumann, a member of the Zionist Executive who had lived in Palestine since 1932, whom he met near the opera house, Neumann replied that he was depressed by the bleak prospects in the political and international sphere and that salvation could only come from the United States.[94]

However, Dr. Shlomo Goldman poured cold water on the great expectations from the Jews of the United States. The American Diaspora, he said, was no different from the other Diasporas and would not be able to offer salvation. Weizmann agreed with him.[95] Goldman accused Britain's civil administration and the police of behaving much like those in Nazi Germany.[96] Shertok reacted to Silver's words with a tough speech:

> How shall the Jew stand before the world? Shall he stand before it as an uninhibited man, murdering, burning and sabotaging, whom you must appease only because you cannot always fight him; or shall we stand the way we have until now, in Palestine — the stance of a man who is building and creating, who is fighting for his freedom, defending his rights, refus-

ing to surrender to injustice, and in the Diaspora—the stance of a persecuted and tortured people, a people whom humanity has sinned against and whom it owes a heavy debt of justice, should injustice continue to be perpetrated against this people, human conscience is unable to rest.[97]

Shertok promised a "political war" and even a "revolt," but directed his harshest words toward the Revisionists, whom he saw as a danger to Zionism. According to the minutes, his speech was greeted with lengthy applause.[98] Golda Meyerson (Meir) did not speak at the Congress. In her autobiography, she wrote that she had spent most of her time "with the delegates of the Labor movement's European youth organizations," who convened in her room, "planning the ways in which we could stay in touch with each other when and if war broke out."[99]

The delegate from Germany, Dr. L. Jacobi, who had to watch what he said, reported that the Jews of Germany were "busy working with vitality and fruitful Jewish energy, and we have an extensive *hachshara* [training] operation in our country and abroad. [. . .] Today, after six years of nonstop immigration, we still have plenty of people who are capable, on a much larger scale than Zionist public opinion imagines, to provide with their physical, economic and spiritual powers a new boost to the building enterprise in Palestine."[100]

The voice of Polish Jewry was barely heard. Only Shlomo Kaplansky, who from 1927 to 1929 headed the Zionist Executive's Settlement Department and in 1932 was appointed principal of the Haifa Technion, and who spoke at the closing session on the evening of August 24 after news of the Ribbentrop-Molotov Pact had become public, mentioned that the danger of war threatened the physical destruction of the Jews of Poland. If war broke out, he declared, the Jewish people would stand "with the democratic countries of the West, with Poland as it fights for its national survival and its liberty."[101]

Only a few of the speakers referred to the situation in Europe and the "Hitlerist evil," and they chose to do so through generalizations and in the context of the situation in Palestine. On the other hand, sharp words were directed at what was described as the "dangerous adventurism" of the Revisionist movement and in particular against the "terrorism" of "Zionist fascism," that is, against the Irgun's terror attacks in Palestine in protest of the White Paper policy. The Revisionist movement and the Irgun were depicted as the biggest threat to Zionism at that fateful hour, as betraying the moral principles of Zionism and endangering its position.

On August 20, Moshe Kleinbaum wrote for the *Haynt*: "The impression is that there is no crucial meaningful topic on this Congress's agenda. There is no need to decide between two options, there is no central question. No one knows, not even one leader in the world, what tomorrow will bring, and obviously the Congress too knows nothing whatsoever."[102]

That same day Shlomo Jacobi, who coordinated the New Zionist Organization's illegal immigration aid in London from the office on Finchley Road, wrote to the South African millionaire Michael Haskell, an ardent supporter of the Revisionist movement, about the desperate situation of about 2,000 Betar members from Poland and the Baltic states who had been stuck in the town of Sniatyń on the Poland-Romania border, holding visas to Peru.[103] The group was carefully organized, and its members were chosen according to their suitability to join the Irgun. The Polish authorities supplied them with passports. They were led by Menachem Begin, the Betar commissioner in Poland; David Yotan; and Shraga Haitin, an emissary from Palestine. To the passengers' surprise their cars were detached from the train at the border station, and they were left in the Polish border town of Sniatyń. The British ambassador to Bucharest had written to London on June 22 that unidentified Romanian officials were allowing illegal immigrants to reach Palestine in large numbers.[104]

Under pressure from the British government, the Romanian government prevented their entry, and they were housed in a camp set up for them near the railway tracks.[105] Jacobi described the camp on June 20 as a "humane prison": "We ordered the refugees to remain at the frontier in the field. They spent there two weeks. Now the Polish authorities do not allow them to remain at the frontier any longer and we are compelled to take them to some place near Warsaw to arrange for them to camp there awhile."[106]

After three weeks, the district governor gave an order to dismantle the camp and sent the convoy back to Poland. Begin had them stand in formation and urged those who still had somewhere to go back to to resist the wish to be among those who were going to cross the border surreptitiously.[107] The author of the book about the Revisionist movement's illegal immigration was impressed by the fact that many of those who could have stolen across the border did not do so "due to the discipline that prevailed at the camp and their reluctance to be separated from the group,"[108] and returned to Poland. About 200 of the camp dwellers managed to steal across the border after bribing the Romanian border police and reached the ship *Naomi Julia* that was anchoring at the Romanian port of Solina. The ship set sail on September 1 and reached Palestine's shores on September 20, 1939, carrying 1,130 illegal immigrants from various countries.[109] British coast guard vessels opened fire on the ship and sprayed the deck with water jets. The ship was led to the port of Haifa and the illegal immigrants onboard were arrested and transferred to the Sarafand camp.

On August 21, Jabotinsky wrote to the party leadership in Palestine wondering whether the Revisionists should take part in the elections to the Knesset (Assembly of Representatives) (these were postponed and eventually held in 1944). His view was that the party did not have the necessary resources to prepare for the elections and that the Mandate government would do all it could to impede it, and if the party won less than a quarter of the votes, the result would be seen as a bad defeat. Therefore, he proposed not to take part in the elections. He added that in the current situation "we have nothing to do in the field of world politics."[110]

On August 22, Hitler summoned his army chiefs to the Eagle's Nest in the Bavarian Alps and declared it was time to attack Poland and that Britain was too weak to prevent the attack. Our enemies are "small worms" (*kleine Würmchen*), he said contemptuously. Germany, he promised, would act against its enemies with ruthless cruelty.

That same evening, King George VI was called back from his summer holiday in Scotland, grumbling about "that villain Hitler" who had cut short his vacation.[111]

The next evening, Hitler decided that the attack on Poland would start at 4:30 a.m. on August 26. On August 24, the British Parliament passed the Emergency Powers (Defense) Act and started partial mobilization. On the morning of August 25, Hitler heard a report on the agreement from von Ribbentrop, who had returned from his successful trip to Moscow. He quickly reported it to his Italian ally, the Duce Benito Mussolini. The latter was alarmed by the possibility of war breaking out. Several hours later, Hitler canceled the order to attack. He promised Henderson, who came to the Chancellor's office at noon, that he was ready to vouch for Britain's independence, and wrote the French prime minister Édouard Daladier that France had no reason to support Poland's insupportable behavior. Daladier's reply, handed to Hitler on August 26, said that Poland was now ready to negotiate and there was no reason for a German-French conflict.

The diplomatic circles still believed that it was only a show of force and that an agreement by the Polish government to give up Danzig and the Corridor would avert war. Many, however, thought differently. On August 24, British and French newspaper correspondents and citizens left Germany. The next evening all of Germany's radio, telegraph, and telephone communication with the outside world were cut off. The American journalist William Shirer wrote in his diary: "War is imminent."[112] That same day Pope Pius XII made an emotional plea for peace on the Vatican's radio. On the evening of August 25, the Anglo-Polish agreement that ratified Britain's commitment to come to Poland's aid if it was attacked by Germany was signed in London. While Hitler canceled the order to start the attack because of Mussolini's objection, the Nazi propaganda used all its outlets to report on the war frenzy that had gripped Poland, on clashes at the border, and on a million and a half Polish soldiers who were moving toward Poland's border with Germany. Anti-aircraft cannons were positioned in Berlin, and Germany's airspace was closed. On August 27 Britain imposed food rationing, and by the end of the month the building of the British Cabinet's bunkers in London, which had begun in 1938, were completed.

Until the morning of August 24, 1939, the discussions at the Zionist Congress's general assembly and political committee took place in the shadow of the British White Paper of May 17. The representatives were divided over how to fight it and how to fight the restrictions it imposed on immigration to Palestine. Placing this subject at the top of the Zionist agenda was not the result of blindness or of ignoring what was happening in Europe. It was well known that the Nazi policy was aimed at driving the Jews out of Germany and its occupied territories, and that it was using methods of cruel terror to achieve this aim. It was also known that in January, at the special Reichstag meeting marking the anniversary of his ascent to power, the Führer stated: "Europe cannot find peace before the Jewish question is out of the way" and blamed the "international finance Jewry" of again "precipitating the nations into a world war." On less heated occasions Hitler explained that what he had meant was getting the Jews out of Europe.[113] The Nazi newspaper *Westdeutscher Beobachter* wrote on April 5 that in Eastern Europe "antisemitism is older than in Germany itself. It has been proved to act like a cure that can bring a unity of feelings and political wishes. The Munich Agreement has done a considerable service to the antisemitic policy that Germany and Italy have been working on in Eastern Europe." Now that Czechoslovakia had been taken, the antisemitic movement would be able to "reach those parts of Eastern Europe that are not yet under its influence."[114]

The Zionist movement saw Britain's policy—justifiably—as an obstacle and a barrier that prevented immigration to the only place that was open and ready to absorb Jewish immigrants and refugees—Palestine. The statement that "what is at stake is the fate of Palestine" did not express a disconnection between Palestine and the Jews of Europe, or an indifference to their fate—quite the contrary. The situation of European Jews was never ignored, even if it did not always receive public expression. The recommendations of the Woodhead Commission of November 1938, which was appointed to examine the possibility of implementing the Partition Plan of July 1937, and the White Paper of May 1939, in effect separated the "Palestine question" from the "Jewish question" in Europe. Then, the issue of how to fight this separation and the great wall that had been erected between European Jews and Palestine had stood at the top of the agenda of the Zionist movement in all its various parts. In light of this, it was no wonder that the Congress delegates argued passionately over the question of how to struggle against Britain's policy and how to prevent the separation between the question of the Jewish refugees and the question of Palestine. Thus, the idea of instigating an "immigration revolt" did not mean giving up on the British Mandate for Palestine. On the contrary, the "revolt" was seen as a means to pressure the British government to remove the White Paper from its agenda. In any case, the "secret" information that Ben-Gurion revealed to his listeners had to do mainly with the strength of the Haganah, while his "revolt plan," whose daring impressed some,[115] was no less imaginary than the "revolt plan" conceived by Jabotinsky on the eve of the war.[116] The collaboration between the Yishuv and the British army in Palestine was not mentioned in the Congress debates.

Selig Brodetsky, a scientist and member of the Zionist Executive and Agency Executive in London, described the dilemma faced by the Zionist movement in his speech at the political committee:

> Many speakers spoke from a perspective of peace, peace around the world, as if there were no upheavals in Japan, Danzig etc., and all we have to do is push ahead with our cause. [. . .] We need two plans: a plan for war and a plan for peace. Even if there is peace for one year, the danger of war under which we have been living in the last years, and of a world war, will not have passed. [. . .] My view is that Ben-Gurion's plan should be examined from this perspective: what can we do now and do in such a way that when war does come Britain will not be skeptical even for a moment and will not doubt that it can trust the Jews?[117]

The mood at the Congress thus vacillated between, on the one hand, helplessness and calls to not be drawn into combative statements and to trust diplomacy and the world's conscience, and, on the other, calls to embark on a determined struggle and even prepare for a revolt against the British Mandate. Those who wanted a struggle could not accept the Jewish-British historian Lewis Namier's contention that Zionism was a very small force, and therefore it had no choice but to wait until the storm subsided—until Hitler and Mussolini were defeated. Then, he promised, a different world would emerge in which the Jews might be saved.[118]

Emanuel Ringelblum wrote in his telegraphic style:

> The Congress is under the cloud of war. The fear [is] of being cut off from [Poland]. The Congress presidium is stalling at the conclusion of the Congress. The state of mind is in the street, not in the assembly hall. The delegates spend more time at the Café Lyrique [which they later dubbed "Café Panic"] and Café National [which they called "Café Tragic"] than at the plenary hall. The tension is rising and reaches a pitch when Germany signs a non-aggression pact. The conversation with the newspaper vendor who sells politics, but does not determine it, in Zurich [it seems that] Poland is disintegrating [according to the estimate in Zurich it is slated for defeat]. My conversations with the Swiss: How will Poland react? Will it capitulate? Great sympathy for Poland and at the same time grumbling about Beck's diplomacy.[119]

On August 23, Shprintzak, who wrote that the Congress "is better than I imagined," described the panic that had seized its participants who felt that they might become cut off from the world: "All the leaders of Zionism are cut off from the people and trapped." While the presidency and the executive discussed how to ensure immediate transportation to Palestine, news came of the Ribbentrop-Molotov Pact. Shprintzak tormented himself: "This is what the Bolshevik conspiracy has brought humanity. The end of all flesh and all spirit!" If earlier he had considered staying for a few days in Geneva and "savoring some of this lovely place's flavor" before returning to Palestine's blistering heat, now "the fear of war drove me to get a ticket for a ship that leaves on 31.8."[120] Moshe Krone recalled: "With tragic irony some people reasoned that the threat of war was merely the clever 'invention' of certain leaders who wanted to achieve some sort of intra-Zionist aims."[121]

In light of the dramatic events, Katznelson proposed to adjourn the Congress immediately. He wrote to Leah Miron that the question was what would become now—after the agreement between Stalin and Hitler—of the Jews of Poland. This question was "more important to me than all the questions that the Congress is dealing with," but "some people love dealing with last year's snow."[122] His proposal was rejected; only the pace of the discussions was accelerated. Weizmann wrote years later:

> The Congress debates pursued their usual course. Every party [had] its say, every resolution was fought out in traditional fashion. The record was scrutinized and criticized, the administration attacked and defended. But in the lobbies of the Congress, and outside the walls of the Geneva Theater where it met, knots of delegates discussed the latest bulletins, and then escaped from the realities by taking refuge within. We went through all the gestures, but felt that nothing said or done at such a moment could have meaning for a long time to come.[123]

The menacing news failed to unite the Zionist movement's ranks, and the rifts did not heal even within the parties themselves. They were manifested in arguments and heckling, but the most extreme manifestation of the disagreement, bitter rivalry, and even hatred were the words uttered against the Revisionist movement and the Irgun's terror attacks in Palestine.

On July 8, 1939, Eliyahu Golomb, a leader in the Haganah, had met with Jabotinsky to discuss security matters and possible cooperation in getting illegal immigrants ashore. He suggested participation in the Zionist Congress, but Jabotinsky put forward conditions, including canceling the shekel as a condition for taking part in the elections. Golomb wrote: "He thinks that the fear of war is exaggerated. There is no panic around the world and there will be no war. In a while people will return to seeking constructive solutions to many questions. This is what we should get ready for." We need "a real Évian," he stated.[124]

Jabotinsky did not change his mind in the following weeks. Prior to its arrival in Geneva, on August 6, the Irgun's delegation had come to see him in Vals-les-Bains, where he was preparing the manuscript of his book *Taryag Millim: 613 (Hebrew) Words* for publication, and privately toying with the idea—probably inspired by the Expedition of the Thousand to Sicily of Giuseppe Garibaldi, one of his heroes—to organize a demonstrative "dramatic landing" on Palestine's shores.[125] Jabotinsky reluctantly agreed to the delegation's departure to Geneva but did not conceal his disapproval of the content of the pamphlets it intended to distribute among the Congress delegates and guests. He wrote to the NZO's presidency in London on August 7 that he could ban the delegation from going to Geneva, but their plan to take advantage of the gathering of Jews and foreign journalists for propaganda purposes was reasonable: "The only problem is that they informed me of their intention instead of proposing it to the Presidency." In any case, he gave his consent, although he believed that "this mentality shows a tendency towards separatism."[126] David Raziel, the Irgun's commander, was much less restrained, calling the group "an anti-Jabotinsky group" bent on stirring up "some villainy."[127]

In Geneva, the delegation met with the chairman of the League of Nations' Mandate Committee, held press conferences that presented the foreign correspondents with the organization's goals, and posted flyers around the city and near the entrance to the theater hall. The flyers included quotations from the French translation of Schiller's play *Wilhelm Tell*.[128] One of the delegation's members, Ila (Lilka) Strasman (Lubinsky), was the driving force behind the group that published the Irgun's periodical *Jerozolima Wyzwolona* (*Jerusalem Delivered*) in Warsaw and contested Jabotinsky's leadership.[129] Years later she proudly recalled that the delegation's talk of the need for the Jews to take their fate into their own hands and fight against the White Paper had made a great impact: finally here were Jews who were not choosing to act with restraint and appeal to the world's—nonexistent—conscience, but were advocating active resistance. According to her, one of the foreign journalists told her: "You are the only Jews who do not arouse in me antisemitic feelings. You are the first Jews in ages whose hands I can touch without feeling dishonored."[130] Like the other delegation members, she returned on one of the last trains that passed through Germany on its way from Switzerland to Poland. Upon arriving in Warsaw she found that her husband Henryk Strasman, an officer in the Polish army, had volunteered for service although he was forty years old and exempt from military service (he was captured by the Russians and murdered with thousands of other Polish officers in Katyn Forest in April and May 1941).

On August 24, Jabotinsky wrote to the NZO members in Ontario, Canada, that whether war broke out or not, the world would have to be reconfigured, and part of the rebuilding would be the creation of a Jewish state by the end of the 1940s.[131] On August 25 he wrote the NZO presidency in London from Pont-Aven that he intended to go to Saint-Malo in Brittany. The panic in Europe, Jabotinsky promised, was unjustified because there was no danger of war.[132]

Early in the morning of August 23 the Greek cargo ship *Parita*, which had been purchased in Marseille by the Revisionist movement's immigration activists, arrived at Palestine's shores. The vessel left Hamburg carrying around a hundred Jews from Germany, anchored in Marseille, where it was boarded by more refugees, and sailed to Constanta, where it was boarded on July 12 by 644 Betar members from Poland and Romania. Now the ship was carrying around 800 passengers, including 200 women and children.

The Italian authorities did not allow the *Parita* to anchor at Rhodes and it was forced to leave the harbor and sail to Izmir. Forty days after setting on its way, on the night of August 22, the *Parita*'s wanderings in the Mediterranean ended when it ran aground opposite the Ritz Hotel on Tel Aviv's beach. A morning storm rocked the ship and some of the passengers jumped overboard. Boats from the Tel Aviv port and the Zevulun Maritime Sports Association rushed to their aid, and as the captain activated the sirens thousands of the city's inhabitants rushed to help transfer the illegal immigrants ashore, applauding them and distributing items of food and clothing.[133] Doctors and paramedics offered medical aid. Pamphlets distributed around town called on the authorities not to arrest the immigrants, but before noon buses began to transport them to the detention camp in Sarafand. The British, reported the *Haynt*, "showed exemplary generosity." The newspaper added: "The large crowd broke through the police chain and managed to get to the buses to release the refugees. The police dispersed the crowd and took down the blue-and-white flag from the ship's mast."[134]

The Zionist diplomacy tried to use the winds of war to its own advantage. On August 24, Shertok left Geneva for Palestine, stopping in London for twenty-four hours to try and find out what would be the British reaction to the agreement that had been signed in Moscow and how the dramatic development would affect its policy in the Middle East. The morning after arriving in London he met with General Sir Henry Pownall, director of Military Operations and Military Intelligence in the War Office, and a day later with the chief of the general staff, General Sir Edmund Ironside, who despite the tense international situation made time for the meeting. Shertok presented them with the proposal to create a Jewish military force in Palestine under British command — a proposal that would become the main topic on the Zionist agenda in the ensuing period. General Ironside reacted dismissively and suspiciously, doubting whether Shertok could vouch for the trustworthiness of the Jews who had immigrated to Palestine from Germany: "After all, many of them have a long-standing German tradition. Might they be hankering after their old country [Germany]?" And another question troubled the general: Would around ten million Jews living in Palestine and the neighboring countries not have too much influence on what was happening in the world? The surprised Shertok thought he had managed to assuage the general's fears of a "world-wide Jewish influence." However, his interlocutor was far from convinced, describing the Yishuv picturesquely as a "half-tamed lion wallowing in its cage." The general's claim that in six months to a year the British would overcome "that chap" [Hitler] failed to reassure

Shertok, who at this point in the conversation brought up the situation of Europe's Jews. He was terrified, he told General Ironside, of the thought of the fate that would befall Polish Jewry should Germany invade: "It means a general massacre of the Jews of Poland."[135] Ironside did not share this concern for the fate of Poland's Jews. "No doubt Jews aren't lovable people. I don't care for them myself, but that is not sufficient to explain the pogrom."

Great Britain and its government had other things to worry about: by the end of March the British government had already reached the conclusion that it would not be able to avoid military intervention on the continent if Germany attacked Poland. On April 27, as already mentioned, the Parliament passed the Military Training Act, and around the island preparations were made to defend against air raids.[136] The British public sphere was permeated with apocalyptic prophecies of the terrible devastation that would be caused by air raids. The Committee for the Scientific Study of Air Defense predicted that in the first twenty-four hours of an air raid on London around 58,000 people would be killed, and in sixty days of ceaseless bombings 600,000 people would be killed in London alone.[137]

While the persecution of German Jews earned condemnation—on November 21, 1938, Parliament decided to condemn the Kristallnacht pogroms—the most the British government was willing to discuss was the possibility of seeking shelter for the Jewish refugees in one of the countries of Equatorial Africa. The government's generosity under public pressure manifested itself in its willingness to relax the immigration policy with regard to children: in the year prior to the war, Britain took in around 40,000 refugees (including around 10,000 children of the Kindertransport)[138]—two and a half times more than in all the preceding five and a half years. At the same time, the British government believed that it should not "cooperate" with Nazi Germany's deportation policy by being willing to absorb masses of Jewish refugees on the British isle.

The proposals of the Yishuv's leadership to join the British war effort did not impress the military commanders. General Archibald Wavell, the general officer commanding of British forces in Palestine and Trans-Jordan, who on the eve of war was named general officer commander in chief of Middle East Command, wrote to the general staff August 24, 1939: "I am sure that they [the proposals] will be more of a hindrance to us, by eliciting the suspicion and hostility of the Arabs, than a help. If we wish to prevent Palestine from becoming as much a source of serious danger to the Empire during wartime as it was during peacetime, we must adhere firmly and decisively to the White Paper policy."[139]

"The situation in Europe is deteriorating," stated the headline of the *Haaretz* newspaper on August 24. As evidence, the newspaper pointed to the British government's instruction to all its representatives in Berlin to leave Germany immediately. The newspaper reported that according to other sources the German army had started to amass its forces along the borders with Belgium and France. That day Katznelson wrote to Leah Miron that he feared for the fate of Poland's Jews, adding: "What will I do the day after the Congress—I do not know. If it were not for the fear of war I would have liked to sit by myself for three or four weeks and write the forewords for Beilinson's book. Now I am thinking of leaving for Palestine immediately. But all these thoughts are futile, because things may well be already out of our hands."[140]

Katznelson left Marseille for London to meet Jabotinsky, who also arrived there. He intended to see whether it was possible to end the internal strife within the Zionist movement. In the report he wrote on August 31 (and according to his words at the Mapai central committee meeting on September 21) about the four long conversations they had at Jabotinsky's hotel, Katznelson said that Jabotinsky had told him with sadness and bitterness: "You managed to capture the rich Jewry of America. I only had the poor Jewry of Poland, and now it is gone. I have lost the game" (it is hard to believe he really made such a confession). According to Katznelson, Jabotinsky proceeded to say that Zionism was for him "the concern of the Jews who are not in Palestine." Katznelson interpreted this as if Jabotinsky "displayed hostility towards the Yishuv," while he himself truly and honestly wished to "save" the Revisionists from "wallowing in errant ways and even false messianism" and bring them back into the fold of the Zionist Organization. Jabotinsky's response brought Katznelson "to despair and total exhaustion." According to him he refrained from replying to Jabotinsky that "our loss is bigger than his," because the Labor movement had lost "the main wellsprings of Hechalutz and the immigration"—the source of the Labor movement and the Zionist enterprise's strength—"and who knows for how long."[141]

Jabotinsky had made his last visit to Poland in May 1939 and knew what dangers were threatening the country's Jews. Weizmann had not visited Eastern Europe after the First World War,[142] and Katznelson had last visited the country at the end of 1933, but his fear of what was in store for its Jews had grown in the previous year. In November 1938, in a closed meeting with the Haganah commanders, he spoke about an impending war and the danger it held for all the Jews of Europe: "I dare not guess the results of the Second World War, whether it will put an end to the dictators' rule or impose the spirit of Fascism and barbarism in their different forms on the entire world. I only think about what might happen at the start of the war. Here the calculation seems simple: the Jews in all the enemy countries are destined for annihilation. They will be the first to be sent to the fire, and there will be no trace of them left."[143]

The Congress delegates continued their discussions, but many of them justifiably feared that the borders of neutral Switzerland would be closed and they would not be able to go back home. Therefore, they used the Congress office to try and leave earlier. Weizmann, who on August 23 reached the conclusion that he belonged in London, took his leave from the Zionist Congress delegates at 10 p.m. on Thursday, August 24, a few hours before its adjournment. The chairman Ussishkin explained that Weizmann had to go back to London, where "he should be at this critical moment in our lives."

Standing tall and regal, the president of the Zionist Organization took the stage "and in a choked and emotional voice" said that heavy clouds were amassing over the future and in his heart there was only one wish: that they would get to see each other again alive, and that if they did, that they would carry on with their work, and maybe a light would still shine from the darkness. His words of solace suggested that he failed to predict the magnitude of the future danger, or that he chose to speak about eternity because he was unable to promise anything else: "Whatever happens [. . .] the eternal people will overcome all the devastations and continue to realize its great dream [. . .] May the God of Zion help us [. . .]." He wished the Congress delegates from Poland that their fate would not resemble that of the Jews beyond their border—the Jews of Germany: "All I can say is this: [. . .] our people is eternal and our land is eternal. We shall work, fight and live until these terrible days are over. See you in peace."[144]

At the end of his speech, his eyes welling up, Weizmann hugged Ben-Gurion, Ussishkin, and the other executive members, and slowly exited the hall. The delegates gave him a standing ovation. Many shed tears, and "the singing of 'Hatikvah' filled the hall." Ussishkin gave Weizmann his good wishes and some words of encouragement, saying that he was now not "alone in fighting for the nation's liberation in such a critical historical moment. All the disagreements on the important and serious questions, in personal relations and in the sins we have committed against each other and that have caused rifts between different sections of the Zionist Organization —are forgotten at a moment like this. [. . .] Go on your new and renewed mission to all the places you see fit, and may the God of Zion be with you!"[145]

His words were greeted with long applause. Years later Weizmann would write that his departure from the Congress had been a sorrowful departure, "mixed with bad premonitions."[146] Dugdale wrote: " I shall never go through a more moving scene. Who can guess the thoughts that filled all our minds, these 600 Jews from all quarters of the world, some of them already cut off from wives and families."[147] Moshe Krone recalled: "Many of the Congress delegates were veterans who had seen wars in their lifetimes, and they were gripped by a special anxiety. But the younger delegates were also [. . .] swept [up] in the general anxiety. The dramatic speeches of Menachem Ussishkin and Chaim Weizmann made my hair stand on end."[148]

Zerach Verhaptig, the Hamizrachi vice president who came from Warsaw to Geneva with his wife, whom he had married about a year and half earlier, for "a kind of honeymoon," would write years later: "The Congress delegates were anxious and concerned, and especially we who had come from Poland, but we were not terrified. Most of us were young, full of energy and hope. Even the most pessimistic did not guess the great devastation that was about to befall us. We were afraid of a great disaster. We did not foresee a devastation."[149]

Marie Syrkin recalled that Weizmann's speech alarmed her, and because of her fears her friends called her "Cassandra" and "Nervous Nellie." The American delegates, she added, debated among themselves whether anything would happen during the Congress, but nobody wanted to give up their place in the General Debate, because they all had to have their say.[150]

On August 24, President Franklin Delano Roosevelt wrote to the Polish president that all the nations of Europe, large and small, wanted peace and did not seek military conquest. They all believed that "all controversies, without exception, can be solved by peaceful procedure if the will on both sides exists to do so."[151]

Many delegates hastened to leave that same night in order to still be able to return through France to their home countries. Some of the Polish delegates set out before Weizmann's speech but were forced to return to Geneva. Ringelblum briefly described the hardships they endured on their way:

> Our epic journey. Near the Swiss-Italian border. [. . .] Sadness. They let us back into Geneva. Fear and trembling in Weizmann's speech to the Congress. The fate of the Jews of Poland in case of war. Komernitzky intervened on our behalf. [. . .][152]
>
> Intervention in Rome, permission from the [Italian] consulate in Berne. We are escorted on the trip through Italy. Our train car was con-

> nected to a different train. We arrive in Yugoslavia. [. . .] We received an enthusiastic reception in Zagreb. In Hungary [. . .] Budapest [. . .] At the Polish border the first signs of a mobilization. We travel three hours in a sleeper car until [. . .] Warsaw.[153]

At 1:40 a.m. on August 25, the delegates dispersed with the closing words of Ussishkin, who did not forget to thank the host city:

> We do not know what tomorrow will bring [. . .]. Now we must leave this hall, leave it without a clear knowledge of where we will be tomorrow. This night is a sleepless night for the whole Jewish and non-Jewish world [. . .]. What will happen to the million Jews in Germany, Austria, Czechoslovakia and Italy? Their blood has already been shed, and their abuse has already gone too far. [. . .] And what will happen to the three and a half million Jews in Poland, to those who will doubtless defend with their lives the country in which they live? What will be the results of the war, how will the Jews be treated once it breaks out? We have not forgotten our brothers' suffering twenty and twenty-five years ago in the same places, when the world war broke out. We have no hope now of being able to help them in any way. [. . .] The Jews of Central Europe, that suffering million—how hard it is to give them any words of encouragement. Only the heavens will have pity on them. For the earthly powers are null. Perhaps the impending catastrophe will bring them salvation. [. . .] And you the Jews of Poland, when you return to our brothers, tell them that we can only help them with our blessing. More than that we are unable to do for you at this time. And our blessing is that you will come out of the war physically unscathed, and what is more important—spiritually unscathed from the crisis that is upon you. Let them not forget that their pain is also our pain even if we are far from them.[154]

His speech was greeted with a long standing ovation, and the crowd sang "Hatikvah" again.

The Congress's closing statement and resolutions reflected the great anxiety on the one hand and the focus on the Palestine question on the other. All the practical resolutions related to settlement, immigration, the relations between the workers' unions, economic matters, and the like, but they opened with a call to the Jewish people:

> The Twenty-First Zionist Congress calls on the Jewish people in all the corners of the Diaspora to intensify their war of liberation. The renewed building of the homeland is an indelible source of the people's power to

> resist the campaign of extermination conducted against them. The Jewish people will not give in to that ferocious attack on their human rights and their dignity.
>
> Surrounded by national hatred and racial loathing, set upon and persecuted, denied their rights and their existence, hundreds of thousands of Jews are trembling in the grip of extinction, and tens of thousands are wandering adrift on ships in the middle of the sea, some on their way to Palestine whose gates have been shut to them and some without a compass or a goal. The Congress sends them words of peace and encouragement and reinspires them with the hope of the Jewish Diaspora: the sovereignty of the Jewish people in its homeland! Despite the persecutions and torments that we are suffering now—our great historical experience gives us the confidence that our people's ancient race will not be broken [. . .].
>
> Let our people not fear the political difficulties that are blocking their way to redemption and freedom. These difficulties will pass if the people rise up for a courageous war, great acts of voluntarism and numerous sacrifices. [. . .] Out of the present predicament and in the face of the impending global storm the Congress calls on the entire Jewish people: Be strong and of good courage! Let every dark corner in Israel be lit by the slogan of confidence and faith: "Let us go forth, for we are well able to overcome!"[155]

The Twenty-First Zionist Congress thus resolved that the White Paper policy was the bitter and dangerous enemy of the Jewish people and of Zionism—and that Palestine was their one and only salvation.

Before the curtain descended on the Congress, an argument still erupted on whether to cancel the double representation accorded to Palestine at the Congress (according to which, one vote in Palestine equaled two votes in the Diaspora). Ussishkin declared that this was not the time for protracted arguments, because all the delegates must return to their respective countries. He intended, he said, to raise a few proposals of his own, but "will wait until the next Congress." Meyerson (Meir) insisted that things should be left as they were because "the Yishuv now stands on the frontline," whereas Nahum Goldmann believed, like Ussishkin, that the Yishuv, now numbering around half a million people, had already passed the romantic and exotic stage and there was no longer any justification for its privileged status. His view won by a majority of 252 to 218 votes.[156]

The journalist Dr. Ezriel Carlebach, who covered the Congress for the newspaper of the religious-national community in Palestine, *Hatzofeh*, reported that Mrs. Dugdale told one of her acquaintances: "I think you are all mad . . . I've just come from London. There is a war on. And here you are arguing as if nothing has happened or is going to happen." Carlebach wrote that the Congress existed in a bubble and that in a day or two its discussions and resolutions would become worthless. The belief that the Congress had the power to influence the Yishuv's fate was funny and strange:

> In our time, when the map of the world changes overnight, in our own country, which is dependent on thousands upon thousands of elements that are represented neither in the Congress nor in the Zionist movement, at this hour, when you do not know if tomorrow or the next day there will still be a remnant or a trace of either the resolutions and the elections or of those electing and resolving [. . . ,] only an ignoramus can delude himself that here the country's fate for the next couple of years is being determined. [. . .] Only a naive person can attribute crucial practical importance to this convention.[157]

Marie Syrkin, by contrast, summed up the Twenty-First Zionist Congress as a success. However, in September, after returning from Geneva to New York, she wrote: "The Congress was faced by two terrible challenges —the crisis in Zionism [the White Paper] and the crisis in European civilization [Adolf Hitler]. I think it is not too much to say that on the whole, the Congress met both challenges with courage and with a high sense of responsibility."[158] But she also observed, "In light of the present, much of what happened at the Zionist Congress seems remote. Geneva became ludicrous and pathetic in retrospect."

Herschel V. Johnson, the U.S. consul general in Geneva, wrote to the secretary of state on August 31 that the Twenty-First Zionist Congress, which was supposed to come to a close on August 28, had been adjourned on August 24 because of "the threatening international situation." Among other things, he reported, the Zionist Congress had decided not to heed the restrictions on immigration and not to oppose illegal immigration. On the other hand the U.S. consul in Jerusalem, Christian T. Steger, wrote on September 4 that the automatic loyalty shown to Britain at the Zionist Congress was not only due to its past friendship or because the Jews expected to gain anything from this loyalty, but also because Britain was standing up against Germany, "the arch-enemy of the Jewish race." Although some harsh criticism of Britain had been heard at the Congress, he remarked, the mood had changed overnight in light of the impending war. According to the consul, neither the British in Palestine nor the Arabs had reacted to the Congress.[159]

On August 26, Willy Cohn wrote in his diary that "Poland allows itself a great deal under the protection of Germany." Two days later he wrote that rationing had begun, and the train schedules were reduced. But there was still hope that Germany would not be isolated and that war would not destroy Europe. On Wednesday, August 30, he wrote: "Perhaps today will decide between peace and war."[160]

The *Haynt* in Warsaw wrote optimistically: "The catastrophe can be averted."

Weizmann, his wife Vera, and Dugdale left Geneva on August 24 at 10:30 p.m. They were driven in a Rolls-Royce and found the border between France and Switzerland closed. Their claims that they were British citizens returning home were met with one answer — *"on ne passe plus"* — no way through. Only after a long delay were they allowed to cross into the neutral zone separating the Savoy region from Switzerland, and they spent the night in the Hotel du Golf in the town of Divonne-les-Bains. The hotel was full of French and British travelers hoping to leave the place as quickly as possible. "What a nightmare," wrote Dugdale in her diary that night, "and what an experience to have been with them all, the Jews, through the Twenty-First Zionist Congress."[161]

Early in the morning they reached the French border, and only after some negotiations with the commanding officer were they allowed to go on. They left the main road, which was blocked by tens of thousands of vehicles, and on the evening of August 27 arrived in Paris and checked in at the Plaza Hotel. Weizmann found the French capital "proud and sure of itself." The next day he met with Léon Blum, until recently the prime minister of France's first socialist government (1936–1937), who maintained that only internal disagreements at the top of the Nazi regime would prevent war, but if Hitler did not withdraw, war would break out on Wednesday; in any case, England and France were standing firm. From Paris the small group continued to London. "A day of vague optimism in the air, I fear not justified by events," wrote Dugdale in her diary on August 29, without specifying whose optimism she was referring to.[162]

On August 24, the High Commissioner left London on his way back to Palestine. All army and police leaves were canceled, and the government officials who were about to go on vacation postponed their plans.

On August 26, at 2:50 p.m., the Irgun assassinated Inspector Ralph Cairns, commander of the Palestine Police CID's Jewish Section, and Ronald Barker, commander of the Arab Section, as they left the Hagina Café in Rehavia, Jerusalem. In response, the authorities closed all the cinemas and cafés in the area, and forty residents from the nearby houses were detained for interrogation. On August 28, the Vaad Haleumi strongly condemned the act, which they called "a despicable murder":

> Whosever criminal hand committed this murder—it is an enemy hand that has struck not only the two victims it intended to strike, but has assassinated the foundations on which the project of our revival in Palestine has been based. In this fateful time for the Jewish people and for the whole world, as grave dangers threaten world peace, as the countries of freedom and democracy are forced to fight for their lives against the attack of the countries led by a regime of violence, our country must hold fast on this international front; the entire Yishuv is required to stand by the institutions authorized to safeguard its existence and its future, and fight against any act that may undermine its vital national interests in Palestine.

The Twenty-First Zionist Congress was a futile Congress. Moreover, there was no substance to the combative talk about an "immigration revolt," about many dozens of ships carrying the Jewish masses of Poland, about taking over the port of Haifa and so on. Likewise, the efforts to convince the British government of its strategic need for the Yishuv's cooperation and the threats that without such cooperation the Empire would come to harm were ineffective for the time being. The danger of impending war mainly intensified the worry for the future of Zionism and of the Yishuv. From a Zionist point of view, Palestine and the immigration of European Jews to the country were the only possible routes of escape from the catastrophe. Now that war was looming, there were also some who hoped and expected that a war would bring a turnaround in Britain's policy toward Zionism and blow a new wind in the Zionist movement's sails. In May 1935, Ben-Gurion had said at the Agency Directorate meeting: "There are also catastrophic forces in Jewish history as there are in world history. Suddenly some storm comes and changes everything."[163] Tragically, the storm that came was a world war.

At that point in time, at the end of August 1939, the Twenty-First Congress thus seemed like a testament to the great powerlessness of the Zionist movement. The Congress would surely not have been held, and the hundreds of delegates would not have made what for many of them was an arduous trip to Geneva and back, if they had guessed that at the end of the month war would break out. There were plenty of dark predictions; the drums of war were rumbling, and many felt that an all-European conflict was imminent. But the atmosphere of uncertainty also engendered hopes that at the end of the day Europe would come to its senses and war would be averted.

7

WILL WAR BREAK OUT?

On May 5, 1935, the *Davar* humor column "Bavat Tzchok" (With a Smile) featured the following joke:

> Hitler once went to a fortuneteller and asked her to tell him about the end of his life.
>
> FORTUNETELLER: Am I allowed to tell you everything?
> HITLER: Yes, by all means, tell me without fear.
> FORTUNETELLER: I see that you will die on the eve of a great Jewish holiday.
> HITLER: Then I will cancel all the Jews' holidays and festivals.
> FORTUNETELLER: Even so, the day after your death will be a great Jewish holiday.[1]

Is this a case of black humor offering refuge from anxiety, or perhaps of blindness regarding the intentions of Nazi Germany—a blindness that marked not only the years that followed 1933, but even the year 1939? Both the leadership and the public relied on news items, rumors, and wishful thinking, and therefore we find contradictory and inconsistent responses to what was to be expected in Europe after the Nazis' rise to power. While talk of the possibility of a great war could be heard as early as 1935—after Nazi Germany violated the Treaty of Versailles by introducing compulsory military conscription on March 16—it did not include the possibility that Poland would be rapidly seized by Nazi Germany, let alone that it would be divided between Germany and the Soviet Union.

On April 13, 1933, about three months after Hitler was appointed chancellor, Winston Churchill said at the House of Commons: "There is a danger of the odious conditions now ruling in Germany being extended by conquest to Poland, and another persecution and pogrom of Jews being begun in this new area."[2] At the beginning of 1934 Ben-Gurion similarly came to the conclusion that the Nazi regime would not be able to survive without a war, thus forecasting that the regime would start a war whenever it was ready. War—he predicted—would break out within four or five years and bring an unprecedented destruction.[3]

The following year, in May 1935, Ben-Gurion said: "The shadow of war is undoubtedly darkening and thickening," and in February 1938 he predicted that after Nazi Germany swallowed Austria, "Czechoslovakia's turn will be next."[4] In May 1935, Meir Yaari spoke before the members of the Hashomer Hatzair General Council about "a new world war," and that year at the Nineteenth Zionist Congress in Lucerne (August 20 to September 4) Yaakov Hazan, Yaari's co-leader, said: "The danger of war, the danger of a new world massacre, is hovering over us and over humanity as a whole, and the most miserable, most shattered people, whose blood is flowing all across the front, are torn to pieces."[5] The fear of what was coming fed on events in the European arena and on press reports.

Ben-Gurion's mood shifted between certainty that war in Europe was unavoidable and relief that it had been thus far avoided. Ben-Gurion gave special attention to the events in the internal British arena, reaching the conclusion that the British did not want war, not because of their pacifism but for fear of defeat and of air raids on their cities.[6] He was especially worried that just as Britain was abandoning Czechoslovakia to its fate, so it might decide to abandon the Yishuv to its fate as well. However, he wrote to his daughter Geula in November 1938, "I am now filled with hope in our future as I have never been before." It was actually the international tension that seemed to offer a lifeline for Zionism. In light of the global upheavals, Ben-Gurion wrote, "England [may] need us."[7] The escalating crisis around Czechoslovakia and Britain's war preparations brought him in December 1938 to the conclusion that "the danger of war in the coming months is *real*. This information comes from an authorized source. This rumor must not be spread in Palestine—but we must get ready."[8] He feared for the fate of Europe's Jews if war broke out, but mostly he was concerned about the fate of the Yishuv. "It would be impossible to save the Jews of Europe from the terrors of war," he wrote, "and therefore the main thing is for us to take root *in this country*, so that even an uncommon storm will not be able to uproot us."[9] Throughout this period Ben-Gurion did not write anything or speak about the military balance of power or Poland's military capabilities and its chances of surviving a German attack. He seems to have shared the assumption that Poland was capable of defending itself.

Weizmann wrote little about Germany's war intentions but thought that it threatened Britain's status. He called the Nazi army's march into the Rhineland "Hitler's new trick," but thought that even those warning sounds that were heard would "quickly die down."[10] He was more worried about the impact of the Italian occupation of Ethiopia on the British Empire and its status in the Mediterranean: Rome destroyed Jerusalem, he wrote, and it will never build it. In any case, Mussolini, like Hitler, was expected to leave the stage after causing sorrow and suffering.[11] In January 1939 the worried Weizmann revealed to Ben-Gurion, who was in the United States at the time, a secret known only to the "closest friends": "Imminent war seriously considered [in] highest quarters."[12] This forecast related to the possibility of war on the western front rather than an attack on Poland.

A week before traveling from London to Poland, on April 10, 1939, Shertok wrote: "Under the boiling surface run cold currents." The English had caught "the disease called 'wishful thinking'" like some kind of malignant leprosy. However, "the atmosphere is that of the eve of war [but] with mental preparation and without panic." Some people were asking him "how I dare to fly to Poland in this situation—what if I am unable to come back?"[13]

Weizmann, Ben-Gurion, Shertok, and others did not engage in military assessments and relied on the available rumors and forecasts. Only few, if any, believed that Germany was indeed about to attack Poland, and even fewer imagined that the "two sworn enemies"—Nazi Germany and the Communist Soviet Union—would sign a "treaty of amity," thus paving the way for an attack on Poland and its partition. It was therefore senseless to speak of "prophecies" or predictions that allegedly showed who among the Zionist movement's leaders foresaw clearer than others what was to come.

Moreover, the heads of the Zionist movement made a distinction between the threat the war held for the Jews of Europe and the threat to the Yishuv from the upheavals caused by a great war in the Middle East. Their main concern was to preserve the Zionist project in Palestine "through terrible times."[14] The Zionist movement's hourglass signaled urgency because of the possible dangers to the Yishuv's future, and mainly due to fears for the fate of the Jews living in the territories of the Reich. The urgency did not stem from a nightmarish vision of Poland's Jews becoming prisoners in what seemed at first like a "Nazi ghetto."

The leaders and newspapers of the Revisionist movement dealt extensively with Germany's military might and its intentions. They had no doubt that Germany was seeking territorial expansion and the annulment of the Treaty of Versailles. A statement published by Hatzohar (acronym for Hatzionim Harevisionistim, the Revisionist Zionists), a political party in Mandatory Palestine, on May 19, 1933, warned that just as in 1914, the current events also revealed "the unrestrained, organic aspiration of the German nation for belligerent violence and territorial annexations," and that Germany was again ready to ignite a global conflagration and arm itself. Therefore, the statement added, it was necessary to tighten the international supervision over Germany and declare an economic boycott of the country. World Jewry should lead the international campaign against Nazi Germany.[15] The movement worked under the assumption that Nazi Germany was weak and would not be able to start a war. In May 1933, Jabotinsky had written: "The only part of Germany's ideology and platform that has any substance" was "the antisemitic part," while all the regime's other slogans were baseless: "All the other slogans with which the National-Socialist movements has poisoned the German minds are unrealizable: it is not even possible to test them—and each of the Nazi leaders knows it. Greater Germany? Taking over the 'corridor,' Danzig? They will be blown to bits within half a month."[16]

Jabotinsky saw Nazi Germany as a weak state whose isolation was a "law of nature" that would soon be realized. It "cannot start a war adventure" because it "lacks the necessary soldiers, guns, warships, airplanes, and with enthusiasm alone you can do nothing in this area."[17] Germany was "the world's besotted country. For a moment it seems as if the world likes the example, but soon it will dislike it." Nevertheless, he did not hide the fact that there was reason to be worried, and that Germany should therefore be restrained so that it stayed "a third- or second-tier country subject to the policing and supervision of others."[18]

In the year prior to the war Jabotinsky kept warning, both in writing and verbally, against the impending disaster that threatened the Jews of Germany and Poland. However, he never warned that Poland might fall to Nazi Germany, and that this was the reason for his great concern for the fate of Poland's Jews. On the contrary, so strong was his confidence in Germany's weakness and Poland's military power to repel a German attack that in his speech at the inaugural conference of the NZO in Vienna in September 1935 he described Germany as a "paper tiger": "Let us not be tempted to think that what we are facing is an iron giant which cannot be bent. This is not true. The giant is not made of iron, its political delusions are delusions, its economy is fundamentally unsound, and inside, behind the screen, there are confusion and quarrels, factions and Praetorians without a guiding idea or a decisive will."[19]

Earlier, in November 1933, Uri Zvi Greenberg wrote: "States are preparing for war? [. . .] True; but preparing for war does not mean wanting war."[20] In April 1934 he wrote about the fear of war that had gripped Europe: "It is likelier that the power of reason of today's mighty states dictates that in the current 'political climate' one should not play with matches. No state is nostalgic for 1914 [. . .]. No one wants to get itself into an atmosphere of gas and blood. Stupid pacifists think differently. But let us leave these idle talkers alone."[21]

In June 1934, when Jabotinsky thought that if war broke out the Jews would not be the only people to face annihilation, "but we will be the first to be annihilated,"[22] he referred to the expected destruction of German Jewry, but believed that such a destruction would strengthen the Zionist movement because it would show the world the need for an overall solution for the "Jewish tragedy."

Enthused by the ban on the import of German goods to Palestine that the Revisionist movement had organized and encouraged by what it saw as signs of distress in Germany, *Hayarden* announced that Germany was approaching an economic catastrophe and that its dying throes could already be seen on the near horizon. After the purge of the SA in June 1934, Jabotinsky wrote, "Measured by the scale of a European war the Reichswehr (the German army), despite all its virtues, is no more than a large and strong police force, and no secret improvements and reinforcements can turn a police force into a modern army." Therefore, the belligerent talk about founding the Third Reich was absurd: "'The Third Kingdom' [The Third Reich] does not exist and will never exist."[23]

Dr. Wolfgang von Weisl thought that Mussolini's intervention on behalf of Austria[24] had isolated Hitler from all sides, "and hopefully he will not be able do the world any harm,"[25] and Dr. Arie Altman, one of the leaders of the Revisionist party in Palestine, wrote at the end of November 1935: "The 'Aryan fool' sitting in the capital's halls, drinking and smiling, does not imagine that perhaps the one who will have the last laugh will be that very Jew, the victim of the current liquidation, who will soon see the total liquidation of German capital [. . .]. The objective observer can already see today that all the roads are closed to Hitler and that there is no escape for him either in a state of peace or in the event of war."[26]

Another Revisionist journalist wrote in a similar vein: "Everybody knows: Germany is nearing an economic catastrophe. Its economic situation is deteriorating by the day. [. . .] This boycott is being felt keenly all over Germany. [. . .] In the war that the Nazis are now conducting to remove the Jews from trade and industry as well, [they] do not see that they are digging their own grave. Germany's death throes can already be seen clearly. When death will arrive it is difficult, of course, to say right now."[27]

The view that Hitler was weakening and that his days in power were numbered was shared by many in the mid-1930s. After the purge of the SA at the end of June 1934, for example, *Davar* published a collection of reports on "the purge in Germany" that estimated: "Hitler is now going through the most serious crisis of his regime," and "Hitler is from now on dependent on the army just like the Weimar community [republic] before him." It was the Brownshirts who had put Hitler in power, and now, on "the bloody day" of June 30, the Nazi revolution had ended with a counterrevolution.[28]

It was risky to make predictions, wrote Jabotinsky in October 1935, because you risk being mistaken. Nevertheless, he was willing to take the risk and predicted that there would be no war in Europe: "Neither half a war nor a quarter of one."[29] Jabotinsky saw the German army's march into the Rhineland in 1936 as the preface for a Nazi takeover of the port of Memel in Lithuania, an act of aggression against Czechoslovakia and a revival of the question of Alsace. However, "I cannot see a campaign against the Ukraine for the time being (it is merely idle talk, the typical imagination of stubborn provincials)."[30] "The Third Reich," he wrote in January 1936, was nothing but "a banal episode in the development of the Jewish plight."[31] Neither should one be too impressed by the daily news of the German policy's successes; whoever claimed that Nazi Germany was going from strength to strength was nothing but an "impressionist"—a pejorative word in his lexicon. He did not budge from this decisive view about the possibility of an all-European war until the night of August 31. In May 1939 Jabotinsky said:

> Until two months ago the world was of the opinion that there is one big fist that can destroy everything—and basta [enough]. And then one country stood up, and not necessarily the largest one, one country [Poland], and for this it will surely be singled out for praise and glory in the annals of history, and it said [in response to Nazi Germany's demands]: "we shall fight," and with these words it finally pierced a hole through that fist. And then the world realized that the fist was not full of power, but full of air![32]

And in a speech in Warsaw, he declared: "I do not believe in the possibility of war. The war jitters will disappear in two or three months."[33] Jabotinsky reproached his listeners for their gloomy outlook, promising them: "Now it turns out that a great European war will not take place. We must not delude ourselves. And here I should say with shame that people are behaving as if their sentence has already been decided. I have not seen such a thing in history, and even in novels I have not read about such a surrender to fate."[34] And in June 1939 he stated that Nazi Germany's threats were empty threats "[and] it is of no consequence if Poland is strong or weak; here we are not talking about physical might but about a scientific experiment [. . .]. Poland has taken a needle and tried to see if the iron armor can be pierced through [. . .]. The fist was never made of iron; it was made of gauze in the minds of a few politicians who allowed themselves to be fooled." Nazi Germany, he said, "has been taught to buy everything on the cheap, without tragic sacrifices, without blood, through poker tricks, through successful threats."[35] Thus, "there is not the remotest chance of war."

These words about Germany's weakness were not, as already noted, completely based on wishful thinking. Rumors about the poor state of Hitler's health and about the opposition of many among the regime's top officials circled around, were included in intelligence reports in the West, and appeared in the press. The Polish government's announcement on March 28, 1939, that it would see any attempt by Germany to change the status quo in Danzig as an act of aggression, and the reiteration of this announcement on May 30 also struck Jabotinsky as conclusive proof that a firm and determined repost would deter Nazi Germany.[36] He wrote to his sister on March 31: "There will be no war; the German insolence will soon subside; Italy will make friends with the British and the Arabs, together with their kings, will lose even the little bit of market value they were supposed to have possessed until now ."[37] On April 6 he wrote to his friend Shlomo Saltzman: "My prediction—war—no; every other form of swinishenss—yes. And in five to seven years—a Jewish state in the whole of Palestine, if there are still any Jews left. I think there will be."[38] A week later, on April 14, he stated with the same conviction that the danger of war in Europe had passed mainly thanks to Poland's announcement of its intention to fight. The cries of war were meant only to intimidate, he wrote, but the countries of Europe will be wary of "the last step"—war. Neither would border disputes kindle the flames of war. The main reason for a European war being "impossible" in his view was modern military technology, which made war destructive even for the civilian home front. It was true that Europe could expect violent attacks and even mass slaughters, but "I 'guarantee' only one thing: there will be no European war."[39]

In the same month, Uri Zvi Greenberg also promised his readers: "The world will not go to war over Prague or Albania."

> The storm! It is in the ink bottle. Among us—the most wretched of all. All the rest have a sense of proportion. We do not. All the rest are enjoying the spring right now [. . .]. Without journalists, losing their heads, they want a well-armed and battle-ready army, but they do not want war.

> Only pacifism wants war—rotting socialism, because it dreams that the war would give it a blood transfusion, and on the ruins and on the shoulders of soldiers who have returned from the battlefields tortured and oppressed, in some shattered and oppressed hinterland, *its own* regime would rise up.[40]

On September 1, Jabotinsky wrote again to the presidium of the movement in London that it was still impossible to know whether the war would spread to Western Europe and what area it would encompass. In any case, the war would revive the idea of creating Jewish regiments in the allied armies, which, among other things, would serve as a barrier against assimilation. At the same time he explained that the Jews were not a factor in the global conflict and that the Jewish problem had not been mentioned in the statements about the war's goals because the prevailing feeling was that the Jews had no choice but to fight against the Nazis.[41]

Dr. Yohanan Bader, a member of the presidency of Hatzohar, who met the movement's leader in June when the latter visited his city, heard from him some cautious yet ambiguous words: "Logic tells me that war is impossible, but too many people believe it will break out; this is dangerous."[42] These words were said in a private conversation, while the statement that war would not break out was published in all of the Revisionist papers. No wonder Jabotinsky's disciples had to justify the false prediction by saying that he did not let himself believe in the impending disaster.

On August 25, before he returned from Pont Aven, Jabotinsky wrote to the presidium of the movement insisting that there was no reason for alarm and that there was "not the remotest chance of war." However, even after the occupation of Poland he still wrote that there was not a remote chance of war "and I don't say it out of stubbornness, but because it is so."[43]

On July 8, 1939, Chajes wrote that Hitler was continuing his blackmailing campaign by spreading fear of his surprising moves: "Complains about Poland. Presents himself as an innocent lamb. Arms himself, arms himself. Our public takes into account the possibility of war [. . .], but despite the public appeal there is no hoarding. The expected good crop is probably creating an optimistic atmosphere. The crops this year in Poland are excellent."[44] He quoted from "Pan Tadeusz" by the Polish national poet Adam Mickiewicz:

> O year of years! and to have seen thee in our land!
> The people call thee still the harvest year,
> The soldier's year of war.[45]

The world was scared of war, he wrote on August 5. "A decisive historic moment is approaching. Hitler is still keeping silent, but is continuing to arm himself. Mussolini is probably afraid of war. The newspapers are full of articles, telegrams, truths and lies. But the whole world is charged with tension."[46]

In Breslau, Willy Cohn continued to be optimistic and wrote on August 18 that although the political situation was quite dangerous, "I continue to believe that it will not lead to war" and "it will be the small remnant of German Jewry who will pay the price for the economic boycott of Germany."[47] The Bund members were full of optimism: the end of the Nazi regime was near due to economic developments and social processes. Karl Marx would triumph over Adolf Hitler! On August 26, after the Ribbentrop-Molotov Pact, one of the movement's leaders, Heinrich Erlich, wrote that it would be possible to defeat Germany with a joint offensive effort from Britain, France, and Poland.[48]

The patent confidence in Poland's power relied, as already noted, on the Polish leadership's determination in the spring and summer of 1939 to firmly reject Germany's demands. At first Colonel Józef Beck, the Polish foreign minister since November 1932, adopted a pro-German foreign policy driven by hostility and fear toward the Soviet Union. After Germany took Prague and the Port of Memel (Klaipėda) in March 1938, Beck was hoping for the support of Britain and France.

Jabotinsky hung on to these declarations, to Chamberlain's statement on March 17 that after Nazi Germany had taken over Bohemia and Moravia Britain would not allow any more German takeovers, and to the British government's pledge on March 31 to guarantee the borders of Poland and other European countries (Ben-Gurion wrote in his diary: "They say that Hitler will not go to war before the end of the summer—when he stocks up enough oil and consolidates his conquests").[49]

Jabotinsky believed wholeheartedly in Poland's military strength and in the weakness of the German "paper tiger." He did not foresee Poland's rapid collapse. Otherwise, he could not have conceived the imaginary plan he described in three coded letters sent via an emissary to the Irgun headquarters in Palestine. The plan outlined a large demonstrative operation, to be carried out on October 1939: a 40,000-strong Jewish force would land on Palestine's shores, seize a few major government buildings, including the High Commissioner's residence in Jerusalem, and declare the foundation of a temporary Jewish government.[50] Such a demonstrative plan, of course, required lengthy preparations and the Polish authorities' cooperation, or at least their turning a blind eye. He found it hard to believe that Germany would invade Poland and that within a short while Poland would cease to exist. To a guest who visited him shortly after the war broke out he said bitterly: "My opponents who have always tried to dismiss my predictions will now use my mistake as proof that Jabotinsky has been wrong again; he was never able to reckon with reality."[51]

The Revisionist movement was taken in by the "lure of militarism" and the "cult of the soldier" (*żołnierz*) that swept over Poland; however, it had good reasons to believe in the power of the country, whose army was considered strong enough to contend with the threat of Nazi Germany. Few people predicted that Poland would be defeated within five weeks. Let us not forget that Poland was trapped between two hostile powers, and that the French army, which was considered even stronger than the Polish army and was moreover aided by a British reinforcement of around a quarter of a million troops, would also display feeble fighting ability and will,[52] collapsing within six weeks. Warsaw surrendered after a siege that destroyed it; Paris surrendered without a fight.

The illusion did not dissipate in the following months. In January 1940, Jabotinsky wrote a piece titled "That Idiot (a friendly conversation)," in which one of the speakers says that difficulties from within would destabilize the Nazi regime and that it would be the army chiefs who would rise against it:[53] "Hallucination? We shall see. I am expecting the beginning of this end every single week. In any event not later than next summer." And he summed up the "friendly conversation" thus: "In a week it might become clear that one of them [the speakers in the conversation] was wrong or that everyone was wrong. Therefore I would like, at the very least, to make it clear to the reader that I am not responsible for the views I hereby recorded and conveyed—neither for the view of Mr. A, nor for that of Sir. B nor for that of Dr. C."[54]

Throughout the period—from January 1933 through September 1939—Jabotinsky and the leaders of the Revisionist movement believed that Germany was a weak, conflicted, and internally divided country. Therefore, they were convinced that the movement could "declare war on Germany" through various means—chiefly by organizing an international boycott on exports from the country that would further the regime's collapse. Moreover, some of them boasted that the Revisionist movement had been the first to declare war on Nazi Germany. The Jewish people, proclaimed a Revisionist statement in May 1933, was going to war against Germany armed with its only weapon—spiritual strength: "And in this war we predict for the Jewish people the complete victory of the principles of justice and peace and the necessary destruction of a regime that has raised its criminal hand against these principles."[55]

After the war broke out, Uri Zvi Greenberg wrote that the world had been struck blind because it had seen the antisemitic aspect of Hitlerism and had failed to understand that it was "a universal Amalek phenomenon [that] has cast its shadow on all the territories and sovereign peoples [. . .] and the Aryan world has started to pay for its mistake [. . .]. Were we not right in guessing what the general world picture would look like if they failed to act in due time against Hitler's expansion instinct?"

It was the Jews, "without guns or armies," who had warned against "Amalek's rise":

> At the time the Jews' early recognition of the face of the western European Amalek did not penetrate the ears and eyes of the Aryan peoples. It has fallen to us to have a prophetic essence: it has no success when it comes with an alarm call and presents a world picture for all to see. Only belatedly, when the danger becomes visible, is it recognized that the prophetic call had been right. [. . .] Neither the great European powers nor the small countries sensed the danger approaching their borders. [. . .] Everywhere the Jews were the only ones to sound the alarm. The Aryan world did not grasp the meaning of the Hitler-Nazism phenomenon. Great countries looked on dismissively and their journalists searched for background materials for political reconnaissance pieces across the Nazi territory.[56]

The Jewish press in Poland and the Hebrew press in Palestine similarly failed to foresee, at least until the middle of 1939, that a pan-European war was imminent. The newspapers printed various forecasts: a war between Germany and the Soviet Union was imminent, the Nazi regime was showing signs of expiring, and so on.[57] Germany's armament might cause a sudden conflagration, *Haaretz* wrote in January 1935, but in May the paper's editorial predicted that when war broke out the German army would be wary of crossing the border into France and Austria but "will pounce with all its force on Soviet Russia together with the Polish armies [*sic*] from south and west and with the Japanese armies"; no country would rush to Russia's aid—and Bolshevism would fall.[58]

After the occupation of Czechoslovakia in March 1939, *Haaretz* wrote that military commentators estimated that the Poles were capable of fighting back: Poland had an army that included around 500,000 soldiers, 25,000 pilots, and 200 aircraft, as well as a large cavalry that "will have a more crucial value in a defensive war on Polish soil." And the reason? There were hardly any paved roads in Poland, and therefore the Polish experts estimated that the cavalry would find it easier to operate than the tanks. The *Times* wrote on September 6 that anyone familiar with the history of Napoleon's wars did not need to be reminded of "the deadly qualities of the Polish mud." The Palestinian newspaper's forecast echoed the Polish army chiefs' view that the tank should not be overestimated, and their confidence that Poland's boggy conditions would be favorable for a cavalry—especially since horses did not require fuel. It did not occur to them that western Poland was a flat country that would not place any obstacles in the way of the German Panzers. In the autumn of 1939, as we shall see, there was not much rain and the road to Warsaw was easy to navigate.

Questions were therefore asked about Nazi Germany's war intentions and its military power. There were many naive illusions and readings of the historical map based on predetermined ideas. However, more than anything else it was a case of interpreting the events according to the available knowledge. The crucial question was the terror regime's nature and its intentions concerning the Jews living under the Reich's rule. The reports that came from Germany, Austria, and Czechoslovakia caused deep anxiety, and although some voices in the Jewish community still believed that Hitler was a passing phenomenon and expressed their confidence that the German barbarism would "finally suffer a deathblow,"[59] many sensed with alarm that "these are times of trouble for the Jewish people."

At the beginning of October 1938, for example, Ben-Gurion wrote from London to the Zionist executive in Jerusalem that abandoning Czechoslovakia to Hitler signified a new turn in world politics; the Jews were not a factor in these global events and could not influence them. What was certain, wrote Ben-Gurion in bitter despair, was that the Jews would be the principal victims of these events, because German antisemitism would spread across Europe: "I see these times as times of trouble for the Jewish people like never before, and Zionism is in for some difficult and bitter days."[60] Although concern for the Zionist movement and the Yishuv was uppermost in Ben-Gurion's thoughts, he did not ignore the harsh fate that awaited the Jews of Europe; those "who [could] not fight for their lives."[61] The danger he foresaw was the spreading of the Nazi-inspired antisemitic fever across Europe. Against this danger he could only declare his faith in the days of the

Messiah: "Evil is not everlasting. Hitler and Chamberlain will not live forever, and there will still be changes and turns in Europe and in the world. Justice, now trampled under foot, will emerge."[62]

Until justice emerged, though, the bitter truth was that the times were "times of power politics." It was the guns that were speaking, "and the Jews in the Diaspora [did] not have guns"—and neither did Zionism.[63] *Haaretz* wrote on August 29: "If evil prevails and in one way or another Nazi Germany's rule is imposed on Poland, on part of it or God forbid on all of it —then their [the Jews'] future is clear: to be eradicated from the country as has been done to the Jews of Germany and Austria and Czechoslovakia and the other places where the Nazis' influence has reached." In "eradicated from the country" the newspaper meant expulsions, oppression, and murder. *Hatzofeh* warned that it was Germany's Jews who were now in terrible peril: if war broke out, it wrote, they would be conscripted for forced labor, and there was a risk of pogroms.

Although grim predictions were heard at the Zionist Congress in Geneva about what was in store for Poland's Jews if war broke out, no one foresaw that by the middle of September Poland would fall into the hands of Nazi Germany and the Soviet Union; much less did anyone foresee the plans that the Nazi regime had prepared for Poland's Jews. From a country that had described the Jews as "superfluous" and had pressured them to leave in droves, Poland turned in August 1939, in the eyes of Zionism as well, if not into a homeland, then certainly into a country that should be unwaveringly defended by all.

The invasion of Poland took all of Europe by surprise and, therefore, one cannot blame the leaders of the Zionist movement or the leaders of the Jewish public for failing to predict it, much less when it would occur. The warnings of impending disaster for the Jews of Poland did not arise out of a fear of Nazi Germany's takeover of Poland, but rather from concerns in the face of Polish antisemitism. Hence, neither Jabotinsky nor his followers predicted that Nazi Germany would conquer Poland; rather, they predicted that Polish antisemitism would lead to a "holocaust," that is to say, the physical elimination of Poland's Jews. This claim was baseless: the Nazi conquest of Poland was what prepared the ground for the realization of Nazi Germany's racist and antisemitic ideology and enabled the implementation of the Final Solution to the Jewish question.

Burdened with backpacks
all kinds of people set out
for the unknown.[1]
Adam Czerniakow,
September 7, 1939

8

"SO EARLY, NO ONE HAS SEEN DEATH YET"

Weizmann left in Geneva an anxious and frightened Zionist Congress: "The terrible panic began. Those who had the chance to flee—packed their suitcases and fled. [. . .] In the afternoon the Congress became largely empty. The Americans had left. The English had left. Many more delegates and guests had fled. The empty seats reminded one of the quake that had shaken the world. The committee heads read out the resolutions. Hands are raised. Here and there comments are made. But all the hearts are beating in contemplation of the foggy future."[2]

It was as if an eternity had passed in the short time between his farewell address to the Congress and the confident and hopeful words with which he had summed up his speech during the Congress's third session on August 17, saying: "Never has all the good and exalted in us as magically arisen as when we have faced difficulties. We are in distress, and I am sure that we will not put our past to shame. And when we meet at the next Congress, we will be able to say that we have moved forward." According to the minutes his words were greeted with "lengthy applause."[3] The delegates dispersed to their places and their fates.

On August 26, 1939, Isaiah Klinov, the *Haaretz* correspondent in Geneva, filed the following piece about the panic. It was printed on September 1:

> The Congress is in turmoil. Today is Thursday, August 24, and in the hall the committees' representatives are still lecturing and the parties' delegates are still making their proclamations, [. . .] but half of the Congress is *outside*, excited, shocked, confused. What is going to happen? What is going to happen? War? Really? [. . .] Pale faces. Dejected eyes. [. . .]

"The trains are full and already terribly crowded, people are standing in the aisles."

"The American delegates have already lost some of their suitcases."

"The French border, they say, is completely shut."

"So is the Italian-Swiss border."

[. . .] A few hours later it turns out that some of the rumors were quite exaggerated. The exodus from the town is certainly not small. But it was exactly the same a year ago, during Munich. My landlady consoles us: "I remember last September. Back then there were no grounds for panic either."

But where should one go? Surely Marseille will be the first to be bombed, in Paris they are evacuating women and children and will not let foreigners stay, and the Italian ships were grounded in their ports; only people with means can try and lease a plane and pay 57 Pp per person.[4]

The Hakibbutz Hameuchad (United Kibbutz Movement) emissaries from Palestine convened on the closing night of the Congress with the Hechalutz emissaries to discuss the dilemma of whether to go back to the countries to which they had been sent or return to Palestine. Katznelson asked one of them, Pini Ginzburg, who held a British passport: "So, back to Germany?" When Ginzburg answered in the affirmative, Katznelson gave him an emotional hug.[5]

The emissaries saw returning to Germany and Poland as a duty and a dictate of conscience, but did not imagine that in a few days' time some of those who had returned to Poland would have to decide whether to stay or join the flight. Some thirty-five members of the Hashomer Hatzair party and its emissaries in Europe gathered in the party's room at the Grand Théâtre to discuss the issue. After a debate it was decided that the emissaries would go back to Palestine and that only two of them—Yaakov Riftin and Avraham Lipsker—would return to Poland.[6] They joined the movement's central seminar in the town of Ol'govskiy in the valley at the foot of the Carpathians, and when general mobilization was announced the camp was dispersed and the two left Poland. The camp's flag was set on fire and the seminar's director parted from its participants with the words: "Would that this flag return to fly on Polish soil."[7]

The Mossad LeAliyah Bet activists waited for a committee made up of Aharon Zisling, Yaakov Hazan, and David Hacohen to decide who among them would return to his duties, who would stay in Switzerland, and who would return to Palestine. Meanwhile, they went rowing on Lake Geneva and smoked cigarettes on the boat; for some of them it was their first ever cigarette. The committee decided that those who had Palestinian passports would not return to the Reich.[8] Zeev Shind and Yehuda Braginsky boarded a train to Paris in Geneva:

> Early in the evening we rushed to the train station. At the station there was chaos. Crowds of tourists swarmed the train cars trying to return to their homelands. We miraculously managed to take hold of a seat in one of the compartments. While sitting there waiting for the train to depart for Paris, we saw Moshe Shertok through the compartment's window, rushing onto the platform. [. . .] We called him into our compartment and offered him the seat we had conquered. He slumped on it and felt somewhat relieved. On a gray and wintry morning we arrived in Paris.[9]

Thanks to the intervention of the head of the Polish delegation to the League of Nations, the Italian government allowed the delegates from Poland to return to their country through Italy and Austria in closed carriages. Emanuel Ringelblum, who described Weizmann's parting speech as a speech full of "terror and anxiety," wrote: "Terrible chaos [. . .] Hanging onto the cars, on the roofs. Some are trying to break into our car. Manifestations of antisemitism in the country. Civic awareness made us decide to return to the country. Those who wanted to stay in the country."[10]

Zerach Warhaftig, one of the leaders of the National Religious Party in Palestine, similarly recorded the Polish delegates' decision to go back: "To Warsaw, to our families and to our duty to our homeland, to Poland, to defend it. Never has a Jew felt so at one with both his civic and Jewish duty as when he stood up against the war threats of Hitler and his troops." In Budapest, the Zionist Organization held a ball and a reception in their honor. The Hamizrachi delegates dined at a kosher restaurant whose owner boasted that Admiral Horthy's son used to come there to eat cholent, a traditional Sabbath stew.[11] The mood improved, wrote Warhaftig, but on the morning of September 2, when the train passed near Lublin, they learned that the day before war had broken out. A train full of refugees from Poznan pulled up next to them. They went up to the train's windows and called out: "Jews to Palestine."[12]

The hundred or so delegates who returned to Poland through Budapest included seven emissaries from Palestine.[13] The *Forverts* reported that several delegates from Poland had gone to France to join its army.[14] Ben-Gurion, Moshe Kleinbaum, and Anschel Reiss, secretary of the World Union of Poalei Zion, discussed the possibility of organizing Jewish units to fight in Poland. According to Reiss, Ben-Gurion took the idea seriously and asked him to return to Poland to promote it. Reiss traveled to Paris intending to catch a flight to Gdynia on September 1, but on the night of August 30 he was told that the flights had been canceled.[15]

Kleinbaum returned from London to Warsaw on August 31 and immediately joined his army unit. When the unit dispersed he left Warsaw for Lublin and joined the regiments retreating east toward Łutzk, where they were captured by the Red Army. During one of the long journeys on which the Soviets marched the captured Polish soldiers he managed to slip away and disappear among the civilian population, thus saving his life. Kleinbaum reached Vilna and rejoined his wife and daughter, who had escaped from Warsaw.[16] The Polish officers were led from the Łutzk camp to the Katyn Forest near Smolensk, where in April and May 1940 they were all executed.[17]

Emanuel Neumann postponed his return to Palestine because he did not know whether it was safe to travel on the Mediterranean. He stayed at "a countryside resort near Geneva." When Britain declared war on Germany, he traveled with his young daughter to Trieste, where they boarded an Italian ship bound for Haifa. When they returned to Palestine he "succumbed" to the pleadings of his relatives in the United States and sailed there with his family.[18]

Some of the 400 delegates and guests who had come to the Zionist Congress from Palestine intended to fly back on two leased planes. However, Switzerland's neighboring countries refused to allow the planes to fly over their territories. Because they could not sail from Italy's ports, most of the delegates took the train to Marseille, where the streetlights had been dimmed several days earlier. The attempts of the Congress delegates and other Jewish travelers who gathered near the Lloyd firm's offices on Rue de Republique to sail from Marseille were documented in an article "We were refugees!" which was published in *Davar* on September 12. At first the Egyptian consul in Marseille forbade the captain of the Egyptian vessel *Quasar* to take on any Palestinian citizens, but in the end he distributed visas free of charge. However, a few Egyptian passengers protested and demanded that the captain remove the passengers from Palestine from the ship: "These Jews are Zionists, they are returning from the Congress in Geneva, where they decided to fight the Arabs, and we are supposed to save them and take them to Palestine?" The delegates and other non-Arab passengers were taken off the ship and returned "to their hotel tired and depressed, and started looking for other vessels." The lesson, summed up the author of the article, was: "Palestinian subjects also need Palestinian ships!"[19]

The delegates waited in town for three days, from August 27 to 29, for the departure of the *Cairo City*, a British-owned vessel that sailed under a Greek flag, onto which some 200 of them boarded. Moshe Krone, the Hamizrachi delegate, described it as a barely manageable "tiny Greek ship": "You had to struggle with tremendous force to climb the stairs that led to the ship's deck. It was also difficult because we were weighed down with several chairs and some vegetables and fruit we had managed to buy during the brief time we had spent in the town. [. . .] The ship sailed the alternately stormy and tranquil seas, carrying a large population of Congress delegates from all the parties. Many of the grandees and leaders of the Yishuv were there, crowded and crammed, worried and scared."[20] Krone's wife Rachel was in Warsaw on a family visit, and at the end of August decided to return to Palestine. Her parents asked: "Stay with us at least for the High Holidays," but she declined.

Ruppin, who was worried about the *Cairo City* being an old merchant ship, bought an easy chair and 300 francs' worth of groceries, but when he boarded the ship he found that it was "a fairly decent passenger ship." "For egalitarian reasons," he noted, he refrained from taking a single room. Eighty of the Labor party delegates boarded the ship. The Mapai and Hashomer Hatzair delegates used the eleven-day voyage to talk about the possibility of uniting the two parties. Meir Yaari, the Hashomer Hatzair leader, reacted noncommittally to the proposal of David Remez, one of Mapai's leaders and the Histadrut secretary, to unite the workers' movement: great effort should be made to achieve unification, but the decision was not entirely in his hands. In fact, Yaari opposed unification for fear that it would damage the Hashomer Hatzair movement's power among Poland's youth.[21] The news about the outbreak of war reached the delegates while they were still far out at sea. Ruppin wrote in his diary: "This morning the radio announced the start of the war—the bombing of Warsaw! Well, a new world war—a turn in the history of the world! This is also where the fate of the Jews will be decided."[22] The ship sailed with its lights dimmed. At the port of Alexandria, from where they sailed to Tel Aviv on September 6, they saw a large number of warships.

Other delegates took the long route to the port of Piraeus in Greece, where they boarded the ships *Har Zion* and *Miriam*. The *Har Zion* sailed with 129 passengers (as well as "two wagons of chickens and 76 bulls") and was detained by the Turkish authorities at Rodosto in the Sea of Marmara, eighty-four miles from Istanbul.[23]

On the last day of the Zionist Congress, Katznelson met Marie Syrkin and was amazed to see that she was still there. The American consul in Geneva advised the delegates from the United States to leave immediately for their ports of departure (one of them said that he had bought a ticket to climb Mont Blanc). On August 27 they left Geneva and traveled to the port of Cherbourg to wait for the arrival of the luxury ship *Queen Mary*, which was about to embark on its final journey.[24] Ben-Gurion and a few other delegates flew from Egypt to Lod airport on a plane operated by the Aviron company. The journey from Geneva to Tel Aviv took eight days. When Ben-Gurion arrived at his home on Keren Kayemet Boulevard on Saturday night, September 2, he was told that Nazi Germany had attacked Poland at 6:30 on the previous morning. The Jewish Agency Executive had convened in Jerusalem in the afternoon and released a public statement. It said that Britain's war against Nazi Germany was also the war of the Jewish people.[25] There was no mention of concern for the fate of Poland's Jews.

Dr. Richard Lichtheim, one of the leaders of Germany's Zionists, a member of the Jewish State Party, which had seceded from the Revisionist movement in 1933, and an activist on behalf of Keren Hayesod, was asked to stay in Geneva to maintain "contact between the Zionist Executive and the Zionist centers in Europe during the war that was about to break out."[26]

Katznelson was called by Shaul Meirov to Marseille for an urgent consultation, and on the evening of August 29 intended to travel to the port city again to try and sail to Palestine. From Paris he wrote to his wife Leah Miron that after the Zionist Congress had adjourned there started "a terrible panic that turned everyone into a frightened herd. A few less-than-wonderful human qualities were revealed [. . .]. The attempts were to no avail, no planes took off. I stayed put without getting too excited and waited for news of a ship, maybe tomorrow they will find a place for me on one."[27]

Instead of going to Marseille, Katznelson traveled to London, where, as already mentioned, he met Jabotinsky for several long conversations.[28] After that Katznelson returned to Paris, where he saw Braginsky and his colleagues at his hotel and told them: "The war will be long, Jews will be annihilated."[29] He sailed from Marseille on the *Marco Polo* and disembarked at the port of Haifa on September 21.

At the end of August the heads of the American Jewish Joint Distribution Committee and the Hebrew Immigrant Aid Society met in Paris. They decided to transfer a large sum of money to Poland by the end of the year and leave only a small sum in the European banks. When the war broke out, Yitzhak Gitelman, the representative of both organizations as well as the Jewish Colonization Association in Poland, who had founded a chain of interest-free loan funds in the country, hastened to return to Warsaw (he was murdered in the Warsaw ghetto on January 18, 1943).[30]

On August 27, the *Haynt* correspondent in Tel Aviv told the newspaper's readers in Poland of his impressions of "life in Palestine in these turbulent times." The article was printed on the August 30:

> Although the atmosphere is quite tense, it does not feel too nerve-wracking. Life goes on almost normally. All day yesterday people swarmed to the beach in great numbers. [. . .] The cafés were full as always. Music was played and young couples were dancing. Until late at night it was almost impossible to make your way down Allenby Street—the traffic in the street was so heavy. All the cinemas bustled with people. The symphony orchestra played under the baton of the guest conductor Simon Parmet. The exhibition hall [Orient Fair] was full [. . .]. So were Habima, Haohel, Hamatateh and so on. This is what Palestine on the eve of war looks like. May it continue in the same way and not get any worse [. . .].

The *Haynt* correspondent reported further that the Tel Aviv municipality had appealed to Palestine's government to pass a law against food profiteering and equip the residents with inexpensive gas masks, and that an office had been opened on 13 Rothschild Avenue to organize air raid defenses.[31]

> "Will there" or "won't there," this was the talk of the day in mid-week. The rumor mill prospered. Baseless or semi-based news were spread around along with alarming rumors. The newspapers' Saturday night editions were practically snatched from the sellers and distributed in thousands of copies. The public breathed a sigh of relief when it learned that efforts —albeit desperate ones—were still made for peace. [. . .] This morning the public was still of the opinion that the last hope had not been lost.[32]

"Peace [*shalom*], pursued by so many yet so elusive, has left Tel Aviv too. Today you no longer hear 'shalom' in inverted commas, even a close friend is no longer greeted with 'shalom,'" wrote *Haaretz* on August 30, "but is immediately addressed with the question: 'will there or won't there (be war).'"[33]

The efforts to preserve peace in Europe, however, continued side by side with the preparations for war. The Palestine press reported on the British ambassador Henderson's flight to Berlin to convey the British government's answer to Hitler, about the closure of the border between France and Germany, about the stoppage of flights and train traffic from France to Germany, about the streets of Paris having been almost totally darkened, about throngs of American citizens leaving Britain, and about Polish citizens in various countries across Western Europe starting to return to their country. They also reported on skirmishes on the Polish-German border and on armies assembling. They further reported that according to Radio Berlin's propaganda broadcasts, while the Polish officers were enjoying excellent food, the rank and file had to beg for potatoes.

From Poland, on the other hand, it was reported that life had not been disrupted and that there was no sense of panic. Germany's Jews were in danger, *Hatzofeh* wrote, because if war broke out they would be conscripted into forced labor.[34] On August 31 *Haaretz*'s main headline read: "Europe continues to look for a way out of the national crisis that is threatening it." Germany and Poland, the newspaper added, were interested in the mediating proposal of the Dutch queen and the Belgian king, but the Polish government had replied that it could not address the matter "as long as Germany does not show signs of willingness to enter negotiations."[35] *Hatzofeh* similarly announced: "The British reply to Hitler leaves the way open for negotiations." At the same time, all the newspapers reported that Poland had announced the general mobilization of its reserves. Civilians in the areas bordering Germany had been evacuated from their homes and the Polish army had taken up positions. On August 27 they reported that an announcement disseminated in Warsaw had proclaimed that the Poles would know how to "fight courageously and to the death to defend every inch of our land and to defend every village destroyed."[36]

Despite the soothing words, the Yishuv became anxious that the war might soon reach it as well. The banks were inundated with customers trying to withdraw their money, and on August 27 the High Commissioner closed the banks for three days. At noon on Friday, August 25, the Tel Aviv city council held a special meeting to discuss the international situation's implications for the city. The general view at the meeting was that there was no room for panic and that even if war broke out, the city's buildings were relatively more solid than in other cities and there were sufficient stockpiles of food in Tel Aviv. The city council decided to turn to Palestine's government and demand that it pass a special bylaw to determine which food products would be supervised. Inspectors were sent to the stores, and stations and food distribution centers were set up. *Haaretz* described the hoarding panic: trucks full of goods were unloaded, the wholesale stores filled with shoppers, and the grocery stores were crammed with women who, gripped by the fear of war, had turned their apartments "into grocery store branches." The shopkeepers demanded cash payments. The war, wrote the newspaper, would start at the wholesale market: "Sometimes you think that the real war will break out here first. [. . .] Here the war has been waged since early morning. The shopkeepers have been desperate to get produce for their customers, to fill the granaries, to hike up the prices because 'if not now, when.'"[37]

Israel Rokach, Tel Aviv's mayor, met with Major Spark, the government expert for air raid defenses. They discussed the readiness of the civilian population and the need to equip it with gas masks. At the beginning of the month he had been preoccupied with a different important matter. He had drafted a municipal ad against the increasing use of foreign languages (that is, Yiddish) in Tel Aviv's public realm: "Even at this difficult and fateful hour, which requires defensive means in all areas of life, the Tel Aviv municipality sees it as its duty to appeal to the city's residents [. . .] about strictly preserving its Hebrew character." On August 29 Spark lectured at the Teachers' Seminar on Ben-Yehuda Street about ways to defend against aerial attacks "and his listeners even got to experience what it was like when they were asked to put on a gas mask and walk through a hall filled with tear gas." Two days later, registration was opened to receive the masks that had been ordered from abroad. Magen David Adom and the Lanoter organization published a brochure with first aid instructions for gas casualties.

The Allenby cinema adapted to the atmosphere with matinee screenings of the film *The Little Man and the Great War*. About a week later, on Saturday night, September 9, it was replaced by the romantic musical *The Devil on Horseback* (1936) starring Lili Damita. The publicity ad announced: "With this movie we have responded to popular demand to offer an amusing and soothing work at this time." The Gan Rina cinema screened the thriller *International Settlement* (1938). The Migdalor cinema showed a Polish film, an adaptation of one of Erich Kästner's books, *Das Doppelte Lottchen* (*The Double Lottie*). The Armon cinema in Haifa screened the picture *Loves of the Dictators* (1935). Ora and Ophir in Tel Aviv showed the musical comedy *Everybody Sing* (1938) with Judy Garland, and the Kikar Dizengoff cinema offered the film *Refugees*. Cinemas in Jerusalem screened *The Good Earth* (1937) and *Yellow Jack* (1938). Ads invited the public to purchase tickets to the performance of the famous cantor Yehoshua Yadlin, who was going to perform at the Kikar Dizengoff cinema over the High Holidays.

One of the city's residents complained that a nonkosher restaurant had been opened on Rambam Street and that there was licentiousness on the beach: the kiosks were open on Saturdays and they were cooking corn on the cob.

A blackout exercise was held in Haifa on August 28 to prepare the city and the port for aerial attacks. The next day the football team Maccabi Tel Aviv left Australia, where it had played nineteen games, on its way back to Palestine. On the same day the immigrants of the illegal immigrant ship *Rim* were released from their detention in Sarafand and transferred to the Immigrants House in Tel Aviv.

An insurance agent from Haaliyah Street in Tel Aviv called on the public to insure their lives and property against the approaching war: "Personal accident insurance—life insurance together with full and complete insurance against the war." On August 29 the trial of eight Jews opened at the military court in Haifa. On July 26 they had shot at nine Arab workers from the village of Abudia who worked for the government's anti-malaria agency; they were suspected of murdering three of them and fleeing from the scene. It was a reprisal for the murder of the farmer Michael Adin from Menachemia. The accused were acquitted.

On that day, a tailor from Damascus, who lived in Jerusalem and worked as the correspondent of the *Al-Qabas* newspaper, was found guilty of leading "a gang of murderous youths" that had perpetrated numerous crimes in and around Jerusalem. Twelve Jews were killed in August and four in September. They were the last to be murdered in the period of the Arab Revolt.

The Nazi government called on all Christian Germans under the age of fifty living in Palestine to return to Germany by August 30. On the evening of August 30 two bombs were thrown into the synagogue of an old people's home. Fortunately, prayer had already ended and no one was hurt. A young couple was shot at while driving their car on their way to Mount Carmel. The next morning a bus was attacked and shot at near the Wadi Rushmia Bridge at the exit from Haifa. None of the passengers was hurt. The graduation ceremony of the Henrietta Szold Nursing School was held at the Hadassah Hospital on Mount Scopus. By contrast, the convention of the Agudat Yisrael party that was supposed to open in Petach Tikva was postponed: "If the tension subsides in the meantime the convention will take place at the same venue and with the same program next Tuesday."

The *Haaretz* editorial on August 29 said:

> Since Poland's sky began to darken after the occupation of Czechoslovakia by Germany, when its aspirations regarding Poland, to which only six months earlier Hitler had sworn friendly relations, became apparent, the Jews of Poland started to show their devotion to the country in which they live. This has been an ancient tradition among the Jewish people: "Seek the peace and prosperity of the city to which I have carried you

into exile. Pray to the Lord for it, because if it prospers, you too will prosper" (Jeremiah 29:7). Poland's Jews have also donated great sums, perhaps more than they were able to, since Poland's Jewry has declined and has become very impoverished in the last fifteen years. And these days, as the shadow of war is practically cast over the country, Poland's Jews have reached the epitome of their patriotism. Out of the three (and perhaps three and a half) million Jews in Poland, the vast majority are devout orthodox Jews, and the leaders of this orthodox Jewry, the rabbis and the Torah scholars among them, have come out and ruled that defending the country takes precedence over the Sabbath [. . .] because Poland's Jews are not foreigners in their country. They have been well integrated in its political and public and economic life for several generations. And they have often proved their devotion and loyalty to the country at times of serious political crises. They have wholeheartedly partaken in the troubles that the country has suffered, they have been tormented together with the Polish people, although they were not always allowed to take similar part in its celebrations, when it experienced days of prosperity and revival. And Poland's Jews also know this: If evil prevails and in one way or another Nazi Germany's rule is imposed on Poland, on part of it or God forbid on all of it—then their [the Jews'] future is clear: to be eradicated from the country as has been done to the Jews of Germany and Austria and Czechoslovakia and the other places where the Nazis' influence has reached.[38]

In July 1937, Jabotinsky had said to the members of the Hatzohar and the Irgun delegation in Palestine who had come to consult him in Alexandria: "If you ask me to give the order for a revolt—I will give it, but only if I am in it with you. Therefore you will have to get me to Machanaim, so that we can fight together, go to prison together and if need be—die together. But I do not think that the British will even try to implement this fantastical plan."[39]

The talk of an uprising and a revolt was part of the internal debate among the various groups in the Revisionist movement. The debate ensued, among other things, from the disappointment with the results of the political and diplomatic activity of the movement's leaders. As for Jabotinsky, he did not believe in a "revolt"; at most he meant a demonstrative act designed to awaken public opinion in Britain. In 1939 Jabotinsky set his sights on a plan to organize a "Zion Sejm," or as he called it, the Jewish "distress parliament," whose aim was to awaken the world's conscience and return Britain to the Charter, that is, to the policy that advocated the implementation of the Balfour Declaration.

Jabotinsky's frustration erupted and he reached the conclusion that now was the time for a dramatic demonstrative act: organizing a fleet of vessels that would transport armed Betar members to Palestine's shores. The latter would take over strategic and governmental facilities and hold fast for at least twenty-four hours. Meanwhile, Jabotinsky would announce the foundation of a Hebrew state and an interim government. He had recently described such actions as "grand gestures." The "plan" reached the Irgun headquarters in Tel Aviv written in code, and was discussed by it on August 31.

Despite their serious doubts, the commanders approved the plan, whereupon British police forces broke into the room and arrested them. On the basis of these four encoded letters, in which Jabotinsky communicated his plan to the members of the Irgun's high command, some of the Revisionist historiographic tradition has called Jabotinsky "the Father of the Revolt." Jabotinsky did not clarify how the "invading force" would be organized in Poland, how the armed fighters would get from Poland to the shores of the Black Sea, how they would obtain vessels, and how they would reach the shores of Palestine undisturbed. In any case, even at the end of August 1939 he was still confident that a world war would not break out.[40]

According to the Lehi version, it was Avraham Stern who was "the Father of the Revolt," because he had conceived the idea as early as 1938 and also received the support of the Poles. The Irgun's military training courses that were held in Poland under his inspiration were designed to train the 40,000 fighters who would seize Palestine. According to the Lehi members, Jabotinsky only adopted Stern's view when he realized that it was a "serious" plan.[41] On August 11 the Polish-language Revisionist newspaper *Trybuna Naradowa*, edited by Dr. Jan (Yohanan) Bader, led with a large picture of Marshal Piłsudski and wrote about "the lesson of August 6"—the day on which the first group from Piłsudski's first brigade had launched its first battle beyond the Russian border.

Wiktor Chajes's diary alternated between uncertainty and illusions. He was deeply occupied with the election campaign for the Lviv municipality, went on a summer vacation, and toyed with the hope that a revolution would erupt in Germany or Italy and that "time [was] on Poland's side."[42] In the last week of August, life in Warsaw proceeded under the shadow of war, but also as usual. A Jewish matchmaker was arrested and accused of fraud; a highflying crook who attached a false beard to his chin and collected donations for Jewish refugees—and immediately after was seen wearing a priest's clothes and asking for donations from Christians—was arrested; a tram struck a young Jewish pedestrian and killed him; Laizer Weinstein from Janów, who came to the community offices to ask for help for his sick eleven-year old daughter, was beaten up in the courtyard and passed out. Avraham Rosenthal who came to his aid and knocked on the office doors to ask for some water was also hit on the head with a stone.

On August 24, the poet and translator Shaul Tchernichovsky stopped at Warsaw on his way to the PEN (international organization of writers) international congress in Oslo. He stayed with the publisher Stybel and they spoke about the political situation. On August 25, a reception was held in his honor by the Union of Yiddish Writers on Karmelicka Street. In his speech, Tchernichovsky talked about the Hebrew revival, "and these were the last words spoken by a Jewish poet in Jewish Warsaw."[43]

On August 25, the play *Yoshe Kalb* (Yoshe Calf) by Israel Yehoshua Singer was performed for the last time at the Scala Theater. On August 28, Zygmunt Turkow's VYKT company staged Abraham Goldfaden's play *Shulamis* for the sixty-second time at the Nowości Theater.

Der Moment published an article by the historian Simon Dubnov: "What shall we do in the days of Haman?" Dubnov wrote that in Central Europe, the whole history of disasters and pogroms from the previous generation was combined with modern murder methods: a million Jews in Germany, Austria, and Czechoslovakia "have been exterminated, robbed and beaten and dozens of refugees from Ashkenaz are knocking on all the countries' doors, but are not allowed in because of immigration laws or plain malice. Therefore, with the sword at their throat, the Jews must unite their forces." This was not the time for internal disagreements and the entire Jewish people should join the "moral siege" against Hitler and Mussolini and enlist for the war once it broke out.

On August 27, the *Haynt* reported that the armies of Europe were standing ready along the borders and that the British navy had been put on high alert and had blockaded the Baltic Sea. The following day it raised its readers' spirits by reporting that in Germany a revolt had erupted against Hitler and that Ukraine was taking Poland's side. The Jews, wrote the newspaper, also saw the independence and integrity of Poland as sacred; Poland was the rock on which the waves of tyranny that sought to take over the world would break. The *Haynt* stated that, confident of its future, Poland was ready and prepared for the fateful battle.

On the evening of August 30, the civil defense sirens in Warsaw were tested. Gas masks were sold for 4 zloty each. The headline of the midday newspaper *Hayntike nayes* (Today's news) on August 31 declared: "Take your hands off Polish soil!" The *Haynt* column "What's happening in Warsaw?" announced the community's intention of opening a military hospital. On August 30, *Davar* quoted Palestine residents who had just arrived from Warsaw as saying that "the mood in Poland is brave and enthusiastic":

> Life in Warsaw and in Poland's other cities has not been disrupted, the factories are working, in the groceries there are large stocks of all the essential products. Prices have remained fixed. Some shopkeepers accused of hiking up prices were imprisoned in Orsza. There is no shortage of food anywhere in Poland. The banks are open, but are supervised. In the financial market there is no sense of panic. [. . .] Despite the numerous mobilizations, train traffic across Poland has not been disrupted, and the postal and telegraph services are working normally. All the news on German radio about disorder in Poland are based on lies.[44]

The newspaper described the Jewish public's enlistment for the war preparations in all the Polish cities: "You can see Orthodox Jews with beards and *payot* (side locks) working side by side with Poles. The view recalls the days of the Polish rebellion against the Russians, when Jews defended Warsaw together with the Poles." In Krakow a group of Jewish youths marched in front of the German consulate building and "the German consul came out and stood for a long time looking at the digging [of trench shelters] done by the Jews."[45]

At the end of the month came a sensational piece of news: the American administration had allocated $200 million for the settlement of 150,000 Jews in Alaska who would serve as the nucleus for a large settlement that would open a new chapter in Jewish history. It was Secretary of the Interior Harold Ickes who was pushing the idea to open Alaska to Jewish immigrants. These immigrants, he claimed, were "men and women with the spirit of our pioneers" and should be given "the opportunity to enlist in the service of the nation, building cities in our last frontier." According to the *Haynt*, the warm part of Alaska, along the Pacific Ocean, was equal in size to Poland. This whole region had a population of only around 60,000 people, and its richness was colossal: fertile fields, abundant forests, gold mines, and other minerals. President Roosevelt, the newspaper informed its readers, was about to reveal the plan, which also had a military aspect: should war break out with Japan, it was better for the United States' defensive line to be inhabited.

Should the Jews agree to Alaska as a destination for mass immigration? The *Haynt* thought that the proposal should be seriously considered, because it was not one of those rumors floated about in times of despair. The "Alaska Program" was mooted as early as November 1938 and was discussed in the highest echelons of the American administration.

In August 1939, the Department of the Interior published a plan to settle around 60,000 people in Alaska, half of whom would be immigrants from Germany. The plan divided public opinion and failed to receive a positive reaction. Far away in Neustadt, Germany, Bruno Rosenthal, who had been arrested on Kristallnacht and spent forty days at the Buchenwald labor camp, read about the plan. On behalf of thirty of the town's Jews he approached the Secretary of the Interior Ickes, who had published the *Alaska Report* on August 16. Rosenthal wrote three letters describing their desire to immigrate to Alaska, because "they cannot stay here [in Germany]," and added: "We know quite well the difficulties of making it in the rough clime of Alaska, but now we have no other choice, we German Jews." The last of the three letters was sent on August 31.[46] Both *Davar* and *Haaretz* thought that this plan was more serious than all the others.[47] President Roosevelt turned the plan down.

On the evening of August 31, a group of sixty Jewish children, along with their adult escorts, set out from Cologne to Kleve, a town on the Germany-Holland border, which they crossed. That same night they sailed across the North Sea to the British port of Harwich. This was the last group of the approximately 10,000 children who left Germany on the Kindertransport.[48] "The minds of the Jews in Poland," wrote the *Zionist Review* on August 31, "are now severely exercised over the war menace. Numerous places thickly populated by Jews are in the possible war zone, and complete ruin threatens them in the event of an outbreak of hostilities."

On August 31, the weather in Warsaw was pleasant: 80°F. The *Haynt* reported that Hitler had had a nervous breakdown. The following day, the *Jewish Chronicle* reported on the conscription of thousands of Jews in Germany for forced labor, but also that the cafés had removed the "No entry for Jews" signs due to the drop in their income. The London newspaper reported in the same issue about the mobilization of Poland's Jews. The Zionist Organization in Poland published a declaration: "A cruel enemy is threatening Poland, the heart of the global Jewish Diaspora for the last thousand years, whose Jews, more than three million in number, are staying loyal to the country and to the Polish nation." The Refugees Committee located on Zamenhoff Street called on all the refugees who had been expelled from

Germany to Poland and were in Warsaw to join in digging air raid shelters: "Jewish refugees! The homeland needs the help and joint effort of all its citizens. Refugees! It is even our urgent duty. Precisely we who have suffered so many injustices and persecutions on foreign soil feel a special gratitude to the homeland that has embraced us."[49]

At 5:40 a.m. on September 1, Hitler broadcasted to his army that the attack had started following Poland's stubborn refusal to hold negotiations. At 10:00 a.m. he spoke again, blaming the Polish government for refusing to accept "reasonable" proposals and initiating "provocations" on its border with Germany: "We will respond to bombings with bombs," the Führer declared.

During the morning Hitler convened the Reichstag in Berlin, stood before it wearing his corporal insignia from the First World War, and announced that he had taken Danzig under his wings. At that time around 2,000 German air force planes were bombing cities across Poland. The Polish president published an address to the nation asking Poland's citizens to rally around the Polish armed forces and defend their liberty, independence, and honor:

> Citizens. During the course of last night, our age-old enemy commenced offensive operations against the Polish state. I affirm this before God and history. At this historic moment, I appeal to all citizens of the country in profound conviction that the entire nation will rally around its commander in chief and armed forces to defend its liberty, independence and honor, and to fire the aggressor a worthy answer, as happened already more than once in the history of Polish-German relations. The entire nation, blessed by God in its struggle for a just and sacred cause, and united with its army, will march as one to aid in the struggle and final victory.[50]

The British ambassador to Poland reported at 8:30 a.m. that Krakow and other cities were being bombed and that the German army had crossed the border. Two hours later, the Polish ambassador arrived at the British Foreign Office with similar information. He demanded the immediate activation of the British-Polish contract and some aerial support. In the afternoon the British government decided to present Nazi Germany with an ultimatum that would expire at midnight. The following morning the British ambassador to Berlin served the ultimatum.

On that day, September 1, Jabotinsky wrote to the NZO activists that the movement's presidency had yet to declare its policy because the political situation was unclear and it was impossible to know whether the war would spread to the western front. The demand to create Jewish regiments in the allied armies would not affect Zionism's status; their creation would be "a step in the struggle against assimilation." The tragic thing right now, Jabotinsky added, was that the Jews were not a factor, and the Jewish problem had remained seemingly unconnected to the global conflict; and the proof: in all the governments' declarations about the war's goals, the tragedy of Polish Jewry and the Jewish problem had not been mentioned even once.[51]

On Friday morning, September 1, the butcher's young apprentice went to the Klemperers' house and told them that the radio had announced "that we already have Danzig and the Corridor, the war with Poland has started, England and France remain neutral." Upon hearing the news, Victor Klemperer said to his wife Eva that if this was so, "then a morphine injection or something similar was the best thing for us." Later he listened to Hitler's urgent voice on the radio, which sounded to him utterly pessimistic. But the people, he wrote, were convinced of an overwhelming, almost unchallenged victory.[52]

Early on the morning of September 1 Willy Cohn heard a succession of heavy squadrons flying in the direction of Upper Silesia and just a few hours later learned that Warsaw and Łódź were bombed. "The calamity has begun. The others will also intervene now and that means world war. [. . .] Air defenses have been mobilized, and from now on, Breslau is under a blackout."[53]

That same day Blanche Dugdale came out of the underground station in Holborn, London, and heard that Germany was bombing the Polish cities. She wrote in her diary: "I felt a kind of relief that the waiting [was] over."[54] President Franklin Delano Roosevelt sent an urgent telegram to the governments of Germany, Poland, Italy, France, and Britain, demanding they refrain from bombing helpless civilian populations from the air.[55] Two days later Dugdale wrote: "The shame is over. We were at war with Germany since 11 a.m., today and France since 5 p.m."[56]

Almost until mid-September a cloud of uncertainty had hung over the situation at the front. On September 19, Klemperer, together with many of Dresden's inhabitants who gathered in Bismarkplatz, listened to Hitler's victory speech as it was played on a loudspeaker: "I had the impression that all the bystanders were completely satisfied, sure of victory, sure even of imminent peace. But every single measure points to a long war. [. . .] One of two things will happen: either Hitler will sign a victorious peace within a week — then we shall perish. Or the war only really starts now and will last for a long time — in that case we shall also perish."[57]

The poet S. Shalom (Shalom Shapira) welcomed the arrival of the writer Max Brod in Palestine. On September 1, he wrote: "Chance is not always calamitous. There is also propitious chance"—and such was the case of Brod chancing to board the train to Prague ten minutes before the occupation of Czechoslovakia, leaving his "second homeland" and coming from a foreign land to the "first homeland."[58] The morning edition of the *Haynt* on September 1 included Israel Stern's poem "Nokha khirurgishn tish" (When the surgery is over). The poem described the Jewish people as haunted and numbed with chloroform, unaware of the lurking catastrophe:

We are sleeping, we are sleeping,
Like buildings late at night
Without knowing what is looming—
So early no one
Has seen death yet.[59]

Ila Strasman returned to Warsaw from Geneva two days before the outbreak of war. On the evening of August 31 she summoned the members of "the club"—a group of Warsovian intelligentsia that supported the Irgun and published the weekly *Jerozalima Wyzwolona* (Jerusalem Delivered)—to report to them on the delegation's activities at the Zionist Congress. On September 1 they published the last issue of the newspaper, which called on the Jews to enlist for the war to defend Poland: "In this historic and fateful moment in the struggle for Poland's independence, we the Jews, citizens of the republic, are ready for the order to join the march of defense and victory that will come from the commander in chief of the armed forces. [. . .] We are the Jewish camp, raised on the tradition of military action [. . .]. We are the good sons of the Polish government, conscious of our civic duty [. . .]. We are ready for the order."

When the air raids started she wrote: "Those strong of character immediately decided to pick up the wandering stick," but others found it difficult to make such a fateful decision and hoped that a miracle would occur and the danger would pass. On September 4, she and her friends packed the weapons the Irgun had accumulated in the warehouse on Ceglana (now Pereca) Street, which included 500 rifles and large amounts of Polish-made R.K.M. machine guns, pistols, and grenades that were intended to be sent to Palestine, and on September 5 she transferred the contents to the Polish army headquarters on Warsaw's Piłsudski square. The Polish officers on the premises gave her an official receipt and promised that one day Poland would reward the Jews for the gesture. The organization's archive was hidden away in milk cans. (Her husband, Dr. Henryk Strasman, a lecturer in medical criminology at the University of Warsaw's Law Department, was captured by the Russians and murdered in Katyn. She remained in Warsaw.) At one point she was arrested on the street by a German patrol but escaped from the detention cell. At the beginning of 1940 she managed to leave with her two small children for Italy holding an entry visa to Honduras, and eventually made it to Palestine.[60]

On the morning of September 1, Willy Cohn wrote in Breslau: "War has become a reality" and expressed concern that a Polish attack from the air was imminent.[61]

On Friday, September 1, the summer break was over and students all across Poland returned to school. Joel Mastbaum described the air raid siren that tore the children away from their games in the courtyard of CENTOS's Vladimir Medem orphanage in Otwock, near Warsaw. Seven children and staff were killed:

> The grating sound of the siren tore through the courtyard, fathers and sons ran around screaming and rushing to the shelters, there was a jumble of voices of adults and little ones—the bustling and muttering and monotonous voices of the whole courtyard, as if the entire world had become one group of toddlers [. . .]. And in the middle of the argument explosions sounded from far and near and terror gripped everyone, and the window lintels and doorposts shook, and windowpanes shattered and there was confusion in the whole courtyard.[62]

Ringelblum recorded laconically: "The news about the children's home in Otwock. Incessant sirens on Polish radio. [. . .] The shelters—living tombs. [. . .] For three weeks there was no bread, only rice. [. . .] [Tenants] are abandoning the upper floors. A disinfection unit collects the casualties. The dead are driven in handcarts with their arms and legs splayed. Around 200 casualties in one building."[63]

Peretz Opoczynski, a journalist and political activist, wrote: "This bombardment [. . .] was a calculated and deliberate murder, an intentional mass murder that has become a symbol: death to the Jewish child, to the offspring of the Jewish people, the physical obliteration of the next generation of Jews!"[64]

The September 1 newspapers in Palestine did not report the outbreak of war but continued to describe the tense atmosphere. They updated their readers that the ultimatum served by Nazi Germany to Poland had been rejected outright and reported on the general mobilization in Britain and

France and on plans for the massive evacuation of London and Paris. They also mentioned the telegram of support sent by Mahatma Gandhi to the Polish government and reproduced in *Haaretz*: "To all those in Poland who believe that only truth and justice will win and who dedicate their best efforts to this goal and sacrifice their lives for it—I send my well wishes and blessings."

The news agencies reported on the military preparations across Europe: general mobilization, the evacuation of civilians from the major cities, and so on.[65] *Haaretz* described the criticism of the Ribbentrop-Molotov Pact in the Soviet Union and Germany and predicted that this friendship would not last. A brief report told of around 4,000 Jewish refugees who were unable to escape to France due to the country having closed its borders, adding that around 500 of them were wandering around the border towns in desperation.[66] More space was devoted by the Friday newspapers to the local news: ships bringing tons of basic food supplies; the electricity situation in Safed; the eighth convention of the union of rail, postal, and telegraph workers; the museum in Ein Harod; the security situation at Kibbutz Negba, founded two months earlier; and so on.

On September 1, the British foreign secretary Halifax sent a message to his country's ambassador to Ankara instructing him to exert pressure on the Turkish government to detain any vessels carrying illegal immigrants.[67] The British banned the Jewish Agency from using around a third of its certificate quota for the months of April through September 1939, claiming that the permits had been given to Jews who were enemy subjects. The temporary office of the Jewish Agency's Immigration Department in Geneva was allowed by the British to authorize its representatives in Trieste to grant entry visas to Palestine to certificate holders who could prove that since the outbreak of war they had not stayed in an enemy country.[68]

On September 2, the Polish Sejm held its last session. Shlomo Seidenman, one of the five Jewish members, proclaimed: "Honored Sejm, this is not the time for debates. I declare again that Poland's Jewish population is putting itself wholly at the disposal of the high command and is ready to make all the sacrifices demanded in this historic moment. A strong and powerful Polish state is the ideal of the Jewish population as citizens with equal rights in this country." According to the minutes his words were greeted with applause.

On September 2, Jabotinsky sent a telegram of support from the French resort town in which he was staying to the Polish president Ignacy Mościcki. The telegram's style recalled the statement released by the Polish president a day earlier:

> Whether Germany's suicidal aggression be destined to end in military debacle, or in a moral collapse now, it will remain engraved in history that Poland's resolve has saved Europe. In the name of a movement which years ago was among the first to realize Poland's mission as one of the world's greatest powers and conceived the provident connection between the renaissance of Jews in Palestine State and the triumph of Poland's victory, I humbly call on God's blessing upon your country, her Marshals, and her soldiers of all creeds united in loyalty and sacrifice.[69]

After the ultimatum it had sent Berlin was rejected, Britain declared war on Nazi Germany at 11:45 a.m. on September 3. France followed Britain in the afternoon. In Warsaw, crowds gathered near the British and French embassies to express their appreciation for the countries' decision to enter the war alongside Poland. On August 26, Chajes had written: "Even the wise men around [Hitler] totally believed him. But now they may sober up and see that they are being led by a confused madman." He expressed his confidence that Foreign Minister Beck was "taking good care of his business." When he returned to his diary on September 3 he wrote: "Alea iacta est [the die has been cast]. On Friday, September 1st, early in the morning, Hitler's bombers attacked Poland in numerous places. [. . .] There are hundreds of innocent civilian victims. [. . .] War, war. The peoples' war against Satan. To think that a fanatical, crazy nomad is setting the world alight [. . .]. I am quiet. I see a bloody war."[70]

On the night of September 1, the illegal immigrant ship *Tiger Hill* reached the Tel Aviv shore. It had sailed from Constanta on August 3 carrying 711 pioneers from Poland, Romania, and Bulgaria. They were detained for several days at the port town's train station under rough conditions. Only after negotiations with the British government did the Romanian government allow the ship to set sail. The Criminal Investigation Department (CID) reported the voyage to the British navy command, but the ship managed to get close to the shore. One hundred and eighty of its passengers were let ashore on a motorboat in Atlit, and the ship sailed to Beirut to collect the 658 passengers of the *Frossoula*, a ship organized by the Revisionist activist Abraham Stavsky. This ship had sailed from Sulina on May 25, and after six weeks at sea had anchored in the port of Beirut, where it was stuck.

British warships followed the *Tiger Hill* as it returned toward Palestine, and opposite Jaffa beach, at 11 p.m. on August 31, troops opened fire on the vessel from the shore. Two illegal immigrants were killed by the shots. The ship's captain on behalf of the Haganah, Katriel Yaffe, steered it to a sandbank in front of the Red House (the Histadrut building) on Hayarkon Street. Around 400 illegal immigrants jumped overboard, swam to the shore, and disappeared among the large crowds that had gathered there. The army and police seized the ship and led the rest of the illegal immigrants to the detention camp in Sarafand (Tzrifin).[71] The notion that soldiers would not "shoot at Jewish refugees" was shown to be false. "Would British public opinion," Selig Brodetsky had asked on the podium of the Zionist Congress in Geneva, "allow English soldiers to shoot at these people? And if the officers ordered the English soldiers to shoot, would they really do it? [. . .] Since English soldiers are not German soldiers, since English soldiers are people, none [of them] would shoot human beings who are trying to save themselves from death."[72]

The *Tiger Hill* was one of twelve illegal immigrant ships that reached Palestine's shores between August 10 and the end of September 1939. MacDonald, Britain's colonial secretary, doubted whether the diplomatic pressure that Britain was exerting on the governments of Poland, Romania, and Greece could stop the illegal immigrants from leaving, "since the power of Jewish money was great." However, he said, "for the present at any rate the results were good."[73]

Plan West—the Polish army's plan of defense—divided the country into three sections: first the army would concentrate along the border with Germany, and if necessary it would retreat to the main defensive line in central Poland. If it were forced to withdraw further, it would withdraw to the last defensive line on the Bug River and fight until Britain and France actively joined the war within about two weeks. This plan quickly fell apart and Poland was taken within eighteen days. The front stretched over some 1,250 miles, in land, air, and sea. The German army included fifty-eight divisions (around 1,850,000 troops and around 3,100 tanks). The air force comprised around 2,000 aircraft, including around 900 bombers. The Poles confronted it with a regular army of around a million troops and more than a million reserves: 30 regular infantry divisions, 9 reserve divisions, 11 cavalry brigades, 900 tanks, and 435 aircraft.[74] This large army was deployed along the long borders and prepared for a defensive battle.

Even the weather betrayed Poland. The fall was mild, the soil dry, and the visibility good. These conditions made it easier for the German tanks and aircraft to operate effectively. Within three days the first Polish defensive line had collapsed and the Polish air force ceased to exist on September 3, after most of it was destroyed on the ground. The dive-bombers, the German Stuka, were able to bombard towns and villages almost at will, as well as the massive numbers of refugees that filled the roads and disrupted the Polish army's movements. Here and there the Polish army mounted some resistance and even launched some nightly attacks, but it was split into several segments and lost around 1,000 tanks and 600 aircraft.

The assumption that the Polish army would be able to hold on for around half a year until the Allies came to its aid turned out to be a false hope and a bitter illusion. The promises of the commander in chief of the French armed forces, Maurice Gamelin — that if Hitler started a war there would be an uprising in Berlin and the forces stationed on the Siegfried Line would have to rush to repress it, and that in any case the French army would cut through Germany like a knife through butter[75] — were a combination of stupidity and arrogance.

It was not only the French commander in chief who overestimated the power of the Polish army. Britain's General Ironside, informed Churchill on August 27 that the Polish army had made a good impression on him. On September 11, he reported to the British Cabinet that the Poles were fighting well and were vigorously determined to defend Warsaw.[76] The thirty-two French divisions that were stationed on the Maginot Line advanced into the Saarland on the night of September 6, encountering no resistance, but remained within the range of the Maginot Line guns, and the French and British air forces made some bombing sorties over Germany.

On September 3, the readers of the Hebrew-language newspapers in Palestine learned that the Polish cities had been bombed from the air and that sixteen German planes, compared to two Polish ones, had been shot down. "Germany stands alone" after Italy and Japan announced their neutrality, the newspapers informed. They also published "emergency orders" by the Palestine government. And *Davar* reported in its sports pages on the local delegation's participation in the University Games in Monaco.

On the third day of the war, Uri Zvi Greenberg burst into the room of the Betar commissioner, Menachem Begin, and shouted: "What are you doing here? Go away immediately. Everything's finished." He pointed at the Bug River on Poland's map: "This is where the Russians will get to, and from the west — the Germans. In a week everything will be over."[77]

On September 5, the Polish general staff ordered all those eligible for conscription to move to the eastern provinces. On the night between September 6 and September 7 Polish radio announced the general staff's decision to evacuate the capital and called on all the men able to carry weapons to go east. Tens of thousands started to flee eastward and southward. The emissaries who had Palestinian passports decided to leave Warsaw in an organized group. They waited many hours for a train, and when it failed to come left with the great crowd of refugees that headed east. After marching for about a fortnight toward the Polish-Romanian border they crossed it safely.

At noon on Thursday, September 5, the representatives of Warsaw's newspapers, including nine Jewish journalists, were invited to a press conference at the government building. Poland's propaganda minister announced that the Germans were getting closer to Warsaw and that the newspapers should move east with all their equipment. Out of sixty to seventy places reserved for the journalists' organized evacuation, fifteen were given to Jews. After an internal debate, sixteen passengers were chosen for the "journalists' train," including Dr. Yehoshua Gottlieb of *Der Moment*. In Łuków some people got off the train and continued toward Lublin. Gottlieb, who made it to Pinsk, went to seek shelter with some relatives, and from then on all traces of him were lost.[78]

The others traveled on a different train toward Lviv. The train on which Greenberg traveled was bombed from the air and its passengers jumped out the windows. Greenberg slipped on the concrete wall on the side of the tracks before managing to climb up to the embankment and with his friend Akiva Baron escaped to a potato field and dug himself into the ground. When the bombers left, the train continued on its way and brought them to safety.[79]

Greenberg crossed the border to Romania and on returning to Palestine wrote an article on September 13 titled "The joint enemy of us all": Now everyone knew what he claimed a long time ago, that Nazi Germany—"the western European Amalek"—did not hate only Jews, but was "a universal Amalek phenomenon." The only country that understood the essence of Nazism was Poland. "The Jewish hands now digging the defensive trenches for Poland and 'against him' [Hitler] are in fact continuing the process of undermining begun by the Jewish people everywhere against the German Amalek." The Jewish people, he added, resembled the Polish people in that they too "had political sovereignty in their blood."[80]

In the evening, after the press conference, the Bund's central committee convened at the building of the *Folktsaytung* newspaper on 7 Nowolpie Street to decide how to proceed. Some people thought that there was no need to panic and that leaving Warsaw would mean "the suicide of the party." They believed the Bund members should stay in town and fight side by side with the Polish working class.

The following day, around 200 activists gathered at the Praga district east of the Visla—the only route out of town—and waited for the party's leadership's decision. Most of them decided to leave without waiting for a decision.

On the morning of September 6, the Bund delegation met with the central committee of the Polish Socialist Party (PPS) to discuss the evacuation order. The general secretary of the PPS, Kazimierz Pużak, had no faith in the government's plan to stabilize and hold a defensive line along the Bug-San. The Bund leadership decided that those members of the central committee who were in real danger for their lives would leave the city. Most of them did so the next day, traveling in different directions.[81]

The Hechalutz leadership got together several times at 34 Dzielna Street to decide what to do. On September 7, the day before the Germans started shelling Warsaw with cannons and incendiary bombs, the leadership decided to leave Warsaw. Most of the comrades went east and made their way on foot at night, avoiding the main roads.[82] The members of the Hashomer Hatzair leadership who reached Vilna wrote to Palestine: "In one moment an organized public turns into human dust, called refugees—without clothes, without food and without a roof over their head. [...] Once people left their nests they made a harsh leap [...] and became a nomadic tribe in the desert."[83]

The movement's leader, Meir Yaari, boasted that its emissaries "stood at their watch until the end and knew to escape in the last minute." However, a few weeks later he described the emissaries' return as a failure because "they did not stay in the battle." Katznelson was more blunt and said that the emissaries from Palestine had not shown "any will for self-sacrifice" and had not told themselves "that there is something sacred that is worth dying for. [...] I would have liked ten emissaries to have fallen in the occupied territory as martyrs."[84]

The emissary Yehuda (Yudka) Helman had written to his wife from Łódź on July 10, 1939, to suggest that the family come from Palestine to Poland for Passover so they could be together for a few months. On August 18 he told her about the mounting tension and the mobilization in Poland, and also that he had sent a package to his children in the kibbutz containing two brooches, a small pocketknife, and a whistle: "And what will happen if war does break out? I myself have the feeling and almost the confidence that it is not so near—but who knows?" At the end of August he wrote from the town of Klevan (Klewań) in east Poland, where he lectured on "Palestine's geography," confessing how lonely he felt: "I felt that I could not bear the loneliness. I felt so bad, and at that moment I only wished that war would break out and force me to return home. Here one lives in great tension about the future, one thinks that any day now an eruption is imminent. And meanwhile I feel as if nothing will happen."

The war caught him in Warsaw, where at a meeting of the Hakibbutz Hameuchad emissaries on September 6 it was decided that the emissaries would return to Palestine. The train that Helman and his friend Moshe Melamed boarded was bombed from the air, and while the other emissaries managed to reach the border with Romania, Helman found himself alone among throngs of refugees and began the march eastward. After many ordeals he reached Kowel in the Soviet territory, where he met his mother and sister. When in January 1940 the Soviet government allowed foreign subjects to cross over to Romania, Helman was among them. From then on, writes his biographer, he lived his life "in the shadow of that internal struggle that raged within him: should he return to his home and his family, to Gvat, or should he stay with the movement members who had gone underground and share their fate."[85]

Most of the leaders and party functionaries joined the throngs of refugees that made their way on the roads under aerial bombardments. Everyone believed that it would be possible to continue their activities in the east. As for Chajes, on September 7, he still refused to believe that the "apocalyptic beast" would take over Poland and hoped that Britain and France would intervene militarily. Hitler's only successes were in the southwest of Poland, he wrote, having no doubt that Germany would be crushed: "Poland will prevail in the end."[86] Victor Alter (Arthur), a leader of the Bund, stayed in Warsaw and was among the twelve hostages handed over to the Nazis who wished to ensure the population's commitment to keeping the order in the city.

At the end of 1939, the central committee of the Tsukunft (Future), the Bund's youth movement in Vilna, convened and declared: "No evil power will manage to uproot us from our homeland of 1,000 years, from Poland. Only recently we fought off some serious dangers, and we will similarly endure the incomparable suffering of the Nazi occupation."[87] Adam Czerniakow, the chairman of Warsaw's Jewish community and Judenrat after the occupation (the 1942 Council), wrote in his diary on September 7: "Burdened with backpacks all kinds of people set out for the unknown." He disapproved of the panicked exodus and on September 10 signed up together with another 200 Jews for the Civil Guard, the militia founded four days earlier by Warsaw's mayor.[88]

After the Irgun's training camp near Mezritch dispersed, Hillel Tzur went to Warsaw and rushed to the British consulate to renew his passport. On August 26, he was issued a new passport. When the air raids began he went to the Latvian consulate and on September 6 and got a transit visa limited to a three-day stay in Latvia. He managed to board a train that was bombed from the air and continued on foot to the Lithuanian border.[89]

Menachem Begin and a few others of the organizers of the convoy that had been stopped in Sniatyń returned to Warsaw on August 31. According to one testimony, Begin proposed to a senior officer in the Polish army to organize battalions of Betar members that would join the army.[90] If there is any truth in this testimony it shows that Begin—like many others—was out of touch with reality. He fled from Warsaw on September 7, on a packed train with his wife and a few members of the Betar commissionership. He would later explain his actions as stemming from his and his colleagues' faith "in Poland's longevity," and from the fact that no one imagined that it would "collapse in such a short time."[91] Like Jabotinsky and the Betar leadership, Begin also believed that Poland had "great strength and [would] be able to stand against the aggressor" until Britain and France rushed to its aid.[92] The train on which they traveled was attacked from the air by German Messerschmitt planes near Garwolin, and the group continued on foot. Ten days later, they crossed the Bug on a boat that took them to the town of Luboml, continued to Ludmir, and from there stole across the border to Vilna, the capital of the independent Lithuania.[93]

Yosef Katznelson, one of the Betar chiefs and the organizers of the Revisionist movement's illegal immigration, stayed behind on his own in Warsaw. He was too sick to join the flight. At the beginning of April he wrote to his wife about "the messianic surge surfacing from the depths of the people in the Diaspora. [. . .] How turbulent are the waves, but we are advancing. Far off, like in a stage play, the promised goal awaits."[94] On May 5, 1939, he wrote: "Everything on the streets of Warsaw strikes me now as prettier, younger, worthier of love and respect. What has happened? [The Poles'] resistance to the Germans? Or is it the intoxication of work? I do not know. But I am in a musical dream." A day later the tone changed: "We live in such a tragic period. [. . .] Oy, what times!"[95] A few months later he died of his illness in occupied Warsaw.

Around 2,900 immigrants who had immigration permits arrived by train in Trieste, from where they sailed to Palestine on ships leased for them by the Jewish Agency.[96]

In contravention of the general staff's decision, the mayor of Warsaw,

Stefan Starzyński, called on September 6 for a general mobilization to defend the capital. An atmosphere of panic spread across the city. The president, the government, and the chief of the general staff fled to the area between the Carpathian mountains and the Zbruch River, while the diplomatic corps was evacuated to Nałęczów, some eighty-five miles southeast of Warsaw. The Polish prime minister, General Sławoj Składkowski, Foreign Minister Beck, and other ministers, who fled from Warsaw, stayed for a while in the lovely guesthouses in the town of Kossów in eastern Galicia at the foot of the Carpathian mountains, near the Romanian border. On the eve of the Jewish New Year, in the middle of the Rosh Hashanah prayers, a few Jews were called out from the synagogue to sweep the foliage from the garden of the house in which the prime minister and his wife were staying.[97] On September 17, Poland's top officials moved to Romania and were placed in detention.

The heads of the Jewish community who remained in Warsaw established a social aid committee in an office on Wielka Street, with Dr. Ringelblum as its general secretary. On January 12, 1940, Y. Kashtan, secretary of the central Palestine office in Warsaw, sent a report from Trieste to Chaim Barlas, director of the Jewish Agency's Immigration Department in Jerusalem, about the situation in Warsaw since the beginning of the war:

> In the first five days of the war we still came to the office under the roar of shooting and the deluge of bombs. We helped the callers, mainly those wishing to return to Palestine, who had risked their lives to come to the office and get the immigration permits in case they managed to escape through Romania on time, which some of them did. Not so the new immigrants. We had a transport [of] around 150 immigrants ready. [. . .] The group's departure could not, of course, take place. It was no longer possible to obtain a train. The immigrants from the provincial towns did not get to Warsaw and the immigrants from Warsaw could not come to the office.[98]

On September 6, the staff collected the documents in order to save them and move them to another city. However, "the city was already under siege. We separated in a panicked flight each to his home, unable to return to the office until it burned down." Three certificates were lost when the building caught fire and was completely destroyed on September 25.[99] The Hebrew teacher Chaim Aaron Kaplan wrote in his diary on September 12: "It is beyond the power of my pen to describe the destruction and ruin that the enemy's planes have wrought on our lovely capital. Entire blocks have been turned into ashes and magnificent palaces into rubble. Every incendiary bomb dropped in the stillness of the night brings havoc and death to hundreds of people."[100]

The *Zionist Review* wrote on September 7 that even Jews who had not been conscripted joined the army and Jewish women volunteered to serve in hospitals. "The Jews' reply to this cruel and criminal attack is to help the government achieve a quick victory for the allies over Hitlerism." The newspaper wrote proudly: "For the first time after many years all the Jews in this country have put aside their party differences and have united as one for the defense of their country against the now commonly acknowledged enemy of humanity, Hitler," and came "to aid the government in all ways that will bring a swift and sure Polish and Allied victory."

On September 8, in an article titled "Poland's Jewish Soldiers," the newspaper described the contribution that Jewish soldiers had made to Poland's wars and their devotion to Poland and its independence. It was thus no wonder, it wrote, that the Polish army was so impressed by Jewish heroism. The whole Jewish community had mobilized for Poland's "defensive war."[101]

Rabbi Yitzchak Menachem Danziger, the so-called Alexander rebbe, released an emotional statement to his disciples in which he said: "There is a short time left for each Jew to fulfil his national duty. [. . .] The Jewish fate has been linked to the Polish soil for hundreds of years. [. . .] Despite the tough situation every Jew must contribute, even beyond his powers."[102] Many testimonies described a surge in the Jews' identification with Poland and a rapprochement toward the Poles, as well as a hope that the joint struggle and suffering would bring an end to antisemitism and discrimination.[103] Willy Cohn, on the other hand, thought that now that the Germans were at Warsaw's gates, the "Polish war" would soon be over and world war might be avoided. In any event, on September 8 he wrote in his diary, "Germany is in the right."[104]

At the end of the first week of the war the Germans stood at Warsaw's gates and were not sparing the civilian population. On September 17, the Red Army crossed the eastern border and the next day it took Vilna. Now all hope was lost. Chajes wrote: "Poland is in a bad way. Warsaw is surrounded. Lviv is defending itself bravely, but hundreds of houses are bombed. There are thousands of civilian casualties. [. . .] The bombers are destroying almost all of Poland's cities. Stalin may enter Poland any day now because he probably has a secret agreement with Hitler, and he will take half of Poland without resistance."[105]

Warsaw surrendered after a siege and battles that went on for about a month. Warsaw, wrote Gruenbaum in Palestine, was not only the capital of Poland, but also "an important Jewish city, the center of the national life [of Poland's Jews], the center of their renaissance and revival, the center of their redemptive aspirations," and if it fell, "Poland would continue to defend its freedom." At that time, he believed, the joint suffering and the common war would strengthen peace and unity between the Polish masses and the Jews. For the situation in the occupied areas there was no other solution but "the expulsion of the occupiers." He still trusted in the power of the Polish army to stop the Nazi invaders in the eastern part of the country, from Vilna to Lviv and the Romanian border. Even if Warsaw fell, Poland would not surrender, he promised. "As long as there is an army in Poland that is ready for battle, it will be hard for the German command to direct all its armed forces against France and England."[106]

After Warsaw surrendered on September 27, the Polish soldiers still left in the destroyed city the following day put down their weapons at Piłsudski Square. On September 28, a German intelligence officer named Walter Schellenberg described it as a "dead city" of ruined and burned houses, without running water, full of starving inhabitants. That day Ribbentrop and Molotov met to amend the map of the August 23rd agreement to divide Poland. Poland ceased to exist.

Around 66,000 Polish soldiers were killed in battle and around 133,000 were wounded. The German losses amounted to around 16,000 killed or missing in action and around 30,000 wounded. Around 16,000 Polish and Jewish civilians and prisoners of war were killed in over 700 mass murders by the Wehrmacht and the Einsatzgruppen.[107] When General Adrian Carton de Wiart, head of the British Military Mission to Poland, returned from Warsaw to London via Romania, he was received by the chief of the general staff, General Ironside, who mockingly commented, "Your Poles haven't put up much of a show," while the prime minister wanted to know what impact had been made by the propaganda leaflets disseminated by British planes in Germany.[108]

A week earlier, on September 13, the sociologist Jacob Leshchinsky wrote in New York: "Human imagination simply cannot comprehend the magnitude of the price that the war will probably exert, or the amount of blood that innocent Jews will shed."[109] Albert Whitton wrote: "Everywhere the Jews are the main victims. [. . .] The impending suffering is limitless. [. . .] Many of the Jews of Central, Eastern and Northern Europe will not be able to save themselves—half of them will certainly be annihilated by the end of the war."[110] It seemed that the writer Aaron Zeitlin's prediction in his 1932 mystery play *Esterke* (in Yiddish) had come true: "Poland, your night and mine / have intertwined."[111]

The vast majority of Poland's Jews were left to their own fate.

After the Anschluss of Austria, Tzila and Romek Rennart traveled from Vienna to Krakow and settled at the Grand Hotel. They attended nightclubs and tea parties that included dancing and bridge games: "We were like dancers dancing on a rumbling volcano." Having started to study medicine in Cologne, Tzila requested to be admitted to the medical school in Krakow but was denied, and she therefore enrolled in the faculty for experimental sciences. After an antisemitic incident at the University of Lviv in which a Jewish student was killed, Tzila started thinking that they should flee Poland as well. However, it was hard to abandon the "sweet life" in Krakow, and the couple stayed on in the villa they had rented on the city's outskirts. Only in summer 1939 did they decide it was time to immigrate with their daughter to France, but first they vacationed in a villa they had rented in the resort town of Zawoja near the border with Czechoslovakia. Border clashes and the atmosphere of panic drove them back to Krakow, but a week passed before they managed to find a small car and take to the road, which was congested with convoys of cars and peasants' carts: "When we came to Krakow we asked ourselves the question that was on everybody's mind: should we keep running, or is it better to stay in the city and wait for what is coming? We knew that if war broke out the Germans [would] immediately take Krakow, which is near the border, and yet we still had some vague hope, borne of a desperate wish, that in spite of everything war would be averted at the last minute."

Despite this faint hope, they—like many other Jews—withdrew their money and securities from the bank. Tzila's husband even moved their belongings to Lviv. Tzila Rennart was reluctant to leave her spacious apartment behind and insisted that war would not break out—until one night when she had a "prophetic dream." In her dream she saw her husband led by two SS troops. She ran after them but did not manage to catch them. Tzila woke up from the dream in tears, ready to leave the city. On the evening of their departure the couple held a farewell dinner for their friends, and the next day, when they arrived at the train station, they found it inundated with people. In Lviv they rented a one-bedroom apartment, and on September 1, Tzila went to the bank to "withdraw all our money ahead of the impending war." It was a pleasant morning and the bank was full of customers who had come to withdraw their money. Suddenly an air raid siren pierced the air and people started to flee from the building. But Tzila stayed in line: "Ah! What a relief I felt when I held the full bag against my body." The trams did not work and she started making her way on foot, when a fancy car stopped beside her and the driver, a well-groomed middle-aged man, offered her a lift. On the way they heard on the radio that Germany had invaded Poland and that all the country's cities were being bombed. When she returned home her husband told her that he had been very worried for her safety and in his mind's eye, "I was already lying under the rubble." The money helped them steal across the border.[112]

Dr. Yohanan Bader was called up to a civil defense commanders' course in 1938 and therefore could not consent to his wife's request to leave Krakow and go to the town of Torczyn in eastern Poland. On August 24, his wife heard on the radio that a Non-Aggression Pact had been signed between the Soviet Union and Nazi Germany, and told her husband she was "sure that the Germans will soon enter Poland." On the last evening of August, Bader was eating at a restaurant with a few journalists. One of them muttered jokingly: "What is Hitler waiting for? There will be no war!" The next day, at 5 a.m., he was awakened by sirens as Krakow was attacked from the air. As part of his duty, Bader patrolled the area he was allocated and remarked that the Poles were "showing their good qualities, and in particular—their love for the homeland." On September 2, the radio reported some victories for the Polish army, but the following day Bader's brother-in-law arrived and told him about the stream of refugees making their way east and about some people driving their cars to Warsaw. The Baders followed suit and left in two cars in the direction of Lviv, while Yohanan returned to the civil defense headquarters and found all the rooms empty. An old clerk urged him to leave the city, which he did. A day and a half later he arrived in his car in Torczyn, and several days later the whole family continued east to the small town of Aleksandriya, near Łutzk.[113]

Krakow was taken by the Germans in the early morning on September 6, and the Rennart family, together with other Jews who had means and vehicles, managed to cross the border into Romania. The question was whether to flee to Lublin or disperse in the nearby towns: "Everyone has gone mad [. . .]. Everyone is fleeing, running away from the Germans [. . .]. The street on which we lived looked like a cemetery."[114] However, the roads were blocked and the Luftwaffe planes flew at low altitudes and shot at the people fleeing. Many made their way back to Krakow "on a road strewn with bodies of men, women and children."[115]

The day before the new school year started the boy Naphtali Lau stood on the corner of Piłsudski and Jerozolimskie Streets in Piotrków and waited for his friends to go to an orientation session with the teacher and the rest of the class. They were just about to cross over to the schoolhouse when the blasting of sirens pierced the air. They froze on the spot. Two trucks passed by. "War!" shouted the Polish soldiers who were sitting in them. On Saturday morning, during prayer, Krakow was bombed, and Naphtali saw dozens of people killed and wounded in the street. Jews flocked to his house to seek advice from his father, the town's rabbi. His advice was based on the verse in Isaiah 26:20: "Hide thyself for a little moment, until the indignation be overpast." Many followed the advice and chose to hide in the nearby towns, in the hope that soon the indignation would be overpast and they would be able to return home. They ran for their lives eastward, and hundreds of families spent the night in Krakow and in the fields near the town of Sulejów. On Monday afternoon, waves of bombers and fighters attacked Krakow, strafing with machine-gun fire the thousands of refugees. The next day the Germans entered the city. On Wednesday afternoon a few military vehicles pulled up outside the house in which the Lau family was staying and soldiers took up positions and opened fire on the Jewish-populated homes. Six Jews were killed and around twenty were wounded. All the houses were set on fire.[116]

On the evening of September 1, Sarah Erlichman-Bank's family was sitting down to have dinner in their home in Lublin, when suddenly they heard a thunderous sound. For a moment they thought it was a training exercise, but the radio announced a German air raid. The sirens went on for a long time and "between the sirens we listen to the radio: What does Europe say?" On September 9 Lublin was attacked from the air again and the family found shelter in the basement of a house together with some soldiers from the air defense service: "What is the point — they ask — Poland has already been sold, the officers have fled and they are moving their belongings to the countryside in army vehicles. They have accumulated money and are hiding like mice." Another attack hit Lublin on September 13, leaving entire families buried under the rubble. Five days later, on September 18, the Germans entered Lublin and assembled the Jewish inhabitants in the city's main square. Polish residents started looting the stores and homes.[117]

The town of Legionowo, around eleven miles from Warsaw, was inundated in May 1939 by more holidaymakers than usual and the vacation business was booming. However, the mobilization of peasants' carts taken from the eastern frontier areas to the west in the middle of the harvest raised concern. On September 1, Daniel Freiberg woke up early and while getting ready to go to Warsaw saw a squadron of airplanes heading toward the capital. Other planes emerged and flew toward them, and one of them burned and dropped to the ground. He naively thought that it was an exercise, but when he got to the train station he found out that there had been a dogfight between German and Polish planes. The trains stopped working and the few that did leave gave precedence to uniformed army personnel. Those who managed to get to their workplaces in Warsaw and come back had terrible stories about aerial bombardments.[118]

In Bolechów, an industrial town at the foot of the Carpathian mountains, nine-year-old Shlomo Adler heard a few explosions. German planes dropped several bombs on the town. Near the window of his uncle's house stood a group of people listening to the radio — the only radio in the vicinity, which his uncle had bought after winning a large sum in the lottery. That was how they found out that the Germans had attacked all along the frontline. The family home was not far from the distillery and some factories, so his parents decided to move to the house of one of the workers in his father's factory in the nearby village of Dolzka. They filled some big sacks with straw and slept in the hayloft. At night the sky turned red; it was the burning distilleries of Boryslav or Drohobych, some twenty miles from the village.

The next day they were dining with their hosts in the courtyard under some bird cherry and chestnut trees, when suddenly they heard the voice of the local policeman roaring on the megaphone. He joyfully announced the obliteration of the Germans on all fronts. In the afternoon the Adlers returned to their home and saw that the neighbors had started boarding up their doors and windows with heavy wooden panels, in fear of a pogrom by the town's Ukrainian inhabitants.[119]

Halina Ashkenazi-Engelhard lived with her family in a large house on Warsaw's Ogrodowa Street. In the second half of August some signs of nervousness started to appear, instructions were given to build shelters, and the tenant's committee appointed to see to the security arrangements also included the only German living in the building. On the morning of September 1, sirens were heard, immediately followed by deafening explosions. The bombardments went on for two weeks, and they hid in the basement: "It was only the hunger that conquered the fear and pushed the people to get out of the basement and get something to eat. Usually it was watery soup or some kind of buckwheat." When they emerged from the basement on quiet moments they saw the horrifying sight of Warsaw going up in flames.[120]

Moshe Margaliot (Margolis) was twelve years old when the war reached

Ludmir (Vladimir-Volynsk). The Poles on the street boasted: "We won't give Hitler even a soldier's button." The family was getting ready to say goodbye to their daughter Shosha, who finally received an immigration permit for Palestine. Her departure was scheduled for Saturday night, September 2, 1939. The war preempted her by thirty-six hours. The next day it transpired that the Polish army had collapsed like a house of cards, and throngs of people started to flee. Overnight Ludmir became one of the escape routes to the east, to the Russian border, and to the south, to the Romanian border. On Sunday, September 10, the city and the refugee convoys passing through it were bombed from the air, and on September 15 the German army, having crossed the Bug River, began to shell Ludmir. On September 17, mobs started to break into shops and a group of Polish officers was getting ready to perpetrate a pogrom against the Jewish inhabitants. Only on the night of September 20, when the Red Army entered the city, was order restored.[121]

Dov Zalmanowicz, born in Będzin, Upper Silesia, spent the months of July and August at a holiday house. The rumors about an impending war sent him back home in the middle of August. On September 1, a rope and steelworks factory in the city was bombed. Saturday passed in great anxiety. On Saturday night two of his cousins got married in a modest ceremony. The following day his father gave the apartment key for safekeeping to the Polish caretaker who had lived in their courtyard for many years, and the family left town in a cart. "All the way to the horizon, along the roads and the fields, throngs of people, horses and vehicles were moving and filling the roads, all gripped by the mania for movement. [. . .] Throngs of depressed and frightened people fled for their lives on the roads, with the planes roaring above their heads. Sometimes the planes lowered their altitude and opened fire. Hundreds fell on the road."

The family returned to Będzin and received the key to their apartment from the caretaker. Immediately after the Germans entered the town they began the executions; they burned the magnificent synagogue and the adjacent beth midrash, shot at residents and passersby who tried to escape or threw them into the flames, and then shot dozens of Jews on the town square.[122]

On the eve of the war the boy Haim Koznitsky cut short his vacation at a summer camp in Wiśniowa Góra and returned home to Łódź. He learned from the newspapers about clashes along the Polish-German border but believed the proclamations that Poland was very strong militarily and therefore was certain to defeat the "quarrelsome Germans." Koznitsky signed up to dig anti-air-raid trenches and helped build a shelter at his home. On

September 1, rumors spread that the Polish army was fending off the German invasion "with fire and sword."[123] The air defense commander said in a radio broadcast that French aircraft were already in Warsaw: "There was a tense quiet, like before a storm. The empty streets were silent. Something menacing hung in the air." On the night between September 5 and 6 the family awoke to the sound of knocking on the apartment's door and a deafening ring. One of the neighbors entered their home sobbing and told them that the Germans were about to enter the city, and that all the men must flee, or "the Germans will kill them." When she dared to leave the basement she saw that the five-story stone house next door had collapsed and was going up in flames. The Wehrmacht soldiers were marching in the wrecked streets singing "Deutschland, Deutschland über alles."[124]

Lily Folman (Goldenberg), who had been admitted to the Hebrew University and was waiting for a certificate, went with her family on a summer holiday in the countryside in Józefów, half an hour from Warsaw. The tense atmosphere and the war preparations did not upset their tranquility and recreational activities. When they returned to Warsaw in peasants' carts there were some siren testings and bombing simulations, but there was no panic. On the morning of September 1, a siren was heard and the residents of the building started running out of their apartments to find shelter in the basement. When the siren stopped the family went up to their apartment and heard on the radio that Nazi Germany had invaded Poland.[125]

In Sosnowiec, eleven-year-old Hadassah Cantor (Wolfovich) woke up at 5:30 in the morning on September 1 to the sound of loud voices outside. The street was full of people running around in a panic. Suddenly there was a siren and a bomb fell near the city's high school and destroyed it. Her mother soothed her: "There is no reason to fear the Germans. They are an enlightened people, and nothing will happen to us." On September 4, the Nazi army entered Sosnowiec and its troops set fire to synagogues, shot at Jewish passersby, and looted houses.[126]

In the summer of 1939 the Fishmans did not spend their summer vacation on the shore of the Baltic Sea, as had been their custom, but at a nearby holiday resort. They stayed in a hut surrounded by greenery, went on walks in the forest, and visited a fair. The danger of war cut the holiday short and the family quickly packed their things and returned to Łódź by train. Immediately on returning they taped paper strips to the windowpanes and set up a room as a shelter against gas bombs. Early on the morning of September 8, they learned that the Nazis had entered the city and taken over the train station. The government radio urged the inhabitants to abandon Łódź and leave for Warsaw. A great deluge of refugees immediately poured out of all the houses and started making their way on foot. The Fishmans' daughter Miriam took along a little sleeping pillow and her father carried a suitcase with a few belongings. Polish soldiers retreating on foot and in carriages filled the roads.[127]

Several months before the war broke out Joseph Korniansky, the secretary of the Grochów Hachshara camp, the largest pioneer training camp in Poland, fell ill and went to convalesce in the spa town of Ciechocinek near the border with Germany. In the last days of August the tension grew and the doctors and convalescents left town. The train station filled with young conscripts. At dawn on September 1, an aircraft squadron bombed the train on which Korniansky was traveling. The passengers jumped out of the windows and doors. The planes returned and opened machine-gun fire on the hundreds of people running for shelter. Early in the morning Korniansky managed to get to Łódź and found the Hachshara members digging defensive trenches. They had also equipped themselves with stockpiles of food, medical supplies, and gas masks. Hundreds of pioneers from the Hachshara camps in west Poland started to congregate in Łódź. On the fourth day of the war, contact with the Hechalutz center in Warsaw was cut off and the responsibility for the Hachshara camp's fate fell on its directors. On September 7, after the government called on the population to leave for the east, they decided to abandon the camp and left behind ten comrades on guard duty:

> Towards evening the hundreds of camp members gathered in the yard, each with his rucksack on his shoulders and his suitcase in his hand. [. . .] We set off. The roads were full to the brim with hordes of people, soldiers and civilians [. . .]. We tried to walk together in an orderly manner, despite the warnings that walking in a tight group might make us an easy target for the pilots of the German bombers and end in disaster. But we wanted to be together, not to be cut off from each other. [. . .] We advanced during nighttime, because the frequent bombings during the day prevented us from marching in daylight.[128]

Only a small number made it to Warsaw. When Korniansky reached the outskirts of the capital he found the entrance closed and turned back.

Bina Garncarska, a worker at a knitting factory in the textile city of Łódź and an activist in the Folkist youth movement, returned from work on Friday evening, September 1. People were congregating around the advertisement poles reading a freshly posted notice announcing a general mobilization. The news did not surprise her because in the last few weeks she had also been recruited to dig trenches around the city. On Saturday night Łódź was bombed. Men who were able to carry weapons were asked to leave for Warsaw and help repel the invaders. Years later she wrote:

> Oh, that night. The city was draped in darkness; it was forbidden to have a light on. Suddenly the streets filled with people. [. . .] Later it was the turn of entire families with their belongings carried in handcarts and children's prams, and pedestrians—everyone was walking, leaving the city. They were mainly Jewish families. [. . .] In the afternoon rumor suddenly spread that the call for men to leave town had been a provocation and that the road to Warsaw, which was full of people, had been bombed from the air and was strewn with thousands of people killed and wounded. Carts loaded with casualties started to arrive one after the other.[129]

Lena Küchler-Silberman was a teacher in the town of Bielsko at the foot of the Carpathian mountains and continuing her PhD studies at the Pedagogical University of Krakow. On Shavuot she went to visit her family in the town of Wieliczka near Krakow. Albert, her husband, was restless, saying: "Hitler is after us. We must run—run where our legs will take us." But there was nowhere to run to. Lena completed her doctorate thesis and sent a copy to Edward Poznansky, secretary of the Society of Friends of the University in Jerusalem, in the hope of receiving a student's immigration permit. The war came before the reply from Jerusalem. Her husband urged her:

> "Pack only one suitcase. Leave everything behind. We must run away."
>
> And I insisted: "Where could we run to?"
>
> "East."
>
> "The Poles have an army," Lena told her husband. "There are airplanes, they will fend off the attack, and the other countries will come to their aid."
>
> "You don't know the Germans. Their army is the strongest army in the world. They want more living space. There's no choice but to run."
>
> We ran.[130]

After visiting her aunt in the village of Zwoleń near Radom, around sixty miles from Warsaw, eleven-year-old Binah Bojman returned to the capital at the end of August to get ready for the new school year. "In Warsaw and all over Poland there is panic buying: they buy food and especially flour, sugar, eggs, potatoes, groats, pulses and lots of tinned food. The prices keep rising." On Friday, September 1, the new school year opened. When Binah went out to the grocery store to buy some bread rolls and other groceries she suddenly heard

> a deafening noise. You can hear it, and you can already see a squadron of planes flying by at a low altitude. A few seconds later you hear fierce explosions. People congregate quickly. Noise and a loud commotion. "These are just our army's exercises," remarks someone in the crowd. [. . .] "These must be those advanced planes we just got from the English and the French, and our pilots are training on them to be ready for war." [. . .] The sounds of explosions intensified, and squadrons of planes appeared one after the other, wave after wave. People started running every which way, looking for shelter. Smoke was rising everywhere. By now everyone already knew that the Germans were attacking from the air, that the city was burning and bombed and that the war had broken out! [. . .] Every day the bombardments became heavier and more frequent; during the day there were air raids, and during the night guns shelled us incessantly.[131]

The Bojmans moved from basement to basement until Warsaw surrendered. The city's streets were impassable due to the fires and the ruins of the destroyed houses. Terrible rumors circulated about the fate of those who had fled from Warsaw and been shot by the diving planes. In the fourth week, the German army crossed the Poniatowski Bridge over the Vistula and entered Warsaw. Now they could leave the basements, into the terror regime that the Germans imposed on the city.

In June 1939 the theater director Jonas Turkow and his wife Diana Blumenfeld finished the season at the Chamber Theater in Warsaw and embarked on their traditional summer tour around the Polish provinces. On August 31, they were in Lviv celebrating Turkow's appointment as the manager of the city's new Yiddish Theater with a dinner at the Jewish restaurant at the Bristol Hotel. One of the guests, the lawyer Dr. Leib Landau, raised a toast and said: "I'm drinking for the war to end as quickly as possible." Turkow was alarmed: "The war hasn't started yet and the great fighter for rights and justice is already drinking for its swift end!" The next day the couple managed to board the last train to Warsaw and discovered that the city had been turned into a military camp. At the beginning of September they saw little dots in the clear sky and heard a big blast: "Our French allies' aircraft are coming to our aid. Finally the dots in the sky become more and more visible, bigger and bigger. An unexpected whistle pierces the air.

Immediately after—strong explosions, until the ground starts to shake. A hailstorm of bombs falls to the ground."

The couple and their five-year-old daughter joined the throngs starting to flee the city to the east. As they crossed the river to Praga, the ground shook under a barrage of bombs. They survived and kept going, the Luftwaffe airplanes all the while continuing to snipe at those fleeing. In Anin some Polish youths shouted, "Jewish lepers," and "Go to Palestine" at them. No one would sell them a glass of water. "Soon Hitler will come, and he will take care of you." In the morning they tried to cross a forest full of army units and cannons while it was bombarded from the air. The roads were blocked and the little Turkow family returned to Warsaw. For three days and nights the city was bombed: "No one could get out into the street. We all lay hidden in the apartments, in the basements, without light, without water, not closing our eyes even for a short nap."[132]

Jonas's brother, the actor Zygmunt Turkow,[133] performed the play *Shulamis*, written by Abraham Goldfaden and based on a Talmudic legend (*Taanit* 8), every night at the Nowości Theater at 5 Bielanska Street. The play opened with a pilgrimage to Jerusalem and was set in Jerusalem and Bethlehem. It began with the following lines:

> Laden with all good things
> with staffs in our hands
> we set forth at this minute
> to our holy land.
>
> . . . .
>
> Oh where are you, oh where are you, you holy Zion?
>
> . . . .
>
> Yes, children, quickly, children, quickly.
> Quickly, children, quickly on our way.[134]

The air raid destroyed the theater building.

Chajes's Polish patriotism did not allow him to give in: the war would be bloody but would bring glory to Poland. "Poland will prevail in the end." However, in the next few days his hope evaporated: "It is bad for my homeland, it is bad for us," he wrote on September 17. On September 22, the city's defenders surrendered to the Soviet army. "Long live Poland!" Chajes ended his diary.[135] He was arrested on April 10, 1940, and exiled to Siberia, where he died.

Hillel Tzur, an Irgun member, left Palestine for Poland on March 29, 1939, to serve as an instructor at the Irgun's training camp near Mezritch. About two months later he was joined in Warsaw by his pregnant wife and his son, who traveled on to his family in Riga, where his wife gave birth. The war separated them, and Tzur stayed in Warsaw. On September 6, he managed to obtain a transit visa and boarded a train that was heading north. The train was bombed from the air. Tzur made his way on foot to the Lithuanian border and from there continued to Latvia.[136]

Sarah Reitberger (Blaustein) and her mother fled Piotrków in the refugee convoys that were bombed from the air:

> Different families got mixed together in the commotion, including me—terrified and lost. As we were running a woman grabbed me; her hair was disheveled and her eyes were darting madly. She started to remove my coat. I tried to resist and held onto it, but she overpowered me, snatched it from my hand, inserted her arms in the sleeves—and quickly pulled the coat inside out and turned it over. She gestured for me to put the coat back on while murmuring hysterically "Red! Red!" The woman kept on murmuring things I did not understand, pointing again and again towards the sky. Suddenly I understood. The Germans could have seen the red color of the coat and the hat I was wearing and used me as a target. I put on my overturned coat and straightened and smoothed out my crumpled hat. I felt guilty.[137]

After many ordeals Sarah and her mother reached Tomaszów, which had already been taken by the Germans. After a while they decided to return to Piotrków and made their way back on a black horse-driven carriage. All the family members returned to the city. The British-Palestinian passport enabled her mother and her to purchase an exit permit. They parted from their family and took the train to Łódź, from where they continued to Breslau and Trieste. Two German soldiers sat in the train car with them. They gave Sarah a picture: a bird that they cut out from the pack of the cigarettes they were smoking. The mother and daughter sailed to Tel Aviv on the ship *Galilea* on November 5 with another 550 immigrants and returning residents; the ship was torpedoed on its way back to Europe and all its crew drowned. When they got to Tel Aviv there was a big crowd of people at the port trying to attract the returnees' attention, waving photographs of family members who had remained in Poland:

> "Have you by any chance met . . . ?" "Excuse me, but maybe . . . ?" Names were called out, photos of people were placed in front of our eyes. "Maybe . . . ," "Maybe . . ." "Sorry, no, I didn't meet, I didn't see, I didn't

hear." [. . .] The circle of people around us gradually dwindled. People left the platform in tears and returned to their homes with their heads bent. "Maybe in the next ship," they tried to console themselves.[138]

Runia Yoachimovich (Levin), born in Kalisz, west Poland, immigrated to Palestine with a student visa in September 1938. With her on the ship *Polonia*, on its final trip to Palestine, were another approximately 1,000 students. In the middle of August 1939, two weeks before the outbreak of war, she went to visit her family in Kalisz. The city was taken in the first days of the German invasion and its Jews were expelled. The family hired a horse-driven cart, loaded it with some of their belongings, and wandered for ten days on the bombarded roads until they reached Warsaw. Three months of efforts and briberies passed before Runia got an exit permit from Poland from the Gestapo, an Italian visa, and a train ticket to Trieste. She reached Haifa in February 1940.[139]

In July 1939, Dvorah Gertz took her five-year-old daughter Dalit to visit her husband's parents in Bialystok. The parents had sent the money for the travel expenses. Haim Gertz was the owner of a textile factory (Bialystok was Poland's second textile city after Łódź) that employed dozens of workers. The family lived in a spacious three-story house. Toward the end of August, Haim Gertz waited for a chimney he had ordered from Sweden that was supposed to increase the factory's productivity. The huge two-story-high chimney arrived by train on August 26. For seven days it rolled slowly on large wooden wheels through the streets of Bialystok until it stopped next to the factory on September 2. That day the Germans entered Częstochowa. Dvorah Gertz followed the discussions at the Twenty-First Zionist Congress in Geneva in the *Haynt*, and on August 26 she learned from the newspaper that the Congress had been dispersed and the emissaries were returning to Palestine. She immediately decided to leave Poland as quickly as possible. Her friend Mika from Warsaw booked her a place on the flight to Palestine: "I left Bialystok in a panic but had time to say good-bye to everyone," she wrote later.

"The trains to Warsaw were full of soldiers. We barely managed to get in among the packages and the kitbags. [. . .] I got to Warsaw with 20 zloty in my purse. In Krasinński Park dozens of men were already digging trenches. Posters on the streets announced a general mobilization." Mika managed to get the last ticket on the Lot airplane — a Zionist Congress delegate from Palestine had canceled his flight at the last minute. "Why don't you leave, too," Dvorah asked Mika, "now that there is a war on here." "We will go for sure," Mika replied. "Once we have finished our business here we will withdraw the money and immigrate to Palestine." On August 28, when Dvorah and her daughter went to the airline's offices to get the flight tickets, they were told that flights from Poland had been stopped. The way to leave was to go by train to Constanta and take a ship from there.

At the Palestine Office Dvorah got a document confirming that they had Palestinian citizenship, and Mika drove them in her car to the train station. When they reached Constanta, they found that they had missed the ship. They took a room in a hotel opposite the port and waited with another few hundred women and children who had been on summer visits to see their families in Europe.

With the Red Army at the gates of Bialystok, the rest of the Gertz family packed their suitcases, withdrew their money from the bank, locked the large apartment on Kupiecka Street, and fled to Sokółka. They were included on the list of large business owners destined for exile in Siberia. In 1941 Haim Gertz wrote to his daughter: "Finally the Russians have left. The Germans have entered Bialystok. We are saved, we can go back."[140]

In the last days of August 1939, there was a busy traffic of ships from the ports of the Black and the Adriatic Sea to Palestine, taking home returning residents: on August 28 the Romanian ship *Dacia* anchored in Tel Aviv with 38 passengers on board. On August 29, the ship *Transylvania* came from Constanta carrying 250 passengers. The next day the ship *Bessarabia* of the shipping company Romanian Maritime Service sailed with several hundreds of returning residents on board, and the Romanian shipping company announced that its services would continue as normal. The ship's passengers complained about the bad treatment from the crew and the inedible food. The ship sailed from Constanta again on the evening of August 31, carrying several hundred passengers. It seems that Dvorah Gertz and her daughter were among them. On September 2, the *Mariette Pacha* arrived with 169 passengers. The *Har Zion* sailed from Constanta on August 26 carrying around 150 passengers, mostly women and children from Poland (as well as slaughter-bound cattle and fowl from Romania). The British navy ordered it to anchor in Rodosto Port, and only on Thursday was it allowed to sail on to Izmir. The passengers endured several days of anxious waiting, planning to take the Taurus Express train and then travel by car to Palestine—a sixty-hour drive. Fortunately, the ship was finally allowed to continue on its way to Haifa, where it anchored on September 10, after sixteen days of sailing. It was followed from Constanta by the ship *Miriam*.[141]

At the beginning of September 1939, Haohel Theater, working under the aegis of the Histadrut, staged the play *The Good Soldier Švejk* by Jaroslav Hašek, which became an instant hit. The theater critic Shmaryahu Gorelik protested on the pages of *Haaretz* against what he saw as a stupid play whose protagonist was not a philosophizing pacifist but "a dangerous fool, a defeatist and a deserter." Had the Haohel directors, he wondered, not considered the contradiction between the audience's enjoyment of the play and their wish "to don the uniform and the hat of a soldier in the great army of liberation. [. . .] Away with this clown."[142]

When Jabotinsky described Poland "as the giant concentration camp occupied by the Germans,"[143] the monstrous meaning that the words "concentration camp" would soon accrue lay beyond the limits of his imagination. In his book *The Jewish War Front*, published in London in July 1940, he repeated his words of appreciation for Piłsudski and his heirs as "the last barrier between the Jews and a general crusade," and his view that Polish antisemitism was an "objective" result of Poland's situation. Jabotinsky wrote about the cruelty of the Nazi occupying regime, which was perpetrating mass murders that felt like they were happening "on a different planet." However, the war struck him as a historic opportunity to turn the Jews into one of the allied nations, hence he warned against turning the "new ghetto" that was being created in Eastern Europe into a "habitable" place. This is the only way to explain the fact that in July 1940 he saw fit to discuss the issue of what would happen to Poland's Jews after the war. In his view, it was therefore already necessary to plan for the solution of "the Jewish problem in Poland" during the times of recovery and rehabilitation. This solution had been and still was the organized evacuation of massive numbers of Jews to Palestine after the victory over the Axis.[144]

These words came in response to the Nazi regime's decision at the beginning of October 1939 to create a "reservation" for the Reich's Jews near the town of Nisko in the Lublin area. Four "transports" of around 6,000 Jews from Austria were sent there under an SS guard. Many of them were forced across the Russian border with intimidation shots. In Lublin, all the city's 45,000 Jews, plus tens of thousands of additional Jews including 6,000 refugees from western Poland, were pushed into the old Jewish quarter. The expulsion of Jews to the area was suddenly stopped, then renewed on February 1, 1940, then stopped completely in March and April.[145] An immigrant who left Nazi Germany in November 1939 testified: "Even though so far not even one person has been transferred from Germany to Lublin, the sound of the word Lublin raises terrifying visions among Germany's Jews. Previously they were afraid of pogroms and concentration camps. Now they are scared of Lublin."[146]

On September 22, 1939, Jabotinsky wrote from London to his friend the millionaire Michael Haskell in South Africa that the situation of the Jews in Poland would force the world to find a solution for them. "I still feel—am convinced—that the outcome of this earthquake will be that those who will have managed to survive will rule Zion." On the other hand, the Jews who were under Soviet rule were lost, but the scale of the plight of the 1.5 million Polish Jews living under the Nazi regime would force a solution in the form of an evacuation.[147]

Three days later, he admitted in a letter to the Betar commissionership in Tel Aviv: "Betar in Poland has been destroyed. I do not have to tell you the magnitude of this loss."[148] On September 29, he repeated these words in another letter: once the war ended the Jews of Eastern Europe would be a strong factor that would force the world to allow an unprecedented exodus of Jews.[149]

In July 1940, Jabotinsky was similarly preoccupied with the question of the fate of Poland's Jews once the war ended. The Nazis wanted to concentrate them in the Lublin district, he remarked, but this plan was merely a "vague improvisation." The Nazi regime had no plans at all: "There is, by the way, a general but stupid tendency to overestimate Germany's ability to 'make plans,' and people are ignoring the clear and obvious fact that very often, in crucial moments, both before and during the war, the Nazi government has embarked on actions without having a definite plan, be it political or strategic, and has changed its plans every single day—and has usually lived 'from hand to mouth.'"[150] If indeed the German government succeeded in realizing its plan to create "a large Jewish ghetto," he added, then at the end of the war there would be hundreds of thousands of Jews in the Lublin district, to which they would have been transferred from the other parts of Poland. Such a territorial-demographic concentration would put the Jews in danger of starvation and the Polish government in a real quandary.[151]

The poet Shlomo Skulski, who was one of those fleeing to Vilna, did not make a distinction between living under Nazi occupation and under a Soviet one either. He wrote in Vilna on December 2, 1939:

> We shall flee neither death nor a lifetime in jail,
> Nor my brother's blood clotted like tar.
> Whether the blood-thirsty swastika be on our trail
> Or likewise—a five-pointed star.[152]

In September 1943, Emanuel Ringelblum analyzed the relations between Poles and Jews "Sine ira et studio" (without anger and bias) and examined "what the Poles did when millions of Poland's Jews burned at the stake." He described the reasons for the antisemitism of the second half of the 1930s, which led to racism, boycott, violence, and anti-Jewish legislation. In September 1939, however, the Polish public became disillusioned and discovered that antisemitism was serving Hitler. At that point, "antisemitism miraculously disappear[ed]" and "the wolf lived with the lamb." He heard testimonies of comradeship and mutual help. With his own eyes he saw Polish and Jewish residents fighting fires together in Warsaw: "Jews are doing all they can to defend the homeland. On the night of the government's evacuation from the capital, between the sixth and the seventh of September, massive numbers of Jews join[ed] together with the general population in digging the defensive trenches, in erecting barricades from overturned trams, carts, broken furniture and boxes."

But at the same time he depicted a different picture:

> The hydra of antisemitism has raised its head before Warsaw fell. It had happened more than once that [during] bombardments Jews shelter[ed] in a house occupied only by Poles. In September 1939 I was an inspector of the civil defense at a particular house on Dluga Street. With my own ears I heard the person in charge of the shelter refusing, on principle, to allow Jewish passersby to find shelter in the new facility under his control. At the time I lived on Leszno Street no. 18. That house had no shelter. The house on the other side of the street, Leszno no. 13 had a shelter [. . .]. On pure antisemitic grounds Jewish tenants were refused entry to this shelter. This was the situation in quite a few houses where the majority of the tenants were Poles.[153]

After the Germans entered Warsaw, he wrote, the "antisemitic filth" volunteered to help the Nazis. Many testimonies suggested that Poles used the days of the war to loot the Jews' homes and violently attack them.

The Polish art expert Dr. Karol Estreicher, who wrote under the pseudonym Dominik Wegierski, had a totally different opinion when he fled to London, writing in 1940 that the Jews had received shelter and hospitality in Poland but had responded with ingratitude. They had disseminated horror stories in the American press, and the Poles could not forgive them for it and had reacted with antisemitism, which had completely disappeared once the war broke out.[154] Roman Reich remembered this period as a pleasant one. Until the summer of 1940, he used to bathe in the Vistula, borrowed books in the library on Saolec Street, and took private lessons.[155]

In secret talks held in September 1939, Ribbentrop and Molotov agreed on the repatriation of the German population that lived in the eastern areas of Poland that had been annexed by the Soviet Union. The USSR agreed to take in Ukrainians, Belarusians, and Russians who lived in the Polish territories that were occupied by Germany. Nothing was said in the agreement about the Jews who lived in those territories. In effect, they were abandoned to their fate. Nazi Germany used terror attacks to encourage Jews to flee into the Soviet territory and in some cases even supplied them with freight carts. In Chełm and Hrubieszów, thousands of Jews were rounded up, driven to the Bug River, and ordered to cross over to the Soviet side. Those who could not swim drowned or were shot. Hundreds of thousands of Jews were expelled or fled eastward.

It is estimated that between 400,000 and 500,000 Jews were pushed out to the Soviet Union, with many of them ending up in the country's remotest regions. Thousands chose to return to the German-held territory, fearing for their safety under the Communist regime. Thousands of others fled toward the southern border—to Romania and Hungary. Around 60 percent of Poland's Jews remained in the German-occupied territory, and around 250,000 Jews managed to flee to the Soviet-occupied territory. Many of them were sent to the cold regions of northern Russia. It is estimated that around 100,000 Jews were killed between September 1939 and the end of 1940.[156]

Around 50,000 Jewish soldiers serving in the Polish army were captured, separated from the other Polish prisoners of war, and held in special prisoner-of-war camps. They were transferred in 1940 and 1941 to the areas of the Generalgouvernement, the territorial unit in Poland with its own administration created by the Nazis on October 26, 1939, and in November 1943 were sent to the Majdanek death camp, where they were murdered.

The Soviet Union stopped its anti-Nazi propaganda. Stalin described the war as a war between two groups of capitalist countries that were fighting and weakening each other. Poland was, in his view, a fascist state that had oppressed Ukrainians, Belarusians, and others. Eradicating it meant having one less bourgeois fascist state! The fate of the Jews left him completely indifferent.

In January, Yitzhak Gruenbaum wrote:

> Let us therefore not mourn the Jewry of Poland as we do that of Germany. The latter has been almost thoroughly uprooted due to the atrocities of

the Nazis, who are forcing Germany's Jews to leave the countries of the Reich. Poland's Jews are also being uprooted, but they are only being uprooted from certain regions of Poland [. . .]. Great numbers of Jews fled Poland after it had fallen to the Germans. Great numbers are fleeing and are yet to flee. But even greater numbers of Jews will still remain in the country despite all the persecutions, oppression and killings [. . .]. And if Poland comes back to life [. . .] the Jews will come back to life with it [. . .]. Of course Polish Jewry will not go back to what it used to be [. . . ,] but it will not be finished and it will not be lost. It will merely enter a new era.[157]

The positive attitude toward Poland among some of its former residents in Palestine found a pathetic expression in the July 29, 1940, issue of the *Hashaa* newspaper. It described a parade of Polish soldiers marching through Tel Aviv's streets:

> A regular Polish army armed with weapons marches in orderly columns through the streets of Tel Aviv and Polish army songs can be heard far in the distance. The children of Warsaw and Poznan, Lviv and Bialystok, Krakow and Vilna—from all over Poland the crumbs of Polish patriotism have gathered here, including even sixteen-year-old boys who have lovingly taken on the difficult and lofty duty of serving their homeland from afar [. . .]. They march along Allenby Street singing: "Homeland, homeland! My heart cries for you homeland! You are bleeding and suffering, but in your suffering you will be saved! We are your watchmen! The longing and the love for you—are our guiding star!" And when they see the hundreds of Polish Jews living in Tel Aviv applauding them and treating them with affection, many of these soldiers must recall the situation of Polish Jewry on the eve of the great disaster that has befallen Poles and Jews alike [. . .]. "In Tel Aviv we feel like we are among our own," boasts one Polish soldier. Would that the Tel Avivians also feel as if they were "among our own" when they visit the future liberated Poland.[158]

EPILOGUE

On September 4, *Davar leyeladim* informed its young readers: "A war has started — the catastrophe has come." The weekly told its young readers that as Hitler spoke at the Reichstag in Berlin "wearing a corporal's uniform [. . . ,] German planes took off and flew over various cities in Poland, bombing houses and killing men, women and children. [. . .] Fleets of German planes continued to shell cities in Poland and set fire to them. Poland defended itself and returned fire toward the attackers." The news item was preceded by a short allegory called "Fish in the Flood," which described some fish that did not drown in the flood but were flung onto the tops of mountains and hills, where they became dehydrated without water. They were crying out in desperation: "Justice, justice! The injustice under the heavens."[1]

No one could have known that on September 1 war would break out, much less imagine that Poland — which many saw as a strong European country — would collapse in a matter of weeks. The Jewish world and its leaders were mainly concerned with the fate of emigrants and refugees[2] from the countries of the Third Reich — Germany, Austria, and Czechoslovakia — and with searching for countries that would be willing to take them in. Of course the great predicament of the Jews of Eastern and Central Europe, and first and foremost the Jews of Poland, was not ignored by the Jewish organizations or Jewish public opinion. In the period discussed in this book, however, it was still possible to present the struggle to defend the civil rights of Poland's Jews as a principal — and realistic — goal, and these Jews, as already mentioned, were not described as "refugees."[3]

Faced with the situation of millions of Eastern and Central European Jews, the world's countries likewise did not display indifference or heartlessness; they rather did not think that resolving the situation was in their interest or that it was possible to find an overall solution. Thus, for example, the president of the United States, Franklin Delano Roosevelt, who in January 1939 had expressed concern that the problem of Eastern European Jews would become as "acute" as that of the Jews of Germany if it was not resolved in time, had also pointed out that it would not be possible to organize the emigration of seven million people, and that the most that could be arranged was the planned emigration of around 150,000 emigrants per year —the majority of them to different world regions (Roosevelt proposed Angola, then under Portuguese rule).[4] Not even immigration destinations on this scale, however, or even a much smaller one, were found.

Simultaneously, the spokespeople of the Zionist movement, who continued to reiterate their belief that the one and only solution for the refugees and potential emigrants was Palestine, must have known that, at least in the short term (and they were not to know how short this term was), it only offered a solution for a few tens of thousands of Jewish immigrants per year. There was no basis to the belief that as the Jews' plight grew and worsened, and as the pressure to emigrate increased and intensified, the governments and the relevant international organizations would reach the unavoidable conclusion that an organized mass emigration was the only solution; nor was there any basis to the wishful or deluded thinking that the "world's conscience," and mainly that of Britain and the United States, could be awakened to recognize this.

In the period of time discussed in this book, the Polish regime presented Jewish emigration as the solution for Poland's difficulties and acted tirelessly in the international arena to include Poland's Jews in the "refugee" question. The Polish government protested against what it described as the "monopolization" of the refugee problem by the Jews of the Reich and sought international cooperation in finding destinations for a large Jewish emigration from Poland. Thus, for example, in a coded telegram sent by the Polish foreign minister Józef Beck to the Polish ambassador to Washington on November 18, 1938, the latter was instructed to inform the American administration that Poland saw "a great urgency in initiating some constructive emigration activity on a large scale." Beck instructed the ambassador to stress that "serious" Jewish circles were also increasingly recognizing the need for an emigration plan—and not necessarily to Palestine.[5] Consequently, a web of connections formed between the Polish regime and the Zionist movement, connections that gave rise to expectations, dramatic plans, and mainly difficult dilemmas. Poland played a significant role in our story because it became one of the sides in the triangle that also included Great Britain on the one hand and the Zionist movement and the Jewish Yishuv in Palestine on the other.

The history of Zionism and of the Yishuv in the period examined in this book is mixed and intertwined with the history of Poland, mainly due to Poland's policy of pushing for a large Jewish emigration in any way possible. In these circumstances, Polish politics and diplomacy were seen as allies of the Zionist movement, and the expectation was that Poland would be able to persuade Britain to change its policy on the Palestine question. Some in the Zionist movement hoped to persuade Poland to support the Partition Plan of July 1937, while others hoped to obtain its help in opposing the plan. Two years later, false hopes were pinned on Poland's ability to change the policy of the White Paper of May 1939. At the same time, it was difficult, and perhaps impossible, to organize illegal emigration from Poland without the help — both overt and covert — of the Polish authorities. The concern for the fate of Poland's Jews was deep and sincere, but the "similarity of interests" between Zionism and Poland could not be of much use. Acknowledging that the Zionist movement was unable to promise a large emigration was tantamount to declaring the ineffectiveness of Zionism at such a crucial time; a declaration that would make it lose its raison d'être. And let us not forget: in the period examined in this book the future of the Yishuv was in danger as a result of the Arab Revolt and of Britain's retreat from the Balfour Declaration and from its commitment to the National Home principle. In these circumstances, the task faced by the Yishuv — and the only one it could perform on its own — was to consolidate its position in all areas and get ready for the coming days.

In June 1937, Ben-Gurion had said that the fate of the Zionist movement lay on the shoulders of one man and one woman, and that Dugdale was now "our Deborah." Dugdale had replied: "This is a terrible responsibility."[6] Now, at the end of August 1939, Weizmann and Dugdale were saddled with an impossible burden. Immediately on returning to London, Weizmann embarked on some vigorous diplomatic activity. On August 29, he sent Chamberlain a letter in which he promised that the Jews stood behind Britain and were ready to do all they could to help, setting aside political disagreements.[7] The prime minister replied politely that while there were certainly differences of opinion between the Mandatory power and the Jewish Agency on the Palestine question, he "willingly" accepted the promises made in the letter.[8] The next day, Weizmann met with Major General Henry Pownall, director of military operations and intelligence, and proposed, among other things, that the Jews of the United States would finance the creation of a weapons manufacturing industry in Palestine that would arm a Jewish military.[9]

At the beginning of September, the NZO presidency published a statement saying, "A cruel enemy is threatening Poland, the heart of the Jewish Diaspora for nearly a thousand years," and declaring its loyalty to the democratic Britain.[10] On September 4, Jabotinsky similarly approached Chamberlain proposing the creation of a Jewish army that would "inject into the war atmosphere a new magnetism of incalculable potency." Two weeks passed before Chamberlain replied on September 21: he frankly and simply wished to inform him that the White Paper policy was still in force.[11] On September 9, Jabotinsky met with the colonial secretary and explained that despite the large flow of refugees fleeing Poland, the illegal immigration might decrease due to the dangers and difficulties of traveling. Equally, however, it might increase, and the government in Palestine would have to use force against it, which would create hostility toward it in U.S. public opinion.[12]

All the promises and arguments fell on deaf ears. Poland's Jews remained imprisoned in what Jabotinsky called "the giant concentration camp occupied by the Germans." On September 17 he instructed the leaders of the party in Palestine (Vaad Hamurshim) to cooperate with the Yishuv's institutions during the war and added that if the war spread to Western Europe "our problem will soon seem important to the whole world, and we will discover some wide-open and far-reaching roads."[13] "Do not overestimate the Palestine front. It is important, but it is not the only one," he wrote on September 29.[14]

Two weeks into the war, on September 15, Weizmann pleaded with the colonial secretary MacDonald to consent to the request of the Polish consul in Palestine and allow 20,000 Jewish children from Poland to immigrate to Palestine as part of the quota of 25,000 refugees allocated in the White Paper:

> I write to ask you to re-consider this decision. In the area already under German occupation in Poland there are already about 1,500,000 Jews; in Warsaw and Lviv another 500,000, and a million further east. Hundreds of thousands of Jews in Poland will have to face the Polish winter without a roof over their heads, dying of starvation. Whatever food can be removed from the Polish countryside will be taken for Germany; little will reach the towns, and still less the Jewish population. Whether the Nazis choose to administer the Occupied Districts themselves, or through a puppet Polish government, the administration will be of the extremist antisemitic character. This is a catastrophe of a magnitude such as not even we have yet experienced. [. . .] It is your decision alone that will determine if the lives of these children will be saved or not.[15]

His request was discussed at the Colonial Office the same day and was denied. It was possible to transfer the children first to Cyprus and then to

Palestine, but this would mean breaking a promise given to the Arabs. In a state of war, the Colonial Office said, "Everything must be subject to the need to win the war. As cruel as it may sound, taking 20,000 children out of Poland at this time would ease the German's economic problem to the same extent. [. . .] Consenting to his [Weizmann's] request might harm the successful running of the war and for this reason it must be denied."[16]

After Ben-Gurion's return from Geneva, on September 3, he went to Jerusalem and summoned a few comrades to discuss the situation. During the discussion they were informed that Britain had declared war on Germany. Twenty minutes later the air raid sirens were sounded in London and a mass evacuation of children and mothers was begun. In the afternoon, the Jewish Agency Directorate convened and released a statement saying that Britain's war against Nazi Germany was also the Jewish Yishuv's war.[17] Tabenkin said that now the defense of Palestine had to "change" and that it was necessary "to mobilize forces and resources" for that purpose.[18] The disaster in Europe was also perceived as a "catastrophe that will bring salvation." The war seemed to have removed Britain's political plans from the agenda, the Arab Revolt had ended, and the military cooperation with Britain in Palestine became stronger once Winston Churchill was appointed prime minister. People in the Yishuv started registering to enlist in the British army, and a debate began on whether they should stay in Palestine or be sent to the front.

Those who were against military cooperation with the "imperialist" Britain that had betrayed Zionism argued that the soldiers from Palestine should not serve as "cannon fodder in foreign killing fields" and become "mercenaries" and a "foreign legion" in overseas battles. The Yishuv's duty was to stand "firm and guard all our economic and political positions in Palestine."[19] Those who were for it argued that the fate of the Jews and of Palestine would be decided on the Rhine river, and that the Yishuv represented a people "who cannot and do not want to give up their right to fight against the hated enemy. But while insisting on this right they must not be choosy as to where they might encounter the enemy."[20]

Britain and France were not prepared to go to Poland's aid far away in the east. Their main concern was a German attack in the west. Poland roused itself with nationalism and patriotic zeal and deceived itself into believing that it could defend its borders. There was no way of knowing whether war would have been averted if the Polish government had agreed to allow a Soviet army to enter its border if Nazi Germany attacked it, and whether Hitler would have overcome his hesitations without the Ribbentrop-Molotov

Pact promising Soviet non-intervention. However, there is no doubt that the pact made it much easier for him to make a decision. The vagaries of history meant that the pact and the occupation of eastern Poland by the Red Army enabled the flight east of around 1.5 million Jews from the German-occupied territory.

On September 12, Shertok said: "This corner of the world [Palestine] may be able to escape the war peacefully." Palestine would not be a front, and Britain would not need the Jews' support as it did in the First World War.[21] Yosef Netz continued his pen war against the Labor movement and the socialist ideology. Ironically, he gave his articles the title "The War Diary."[22] The Mugrabi cinema in Tel Aviv screened the film *Confessions of a Nazi Spy*. *Hamashkif*'s film critic wrote that the movie was remarkable for its realism: "When you leave the theater you imagine that you will soon be able to see the continuation. Because life continues as well."[23]

On September 8, Ben-Gurion spoke before some "security chiefs" and explained that the war might bring a change in Britain's policy because the Yishuv could join its war effort. On the Yishuv's ability to offer help to the Jews of Europe, however, he had no words of encouragement. At the meeting of the Jewish Agency Directorate on September 13 he outlined a grim prospect: "Helping the Jewish people in the Diaspora today is beyond human powers," and therefore "we must concentrate mainly on dealing with Palestine matters."[24] A day earlier, at the meeting of Mapai's Central Committee, he estimated that the world's fate would be decided on the French front and "the fate of Poland will be decided by a French victory, but our own fate will be decided here, in Palestine. [. . .] On this war, on its results, depends the fate of the world; we have a small war, which for us is everything."[25] On the future of the illegal immigration he could only say: "Tens and hundreds of thousands in Poland are already facing massacre, and who can guarantee that the hand of destruction would not reach other countries." "The call for immigration must continue to be heard,"[26] he declared, but his words were an admission that the Zionist movement and the Yishuv were standing helpless against the destruction of European Jewry, a destruction whose magnitude they could not have imagined. In September 1939—and later as well—it was impossible to know what the war's results would be.

The Jews of Eastern Europe were now beyond the Sambatyon, the unnavigable legendary river. In order to bring them across the river it was necessary to try and change the immigration policy of the British government, which allocated a meager quota of immigration permits and made considerable efforts to block the channels of illegal immigration. At the same time, in the first two years of the war more Jews managed to leave Poland in various ways—not necessarily on illegal immigrant ships—and reach Palestine. Exit, flight, and escape routes from occupied Europe still remained open through 1940 and 1941. Some individuals and groups managed to take them; the majority were left to their fate. That year two ships of the Mossad LeAliyah Bet reached Palestine's shores carrying around 1,500 immigrants, two ships organized by the Revisionist movement's offshoots brought around 2,900 immigrants, and another six ships organized by private people and various public bodies arrived as well. The war did not put a stop to the British pursuit of the ships and the illegal immigrants.

Ben-Gurion and Jabotinsky, and not only they, believed that the catastrophe that had befallen Europe's Jews would blow wind and momentum in Zionism's sails and strengthen the Yishuv. In the years before August 1939 Ben-Gurion put his trust mainly in the Yishuv's strength and even thought that it was approaching the "times of greatness" when it would prove its capability to the fullest.[27] Jabotinsky believed in the strength of the Jewish people and in the ability of his movement to change the British government's view or alternatively acquire other allies for Zionism. He worked indefatigably for that purpose, without registering any real achievements.

Greater Israel on both sides of the Jordan River and an organized mass immigration were combined goals in the Revisionist movement's worldview. The independent diplomacy it pursued earned it declarations of support and sympathy—some sincere and others hollow, stemming from the wish to see the Jews leave by any means possible—but failed to register any achievements. There is no way of knowing what routes history would have taken if the Second World War had not broken out on September 1, 1939, or if Poland had managed to withstand the aggressor. Both leaders, from the two sides of the political divide, as well as countless others, did not imagine that Poland would be defeated so quickly, and both were unable to offer a response to the disaster. Palestine was worlds apart from Poland.

Ben-Gurion's words cited above can be interpreted as a conscious "abandonment" of Europe's Jews to their fate, and as expressing the primacy of the Jewish Yishuv in Palestine; evidence suggests that the Zionist parties did not instigate rescue efforts or pool all their resources for that purpose. It was not, however, due to indifference or unwillingness that "the Zionist parties stopped being parties of immigration,"[28] but rather due to their inability to increase the pace of immigration. The fear of weakening the strength and status of the Zionist movement did not stem from a "narrow interest," from a "Palestinocentrism," or from indifference to the fate of

Europe's Jews. A weakened Zionist movement on the eve of war would have put the Yishuv in real danger. In September 1939, and earlier, its future did not seem certain by any means. However, only in Palestine was the Yishuv able to act and record achievements: to purchase land, found around sixty new settlements, consolidate and strengthen the Jewish defense force (in part in collaboration with the British army in Palestine), and so on. The Yishuv became a "state in the making," and after the defeat of Nazi Germany could do what it was unable to do in the previous years: bring the refugees and the displaced persons to Palestine.

On October 1, 1939, Moshe Shertok left Palestine for London, stopping for half a day in Geneva. He flew from Lod to Athens, which was "happy and gay," celebrating some inter-Balkan sporting events, and continued to Rome, from where he flew to Milan and took a sleeper train to Switzerland. On his way he saw that the train stations were filled with military personnel and freight cars packed with "war paraphernalia." In Geneva he met Nahum Goldmann and discussed the attempt to get the French government's agreement to form a Jewish army to help France on the western front, as well as Weizmann's success in revoking the ban on the immigration of 2,900 permit holders from Germany who had not yet set out on their way. The two then drove to Lichtheim's office in rue de Lausanne, where they discussed the future of illegal immigration. Lichtheim wondered: "What good is it to us in a state of war? [. . .] Do we have the resources to finance Aliyah Bet?" Shertok replied, "*Immigration* is imperative under any conditions: Where would Poland's refugees who have found themselves in the neighboring countries go if not to Palestine? If we can get more and more people out of Germany —well, this is their sole salvation. Offering the government that we put a stop to illegal immigration (this was in fact his [Lichtheim's] suggestion, in order to obtain a quota for legal immigration in this half a year) means first of all admitting our responsibility for Aliyah Bet without any guarantee of a positive result. On the contrary, chances are we will be refused."[29]

From Geneva, Shertok took the train to Paris, from where he continued to London. On October 9, 1939, he surveyed the state of the Yishuv and the prospects for the future before the members of the London branch of the Agency Directorate and other invited dignitaries from the Jewish community:

> Half of Polish Jewry is being ground to dust—it will turn into a refugee camp but will no longer be a constructive element in terms of resources;

> the other half has entered the Soviet prison—a million and a half Jews erased from the national balance sheet; their international weight as an element demanding the realization of Zionism has been wiped out. Hitler's defeat will improve the Jews' position in the world [. . .] but it will not necessarily reinforce Zionism. On the contrary, there could be a movement of return from Palestine to Germany and from Zionism to Diasporism [. . .]. Hitler's defeat and Britain's victory in the war are by no means certain to bring the revocation of the White Paper policy—the elements that led to this policy will remain in place even if the terrifying shadow of the Nazi danger is removed from the east. In light of all this our main support will be the success we will achieve and the power we will accumulate in Palestine, figuratively and literally, and this is what we must concentrate all our efforts on.[30]

In his home in Geneva, Richard Lichtheim, the Agency Directorate's representative in Europe, felt "like old Noah in his ark, as the water continues to rise all around it," and could only hope "that the water will subside in time, that is, before our Jews in Europe run out of their staying power." Less than a year later, in August 1941, he wrote from "the Happy Island of Switzerland":

> Are you aware how happy you are under the sun in Palestine? Just think of the 500,000 Jews languishing behind the walls of the Warsaw Ghetto, of the 20,000 German and Polish Jews rotting on abject straw in the concentration camps in France, of the nameless masses in the areas of Poland occupied by the Russians now being trampled under the war machine, of the miserable Jews in Croatia, Bulgaria and Romania who have been recruited to forced labor regiments under inhuman conditions [. . .]. Sometimes when I get letters or telegrams from Palestine, I wonder if our friends there *really* understand what is happening in Europe.[31]

ACKNOWLEDGMENTS

In writing this book we received help from colleagues who read all or portions of the Hebrew and also English manuscripts, made important comments and suggestions, and graciously pointed out errors of commission as well as omission. First and foremost we thank Professor Meir Chazan, who much improved an early draft. Professors Havi Dreifuss and Aviva Halamish, and Dr. Scott Ury read portions of the manuscript and contributed significantly. Professor Antony Polonsky read the final draft in English and answered our many questions and shared his expert knowledge with us. Thanks also to Dr. Raphael Witkowski at the Adam Mickiewicz University in Poznań. Aviv Livnat translated the Yiddish texts for the Hebrew edition and was most helpful in locating valuable sources, as were Eran Eldar, David Motzafi-Haller, Dr. Maya Shabbat, and Elit Guberman. Avital Ganit and Irit Halevi were involved in the research from the very start and until the book went to press.

Golan Moskowitz is to be commended for his relentless efforts to track English sources and edit the footnotes and bibliography. The assistance of the Tauber Institute for the Study of European Jewry and its executive director, Sylvia Fuks Fried, is much appreciated.

NOTES

PREFACE. "THE BIRDS LEFT EARLY"

1. "At the Tel Aviv Zoo," *Davar LeYeladim*, September 4, 1939, p. 14. The small Tel Aviv Zoo, which included two lion cubs and two bear cubs, moved from the house on Hayarkon Street in which it had been located since 1936 to an area of 2,500 square meters on Keren Kayemet Boulevard (Hadassah Park) and became a point of attraction for the city's residents and for outside visitors. In 1939 it hosted around 50,000 visitors and in the first year of the war—in 1940—around 70,000 visitors.

2. Blaustein (2004), 11–24. Aryeh Dayan, "Bayom bo palshu hagermanim lepolin," *Haaretz*, April 19, 2004.

3. Melchior (2006), 27–28.

4. Reich (1995), 63.

5. Bader (1999), 226.

6. N. von Weisl (2009), 12–13.

7. Bader (1999), 175–176.

8. Chajes (1998), 267.

9. W. Cohn (2014), 563.

10. JIA. 2/29/2-1a: letter from 1939. Also see: Schechtman (1961), 366. Pont-Aven is known, among other things, thanks to the group of painters who worked there, including Paul Gaugin, as École de Pont-Aven. The town Vals-les-Bains is in the Rhône-Alpes region, on the river Rhône.

11. Schechtman (1961), 366–367.

12. Klemperer (2009), 305–306.

13. W. Cohn (2014), 533–536.

14. Weizmann (1979), Vol. 19, 147: letter from August 30, 1939.

15. Shaltiel (2000), 99.

16. Ringelblum (1992), 5.

17. "The Polish Corridor" was Poland's access to the Baltic Sea. It was created under the Treaty of Versailles, following Danzig becoming a "Free City" on the border of East Prussia, and the link from Germany (Pomerania) to the city passed through the "corridor." The Free City was under the authority of the League of Nations and its High Commissioners. West of Danzig the Poles built the port of Gdynia—Poland's only access to the sea.

18. "The mood in Poland is brave and enthusiastic," *Davar*, August 30, 1939.

19. *Hazofeh*, August 30, 1939.

20. LPA. 4-6-1920-98: letter from October 7, 1938.

21. On Germany, see Friedländer (1997).

22. The Fifth Aliyah included around 76,000 immigrants from Poland. Gurevich and Gertz (1945), 61. Weinryb (1997), 369–398.

	Immigrants from Poland		Immigrants from Germany*	
Year	Number	Percentage of Total Immigrants (%)	Number	Percentage of Total Immigrants (%)
1933	13,251	45	7,510	26
1934	17,723	45	9,729	25
1935	30,593	52	8,460	14
1936	13,256	47	8,664	30
1937	3,708	37	3,680	37
1938	3,642	29	6,895	55
1939	4,532	18	16,400	65
Total	86,705	43	61,338	30

*Immigrants from Germany also include around 7,000 people who were not German citizens, and 2,500 without citizenship or whose citizenship was unspecified.
Source: Gertz (1947), 104–105. See also Cherniavsky (2010), 63–78.

23. Weizmann (1979), Vol. 17, 363: letter to Shertok from October 14, 1936.

24. Ben-Gurion (1982), Vol. 5, 114.

25. Shapira (1985), pp. 21–39; Avizohar (1984), 95–127. The literature about the history of Polish Jews between the two World Wars and about the Zionist movement in Poland is very extensive. Because this chapter does not intend to be a summary of this broad subject, we cite here only a handful of the research literature. We should note, however, that we relied heavily on Melzer (1997).

1. "A MILLION SUPERFLUOUS JEWS"—AND MORE

1. Chajes (1998), 262.

2. Gruenbaum (1940), 450.

3. Chajes (1998), 202–203.

4. In Michael Burstein's novel *Bay di taykhn fun Mazovye* (1937), the author refers to Piłsudski's death in the biblical words: "And Joseph died" [Exodus 1:6]. See Chone Shmeruk, *Sifrut Yiddish b'Polin: mehkarim v'iyunim historim* (1999), 212–213.

5. Jabotinsky (2007–2009), vol. 10, 114: letter from May 12, 1935 (in Polish).

6. See Kapiszewski (2007), 108.

7. Melzer (1997), 42.

8. *Tempo Dnia*, May 14, 1935. The newspaper was published in Krakow.

9. Chajes (1998), 203.

10. Goering wrote in the introduction to the German translation of Piłsudski's writings in 1935 that Piłsudski and Hitler were "people who make history" (*Männer, die Geschichte machen*). See Shavit (1986), 15–62.

11. Pierre Laval was the prime minister of France from 1934 to 1936. He collaborated with the Nazi occupation during World War II and was subsequently executed as a traitor by a firing squad.

12. Chajes (1998), 203–204.

13. On the tension between nationalism, citizenship, and autonomy in the First World War. See Silber (2014).

14. Bronisław Pieracki, the minister of the interior, expressed his position thus in March 1932: "The ethnic Polish group enjoys in the state, by the nature of things, the greatest privilege—that is, the privilege of being in the majority. The state is thus eo ipso the most important organ of the Polish *raison d'etat*. This is why every privilege can derive from the service rendered to the state by any given individual and not at all from the fact that he belongs to this or that ethnic group" (Polonsky (2012), 78.

15. Eli Tzur (2010), 135–181.

16. Melzer (1973), 211–249: encoded letters from November 14 and 18, 1938.

17. The eleventh Olympiad took place in Berlin on June 1–16, 1936.

18. Chajes (1998), 225.

19. Krotoshinsky (2002), 16.

20. *Davar*, May 15, 1935.

21. Ben-Gurion (1971–1987), vol. 1, 672: meeting between the heads of the Jewish Agency and head of state on October 17, 1933.

22. *Hayarden*, May 15, 1935.

23. Ibid., January 10, 1935.

24. *Haaretz*, May 17, 1935, in Gruenbaum (1940), 302–316.

25. Ben-Gurion responded that he feared "that even the Zionists in Poland will stop being Zionist if Palestine cannot offer Polish Jewry any help. Zionist ideology cannot oppose reality. We must act decisively." Ben-Gurion (1971–1987), vol. 3, 93–94: meeting of the Jewish Agency on March 22, 936.

26. *Ha'olam lifnei ha'ason: Yehudei Kraków bishnei ha'asorim shebein hamilhamot* (2008), 120.

27. In the revolt against the Tsarist regime led by Tadeusz Kościuszko. See Bartal (1997), 357–359.

28. *Ha'olam* (2008), 122–123.

29. Ibid.

30. Chajes (1998), 204.

31. Shavit (1986), 15–62.

32. The district southeast of the Wawel, which was Krakow's Jewish district.

33. *Hayarden*, August 25, 1935.

34. Jabotinsky (1941), 61.

35. *Razswiet*, March 18, 1928.

36. Jabotinsky (1941), 62. Emphasis in the original.

37. There is no basis for the argument that Zionism "tended to deter the Jews from loyalty and involvement in the new Polish state" (Kochanski, 2012, 31). On trends toward Polonization, see Joseph Lichten, "Notes on the Assimilation and Acculturation of Jews in Poland, 1863–1943," in Abramsky, *The Jews in Poland*, 106–129; the same is true for the exaggerated claims made by Bashevis Singer on whom the author bases herself: "Rarely did a Jew think it necessary to learn Polish; rarely was a Jew interested to learn Polish history." This may be true of a large number of Polish Jews but it is not true of all.

38. Weinbaum (1993), 6.

39. League of Nations (1935) *Official Journal*, Special Supplement 1935, No. 143. See

also Melzer (1997), 212. The historian Timothy Snyder recently argued in his book *Black Earth: The Holocaust as History and Warning* (2015) that the government of Poland was pro-Zionist and sought to support the establishment of a Jewish state in Palestine. This is a distorted description of the complex relations between colonial powers and various elements in the Zionist movement.

40. Kahn (1988), 25–26.

41. Jabotinsky (2007–2009), vol. 10, 139: letter from February 2, 1935 (in Russian).

42. Ibid., 137: letter from June 15, 1935. French in the original.

43. Ibid., 143: letter from June 19, 1935.

44. Ibid., 140: letter from June 16, 1935.

45. Schechtman (1959), 93 [only in the Hebrew version].

46. Jabotinsky first proposed to hold the New Zionist Organization's inauguration congress in Trieste, envisaging an exhibition that would show the Arch of Titus, views of Betar fortress, and so on. He also suggested that the delegates would sail on the ship *Sarah* from Trieste to the Adriatic port town of Abbazia—"every passenger would get a bucket, in case of seasickness," he added. Jabotinsky (2007–2009), vol. 10, 119: letter from 1935.

47. At the same time he wrote to his sister, Tamar Jabotinsky-Kop, that if the situation arose and he had to negotiate with England to get independent certificates, he would not try to lobby for "England's enemies," by which he meant the members of the movement's maximalist faction. Ibid., 55–56: letter from March 19, 1935.

48. Ibid., 268: letter from February 11, 1935.

49. Ibid., 185: letter from July 20, 1935.

50. In April 1935, after Nazi Germany had decided on the conscription of more than half a million soldiers, Jabotinsky wrote Leopold Amery that the Jewish people could offer Britain a 100,000 trained youths. In September, a fortnight before Fascist Italy invaded Ethiopia on October 3, Jabotinsky proposed that the Revisionist movement would commit to the British regime to bring up to 20,000 "well-trained" youths to Palestine to take part in its defence. Ibid., 82–83: letter from 1935. See also Ibid., 231–232: letter from September 19, 1935.

51. Letter to Joseph Beck, June 21, 1936, in French. Vol. 11, 2011, 182–184.

52. After World War I and until 1924, around 100,000 Poles returned to Poland from various countries outside Europe; from 1925 to 1930, around 11,000 Poles returned to the country from the United States. See Erdmans (1998), 31; Znaniecki Lopata (1976), 85–107.

53. See Cherniavsky (2010), 68–76.

54. Halamish (2006), 243.

55. Gertz (1947), 104–105.

56. Ben-Gurion (1971–1987), vol. 1, 611. Ben-Gurion called Poland "the great unknown" and described the election campaign for the Eighteenth Zionist Congress as "a crusade against Revisionism in Poland." Ibid., 586, 592.

57. JIA, 74/c10.

58. *Minutes of the Twenty-First Zionist Congress* (1939), 7.

59. Ben-Gurion (1971–1987), vol. 2, 524: meeting from November 23, 1935.

60. Chajes (1998), 212.

61. Ibid., 222.

62. Melzer (1997), 53. Tomaszewski (1997), 415–426.

63. Chajes (1998), 228–231.

64. Melzer (1997), 30.

65. Ben-Gurion (1971–1987), vol. 1, 674: letter to Weizmann, October 26, 1933.

66. Ibid.

67. Ibid., 672.

68. Ibid., emphasis ours.

69. Kapiszewski (2007), 99.

70. *Ha'olam lifnei ha'ason* (2008), 112–113. On antisemitic cartoons in Poland between the world wars and an exhibition on the subject in the Ringelblum Historical Institute in Warsaw in 2013, see Dariusz Konstantynow, *Kesher* 46, spring 2014, 139–146.

71. *Nowy Dziennik*, June 24, 1939.

72. Melzer (1997), 55. After escaping from Poland, Sławoj-Składkowski spent some time in Tel Aviv.

73. Chajes (1998), 221.

74. Kapiszewski (2007), 109.

75. Gruenbaum (1940), 347. See also Wynot (1971), 1035–1058.

76. Weiss (2000), 104.

77. *Ha'olam*, March 26, 1936, quoted in Halamish (2006), 336.

78. Ben-Gurion (1971–1987), vol. 3, 105: conversation in *Ein hanatziv ha'elion* from April 12, 1936.

79. "The Evacuation Plan" in *Unzer Velt*, no. 3 (63), Warsaw, October 1933.

80. Quoted in Weiss (2000), 155.

81. Quoted in Melzer (1997), 56.

82. Weizmann (1936), vol. 4, 788-794. Chaim Weizmann, *The Letters and Papers of Chaim Weizmann* (Jerusalem, 1984), Series A, edited by Barnet Litvinoff, vol. 18, 55–58.

83. Weizmann also told the Royal Commission: "The German tragedy is in size much smaller than the Polish; it is of manageable proportions and, moreover, the German Jews are stronger, economically stronger; they can resist the onslaught much better than the Polish Jews, who have been ground down for almost a century, first in Russia and now in Poland." Weizmann testified before the Peel Commission publically on November 25 and 26, 1936, and in camera on December 18 and 23, 1936, and January 8, 1937. Weizmann (1984), vol. 2, 100–264. The Polish government denied that Beck had made this statement. See Weizmann (1979–1984), vol. 17, 55–58: letter from 1937.

84. Gruenbaum (1940), 272–276.

85. *Letters*, March 10, 1935, vol. 18, 55–58.

86. *Unzer Velt* 63 (3), October 1936. Jabotinsky (1958), 212–217.

87. Jabotinsky (1941), 60.

88. See Engel (2006), 55–79.

89. Katz (1993), 1068–1069.

90. Ibid.

91. Greenberg, U. Z. (1924), 3. Emphasis in the original.

92. Halamish (2006), 416.

93. *Minutes of the Twenty-First Zionist Congress* (1939), 149–152.

94. Halamish (2006), 245–249.

95. Chajes (1998), 222.

96. Leichter and Milkov (1993), 125.

97. Saadia (2008), 21–23.

98. Werber (2014), 20.

99. Goldenberg (1986), 29.

100. Pollack (1997), 399–412.

101. Olitzer (1939).

102. *Minutes of the Nineteenth Zionist Congress* (1937), 23.

103. Bauer (1974), 306. See also Szajkowski (1974), 171–174.

104. Yunas-Dinovitz (2004), 90.

105. Pollack (1997), 399–412.

106. Achimeir, A. (1974), 90–91. Nalewki was the main street in the large Jewish district in Warsaw.

107. *Davar*, "Baderekh," September 8, 1937.

108. *Davar*, "Tsefifut veantishmiut be'oniot ramaniot," November 22, 1935.

109. *Davar*, "Rishme masa Polin," July 7, 1937, July 20, 1937.

110. Melzer (1997), 148.

111. Protocol of the Zionist Executive Committee, October 13–14, 1936, quoted in Frankel (1994), 243.

112. Blatman (1996), 25, note 28.

113. Gorny (2005), 159.

114. Blatman (1996), 25.

115. *Das Jüdische Tageblatt*, September 22, 1936.

116. Ibid. September 11, 1936. Quoted in Blatman (2004), 381.

117. Chajes (1998), 244–245.

118. Ibid. 252.

119. Ibid. 262.

120. AZIH, 218.302. We would like to thank Professor Havi Dreifus for this source.

121. Polish Jews, as well as the Zionist public, were also divided along regional-cultural lines, but here we have not considered these differences.

122. Ben-Gurion (1971–1987), vol. 2, 542: press conference from December 9, 1935.

123. The data are taken from the minutes of the Zionist Congresses.

124. See Engel (2001), 649–665.

125. Ben-Gurion (1971–1987), vol. 1, 613: meeting from 1933.

126. Ibid., 524–539.

127. Ibid., 600–643.

128. Ibid., 621.

129. Ben-Gurion (1971–1987), vol. 3, 253–254.

130. See Engel (2001).

131. Sokolow (1961), 240–335.

132. Brit Hahayal: an association of Jewish ex-soldiers in the Polish Army.

133. *Hazit Haam*, November 10, 1933.

134. *Hayarden*, November 15, 1938.

135. Chajes (1998), 178–181.

136. Mendelsohn, "Jewish Politics in Interwar Poland: An Overview," 9–19. See also

idem "Interwar Poland: Good for the Jews or Bad for the Jews?" 1986, 130–139, and "The Jews of Poland between the Two World Wars—Myth and Reality," 1–6.

137. Döblin (1991), xii.

138. Ibid., 50.

139. Albert Londres, *Le Juif errant est arrivé*, 1938, 126.

140. Bojman (2007), 12.

141. Peltz (2009), 19–20.

142. Werber (2009), 19–23.

143. The data is from Mahler (1968), 189. See also Marcus (1983).

144. Bader (1999), 212.

145. Shaltiel (2000), 52.

146. Goldenberg (1986), 18–19. The history teacher in her gymnasium was Emanuel Ringelblum.

147. Novershtern (2008), 255–298.

148. Glatstein (2010), 226.

149. Glatstein (2010), 338–39.

150. Ibid., 262.

151. Novershtern (2003).

152. See *Haynt*, November 20, 1931 (1948), 339–344. Jabotinsky (n.d.), 57.

153. Hacohen (1956), 187–188.

154. Ibid., 180–181.

155. Katznelson (1984), vol. 6, 136. See Shapira, A. (1980), vol. 2, 431–435.

156. *Davar*, October 21, 1937.

157. *Davar*, June 1, 1937. Ibid., September 12, 1937.

158. *Davar*, July 20, 1937. See also Ibid., June 14, 1937.

159. *Davar*, June 24, 1937

160. *Davar*, June 30, 1937.

161. Ruppin (1968), 291–297.

162. Kanari (2003), 446.

163. Sharett (1968–1979), vol. 4, 230–232.

164. Ibid., 230–246.

165. Armoni (2010), 117.

166. Schechtman (1959), 107.

167. London (2000), 256.

168. Gilbert, M. (1978), 215

169. *Auswärtiges Amt, abt. Iva (Juden in Polen, allgemeines, January 1921–December 1935)*, Bd. 2, L360836.

170. Weizmann (1979–1984), vol. 17, 199–202. See also Melzer (1997), 102.

171. Buber (1975), 124: letter from 1939.

172. Lord Melchett, a British Zionist, described it in 1933 as "economic antisemitism" and believed that it was the "state's problem." He thought that the government should solve it together with the Jews. Quoted in Weiss (2000), 151.

173. Jabotinsky (1941). His view was different before Poland gained its independence. In March 1911, for example, he wrote Maxim Gorky about the intensifying "antisemitic

incitement in Polish society" (Jabotinsky [2007–2009], vol. 1, 124) and reiterated this position more than once.

174. See Feinberg (1967), 113–131.

175. In Cohen, N. (2003), 266: letter from 1933.

176. Melzer (1989), 126–137.

177. Ben-Gurion (1971–1987), vol. 5, 416: meeting from December 15, 1938.

178. Lofban, Y., "Leheshbon hayamim." *Hapoel hatzair*, September 11, 1931. See also Halamish (2006), 28.

179. Bornstein-Bilitzka (2003), 53–54.

180. Penkower (2013), 173–174.

181. Melzer (1997), 83.

182. Vinkovetzky, A. (1987), 62.

183. There are different estimations of the number of Jews who were murdered or killed in the period under discussion. For background to the violent anti-Jewish riots and a full description, see Polonsky (2012), 85–90. The Polish government censored reports of attacks on Jews so that the numbers of killed and wounded vary from source to source. Apparently approximately twenty or so Jews were killed. See Melzer (1997), 78–96, 436–438. Gutman (2001), vol. 2, 631. Polonsky (2012). We would like to thank Professor Polonsky for allowing us to read the manuscript before its publication. Norman Davies dismisses the description of these events as pogroms, further adding that the Jews in Poland suffered less than the Jews in any other country. See Davies (1981), 261.

184. Feinberg (1967), 113–115. See also Wasserstein (2012), 35–50.

185. Leszczynski (1952), 36–72.

186. Chajes (1998), 243.

187. Ibid., 245.

188. Gruenbaum (1940), 363–364.

189. Melzer (1997), 97–110. On the proportion of Jews who needed kosher slaughter see Kaniel (2010), 75–106. Weiss (2000), 86–106.

190. *Davar*, March 16, 1936.

191. *Haaretz*, July 18, 1939.

192. *Haaretz*, July 2, 1939.

193. Wasserstein (2012), 329–330.

194. Melzer (1997), 111–117.

195. Chajes (1998), 260–261.

196. Ibid., 261: note 20, 291.

197. Polonsky (2012), 87.

198. Melzer (1997), 230–242.

199. *Haaretz*, July 2, 1939.

200. Mahler (1968), 172–173.

201. Lily Goldenberg, in Leichter and Milkov (1993), 98–99. Goldenberg (1986), 120–121.

202. Ella Goral, in Leichter and Milkov (1993), 99–101.

203. Chajes (1998), 222.

204. David Shimonovich, in Habas (1937), 51. The poem has no name.

205. Shalom, S., "Leilotenu bamatsor" (Our Nights Under Siege), in Habas (1937), 503.

206. Slutzky (1973), 631–663.

207. Ruppin (1968), 258–260. Diary entry on April 25, 1936.

208. See Shavit (1983).

209. "El ha'am hayehudi" (To the Jewish people), April 24, 1936, in Habas (1937), 53.

210. "Sikum hadamim," (Death Toll) in Habas (1937), 254.

211. *Hazit Haam*, May 5, 1933. On "Our campaign against Hitler" see Schechtman (1961), 282. S. Katz (1993), 873.

212. *Daily Express*, March 24, 1933.

213. Shamir (1974), 78–82.

214. Melzer (1997), 26–30.

215. AWA, Juden in Poland II, J. nr 951/34, PL 360949.

216. *Geheimes Staatspolizeiamt*, February 6, 1935.

217. Melzer (1997), 26–30.

218. Chajes (1998), 262.

219. Eilati (1987), 127–138.

220. We would like to thank Professor Piotr Muchowski of Adam Mickiewicz University in Poznan for obtaining the copy of the periodical from the library of the University of Warsaw, and Ms. Anat Vatori for the translation.

221. Sharett (1968–1979), vol. 4, 234–236.

222. See Tzur (2004), 389–415.

223. Letter from Jabotinsky to Beck, Jabotinsky, *Igrot* (1986), vol. 11, 197–198.

224. Schechtman (1961), 354–360.

225. Jabotinsky (2007–2009), vol. 11, 197–199: letter from July 1, 1936.

226. Ibid., 184–186: letter from June 21, 1936.

227. Ibid., 197–198: letter from 1936.

228. CZA, S25/10004/152.

229. Schechtman (1961), 337.

230. See Tomaszewski (1988), 276–293. Weinbaum (1990), 156–172.

231. On the weakness of the Polish navy see Baginski (1942), 300.

232. Kahn recounted that these negotiations formed the basis for the "revolt plan" at the end of 1939. Kahn (1988), 43–44.

233. Weinbaum (1993), 221.

234. "A Marriage of Convenience" is how Weinbaum described this relationship.

235. See Weinbaum (1993), 62.

236. JIA, 1/2/29/1a: letter from February 2, 1939.

237. Weinbaum (1993), 198.

238. Ben-Gurion (1971–1987), vol. 6, 292: diary entry from May 4, 1939.

239. See Schechtman (1961), 338–353. Weinbaum (1993), 164–199.

240. Benari (1969). Mechman (1980), 119–127. Melzer (1997), 148–154.

241. Jabotinsky (1937), 115.

242. Jabotinsky (1958), 335–336. Printed in *Der Moment* on May 16–17, 1939.

243. Weinbaum (1993), 211–213.

244. See Schechtman (1961), 89–127.

245. Melzer (1997), 140–163, 334–338. Niv (1965), 337.

246. Gilboa (1986), 58. See also Weinbaum (1993), 123–165.

247. Gilboa (1986), 50.

248. Kahn (1988), 37.

249. The Haganah and the Irgun funded weapons acquisition with the aid of sympathetic Jewish donors in western Europe.

250. Boaz (2001), 332, note 73.

251. Ibid., 94. See also Slutzky (1973), 999–1002.

252. Ibid., 968–974.

253. Ringelblum (1994), 304–306. English translation: Yad Vashem, The Holocaust Martyrs and Heroes Remembrance Authority Website. "Emmanuel Ringelblum's Notes of the Refugees in Zbąszyń," Documents of the Holocaust, part 1. Copyright 2003. From R. Mahler, "Mikhtavei E. Ringelblum mi-Zbąszyń veal Zbąszyń" (Letters of E. Ringelblum from and about Zbąszyń), *Yalkut Moreshet*, no. 2 (1964), 24–25. (Accessed November 16, 2013.) www.jewishvirtuallibrary.org/jsource/Holocaust/Zbaszyn1.html. See also Wasserstein (2012), 372–76, 398–99; Kassow (2007), 100–103.

254. The number of Jews with Polish citizenship who lived in Germany is estimated at around 56,000.

255. Reich-Ranicki (2004), 119–120.

256. See the research and testimonies in Skórzyńska (2011).

257. Weiss (2000), 236–237.

258. Melamed, David (2008). "Gerush Zbąsyń be'enayim shel terem shoah," *Makor Rishon*, December 12, 2008.

259. Bauer (1974), 243–247.

260. Melzer (1973), 242–243.

261. Ibid., 230–231.

262. Ibid., 226–247.

263. AZIH, 302.218.

264. *Haaretz*, November 7, 2008.

265. Tzur, E. (2006), 306.

266. *Haaretz*, July 2, 1939.

267. PRO FO 7031/46/98/39 W10603: letter from May 12, 1939.

268. PRO FO 7031/12/39 W10943: comment from 1939.

269. Friedländer (1997), 304.

270. *Haynt*, March 19, 1939. Melzer (1997), 334–337.

271. Shaltiel (2000), 84–85. Reiss (1982), 192–193.

272. Shaltiel (2000), 85–86.

273. Tzur, E. (2006), 310.

274. Chajes (1998), 258.

275. Weinbaum (1993), 216.

276. See Garlicki and Weinbaum (1991), 93–106.

277. Ben-Yeruham (1976), 864.

2. "THE DREAM OF A JEWISH STATE"

1. Katznelson (1984), vol. 6, 384: letter from 1937.

2. Rippel also published his plan in the antisemitic newspaper *Merizujus Polki* in March 1937. See Weinbaum (1993), 89.

3. Rippel was murdered by the Nazis in 1940. See Lazar-Litai (1957), 70–72.

4. *Der Moment*, July 30, 1937. Ben-Yeruham (1976), 679.

5. Lazar-Litai (1957), 72.

6. Kanari (2003), 429.

7. *Der Moment*, July 4, 1937.

8. Ibid., July 8, 1937.

9. Chajes (1998), 240: diary entry from July 3, 1937.

10. See Dotan (1979), 205–271.

11. Gurevich and Gertz (1945), 13.

12. Martin Gilbert, Winston S. Churchill, vol. 5, republished in AZ A-1 -2/27; see Gilbert, M. (2007), 124–126.

13. Ben-Gurion (1971–1987), vol. 4, 344: speech from July 29, 1937.

14. Ibid., vol. 5, 144: letter from March 16, 1938.

15. Melzer (1982), 323.

16. Ben-Gurion (1971–1987), vol. 4, 384: speech from August 4, 1937.

17. Jabotinsky (2007–2009), vol. 11, 272: letter from September 15, 1936.

18. Ibid., 231: letter from June 30, 1936.

19. On the route to the Partition Plan and on the "Partition Debate" see, for example, Dotan (1979). Gal-Nur (1994). Katzburg (1974). Katzburg (1994), 381–399. Klieman (1983). Cohen, M. J. (1978), 32–49.

20. Ben-Gurion (1971–1987), vol. 3, 203: speech from May 19, 1936.

21. Ibid., 366: letter from August 18, 1936.

22. Ibid., 386: letter from August 11, 1936.

23. Jabotinsky (2007–2009), vol. 9, 61–63: letter to King George V from March 6, 1934.

24. Weizmann (1979–1984), "The Jewish Cases: Testimony before Royal Commission," series B, 102: testimony from November 25, 1936.

25. Gilbert, M. (2007), 121.

26. On Weizmann's perception regarding the pace of immigration and the character of the immigrants, see Aviva Halamish, "Yachaso shel Weizmann l'aliya ben milhamot ha'olam," *Weizmann manhig hatzionut*, edited by Uri Cohen and Meir Chazan (2016), 261–298.

27. Frankel (1994), 242–253.

28. Meeting of the Zionist Executive Committee in Jerusalem, March 31, 1935, 121, 127. Quoted in Frankel (1994), 115.

29. Ben-Gurion (1971–1987), vol. 3, 105: conversation from April 2, 1936.

30. Ibid., vol., 2, 399: speech from August 21, 1935. Emphasis in the original.

31. Ibid., vol., 4, 342–343: speech from July 7, 1937.

32. *Minutes of the Nineteenth Zionist Congress* (1937), 95–110. See also Teveth (1987), 215–230.

33. Sharett (1968–1979), vol. 1, 366–367.

34. *Palestine Royal Commission Report*, July 1937.

35. Ibid., 216–221.

36. Melzer (1973), 215.

37. Weizmann (1979–1984), vol. 18, 131–136: letter to Stephen Wise from June 29, 1937.

38. Ibid., 145–146: letter from July 7, 1937.

39. Ibid.

40. Sharett (1968–1979), vol. 2, 238: speech from July 7, 1937.

41. Ibid., 240–241.

42. Ibid., 259–260: speech from July 9, 1937.

43. Ruppin (1968), 280.

44. Northwest of Bolzano.

45. Teveth (1987), 202–206.

46. Ben-Gurion (1971–1987), vol. 4, 226: diary entry from June 11, 1937.

47. Ibid., 279: letter from July 3, 1937.

48. See Teveth (1987), 206–211.

49. Ben-Gurion (1971–1987), vol. 4, 291: diary entry from July 9, 1937.

50. Ibid., 297–299: diary entry from July 12, 1937.

51. Ibid., 296: diary entry from July 10, 1937.

52. Schechtman (1961), 321. *Davar* cited the assessment of Chaim Greenberg, one of the leaders of Mapai's sister party in the United States and the editor of its organ, *Der Yiddisher Kempfer*, that Jabotinsky's words to the Peel Commission "did not stand to make any impression on the Royal Commission." Zionism was not interested in a Jewish state right away, but rather in a long transition period, in which it would be possible to bring to Palestine "hundreds of thousands, and perhaps millions of Jews." The members of the Commission, wrote Greenberg, "were probably thinking to themselves: if all the Jews are like Jabotinsky, they are surely *incapable of having a state*." *Davar*, March 17, 1937. Emphasis in the original.

53. On July 16, 1937, Jabotinsky wrote to Churchill that even if the territory for the Jewish state in the Partition Plan were to be enlarged it would not suffice for massive Jewish immigration; moreover, that state would be subject to attack by the Arab states and its takeover would be a foregone conclusion. In Zeev Jabotinsky (2013), *Igrot*, vol. 12, 124–27. The memorandum submitted by the presidency of the new Zionist Organization to the Permanent Mandates Commission was written in the same spirit, its main argument being that the borders of the proposed partition would make it impossible to integrate a Jewish immigration; the result would be increased antisemitism in Europe and could affect the balance of power (ibid., 140–53).

54. Katznelson (1984), vol. 6, 319: letter from April 27, 1937.

55. Ibid., 336–346: letters to Mapai's executive from June 12, 16, 1937. Emphasis in the original.

56. Ruppin (1968), 276.

57. Ibid., 280.

58. Melzer (1997), 324.

59. Ibid.

60. See the articles in the booklet *Al churban bait shlishi!* (1937). Emphasis in the original.

61. Jabotinsky (1937), 105. The book was published in Polish at the beginning of 1937 in order to convince the Polish government that the Revisionists opposed the Partition Plan on the grounds that it would interfere with a massive immigration of Polish Jews to Palestine.

62. Ibid., 106. Jabotinsky (1941), 170–171.

63. Shavit (1986), 63–84.

64. Weizmann, testimony, November 25 (1937).

65. Ben-Gurion (1971–1987), vol. 4, 386: testimony before the Peel Commission, August 7, 1937.

66. Ibid., 290: letter from July 6, 1937.

67. Katz, Y. (2000), 110–123.

68. Fein (2009), 32–107.

69. *Minutes of the Nineteenth Zionist Congress* (1937), 32.

70. *Davar*, August 30, 1937.

71. *Davar*, August 3, 1937.

72. Kanari (2003), 428.

73. Ben-Gurion (1971–1987), vol. 4, 334: diary entry from July 29, 1937. See also Teveth (1987), 215.

74. Teveth (1987), 216.

75. See *Minutes of the Nineteenth Zionist Congress* (1937).

76. Ibid., 23–33.

77. Rose (1973), 57.

78. Katz, S. (1993), 1008. Locker (1963), 264.

79. Weizmann (1979–1984), vol. 18, 185–187: letter to Pierre Orts, chairman of the Permanent Mandates Commission of the League of Nations, from August 14, 1937.

80. Ibid., 387–390: letter to Pierre Orts from 1938.

81. *Davar*, August 19, 1938.

82. *Minutes of the Nineteenth Zionist Congress* (1937), 170–177.

83. Sharett (1968–1979), vol. 2, 277.

84. *Minutes of the Nineteenth Zionist Congress* (1937), 79. Emphasis in the original. The important speeches in the Congress were given when it sat as a political committee, and therefore *in camera*.

85. Sharett (1968–1979), vol. 2, 278–279.

86. *Minutes of the Nineteenth Zionist Congress* (1937), 95–110.

87. Katznelson (1984), vol. 6, 393–394: letter from 1937.

88. Sharett (1968–1979), vol. 2, 274–275.

89. Ussishkin, *Haolam*, April 4, 1937.

90. *Minutes of the Nineteenth Zionist Congress* (1937), 185–193.

91. Goldstein, Y. (2001), vol. 2, 186.

92. Ibid., 188: letter from January 16, 1937.

93. Ibid., 186.

94. Ruppin (1968), 282. *Iton meyuhad*, published in Tel Aviv, reported extensively on Nazi demonstrations in front of the theater and on attacks on delegates and "guests." *Iton meyukhad*, August 18, 1937.

95. *Davar*, August 15, 1937.

96. *Minutes of the Nineteenth Zionist Congress* (1937), 39.

97. Ibid., 54.

98. Ibid., 40.

99. Ibid., 41.

100. Albert Hyamson's letter to the *Times*, August 18, 1937, published in *Davar*, August 27, 1937. Hyamson was a non-Zionist and had been director of immigration to Palestine.

101. Schechtman (1961), 329. A rumor spread that Jabotinsky intended to give a public speech on the evening of Weizmann's speech at the Zionist Congress, but he settled for a meeting with Joseph Schechtman.

102. Ben-Gurion (1971–1987), vol. 5, 7: letter from January 4, 1938.

103. *Davar*, August 16, 1937.

104. *Minutes of the Nineteenth Zionist Congress* (1937), 202.

105. Ibid., 218.

106. Ibid., 352.

107. Ibid., 366–367.

108. *Davar*, August 25, 1937.

109. Ruppin (1968), 282.

110. *Davar*, Evening supplement, August 16, 1937.

111. Chajes (1998), 241: diary entry from August 21, 1937.

112. *Davar*, August 16, 1937.

113. Ben-Gurion (1971–1987), vol. 4, 425.

114. Teveth (1987), 231.

115. Shapira, A. (1980), vol. 2, 562.

116. Sharett (1968–1979), vol. 2, 319.

117. Ibid., 320.

118. Ibid., 326.

119. Ibid., 340.

120. Melzer (1973), 216–217.

121. Sharett (1968–1979), vol. 2, 345–346.

122. See Katzburg (1994), 399–403.

123. Ben-Gurion (1971–1987), vol. 4, 11: testimony from January 7, 1937.

124. Halamish (2006), 119–122.

125. Weizmann (1979–1984), vol. 18, 281–286: letter to Sir John Shuckburgh from December 31, 1937.

126. Ben-Gurion (1971–1987), vol. 5, 6: letter from January 4, 1938. Emphasis in the original.

127. Ibid., 28: speech from 1938.

128. Ibid., 90: diary entry from January 29, 1938.

129. Sharett (1968–1979), vol. 3, 248: speech from August 17, 1938.

130. On July 20, 1937, Dugdale wrote, "I trust no mad Revisionist will make an attempt at Zurich. Chaim, himself, said to me today, that if he is ever 'bumped off' it will be by a Jew, not by an Arab." Rose (1973), 53.

131. JIA, 2/29/2–1a.

132. Ben-Gurion (1971–1987), vol. 5, 144: letter from March 16, 1938.

133. Rose (1973), 99.

134. Ben-Gurion (1971–1987), vol. 5, 264: letter from September 20, 1938.

135. Schechtman (1961), 334–346. Robinson (2010), 153–174.

136. Kanari (2003), 458–459.

137. Teveth (1987), 243.

138. See Von Weisl (1967), 165–176. Bentwich (1967), 467–488. Rosenkranz (1967), 497–526.

139. *Parliamentary Debates*, vol. 110, No. 95, 1220–1221.

140. Braginsky (1965), 19–35.

141. Lazar-Litai (1957), 69.

142. Ibid.

143. *Idan*, vol. 1: Aliyah B (1982), 11–29.

144. Braginsky (1965), 36–52.

145. Ben-Gurion (1971–1987), vol. 3, 507: meeting from November 11, 1936.

146. Avneri (1985), 14–15.

147. Ben-Gurion (1971–1987), vol. 5, 407–408: meeting from December 11, 1938.

148. Ofer (1990b), 44–60. Robinson (2010), 215–281.

149. Robinson (2010), 248.

150. There is disagreement in the various sources as to the numbers of immigrants in the different ships mentioned here and below.

151. *Haynt*, March 26, 1932. *Hazit Haam*, March 11, 1932.

152. Jabotinsky (2007–2009), vol. 9, 200: letter from September 3, 1934.

153. Ibid., 213: letter from November 28, 1934. In Jabotinsky's view, 350 pounds sterling should have been earmarked for this purpose.

154. Ibid., 322: letter from 1934.

155. Lazar-Litai (1957), 94.

156. Ben-Yeruham (1976), 801–802.

157. Ibid., 889–900.

158. Lazar-Litai (1957), 138.

159. Ibid., 100. See also Ofer (1990b), 44–60.

160. Braginsky (1965), 49.

161. Carpi (1962), 186–194.

162. We would like to thank his granddaughter, Dr. Gabriella Moscati, for this information.

163. That is, "the principle of economic absorption capacity." See *Haaretz*, Evening supplement, December 6, 1938. Ibid., December 9, 1938. We learned about the arrival of these immigrants and about Alterman's poem from Professor Meir Chazan.

3. "THE WAILING WALL IN ÉVIAN" AND KRISTALLNACHT

1. *Der Moment*, August 7, 1938.

2. Ruppin (1968), 218.

3. Ibid., 219.

4. Chajes (1998), 171.

5. Yahil (1990) vol. 1, 135, Emphasis in the original.

6. For a detailed discussion of the immigration of German Jews, see Gelber (1990), 51–151.

7. Ibid., 101.

8. *Hazit Haam*, April 21, 1933.

9. Chajes (1998), 240–241.

10. Teveth (1987), 68. Teveth does not mention whether Ben-Gurion read the whole book. *Mein Kampf* was "required reading" at the British Foreign Office and awakened engrained anti-Jewish views in at least some of its readers. Horace Rumbold, for example, believed that the "good Jews" in Germany were suffering because of the actions of the "bad Jews." See Gilbert, M. (1973), 377–381.

11. Ibid., 437.

12. Ben-Gurion (1971–1987), vol. 2, 161.

13. Ibid., 139.

14. Ibid., 14.

15. Weizmann (1979–1984), vol. 16, 12–14: letter from July 27, 1933.

16. *Minutes of the Twenty-First Zionist Congress* (1939), 42.

17. See Carpi (1971), 179, 205. At that time, Mussolini gave orders to grant permits more readily to Jewish refugees from Germany and helped the tens of thousands of Jews who passed through Italy's ports. Weizmann was naive enough to propose that Mussolini explain to Hitler that the anti-Jewish boycott would not benefit Germany, and in return to offer aid to the Italian chemical industry in order to release it from its dependency on the German industry.

18. Weizmann's exact words in Munich were not recorded in writing. Rose (1987), 91.

19. *Hazit Haam*, February 24, 1933.

20. Heinrich Brüning served as German prime minister from 1930 to 1932, and in 1934 fled from Germany. Gustav Stresemann was prime minister in 1923 and served as a minister until his death in 1929. In 1926 he won the Nobel Peace Prize.

21. *Hayarden*, "Germany after the Slaughter," July 29, 1934.

22. *Haaretz*, March 7, 1933.

23. *Doar hayom*, February 1, 1933.

24. Ibid., February 10, 1933.

25. *Hazit Haam*, March 17, 1933. Emphasis ours.

26. *Davar*, March 17, 1933. Emphasis in the original.

27. *Haaretz*, June 28, 1932.

28. *Haaretz*, November 11, 1932.

29. Bialik (1939), vol. 5, 224: letter from May 10, 1933. Emphasis in the original. Ibid. 307: letter from January 1, 1934: letter to Judisk Tiskriff. Stockholm.

30. *Minutes of the Nineteenth Zionist Congress* (1937), 472.

31. Ibid., 151–153.

32. Israeli (1974), 122, 274–275, notes 69–70.

33. Stein (1953), 136–137.

34. Cohen, M. J. (1978), 263–289.

35. See Cohen, N. (2006), 101–111.

36. Ben-Gurion (1971–1987), vol. 2, 161.

37. Ibid. Among other things, Ben-Gurion asserted that there was no objective "necessity" for "those clowns to become the leaders of the Jewish people."

38. *Hayarden*, October 24, 1934.

39. Plugot Hapoel were formed in the early 1930s as the operational arm designed to demonstrate the Histadrut's control over "the street," and at times also served as cover

for Haganah activities. Plugot Hapoel were activated first and foremost against the Revisionist circles, as well as against Communist elements in the Yishuv.

40. *Hayarden*, October 17, 1934.

41. *Hazit Haam*, March 16, 1934.

42. Friedländer (1997), 143.

43. Ruppin (1968), vol. 3, 242.

44. Améry (1980), 85. Améry fled from Vienna in 1938, was caught in Brussels in 1943 by the Gestapo, and tortured for weeks before being sent to Bergen-Belsen and Auschwitz, from which he survived.

45. See Livnat (2009), 98–104.

46. *Times*, September 11, 1935; *Manchester Guardian*, September 17, 1935, quoted in Shamir (1974), 203.

47. Ben-Gurion (1971–1987), vol. 2, 360–363.

48. Ibid.

49. Ibid., 395–396: speech from August 21, 1935, at the Nineteenth Zionist Congress.

50. Quoted in Gelber (1988), 56.

51. Ben-Gurion (1971–1987), vol. 2, 520.

52. Dispersing them in countries other than Palestine is a "harmful illusion," he wrote. Ibid., 570–571: letter from December 31, 1935.

53. Ibid., 520–521.

54. See Frankel (1994). Halamish (2006), 312–315, 325–338.

55. Dobkin quoted in Gelber (1988), 57.

56. Margaliot (1990), 83.

57. Gruenbaum (1940), 524.

58. Ben-Gurion (1971–1987), vol. 2, 520: protocol from January 1, 1935.

59. *Hazit Haam*, May 26, 1933.

60. Cohn (2014), 222.

61. Ben-Gurion (1971–1987), vol. 5, 282: letter from October 1, 1938.

62. Ibid., 346: letter from October 20, 1938.

63. See in Friling (1998), vol. 1, 26.

64. Ibid., 26–27.

65. Gelber (1990), 131.

66. Tuvin (1986), 81–110.

67. *Hazit Haam*, "Germany." February 24, 1933.

68. Ibid.

69. *Doar Hayom*, May 3, 1933.

70. *Der Moment*, April 14, 1933.

71. *Doar Hayom*, May 3, 1933.

72. Jabotinsky (1934), 2.

73. *Hayarden*, August 4, 1935.

74. *Hayarden*, January 31, 1936.

75. *Hazit Haam*, May 19, 1933.

76. *Hazit Haam*, May 26, 1933.

77. See Weiss (1998), 126.

78. *Hazit Haam*, March 10, 1933.

79. *Hazit Haam*, March 17, 1933.
80. *Hazit Haam*, June 30, 1933.
81. Albania was captured by Fascist Italy in April 1939.
82. *Hamashkif*, April 25, 1939.
83. *Der Moment*, May 2, 1939.
84. *Hamashkif*, February 3, 1939.
85. JIA, *The NZO in Palestine, 1938–1940*, 9–10: resolutions from 1939.
86. *Hamashkif*, February 3, 1939.
87. Barkai (2009), 123–150.
88. *Hazit Haam*, May 12, 1933.
89. Jabotinsky (1934).
90. *Hazit Haam*, May 12, 1933.
91. See Tenenbaum (1959), 129–146. Gottlieb (1982).
92. *Hayarden*, November 22, 1934.
93. Shamir (1974), 68–95.
94. Israeli (1974), 125.
95. See memorandum from February 28, 1934, Auswärtiges Amt, Inland 11 A/R, Bd. 1, 9. See also Weiss (1997), 151–179.
96. Krikler (1969), 26–32.
97. Israeli (1974), 125–129. Nicosia (1985), 33–49. Black (1984). Yahil (1990), 141–2. Bauer (1994), 11–19.
98. Auswärtiges Amt: *Referat Deutschland Inland*, II, A/B, Bd. 2, January 29, 1935.
99. *Hazit Haam*, April 17, 1933.
100. *Hazit Haam*, May 5, 1933.
101. Jabotinsky (2007–2009), vol. 9, 196: letter from August 17, 1934.
102. *Hayarden*, September 30, 1934.
103. *Hayarden*, October 12, 1934.
104. Jabotinsky (1934).
105. Israeli (1974), 125–126.
106. Ibid., 142. Gelber (1990), 152–175. Feilchenfeld (1972).
107. Israeli (1974), 123–124. Halevy (1977), 176–178.
108. Weiss (2000), 213.
109. Jabotinsky (2007–2009), 91: letter from April 25, 1935.
110. A. Kolisher, "Mazavo shel hareich vehapeulah hayehudit," *Hayarden*, July 17, 1934.
111. Israeli (1974), 133.
112. Ben-Gurion (1971–1987), vol. 2, 522: meeting from November 23, 1935.
113. Ibid., 570–571: letter from December 31, 1935.
114. Weizmann (13:2), 102: testimony from November 6, 1936.
115. In 1938 and 1939, around 100,000 Jews emigrated from Germany, around 111,000 emigrated from Austria, around 35,000 emigrated from Bohemia and Moravia, and around 5,500 emigrated from Danzig. The data here and below are taken from Niederland (1998), 239–240.
116. Friedländer (1997), 68.
117. See Margaliot (1990), 77–91, 93–106.
118. Shamir (1974), 299–300. The final goal (*das letzte Ziel*) of German politics, the

memorandum said, was to bring about the emigration of all the Jews. Until 1938, the Jews preferred to stay in Germany "hoping for better times" as long as they could support themselves, in which they had the wide support of international Jewry, which did not seriously want to encourage the mass emigration of its "racial kin" from Germany. Moreover, almost all the world's countries had closed their gates to Jewish immigration, and those who did agree to receive immigrants conditioned their agreement on an official German statement that nothing would prevent their return. And as for Palestine—the British government had imposed restrictions that had reduced incoming migration considerably, and the Transfer Agreement had only resulted in the immigration of rich Jews, but left massive numbers of poor Jews behind. From Germany's point of view, creating a Jewish state in Palestine, even a tiny one, would only boost the international status of the Jews, Germany's enemies. The report is printed in *Der Prozess gegen die Hauptkriegsverbrecher vor dem Internationalen Militärgerichthof* (1948), 237–245.

119. The letter was translated in *Haaretz*, July 5, 1936. Lux had published four pieces under the penname Peter Strumbusch and had worked as a journalist for the pacifist weekly *Weltbühne* (*World Stage*).

120. Sargent (1989), 187–201.

121. Gelber (1990), 118–120.

122. JIA, 1/29/2–1a: letter from January 1, 1938.

123. Ruppin (1968), 298–299.

124. Landau (2006), 137–140.

125. On the Évian Conference, see Wymann (1968), 43–513; Sherman (1973), 112–136; Feingold (1979), 22–44; Adler-Rudel (1968), 235–273; Weingarten (1981); Weiss (2000), 197–204. See also Bartrop (1995) and Wasserstein (2012), 364–71.

126. Israeli (1974), 145.

127. Ibid.

128. *Haaretz*, July 13, 1938.

129. *Der Moment*, July 12, 1938.

130. Habe (1966), 71.

131. Ibid., 72.

132. Sharett (1968–1979), vol. 3, 250–251.

133. *Haaretz*, July 6, 1938.

134. *Hayarden*, April 21, 1938.

135. *Davar*, July 14, 1938.

136. *Davar*, July 6, 1938.

137. *Der Moment*, July 6, 1938.

138. Zaïd's commemoration owed a lot to his diary, which was published in 1942, and to the book for young adults written about him by Eliezer Smoly, *Anshei Bereshit*. His murderer was executed by a Palmach squad in 1943.

139. Habe (1966), 94–5.

140. *Davar*, July 14, 1938.

141. *Haaretz*, July 13, 1938.

142. Quoted in Friedländer (1997), 301, note 121.

143. *Haaretz*, July 13, 1938.

144. Bauer (1994), 30–32, 262–63, note 3.

145. On the British Dominions' position, see Bartrop (1995).

146. Ruppin (1968), 302–303.

147. Akzin (1989), 300–302.

148. Ruppin (1968), 303–304.

149. Ibid., 302. CZA, L379/1/22: report from 1938, quoted in part in Weiss (2000), 198.

150. Meir (1975), 158–9.

151. *Davar*, July 14, 1938.

152. Melzer (1973), 223–225.

153. Shamir (1974), 274.

154. *Davar*, July 10, 1938. Ibid., July 13, 1938.

155. *Der Moment*, July 15, 1938. Cohen, N. (2003), 274.

156. See Cohen, N. (2006).

157. *Davar*, July 12, 1938.

158. *Haaretz*, July 12, 1938.

159. *Davar*, July 17, 1938.

160. *Parliamentary Debates*, vol. 111, No. 16; vol. 338, No. 159; vol. 110, No. 95: debates from July 27, July 29, and December 14, 1938.

161. See Shamir (1974), 262–274.

162. Melzer (1997), 328–334. Bauer (1974), 243–250.

163. Weiss (2000), 199–202. Kochavi (1984), 97–121.

164. Ben-Gurion (1971–1987), vol. 5, 219–220.

165. Halamish (2006), 318–321.

166. Frankel (1994), 283.

167. Ben-Gurion (1971–1987), vol. 5, 219–220.

168. CZA, Protocol of the Jewish Agency Directorate, December 11, 1938.

169. As announced by Benjamin Akzin at a press conference in Tel Aviv. *Hayarden*, April 21, 1938. Emphasis in the original.

170. CZA, S25/9778.

171. Weizmann (1979–1984), vol. 18, 431–432: letters from 1938.

172. Ruppin (1968), 304.

173. Frankel (1994), 284.

174. *Minutes of the Twenty-First Zionist Congress*, 2–3.

175. Rose (1973), 92.

176. Cited in Rose (1986), 301.

177. Weizmann (1979–1984), vol. 18, 486–487: letter from November 16, 1938.

178. Margaliot (1990), 107–133.

179. Ben-Gurion (1946), vol. 2, 85–87: speech from December 12, 1938.

180. Jabotinsky dedicated a chapter to the Évian Conference and to the Intergovernmental Committee for Refugees in his 1940 book, *Jewish War Front*. He listed the various governments' announcements at the conference and their subsequent reports on refugees entering their countries, and concluded that a concerted attack on public opinion, "powerfully supported by the facts drawn from the tragedy currently unfolding in Eastern Europe [. . .] will sweep away the obstacles" and force the world "to concentrate on the problem of the Jewish state." Jabotinsky (1941).

181. See Weingarten (1981).

182. Ruppin (1968), 302.

183. *Minutes of the Twenty-First Zionist Congress*, 2–3.

184. Tamir (1967), 63–65.

185. *Davar*, July 21, 1938.

186. Katz (1993), 1068.

187. Bondy (1989), 110–111.

188. The first conversation took place on July 10, 1938. JIA, 2/19-43. The second took place on July 8–9 1939. Golomb (1955), 92–98.

189. *Hamashkif*, February 9, 1940.

190. See "New Zionist Organization: Palestine Emergency Plan": November 33, 1938, JIA, 2/28/2.

191. Robinson (2010), 183–185.

192. Sharett (1968–1979), vol. 3, 186.

193. *Davar*, July 17, 1938.

194. Carpi (1969), 79–88.

195. Rose (1973), 93.

196. John Hope Simpson was chairman of the commission appointed in 1930, in the wake of the 1929 riots, to examine the possibilities of land development in Palestine. In 1939 he published a survey of the refugee problem.

197. Gilbert, M. (1979), 215.

198. Ben-Gurion (1971–1987), vol. 5, 373.

199. Grynszpan was extradited by the Vichy government to Germany and Goebbels planned a great show trial, which never took place.

200. Hermann (2008), 603–619. Friedländer (1997), 305–315.

201. Gilbert, M. (2006), 13. Kristallnacht is described extensively in this book and in others. See for example Friedländer (1997), 269–76; Yahil (1990), 305–316.

202. See Kaufman (1985), 114.

203. Shedletzky (1998), 518.

204. Gilbert, M. (2006). Ball Kaduri (1968), 106–110. Ball Kaduri (1985), 153–155. Friedländer (1997), 305–316. Yahil (1990), 161–164.

205. Cohn (2014), 514.

206. Galezer (1984), 98–100.

207. Shprintzak (1969), vol. 2, 377–379. Ben-Gurion (1971–1987), vol. 5, 423.

208. See Kulka (1975), 186–290. Kershaw (2008), 221.

209. Ruppin (1968), 308–309.

210. Chajes (1998), 260.

211. Ibid., 262.

212. London (2000), 32–33.

213. Ibid., 100–105.

214. Ben-Elissar (1978), 160.

215. The director general of the Foreign Office, Sir Alexander Cadogan, cited in Gilbert, M. (1979), 101, note 12.

216. Shamir (1974), 292. Shamir relied on Parliamentary Debates vol. 341, col. 142.83.

217. *Davar*, November 11, 1938.

218. *Haaretz*, November 13, 1938.

219. See Cohen, N. (2006).

220. Mechman (1980), 119–127. Mechman cites the telegram sent to the Dutch government, but estimates that it was sent to other governments as well.

221. See Harris and Oppenheimer (2008).

222. Sharett (1968–1979), vol. 3, 334–335.

223. Shprintzak (1969), vol. 2, 378.

224. Katzburg (1994), 413.

225. Ben-Gurion (1971–1987), vol. 5, 416–418: meeting with Mapai Central Committee from December 15, 1938.

226. Ibid., 417.

227. Braginsky (1965), 130.

228. Rülf (1969), 66–67.

229. McClure (2003). Bauer (1994), 37–39. Israeli (1974), 149–150. Zariz (1990), 20–22.

230. Cohen, R. (1999), 19.

231. Friedländer (1997), 303.

232. Quoted in Zariz (1990), 63.

233. By November 1938, around 160,000 Jews had emigrated from Germany, and around 90,000 additional Jews emigrated between November 1938 and October 1941, when emigration stopped. Around 150,000 were left of the approximately 560,000 Jews living in Germany in 1933. Toury (1987), 65–98. Zariz (1990). Strauss (1960), 326–328. Seventeen or eighteen refugees ended up in China.

234. Quoted in Shelach (1994), 11.

4. FUNERAL MARCH AT ST. JAMES'S PALACE

1. Kanari (2003), 447.

2. Cohen, M. J. (1978), 66–87.

3. The palace had already hosted several international conferences, such as after the second Balkan war in 1912, and regarding the future of India in 1930–1931. See Scott (2010).

4. Ibid., 114–115.

5. Ben-Gurion (1971–1987), vol. 5, 110: letter from February 18, 1938.

6. Ibid., 114–115.

7. Ibid., 360–364: letter from February 18, 1938.

8. Gilbert, M. (2006), 121–134.

9. Sharett (1968–1979), vol. 3, 262.

10. Ibid., 308.

11. Ruppin (1968), 304–305.

12. Ibid., 306.

13. Cohen, M. J. (1978), 73.

14. In Yahil (1990), 115.

15. On March 7, 1938, Jabotinsky wrote: "We anticipate great changes in the world, and particularly in the Jewish world; I do not know what these changes will be, but I feel like they will be constructive, positive and uniting" (Jabotinsky, *Igrot*, 13, 2014, 4). Throughout 1938 Jabotinsky never wrote about the Munich Pact or the takeover of Czechoslovakia.

16. Ben-Gurion (1971–1987), vol. 5, 258–265: letter from September 20, 1938.

17. Sharett (1968–1979), vol. 3, 311.

18. Ben-Gurion (1971–1987), vol. 5, 276: diary entry from 1938.

19. Ibid., 290: letter to the Zionist Executive from October 3, 1938. See also ibid., 281–283: letter from October 1, 1938.

20. Overy and Wheatcroft (2009).

21. Ben-Gurion (1971–1987), vol. 5, 281: letter from October 1, 1938. Teveth (1987), 251–252.

22. The 1938 events that led to the Munich Agreement are described in detail in Faber (2009).

23. Weizmann (1979–1984), vol. 18, 465–466: letter from October 3, 1938.

24. Ben-Gurion (1971–1987), vol. 5, 272: letter to Ussishkin from October 24, 1938.

25. Braginsky (1965), 119–120.

26. Shapira, A. (2008), II, 570.

27. Rose (1973), 103.

28. LPA, 4-6-1920-98: letter from September 28, 1938.

29. Ben-Gurion (1971–1987), vol. 5, 284. Bondy (1989), 121–22.

30. Ben-Gurion (1971–1987), vol. 5, 286.

31. LPA, 4-6-1920-98: letter from 1938.

32. Shapira, A. (2008), 273–4. By contrast, Katznelson, added Shapira, "thought that preparations should be made for a world war, on the one hand, and a struggle against the Mandatory Government, on the other." It is unclear, however, how he intended to prepare for a world war.

33. Masaryk told Benjamin Akzin about Foreign Secretary Halifax: "How can you expect any consideration for the troubles of another nation from a person who spends half his day riding horses and killing foxes, and the minute he gets off his horse kneels and spends the other half of the day praying? In diplomatic circles we don't call him Halifax, we call him holy fox." Akzin (1989), 269.

34. Edvard Beneš served as president of the Czechoslovakian Republic from 1935 to 1938.

35. Rose (1973), 140.

36. Ibid., 99.

37. Ben-Gurion (1971–1987), vol. 5, 1982, 259: letter from August 29, 1938.

38. Rose (1973), 99.

39. Sharett (1968–1979), vol. 3, 312–314.

40. Chajes (1998), 257–258.

41. Roos (1965), 356.

42. Rothkirchen (2006), 78–79.

43. Ben-Elissar (1978), 134.

44. Rothkirchen (2006), 79.

45. Bondy (1989), 120–21. Faber (2009), 436–437.

46. Messenger (2009), 31.

47. Gai (1995), 194–195.

48. Achimeir, Y. (1983), 251–252.

49. Klemperer (2009), 296.

50. Sharett (1968–1979), vol. 4, 161.

51. Ibid., 164–165.
52. Ben-Gurion (1971–1987), vol. 6, 202.
53. Rose (1973), 130.
54. Bondy (1989), 114–15.
55. *Haaretz*, September 29, 2008.
56. Brod (1967), 255.
57. Ben-Yeruham (1976), 232, 284.
58. Leichter (1993), 253–257.
59. Galezer (1984), 86–96.
60. *Hamashkif*, March 16, 1939.
61. *Der Moment*, March 17, 1939.
62. *Hamashkif*, March 19, 1939.
63. Ruppin (1968), 312–313.
64. Winton, a stockbroker, arrived in Prague at the end of 1938 and single-handedly organized the children's rescue as well as their placement with foster families in England. See *Haaretz*, September 2, 2009.
65. Hope Simpson (1939), 5.
66. Gilbert, M. (1978), 216.
67. Rothkirchen (1979), 211–235.
68. Bondy (1989), 125.
69. *Jewish Chronicle*, August 11, 1939.
70. Ibid.
71. Bader, M. (1954), 15, 25.
72. Friedländer (1997), 358.
73. Rothkirchen (2006), 107.
74. Rosenblit's letter to the Palestine Office in Prague, August 19, 1938, quoted in Gelber (1990), 144.
75. Gort served as High Commissioner in Palestine from October 1944 to November 1945.
76. Gilbert, M. (1979), 223.
77. Wasserstein (1979), 26–27.
78. Hope Simpson (1939), 5.
79. Ben-Gurion (1971–1987), vol. 5, 169: speech from April 4, 1938.
80. Ibid., 273: letter from 1938. Teveth (1987), 250.
81. Ben-Gurion (1971–1987), vol. 5, 281: letter from October 30, 1938.
82. Cohen, M. J. (1978), 68.
83. Ibid., 74–87.
84. WA, ADA 15-2099: secret telegram from Jerusalem to Weizmann, October 21, 1938.
85. He is referring to the talks between Poland and the USSR in 1938.
86. Ben-Gurion (1971–1987), vol. 5, 421–423: letter from December 21, 1938. Emphases in the original.
87. Ben-Gurion (1971–1987), vol. 6, 121.
88. Ibid., 127.
89. Rose (1973), 96.
90. LPA, 4-6-1920-98: letter from February 6, 1939.

91. Kanari (2003), 447.
92. *Hamashkif*, February 17, 1939.
93. Rose (1973), 119.
94. Report from January 11, 1939, quoted in Shapira, D. H. (1976), 114.
95. Gilbert, M. (1978), 218.
96. WA:19, 8–9.
97. Ben-Gurion (1971–1987), vol. 6, 122.
98. WA, ADA 15-2122.
99. WA, ADA 17-21/OA. Minutes of the Fifth Meeting of the Executive, December 16, 1938.
100. *Hamashkif*, February 6, 1939.
101. *Hamashkif*, "The *Star* is Derisive," February 7, 1939.
102. Gal (1985), 29–30.
103. For a description of the conference proceedings, see Katzburg (1994), 420–426.
104. *Hamashkif*, February 7, 1939.
105. Sharett (1968–1979), vol. 4, 24.
106. LPA, 4-6-1920-98: letter from February 2, 1939.
107. Sharett (1968–1979), vol. 4, 25.
108. Ibid., 25–26.
109. *Hamashkif*, February 24, 1939. Emphases in the original.
110. Sharett (1968–1979), vol. 4, 83. Weizmann prepared notes for his speech.
111. Weizmann (1979–1984). "The St. James Conference: Opening Statement for Jews," February 8, 1939, 341–360.
112. Sharett (1968–1979), vol. 4, 26.
113. Ibid., 30.
114. Ben-Gurion (1971–1987), vol. 6, 134–136: letter from February 9, 1939.
115. LPA, 4-6-1920-98: letter from February 14, 1939.
116. LPA, 4-6-1920-98: letter from March 6, 1939.
117. LPA, 4-6-1920-98: letter from March 6, 1939.
118. *Forverts*, August 26, 1939.
119. Schwartz (1949), 25.
120. Ben-Gurion (1971–1987), vol. 6, 164.
121. Asch (1980), 110.
122. CZA, A116/52/1: Yitzhak Ben Zvi's diary, entry from 1939. See Sarid (2008), 215.
123. Katzburg (1974), 48–74.
124. WA, ADA 18-2126.
125. WA, ADA 8-2/30.
126. Cohen, M. J. (1978), 74.
127. Rose (1973), 124.
128. Avneri (1985), 59–60. Braginsky (1965), 144–148.
129. Gilbert, M. (1978), 223.
130. Weizmann (1949), 395.
131. Ibid.
132. Ben-Gurion (1971–1987), vol. 6, 147.
133. Sharett (1968–1979), vol. 4, 68–71.

134. Ben-Gurion (1971–1987), vol. 6, 155–164. Sharett (1968–1979), vol. 4, 68–71.

135. Ibid., 79.

136. Ben-Gurion (1971–1987), vol. 6, 163–166.

137. Ibid., 169.

138. Sharett (1968–1979), vol. 4, 99.

139. Ibid., 100.

140. Yarkoni (2005), 55–57.

141. Ben-Gurion (1971–1987), vol. 6, 548–549.

142. Sharett (1968–1979), vol. 4, 105.

143. Teveth (1987), 299.

144. Ibid., 310.

145. Gilbert, M. (1978), 225.

146. Sharett (1968–1979), vol. 4, 123.

147. Asch (1980).

148. Ruppin (1968), 312.

149. Sharett (1968–1979), vol. 4, 171.

150. The vessel made five voyages.

151. Braginsky (1965), 152–163.

152. July 13, quoted in Gelber (1990), 137.

153. Weizmann (1949), 392.

154. Ben-Gurion (1971–1987), vol. 6, 205.

155. Ibid., 208.

156. Ibid., 213.

157. Shprintzak (1969), vol. 2, 386: letter from March 15, 1939.

158. WA, ADA 5–2137A.

159. LPA, 4-6-1920–98: letter from March 19, 1939.

160. Cohen, M. J. (1978), 83–84.

161. *Hamashkif*, March 17, 1939.

162. Sharett (1968–1979), vol. 4, 179.

163. Ben-Gurion (1971–1987), vol. 6, 208.

164. Ibid., 218–219.

165. Chajes (1998), 263–264.

166. Sharett (1968–1979), vol. 4, 161.

167. Ibid., 171. At the third session of the Twenty-First Zionist Congress, on August 17, Weizmann said: "When we meet in better times, and if you are allowed to read the minutes of these talks, you will spend a pleasant hour seeing how they received us, who were fighting for the lives of tens of thousands of people and an ancient tradition." *Minutes of the Twenty-First Zionist Congress*, 43.

168. Weizmann to Chamberlain (1939), vol. 19, 32–34: letter from March 24, 1939.

169. Gal (1985), 31.

170. *Forverts*, August 14, 1939.

171. Sharett (1968–1979), vol. 4, 187.

172. Sharett (1968–1979), vol. 4, 189.

173. LPA, 4-6-1920–98: letters from March 19 and 24, 1939.

174. After the protagonist of Alexandre Dumas's novel *The Count of Monte Cristo*.

175. Rose (1973), 132. Ben-Gurion (1971–1987), vol. 6, 220–221, 136.
176. Weizmann (1979–1984), vol. 19, 43–44: letter from April 25, 1939.
177. Gilbert, M. (1979), 238–239.
178. Sharett (1968–1979), vol. 4, 202. Bentov (1984), 57–58.
179. Sharett (1968–1979), vol. 4, 223–230.
180. *Hamashkif*, March 24, 1939.
181. *Hamashkif*, February 10, 1939.
182. *Davar*, April 6, 1939.
183. *Hamashkif*, March 31, 1939.
184. Testimony of Yechezkel Sacharov in Sykes (1965), 185.
185. Rose (1973), 138–139.
186. *Parliamentary Debates: House of Commons* (April 6, 1939), vol. 345, no. 6, 3049–3093.
187. Avizohar (1987), 51, n. 24.
188. Ruppin (1968), 313.
189. Ben-Gurion (1971–1987), vol. 6, 279.
190. Schechtman (1961), 366.
191. Ben-Gurion (1971–1987), vol. 6, 293, 540.
192. Niederland (1998), 240.

5. A BRIDGE OVER THE WHITE PAPER?

1. Zeev Jabotinsky at the Betar world conference in Warsaw, September 11–16, 1938, Ben-Yeruham (1976), 864.
2. Sharett (1968–1979), vol. 4, 284.
3. Boris Smolar, "Tragedy of the *St. Louis*," May 29, 1939, in Penkower (2013), 244–246.
4. *Davar*, June 7, 1939.
5. Kochavi (1984), 109.
6. Gelber (1990), 136–137.
7. Thomas (1974). Gellman (1971), 144–156.
8. Zariz (1990), 171–172.
9. *Parliamentary Debates* (April 6, 1939), vol. 345, No. 6, 3049–3093. Other speakers argued that they needed to remember the fate of other refugees, for example the quarter of a million Spaniards who fled Franco's Spain.
10. *Haaretz*, May 14, 1939.
11. *Haaretz*, May 15, 1939. The poem's ending alludes to Laban, the Aramean who deceived Jacob (Genesis 29–31).
12. *Haaretz*, May 10, 1939.
13. *Haaretz*, May 11, 1939.
14. *Davar*, May 18, 1939.
15. "Palestine Trembles Tonight," address to E.Z.F. Conference, May 18, 1939, in Weizmann (1979–1984), series B:2, 364–65.
16. POR 701/13/19. Gilbert, M. (1979), 119–120.
17. Katz, S. (1993), 1092. Weinbaum (1993), 241.
18. *Minutes of the Twenty-First Zionist Congress*, 123.
19. Sharett (1968–1979), vol. 4, 296.

20. *Foreign Relations of the United States* (1955), vol. IV, 7771.

21. Katz (1993), 1103.

22. Ibid., 1093.

23. Ibid., 1097.

24. *Minutes of the Twenty-First Zionist Congress*, 125.

25. Ibid., 141–142.

26. Weinbaum (1993), 221–222.

27. After Poland ceased to exist, the only possible ally left was Nazi Germany. The story of the contacts between the envoy of Lehi (the group that broke away from the Irgun under Yair's leadership) and the Nazi diplomat von Hentig has been described extensively in the literature. The memorandum (as cited by the Nazi diplomat) talked about an alliance and a cooperation between the "new Germany" and the "renewed national-popular Hebrew movement" (eine Kooperation zwischen dem Neuen Deutschland und einen erneuertem, völkisch-nationalen Hebräertum möglich wäre). The memorandum presented Lehi as a fighting force that Nazi Germany would do well to cooperate with.

28. Ben-Yeruham (1976), 850–864.

29. Kahn (1988), 27–31.

30. JIA, 2/29/2/1a.

31. See Golomb (1955), 92–98. JIA, 2/19–43, in Shavit (1983), 121–134.

32. Ben-Yeruham writes: "The directive was very difficult to implement in practice, and this was explained to Jabotinsky." Ben-Yeruham (1976), 955. Emphases in the original.

33. These raids, which came in reaction to air raids on London and Folkstone Harbor, from where British soldiers left for the western front, included 675 strategic bombings in which 746 German soldiers and civilians were killed. Britain's air force lost 352 aircraft and 264 aircrew were killed or declared missing in action. The damage was minimal and the bombings had no influence on the population's morale.

34. Sharett (1968–1979), vol. 4, 313. Meeting of the Central Committee of Mapai.

35. Shapira, D. H. (1976), 96–160. See also Ilan (1979), 26–59.

36. PRO, FO 371/24084, in Melzer (1973), 249.

37. Gilbert, M. (1979), 239.

38. Parliamentary Papers; 1939, CMD. 6019.

39. Minutes of the Histadrut Executive Committee meeting, March 16, 1939. Quoted in Kochavi (1984), 107.

40. Ben-Gurion (1971–1987), vol. 6, 236: meeting from April 16, 1939.

41. Ibid., 282: meeting from April 30, 1939.

42. Ibid., 222: meeting from April 5, 1939.

43. Ibid., 404: meeting from April 28, 1939.

44. Katznelson (1947), 44–45: meeting from 1939. On Ben-Gurion's position on illegal immigration, see Tzahor (1987), 422–447.

45. Weizmann (1979–1984), vol. 19, 61–65: letter from May 5, 1939.

46. Gilbert, M. (1978), 235.

47. Braginsky (1965), 76–77.

48. Ibid., 53–79. Avneri (1985), 36–47. Yarkoni (2005), 205–206.

49. See Chazan (2010), 139.

50. Ben-Gurion (1971–1987), vol. 6, 374–375.

51. Boaz (2001), 108–118.

52. Meir Avizohar considered these proposals as practical "plans" that were mostly not realized due to internal opposition. Avizohar (1987), 17–60.

53. Kanari (2003), 446..

54. Ibid., 458.

55. Ibid., 447. Emphasis ours.

56. *Foreign Relations of the United States* (1939), vol. IV, 771–773.

57. Ben-Gurion (1971–1987), vol. 4, 51: meeting from January 23, 1937.

58. We do not know how many graduates of this naval school took part in the voyages of the illegal immigrant ships brought to Palestine's shores by the various branches of the Revisionist movement.

59. Ben-Yeruham (1976), 685.

60. Ben-Gurion (1971–1987), vol. 5, 236: diary entry from August 25, 1938.

61. Ben-Gurion (1971–1987), vol. 6, 255–258: diary entry from April 22, 1939.

62. Ibid., 260.

63. Ibid., 243–244: meeting from April 16, 1939.

64. Zertal (1990), 87–107.

65. Avneri (1985), 73.

66. Ibid., 251–252.

67. Yarkoni (2005), 51–52. Avneri (1985), 263.

68. Yarkoni (2005), 55–57.

69. Ofer (1990a), 133–34. Ramba (1944), vol. 2, 123–124.

70. Ben-Yeruham (1976), 897.

71. Yarkoni (2005), 216–217. Avneri (1985), 213–218. Galezer (1984), 71–85.

72. In the article "The National Sport," which he published in *Der Moment* on April 28, 1939, and in other newspapers (in *Hamashkif* on May 5, 1939), Jabotinsky wrote that any project involves risk taking: "The Jewish merchant today lives in a romantic period. Any new trade is a romance that might end in drama."

73. "Tertium non datur," *Hamedina*, April–May, 1939.

74. Ben-Yeruham (1976), 963–965. Galezer (1984), 123–135.

75. The piece was published in *Haboker* in September 1944, and is quoted in Lazar-Litai (1957), 235–250.

76. *Davar*, April 27, 1939. On June 15, 1939 *Haolam*, the organ of the World Zionist Organization, also published a "horrifying letter" in which an immigrant on the *Agios Nikolaus* wrote that the passengers had suffered abuse. Other disturbing reports described what the passengers of the *Astir* went through. On the *Agios Nikolaus*, see JIA, 4/8/6-4k. Robinson (2010), 257–278.

77. *Davar*, April 27, 1939.

78. Gilbert, M. (1978), 238.

79. Katznelson (1960), 438–447.

80. Harsh words about the immigration enterprise of the Revisionists and the private groups continued to be heard after the war broke out. On February 4, 1940, Shertok wrote in his diary that the "wolves" (the Revisionists) were continuing to amass hundreds of refugees, "the blind and the lame etc., including an entire old people's home, the wretched Viennese Jewish community's gift to Palestine." The sphere of immigra-

tion, he added, has been abandoned to the "rabbles' exploits." Sharett (1968–1979), vol. 5, 15–19.

81. Braginsky (1965), 216.

82. Ibid., 225–226.

83. Ofer (1990), 14.

84. Ibid., 457.

85. Zweig (1981), 292–323.

86. Wasserstein (1979), 31–32.

87. Avneri (1985), 92.

88. *Der Moment*, April 28, 1939.

89. Ben-Yeruham (1976), 862–864.

90. Ibid., 973–974.

91. Ibid.

92. Ofer (1990) 14.

93. Wasserstein (1979), 47.

94. To these should be added illegal immigrants who arrived as tourists, on the basis of fictive marriages, and so on.

95. Gelber (1990), 138.

96. *Foreign Relations of the United States* (1939), vol. IV, 802–806.

97. Ofer (1990), 57.

98. As mentioned above, the memoirs and the research literature do not always concur on the passenger numbers and the dates of setting off and arriving in Palestine.

99. Galezer (1984), 114–116.

100. Flying in the face of historical reality and of the facts, the Revisionist movement and its heirs have nurtured the claim that "if certain circles had not tried to hinder it [the movement's immigration endeavor], the organizers would have brought not tens of thousands, but maybe hundreds of thousands of Jews." Letter from Menachem Begin to Eliyahu Galezer, February 1, 1982, in Galezer (1984), 9.

101. See Krzykalski (1995), 67–88.

102. Buber (1939), 27–29.

6. THE FORGOTTEN CONGRESS (GENEVA, AUGUST 16–25, 1939)

1. The number of shekel payers in 1939 was around a million, approximately a quarter of whom were in Palestine and a third in Poland. Of the delegates, 134 were elected in Palestine and 109 were elected from Poland and the two Galicias. The Labor party had 216 delegates, Hamizrachi had 65, the Medina Ivrit party had 8, the Poalei Zion Left had 13, and there were a number of delegates from thirty-five countries. For data on the composition of the Congress, see *Minutes of the Twenty-First Zionist Congress* (1939), 13–39.

2. LPA, 4-6-1920-98: letter from August 28, 1938.

3. LPA, 4-6-1920-98: letter from August 16, 1938.

4. Ben-Gurion (1971–1987), vol. 6, 497. When Ben-Gurion went out to vote on July 30 he found that his name was absent from the voter register at his ballot box. He was sent from one ballot box to another and in the end went to vote in Jerusalem. Ibid., 483.

5. Katznelson wrote: "The parties that wished to gain from riggings now want to gain from crying foul against the riggings—but I believe this too will blow over." LPA, 4-6-1920–98: letter from August 16, 1939.

6. Ben-Gurion (1971–1987), vol. 6, 497. Perhaps this is why the Twenty-First Zionist Congress was mentioned only briefly in the memoirs of most of its participants, as well as in the research literature. Similarly, in the long novella by Natan Shaham, "Oniyat Kitur: Cairo City," in *Kirot etz dakim*, Tel Aviv, 1977, 7–79, there is a detailed and accurate description of the Congress, probably based on an eyewitness report.

7. *Jewish Chronicle*, August 11, 1939.

8. Overy (2009), 19.

9. Arad (2010), xxiii. Stalin's words are based on a release by the French news agency Havas. At the time in question there were no Politburo meetings, but the words reflect Stalin's intentions at the time.

10. Quoted in Yahil (1990), I, 185. The quote is from Albert Speer (1969), 12.

11. Yahil (1990), 186.

12. Thorne (1967), 175.

13. Many books describe the chain of events leading to the Second World War. See for example: Aster (1973), Watt (1989), Bethell (1972), Overy and Wheatcroft (2000), Ben-Arie (1987), Batowski (1979), and Carley (1999).

14. Ford and Schorske (1953), 547. Stachura (2004), 23.

15. Maisky and Gorodetsky (2015), 219.

16. Mintz (2010), 268–84.

17. *Haaretz*, August 23, 1939.

18. Chajes (1998), 267–268. Józef Beck was Poland's foreign minister from 1932 to 1939.

19. Ben-Gurion (1971–1987), vol. 4, 224. Ben-Gurion wrote to his wife Paula on March 23, 1938: "Mrs. Dugdale is very dedicated and has some influence and contacts, but I do not trust her thinking or her opinion on political matters." Ibid., vol. 5, 167.

20. Rose (1973), 146. The diary entry is from August 22 but the date is probably mistaken, because Dugdale wrote that she had read about the agreement in the Swiss papers over breakfast, while the agreement was signed the next day.

21. Cohn (2012).

22. Gilbert, F. (1953), 537–554.

23. Ruppin (1968), 316–317. *Davar* wrote that day that the German-Soviet agreement might "help to preserve peace." *Haboker*, the General Zionists' newspaper, wrote that the entire system of European alliances had collapsed and that Britain and France's promises to Poland were worthless without the Soviet Union's support. It turned out, the newspaper noted, that the "prophecy" that the two dictatorships—"the red one and the brown one"—were destined to unite had come true. The Ribbentrop-Molotov Pact had brought the world to the brink of war.

24. Weizmann, like other writers, gave the wrong date for the signing of the agreement. Incidentally, in the course of the Congress, Weizmann wrote very few letters. Weizmann (1949), 413. Weizmann, of course, could not have known in August 1939 about the secret agreement.

25. *Davar*, July 4, 1939.

26. Shprintzak (1969), vol. 2, 392: letter from August 11, 1939.

27. Mowrer was the correspondent for the *Chicago Daily News* and after his book appeared he received death threats from the Nazi regime. Larsen (2011), 74–76.

28. Ruppin (1968), 315–316.

29. Meir (1975), 161.

30. *Hamashkif*, August 18, 1939.

31. *Davar*, August 15, 1939.

32. *Hamashkif*, August 18, 1939. Emphasis in the original.

33. The New York *Forverts* published a series of photographs on August 21, 1939, boasting that they had been sent by a "Yankee Clipper" airplane on August 18 and reached the newspaper "three days later."

34. *Minutes of the Twenty-First Zionist Congress* (1939), 32. The *Davar* correspondent reported on "the excellent Spanish exhibition" of paintings that had been sent for safekeeping "in the League of Nations city" during the Spanish Civil War. "The early birds among the Zionist Congress delegates will visit it even if art is not their thing—for lack of anything else to do." *Davar*, August 15, 1939.

35. Around 40,000 German Jews were held in concentration camps. See Frankel (1994), 286–287.

36. *Der Moment*, August 20, 1939.

37. Bondy (1989), 147.

38. Ringelblum (1999), 3. Kassow (2007), 103–104.

39. The first prize was 5 Pp. CZA, KL10/87. The badges were made of gold, silver, and bronze, and the Agency had to negotiate with the Swiss authorities over the custom imposed on them. At the beginning of September, Kretschmer, the owner of a workshop for artistic engraving and enamel on Hassolel Street in Jerusalem, who had manufactured the symbol of the Twenty-First Zionist Congress, approached the Jewish Agency's organization department asking for its permission to use the symbol for commercial purposes and for propagating Palestine-made products, while omitting the designation "21." Kretschmer threatened that if he did not get the permission he would have to close the workshop and lay off the workers. The correspondence on this matter between Kretschmer, Gumbel, and the organization department continued for more than five months. CZA, KL14.

40. Shertok dubbed the newspaper a slanderous and sensationalist "national criminal," calling for an atmosphere that would stifle it. Sharett (1968–1979), vol. 4, 241.

41. *Der Moment*, August 11, 1939.

42. Shprintzak (1969), vol. 2, 393: letter from August 11, 1939.

43. Ringelblum (1993), 3.

44. *Der Moment*, August 15, 1939.

45. Braginsky (1965), 240–241.

46. Ruppin (1968), 316–317.

47. Weizmann invited him to attend the Congress's opening session. Weizmann (1979–1984), vol. 19, 142: letter from July 23, 1939, 128–34.

48. Feinberg (1936), 149, note 119.

49. Katznelson (1947), 61–62: article from 1939.

50. Klemperer (2009), 370.

51. *Dvar Hapoelet*, August 15, 1939, 140.

52. Boaz (2001), 116–120. Braginsky (1965), 188–203. Yarkoni (2005), 75–77.

53. Ben-Gurion (1971–1987), vol. 6, 120.

54. Weizmann (1979), vol. 19, 144: letter from August 13, 1939.

55. The speeches of the Congress speakers are based on the minutes, the summaries in the *Zionist Review*, and the coverage in the daily newspapers.

56. *Minutes of the Twenty-First Zionist Congress*, 1–8, 6. See also *Zionist Review*, August 17, 1939, 5.

57. Shprintzak (1969), vol. 2, 394: letter from August 18, 1939.

58. *Zionist Review*, August 17, 1939.

59. Ben-Gurion (1971–1987), vol. 6, 500.

60. *Minutes of the Twenty-First Zionist Congress*, 42–47.

61. Ibid., 14–25. See also *Davar*, August 24, 1939.

62. Burg (2000), 91.

63. Ben-Gurion (1971–1987), vol. 6, 494–495.

64. Ibid., 514. *Minutes of the Twenty-First Zionist Congress*, 80–87.

65. Ben-Gurion (1971–1987), vol. 6, 516–524.

66. See Chazan (2010), 118–146.

67. Ben-Gurion (1971–1987), vol. 6, 495.

68. *Minutes of the Twenty-First Zionist Congress*, 87–91.

69. Ibid., 91–97.

70. Ben-Gurion (1971–1987), vol. 3, 105–106.

71. Avizohar (1984), 17–60.

72. Ben-Gurion (1971–1987), vol. 5, 402–404.

73. Kessner (2008), 310.

74. Mardor (1957), 37–40.

75. Norden was one of Kaf-Gimel Yordei Hasira—the twenty-three commandos who went missing in action in May 1941.

76. *Minutes of the Twenty-First Zionist Congress*, 104–108.

77. Ibid., 243–244. Goldstein, Y. (2001), vol. 2, 208–209.

78. We have been unable to identify the film in question.

79. Katznelson (1947), 61–82: article from 1939. *Minutes of the Twenty-First Zionist Congress*, 142–156.

80. Katznelson (1947), 72.

81. *Zionist Review*, August 24, 1939, 19.

82. JIA, 2/124/42. See also Avneri (1985), 255.

83. Avneri (1985), 254–256. Yarkoni (2005), 37–40, 226–228. Lazar-Litai (1957), 290–292.

84. See chapter 4.

85. *Minutes of the Twenty-First Zionist Congress*, 149–152. Shapira, A. (2008), 279.

86. Kessner (2008), 311.

87. Shapira, A. (2008), I, 279. Rose (1973), 145.

88. Krone (1987), 198.

89. Rose (1973), 144–145.

90. Avneri (1985), 147.

91. Zertal (1990), 106.

92. Gal (1985), 39.

93. *Minutes of the Twenty-First Zionist Congress*, 134–136.
94. Neumann (1976), 188.
95. *Minutes of the Twenty-First Zionist Congress*, 113.
96. *Forverts*, August 14, 1939.
97. *Minutes of the Twenty-First Zionist Congress*, 170.
98. Ibid., 165–176.
99. Meir (1975), 165.
100. *Minutes of the Twenty-First Zionist Congress*, 119–120.
101. Ibid., 223–227.
102. *Haynt*, August 23, 1939.
103. Weinbaum (1993), 197–198.
104. Ibid., 198.
105. Ibid., 196–199.
106. Ibid., 197–198.
107. Lazar-Litai (1957), 272–275.
108. Ibid., 275.
109. Ben-Yeruham (1976), 965. Yarkoni (2005), 181–182.
110. JIA, document 1313. See Sarid (2008), 268–269.
111. Overy (2009), 24.
112. Shirer (1960), 550.
113. Friedländer (1997), 309–10.
114. Ben-Elissar (1978), 136.
115. Teveth (1987), 271–276.
116. Shavit (1986), 102–110. See also chapter 8.
117. Gelber (1979), 17.
118. Sharett (1968–1979), vol. 4, 226.
119. Ringelblum (1993), 3.
120. Shprintzak (1969), vol. 2, 396: letter from 1939.
121. Krone (1987), 198.
122. LPA, 4-6-1920-98: letter from 1939.
123. Weizmann (1949), 413.
124. Golomb (1955), 93–98.
125. Shavit (1986), 102–110.
126. JIA, 1/2/29/2א. See *The Irgun* (1990), 94.
127. JIA, 1/5/211/ה.
128. Niv (1965), 194–195.
129. In March 1939 some of the group's members said at a press conference they held in Warsaw that Jabotinsky was a former activist who was now conducting a policy that promoted complacency. Schechtman (1961), 460.
130. Spielman (1960), 122. See also Freilich (1999), 206–232.
131. JIA, 2/29/2-1א: letter from 1939.
132. JIA, 2/29/2-1א: letter from 1939.
133. Ben-Yeruham (1976), 964–965. Lazar-Litai (1957), 222–250.
134. Yarkoni (2005), 203–205. *Haynt*, August 23, 1939.
135. Sharett (1968–1979), vol. 4, 331–338.

136. Bialer (1980).
137. Melman (2009), 271–275.
138. See chapter 6.
139. Gelber (1979), 60.
140. LPA, 4-6-1920-98: letter from 1939.
141. Katznelson (1960). See also Shapira, A. (2008), II, 589–592.
142. In July 1922 Weizmann wrote to his sister that he may come to Poland in the winter, "since it has been my hidden wish for several years," but "our Zionist friends are afraid that my trip will cause irregularities in Warsaw," he added without further explanation. Weizmann (1979), vol. 11, 174: letter from 1922.
143. Katznelson (1947), 25: article from December 31, 1938.
144. In the minutes of the Twenty-First Zionist Congress the wording is slightly different, but the gist is similar. *Minutes of the Twenty-First Zionist Congress*, 222–223.
145. Ibid., 223.
146. Weizmann (1949), 403.
147. Rose (1973), 147.
148. Krone (1987), 198.
149. Warhaftig (1984), 4.
150. Kessner (2008), 313.
151. Stachura (2004), 125.
152. Head of the Polish delegation to the League of Nations in Geneva.
153. Ringelblum (1993), 4–5.
154. *Minutes of the Twenty-First Zionist Congress*, 242–245. Goldstein, Y. (2001), vol. 2, 209.
155. *Minutes of the Twenty-First Zionist Congress*, 249.
156. Ibid., 190–192. *Davar*, August 25, 1939.
157. *Hatzofeh*, August 25, 1939.
158. Kessner (2008), 309.
159. *Foreign Relations of the United States* (1955), 799–802.
160. Cohn (2014), 635–637.
161. Rose (1973), 147.
162. Rose (1973), 148.
163. Minutes of the Agency Directorate, May 22, 1936, CZA, quoted in Heller (1987), 150.

7. WILL WAR BREAK OUT?

1. *Davar*, Evening Supplement, May 5, 1935.
2. Gilbert, M. (2007), 100.
3. Friling (2005), vol. 1, 19. See also Teveth (1996).
4. Friling (1998), vol. 1, 19.
5. Yaakov Hazan's words at the Nineteenth Zionist Congress are quoted in Halamish (2009), 204.
6. Ben-Gurion (1971–1987), vol. 5, 169.
7. Teveth (1987), 250.

8. Ben-Gurion (1971–1987), vol. 5, 423: letter from December 21, 1938. Emphasis in the original.

9. Ben-Gurion's words at the Zionist Executive Committee, October 26, 1936, CZA, 117. Emphasis in the original.

10. Weizmann (1979–1984), vol. 17, 205: letter to Ormsby Gore from July 19, 1936.

11. Ibid., 312–316: letter from 1936.

12. Weizmann (1979–1984), vol. 19, 8–9: letter from January 20, 1939.

13. Sharett (1968–1979), vol. 4, 223.

14. See Halamish (2009), 204–205.

15. *Hazit Haam*, May 19, 1933.

16. *Der Moment*, May 10, 1933. See Shavit and Steir-Livny (2004), 345–369.

17. Ibid.

18. *Der Moment*, July 9, 1933.

19. Jabotinsky (1958), 187–188.

20. *Hazit Haam*, November 10, 1933.

21. *Hayarden*, October 24, 1934.

22. Jabotinsky (1934).

23. *Hayarden*, June 23, 1934.

24. After Mussolini's intervention the German army's entry into Austria was prevented in 1934.

25. *Hayarden*, September 9, 1934.

26. *Hayarden*, October 29, 1935.

27. *Hayarden*, November 28, 1935.

28. *Davar*, July 6, 1934.

29. *Hayarden*, October 11, 1935.

30. *Hayarden*, March 27, 1936.

31. *Hayarden*, January 31, 1936. In August 1935 Jabotinsky compared the Nazis to the Chicago gangs, claiming that the violence against Jews in Germany was not connected "to any kind of politics, nor even to antisemitism," and in any case, the Nazi regime was a "gangrene" that ended with "surgery." *Hayarden*, August 4, 1935.

32. The speech by Jabotinsky was printed in numerous places, including *Hamashkif*, June 2, 1939.

33. Schechtman (1961), 130.

34. Jabotinsky (1939), note 32, 35.

35. Ibid. *Hamashkif*, June 18, 1939; *Der Moment*, June 9, 1939. See also Shavit and Steir-Livny (2004).

36. *Hamashkif*, June 18, 1939. *Der Moment*, June 9, 1939.

37. Jabotinsky's letter to his sister, August 11, 1939, quoted in Schechtman (1961), 366.

38. Jabotinsky's letter to Shlomo Saltzman, April 6, 1939, quoted in Schechtman (1961), 366.

39. *Hamashkif*, April 14, 1939.

40. *Hamashkif*, April 24, 1939. Emphasis in the original.

41. JIA, 2/29/2–1א: letter from September 1, 1939.

42. Bader (1999), 220.

43. Schechtman (1961), 367.

44. Chajes (1998), 265.

45. Ibid. Adam Mickiewicz, *Pan Tadeusz*, trans. Kenneth R. MacKenzie (New York: Hippocrene, 2007), 484.

46. Chajes (1998), 265.

47. Cohn (2014), 631–632.

48. See Gorny (2005), 158.

49. Ben-Gurion (1971–1987), vol. 6, 219: diary entry from March 24, 1939.

50. Shavit (1986), 106–110.

51. Schechtman (1961), 131.

52. Horne (1969). Sebag-Montefiore (2006).

53. Jabotinsky must have based this opinion on rumors about a disagreement between Hitler and some of his generals, the war minister von Blomberg, the foreign minister Neurath, and the army commander in chief General von Fritsch, who were dismissed for various reasons. See Deutsch (1974).

54. *Hamashkif*, January 26, 1940.

55. *Hazit Haam*, May 19, 1933.

56. *Hamashkif*, September 13, 1939.

57. *Haaretz*, July 9, 1934.

58. See *Haaretz*, July 17, 1935.

59. *Der Tag*, November 18, 1938.

60. Ben-Gurion (1971–1987), vol. 5, 290–291.

61. Ibid., 292.

62. Ibid., 294.

63. Ibid., 295.

8. "SO EARLY, NO ONE HAS SEEN DEATH YET"

1. Czerniakow (1979), 73. Czerniakow became head of the Judenrat in the Warsaw Ghetto and was murdered in 1942.

2. *Hatzofeh*, August 31, 1939.

3. *Minutes of the Twenty-First Zionist Congress*, 47.

4. *Haaretz*, September 1, 1939. Emphasis in the original.

5. Weitz (1990), 109.

6. Borenstein (1996), 23–24. Yitzhak Tabenkin wrote in his diary on September 3: "Right now we need to leave pivotal people abroad." Kanari (2003), 475.

7. Bornstein-Bielicka (2003), 55–56.

8. Avriel (1976), 70.

9. Braginsky (1965), 242. Shertok traveled from there to London.

10. Ringelblum (1992), 5.

11. Admiral Miklós Horthy was regent of Hungary from 1920 to 1944. His rule was characterized by an antisemitic policy.

12. Warhaftig (1984), 4–5.

13. Tamir (1967), 84–85.

14. *Forverts*, August 27, 1939.

15. Reiss (1982), 191–192.

16. Shaltiel (2000), 88–91.

17. Mass murder was in fact committed in two other places.

18. Neumann (1976), 147–48.

19. *Davar*, September 12, 1939.

20. Krone (1987), 199.

21. Halamish (2009), 153–154.

22. Ruppin (1968), 318.

23. *Davar*, September 11, 1939.

24. Kessner (2008), 314–315.

25. Ben-Gurion (1971–1987), vol. 6, 41.

26. Cohen, R. (1999), 29.

27. LPA, 4-6-1920-98: letter from 1939.

28. Katznelson (1960), 438–441. See also Shapira, A. (2008), II, 589–592.

29. Braginsky (1965), 245.

30. Bauer (1981), 34.

31. *Haynt*, August 30, 1939.

32. *Haaretz*, August 28, 1939.

33. *Haaretz*, August 30, 1939.

34. *Hatzofeh*, August 30, 1939.

35. *Haaretz*, August 31, 1939.

36. *Hatzofeh*, August 31, 1939.

37. *Haaretz*, August 30, 1939.

38. *Haaretz*, August 29, 1939.

39. Niv (1965), 14.

40. See Shavit (1986), 106–110. Shmuel Katz, who discusses the plan, treats it as a serious, real, and plausible plan "with all the great dangers involved." See Katz, S. (1993), 1124–1125. Niv (1965), 279. Schechtman (1961), 482–484; Schechtman calls this chapter "The Great Mistake." Stern objected to Jabotinsky's plan because according to his own plan another year or two were required to organize a fleet of vessels to transport the regiments assigned to pry Palestine from the British. Stern's followers saw the plan as a "strategic plan" as opposed to Jabotinsky's plan, which they saw as a "tactical episode." See Yellin-Mor (1974), 55–56.

41. Gilboa (1986), 46–50. There are even those who let their imaginations run loose and wrote in their memoirs that by the eve of the Second World War many vessels had been purchased to bring the 40,000 Irgun soldiers to Palestine, and that aircraft had also been purchased for that purpose. See Spielman (1974), 80. Niv (1965), 279.

42. Chajes (1998), 264–268.

43. Mastbaum (n.d.), 162–163.

44. *Davar*, August 30, 1939.

45. Ibid.

46. On the Alaska Plan, see Wyman (1968), 97–115. Feingold (1979), 94–99. Berman (1982), 271–283. Chava Eshkoli Wegman, "Tochnit Alaska: veyozmot shel yehudim l'hatzalat plitim migermanyah hanatzit," Yad Vashem, *Kovetz Mehkarim*, 39, Jerusalem 2011, 197–23.

47. *Anchorage Daily News*, May 16–19, 1999.

48. Gilbert, M. (2006), 226.

49. *Jewish Chronicle*, September 1, 1939. Uri Zvi Greenberg wrote before he left Poland: "Anyone who sees the daily march of old and young Jews, keenly and swiftly joining the work of defending the country, realizes that we Jews do not intend 'to rake the fire with someone else's hands.' No, our intentions and our desire for war are serious. [. . .] Like the Polish people in the days of their exile, we are truly ready for a call to arms [. . .]. The Jewish hands now digging the defensive trenches for Poland and 'against him' [Hitler] are in fact continuing the process, begun by the Jewish people everywhere, of undermining the German Amalek." *Hamashkif*, September 13, 1939.

50. Stachura (2004), 126–127.

51. JIA, 2/29/2–2א.

52. Klemperer (2009), 373–374.

53. Cohn (2012), 271–72; Cohn (2014), 638–39.

54. Rose (1973), 149.

55. Baker (2008), 134.

56. Rose (1973), 150.

57. Klemperer (2009), 380–381.

58. *Davar*, September 1, 1939.

59. Cohen, N. (2003), 285.

60. Spielman (1960), 24–26. When Ila Strasman arrived in Trieste she received a letter from Jabotinsky in which he expressed the hope that her husband would join her unharmed and then added: "Nobody will ever again believe in my intuition, after my not believing in the war." Thanks to her son, Gabriel Strasman, for providing us with the letter.

61. Cohn, W. (2014), 638–39.

62. Mastbaum (n.d.), 192–195.

63. Ringelblum (1992), 5.

64. Opochinsky (1970), 113.

65. *Haaretz*, September 1, 1939.

66. *Haaretz*, September 1, 1939.

67. Gilbert, M. (2006), 124.

68. Cohen, R. (1999), 30.

69. JIA, 2/29/2–1א.

70. Chajes (1998), 267–268.

71. Avneri (1985), 133–144. Yarkoni (2005), 117. Braginsky (1965), 244–245. Two other female illegal immigrants died on the *Tiger Hill* during the voyage.

72. *Minutes of the Twenty-First Zionist Congress*, 130.

73. Gilbert, M. (2006), 222.

74. *The Historical Encyclopaedia of World War II* (1980), 300. Hempel (2000), 23. Roberts (2009). Pruszynski (1944). Prenatt (2015).

75. Bethell (1972), 5–6.

76. Ibid., 106.

77. Eldad (1975), 39.

78. Cohen, N. (2003), 297–299.

79. Arnon (1983), 330–331. See also Eldad (1975), 39.

80. *Hamashkif*, September 13, 1939.

81. Blatman (1996), 33–35. Stein (1953), 133.
82. Gutterman (2011), 64–69.
83. Tzur, E. (2006), 331.
84. Halamish (2009), 209.
85. Armoni (2010), 117–135.
86. Chajes (1998), 269.
87. Stein (1953), 142–143.
88. Hilberg (1999), 88. Czerniakow (1979), 73.
89. Tzur, Y. (2010), 38–39.
90. Temko (1987), 54.
91. JIA, 106-פ: letter from 1940.
92. Shavit (1986), 43.
93. Chrust (1974), 20.
94. Achimeir, Y. (1983), 253.
95. Ibid., 257.
96. Eshkoli (1993), 189–209. Zariz (1991), 109–127.
97. Gertner and Gertner (2000), 51.
98. CZA, S6/1531/1.
99. TAA, section 4, folder 589, file ג4.
100. Kaplan (1999), 29.
101. "Poland's Jewish Soldiers," *Jewish Chronicle*, September 8, 1939.
102. Ibid.
103. Dreyfus (2007), 49–76.
104. Cohn (2014), 644–646.
105. Chajes (1998), 270.
106. Gruenbaum (1940), 432.
107. *The Encyclopaedia of the Holocaust* (1990), vol. 4, 932.
108. Davies (1981), 439.
109. Grobman (1976), 162.
110. Ibid.
111. Shmeruk (1981), 270–271.
112. Rennart (1987), 51–67.
113. Bader, Y. (1999), 226–229.
114. Feldman (2002), 113. See also Peled (1993), 37.
115. Kornblum-Rosenberger (1986), 16.
116. Lau-Lavie (1993), 43–46.
117. Erlichman-Bank (1976), 14–19.
118. Freiberg (1970), 10–13.
119. Adler, Sh. (2008), 25–27.
120. Ashkenazi-Engelhard (1976), 7–11.
121. Margaliot (2000), 42–54.
122. Zalmanowicz (2003), 39–47.
123. As in the title of the historical novel by the Polish writer Henryk Sienkiewicz, *With Fire and Sword* (*Ogniem Mieczem*).
124. Koznitsky (1999), 37–39.

125. Goldenberg (1987), 86–95.
126. Wolfovich-Cantor (2007), 12–22.
127. Saadia (2008), 101–114.
128. Korniansky (1979), 11–17.
129. Garncarska-Kadari (2008), 120.
130. Küchler-Silberman (1985), 175–176.
131. Bojman (2007), 9–44.
132. Turkow (1948), 9–13.
133. The Turkow family included four brothers.
134. Goldfaden (1921), 5–6. English translation: Avrom Goldfaden's *Shulamis: A Critical Edition*. Translation by Nahma Sandrow. Edited by Alyssa Quint and Ronald Robboy. Forthcoming from Dusseldorf University Press. The play included the song "Raisins with Almonds" (Rozhinkes mit mandlen), a lullaby in which the mother imagines her son's future as a great merchant.
135. Chajes (1998), 268–270.
136. Tzur, Y. (2010), 29–47.
137. Blaustein (2004), 27–28.
138. Ibid., 93–94.
139. Yoachimovich-Levin, in Leichter and Milkov (1993), 141–142.
140. Gertz and Gertz (1997), 91–98.
141. *Davar*, September 11, 1939.
142. *Haaretz*, September 13, 1939. See also *Haaretz*, *Tarbut Vesifrut*, May 9, 2011.
143. Robinson (2010), 305.
144. Jabotinsky (1941), 62–79.
145. Bondy (1989), 202–209.
146. *Haaretz*, December 4, 1939.
147. JIA, 1/2/29/2א: letter from September 22, 1939.
148. Ibid.: letter from September 24, 1939.
149. Ibid.: letter from September 25, 1939.
150. Jabotinsky (1941), 71.
151. Ibid., 72.
152. *Hamashkif*, February 9, 1940.
153. Ringelblum (1992), 177–179, 190–193.
154. Wegiersky (1940), 147–154.
155. Reich (1995), 83–84.
156. Prager (1941), 19–27.
157. Gruenbaum (1940), 447–448.
158. *Hashaa*, July 29, 1940.

EPILOGUE

1. *Davar Leyeladim*, September 4, 1939.
2. On the term "refugees" and its suitability for describing the Jews who for various reasons left the Reich countries, see Tartakower and Grossmann (1944), 2–6. See also the extensive bibliography on the subject: Ibid., 597–659.

3. *World Jewish Congress Memorandum for the Évian Conference* (1938), 531.
4. Melzer (1973), 233–235.
5. Ibid., 242–243.
6. Ben-Gurion (1971–1987), vol. 4, 227: diary entry from June 11, 1937.
7. Weizmann (1979–1984), vol. 19, 145: letter from August 29, 1939 to Neville Chamberlain: "The Jews stand by Great Britain and will fight on the side of the democracies. Our urgent desire is to give effect to these declarations. We wish to do so in a way entirely consonant with the general scheme of British action, and therefore would place ourselves, in matters big and small, under the co-ordinating direction of His Majesty's Government. The Jewish Agency is ready to enter into immediate arrangements for utilizing Jewish man-power, technical ability, resources, etc."
8. Kedem (1983), 25.
9. Weizmann (1979), vol. 19, 145–146: letter from August 30 1939.
10. JIA, 2/29/2-1א.
11. Katz, S. (1993), 1127–1129, 1738.
12. Robinson (2010), 305.
13. JIA, 2/29/2-1א.
14. JIA, 2/29/2-1א.
15. Weizmann (1979), vol. 19, 157–8: letter from September 15, 1939.
16. Gilbert, M. (1979), 125–126.
17. Ben-Gurion (1971–1987), vol. 6, 41.
18. Kanari (2003), 445.
19. *Hashomer hatzair*, September 28, 1939. See Spiegel (2010), 90–100.
20. *Hapoel hatzair*, September 27, 1939, quoted in Gelber (1979), 150–151.
21. Sharett (1968–1979), vol. 4, 341.
22. *Hamashkif*, November 10, 1939; November 17, 1939.
23. *Hamashkif*. November 29, 1939.
24. CZA, S100/28b, in Goldstein, Y. (2001), vol. 2, 210.
25. *Minutes of Mapai Central Committee*, September 12, 1939, LPA.
26. Ben-Gurion (1957), vol. 3, 1.
27. Letter to Weizmann October 26, 1933 in Ben-Gurion (1971–1987), vol. 1, 674–675.
28. Mintz (1984), 153.
29. Sharett (1968–1979), vol. 4, 363–366. Emphasis in the original.
30. Ibid., 380–381. Shertok addressed his politically oriented words to the senior figures in the Agency and his financially oriented words to the representatives of the Marks and Spencer families.
31. Cohen, R. (1999), 41–42, 47. Emphasis in the original.

BIBLIOGRAPHY

ARCHIVES

Labor Party Archive (LPA)
Central Zionist Archives (CZA)
Weizmann Archive (WA)
Jabotinsky Institute Archive (JIA)
Tel Aviv-Yafo Municipal Historical Archive (TAA)
German Foreign Office Archive, Auswärtiges Amt
Polish Foreign Office Archive (AWA)
Jewish Historical Institute (AZIH)
Public Record Office, London (PRO)
YIVO, New York
Minutes of the Nineteenth Zionist Congress and the Fourth Session of the Jewish Agency Council (1937). Lucerne, August 20–September 4, 1935 (Jerusalem)
Minutes of the Twentieth Zionist Congress and the Fifth Session of the Jewish Agency Council, August 3–21, 1937 (Jerusalem)
Minutes of the Twenty-First Zionist Congress, August 16–25, 1939 (Jerusalem)
Foreign Relations of the United States, 1939, vol. IV
Parliamentary Debates: House of Commons (April 6, 1939), 345(6)
Parliamentary Debates: House of Lords (21 June 1938), 110 (95)

PRESS AND PERIODICALS

Das Jüdische Tageblatt; Davar; Davar Leyeladim; Der Moment; Der Tag; Der Yiddisher Kempfer; Doar Hayom; Dvar Hapoelet; Forverts; Gal-Ed; Haaretz; Haboker; Hamashkif; Hamedina; Haolam; Hapoel Hatzair; Hashaa; Hashomer Hatzair; Hatzofeh; Hayarden; Haynt; Hazit Haam; Iton Meyuhad; Makor Rishon; Nowy Dziennik; Polin; Razsviet; Sadan; Unser Velt; Yad Vashem; Yalkut Moreshet; Zion
Anchorage Daily News; Geheimes Staatspolizeiamt; Jewish Chronicle; Merizujus Polki; Tempo Dnia; The Daily Express; The Manchester Guardian; The Times; Zionist Review

SECONDARY SOURCES, MEMOIRS, AND DIARIES

Abramsky, Chimen, et al., eds. (1986). *The Jews in Poland* (Oxford).
Achimeir, Aba (1974). *Ktavim nivharim: moto shel Yosef Katznelson* (Tel Aviv).
Achimeir, Yosef, ed. (1983). *Hanasikh hashahor: Yosef Katznelson vehatnuah haleumit bishnot hashloshim* (Tel Aviv).
Adler, Shlomo (2008). *Ani shuv yehudi: mibolchov el polin hacomunistit vehazarah layahadut* (Jerusalem).

Adler, Susie (2004). *Hohevet veha'ahuvah: Yomana shel Susie Adler* (Jerusalem).
Adler-Rudel, S. (1968). "The Évian Conference on the Refugee Question." *LBL Year Book* 12: 235–273.
Akzin, Benjamin (1989). *Meriga leyerushalayim: pirkei zikhronot* (Jerusalem).
Alfasi, I., ed. (1990). *Ha'irgun hatzva'i haleumi be'eretz yisrael*. Vol. 1 (Tel Aviv).
Améry, Jean (1980). *At the Mind's Limits: Contemplations by a Survivor on Auschwitz and Its Realities*. Translated by Sidney and Stella P. Rosenfeld (Bloomington).
Arad, Yitzhak (2010). *In the Shadow of the Red Banner: Soviet Jews in the War Against Nazi Germany* (Jerusalem and New York).
Armoni, Ora (2010). *Kmo shnei slaim: sipuram shel Batya veYudka Helman* (Jerusalem).
Arnon, Yochanan (1983). "Kol hakavod bo bamahapekhan (U. Z. G.)." *Hanasikh hashahor: Yosef Katznelson vehatnuah haleumit bishnot hashloshim*. Edited by Yosef Achimeir (Tel Aviv), 320–331.
Asch, Sholem (1980). *Briv fun Sholem Asch* (Bat-Yam).
Ashkenazi-Engelhard, Halina (1976). *Ratziti lihyot* (Tel Aviv).
Aster, Sidney (1973). *1939: The Making of the Second World War* (London). Avigur, Shaul (1964). "Im Yehuda Arzi: kta'ei zikhronot." *Molad* 2, 394–414.
Avizohar, Meir (1984). "Tokhnit hamedina vehatziyonut halohemet etzel Ben-Gurion." In *Iyunim betokhnit hahalukah, 1937–1947*. Edited by Meir Avizohar and Isaiah Friedman (Kiryat Sdeh-Boker), 95–127.
——— (1987). "Hatziyonut halohemet: mavo leyoman Ben-Gurion, 1939." In David Ben-Gurion, *Zikhronot*. Vol. 6 (Kiryat Sdeh-Boker), 17–60.
Avneri, Arie L. (1985). *Mivelus ad Taurus: asor rishon lahaapalah, 1934–1944* (Tel Aviv).
Avriel, Ehud (1976). *Pithu she'arim* (Tel Aviv).
Bader, Menachem (1954). *Shlihuyot atzuvot* (Tel Aviv).
Bader, Yohanan (1999). *Darki letzion, 1901–1948* (Jerusalem).
Baginski, Henryk (1942). *Poland's Freedom of the Sea* (Kirkadly).
Baker, Nicholson (2008). *Human Smoke: The Beginning of World War II, the End of Civilization* (New York).
Ball Kaduri, K. J. (1968). "Leil habdolah vereshimat hamekomot hameyuadim leharisah." *Yalkut Moreshet* 9: 153–155.
——— (1985). "Hatikhnun hamukdam shel leil habdolah." *Yalkut Moreshet* 39: 109–121.
Barkai, Avraham (2009). "Ha'interes hagermani beheskem hahaavarah, 1933–1939." *Tikvah vekilayon: iyunim betoldot yehudei germanyah bameot ha-19 veha-20* (Jerusalem), 123–150.
Bartal, Israel (1997). "Giborim o mugei lev: yehudim betzvaoteha shel polin (1794–1863)." In *Kiyum vashever: yehudei polin ledoroteihem*. Vol. 1. Edited by Israel Bartal and Israel Gutman (Jerusalem), 605–639.
Bartal, Israel, and Israel Gutman, eds. (1997, 2001). *Kiyum vashever: Yehudei polin ledoroteihem* (Jerusalem).
Bartrop, Paul R., ed. (1995). *False Havens: The British Empire and the Holocaust, Studies in the Shoah*. Vol. X (Lanham).
Batowski, Henryk (1979). *Agonia Pokoju i poczatek Wojny (Sierpień-Wrzesień 1939)* (Poznan).
Bauer, Yehuda (1974). *My Brother's Keeper: A History of the American Jewish Joint Distribution Committee, 1929–1939* (Philadelphia).

—— (1981). *The American Jewish Joint Distribution Committee, 1939–1945* (Detroit).
—— (1994). *Jews for Sale?: Nazi-Jewish Negotiations* (New Haven).
Benari, Y. (1969). *Tokhnit haevakuatzyah shel Jabotinsky vehazoto et goral yahadut polin* (Tel Aviv).
Ben-Arie, Katriel (1987). *September 1939* (Tel Aviv).
Ben-Elissar, Eliyahu (1978). *Kesher hahashmadah: mediniyut hahutz shel hareich hashlishi vehayehudim, 1933–1939* (Jerusalem).
Ben-Gurion, David (1946). *Bamaarakhah*. Vol. 2 (Tel Aviv).
—— (1957). *Bamaarakhah*. Vol. 3 (Tel Aviv).
—— (1971–1987). *Zikhronot*. Vol. 1–6 (Tel Aviv).
Bentov, Mordechai (1984). *Yamim mesaprim: zikhronot mehatkufah hamakhraat* (Tel Aviv).
Bentwich, Norman (1967). "The Destruction of the Jewish Community in Austria 1938–1942." In *The Jews of Austria: Essays on their Life, History and Destruction*. Edited by Josef Fraenkel (London), 467–488.
Ben-Yeruham, Ch. (1976). *Sefer betar: korot umekorot*. Vol. 2, part 2 (Jerusalem and Tel Aviv).
Berman, Gerald S. (1982). "Reaction to the Resettlement of World War II Refugees in Alaska." *Jewish Social Studies* 44: 271–283.
Bethell, Nicholas (1972). *The War Hitler Won: The Fall of Poland, September 1939* (New York).
—— (1979). *The Palestine Triangle: The Struggle for the Holy Land, 1935–48* (London).
Bialer, Uri (1980). *The Shadow of the Bomber: The Fear of Air Attack and British Politics, 1932–1939* (London).
Bialik, Chaim Nachman (1939). *Igrot*. Vol. 5 (Tel Aviv).
Black, Edwin (1984). *The Transfer Agreement: The Untold Story of the Secret Pact between the Third Reich and Jewish Palestine* (New York).
Blatman, Daniel (1996). *Lemaan herutenu veherutkhem: habund bepolin, 1939–1949* (Jerusalem).
—— (2004). "Havikuah bepolin be-1936 al tokhnit haevakuatzyah shel Jabotinsky." In *Ish basaar: masot umehkarim al Zeev Jabotinsky, iyunim betkumat yisrael*. Edited by Avi Bareli and Pinchas Genosar (Sde Boker), 371–387.
——, ed. (2014). *Hahistoriyah mitnageshet vekiyum meshutaf: perspectivot hadashot al hamifgash hayehudi polani* (Jerusalem).
Blaustein, Sarah (2004). *Shloshah meyilim: yaldah tzabarit bepolin hakvushah* (Jerusalem).
Boaz, Arie (2001). *Alum venokhah bakol: sipur hayav shel Shaul Avigur* (Tel Aviv).
Bojman, Binah (2007). *Yaldei hakorpus hasheni: yatmut besibir ube'arvot Kirgizia* (Jerusalem).
Bondy, Ruth (1989). *Elder of the Jews: Jacob Edelstein of Theresienstadt* (New York).
Borenstein, Heini (1996). *Hayei schweitz: peulot ezrah vehatzalah bashanim 1939–1946* (Tel Aviv).
Bornstein-Bilitzka, Chasia (2003). *Ahat mima'atim: darka shel lohemet umehanekhet, 1939–1948* (Tel Aviv).
Bracher, Karl Dietrich (1970). *The German Dictatorship* (New York).
Braginsky, Yehuda (1965). *Am hoter el hof: hamesh esreh shana besherut aliyah bet* (Tel Aviv).

Brod, Max (1967). *Hayei merivah* (Jerusalem).
Brykczynski, Paul (2016). *Primed for Violence: Murder, Antisemitism, and Democratic Politics in Interwar Poland* (Madison, WI).
Buber, Martin (1939). "Hashimshonim." In *Neged hateror: maamarim, reshimot, neumim, giluyei daat*. Edited by R. Binyamin and Yaacov Peterzeil (Jerusalem), 25–29.
——— (1975). *Briefwechsel aus sieben Jahrzehnten*. Vol. III: 1938–1965 (Heidelberg).
Burg, Yosef (2000). *Prakim meotobiografyah*. Interviewed and written by Meir Hovav (Jerusalem).
Carpi, Daniel (1962). "Habe'ayah hayehudit bamediniyut ha'italkit bein shtei milhamot olam." *Molad* 166–167: 186–194.
——— (1969). "Hitpathutah umahalakheha shel haantishemiyut hafashistit be'italyah (1922–1945)." *Yalkut Moreshet* 10: 79–88.
——— (1971). "Peiluto hamedinit shel Weizmann be'italyah bashanim 1923–1934." *Hatziyonut* 2: 169–207.
Chajes, Wiktor, and Pnina Meizlish, eds. (1998). *Gam yehudi gam polani: yomano shel Victor Chayut* (Ramat Gan).
Chazan, Meir (2010). "Mapai betadhemah: Ben-Gurion mul miflagto bemashberei shnot hashloshim." *Cathedra* 135: 118–146.
Cherniavsky, Irith (2010). *Yehudei polin baaliya hahamishit 1932–1939* (PhD Dissertation, Hebrew University in Jerusalem).
Chrust, Yosef, ed. (1974). *Ha'ish shekiyem et haneder* (Tel Aviv).
Cohen, Michael J. (1978). *Palestine: Retreat from the Mandate—The Making of British Policy 1936–1945* (London).
Cohen, Nathan (2003). *Sefer, sofer ve'iton: merkaz hatarbut hayehudi bevarshah, 1918–1942* (Jerusalem).
——— (2006). "'Yehudi akshan she'eino nitan letikun': Yitzhak Katznelson hapublitzist lenohah hitbasesut hashilton hanatzi begermanyah (1933–1939)." *Gal-Ed* 20: 101–111.
Cohen, Raya (1999). *Bein "sham" lekan": sipuram shel edim lahurban, Switzerland 1939–1942* (Tel Aviv).
Cohn, Willy (2012). *No Justice in Germany: The Breslau Diaries, 1933–1941*. Edited by Norman Conrads (Stanford).
——— (2014). *Betzipornei hareich hashlishi: yomano shel Willy Cohn 1933–1941* (Jerusalem).
Czerniakow, Adam (1979). *Warsaw Ghetto Diary of Adam Czerniakow: Prelude to Doom* (New York).
Davies, Norman (1981). *God's Playground: A History of Poland*. Vol. II: 1795 to the Present (Oxford).
——— (1986). *Heart of Europe: A Short History of Poland* (Oxford).
Der Prozess gegen die Hauptkriegsverbrecher vor dem Internationalen Militärgerichthof (1948) Band XXXI (Nürnberg).
Deutsch, Harold C. (1974). *Hitler and His Generals: The Hidden Crisis, January–June 1938* (Minneapolis).
Döblin, Alfred (1991). *Journey to Poland* (New York).
Dotan, Shmuel (1979). *Pulmus hahalukah bitkufat hamandat* (Jerusalem).
Dreifuss (Ben-Sasson), Havi (2007). "'Eleh, she'al ezratam haitah lanu hazkhut lismokh':

yahasim bein yehudim lepolanim bereshit milhemet haolam hashniyah le'or ktavim yehudiyim bnei-hazman." *Gilad* 21: 49–76.
Eilati, Naphtali (1987). "Tokhnit hagirat hayehudim lemadagascar ukishlonah." *Kivunim* 34: 127–138.
El hurban ba'it shlishi! (1937). Booklet for Tisha B'Av.
Eldad (Scheib), Israel (1975). *Maaser rishon: pirkei zikhronot umusar haskel* (Tel Aviv).
Engel, David (2001). "Masoret nega'im? Al hamegamot hapolitiyot vehatarbut hapolitit shel yahadut polin bein shtei milhamot haolam." In *Kiyum vashever: yehudei polin ledoroteihem*. Vol. 2. Edited by Israel Bartal and Israel Gutman (Jerusalem), 649–665.
——— (2006). "'Hameser hakaful': hatziyonut haklalit bepolin lenokhah medinat hale'om." *Gal-Ed* 20: 55–79.
——— (2009). "On Reconciling the Histories of Two Chosen Peoples." *American Historical Review* 114(4): 914–929.
Erdmans, Mary Patrice (1998). *Opposite Poles: Immigrants and Ethnics in Polish Chicago, 1976–1990* (University Park, PA).
Erlichman-Bank, Sarah (1976). *Biyedei tme'yim* (Tel Aviv).
Eshkoli (Wagman), Hava (1993). "Lesheelat yetziatam shel hapeilim hatziyonim meeropah." *Hatziyonut* 17: 189–209.
Faber, David (2009). *Munich: The 1938 Appeasement Crisis* (London).
Feilchenfeld, Werner, Rolf Michaelis, and Ludwig Feinert (1972). *Haavara-Transfer nach Palästina und Einwanderung Deutscher Juden 1933–1939* (Tübingen).
Fein, Yonatan (2009). *Kakh noldah: hakamat maarekhet hamimshal hayisraelit, 1947–1951* (Jerusalem).
Feinberg, Nathan (1936). *Some Problems of the Palestine Mandate* (Tel Aviv).
——— (1967). *Haagudot hayehudiyot lemaan hever haleumim: perek betoldot maavakam shel hayehudim al zkhuyoteihem* (Jerusalem).
Feingold, Henry L. (1979). *The Politics of Rescue: The Roosevelt Administration and the Holocaust 1938–1945* (New Brunswick, NJ).
Feldman, Julius (2002). *The Krakow Diary of Julius Feldman*. Translated by William Brand (Mansfield, UK).
Ford, Franklin L., and Carl E. Schorske (1953). "The Voice in the Wilderness: Robert Coulondre." In *The Diplomats, 1919–1939*. Edited by Gordon A. Craig and Felix Gilbert (Princeton), 555–578.
Frankel, Daniel (1994). *Al pi tehom: hamediniyut hatzionit vesheelat yehudei germanyah, 1933–1938* (Jerusalem).
Freiberg, Daniel (1970). *Hoshekh kisa eretz* (Tel Aviv).
Freilich, Miri (1999). *Hitbolelut vepolanizatzyah bekerev yehudim bepolin (1918–1939): hebetim irguniyim, politiyim vehevratiyim* (PhD Dissertation, Hebrew University in Jerusalem).
——— (2010). *Ahim bemivhan: hamaavak haideologi veha'irguni al dmutah shel tnuat Betar be'eropa, 1939–1946* (Ramat Gan).
Friedländer, Saul (1997). *Germanyah hanazit vehayehudim: shnot haredifot, 1933–1939* (Tel Aviv).
——— (2009). *Germanyah hanazit vehayehudim: shnot hahashmada, 1939–1945* (Tel Aviv).
Friling, Tuvia (1998). *Hetz ba'arafel*. Vol. 1 (Sde Boker).

Gai, Carmit (1995). *Hamalkah nasah beotobus: Rovina vehabimah* (Tel Aviv).
Gal, Alon (1985). *David Ben-Gurion—likrat medinah yehudit: he'arkhut hamedinit nokhah hasefer halavan ufrotz milhemet haolam hashniyah, 1938–1941* (Kiryat Sdeh-Boker).
Galezer, Eliyahu (1984). *Beterem zarkhah hashemesh: besherut tnuat Jabotinsky* (Jerusalem).
Gal-Nur, Yitzhak (1994). *Veshavu banim ligvulam: hakhraot al medinah ushtahim batnuah hatziyonit* (Kiryat Sdeh-Boker and Jerusalem).
Garlicki, Andrzej, and Laurence Weinbaum (1991). "The Zionist Revisionists, the Sanacja Regime, and the Polish Press, 1936–1939." *Gal-Ed* 12: 93–106.
Garncarska-Kadari, Bina (2008). *Hameah haesrim sheli: resisei zikhronot* (Tel Aviv).
Gelber, Yoav (1979). *Toldot hahitnadvut*. Vol. 1 (Jerusalem).
——— (1988). "Tguvat hahanhagah hatziyonit al hukei Nuremberg." *Dapim leheker hashoah* 6: 49–79.
——— (1990). *Moledet hadasha: aliyat yehudei merkaz eropah uklitatam, 1933–1948* (Jerusalem).
Gellman, I. F. (1971). "The *St. Louis* Tragedy." *American Jewish Historical Quarterly* 61(2): 144–156.
Gertner, Jehoschua, and Danek Gertner (2000). *Home Is No More: The Destruction of the Jews of Kosow and Zabie* (Jerusalem).
Gertz, A. (1947). *Statistical Handbook of Jewish Palestine, 1947* (Jerusalem).
Gertz, Nurit, and Dvorah Gertz (1997). *El ma shenamog* (Tel Aviv).
Gilbert, Felix (1953). "Two British Ambassadors: Perth and Henderson." In *The Diplomats, 1919–1939*. Edited by Gordon A. Craig and Felix Gilbert (Princeton), 537–554.
Gilbert, Martin (1978). *Exile and Return: The Struggle for a Jewish Homeland* (London).
——— (1979). "Mediniyut hamemshala habritit klapei haplitim hayehudim (November 1938–September 1939)." *Yad vashem: kovetz mehkarim*. Vol. 13 (Jerusalem), 99–129.
——— (2006). *Kristallnacht: Prelude to Destruction* (New York).
——— (2007). *Churchill and the Jews: A Lifelong Friendship* (London).
Gilboa (Polani), Yaakov (1986). *Belekhtekha bisdot eima . . . : al olam sheharav, al Yair umahteret lehi* (Tel Aviv).
Glatstein, Jacob (1962). *Homecoming at Twilight* (New York).
——— (2010). *The Glatstein Chronicles* (New Haven).
Goldenberg, Lily (1986). *Beredet hamasakh* (Tel Aviv).
Goldfaden, Abraham (1921). *Shulamis* (Warsaw).
Goldstein, Bernard (2016). *Jewish Life, Struggle, and Politics in Interwar Poland Twenty Years with the Jewish Labor Bund in Warsaw, 1919–1939*. Translated and edited by Mavin S. Zuckerman (West Lafayette, IN).
Goldstein, Yossi (2001). *Ussishkin: biografyah* (Jerusalem).
Golomb, Eliyahu (1955). *Hevion az*. Edited by Yehuda Erez (Tel Aviv).
Gorny, Yosef (2005). *Halufot nifgashot: mifleget habund, tnuat hapoalim haivrit uklal yisrael, 1897–1985* (Jerusalem and Haifa).
Gottlieb, Moshe R. (1982). *American Anti-Nazi Resistance, 1933–1941: An Historical Analysis* (New York).
Greenberg, Uri Zvi (1924). "Manifest lebitui," *Sadan*, no. A-B: 3.
Grobman, Alex (1976). "Ha'im hegivu? Tguvatah shel ha'itonut haamerikanit haklalit vehayehudit al redifot hayehudim bereshit milhemet haolam hashniyah." In *Pirkei*

mehkar betoldot hatziyonut: mugashim leIsrael Goldstein behagioh legvurot. Edited by Yehuda Bauer, Moshe Davis, and Israel Kolatt (Jerusalem), 161–187.

Gruenbaum, Yitzhak (1940). "Al horban yahadut polanyah." In *Milhemet yehudei polanyah tarad-tash* (Jerusalem and Tel Aviv), 450.

Gurevich, David, and Aaron Gertz (1945). *Haaliyah, hayishuv vehatnuah hativit shel haukhlusiyah beeretz yisrael* (Jerusalem).

Guterman, Bela (2011). *Tzvia haahat: sipur hayeha shel Tzvia Lubatkin* (Tel Aviv).

Gutman, Israel (2001). "Yehudim—polanim—antishemiyut." In *Kiyum vashever: yehudei polin ledoroteihem*. Vol. 2. Edited by Israel Bartal and Israel Gutman (Jerusalem), 605–639.

Gutman, Israel, ed. (1990). *Encyclopedia of the Holocaust* (Jerusalem).

Gutman, Israel, et al., eds. (1989). *The Jews of Poland between Two World Wars* (Hanover).

Habas, Bracha, ed. (1937). *Sefer meoraot tartzav* (Tel Aviv).

Habe, Hans (1966). *The Mission* (London).

Hacohen, David (1956). *Hessed neurim: dapim misefer hanoar haoved* (Tel Aviv).

Halamish, Aviva (2006). *Bemerutz kaful neged hazman: mediniyut haaliyah hatziyonit bishnot hashloshim* (Jerusalem).

—— (2009). *Meir Yaari: biografyah kibbutzit—hamishim hashanim harishonot, 1897–1947* (Tel Aviv).

—— (2016). "Yahaso shel Weizmann la'aliya ben milhamot ha'olam." In *Weizmann manhig hatziyonut*. Edited by Uri Cohen and Meir Chazan (Jerusalem), 261–298.

Halevy, Nadav (1977). "Tahat shilton habritim." In *Bankai le'umah behithadshutah: toldot bank leumi leyisrael* (Ramat Gan), 113–201.

Ha'olam lifnei ha'ason (2008). *Yehudei krakov bishnei haasorim shebein hamilhamot* (Krakow/Jerusalem).

Harris, Mark Jonathan, and Deborah Oppenheimer (2008). *Into the Arms of Strangers: Stories of the Kindertransport* (New York and London).

Hartzaat havaadah hamalkhutit lepalestina (1937). (Jerusalem).

Heller, Yosef (1987). *Bemaavak lemedinah: hamediniyut hatziyonit bashanim 1936–1948* (Jerusalem).

Hempel, Andrew (2000). *Poland in World War II: An Illustrated Military History* (New York).

Hermann, Angela (2008). "Hitler und sein Strasstrupp in der 'Reichskristallnacht.'" *Vierteljahrshefte für Zeitgeschichte* 56(4): 603–619.

Hilberg, Raul (1999). *The Warsaw Diary of Adam Czerniakow: Prelude to Doom* (Chicago).

The Historical Encyclopedia of World War II (1980). (New York).

Hope Simpson, John (1939). *Refugees: A Review of the Situation since September 1938* (London).

Horne, Alistair (1969). *To Lose a Battle: France 1940* (London).

Ilan, Amitzur (1979). *America, britanyah ve'eretz yisrael: reshita shel me'uravut artzot habrit bamediniyut habritit be'eretz yisrael, 1938–1947* (Jerusalem).

Israeli, David (1974). *Hareich hagermani ve'eretz yisrael: be'ayot eretz yisrael bamediniyut hagermanit bashanim 1889–1945* (Ramat Gan).

Jabara Carley, Michael (1999). *1939: The Alliance That Never Was and the Coming of World War II* (Chicago).

Jabotinsky, Zeev (n.d.). *Zikhronot bnei dori* (Jerusalem).
——— (1933). "The Evacuation Plan" (Yiddish). *Unzer Velt*, October 1933.
——— (1934). *Ura yisrael!* (Tel Aviv).
——— (1937). *Medinah ivrit: pitron sheelat hayehudim* (Tel Aviv).
——— (1939). "Zion Seym lehatzalah atzmit," *Hamashkif*, April 3.
——— (1941). *Hazit hamilhamah shel am yisrael* (Jerusalem).
——— (1948). *Al sifrut ve'omanut* (Jerusalem).
——— (1958). *Ne'umim, 1927–1940* (Jerusalem).
——— (2007–2016). *Igrot*. Vol. 9–13. Edited by Moshe Halevi (Jerusalem).
Kahn, Meir (Alex) (1988). *Sa esh lehatzit*. Edited by Yitzhak Elfasi (Tel Aviv).
Kanari, Baruch (2003). *Tabenkin be'eretz yisrael* (Ramat Efal and Kiryat Sdeh-Boker).
Kaniel, Assaf (2010). "Bein hilonim, masortiyim veortodoxim: shmirat mitzvot bere'i hahitmodedut im 'gzerat hakashrut,' 1937–1939." *Gilad* 22: 75–106.
Kapiszewski, Andrzej (2007). "The American Federation of Polish Jews in Polish-Jewish Relations, 1924–1939." *Polin* 19: 97–116.
Kaplan, Chaim A. (1999). *Scroll of Agony: The Warsaw Diary of Chaim A. Kaplan* (Bloomington).
Kassow, Samuel (2007). *Who Will Write Our History?: Emanuel Ringelblum, the Warsaw Ghetto, and the Oyneg Shabes Archive* (Bloomington).
Katz, Shmuel (1993). *Jabo: biografyah shel Zeev Jabotinsky*. Vol. 2 (Tel Aviv).
Katz, Yossi (2000). *Medinah baderekh: hatokhniyot hatzioniyot lehalukat eretz yisrael ulehakamat medinah yehudit* (Jerusalem).
Katzburg, Nathaniel (1974). *Mihalukah lesefer lavan: mediniyut britanyah be'eretz yisrael, 1936–1940* (Jerusalem).
——— (1994). "Ha'asor hasheni lemishtar hamandat be'eretz yisrael, 1931–1939." In *Toldot hayishuv hayehudi be'eretz yisrael me'az haaliyah harishonah: tkufat hamandat habriti*. Edited by Moshe Lissak, Part 1 (Jerusalem), 329–432.
Katznelson, Berl (1947). *Ktavim nivharim*. Vol. 9 (Tel Aviv).
———. (1960). "Sicha im Jabotinsky bestav 1939," *Molad*, October, 1960: 438–447.
——— (1961–1984). *Igrot B. Katznelson*. Edited by Yehudah Sharett (Tel Aviv).
Kaufman, Menachem (1985). "Leil-habdolah ba'ayarah Groß-Gerau: November 1938." *Yalkut Moreshet* 39: 109–121.
Kedem, Menachem (1983). *Chaim Weizmann bemilhemet haolam hashniyah* (n.p.).
Kershaw, Ian (2008). *Hitler, the Germans, and the Final Solution* (New Haven).
Kessner, Carol S. (2008). *Marie Syrkin: Values beyond the Self* (Hanover).
Klemperer, Victor (2009). *I Shall Bear Witness: The Diaries of Victor Klemperer, 1933–41* (London).
Klieman, Aaron (1983). *Hafred umshol: mediniyut britanyah vehalukat eretz yisrael hizdamnut shehuhmetza?* (Jerusalem).
Kochanski, Halik (2012). *The Eagle Unbowed: Poland and the Poles in the Second World War* (Cambridge, MA).
Kochavi, Arik (1984). "Hanhalat hasokhnut umetzukat yehudei germanyah veostriyah meha 'anschluss' ve'ad protz milhemet haolam hashniyah." *Dapim leheker tkufat hashoah* 3: 97–121.
Kolat, Shifrah, ed. (1994). *Hakiyum hayehudi batfutzot bameah ha'esrim* (Tel Aviv).

Konstantynow, Darriusz (2014). *Kesher* 46 (spring): 139–146.
Kopstein, Jeffrey S., and Jason Wittenberg (2012). "Between State Loyalty and National Identity Electoral Behaviour in Inter-War Poland." *Polin* 24: 171–185.
Kornblum-Rosenberger, Ruth (1986). *Neder: zichronot 1939–1945* (Tel Aviv).
Korniansky, Joseph (1979). *Beshlihut halutzim* (Tel Aviv).
Kozińska-Witt, Hanna (2017). "Ha'alimut ha'anti yehudit bekrakuv bein shtei milhamot ha'olam veteguvot ha'iriyah vemoetzet ha'ir aleha," *Gal-Ed* 25: 131–157.
Koznitsky, Chaim (1999). *Ratziti lichyot*.
Krikler, Bernard (1969). "Boycotting Nazi Germany." *The Wiener Library Bulletin* 22(4): 26–32.
Krone, Moshe (1987). *Morai verabotai, ahai vere'ai: pirkei zikhronot* (Tel Aviv).
Krotoshinsky, Isaiah (Sevek) (2002). *Noladeti belodz* (Tel Aviv).
Krzykalski, Kazimiez (1995). "Martin Bubers Reise nach Polen am Vorabend des II. Weltkrieges (März–April 1939) Im Spiegel der polnischsprachigen jüdischen Presse." *Judaica* (Basel), 51(2): 67–88.
Küchler-Silberman, Lena (1985). *Beit Imi* (Tel Aviv).
Kulka, O. D. (1975). "'Daat hakahal' begermanyah hanatzional-sotzyalistit vehabe'ayah hayehudit.'" *Zion* 40(3–4): 186–290.
Landau, Ronnie S. (2006). *The Nazi Holocaust* (London).
Larson, Erik (2011). *In the Garden of Beasts* (New York).
Lau-Lavie, Naphtali (1998). *Balaam's Prophecy: Eyewitness to History, 1939–1989* (New York).
Lazar-Litai, Chaim (1957). *Af al pi: sefer aliyah bet* (Tel Aviv).
League of Nations (1935). *Official Journal*, Special Supplement, No. 143.
Leichter, Sinai, and Chaim Milkov, eds. (1993). *Sefer olei hasertificatim: zikhronot, te'udot, igrot* (Jerusalem).
Leszczynski, Yaacov (1952). "Hapraot bepolin (1935-1937)." *Dapim leheker hashoah vehamered*, 36–72.
Lichten, Joseph (1986). "Notes on the Assimilation and Acculturation of Jews in Poland, 1863–1943." In *The Jews in Poland*. Edited by C. Abramsky et al. (Oxford), 106–129.
Livnat, Hannah (2009). *Kamah yafeh lihiyot yehudi: itzuv zehut leyeladim yehudim begermanyah bashanim 1933–1938* (Jerusalem).
Locker, Berl (1963). *Behevlei kiyum vetkumah* (Tel Aviv).
London, Louise (2000). *Whitehall and the Jews: British Immigration Policy, Jewish Refugees, and the Holocaust, 1933–1948* (Cambridge).
Londres, Albert (1938). *Le Juif errant est arrivé* (Lyon).
MacDonogh, Giles (2009). *1938: Hitler's Gamble* (London).
Mahler, Raphael (1968). *Yehudei polin bein shtei milhamot olam: historyah kalkalit-sotzyalit leor hastatistikah* (Tel Aviv).
Maisky, Ivan, and Gabriel Gorodetsky, eds. (2015). *The Maisky Diaries: Red Ambassador to the Court of St. James's, 1932–1943* (New Haven).
Marcus, Joseph (1983). *Social and Political History of the Jews in Poland, 1919–1939* (Berlin).
Mardor, Munya (1957). *Strictly Illegal* (London).
Margaliot, Abraham (1990). *Bein hatsalah leovdan: iyunim betoldot yehudei germanyah, 1932–1938* (Jerusalem).

Margalit (Margolis), Moshe (2000). *Yaldut belehavot* (Tel Aviv).
Mastbaum, Yoel (n.d.). *Varsha 1939: sefer hazikaron* (Tel Aviv).
McClure, Marc Eric (2003). *Earnest Endeavors: The Life and Public Work of George Rublee* (Westport, CT).
Mechman, Dan (1980). "Zeev Jabotinsky—tokhnit haevakuatzyah ube'ayat tzfiyat hashoah." *Kivunim* 7: 119–127.
Meir, Golda (1975). *My Life* (New York).
Melchior, Dan (2006). *Ubaharti bahaim: sipuro shel sored* (Jerusalem).
Melman, Billie (2009). *London: makom, anashim veimperyah (1800–1960)* (Tel Aviv).
Melzer, Emanuel (1973). "Hadiplomatyah hapolanit ube'ayat hahagirah hayehudit bashanim 1935–1939." *Gal-Ed* 1: 211–249.
——— (1989). "Antisemitism in the Last Years of the Second Polish Republic." In *The Jews of Poland between Two World Wars*. Edited by Israel Gutman, et al. (Hanover), 126–130.
——— (1997). *No Way Out: The Politics of Polish Jewry, 1935–1939* (Cincinnati).
Mendelsohn, Ezra (1986). "Interwar Poland: Good for the Jews or Bad for the Jews?" In *The Jews in Poland*. Edited by Chimen Abramsky, et al. (Oxford). 130–139.
——— (1989). "Introduction: The Jews of Poland between Two World Wars—Myth and Reality." In *The Jews of Poland Between Two World Wars*. Edited by Israel Gutman, et al. (Hanover), 1–6.
——— (1989). "Jewish Politics in Interwar Poland: An Overview." In *The Jews of Poland Between Two World Wars*. Edited by Israel Gutman, et al. (Hanover and London), 9–19a.
Messenger, Charles (2009). *Rommel: Leadership Lessons from the Desert Fox* (New York).
Mickiewicz, Adam (2007). *Pan Tadeusz*. Translated by Kenneth R. Mackenzie (New York).
Mintz, Matityahu (1984). "Avodat eretz yisrael ve'avodat hahoveh: konseptzyah shel ahdut umamashut shel stirah." *Hatziyonut* 9: 147–155.
——— (2010). "Klum nidonah sheelat hayehudim besihot Molotov-Ribbentrop?" *Gal-Ed* 22:107, 129. "Hamedinah hasovietit umetzukat hayehudim ba'idan hamesuvag, September 1939–June 1941: hatzalah o hafkarah?" *Yalkut moreshet* 89: 53–74.
Morris, Benny (1998). "Ha'itonut hayehudit hayomit be'eretz-yisrael nokhah aliyat Hitler lashilton, 1933." *Yad vashem kovetz mekhkarim* 27: 287–319.
——— (1999). "Response of the Jewish Daily Press in Palestine to the Accession of Hitler, 1933." *Yad Vashem Studies* 27: 363–407.
Morse, Arthur D. (1968). *While Six Million Died: A Chronicle of American Apathy* (New York).
Muñoz Molina, Antonio (2003). *Sepharad* (Orlando).
Neumann, Emanuel (1976). *In the Arena: An Autobiographical Memoir* (New York).
Nicosia, Francis R. (1985). *The Third Reich and the Palestine Question* (London).
Niederland, Doron (1998). *Yehudei Germania: mehagrim o plitim?: iyun bidfusei hahagirah ben shtei milhamot haolam* (Jerusalem).
Niv, David (1965). *Maarakhot ha'irgun hatzva'i haleumi*. Vol. 2 (Tel Aviv).
Novershtern, Avraham (2003). *Kesem hadimdumim: apocalipsah umeshihiyut besifrut yiddish* (Jerusalem).

——— (2008). "The Open Suitcases: Yankev Glatshteyn's *Ven Yash Iz Gekumen*." In *Arguing in Modern Jewish Canon: Essay on Literature and Culture*. Edited by Justin Cammy, et al. (Cambridge, MA), 255–298.

Ofer, Dalia (1990a). *Escaping the Holocaust: Illegal Immigration to the Land of Israel, 1939–1944* (New York).

——— (1990b). "Haaliyah haatzma'it shel hatnuah harevizionistit." In *Haapalah: measef letoldot hahatzalah, habrihah, hahaapalah ushe'erit hapletah*. Edited by Anita Shapira (Tel Aviv), 44–60.

Olitzer, A. (1939). *Hahon haleumi ubinyan ha'aretz: uvdot umisparim 1918–1937* (Jerusalem).

Opochinsky, Peretz (1970). *Reshimot* (Tel Aviv).

Overy, Richard (2009). *1939: Countdown to War* (London).

Overy, Richard, and Andrew Wheatcroft (2009). *The Road to War*. Revised and Updated (3rd ed.) (London).

Palestine Royal Commission Report (1937). (London).

Peled (Margolin), Yael (1993). *Krakov hayehudit, 1939–1943: amidah, mahteret, maavak* (Tel Aviv).

Peltz, Mordechai (2009). *Shover shtikah: masa hisardut* (Jerusalem).

Penkower, Monty Noam (2013). *The Swastika's Darkening Shadow: Voices Before the Holocaust* (New York).

Pickhan, Gertrud (2009). "Yiddishkayt and Class Consciousness. The Bund and Its Minority Concept." *East European Jewish Affairs* 39(2): 249–263.

Pollack, Avraham N. (1997). "Yehudei polin be'eretz yisrael." In *Kiyum vashever: yehudei polin ledoroteihem*. Vol. 1. Edited by Israel Bartal and Israel Gutman (Jerusalem), 399–412.

Polonsky, Antony (2012). *The Jews in Poland and Russia*. Vol. 3 (London).

Prager, Moshe (1941). *Yeven metzulah hehadash: yahadut polanyah betzipornei hanatzim* (Tel Aviv).

Prażmowska, Anita (2010). *Poland: A Modern History* (London and New York).

Prenatt, Jamie (2015). *Polish Armor of the Blitzkrieg* (Oxford and New York).

Pruszynski, Ksawery (1944). *Poland Fights Back: From Westerplatte to Monte Cassino* (New York).

Ramba, Isaac (1944). *Jabotinsky laolam ule'amo*. Vol. 2 (Tel Aviv).

Reich, Roman (1995). *Zichronot, 1928–1951* (Tel Aviv).

Reich-Ranicki, Marcel (2001). *The Author of Himself: The Life of Marcel Reich-Ranicki* (Princeton, NJ).

Reiss, Anschel (1982). *Besa'arot hatkufah* (Tel Aviv).

Rennart, Tzila (1987). *Shloshah kronot bakar, 1914–1945* (Jerusalem).

Ringelblum, Emanuel (1999). *Yoman vereshimot mitekufat hamilhamah: geto Varsha, September 1939–December 1942* (Jerusalem).

——— (1992). *Yoman ureshimot mitkufat hamilhamah: Geto varsha, September 1939–December 1942* (Jerusalem).

——— (1994). *Ktavim ahronim: yahasei polanim-yehudim, Yanuar 1943–April 1944* (Jerusalem).

Roberts, Andrew (2009). *The Storm of War: A New History of the Second World War* (New York).

Robinson (Gorodentschik), Rinat (2010). *Seara mesayaat: hatnuah harevizionistit bashanim 1925–1940* (Jerusalem).
Roos, Hans (1965). *Polen und Europa: Studien zur polnischen Aussenpolitik, 1931–1939* (Tübingen).
Rose, Norman A. (1973). *The Diaries of Blanche Dugdale, 1936–1947* (London).
——— (1987). *Chaim Weizmann: A Biography* (London).
Rosenblum, Howard (Hanoch) (1991). "Promoting an International Conference to Solve the Jewish Problem: The New Zionist Organization's Alliance with Poland, 1938–1939." *Slavonic and East European Review* 69.3: 478–501.
Rosenkranz, Herbert (1967). "The Anschluss and the Tragedy of Austrian Jewry, 1938–1945." In *The Jews of Austria: Essays on their Life, History and Destruction*. Edited by Josef Fraenkel (London), 497–526.
Rothkirchen, Livia (1979). "Yahasam shel hatshekhim klapei hayehudim biyemei shilton hanatzim." *Yad vashem: kovetz mehkarim* (Jerusalem) 13: 211–235.
——— (2006). *The Jews of Bohemia and Moravia: Facing the Holocaust* (Lincoln and Jerusalem).
Rülf, Schlomo (1969). *Bamidbar mayim* (Jerusalem).
Ruppin, Arthur (1968). *Pirkei hayai*. Vol. 3 (Tel Aviv).
Saadia, Miriam (2008). *Lisrod kedei lesaper: na'arah nodedet bein minzarim bepolin* (Jerusalem).
Sargent, Betty (1989). "The Desperate Mission of Stefan Lux." *The Georgia Review* 55–56(4): 187–201.
Sarid, Menachem (2008). *Herev ledavid: hamahteret bein havlagah letagmul (1920–1942)* (Herzliya).
Schechtman, Joseph B. (1959). *Zeev Jabotinsky: parshat hayav* (Tel Aviv).
Schwartz, Shalom (1949). *Ussishkin be'igrotav: mimoskva ve'ad yerushalayim* (Jerusalem).
Scott, Kenneth (2010). *St. James's Palace: A History* (London).
Sebag-Montefiore, Hugh (2006). *Dunkirk: Fight to the Last Man* (Cambridge, MA).
Segal, Simon (1938). *The New Poland and the Jews* (New York).
Shaham, Natan (1977). *Kirot etz dakim* (Tel Aviv).
Shaltiel, Eli (2000). *Tamid bemeri: Moshe Sneh, biografyah, 1909–1948* (Tel Aviv).
Shamir, Haim (1974). *Beterem Shoah: redifat yehudei germanyah vedaat hakahal bemaarav eropah, 1933–1939* (Tel Aviv).
Shandler, Jeffrey, ed. (2002). *Awakening Lives: Autobiographies of Jewish Youth in Poland before the Holocaust* (New Haven).
Shapira, Anita (1985). "The Concept of Time in the Partition Controversy of 1937." *The Journal of Israeli History: Politics, Society, Culture* 6(2): 211–228.
——— (1980). *Berl: Biografyah*, vols. 1 and 2 (Tel Aviv).
Shapira, David H. (1976). "Hatguvah hamedinit shel tzionei artzot habrit al hasefer halavan bashanim 1938–1939." In *Pirkei mehhkar betoldot hatziyonut: mugashim leIsrael Goldstein behagioh legvurot*. Edited by Yehuda Bauer, Moshe Davis, and Israel Kolatt (Jerusalem), 96–160.
Sharett, Moshe (1968–1979). *Yoman Medini*. Vols. 1–5 (Tel Aviv).
Shavit, Yaakov, ed. (1983). *Havlagah o tguvah: havikuah bayishuv hayehudi tartzav-tartzat* (Ramat Gan).

—— (1986). *Hamitologiot shel hayamin* (Beit Berl).
Shavit, Yaacov, and Liat Steir-Livny (2004). "Mi karah zeev? Eikh hevin Zeev Jabotinsky et tivah shel germanyah hanatzit ve'et kavanoteha?" In *Ish basaar: masot umehkarim al Zeev Jabotinsky, iyunim betkumat yisrael*. Edited by Avi Bareli and Pinchas Genosar (Sde Boker), 345–369.
Shedletzky, Itta, ed. (1998). *Gershom Scholem ve'imo: mikhtavim, 1917–1946* (Jerusalem and Tel Aviv).
Shelach, Menachem (1994). *Hakesher hayugoslavi: Yugoslavia ve'aliyah bet, 1938–1948* (Tel Aviv).
Sherman, A. J. (1973). *Island Refuge: Britain and Refuge from the Third Reich* (London).
Shirer, William L. (1960). *The Rise and Fall of the Third Reich* (New York).
Shmeruk, Chone (1981). *Sifrut yiddish bepolin: mekhkarim ve'iyunim historyim* (Jerusalem).
—— (1999). *Hakriah lenavi: mehkarei historyah vesifrut* (Jerusalem).
Sprinzak, Yosef (1969). *Igrot*. Edited by Yosef Shapira (Tel Aviv).
Silber, Marcos (2014). *Leumiyut shonah, ezraḥut shayah!: hama'amatz le-haśagat oṭonomyah li-yehudei polin bemilhemet ha'olam* (Jerusalem).
Skórzyńska, Izabela, and Wojciech Olejniczak (2011). *See You Next Year in Jerusalem: Deportations of Polish Jews in 1938 from Germany to Zbaszyń* (Poznan).
Slutzky, Yehuda (1973). *Sefer toldot hahaganah*. Vol. 2, part 2 (Tel Aviv).
Snyder, Timothy D. (2015). *Black Earth: The Holocaust as History and Warning* (New York).
Sokolow, Nahum (1961). *Hatzofeh lebeit yisrael: ktavim nivharim* (Jerusalem).
Speer, Albert (1969). *Erinnerungen* (Frankfurt am Main).
Spiegel, Yair (2010). *Al hamishmar: hashomer hatzair bemaarakhot hahaganah vehabitahon, 1920–1947* (Jerusalem).
Spielman, A. (1960). *Sefer Ila (Lily) Lubinsky* (Tel Aviv).
—— (1974). "Avraham kiyem et haneder." In *Ha'ish shekiyem et haneder: dmuto shel Avraham Amper lohem herut yisrael*. Edited by Yosef Crost (Tel Aviv).
Stachura, Peter D. (2004). *Poland, 1918–1945* (London).
Stein, A. Sh. (1953). *Haver Arthur: dmuyot ufrakim mehayei habund* (Tel Aviv).
Strauss, H. A. (1960). "Jewish Emigration from Germany." *Leo Baeck Institute Year Book* 25: 326–328.
Sykes, Christopher (1965). *Crossroads to Israel: Palestine from Balfour to Bevin* (London).
Szajkowski, Z. (1974). "Western Jewish Aid and Intercessions for Polish Jewry, 1919–1939." In *Studies on Polish Jewry, 1919–1939*. Edited by Joshua A. Fishman (New York), 171–174.
Tamir (Lipsky), Shlomo (1967). *Pirkei shlihut* (Tel Aviv).
Tartakower, Arieh, and Kurt R. Grossmann (1944). *The Jewish Refugee* (New York).
Temko, Ned (1987). *To Win or to Die: A Personal Portrait of Menachem Begin* (New York).
Tenenbaum, Jospeh (1959). "Tnuat haherem haanti-natzi be'artzot habrit." *Yad vashem: kovetz mehkarim* 3: 129–146.
Teveth, Shabtai (1987). *Kinat David: hayei David Ben-Gurion*. Vol. 3 (Jerusalem).
—— (1996). *Ben-Gurion and the Holocaust* (New York).
Thomas, Gordon, and Max Morgan Witts (1974). *Voyage of the Damned* (New York).
Thorne, Christopher (1967). *The Approach of War, 1938–1939* (New York).
Tomaszewski, Jerzy (1988). "Vladimir Jabotinsky's Talks with Representatives of the Polish Government." *Polin* 3: 276–293.

—— (1997). "Hayehudim bemeshek polin bashanim 1918–1939." In *Kiyum vashever: yehudei polin ledoroteihem*. Vol. 1. Edited by Israel Bartal and Israel Gutman (Jerusalem), 415–426.

Toury, Jacob (1987). "Mehagirah kfuyah legerush." *Yad vashem: kovetz mehkarim* 17–18: 65–98.

Tovy, Jacob (2011). *Milhamah beli gevulot: hatnuah hatsiyonit harevizyonisttit vesugyat haaliyah le'erets Yisrael bashanim 1930–1940* (Haifa).

Turkow, Jonas (1948). *This Is How It Was . . .* (Buenos Aires).

Tuvin, Yehuda (1986). "Berl Katznelson beterem shoah: bhinat hashkafotav." *Yalkut Moreshet* 42: 81–110.

Tzahor, Zeev (1987). "Ben-Gurion vehahaapalah." In *Yahadut mizrah eropah bein shoah letkumah*. Edited by Binyamin Pinkus (Kiryat Sdeh-Boker), 422–447.

Tzur, Eli (2004). "Yahasim mesukanim: Zeev Jabotinsky umisrad hahutz shel polin." In *Ish basaar: masot umehkarim al Zeev Jabotinsky, iyunim betkumat yisrael*. Edited by Avi Bareli and Pinchas Genosar (Sde Boker), 389–415.

—— (2006). *Lifnei bo haafelah: hashomer hatzair bepolin ubegalitzyah, 1930–1940* (Sde Boker and Givat Haviva).

—— (2010). "Palganut, tikvot vetiskulim: hatziyonut hapolanit 1915–1939." In *Hatziyonut leezoreha*. Vol. 1. Edited by Alon Gal (Jerusalem), 135–181.

Tzur, Yaakov (2010). *Yemei hatzrif: sipura shel mishpahah lohemet veohevet, 1936–1949* (Tel Aviv).

Von Weisl, Niva (2009). "Eikh nishkah Wolfgang von Weisl." *Yakinton* 234: 12–13.

Von Weisl, Wolfgang (1967). "Illegal Transport." In *The Jews of Austria: Essays on Their Life, History, and Destruction*. Edited by Josef Fraenkel (London), 165–176.

Warhaftig, Zerach (1984). *Palit vesarid beyemei hashoah* (Tel Aviv).

Wasserstein, Bernard (1979). *Britain and the Jews of Europe, 1939–1945* (London and Oxford).

—— (2012). *On the Eve: The Jews of Europe Before the Second World War* (New York).

Watt, Donald Cameron (1989). *How War Came: The Immediate Origins of the Second World War, 1938–1939* (New York).

Wegierski, Dominik (1940). *September 1939* (London).

Weinbaum, Laurence (1990). "Jabotinsky and the Poles." *Polin* 5: 156–172.

—— (1993). *A Marriage of Convenience: The New Zionist Organization and the Polish Government, 1936–1939* (New York).

Weingarten, Ralph (1981). *Die Hilfeleistung der westlichen Welt bei der Endlösung der deutschen Judenfrage* (Bern).

Weinryb, Dov (1997). "Yehudei polin el mihutz lepolin." In *Kiyum vashever: yehudei polin ledoroteihem*. Vol. 1. Edited by Israel Bartal and Israel Gutman (Jerusalem), 369–398.

Weiss, Yifat (1997). "Projektionen vom 'Weltjudentum': die Boykottbewegung der 1930er Jahre." In *Tel-Aviver Jahrbuch für deutsche Geschichte* XXVI: 151–179.

—— (1998). "Heskem hahaavarah utnuat haherem: dilema yehudit bashoah." *Yad vashem: kovetz mechkarim* 26: 99–130.

—— (2000). *Etniyut ve'ezrahut: yehudei germanyah veyehudei polin 1933–1940* (Jerusalem).

Weitz, Yechiam (1990). "Hahzarat shlichei hakibbutz hameuchad me'eropah, 1939–1941." In *Haapalah: meassef letoldot hahatzalah, habrihah, hahaapalah ushe'erit hapletah*. Edited by Anita Shapira (Tel Aviv), 108–123.
Weizmann, Chaim (1936). *Am yisrael veeretz yisrael*. Dr. Chaim Weizmann's testimony before the Royal Commission for Palestine on November 25, 1936 (Jerusalem).
——— (1937). *Dvarim: neumin, maamarim umikhtavim* (Tel Aviv).
——— (1949). *Trial and Error: The Autobiography of Chaim Weizmann* (New York).
——— (1979–1984). *The Letters and Papers of Chaim Weizmann*. Series A+B. Edited by Barnet Litvinoff, et al. (Jerusalem).
Werber, Jack, and William B. Helmreich (2014). *Saving Children: Diary of a Buchenwald Survivor and Rescuer* (Piscataway, NJ).
Wolfovich-Cantor, Hadassah (2007). *Mi yiftah et hashe'arim? Korotehah shel naarah besosnowiec ubemahanot avodah* (Jerusalem).
World Jewish Congress Memorandum for the Évian Conference (1938).
Wymann, David S. (1968). *Paper Walls: America and the Refugee Crisis 1938–1941* (Amherst).
Wynot, Edward D. Jr. (1971). "'A Necessary Cruelty': The Emergence of Official Anti-Semitism in Poland, 1936–1939." *The American Historical Review* 76(4): 1035–1058.
Yahil, Leni (1990). *The Holocaust: The Fate of European Jewry, 1932–1945* (New York).
Yarkoni, Hillel (2005). *Sfinot maapilim me'alef ad tav* (Tel Aviv).
Yellin-Mor, Nathan (1974). *Lohamei herut yisrael: anashim, raayonot, alilot* (Jerusalem).
"Yoman Velus" (1982). Translated and edited by Musya Lipman. *Idan* 1: 11–29.
Young, Peter (1980). *World War II* (Secaucus, NJ).
Yunas-Dinovitz, Yael (2004). *Bein hishtalvut letlishut: hamehagrim mipolin le'eretz yisrael bein shtei milhamot haolam bemifgash im "kur hahitukh" hatzioni* (MA Thesis, Hebrew University in Jerusalem).
Zalmanowicz, Dov (2003). *Aviv baalatah: ovdan haneurim bebendin ubamahanot* (Jerusalem).
Zariz, Ruth (1990). *Brihah beterem shoah: hagirah migermanyah bashanim 1938–1941* (Tel Aviv).
——— (1991). "Nisyonot aliyah mipolin hakvushah." *Dapim leheker tkufat hashoah* 9: 109–127.
Zertal, Idith (1990). "Bein musar lepolitikah: haaliyah habilti-legalit betfisoteihem shel manhigei hayishuv bein hakongres hatzioni ha'esrim lakongres ha'esrim ve'ehad." In *Haapalah: measef letoldot hahatzalah, habrikhah, hahaapalah ushe'erit hapletah*. Edited by Anita Shapira (Tel Aviv), 87–107.
Zilber, Marcus (2015). "Umah netulat medinah: haavarah hadadit shel raayonot bein haleumiut hapolanit vehayehudit." *Zion* 80: 473–502.
Zimmerman, Moshe (2013). *Germanin neged germanim: Goralam shel yehudim 1938-1945* (Tel Aviv).
Znaniecki Lopata, Helena (1976). "Polish Immigration to the United States of America: Problems of Estimation and Parameters." *The Polish Review* 21: 85–107.
Zweig, Ronald (1981). "Mediniyut veyisumah: misrad hamoshavot, hasefer halavan vehaaliyah habilti legalit, 1939–1940." *Hatziyonut* 7: 292–323.

INDEX

Note: page numbers followed by n refer to notes, with note number.

COVER ILLUSTRATIONS

Front: Zbąszyń, Poland. October 1938. Jewish refugees outside an abandoned military barracks. Courtesy of Wikimedia Commons.

Back: The 15,000-ton *Polonia*, the largest ship on the Haifa–Piraeus and Constantinople–Constantza line. Courtesy of the Central Zionist Archives, Jerusalem.